in *Selling Today*

CUSTOMER RELATIONSHIP MANAGEMENT WITH TECHNOLOGY

Learning CRM Software
Communicating through CRM
Exercising Care with CRM Data
Starting Fast with CRM
Managing New Product Information with CRM
Managing Multiple Contacts with CRM
Using the Same CRM Software as AT&T
Planning Personal Visits
Reviewing Account Status
Automated Sorting and Productivity
Adding and Deleting Prospects
Islands of Information
Confirming Immediately
Being Prepared
Staying Informed

PARTNERSHIP SELLING: A ROLE-PLAY/SIMULATION

Developing a Product Strategy
Developing a Relationship Strategy
Understanding Your Customer's Buying
*   Strategy*
Developing a Sales Presentation Strategy—
*   The Demonstration*
Developing a Presentation Strategy—
*   Negotiation*
Developing a Presentation Strategy—
*   Closing the Sale*
Developing a Presentation Strategy—
*   Servicing the Sale*

An Investment in the Future

Charles Schwab the great industrialist and entrepreneur said, "We are all sales-people every day of our lives, selling our ideas and enthusiasm to those with whom we come in contact." As authors, we suggest that you retain this book for future reference. Periodic review of the ideas in this text will help you daily in areas such as:

- interacting more effectively with others
- interviewing for new jobs in the future
- understanding and training salespeople who work for you or with you
- selling new ideas to senior management, co-workers, or employees you might be supervising
- selling products or services that you represent as a salesperson

We wish you much success and happiness in applying your knowledge of personal selling.

Gerald L. Manning   *Barry L. Reece*

SELLING TODAY

Building Quality Partnerships

SELLING TODAY

Building Quality Partnerships

8TH EDITION

Gerald L. Manning
Des Moines Area Community College

Barry L. Reece
Virginia Polytechnic Institute and State University

Prentice
Hall

Upper Saddle River, New Jersey

Acquisitions Editor: Leah Johnson
Editorial Assistant: Rebecca Calvert
Editor-in-Chief: Natalie Anderson
Marketing Manager: Shannon Moore
Managing Editor (Editorial): Bruce Kaplan
Marketing Assistant: Kathleen Mulligan
Managing Editor (Production): John Roberts
Senior Production Editor: Mary Ellen McCourt
Production Manager: Arnold Vila
Associate Director, Manufacturing: Vincent Scelta
Design Manager: Patricia Smythe
Interior Design: Christine Cantera
Photo Research Supervisor: Elizabeth Boyd
Image Permission Supervisor: Kay Dellosa
Photo Researcher: Melinda Alexander
Cover Design: Michael Fruhbeis

Composition: Progressive Publishing Alternatives

Library of Congress Cataloging-in-Publication Data

Manning, Gerald L.
   Selling today : building quality partnerships / Gerald L. Manning, Barry L. Reece.--8th ed.
     p. cm.
   Includes bibliographical references (p. 482-498) and indexes.
   ISBN 0-13-027477-1
   1. Selling.   I. Reece, Barry L. II. Title.

HF5438.25 .M35 2000
658.85--dc21

                00-023065

Printed in the United States of America
10 9 8 7 6 5 4 3
ISBN 0-13-027477-1

We wish to dedicate this book to our wives whose patience and support make our work possible.

Beth Hall Manning and Vera Marie Reece

Brief Contents

CONTENTS

PART IV

*D*eveloping a Customer Strategy

PART V

Developing a Presentation Strategy

PART VI

*M*anagement of Self and Others

➤ A personal selling textbook suitable for the twenty-first century must offer students a blend of time-proven fundamentals and new practices needed to succeed in today's information economy. The eighth edition of *Selling Today—Building Quality Partnerships* provides comprehensive coverage of consultative selling, strategic selling, partnering, value-added selling and sales force automation. These are the major developments that have transformed personal selling from "peddling" to a new level of professionalism that has dramatically changed the way products are sold around the world.

The new age of personal selling requires that we build on past improvements and adjust to the changes that have accompanied the age of information. Learning how to manage and communicate information to customers within a high-trust working relationship is one of the major challenges facing salespeople today. Personal selling in the age of information also involves fulfilling customer expectations through strategic alliances. These alliances, which represent the highest form of partnering, are growing in importance. Strategic alliances have created a new selling environment that requires the use of advanced customer relationship management (CRM) technology. The fundamentals of CRM represent an important new feature of the eight edition of *Selling Today—Building Quality Partnerships.*

The new edition recognizes that information has become a strategic resource in personal selling. The growth of electronic commerce has, in many cases, rearranged relationships among buyers and sellers. The changes brought about by the Internet are addressed in several chapters.

As in earlier editions, the eighth edition includes a number of important components that have been praised by instructors and students during the past two decades.

1. The four broad strategic areas of personal selling, introduced in Chapter 1, serve as a catalyst for skill development and professional growth throughout the textbook. Success in selling depends heavily on the student's ability to develop relationship, product, customer and presentation strategies. Salespeople who have achieved long-term success in personal selling have mastered the skills needed in each of these four strategic areas.
2. The partnering era, which evolved during the past decade, is described in detail. A series of partnering principles are presented in selected chapters.
3. Value-added selling strategies are presented throughout the text. A growing number of customers are seeking a cluster of satisfactions that include a quality product, a salesperson who is truly a partner, and outstanding service after the sale. The salesperson is usually in the best position to discover what adds value (in the mind of the customer) and then determine ways to add value.
4. A hallmark of this edition, and all previous editions, is the use of many real world examples that build the reader's interest and promote understanding of major topics and concepts. Examples have been obtained from a range of progressive organizations (large and small) such as Baxter Healthcare, Xerox Corporation, Maytag Corporation, Mutual of Omaha, Nordstrom, and Marriott Hotels.
5. *Selling Today* provides a three-dimensional approach to the study of ethical decision making. One dimension is a chapter on ethics (Chapter 4) titled "Ethics: The Foundation for Relationships in Selling." Chapter 4 provides a contemporary examination ethical considerations in selling. The second dimension involves the discussion of ethical issues in selected chapters throughout the text. The authors believe that ethics in selling is so important that it cannot be covered in a single chapter. The third dimension is an exciting business game entitled, *Gray Issues—Ethical Decision Making in Personal Selling.* Participation in this game provides students with an introduction to a range of real-life ethical dilemmas. It stimulates in-depth thinking about the ethical consequences

of their decisions and actions. Students play the game to learn without having to play for keeps.

6. The knowing-doing gap, common in personal selling classes, is closed when students participate in the comprehensive role play/simulation included in recent editions of *Selling Today*. Students assume the role of a new sales trainee employed by the Park Inn International Convention Center. In this role, they develop the skills needed to apply relationship, product, customer and presentation strategies. The role play/simulation serves as an excellent capstone experience because the learning activities move the student very close to the real world of personal selling.

Improvements in the Eighth Edition

The age of information is creating a new economy that offers salespeople many challenges and exciting employment opportunities. The eighth edition of *SellingToday—Building Quality Partnerships* describes how sales professionals are adjusting to this new economy. Several important improvements appear in this edition and in the support materials. The most significant changes include:

1. Personal selling is presented as a set of transferable employment skills needed by four groups of knowledge workers who often do not consider themselves salespeople: customer service representatives; professionals (accountants, consultants, lawyers, etc.); entrepreneurs; and managerial personnel. Success in each of these employment areas requires mastery of many of the skills used by sales professionals. This new feature helps develop a higher level of motivation among class members who may be uncertain about a career in personal selling.

2. The role of technology in personal selling has been updated and expanded. All ACT! Sales Force Automation exercises have been updated with a new customer database and converted to the Windows operating system. These exercises, featured in every chapter, are now described as Customer Relationship Management (CRM) exercises. The textbook includes new material on how to use PowerPoint and Excel software to create attractive and effective sales demonstration materials. The impact of the Internet on personal selling is described in detail. Internet exercises are featured at the end of each chapter.

3. The growth of strategic alliances used in business to business selling situations is explained and students learn about the new selling environment created by these alliances. The result of most strategic alliances is a complex sale that requires the approval of several people before the sale can be closed. Information on team selling, an approach commonly used in conjunction with complex sales, has been expanded in this edition.

4. The use of sales planning forms, a popular feature of previous editions, has been expanded. These forms provide the student with important skill development opportunities.

5. The new edition is a more concise, tightly focused textbook. Information not essential to coverage of the topic or concept has been removed. The finished product is very "reader friendly" because the text is focused on important "must know" information. In most cases a real-world example is provided to enhance student interest and clarify important concepts.

6. A new and expanded Web site has been developed for use by students and professors. One new feature is an interactive study guide/pretest for students who want to check their comprehension of key concepts in the book.

Special Acknowledgments

Selling Today has been the recipient of many accolades over the years. Three of the most important honors will be of interest to current and potential adopters. *Selling Today* was selected by Intelecom for use in its telecourse entitled, *The Sales Connection.* An esteemed panel of business and academic professionals spent over 2 years developing this important new college course. *Selling Today* was also selected by Certified Marketing Services International (CMSI) for use with the first international program for sales certification. The International Organization for Standardization (ISO) authorized CMSI to develop and administer this important new program. The major objective of this certification program is to increase the standard of excellence in the field of personal selling. Sales Links/Mentor Associates, a popular Internet Web site for persons involved in major account selling, sales training, and sales optimization selected *Selling Today* as the best overall textbook covering the field of personal selling.

Organization of This Book

The material in *Selling Today* is organized around the four pillars of personal selling: relationship strategy, product strategy, customer strategy, and presentation strategy. The two chapters that make up Part I set the stage for an in-depth study of the four strategies. The first chapter describes the evolution of personal selling from 1950 to the present and introduces the four strategies. The second chapter gives students an opportunity to explore specific career opportunities in the four major employment areas: service, retail, wholesale, and manufacturing. Career-minded students will also find the first appendix, "Finding Employment: A Personalized Marketing Plan for the Age of Information," very helpful.

Research indicates that high-performance salespeople are better able to build and maintain relationships than are moderate performers. Part II, "Developing a Relationship Strategy," focuses on several important person-to-person relationship-building practices that contribute to success in personal selling. Chapter 4 examines the influence ethics on relationships between customers and salespeople.

Part III, "Developing a Product Strategy," examines the importance of complete and accurate product, company, and competitive knowledge in personal selling. A well-informed salesperson is in a strong position to configure value-added product solutions for complex customer needs.

Part IV, "Developing a Customer Strategy," presents information on why and how customers buy and explains how to identify prospects. With increased knowledge of the customer, salespeople are in a better position to understand complex customer wants and needs.

The concept of a salesperson as advisor, consultant, and partner to buyers is stressed in Part V, "Developing a Presentation Strategy." The traditional sales presentation that emphasizes closing as the primary objective of personal selling is abandoned in favor of three types of need-satisfaction presentations. As in the seventh edition, the salesperson is viewed as a counselor and consultant. Part VI includes three chapters: "Management of Self: The Key to Greater Sales Productivity," "Communication Styles: Managing the Relationship Process," and "Management of the Sales Force."

Learning Tools That Enhance Instruction

The eighth edition of *Selling Today* includes several learning tools that will aid both teaching and learning. The design and development of these learning activities was influenced by experiences acquired by the authors in over 1000 seminars, workshops and conferences.

1. Six challenging video case problems are provided. Each video case problem (10–13 minutes in length) is introduced in the text. These introductions take the form of an opening vignette provided at the beginning of selected chapters. Once students view the video, they study additional case information at the end of the chapter and then prepare answers to thought-provoking questions. The video introduces the student to salespeople employed by real companies. These

real world examples enhance the students understanding of various career opportunities in personal selling. Video case problems are provided for Chapters 1, 3, 5, 7, 9, and 12.

2. An optional role play/simulation provides students with a realistic opportunity to apply major concepts presented in selected chapters. They are given information about a selling position in the service industry and required to make several critical decisions and complete a number of tasks. All materials needed for both salesperson and customer roles are provided in this easy-to-use exercise. Easy-to-follow instructions are provided in the text (and the Instructors Resource Manual) at the end of Chapters 1, 5, 9, 10, 11, 12, 13, and 14. These instructions refer to assignments in Appendix 3. The role play/simulation provides a bridge between classroom instruction and the real world of personal selling.

3. Most chapters feature three or four insights that focus on the themes "Building Quality Partnerships," "Building Partnerships in a Diverse World," "Selling in Action" or "Customer Relationship Management with Technology." These insights explore current real-world examples of what the student is learning throughout the text. This feature gives students a contemporary look at personal selling. Each chapter includes the following special features that aid the teaching and learning process:

   • A list of learning objectives to help the student focus on the important concepts.

   • A summary that provides a brief review of the most important ideas presented.

   • A list of key terms that follows the chapter summary.

   • A set of review questions that reinforce the student's understanding of the major concepts presented in the chapter.

   • A series of application exercises that will provide the reader with an opportunity to apply concepts and practices presented. Each chapter includes one "Internet Exercise."

   • A case problem that permits the reader to analyze and interpret actual selling situations. Each case problem is based on a real-life situation.

4. Every chapter features an insight on the use of sales force automation, now referred to as Customer Relationship Management (CRM). The trend toward greater use of technology to improve personal selling effectiveness has grown extensively during the past three years and will continue to in the years ahead. In response to this important trend the eighth edition features 17 "Building Customer Relationships with Technology" insights. Each insight explains how salespeople use sales automation to improve quality in the selling process. Optional, easy to complete "Customer Relationship Management Application Exercises" have been expanded in this edition to 16 chapters. These interactive exercises give students the opportunity to use the "Windows" version of the highly acclaimed ACT! Contact Management Software program developed by Pat Sullivan and Mike Muhney, leaders in the field of sales force automation.

See the *Selling-Today* home page at http://www.prenhall.com/manningreece. The student can use the *Selling-Today* home page to access the ACT! Contact Management System that features a prospect database and other information to be used by students as they make a range of decisions regarding qualifying prospects, approaching prospects, the sales presentation, demonstration, negotiation, closing, and servicing the sale. Students can print prospect profiles, sales letters, and telephone contact lists; conduct key word searches to find important references in the database; and do many other things. Simple single-stroke instructions are provided that enable students to experience the many advances in sales automation.

Intelecom Telecourse

The eighth edition of *Selling Today,* as noted previously, has been selected by Intelecom for use in its video course entitled, "The Sales Connection." A growing number of colleges and universities are embracing distance learning, so this telecourse will likely enjoy continued popularity in the academic community. Intelecom spent over 24 months and invested in excess of $1,000,000 to develop the telecourse. The 26 *Selling Today/Sales Connection* videos present strategies and techniques of top rated sales oriented companies and their high performing individual salespeople. In addition, over 25 recognized college and university professors are featured in the videos.

Supplements Available with the Textbook

A complete supplements package is available to adopters including 100 color acetates. New to this edition is the interactive power point presentation software with over 170 slides covering key concepts presented in the text. Also included in this package is a complete Instructors Resource Manual that contains:

- Detailed presentation outlines
- Answers to review questions
- Copies to be printed for students, and a trainer's guide for the "gray issues" ethics game
- Suggested responses to learning activities
- Copies of printouts for CRM sales automation exercises
- Detailed instructions for using the video case problems
- A complete trainers guide for using the role play/simulation
- A video tape supplement keyed to learning activities in the text.

A completely revised author-developed test bank that includes over 1,000 questions is available, as is a computerized test bank, Prentice Hall Custom Test.

Prentice Hall Test Manager 4.2: This powerful computerized testing package is available for Windows-based computers. It offers full mouse support, complete question editing, random test generation, graphics and printing capabilities. Toll free technical support is offered to all users, and the Test Manager is free. You may contact your local rep or call our Faculty Support Services department at **1-800-333-7945.** Please identify the main text author, title, and disk size. Some test item files are also available on Macintosh.

For those instructors without access to a computer, we offer the popular **Prentice Hall Telephone Testing Service.** It is simple, fast, and efficient. Simply pick the questions you would like on your test from this bank and call our College Media department at **1-800-842-2958;** outside the United States call 1-201-592-3263. Identify the main text and test questions you would like, as well as any special instructions. We will create the test (or multiple versions, if you wish) and send you a master copy for duplication within 48 hours. Free to adopters for life of text use.

The Search For Wisdom in the Age of Information

The search for the fundamentals of personal selling has become more difficult in the age of information. The glut of information (information explosion) threatens our ability to identify what is true, right, or lasting. The search for knowledge begins with a review of information, and wisdom is gleaned from knowledge (see model below). Books continue to be one of the best sources of wisdom. Many new books, and several classics, were used as references for the eighth edition of *Selling Today*. A sample of the more than 60 books used to prepare this edition follows.

Blur: The Speed of Change in the Connected Economy by Stan Davis and Christopher Meyer.
Data Smog: Surviving the Information Glut by David Shenk
Strategic Selling by Robert B. Miller and Stephen E. Heiman
Selling the Invisible by Harry Beckwith
Working With Emotional Intelligence by Daniel Goleman
Psycho-Cybernetics by Maxwell Maltz
The Double Win by Denis Waitley
Zero-Resistance Selling by Maxwell Maltz, Dan S. Kennedy, William T. Brooks, Matt Oechsli, Jeff Paul and Pamela Yellen
Messages: The Communications Skills Book by Matthew McKay, Martha Davis and Patrick Fanning
Spin Selling by Neil Rackham
The Power of 5 by Harold H. Bloomfield and Robert K. Cooper
Secrets of Closing the Sale by Zig Ziglar
Sales Magic by Kerry L. Johnson
The New Professional Image by Susan Bixler and Nancy Nix-Rice
Complete Business Etiquette Handbook by Barbara Pachter and Marjorie Brody
The 7 Habits of Highly Effective People by Stephen R. Covey
Integrity Selling by Ron Willingham
Selling With Integrity by Sharon Drew Morgan
Thriving on Chaos by Tom Peters
Changing the Game: The New Way to Sell by Larry Wilson
The Circle of Innovation by Tom Peters
Business @ The Speed of Thought by Bill Gates
Consultative Selling by Mack Hanan
The 10 Natural Laws of Successful Time and Life Management by Hyrum W. Smith
Personal Styles and Effective Performance by David W. Merrill and Roger H. Reid
The Versatile Salesperson by Roger Wenschlag
Management Information Systems for the Information Age by Stephen Hagg, Maeve Cummings and James Dawkins
Megatrends and *Megatrends 2000* by John Naisbitt

➤ Many people have made contributions to *Selling Today: Building Quality Partnerships.* We are very grateful to Jack W. Linge, who contributed significantly to the development of the CRM case study, which is an important addition to this textbook. Special recognition is also extended to Park Inn International and Contact Software International for assistance in developing materials used in conjunction with the eighth edition. Throughout the years the text has been improved as a result of numerous helpful comments and recommendations. We extend special appreciation to the following persons.

Robert Bochrath
Gateway Technical Institute

Jim Boespflug
Arapahoe Community College

Jerry Boles
Western Kentucky University

Jim Boles
Georgia State University

Duane Brickner
South Mountain Community College

Don Brumlow
St. Johns College

Murray Brunton
Central Ohio Technical College

William R. Christensen
Community College of Denver (North Campus)

Larry Davis
Youngstown State University

Lynn Dawson
Louisiana Technical University — Ruston

Dayle Dietz
North Dakota State School of Science

Casey Donoho
Northern Arizona University

Wendal Ferguson
Richland College

Dean Flowers
Waukesha County Technical College

Victoria Griffis
University of South Florida

Donald Hackett
Wichita State University

Jon Hawes
The University of Akron

Ken Hodge, Marketing Manager
Nordson

Norm Humble
Kirkwood Community College

Michael Johnson
Chippewa Valley Tech College

Richard Jones
Marshall University

Katy Kemp
Middle Tennessee State University

Wesley Koch
Illinois Central College

Stephen Koernig
University of Illinois — Chicago

Wilburn Lane
Lambuth University

R. Dale Lounsburg
Emporia State College

George H. Lucas, Jr.
Texas A & M University

Alice Lupinacci
University of Texas at Arlington

Leslie E. Martin
University of Wisconsin, Whitewater

Jack Maroun
Herkimer County Community College

Tammy McCullough
Eastern Michigan University

Bob McMahon
Appalachian State University

Darrel Millard
Kirkwood Community College

Ron Milliaman
Western Kentucky University

Irene Mittlemark
Kingsborough Community College

Rita Mix
Our Lady of the Lake University — Dallas

Mark Mulder
Grand Rapids Junior College

Gordon Myron
Lucent Technologies

John Odell
Merketing Catalysts

Jim Parr
Louisiana State University

James Randall
Georgia Southern University

Stan Salzman
American River College

Donald T. Sedik
William Rainey Harper College

Robert E. Smiley
Indiana State University, Terra Houte

C. Phillip Smith
John C. Calhoun, State Community College, Alabama

Robert Thompson
Indiana State University

Rae Verity
Southern Alberta Institute of Technology

Curtis W. Youngman
Salt Lake Community College

Donald A. Zimmerman
University of Akron

Finally, we thank the people on the book team at Prentice Hall: Leah Johnson, Rebecca Calvert, Shannon Moore, John Roberts, and Mary Ellen McCourt.

Dr. Barry L. Reece, Professor
Virginia Polytechnic Institute and State University

Dr. Reece has devoted more than three decades to teaching, research, consulting, and the development of training programs in the areas of sales, supervision, human relations, and management. He has conducted over 600 seminars and workshops for public and private sector organizations. He has written several textbooks and articles in the areas of sales, supervision, communications, and management. Dr. Reece was named "Trainer of the Year" by the Valleys of Virginia Chapter of the American Society for Training and Development and was awarded the "Excellence in Teaching Award" by the College of Human Resources and Education at Virginia Polytechnic Institute and State University.

Dr. Reece has contributed to numerous journals and is author or co-author of twenty-five books including *Business, Human Relations—Principles and Practices, Supervison and Leadership in Action,* and *Effective Human Relations in Organizations.* He has served as a consultant to Lowe's Companies, Inc., First Union, WLR Foods, Kinney Shoe Corporation, Carilion Health System, and numerous other profit and not-for-profit organizations.

Gerald L. Manning
Des Moines Area Community College

Mr. Manning has served as chair of the Marketing/Management Department for more than 30 years. In addition to his administrative duties, he has served as lead instructor in sales and sales management. The classroom has provided him with an opportunity to study the merits of various experiential learning approaches such as role-plays, simulations, games, and interactive demonstrations. *Partnership Selling: A Role Play/ Simulation for Selling Today,* included in the eighth edition of *Selling Today,* was developed and tested in the classroom by Mr. Manning. He has also applied numerous personal selling principles and practices in the real world as owner of a real estate development and management company.

Mr. Manning has served as a sales and marketing consultant to senior management and owners of over 500 businesses, including several national companies. He appears regularly as a speaker at national sales conferences. Mr. Manning has received the "Outstanding Instructor of the Year" award given annually by his college.

Keeping Current in a Changing World

Throughout the past decade, Professors Manning and Reece have relied on three strategies to keep current in the dynamic field of personal selling. First, both are actively involved in sales training and consulting. Frequent interaction with salespeople and sales managers provides valuable insights regarding contemporary issues and developments in the field of personal selling. A second major strategy involves extensive research and development activities. The major focus of these activities has been factors that contribute to high-performance salespeople. The third major strategy involves completion of training and development programs offered by America's most respected sales training companies. Professors Manning and Reece have completed seminars and workshops offered by Learning International, Wilson Learning Corporation, Forum Corporation, Franklin Covey, and several other companies.

DEVELOPING A PERSONAL SELLING PHILOSOPHY FOR THE NEW ECONOMY

➤ The two chapters that make up Part I explain the important role of personal selling in organizations, in economic systems, in social reform movements, and most importantly in the personal lives of millions of men and women enjoying rewarding sales careers in the new global marketplace.

Every employee at Federal Express must be sales oriented and each manager must be an outstanding individual salesperson.

FEDERAL EXPRESS

Personal Selling and the Marketing Concept

LEARNING OBJECTIVES

ℬody Glove International (www.bodyglove.com), a leading manufacturer of wet suits for a variety of water sports, had a humble beginning. Bill and Randy Meistrell, founders of the company, were active in surfing and scuba diving in the early 1950s when good quality wet suits were hard to find. They decided to turn this problem into an opportunity and developed their own wet suit design. The first suits were sold at a small dive shop in Redondo Beach, California. Today Body Glove International is a multimillion dollar global company that is recognized worldwide for its quality products and outstanding customer service.

The company also provides opportunities for career advancement. Celeste Berouty, for example, began her career at Body Glove as a customer service representative and soon was promoted to customer service manager. Then she was promoted to sales coordinator where she served as liaison between sales representatives and the national sales manager. Today Celeste is national sales manager of the Wet Suit Division and has helped develop and maintain over 30 partnerships with Body Glove International distributors. At the present time 250 salespeople employed by these distributors sell Body Glove products to 1500 retailers.[1]

Sales professionals who represent the Body Glove line of products are experiencing changes in selling that are shared with salespeople around the world. One area of change is the scope of the competitive selling environment. Today a one-world market exists for products ranging from consulting services to automobiles. To stay competitive, salespeo-

The gorgeous Ferrari 360 Spider competes with Porsche, Jaguar, BMW, Lamborghini, Aston Martin and other high performance sports cars in a one-world market.

ple need to adopt a global perspective. A sales representative employed by United Parcel Service, for example, must compete with Federal Express, DHL Worldwide Express, and Emery for the opportunity to serve customers throughout the world.

A second area of commonality is the need for salespeople to develop the skills needed to sell intangibles. A majority of today's salespeople sell services. Salespeople employed by Cisco Systems, New York Life, Dun & Bradstreet, Federal Express, NationsBank Corporation, A. G. Edwards & Sons, Marriott Hotels, and ADT Security Systems sell services, not physical products. As our service economy continues to expand, so will employment opportunities for salespeople in the service sector.

A third area of commonality is the need for all sales professionals, regardless of employer, to adjust to the changes that accompany the age of information. These changes are creating a new economy that offers salespeople many challenging and exciting employment opportunities. Learning how to manage and communicate information to customers within a high-trust work relationship is one of the major challenges facing today's salesperson.

PERSONAL SELLING IN THE AGE OF INFORMATION

The restructuring of America from an industrial economy to an information economy began in the 1950s (Fig. 1.1). John Naisbitt, author of the popular book *Megatrends* noted that during this period our economy began shifting from an emphasis on industrial activity to an emphasis on information processing. He recognized that industrial America was giving way to a new society where most of us would work with information instead of producing goods.[2] We live in an age in which the effective exchange of information is the foundation of most economic transactions. Today we are in the latter stages of the age of information, and the implications for personal selling are profound. We will describe the three major developments that have shaped the information economy and discuss the implications for personal selling.

Major Advances in Information Technology

The information age has spawned the information technology revolution. Salespeople and other players in the information age use personal computers, e-mail, faxes, mobile phones, and other forms of technology to obtain and process information. Explosive growth of electronic commerce and other Internet activities has changed the way in which computers are used. Stan Davis, futurist and co-author of *Blur: The Speed of Change in the Connected Economy*, says that we now use the computer less for data crunching and more for connecting. These connections involve people to people, machine to machine, product to ser-

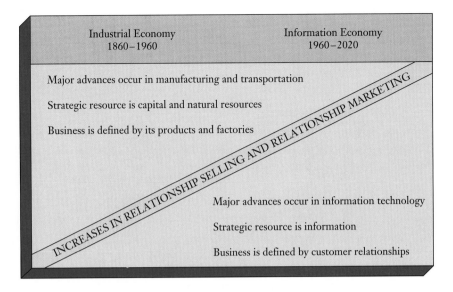

Industrial Economy 1860–1960	Information Economy 1960–2020
Major advances occur in manufacturing and transportation	
Strategic resource is capital and natural resources	
Business is defined by its products and factories	
	Major advances occur in information technology
	Strategic resource is information
	Business is defined by customer relationships

INCREASES IN RELATIONSHIP SELLING AND RELATIONSHIP MARKETING

Figure 1.1
The age of information has greatly influenced personal selling. Today, salespeople use a variety of information technology tools to gather and process information of value to the customer. They recognize that information is a strategic resource and relationship skills are needed to build a conduit of trust for information acceptance.

vice, organization to organization, and all these in combination.[3] Without these connections, information age workers cannot do their jobs. People who work extensively with information, such as salespeople, need these connections to conduct their information gathering and information management responsibilities.

Strategic Resource Is Information

Advances in information technology have increased the speed at which we acquire, process, and disseminate information. David Shenk, author of *Data Smog: Surviving the Information Glut*, notes that we have moved from a state of information scarcity to one of information overload.[4] The information age is dynamic, but it also can be disorienting. In an era of limitless data, informed salespeople are expected to help us decide which information has value and which information should be ignored. Customers who have less time to adjust to new products and circumstances value this assistance.

Business Is Defined by Customer Relationships

On the surface, the major focus of the age of information seems to be the accumulation of more and more information and the never-ending search for new forms of information technology. It's easy to overlook the importance of the human element. Humans, not computers, have the ability to think, feel, and create ideas. It is no coincidence that relationship selling and relationship marketing, which emphasize long-term, mutually satisfying buyer–seller relationships, began to gain support at the beginning of the information age. Personal selling provides a counterbalancing human response to the impersonal nature of technology.

Today's salespeople are competing in a service-oriented, information-saturated global economy. They must spend considerable time acquiring, processing, and delivering information to customers who often are experiencing information overload. Success can be achieved by those salespeople who employ relationship skills to build a conduit of trust for information acceptance. As the level of trust builds, the customer becomes more willing to share information that the salesperson must have to satisfy the customer's needs.

"One question: If this is the Information Age, how come nobody knows anything?"

PERSONAL SELLING—A DEFINITION AND A PHILOSOPHY

Personal selling involves person-to-person communication with a prospect. It is a process of developing relationships; discovering needs; matching the appropriate products with these needs; and communicating benefits through informing, reminding, or persuading. The term **product** should be broadly interpreted to encompass information, services, ideas, and issues. Increasingly, personal selling is viewed as an important form of customer service. In an ideal situation the salesperson diagnoses the customer's needs and custom fits the product to meet these needs.

Preparation for a career in personal selling begins with the development of a personal philosophy or set of beliefs that provides guidance. To some degree this philosophy is like the rudder that steers a ship. Without a rudder the ship's direction is unpredictable. Without a personal philosophy the salesperson's behavior also is unpredictable.

The development of a **personal selling philosophy** for the information age involves three prescriptions: adopt the marketing concept, value personal selling, and assume the role of a problem solver or partner in helping customers make buying decisions (Fig. 1.2).

Figure **1.2**
Today, salespeople use a strategic plan based on a personal philosophy that emphasizes adopting the marketing concept, valuing personal selling, and becoming a problem solver/partner.

Strategic/Consultative Selling Model	
Strategic step	Prescription
DEVELOP A PERSONAL SELLING PHILOSOPHY	☐ ADOPT MARKETING CONCEPT ☐ VALUE PERSONAL SELLING ☐ BECOME A PROBLEM SOLVER/PARTNER

These three prescriptions for success in personal selling are presented here as part of the Strategic/Consultative Selling Model. This model is expanded in future chapters to include additional strategic steps in the selling process.

PERSONAL SELLING AS AN EXTENSION OF THE MARKETING CONCEPT

A careful examination of personal selling practices during the past 40 years of the information age reveals some positive developments. We have seen the evolution of personal selling from an era that emphasized *pushing or peddling products* to an era that emphasizes *partnering*. Throughout this period we have seen the emergence of new thinking patterns concerning every aspect of sales and sales management. Today, salespeople are no longer the flamboyant product "pitchmen" of the past. Instead they are increasingly becoming diagnosticians of customers' needs and problems. A growing number of salespeople recognize that the quality of the partnerships they create is as important as the quality of the products they sell.

Evolution of the Marketing Concept

What is the **marketing concept**? When a business firm moves from a product orientation to a consumer orientation, we say that it has adopted the marketing concept. This concept springs from the belief that the firm should dedicate all of its policies, planning, and operation to the satisfaction of the customer.

The era of marketing and the age of information began in the 1950s (Table 1.1). J. B. McKitterick, a General Electric executive, is credited with making one of the earliest formal statements indicating corporate interest in the marketing concept. In a paper written in

Establishing and building a quality relationship begins during the initial contact.

Table 1.1   **EVOLUTION OF PERSONAL SELLING (1950 TO PRESENT)**

SALES AND MARKETING EMPHASIS	TIME PERIOD	IMPORTANT EVENTS	SELLING EMPHASIS
Marketing Era Begins Organizations determine needs and wants of target markets and adapt themselves to delivering desired satisfaction; product orientation is replaced by a customer orientation	Middle 1950s	• John Naisbitt cites 1956–1957 as the beginning of the information age • J. B. McKitterick, General Electric executive, presents a paper in 1957 on applications of the marketing concept	• More organizations recognize that the salesperson is in a position to collect product, market, and service information concerning the buyer's needs
Consultative Selling Era Salespeople are becoming diagnosticians of customers' needs as well as consultants offering well-considered recommendations; mass markets are breaking into target markets	Late 1960s to early 1970s	• In the late 1960s Wilson Learning Corporation developed a sales training course entitled "Counselor Selling" • In 1973 Mack Hanan writes *Consultative Selling*	• Buyer needs are identified through two-way communication • Information giving and negotiation tactics replace manipulation
Strategic Selling Era The evolution of a more complex selling environment and greater emphasis on market niches creates the need for greater structure and more emphasis on planning	Early 1980s	• *Strategic Selling* is written by Robert Miller and Stephen Heiman in 1985 • Learning International, The Forum Corporation, and Wilson Learning Corporation develop sales training courses that emphasize strategic selling	• Strategy is given as much attention as selling tactics • Product positioning is given more attention
Partnering Era Salespeople are encouraged to think of everything they say or do in the context of their long-term, high-quality partnership with individual customers; sales force automation provides specific customer information	1990 to the present	• Tom Peters, Larry Wilson, and others popularize the "Lifetime" customer concept • American Media, Incorporated produces a training film titled "Partnering: The Heart of Selling Today"	• Customer supplants the product as the driving force in sales • Greater emphasis is on total quality relationships that result in repeat business and referrals

1957 he observed that the principal marketing function of a company is to determine what the customer wants and then develop the appropriate product or service. This view contrasted with the prevailing practice of that period, which was to develop products and then build customer interest in those products.

The foundation for the marketing concept is a business philosophy that leaves no doubt in the mind of every employee that customer satisfaction is of primary importance. All energies are directed toward satisfying the customer. As Peter Drucker once observed, "The customers define the business."

Business firms vary in terms of how strongly they support the marketing concept. Some firms have gone the extra mile to satisfy the needs and wants of their customers:

▶ Nordstrom, a Seattle-based department store chain, has turned exacting standards of customer service into a billion-dollar annual business. A major key to Nordstrom's success is the quality of the sales staff. They are well trained and encouraged to do almost anything within reason to satisfy customers.

▶ Marriott Hotels uses a blend of "high tech" and "high touch" to build customer goodwill and repeat business. Each of the 5,500 sales representatives can sell the services of 10 motel brands in Marriott's portfolio. The customer with a small meeting budget might be encouraged to consider a Fairfield Inn property. The customer seeking luxury accommodations might be introduced to a Ritz-Carlton hotel (acquired a few years ago). All reservations go through the same system, so if one Marriott hotel is full, the sales representative can cross-sell rooms in another Marriott hotel in the same city.[5]

Nordstrom views personal selling as an important dimension of its marketing program. This company also realizes the value of relationships in creating repeat business.

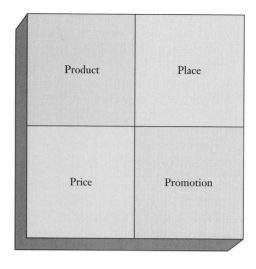

Figure 1.3
Each of the elements that make up the marketing mix must be executed effectively for a marketing program to achieve the desired results.

Marketing Concept Yields Marketing Mix

Once the marketing concept becomes an integral part of a firm's philosophy, its management seeks to develop a network of marketing activities that maximize customer service and ensure profitability. The combination of elements making up a program based on the marketing concept is known as the **marketing mix** (Fig. 1.3). According to Jerome McCarthy, these elements are product, promotion, place, and price.[6] For a marketing program to achieve the desired results, each function must be executed effectively.

One of the four P's shown in Figure 1.3—promotion—can be further subdivided into advertising, public relations, sales promotion, and personal selling. When a company adopts the marketing concept, it must determine how some combination of these elements can result in maximum customer satisfaction.

Important Role of Personal Selling

Every marketer must decide how much time and money to invest in each of the four areas of the marketing mix. The decision must be objective; no one can afford to invest money in a marketing strategy that does not provide continuing customer satisfaction. *Personal selling is the major promotional method used in American business—whether measured by people employed, by total expenditures, or by expenses as a percentage of sales.*[7] Firms make large investments in personal selling in response to several major trends: products and services are becoming increasingly sophisticated and complex; competition has greatly increased in most product areas; and demand for quality, value, and service by customers has risen sharply. In response to these trends, personal selling has evolved to a new level of professionalism. Since the beginning of the information age, personal selling has evolved through three distinct developmental periods: the consultative selling era, the strategic selling era, and the partnering era. Next we examine each of these developments.

EVOLUTION OF CONSULTATIVE SELLING

Consultative selling, which emerged in the late 1960s and early 1970s, is an extension of the marketing concept (see Table 1.1). This approach emphasizes need identification, which is achieved through effective communication between the salesperson and the cus-

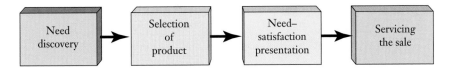

Figure 1.4
THE CONSULTATIVE SALES PRESENTATION GUIDE
This contemporary presentation guide emphasizes the customer as a person to be served.

tomer. The salesperson establishes two-way communication by asking appropriate questions and listening carefully to the customer's responses. The salesperson assumes the role of consultant and offers well-considered recommendations. Negotiation replaces manipulation as the salesperson sets the stage for a long-term partnership. Salespeople who have adopted consultative selling possess a keen ability to listen, define the customer's problems, and offer one or more solutions.[8]

Although consultative selling is emphasized throughout this text, it is helpful to understand the role of transactional selling in our economy. **Transactional selling** is a sales process that most effectively matches the needs of the value conscious buyer who is primarily interested in price and convenience. Because the transaction-based buyer tends to focus primarily on low price, some marketers are adopting lower cost selling channels. Low cost transaction selling strategies include telesales, direct mail, and the Internet. This approach to selling is usually used by marketers who do not see the need to spend very much time on customer need assessment, problem solving, relationship building, or sales follow-up.[9] It is an unattractive alternative to consultative selling in situations involving high-value customized products with relatively long and complex decision-making processes.

Service, retail, manufacturing, and wholesale firms that embrace the marketing concept already have adopted or are currently adopting consultative selling practices. The major features of consultative selling are as follows:

1. The customer is seen as a *person to be served*, not a prospect to be sold. Consultative salespeople believe their function is to help the buyer make an intelligent decision. They use a four-step process that includes need discovery, selection of the product, a need–satisfaction presentation, and servicing the sale (Fig. 1.4). These customer-centered strategies are fully developed and explained in Chapters 9–14.
2. The consultative salesperson, unlike the peddler of an earlier era, does not try to overpower the customer with a high-pressure sales presentation. Instead the buyer's needs are identified through *two-way* communication. The salesperson asks the potential buyer questions in an attempt to learn as much as possible about the person's needs and perceptions.
3. Consultative selling emphasizes *information giving, problem solving, and negotiation instead of manipulation*. This approach leads to a more trusting relationship between buyer and seller. Helping the buyer make an informed and intelligent buying decision adds value to the product.
4. Consultative selling emphasizes *service* after the sale. Theodore Levitt, author–consultant, recognizes that the relationship between a seller and a buyer seldom ends when a sale is made. In an increasing number of transactions the relationship actually intensifies because the customer has higher expectations after the sale. The personalized service provided after the sale may include making credit arrangements, supervising product delivery and installation, servicing warranties, and following up on complaints.

At first glance, it may appear that consultative selling practices can be easily mastered. The truth is, consultative selling is a complex process that puts great demands on sales personnel.[10] This approach to personal selling requires an understanding of concepts

In consultative selling, negotiation replaces manipulation as the salesperson sets
the stage for a long-term
relationship.

and principles borrowed from the fields of psychology, communications, and sociology. It takes a great deal of personal commitment and self-discipline to become a sales consultant/advisor.

Enhancement of Consultative Selling

Throughout the past 30 years consultative selling has evolved into a more mature and more focused approach to meeting the customer's needs. With each passing year we have learned more about high-performance salespeople who use this approach; and this information has been incorporated into many sales training programs, training videos, and books devoted to personal selling.

The early consultative sales training programs emphasized the development of face-to-face selling skills. These skills continue to be important today, but they must be enhanced with strategic planning and a strong commitment to building partnerships. Today, salespeople are encountering better educated and more demanding customers who are asking harder questions and seeking more precise solutions to their buying problems. Time is a precious commodity for most of today's customers. They want to partner with a salesperson who is well organized, well informed, and able to use strategic thinking to meet their complex needs. The remainder of this chapter is devoted to an introduction of strategic selling and partnering.

EVOLUTION OF STRATEGIC SELLING

Strategic selling began receiving considerable attention during the 1980s (see Table 1.1). During this period we witnessed the beginning of several trends that resulted in a more complex selling environment. These trends, which include increased global competition, broader and more diverse product lines, more decision makers involved in major purchases, and greater demand for specific, custom-made solutions, continue to influence personal selling and sales training in the age of information.

As companies face increased levels of complexity in the marketplace, they must give more attention to strategic planning. The strategic planning done by salespeople is often influenced by the information included in the company's strategic market plan. A **strategic**

market plan is an outline of the methods and resources required to achieve an organization's goals within a specific target market. It takes into consideration all the major functional areas of the business that must be coordinated, such as production, marketing, finance, and personnel.[11] Almost every aspect of the plan directly or indirectly influences the sale of products.

The strategic market plan should be a guide for a strategic selling plan. This plan includes strategies that you use to position yourself with the customer before the sales call even begins.[12] The authors of *Strategic Selling* point out that there is a difference between a *tactic* and a *strategy*. **Tactics** are techniques, practices, or methods you use when you are face to face with a customer. Examples are the use of questions to identify needs, presentation skills, and various types of closes. These and other tactics are discussed in Chapters 9–14.

A **strategy**, on the other hand, is a prerequisite to tactical success. If you develop the correct strategies, you are more likely to make your sales presentation to the right person, at the right time, and in a manner most likely to achieve positive results.

A selling strategy is a carefully conceived plan that is needed to accomplish a sales objective. Let's assume you are a sales representative employed by a food service distributor (wholesaler) and you call on full-service restaurants. A strategy might include careful analysis of restaurant menus prior to sales calls. Menu analysis helps you determine what products the restaurant needs to prepare the items served to customers.[13] With this information you can select the most appropriate selling tactic (method), which might be to present samples of food and beverage items the restaurant is currently not buying from you.

Strategic planning sets the stage for a value-added form of consultative selling that is more structured, more focused, and more efficient. The result is better time allocation, more precise problem solving, and a greater chance that there will be a good match between your product and the customer's needs. Andrew Parsons, director of consumer marketing for McKinsey and Company, notes that in the current selling environment salespeople must choose from a sophisticated range of alternatives. He points out in general terms that personal selling has moved from "a game of checkers to a game of chess." For many salespeople, strategic planning is not an option, but the key to survival.

Today's customer wants a quality product and a quality relationship. Salespeople who build partnering relationships are rewarded with repeat business and referrals.

Strategic/Consultative Selling Model

When you study a value-added approach to personal selling that combines strategic planning, consultative selling practices, and partnering principles, you experience a mental exercise that is similar to solving a jigsaw puzzle. You are given many pieces of information that ultimately must form a complete picture. Putting the parts together isn't nearly as difficult if you can see the total picture at the beginning. Therefore, a single model has been developed to serve as a source of reference throughout the entire text. Figure 1.5 shows this model.

Strategic/Consultative Selling Model*

Strategic step	Prescription
DEVELOP A PERSONAL SELLING PHILOSOPHY	☐ ADOPT MARKETING CONCEPT ☐ VALUE PERSONAL SELLING ☐ BECOME A PROBLEM SOLVER/PARTNER
DEVELOP A RELATIONSHIP STRATEGY	☐ ADOPT DOUBLE-WIN PHILOSOPHY ☐ PROJECT PROFESSIONAL IMAGE ☐ MAINTAIN HIGH ETHICAL STANDARDS
DEVELOP A PRODUCT STRATEGY	☐ BECOME A PRODUCT EXPERT ☐ SELL BENEFITS ☐ CONFIGURE VALUE-ADDED SOLUTIONS
DEVELOP A CUSTOMER STRATEGY	☐ UNDERSTAND BUYER BEHAVIOR ☐ DISCOVER CUSTOMER NEEDS ☐ DEVELOP PROSPECT BASE
DEVELOP A PRESENTATION STRATEGY	☐ PREPARE OBJECTIVES ☐ DEVELOP PRESENTATION PLAN ☐ PROVIDE OUTSTANDING SERVICE

*Strategic/consultative selling evolved in response to increased competition, more complex products, increased emphasis on customer needs, and growing importance of long-term relationships.

Place	Promotion
Product	Price

Figure 1.5
The Strategic/Consultative Selling Model is an extension of the marketing concept.

The Strategic/Consultative Selling Model features five steps, and each step is based on three prescriptions. The first step involves the development of a personal selling philosophy. Each of the other steps relates to a broad strategic area of personal selling. Each makes an important and unique contribution to the selling/buying process. A brief introduction to each strategic area follows.

DEVELOPING A RELATIONSHIP STRATEGY

Success in selling depends heavily on the salesperson's ability to develop, manage, and enhance interpersonal relations with the customer. People seldom buy products or services from someone they dislike or distrust. Harvey B. Mackay, chief executive officer of Mackay Envelope Corporation, says, "People don't care how much you know until they know how much you care." Most customers are more apt to openly discuss their needs and wants with a salesperson with whom they feel comfortable.

A **relationship strategy** is a well-thought-out plan for establishing, building, and maintaining quality relationships. This type of plan is essential for success in today's marketplace, which is characterized by vigorous competition, look-alike products, and customer loyalty dependent on quality relationships as well as quality products. The relationship strategy must encompass every aspect of selling from the first contact with a prospect to servicing the sale once this prospect becomes an established customer. The primary goal of the relationship strategy is to create rapport, trust, and mutual respect, which ensures a long-term partnership. To establish this type of relationship, salespeople must adopt a double-win philosophy, that is, if the customer wins, I win; project a professional image; and maintain high ethical standards (see Fig. 1.5). These topics are discussed in detail in Chapters 3 and 4.

Some people think that the concept of *relationships* is too soft and too emotional for a business application; these people think that it's too difficult to think about relationships in strategic terms. In fact, this is not the case at all. Every salesperson can and should formulate a strategic plan that builds and enhances relationships.

DEVELOPING A PRODUCT STRATEGY

Products and services represent problem-solving tools. The **product strategy** is a plan that helps salespeople make correct decisions concerning the selection and positioning of products to meet identified customer needs. The development of a product strategy begins with a thorough study of one's product (see Fig. 1.5) using a feature–benefit analysis approach. Product features such as technical superiority, reliability, fashionableness, design integrity, or guaranteed availability should be converted to benefits that appeal to the customer. Today's high-performance salespeople strive to become product experts. Chapter 5 focuses on company, product, and competition knowledge needed by salespeople.

A well-conceived product strategy for the information age also requires that decisions be made concerning product positioning. The positioning of a product refers to the decisions, activities, and communications that establish and maintain a firm's intended product concept in the customer's mind. The goal of salespeople at a Lexus dealership, for example, is to create the perception that their automobiles are the best in the high-performance luxury category and the company stands behind its products with an excellent customer service program. The brokers at Paine Webber Incorporated strive to create the perception that they are well-informed consultants and that the company is able to service its accounts to maximize customer satisfaction. The positioning of products and other product-related sales strategies is the major focus of Chapter 6.

The development of a product strategy often requires thoughtful decision making. Today's more knowledgeable customers seek a cluster of satisfactions that arise from the product itself, from the manufacturer or distributor of the product, and from the salesper-

>> Building Quality Partnerships

Adding Value in Commodity Sales

We use the term **commodity** to describe products that are nearly identical or appear to be the same in the customer's mind. A good example of a commodity is the standard business envelope. There are over 200 envelope companies selling basically the same product. Mutual funds have become a modern day commodity. Investors can choose from several hundred different funds that have basic similarities.

Commodities are often sold by marketers who have adopted a transactional selling strategy. A common way to increase market share in a competitive commodity industry, and thus escape a transactional sale, is to use a form of personal selling that adds value to look-alike products. This can be accomplished by creating a truly distinctive offering, either by product innovation or by developing truly distinctive services that appeal to customers. Dennis Courtney, chief information officer of Dunlop Tire Corporation, offers this advice on how to add value to commodity sales:

The products that a supplier offers are only a small part of the equation. Generally we could get what we need from several places, so it's not unique. What we're looking for goes beyond the product. We're looking for business understanding, we're looking for whether they can adapt to our special needs or whether they can advise and help us. We want their salespeople to add something worthwhile on their own account.

As Courtney notes, salespeople are in a position to add value to commodities. For example, a salesperson that is viewed as a trusted advisor, capable of giving prompt and dependable service, can give a product a measure of uniqueness in the eyes of the customer. When customers face increasing choices, and feel overwhelmed by information overload, they value the assistance of a well-informed salesperson. Knowledge can add value.[a]

son. The "new" product that customers are buying today is the sum total of the satisfactions that emerge from all three sources. The cluster of satisfactions concept is discussed in more detail in Chapter 6. The three prescriptions for the product strategy are become a product expert, sell benefits, and configure value added solutions.

DEVELOPING A CUSTOMER STRATEGY

Customers have become increasingly sophisticated in their buying strategies. More and more, they have come to expect value-added products and services and long-term commitments.[14] Selling to today's customers starts with getting on the customers' agenda and carefully identifying their needs, wants, and buying conditions.

A **customer strategy** is a carefully conceived plan that results in maximum responsiveness to the customer's needs. This strategy is based on the fact that success in personal selling depends, in no small measure, on the salesperson's ability to learn as much as possible about the prospect.[15] It involves the collection and analysis of specific information on each customer. When developing a customer strategy, the salesperson should develop a broad understanding of buying behaviors, discover individual customer needs, and build a strong prospect base (see Fig. 1.5). The first two parts of the customer strategy are introduced in Chapter 7. Suggestions concerning ways to build a solid prospect base are discussed in Chapter 8.

Many of the most progressive companies in the United States have well-established customer strategies. Baxter Healthcare, a company based in Deerfield, Illinois, provides a good example of a marketer who has adopted a unique customer strategy.

Baxter's salespeople are encouraged to continuously collect information from those who use their products, or prospective customers in the medical field, and then use this information to refine existing products or develop new products (Fig. 1.6). The collection and analysis of information results in better management of orders and deliveries. Baxter is helping many hospitals make progress toward just-in-time supply management.[16]

DEVELOPING A PRESENTATION STRATEGY

Typical salespeople spend about 30 percent of their time in actual face-to-face selling situations. However, the sales presentation is a critical part of the selling process. The **presentation strategy** is a well-developed plan that includes preparing the sales presentation objectives, preparing a presentation plan that is needed to meet these objectives, and renewing one's commitment to provide outstanding customer service (see Fig. 1.5).

The presentation strategy usually involves developing one or more objectives for each sales call. For example, a salesperson might update personal information about the customer, provide information on a new product, and close a sale during one sales call. Multiple-objective sales presentations, which are becoming more common, are discussed in Chapter 9.

Presale presentation plans give salespeople the opportunity to consider those activities that take place during the sales presentation. For example, a salesperson might preplan a demonstration of product features to use when meeting with the customer. Presale planning ensures that salespeople are well organized during the sales presentation and prepared to offer outstanding service.

INTERRELATIONSHIP OF BASIC STRATEGIES

The major strategies that form the Strategic/Consultative Selling Model are by no means independent. The relationship, product, and customer strategies all influence development of the presentation strategy (Fig. 1.7). For example, one relationship-building practice might be developed for use during the initial face-to-face meeting with the customer and another for possible use during the negotiation of buyer resistance. Another relationship-building method might be developed for use after the sale is closed. The discovery of customer needs (part of the customer strategy) greatly influences planning for the sales presentation.

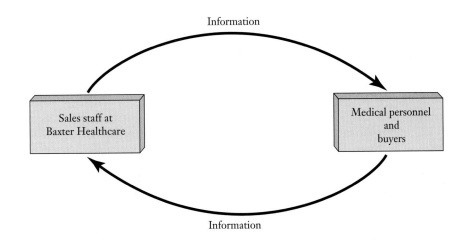

Figure **1.6**
Baxter's customer strategy loop illustrates how salespeople obtain information on ways to better serve their customers.

Figure 1.7
The major strategies that
form the Strategic/
Consultative Selling Model
are by no means indepen-
dent of one another. The
focus of each strategy is to
satisfy customer needs and
build quality partnerships.

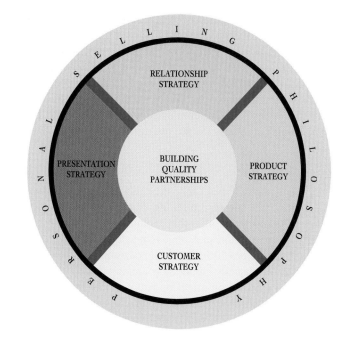

Electronic Commerce and the Complex Sale

Electronic commerce is a modern methodology that addresses the use of information technology as an essential business enabler.[17] Most organizations involved in sales and marketing use electronic commerce to support external business activities, such as personal selling, and internal activities, such as customer service. A complex sale will almost always require the use of several forms of information technology to gather and distribute information to customers. These tools, described in selected chapters, include electronic product catalogs, product configurators, and sales proposal writers (Chapter 5), contact management systems (see ACT! references throughout the book), Power Point and Excel spreadsheet software (Chapter 11), Internet applications (references throughout the book), and electronic mapping software (Chapter 15).

Electronic commerce, in its many forms, promises to enhance strategic selling in the years ahead. A recent survey conducted by *Sales & Marketing Management* magazine reports that 85 percent of the respondents regard electronic commerce strategies as vital to their marketing and sales success.[18]

EVOLUTION OF PARTNERING

In the early 1990s, we witnessed the demise of the product solution in many major industries. A growing number of customers began buying relationships, not products. This trend is the result of a situation where the products of one company in an industry are becoming nearly identical to those of the competition. When a given industry (service, retail, whole-sale, or manufacturing) is dominated by look-alike products, the product strategy becomes less important than the relationship strategy.

The term **relationship selling**, popularized over the past several years, recognizes the growing importance of relationships in selling. Salespeople who have adopted relationship selling work hard to build and nourish long-term partnerships. They rely on a personal, customized approach to each customer.[19] This approach stands in stark contrast to the more traditional *transaction-oriented* selling.

Today's customer wants a quality product *and* a quality relationship. Salespeople willing to abandon short-term thinking and invest the time and energy needed to develop a high-quality, long-term relationship with customers are greatly rewarded. A strong partnership serves as a barrier to competing salespeople who want to sell to your accounts. Salespeople who are able to build partnerships enjoy more repeat business and referrals. Keeping existing customers happy makes a great deal of sense from an economic point of view. Experts in the field of sales and marketing know that it costs four to five times more to get a new customer than to keep an existing one. Therefore, even small increases in customer retention can result in major increases in profits.[20]

Partnering is a strategically developed, long-term relationship that solves the customer's problems. A successful long-term partnership is achieved when the salesperson is able to skillfully apply the four major strategies and thus add value in various ways (Fig. 1.8). Successful sales professionals stay close to the customer and constantly search for new ways to add value. The salespeople at Mackay Envelope Corporation achieve this goal by making sure they know more about their customers than the competitors know. Salespeople who work for Xerox Corporation are responding to a sales orientation that emphasizes postsale service. Bonuses are based on a formula that includes not only sales but also customer satisfaction.

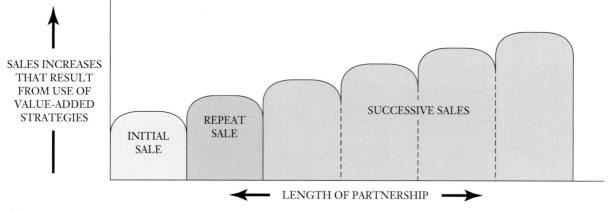

Figure 1.8
Partnering is a strategically developed, long-term relationship that solves the customer's problems. A successful partnering effort results in repeat sales and referrals that expand the prospect base. The strength of the partnership increases each time the salesperson uses value-added selling strategies.

Partnering Is Enhanced with High Ethical Standards

In the field of selling there are certain pressures that can influence the ethical conduct of salespeople, and poor ethical decisions can weaken or destroy partnerships. To illustrate, let us assume a competitor makes exaggerated claims about a product. Do you counteract by promising more than your product can deliver? What action do you take when there is a time management problem and you must choose between servicing past sales and making new sales? What if a superior urges you to use a strategy that you consider unethical? These and other pressures must be dealt with every day.

Although pressures exist in every selling position, most salespeople are able to draw the line between ethical and unethical behavior. This is especially true of those who have taken a long-range view of sales work that emphasizes building partnerships. These people know that the best way to ensure repeat business is to deal honestly and fairly with every customer. Most customers today are reaching out for a partner they can trust.

►► CUSTOMER RELATIONSHIP MANAGEMENT (CRM) WITH TECHNOLOGY

INTRODUCING CRM

Today, many sales professionals use computers to help them better perform the tasks associated with successful personal selling. Various software programs are used, including e-mail, electronic spreadsheets, word processors, configuration systems, presentation packages, fax managers, and customer relationship management (CRM) systems. A basic CRM system consists of a database containing information about the people with whom a salesperson maintains relationships, such as customers, prospects, co-workers, and suppliers. For your use with the CRM studies in this text, a basic Windows-based CRM system is available for you to download at *www.prenhall.com/manningreece.* You can learn the fundamentals of CRM with this software, including searching for customer and product-related information, managing time and priorities, communicating, forecasting sales, and estimating your commissions. (See the exercise, Downloading CRM, on p. 24 for more information on the Windows-based CRM system and its fundamentals.)

Although Chapter 4 is devoted entirely to ethical considerations in personal selling, it should be noted that ethics is a major theme of the text. The topic of ethics has been interwoven throughout several chapters. The authors believe that ethical decisions must be made every day in the life of a salesperson, so this important topic cannot be covered in a single chapter.

Partnering Is Enhanced with Sales Automation

Many companies are using some form of sales automation to enhance partnerships with customers. **Sales automation** is the term used to describe those technologies used to improve communications in a sales organization and to enhance customer responsiveness. Improvements in sales automation reflect the changes taking place in the age of information. New technologies are needed to process the massive amounts of information available to salespeople. New technologies also help salespeople stay connected to customers, sales support personnel, and other key people.

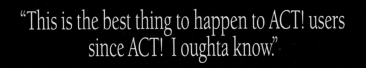

"This is the best thing to happen to ACT! users since ACT! I oughta know."

"For the three million of you who rely on ACT! to keep your professional lives in order, the history of contact management began the day ACT! arrived on the market.

On that day, the PC changed from a thing you reluctantly learned to live with into something you couldn't live without.

Well, if you think that was neat, wait'll you see what we've got in store for you now that ACT! has joined the SalesLogix™ family.

The world's favorite contact manager is now Internet Activated.

Through the magic of Interact.com, ACT! can be dynamically linked to an astonishing array of Web-based services designed to get you more sales with less work.

And what, you ask, does

As co-founder of the company that originally developed and marketed ACT!, Pat Sullivan created the contact management category. Today he's creating a whole new way of selling as President/CEO of SalesLogix Corp., the world's fastest-growing front office and e-commerce software company – and the new publisher of ACT!

ACT NOW!
YOU COULD BE A BIG WINNER!

Visit Interact.com to check out the new Internet Activated ACT! Thousands of dollars worth of great prizes are being awarded daily, so don't miss out! Or call us at 888-655-5791.

'dynamically linked' mean?

It means that stuff you do in ACT! – like entering contact information or scheduling appointments – triggers powerful Internet commerce services that you can use *without ever leaving ACT!*

How'd you like to view everything on the Web that's relevant to that account you've got on your screen right now? Company and category news? Credit history? How about the stock price?

You got it. Want to book a trip to see that account? Flights? Hotels? How about a rental car?

It's done. Want to buy leads that fit your criteria? Generate automatic e-marketing campaigns?

You can do it all – and much more – right from your favorite place.

I know. You could get used to this."

©2000 SalesLogix Corporation. ACT! and SalesLogix are registered trademarks of SalesLogix Corporation. No purchase necessary. Please see Interact.com for contest rules.

The ACT! contact management program has been improved with a new technology called Internet Activated. This new technology, available to the three million ACT! users, links the salesperson to an array of Web-based services.

STRATEGIC ALLIANCES — THE HIGHEST FORM OF PARTNERING

Throughout the past decade we have seen the growth of a new form of partnership that often is described as a **strategic alliance**. The goal of strategic alliances is to achieve a marketplace advantage by teaming up with another company whose products or services fit well with your own.[21] Alliances often are formed by companies that have similar business interests and thus gain a mutual competitive advantage. It is not uncommon for a company to form several alliances. Corning, a maker of glass products, has formed partnerships with several companies that need innovative glass technology. For example, Corning formed an alliance with Samsung, a Korean manufacturer of television screens. Digital Equipment Corporation has partnered with several small companies that have been able to deliver technological breakthroughs. Rosabeth Moss Kanter, Harvard Business School professor says that "do-it-together" is the next great growth strategy.

Strategic alliances have created a new selling environment. The first step in building an alliance is to learn as much as possible about the proposed partner. This study takes place long before face-to-face contact. The second step is to meet with the proposed partner and explore mutual benefits of the alliance. At this point the salesperson (or account manager) is selling advice, assistance, and counsel, not specific products.[22] Strong interpersonal and communication skills are needed to build an alliance that has long-term benefits to both partners. Building win–win partnerships requires the highest form of consultative selling. Very often, the salesperson is working with a company team made up of persons from such areas as research and development (R&D), finance, and distribution. Presentations and proposals usually focus on profit impact and other strategic account benefits.

Summary

As the global economy has shifted from one of excess demand to one of excess supply, competition has increased, both from organizations within the United States and from those in foreign countries. Vigorous sales promotion, including personal selling, are key factors in stimulating global demand for products.

Personal selling is the process of developing customer relationships; discovering customer needs; matching the appropriate products with those needs; and communicating benefits through informing, reminding, or persuading. (A *product* can be information, a service, an idea, an issue, or an item.) The *marketing concept* is the belief that a firm should dedicate all its policies, planning, and operation to the satisfaction of the customer. The marketing concept has grown in popularity throughout the age of information.

The *marketing era* that began in the United States in the 1950s looked first at customer needs and wants, and then created goods and services to meet those needs and wants. (During the industrial age, the emphasis first was on creating products and then on building customer interest in those products.) *Consultative selling* emerged in the late 1960s and early 1970s as an approach that emphasizes identification of customer needs through effective communication between the salesperson and the customer. *Strategic selling* evolved in the 1980s and involves the preparation of a carefully conceived plan to accomplish sales objectives. In the 1990s, the development of *partnership selling* involves providing customers with a quality product *and* a quality, long-term relationship.

Strategic selling is based on a company's *strategic market plan*, which takes into consideration the coordination of all the major functional areas of the business—production, marketing, finance, and personnel. The four broad strategic areas in the strategic/consultative selling model (after development of a personal selling philosophy) are developing a relationship strategy, developing a product strategy, developing a customer strategy, and developing a presentation strategy.

Partnering is the creation of long-term relationships with customers, which requires salespeople to continuously search for ways to add value to their selling relationships. The quality improvement process reinforces partnering through the firm's search for ways to provide a higher quality, lower cost product, and the salesperson's attempt to continuously improve the quality of customer service.

Ethical considerations are particularly important in the field of personal selling because the salesperson represents his company to the buyer. The salesperson may encounter pressures to "bend" principles of honesty or straight-forwardness, so it is necessary to consider and develop ethical principles that serve as the guidelines for one's entire career.

KEY TERMS

Personal Selling
Product
Personal Selling Philosophy
Marketing Concept
Marketing Mix
Consultative Selling
Transactional Selling
Strategic Market Plan
Tactics
Strategy

Relationship Strategy
Product Strategy
Customer Strategy
Commodity
Presentation Strategy
Electronic Commerce
Relationship Selling
Partnering
Sales Automation
Strategic Alliance

REVIEW QUESTIONS

1. Explain how personal selling can help solve the problem of information overload.
2. According to the Strategic/Consultative Selling Model (see Fig. 1.2), what are the three prescriptions for developing a successful personal selling philosophy?
3. Why is peddling or "pushing products" inconsistent with the marketing concept?
4. What is consultative selling? Give examples.
5. Diagram and label the four-step Consultative Sales Presentation Guide.
6. List and briefly explain the four broad strategic areas that make up the selling process.
7. Briefly describe the evolution of partnering. Discuss the forces that contributed to this approach to selling.
8. Read the Building Quality Partnerships boxed insight on page 16 and then discuss ways to add value when selling a commodity.
9. Briefly describe why some organizations are developing strategic alliances.
10. Explain why the ethical conduct of salespeople has become so important today.

APPLICATION EXERCISES

1. Assume that you are an experienced professional salesperson. A professor who teaches at a nearby university has asked you to speak to a consumer economics class about the social and economic benefits of personal selling. Make an outline of what to say.

2. A friend of yours has invented a unique and useful new product. This friend, an engineer by profession, understands little about marketing and selling this new product. She does understand, however, that "nothing happens until somebody sells the product." She has asked you to describe the general factors that need to be considered when you market a product. Prepare an answer to her question.

3. Sharon Alverez has been teaching college biology courses. She is offered a position selling pharmaceutical products. This position requires that she call on doctors and pharmacists to explain her product line. Describe the similarities and the differences between her two positions.

4. To learn more about an industry-based sales training program, access *www.wilson-learning.com.* Click on the "Sales Effectiveness" link and examine the content of the various sales courses offered.

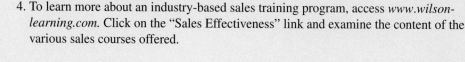

CRM APPLICATION EXERCISE

Downloading CRM Software

The CRM system that is available for you to download is a demonstration version of the best selling software called ACT!. This version of ACT! includes a database of information about prospective customers for a company selling network systems. In the case study and exercises ahead, you assume the role of a salesperson who is selling these network systems. The emphasis in these exercises is customer relationship management. No prior experience or prior knowledge of networking systems is required to complete these exercises. To download this software, enter *www.prenhall.com/manningreece* into your browser and follow the instructions found on that page.

ACT! is a database program, which means that it uses records and fields. Records are the screens that contain information about each person. Fields are the boxes on the records for entering and displaying data, such as the name of the person (e.g., Bradley Able). ACT! also is known as a contact management program because it maintains a record for each contact (person). Some CRM systems offer a separate record for each organization.

You can experiment with ACT! without concern about damaging the program. If you inadvertently delete information in the database, you can simply download the software again. To get acquainted with the ACT! version of CRM, click on the various menu items and icons and observe the functions that are available to you. Experimenting with this software gives you a feel for the potential power of using technology to enhance your sales career. Test ACT!'s report capabilities by printing a phone list: Select Report and Phone; in the Prepare Report box, choose Active Group, and Printer; then print the list.

As you experiment with ACT!, you can obtain help at any time by pressing the F1 function key. (See the exercise, Learning CRM Software, at p. 45 for more information.)

VIDEO CASE PROBLEM

This chapter opens with an introduction to Body Glove International (bodyglove.com), a global company that manufactures a quality line of wet suits for persons who like water sports. Many of the consumers who are involved in water skiing, scuba diving, surfing, or jet skiing purchase Body Glove products because they represent both quality and value. The company was started in 1953 by Bill and Randy Meistrell, two persons who shared a passion for surfing and diving. The first suits were custom made for customers who responded to ads placed in local publications. As sales increased the Meistrell brothers developed a small manufacturing facility and began distributing their products through retail stores on the West Coast. Soon Body Glove became a national company and later an international company. The success of Body Glove can be traced to several factors:

- A company philosophy that is based on the belief that you never sacrifice quality. A product that is comfortable and well made attracts the customer who is willing to spend a little more to get the best product. The company used to manufacture its own products, but now it outsources all manufacturing. These companies must maintain high-quality standards established by Body Glove.

- A belief that brand management is very important. Today Body Glove International is placing more emphasis on brand management. The company wants to influence the perception of Body Glove products in the minds of customers. Company officials recognize that in a world of sensory overload caused by too much information, brands are more important than ever. Customers think about what matters to them, analyze their choices, and usually select a brand that meets their needs.

- Innovations in sales and marketing strategies that enhance product distribution and sales. Body Glove International has developed over 30 partnerships with distributors. These distributors (called marketing intermediaries) employ salespeople who call on retail stores. At the present time distributors employ about 250 salespeople. The company now has a stronger global sales organization with special emphasis on South America, New Zealand, and Australia.

- Investment in a first-class customer service center. The people at Body Glove believe that excellent customer service adds value to the product. Celeste Barouty, national sales manager for the Wet Suit Division, makes sure that all orders are carefully processed. With the aid of modern computers, Celeste can check on the status of any order. She and her staff also can process special orders quickly. The customer service staff works hard to build the strongest possible partnership with the customer.

Questions

1. Does it appear that the management team at Body Glove International and members of the sales force have adopted the three prescriptions of a personal selling philosophy? (See Strategic/Consultative Selling Model.) Explain your answer.

2. What prescriptions of the relationship strategy (see Strategic/Consultative Selling Model) have been adopted by Body Glove International? How does this strategy contribute to the company's long-term success?

3. The company officers have made a decision to develop partnerships with a group of distributors. These distributors will employ salespeople to call on retailers who sell Body Glove products. What steps can Body Glove take to ensure that retailers and retail customers receive excellent service? Do you think this was a good decision? Explain.

4. Body Glove International is currently placing a great deal of emphasis on brand management. What role can salespeople play in building brand identification and brand acceptance?

PARTNERSHIP SELLING: A ROLE PLAY/SIMULATION
(see Appendix 3, p. 406)

[If your instructor has chosen to use the *Partnering Role Play/ Simulation* exercise that accompanies this text, these boxes alert you to your *Role Play/Simulation* assignments. Your instructor will also provide you with needed information.]

Preview the role play/simulation materials in Appendix 3. These materials are produced by the Park Inn International Hotel and Convention Center, and you will be using them in your role as a new salesperson (and, at times, as the customer) for the hotel and its convention services.

The role play exercises begin in Chapter 5, as you begin to create your product strategy. However, in anticipation of the role play, you can begin to imagine yourself in the role of an actual salesperson. Start to think about how you can develop your personal selling philosophy. What are some ethical guidelines that you may wish to adopt for yourself? (Ethics is also the subject of Chapter 4, Ethics—The Foundation for Relationships in Selling.) What skills do you need to develop to become a partner with your prospective customers? (Refer to the position description on page 414.)

The Park Inn has implemented a Quality Improvement process. How does this affect your role as a sales representative? (Refer to the Total Quality Customer Service Glossary on page 415.)

Personal Selling Opportunities in the Age of Information

When you finish reading this chapter, you should be able to

1. Describe how personal selling skills contribute to work performed by knowledge workers

2. Discuss the rewarding aspects of personal selling careers

3. Describe the opportunities for women and minorities in the field of personal selling

4. Discuss the characteristics of selling positions in four major employment settings: service, retailing, wholesaling, and manufacturing

5. Identify the four major sources of sales training

*P*ersonal selling attracts people from many different professions. Todd Natenberg prepared for a career in journalism and worked as a newspaper reporter for the Arizona Republic. Today he is an account representative for LCI International, a telecommunications company located in Rosemont, Illinois. Natenberg has discovered that many of the communication skills he learned in journalism classes have application in personal selling. As a reporter, he found that people would not talk to him openly unless they trusted him. Building trust in no less important in his sales work.[1]

For many years Catherine Leonard was a teacher helping students. Today she is a salesperson helping customers. The decision to make a career transition began when she was working on a graduate degree in apparel merchandising. She began to question whether a college teaching career would provide the financial stability and job security she desired. Soon after completing her Ph.D. she obtained a sales position with Freudenberg Nonwovens, a textile supplier serving such customers as Levi Strauss and Liz Claiborne. She pursued a sales career with Freudenberg because the company rewards professional development and integrity.[2]

Personal selling skills are no less important in the life of Bob Nelson, co-founder, chairman, and CEO of CrossMedia Networks Corporation in McLean, Virginia. For over two years this entrepreneur has struggled to build a profitable company based on a simple idea: Give people a way to listen to e-mail over the telephone. He and Bill Livingston, a speech–technology expert, founded CrossMedia in the basement of Mr. Nelson's rented

Successful knowledge workers understand Stanley Marcus' views that "sooner or later in business, everybody has to sell something to somebody."

Washington, D.C., home. To finance the new company he has had to sell his idea to many potential investors. To launch his dream, he needs to sell his service to customers. Every day Nelson uses his personal selling skills to keep his dream alive.[3]

PERSONAL SELLING OPPORTUNITIES IN THE AGE OF INFORMATION

Stanley Marcus, Chairman Emeritus of the prestigious Neiman Marcus retail company, said, "Sooner or later in business, everybody has to sell something to somebody." He noted that even if you are not in sales, you must know how to sell a product, a service, an idea, or yourself.[4] Marcus's views have garnered a great deal of support among observers of the information age. Today's workforce is made up of millions of knowledge workers who succeed only when they add value to information. The new economy is about the growing value of knowledge, making it the most important ingredient of what people buy and sell.[5] One way to add value to information is to collect it, organize it, clarify it, and present it in a convincing manner. This skill, used everyday by professional salespeople, is invaluable in a world that is overloaded with information.

As noted in Chapter 1, relationships began to become more important at the beginning of the information age. In many cases, information does not have value unless people interact effectively. Bob Nelson possesses information concerning an important new technology, but that information has no value until it is communicated effectively to an investor, a customer, or someone else who can benefit from knowing more about his product. A bank loan officer may have the resources needed to assist Nelson reach his dream, but in the absence of a good relationship, communications may break down. John Naisbitt was right on target when he noted that in the information age, ". . . the game is people interacting with other people."[6]

Today personal selling skills contribute in a major way to four groups of knowledge workers who usually do not consider themselves salespeople:

- Customer service representatives
- Professionals (accountants, consultants, lawyers, etc.)
- Entrepreneurs
- Managerial personnel

According to John Naisbitt, well known author of MEGATRENDS and MEGATRENDS 2000 "the game of life in the information age is people interacting with other people." Today's personal selling skills contribute to successfully interacting with people in business.

Customer Service Representatives

The assignment of selling duties to employees with customer service responsibilities has become quite common today. The term **customer service representative** (CSR) is used to describe people who process reservations, accept orders by phone or other means, deliver products, handle customer complaints, provide technical assistance, and assist full-time sales representatives. Some companies are teaming CSRs and salespeople. After the sale is closed, the CSR helps process paperwork, check on delivery of the product, and engage in other customer follow-up duties. Some examples of companies that are moving customer service representatives into the proactive role of selling follow:

Item: Nick Nicholson, CEO of Ecology Group, a $40 million recycling and waste-management company in Columbus, Ohio, believes that each of his employees should possess selling skills. All his staff members receive sales training. To illustrate how sales training makes a difference, he points to a member of his accounting staff who received a call from a customer concerning an overbilling problem. In the process of clarifying the problem, the staff member identified an opportunity to expand the Ecology Group's agreement with the client. This involved extending service to more locations.[7]

Item: Western Kansas Xpress (WKX), a highly successful freight company based in Wichita, Kansas, encourages all its drivers to carry business cards to distribute to potential customers. Every employee is expected to discover needs and sell WKX services.[8]

Item: Tampa-based Fort Brooke Bank discovered that tellers had many opportunities to sell the bank's services. Seventeen tellers attended a series of selling seminars where they learned how to identify customer needs and suggest specific bank services. The selling strategy has been successful at this community bank.[9]

Assigning sales duties to customer service representatives makes sense when you consider the number of contacts customers have with CSRs. When a customer seeks assistance with a problem or makes a reservation, the CSR learns more about the customer and often provides the customer with needed information. Customer needs often surface as both parties exchange information. It is important to keep in mind advice offered by the authors of *Selling the Invisible*: "Every act is a marketing act. Make every employee a marketing person."[10]

Professionals

Today's professional workers include lawyers, designers, programmers, engineers, consultants, dietitians, counselors, doctors, accountants, and many other specialized knowledge workers. Our labor force includes nearly 20 million professional service providers, persons who need many of the skills used by professional salespeople. Clients who purchase professional services are usually more interested in the person who delivers the service than in the firm that employs the professional. They seek expert diagnosticians who are truly interested in their needs. The professional must display good communication skills and be able to build a relationship built on trust.

Technical skills are not enough in the information age. Many employers expect the professional to bring in new business in addition to keeping current customers satisfied.[11] Employers often screen professional applicants to determine their customer focus and ability to interact well with people.

Many firms are providing their professional staff with sales training. The accounting firm Ernst & Young sets aside several days each year to train its professional staff in personal selling. The National Law Firm Marketing Association recently featured Neil Rackham, author of *Spin Selling*, as keynote speaker at its national conference. Faced with increased competition and more cost-conscious customers, a growing number of law, accounting, engineering, and architectural firms are discovering the merits of personal selling as an auxiliary activity.[12] Providers of financial planning services, property management, landscape design, and health care services also are discovering that personal selling can be used to obtain and keep customers.

While many professional service firms are trying to train their employees to sell, others have been hiring professional salespeople to assist or team up with their service professionals. A common approach is to use a team selling approach that involves a salesperson and a service professional who has received training in the area of team selling.[13]

Entrepreneurs

About 3 million new businesses are started each year in the United States.[14] As noted previously, people who want to start a new business frequently need to sell their plan to investors and others who can help get the firm established. Once the firm is open, owners rely on personal selling to build their businesses.

James Koch, chief executive officer of the Boston Beer Company (brewer of the popular Samuel Adams beer), makes a strong case for personal selling. Like most new companies, his started with no customers. To get established, he assumed the role of salesperson and set a goal of establishing one new account each week. He recalls the ecstasy he felt when he closed his first sale:

> When I got home that evening, the vision in my head was that it's really selling that drives most businesses; the direct interface between the product and customer; the crucial feedback loop. And if more CEOs had to go out and sell their products, day in and day out, they'd pay a lot more attention to what they were making.[15]

Today, James Koch's company is very successful. Like so many other business owners he discovered that no matter how sophisticated your marketing plan, nothing really happens until somebody sells the product.

Managerial Personnel

People working in managerial occupations represent another large group of knowledge workers. They are given such titles as executive, manager, or administrator. Leaders are constantly involved in capturing, processing, and communicating information. Some of the most valuable information is acquired from customers. This helps explain the rapid growth in what is being described as "executive selling." Chief executive officers and other executives often accompany salespeople on sales calls to learn more about customer needs and in some cases to assist with presentations. Manny Fernandez of the Gartner Group, a technology consulting firm based in Stanford, Connecticut, spends more than half his time traveling on sales calls.[16] Leaders also must articulate their ideas in a persuasive manner and win support for their vision.

Increasingly, work in the information economy is understood as an expression of thought. At a time when people change their careers eight times during their lives, selling skills represent important transferable employment skills.[17]

YOUR FUTURE IN PERSONAL SELLING

According to the Bureau of Labor Statistics there are 15.7 million sales jobs in America.[18] In addition, the number of sales positions is increasing in most industrialized countries. A close examination of these positions reveals that there is no single "selling" occupation. Our labor force includes hundreds of different selling careers and chances are there are positions that match your interests, talents, and ambitions. The diversity within selling becomes apparent as you study the career options discussed in this chapter.

Although many college students ultimately become salespeople, often it's not their first career choice. Students tend to view sales as dynamic and active, but believe a selling career requires them to engage in deceitful or dishonest practices. The good news is that old stereotypes about sales are gradually going by the wayside.[19] Students who study the careers of highly successful salespeople discover that ethical sales practices represent the key to long-term success.

A professional selling position encompasses a wide range of tasks (Fig. 2.1), and therefore salespeople must possess a variety of skills. A salesperson representing Federal Express (FedEX) makes numerous sales calls each day in an attempt to establish new accounts and provide service to established accounts. There are a wide range of potential customers who can use FedEX delivery services. A salesperson working for a Caterpillar construction equipment dealer may make only two or three sales calls per day. The products offered by the dealer are expensive and are not purchased frequently.

Just as selling occupations differ, so do the titles by which salespeople are known. Their titles reflect, in part, the variety of duties they perform. A survey of current job announcements indicates that fewer and fewer companies are using the word *salesmen* to refer to the people they employ to sell their products. Instead they are using such titles as these:

Account Executive	Sales Consultant
Account Representative	Client Development Manager
Sales Account Manager	Sales Associate
Relationship Manager	Marketing Representative
District Representative	Territory Manager

Salespeople, regardless of title, play an important role in sustaining the growth and profitability of organizations of all sizes (Table 2.1). They also support the employment of many nonselling employees. One study indicates that in service and manufacturing firms, one salesperson creates enough sales revenue to pay for nine other jobs within the company.[20]

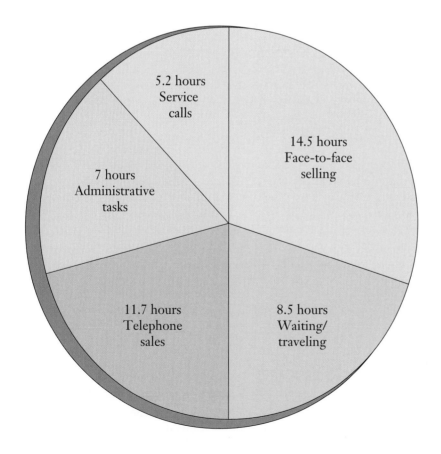

Figure 2.1
HOW SALESPEOPLE SPEND THEIR TIME DURING AN AVERAGE 46.9-HOUR WORKWEEK

(Source: *Selling,* February 1997, p. 4.)

Table 2.1	SELECTED LARGE U.S. SALES FORCES (MANUFACTURING, SERVICE, AND INSURANCE)	
COMPANY	CATEGORY	U.S. SALESPEOPLE
PepsiCo	Manufacturing	36,000
DaimlerChrysler	Manufacturing	31,280
Schlumberger	Manufacturing	24,000
Interstate Bakeries	Manufacturing	16,700
General Electric	Manufacturing	14,000
Microsoft	Manufacturing	13,547
International Paper	Manufacturing	13,225
Schering-Plough	Manufacturing	10,975
IBM	Manufacturing	10,000
Primerica	Service	150,000
TransAmerica	Service	52,600
BankAmerica	Service	30,000
Ameritech	Service	25,000
American Express	Service	22,467
A.C. Nielsen	Service	17,000
Merrill Lynch	Service	15,327
Citigroup	Service	12,685
The Hartford (IA)	Insurance	157,000
Conseco	Insurance	150,000
Aegon USA	Insurance	100,000
Life USA	Insurance	75,000
Torchmark	Insurance	49,000
Humana	Insurance	45,600

Source: "The Selling Power 500," *Selling Power*, 1999, pp. 74–92.

Rewarding Aspects of Selling Careers

Gene Fay, account manager for Avid Sports, sells digital video and software systems to professional and college baseball, basketball, football, and hockey teams in the United States and Canada. The job offers him many rewards. Not only does he sell a very innovative product that improves team play but also he gets to meet well-known sports executives he has admired for years. His most memorable sale was to Wes Unseld, the Hall of Fame basketball center who is now vice president of basketball operations for the Washington Wizards. His biggest sale to date was to the Orlando Magic, a $370,000 deal.[21]

From a personal and economic standpoint, selling can be a rewarding career. Careers in selling offer financial rewards, recognition, security, and opportunities for advancement to a degree that is unique, compared with other occupations.

ABOVE-AVERAGE INCOME

Studies dealing with incomes in the business community indicate that salespeople earn significantly higher incomes than most other workers. Some salespeople actually earn more than their sales managers and other executives within the organization. This high level of compensation (whether from base salary, bonus, or incentives) is justified for good performance. Definitions for three major sales position categories and the compensation (salary plus incentives) earned by each type of salesperson follow:

> **Entry level sales representative.** An entry level sales representative has acquired knowledge of the company's products, services, policies, and successful sales techniques. Estimated compensation range is from $36,800 to $42,800.

> **Intermediate sales representative.** An intermediate sales representative (midlevel salesperson) is a salesperson who has broad knowledge of the company's products and services and sells in a specifically assigned territory. He or she maintains contact with established customers and develops new prospects. Estimated compensation range is from $47,700 to $53,700.

> **Senior sales representative.** A senior sales representative is a salesperson at the highest nonsupervisory level of selling responsibility. He is completely familiar with the company's products, services, and policies; usually has years of experience; and is assigned to major accounts and territories. Estimated compensation range is from $65,300 to $71,300.

The amount earned by salespeople is clearly tied to their selling skill and the amount of effort put forth. Unlike many other workers, salespeople are rewarded financially when they give extra effort. This effort is often triggered by commissions, bonuses, incentives, and other rewards.

ABOVE-AVERAGE PSYCHIC INCOME

Two major psychological needs common to all people are recognition and security. **Psychic income**, which consists of factors that provide psychological rewards, help satisfy these important needs and motivates us to achieve higher levels of performance. The need for recognition has been established in numerous studies that have examined human motivation. Workers from all employment areas indicate that recognition for work well done is an important morale-building factor.

In selling, recognition occurs more frequently and with greater intensity than it does in most other occupations. Because selling contributes so visibly to the success of most business firms, the accomplishments of sales personnel seldom go unrecognized.

Most people want to achieve some measure of security in their work. Selling is one of those occupations that usually provides job security during both good and bad times. A survey of more than 1,100 human resources managers reveals that sales professionals and marketers are among the most sought after employees.[22] An increasing number of companies are reducing the size of their labor force, and this trend should continue. Workers who contribute directly to the value of the enterprise through research, product development, manufacturing, and sales are most likely to avoid these layoffs.

OPPORTUNITY FOR ADVANCEMENT

Each year, thousands of openings appear in the ranks of supervision and management. Because salespeople work in positions of high visibility, they are in an excellent position to be chosen for advancement to positions of greater responsibility. The presidents of many of today's companies began their marketing careers in the ranks of the sales force.

Of course, not all salespeople can become presidents of large corporations, but in the middle-management ranks there are numerous interesting and high-paying positions in which experience in selling is a prime requisite for advancement. Information on careers in sales management are presented in Chapter 17.

Opportunities for Women

Opportunities for minorities exist in a variety of selling careers.

Prodded by a growing awareness that gender is not a barrier to success in selling, business firms are recruiting qualified women in growing numbers. The percentage of women in the sales force has increased considerably. Although women are still relative newcomers to industrial sales, they have enjoyed expanded career opportunities in such areas as real estate, insurance, advertising services, investments, and travel services. A growing number of women are turning to sales employment because it offers excellent economic rewards and in many cases a flexible work schedule. Flexible schedules are very appealing to women who want to balance career and family.

Opportunities for Minorities

From a historical perspective, the field of selling has not provided equal opportunity to minorities. In the past it was not easy for a member of a minority group to obtain a sales position. Today the picture has changed, and more firms are actively recruiting employees from minority groups. Although state and federal equal opportunity legislation can be credited, in part, for bringing about changes in hiring practices, many firms now view the recruitment and training of minority employees as simply good business. Minority salespeople have become top producers in many organizations.

In recent years, several trade journal reports have highlighted the under representation of minority employees in sales. Many companies recognize that shifting population demographics require a reexamination of hiring practices. The biggest population gains have

▶▶ *Building Relationships in a Diverse World*

OPPORTUNITIES FOR WOMEN IN SALES

In a world that is beginning to value diversity we are seeing growing opportunities for women in sales. However, some misinformation concerning women in sales still exists. Four common myths follow:

Myth: Women will not relocate or stick around long enough to repay the firm's hiring and training expenses. Today, working women make up nearly half of the workforce and they have made significant gains in a wide range of traditionally male-dominated areas. About 50 percent of the working women contribute more than half of their family's income. Most of the women in this group need to work, want to work, and seek rewarding career opportunities.

Myth: Women earn significantly less in sales than their male counterparts. Although a pay gap between men and women exists in the field of sales, it is relatively small compared with the earnings gap for women who work full-time in the workforce as a whole.

Myth: Buyers are less accepting of female salespeople. In the field of personal selling perceived expertise, likability, and trustworthiness can have a major influence on purchase decisions. Women who project these qualities seldom face rejection based on gender.

Myth: Women face special problems when assigned to selling positions in foreign countries. The truth is, recent research suggests that businesswomen often enjoy a significant edge over their male counterparts when given overseas assignments.[a]

Diane Elder, sales representative for the Hotel Roanoke and Conference Center, loves her work and loves her family. As a telecommuter, she can achieve her sales goals and still spend quality time everyday with her children. "All my life I wanted to be the one to take my kids to school and pick them up," says Diane. Supported by modern technology, she is able to keep in touch with the hotel staff and her customers. With the flip of a switch she can check her two electronic mailboxes, review any new voice-mail messages on her telephone, and log into the hotel's automated booking network. Prior to becoming a telecommuter, Diane worked out of an office at the hotel. Since moving into her home office, she has reduced her commute from an hour to 30 seconds, and she no longer struggles with "guilty mom syndrome."

been made by women, minorities, and immigrants. Many companies realize the need for a diverse sales force that can gain access to the diverse clientele that make up certain market segments.[23] This philosophical shift should open doors for our growing population of minorities.

EMPLOYMENT SETTINGS IN SELLING TODAY

Careers in the field of selling may be classified in several ways. One of the broadest differentiations is based on whether the product is a tangible or an intangible. Tangibles are physical goods such as furniture, homes, and data processing equipment. Intangibles are nonphysical products or services such as stocks and bonds, insurance, and consulting services. This chapter classifies selling careers according to employer. We explore the following four major employment settings and identify some of the unique characteristics of each:

Selling a service

Selling for a retailer

Selling for a wholesaler

Selling for a manufacturer

Selling a Service

What do Ernst & Young, AT&T, Radisson Hotels, Mayflower Transit, and Manpower have in common? Each of these companies is selling services. In recent years the number of consumer and business dollars spent on services in our society has steadily increased. Nearly 80 percent of the U.S. labor force is now employed in the service sector. Customers feel the need for assistance from a knowledgeable salesperson when making purchases in such areas as insurance, real estate, vacation planning, business security, and advertising.

Brian Stutzman is typical of the many salespeople who sell services. As an account executive for Lucent Technologies, he sells telecommunications services to organizations. He recently sold an $800,000 telephone system to the Colorado Springs public schools. After a careful study of the school district's communication needs, he recommended a system that was custom designed to meet the schools needs.[24]

We will look briefly at some of the career opportunities in the service field.

FINANCIAL SERVICES

At the present time there are over 1 million sales jobs in the securities and financial services field, and employment is expected to increase at least 35 percent by the year 2005.[25] Banks, brokerage firms, and other businesses are branching out, selling a broader range of financial planning and investment services.

RADIO AND TELEVISION

Revenue from advertising supports the radio and television broadcasting industry. Every station must employ a force of salespeople whose job is to call on current and prospective advertisers. Each client's needs are unique, and meeting them makes the work of a media sales representative interesting. Additionally, there is a creative side to media sales, for members of the sales staff often help develop commercials.

NEWSPAPER ADVERTISING

There are several thousand daily and weekly newspapers in this country. Each newspaper is supported by both local and national advertisers and must sell advertising space to stay in business. Many business firms rely heavily on media sales personnel for help in developing effective advertising campaigns.

HOTEL, MOTEL, AND CONVENTION CENTER SERVICES

Each year, thousands of seminars, conferences, and business meetings are held throughout the United States. Most of these events are hosted by hotels, motels, or convention centers. By diversifying their markets and upscaling their services these marketers are catering to

Hotel, Motel, and Convention Center salespeople play a key role in attracting meetings. They are often rewarded with repeat business and referrals.

business clients in many new and exciting ways. The salespeople employed by these firms play an important role in attracting meetings. They sell room space, food, beverages, and other services needed for a successful meeting. (See the job description of a Convention Center Salesperson on p. 414 of Appendix 3.)

REAL ESTATE

Buying a home is a monumental undertaking. It is usually the single largest expenditure in the average consumer's lifetime. The purchase of commercial property by individual investors or business firms also is a major economic decision. Therefore, the people who sell real estate assume an important responsibility. Busy real estate salespeople often hire assistants who help hold open houses or perform other duties.

INSURANCE

Selling insurance always has been one of the most rewarding careers in sales. Common forms of insurance sold include fire, liability, life, health, automobile, casualty, and home-owners. There are two broad groups of insurance salespeople. One group is employed by major companies such as Allstate, Prudential, Travelers, State Farm, and Mutual of Omaha. The second group is made up of independent insurance agents who serve as representatives for a number of various companies. The typical independent agency offers a broad line of personal and business insurance services.

BANKING

The banking industry is very competitive today. Most banks have a sales promotion program, and personal selling is one of their key strategies. An increasing number of bank officers and customer service representatives are involved in personal selling activities. They develop new accounts and service established accounts. Bank personnel are completing sales training courses in record numbers these days.

➤➤ Selling in Action

PITNEY BOWES CERTIFICATION SETS HIGH STANDARDS

Kevin Kercheval is a proud graduate of the Pitney Bowes Certified Postal Consultant (CPC) program. The goal of this intensive certification program is to improve the level of assistance given to customers who want to upgrade their mail process. The CPC program has been endorsed by the U.S. Postal Service. Members of the 4,000-person Pitney Bowes sales force sell both products (postage meters) and services. Before sales representatives are allowed to register for the CPC program they must work in a postal distribution center, review a series of informational videos, and write case studies that explain how postal knowledge can be used to save customers money. Once enrolled in the program, salespeople study materials that cover every aspect of the mail process. They then must pass a 50-question written exam. Those who can answer at least 49 questions correctly can advance to the final oral examination. Earning the CPC certification has given Kercheval greater confidence and improved earnings. He says, "The investment in knowledge has really paid off for me."[b]

The heavy volume of business mergers and corporate downsizing has increased demand for business services provided by outside contractors. Some of the business services purchased today are computer programming, training, printing, credit reporting, payroll, and recruiting. Sales positions in the business services field are expected to increase by at least 50 percent by the year 2005.[26]

The list of careers involving the sales of services is much longer. We have not explored the expanding fields of home and business security, travel and recreation, pest control, and transportation. As the demand for services increases, so do the employment opportunities for salespeople.

Selling for a Retailer

Harolds, a multimillion dollar clothing store in Houston, Texas, has been growing by more than 10 percent a year. This progressive retailer sells top-of-the-line men's and women's apparel to a group of discriminating customers who understand the difference between price and value. The success of Harolds is due in large part to an expert staff of full-time career salespeople who know their customers by name and are knowledgeable concerning clothing. Customers are willing to pay full price because they value the quality products and assistance offered by Harolds.[27]

The **retail salesperson** usually engages in full-time professional selling and is paid well for her contributions to the business. Products sold at the retail level range from exotic foreign automobiles to fine furniture. A partial list of retail products that usually require a high degree of personal selling follows:

Automobiles	Recreational vehicles
Musical instruments	Television and radio receivers
Photographic equipment	Furniture/decorating supplies
Fashion apparel	Tires and related accessories
Major appliances	Microcomputers

Today, traditional retailers are facing new competition from on-line retailers. Consumers are spending billions of dollars on Internet purchases, a clear sign that electronic commerce is here to stay. Traditional retailers must offer customers more than products. Wendy Liebmann, president of WSL Strategic Retail, a retail consulting firm, says, "In order to get someone to come into the store, retailers really need to create a compelling environment; a combination of product, value, and experience."[28] Well-trained salespeople can add value to the traditional shopping experience.

Selling for a Wholesaler

Jerry Upchurch is a field representative for Super Valu, a wholesaler of grocery products. Jerry's career in food marketing began when he obtained a part-time job in a supermarket while attending high school. He worked his way up to assistant store manager, a position he held for two years. Later he was promoted to store manager with the Kroger chain. With a background in food retailing, Jerry was able to obtain a sales job with Super Valu. His title is retail counselor, a name that reflects the type of consultative selling he does.

Jerry Upchurch is one of more than a million wholesale salespeople who are employed in the United States. Wholesalers play an important role in making channels of distribution efficient. A full-service wholesaler offers a wide variety of services to its customers, including maintaining inventories, gathering and interpreting market information, extending credit, distributing goods, and providing promotional activities. Wholesalers employ two kinds of salespeople: "inside" and "outside."

INSIDE SALESPERSON

The **inside salesperson** relies almost totally on telephone orders and follows a strict timetable of customer contact. Because of the escalating cost of personal selling, selling by telephone is growing in popularity. This selling method has become so popular that some companies are taking their salespeople off the road and bringing them back to headquarters, where they are retrained to sell by telephone. Ellett Brothers, a South Carolina-based wholesale firm specializing in the sale of guns and shooting supplies, uses inside sales personnel exclusively. This company employs 125 inside salespeople who average a total of 4,400 calls a day and generate in excess of $50 million in sales each year. Chilton Ellett, president of the company, reports that new employees complete a 10-week training program before they begin contacting customers.

OUTSIDE SALESPERSON

The duties of an **outside salesperson** vary from one wholesale firm to another. Some specialize in a single area such as electronics or small appliances, while others sell a wide range of product lines. The typical outside salesperson must have knowledge of many products and be able to serve as a consultant to the customer. For example, a sales representative for a pharmaceutical wholesaler calling on retail stores needs to be familiar with advertising and display techniques, store layout, and other merchandising strategies. Most important, this person must be completely familiar with the customer's operation.

Selling for a Manufacturer

Although Donna Crowell is a member of the Hewlett Packard sales force, she spends much of her time at Texas Instruments. Texas Instruments makes software that runs on Hewlett Packard hardware. Hewlett Packard stands to sell more if Texas Instruments recommends its hardware. Thus, Crowell spends a lot of time making sure there is a good relationship between the two large companies. She says, "It's more than traditional selling. I'm really a business relationship manager."[29]

Manufacturers employ sales and sales support personnel in many different capacities. Field salespeople, sales engineers, and detail salespeople are outside salespeople who interact face to face with prospects and customers. Inside salespeople rely primarily on the telephone to identify prospects and engage in other selling activities.

FIELD SALESPERSON

A **field salesperson** sells to new customers and increases sales to current ones. These salespeople must be able to recognize buyer needs and prescribe the best product or service to meet these needs. Field salespeople who provide excellent service find their customers to be a good source of leads for new prospects.

SALES ENGINEER

A **sales engineer** must have detailed and precise technical knowledge and the ability to discuss the technical aspects of his products. Expertise in identifying, analyzing, and solving customer problems is of critical importance. A sales engineer may be responsible for

Sales engineers must have detailed and precise technical knowledge.

introducing a new product that represents a breakthrough in technology and must be prepared to answer a wide range of highly technical questions with conviction.

DETAIL SALESPERSON

The primary goal of a **detail salesperson** is to develop goodwill and stimulate demand for the manufacturer's products. This person is usually not compensated on the basis of the orders obtained, but receives recognition for increasing the sale of goods indirectly. The detail salesperson calls on wholesale, retail, and other customers to help improve their

►► CUSTOMER RELATIONSHIP MANAGEMENT WITH TECHNOLOGY

LEARNING CRM SOFTWARE

Many salespeople are at first apprehensive about using computers; yet research shows a high degree of acceptance, with this comment often heard, "I don't know how I got along without it."

Following the instructions in this text's customer relationship management (CRM) application exercises and case study gives you a good understanding of basic CRM. This knowledge can be valuable as you enter today's selling environment. Many sales organizations are using CRM and your understanding of the basics can help you learn more rapidly any system in use by your potential employers. Some people, after following these instructions, list their use of CRM on their resumés.

Many users of CRM enter information about friends and family into their databases and use it to enhance all their relationships. CRM helps people remember the status of relationships, steps to take, and pending events, such as anniversaries and birthdays. (See the exercise, Learning CRM Software, at p. 45 for more information.)

A growing number of professionals such as architects, accountants, and interior designers have discovered that personal selling is a very important "auxiliary" activity.

marketing. In a typical day this salesperson may help train a sales staff or offer advice to a firm that is planning an advertising campaign. Detail salespeople also collect valuable information concerning customer acceptance of products. They must be able to offer sound advice in such diverse areas as credit policies, pricing, display, store layout, and storage. The detail salesperson is sometimes referred to as a missionary salesperson.

INSIDE SALESPERSON

As face-to-face sales costs increase, many manufacturers have developed an inside sales force. At IBM, about 15 percent of the sales force never leave the office. They make calls to smaller customers, take orders, and in some cases provide support to field sales people.[30] Some marketers are finding that only the initial sale of the product requires face-to-face contact. Inside salespeople can handle repeat contacts.

LEARNING TO SELL

"Are salespeople made or are they born?" This classic question seems to imply that some people are born with certain qualities that give them a special advantage in the selling field. This is not true. The principles of selling can be learned and applied by people whose personal characteristics are quite different.

In the past few decades, sales training has been expanded on four fronts. These four sources of training are corporate-sponsored training, training provided by commercial vendors, certification studies, and courses provided by colleges and universities.

Hundreds of business organizations, such as Xerox Corporation, IBM, Maytag, Western Electric, and Zenith, have established or expanded training programs. These large corporations spend millions of dollars each year to develop their salespeople. *Training*

Sales and customer service training programs such as those offered by AchieveGlobal, Inc. (formerly Learning International) are very popular. This type of training is viewed as a good investment by firms that want to establish a long-term relationship with the customer.

You've improved product quality, invested in new technology, even lowered your prices...

So why is the competition gaining on you?

A critical element may be missing from your competitive strategy—a focus on your relationships with your customers.

In a world of parity products and services, the quality of your customer relationships may be the only thing that can set you apart.

The key question: How do you ensure that your sales and service people have the skills they need to build and maintain lasting partnerships with your customers?

The very survival of your company depends on the answer to that question. And we can help you.

We're Learning International, the world's leading training company dedicated to strengthening clients' sales and service performance. For more than 30 years, we've been helping the world's most successful organizations to outdistance the competition.

We provide market-tested training programs for both sales and service professionals. Training that will help you leverage every point of customer contact to your advantage.

Training that will help your people develop the skills needed to win new business — and build customer loyalty.

Training that will help you not only achieve a competitive advantage, but sustain it. In a word, training that gets results.

If you'd like to know more about what Learning International can do for you, or to obtain a copy of our white paper on the new buyer-seller relationships, *Profiles in Customer Loyalty*, call or write today.

Learning International
225 High Ridge Road
Stamford, CT 06905
**1-800-456-9390,
extension 85**

Circle No. 120 on Reader Service Card

magazine, which conducts annual analysis of employer-provided training in U.S. organizations, indicates that salespeople are among the most intensively trained employee groups. The typical salesperson completes 38 hours of training a year, which is 10 hours more than senior executives receive.[31]

The programs designed by firms specializing in the development of sales personnel are a second source of sales training. Some of the most popular courses are offered by Wilson Learning Corporation, the Forum Corporation, Dale Carnegie Training, and Zig Ziglar Corporation. At the present time, there are several hundred sales training courses offered by vendors. These training programs have proved to be a good investment for many individuals and business firms.

The trend toward increased professionalism in personal selling has been the stimulus for a third type of training and education initiative. Many salespeople are returning to the classroom to earn certification in a sales or sales related area. In the pharmaceutical industry many salespeople earn the Certified Medical Representative (CMR) designation. The National Automobile Dealers Association sponsors the Code of Conduct Certification program for automotive sales representatives. Both of these certification programs require extensive study of modules and completion of rigorous examinations. Sales & Marketing Executives–International offers the Certified Sales Executive (CSE) designation to sales professionals who meet the highest standards of education, experience, and ethical conduct.

The International Organization for Standardization (ISO) authorized Certified Marketing Services International (CMSI) to launch an international program for marketing and sales certification. The CMSI program grants certification to those individuals who have reached certain achievement levels during their careers, as attested by their experience and personal references. Recipients also must complete an authorized training program and pass a comprehensive monitored examination. The major objective of this certification program is to increase the standard of excellence in the field of personal selling.[32]

The fourth source of sales training is personal selling courses offered by colleges and universities throughout the United States. A large majority of the nation's undergraduate business schools offer this course, and it is attracting more interest among business majors. Some two- and four-year colleges have developed extensive education programs for students interested in a sales career. Cardinal Stritch College offers a Sales Certificate Program that includes a five-course sequence. Weber State University, located at Ogden, Utah, offers a bachelor of science degree in technical sales. The University of Akron, the University of Houston, Western Carolina University, Ball State University, Baylor University, the College of St. Catherine, and the University of Memphis offer undergraduate programs for students who are preparing for a career in personal selling.

Summary

Today's workforce is made up of millions of *knowledge workers* who succeed only when they add value to information. The new economy rewards salespeople and other knowledge workers who collect, organize, clarify, and present information in a convincing manner. Selling skills contribute in a major way to four groups of knowledge workers who usually do not consider themselves salespeople: customer service representatives, professionals (accountants, consultants, lawyers, etc.), entrepreneurs, and managerial personnel.

Selling careers offer many rewards not found in other occupations. Income, both monetary and psychic, is above average, and there are many opportunities for advancement. Salespeople enjoy job security, mobility, and independence. Opportunities in selling for members of minority groups and for women are growing. In addition, selling is very interesting work, because a salesperson is constantly in contact with people. The redundant adage "no two people are alike" reminds us that sales work is never dull or routine.

The text describes each of the four major career options in the field of personal selling. We provide a brief introduction to the variety of employment opportunities in service, retail, wholesale, and manufacturer's sales. Keep in mind that each category features a wide range of selling positions, varying in terms of educational requirements, earning potential, and type of customer served. The discussion and examples should help you see which kind of sales career best suits your talents and interests.

KEY TERMS

Customer Service Representative
Entry Level Sales Representative
Intermediate Sales Representative
Senior Sales Representative
Psychic Income
Retail Salesperson

Inside Salesperson
Outside Salesperson
Field Salesperson
Sales Engineer
Detail Salesperson

REVIEW QUESTIONS

1. List and describe the four employment settings for people who are considering a selling career.
2. Explain the meaning of *psychic income.*
3. Explain why personal selling is an important auxiliary skill needed by lawyers, engineers, accountants, and other professionals.
4. What future is there in selling for women and minorities?
5. Develop a list of retail products that require well-developed personal selling skills.
6. Some salespeople have an opportunity to earn certification in a sales or sales-related area. How can a salesperson benefit from certification?
7. Describe the two types of wholesale salespeople.
8. List three titles commonly used to describe manufacturing salespeople. Describe the duties of each.
9. Develop a list of eight selling career opportunities in the service field.
10. List and briefly describe the four major sources of sales training.

APPLICATION EXERCISES

1. Examine a magazine or newspaper ad for a new product or service that you have never seen before. Evaluate its chances for receiving wide customer acceptance. Does this product require a large amount of personal selling effort? What types of salespeople (service, manufacturing, wholesale, or retail) are involved in selling this product?
2. For each of the following job classifications, list the name of at least one person you know in that field:
   a. Full-time retail salesperson
   b. Full-time wholesale salesperson
   c. Full-time manufacturer's salesperson
   d. Full-time person who sells a service

   Interview one of the people you have listed, asking the following questions concerning her duties and responsibilities:
   a. What is your immediate supervisor's title?
   b. What would be a general description of your position?
   c. What specific duties and responsibilities do you have?
   d. What is the compensation plan and salary range for a position like yours?

   Write a job description from this information.

3. Shelly Jones, a vice president and partner in the Chicago office of the consulting firm Korn/Ferry International, has looked into the future and he sees some new challenges for salespeople. He recently shared the following predictions with *Selling* magazine:

   a. Salespeople will spend more time extending the range of applications or finding new markets for the products they sell.

   b. The selling function will be less pitching your product and more integrating your product into the business equation of your client. Understanding the business environment in which your client operates will be critical.

   c. In the future you will have to be a financial engineer for your client. You need to understand how your client makes money and be able to explain how your product or service contributes to profitable operation of the client's firm.

   Interview a salesperson who is involved in business-to-business selling, a manufacturer's representative, for example, and determine if this person agrees with the views of Shelly Jones.

4. There are many information sources on selling careers and career opportunities on the Internet. *Search the Internet for information on selling careers.*

   Use your search engine to find career information on a pharmaceutical representative, a field sales engineer, and a retail salesperson.

CRM APPLICATION EXERCISE

Learning CRM Software

After downloading and launching the CRM software from *www.prenhall.com/ manningreece,* you will become acquainted with the layout and features of the ACT! program. Start by pressing the F1 function key that displays the contents of the help file. Clicking on the first entry, ACT! Screens, shows information about the program's three main screens: Contact Screens (records with information about people), Word Processing Screens, and the Query Screen. Print the ACT! Screens page by selecting File, Print Topic. At the bottom of this page is a row of icons, a small version of the tool bar icons found on the main contact screen. Click on each of these icons for an explanation of its function.

Next select the underlined link, The Contact Screens, to learn about the two screens that are available to view information about a contact (person). At the top of this screen, click on the link labeled Status Area to read a description of the information found along the side of the contact screens. Here you learn to determine the number of records in the database; how to use the card index icon to navigate; and how to discover whether there are notes, history information, or activities scheduled for this contact.

Browse through the help screens to learn more about the structure and functions of this CRM software.

CASE PROBLEM

Ronald McMains is 23 years old and works for Metropolitan Financial Bank in the information services department. He was employed part-time while attending college and decided to accept a full-time position after graduation.

The position in information services offers an opportunity to learn a great deal about banking, a secure income, a good insurance and retirement program, 2 weeks of vacation a year, and 15 days of sick leave a year if needed. There also will be opportunities to move into supervision within the next couple of years, because the company is expanding rapidly.

Ron has been thinking about changing jobs and has been described by his friends as an opportunist—a person who seeks out opportunities and takes advantage of them. He sees himself the same way and someday hopes to earn well above the average income.

Ron has been interviewing for several positions. One company has offered him a position that involves calling on potential dealers for a new line of fiberglass boats. The manufacturer has a patent on an improved fiberglassing technique that is setting new standards for boat strength. The boat has proved to be a success and has sold extraordinarily well in the five territories that the company already has opened. Letters are coming from dealers all over the country expressing an interest in taking on a dealership. The company has decided to open up new territories in the southern half of Wisconsin and northern half of Illinois. The latter is the territory they have offered to Ron.

The specific responsibilities of the position include calling on marinas and boat dealers in the territory and setting up the better ones as distributors of the new line of boats. Ron would evaluate each potential distributorship and would select and appoint the new distributors. The company's excellent training program would teach Ron how to help each new dealer set up a promotional program to sell the boats.

The company has offered Ron a commission program that includes a "draw against commission" form of compensation. In this type of program a drawing account enables the salesperson to receive a set amount either weekly or monthly that is later subtracted from earned commissions. Ron's draw would equal his present salary, including his overtime pay. Ron's commissions would be based on the number of boats his dealers sold. The company expects this territory to be one of the best; and if Ron is successful, his income could be well into the $50,000 to $60,000 range within the second year, if not sooner.

Ron would have to relocate about 100 miles from where he now lives. The company has offered relocation expenses to cover the cost of the entire move. Ron realizes he would be away from home on the average of one night a week, and this poses no problems. The company will cover all of Ron's travel and lodging expenses and will provide him with a new car.

Questions

1. List the pros and cons of this job opportunity.
2. On the basis of the information given, should Ron accept the new job? Why or why not?

DEVELOPING A RELATIONSHIP STRATEGY

➤ High-performance salespeople are generally better able to build and maintain relationships than moderate performers. Part II focuses on the person-to-person–relationship-building strategies that are the foundation for personal development and relationships with customers that result in long-term partnerships. The influence of ethical decisions on relationships in selling is also discussed in Part II.

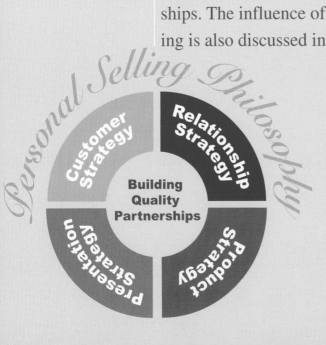

Personal Selling Philosophy

Customer Strategy

Relationship Strategy

Building Quality Partnerships

Presentation Strategy

Product Strategy

The manner in which high-performance salespeople establish, build, and maintain relationships is a key ingredient of success.

DR. WILLIAM M. DEMARCO
AND
DR. MICHAEL D. MAGINN
SALES COMPETENCY
RESEARCH REPORT

3

Creating Value with a Relationship Strategy

The salespeople who work for Fred Sands Realtors (fredsands.com) understand the importance of developing relationship strategies. This successful company, with offices throughout the United States and in many parts of the world, strives to build a long-term partnership with each customer. Sandra Khadra, vice president of marketing at Fred Sands Realtors, encourages salespeople to begin building rapport during the first contact. She teaches salespeople the basics of creating a professional image and stresses the importance of empathy with the customer. She knows that when you sincerely care about the welfare of the customer, you add value to the sale.[1]

Helping people buy a home requires a multitude of skills. You must assume the roles of financial adviser, educator, and counselor. Above all, you must listen closely to everything that prospects say to accurately identify their wants and needs.

DEVELOPING A RELATIONSHIP STRATEGY

Developing and applying the wide range of interpersonal skills needed in today's complex sales environment can be challenging. Daniel Goleman, author of the best selling books *Emotional Intelligence* and *Working with Emotional Intelligence*, notes that there are many forms of intelligence that influence our actions throughout life. One of these, **emotional intelligence**, refers to the capacity for recognizing our own feelings and those of others, for

Strategic/Consultative Selling Model	
Strategic step	Prescription
DEVELOP A PERSONAL SELLING PHILOSOPHY	☑ ADOPT MARKETING CONCEPT ☑ VALUE PERSONAL SELLING ☑ BECOME A PROBLEM SOLVER/PARTNER
DEVELOP A RELATIONSHIP STRATEGY	☐ ADOPT DOUBLE-WIN PHILOSOPHY ☐ PROJECT PROFESSIONAL IMAGE ☐ MAINTAIN HIGH ETHICAL STANDARDS

motivating ourselves, and for managing emotions well in ourselves and in our relationships. People with a high level of emotional intelligence display many of the qualities needed in sales work: self-confidence, trustworthiness, adaptability, initiative, optimism, empathy, and well-developed social skills.[2] The good news is that emotional intelligence can be enhanced with a variety of self-development activities. We discuss many of these activities in this chapter.

Information age selling involves three major relationship challenges. The first major challenge is building new relationships.[3] Salespeople who can quickly build rapport with new prospects have a much greater chance of achieving success in personal selling. Building new relationships starts with the communication of positive impressions during the initial contact. The second major challenge is transforming relationships from the personal level to the business level. Once rapport is established, the salesperson is in a stronger position to begin the need identification process. The third major challenge is management of relationships. Dr. Charles Parker—noted consultant and sales trainer—says, "In order to achieve a high level of success salespeople have to manage a multitude of different relationships."[4] Salespeople must develop relationship management strategies that focus on four key groups. These groups are discussed later in this chapter.

Ongoing development of a relationship strategy should be the goal of every salesperson; customers tend to buy from people they like and trust, so we must learn how to establish and build relationships. In this chapter we introduce the double-win philosophy and discuss the importance of projecting a professional image. Chapter 4 focuses on the importance of maintaining high ethical standards to build long-term relationships with the customer (Fig. 3.1). Chapter 16 explains how an understanding of communication styles can help us better manage the relationship process.

Relationships Add Value

Denis Waitley, in his book *Empires of the Mind*, describes developments in the business community. He says, "Yesterday value was extra. Today value is everything."[5] Customers have become more sophisticated and more demanding in their buying strategies. They have come to expect partnering, and selling strategies that add value to the purchase. Consequently, salespeople need to become more sophisticated in their selling strategies. Learning International, Wilson Learning Corporation, Dale Carnegie Training, Zig Ziglar

Corporation, and the Forum Corporation offer sales training that stresses a style of selling that favors a close, trusting, long-term relationship over the quick sell. A representative of Forum noted, "The philosophy is to serve the customer as a consultant, not as a peddler."

The manner in which salespeople establish, build, and maintain relationships is no longer an incidental aspect of personal selling; in the information age it is a key to success. A satisfied customer can recommend you to many other prospects, and a disgruntled customer can be counted on to complain about you to numerous prospects.[6]

The salesperson who is honest, accountable, and sincerely concerned about the customer's welfare brings added value to the sale. These characteristics give the salesperson a competitive advantage—an advantage that is becoming increasingly important in a world of "look-alike" products and similar prices.

Partnering—The Highest Quality Selling Relationship

Salespeople today are encouraged to think of everything they say or do in the context of their relationship with the customer. They should constantly strive to build a long-term partnership. In a marketplace characterized by increased levels of competition and greater product complexity, we see the need to adopt a relationship strategy that emphasizes the "lifetime" customer. High-quality relationships result in repeat business and those important referrals. A growing number of salespeople recognize that the quality of partnerships they create is as important as the quality of the products they sell. Today's customer wants a quality product *and* a quality relationship. One example of this trend is the J. D. Power and Associates Automotive Studies research. The Initial Quality Study conducted by this marketing information firm measures the number and type of problems experienced by new car owners. The Sales Satisfaction Study, also conducted by J. D. Power, examines factors that impact on sales satisfaction such as treatment by auto sales representatives and customer experience when the auto was delivered.[7]

This salesperson's clothing and facial expression project a professional image. A pleasant smile and eye contact convey friendliness to the customer.

Partnering can be defined as a strategically developed, high-quality, long-term relationship that focuses on solving the customer's buying problems.[8] This definition is used in the sales training video entitled "Partnering—The Heart of Selling Today," which was produced by American Media. Traditional industrial age sales training programs emphasized the importance of creating a good first impression and then "pushing" your product. Partnering emphasizes building a strong relationship during every aspect of the sale and working hard to maintain a quality relationship with the customer after the sale. Today, personal selling must be viewed as a process, not an event.[9]

Larry Wilson, noted author and sales consultant, identifies partnering as one of the most important strategic thought processes needed by salespeople. He points out that the salesperson who is selling a "one-shot" solution cannot compete against the one who has developed and nurtured a long-term, mutually beneficial partnership. Wilson believes there are three keys to a partnering relationship:

▶ The relationship is built on shared values. If your client believes that you both share the same ideas and values, it goes a long way toward creating a powerful relationship.

▶ Everyone needs to clearly understand the purpose of the partnership and be committed to the vision. Both the salesperson and the client must agree on what they are trying to do together.

▶ The role of the salesperson must move from selling to supporting. The salesperson in a partnership is actively concerned with the growth, health, and satisfaction of the company to which she is selling.[10]

Salespeople willing to abandon short-term thinking and invest the time and energy needed to develop a high-quality, long-term relationship with customers are rewarded with greater earnings and the satisfaction of working with repeat customers. Sales resulting from referrals also increase.

➤➤ CUSTOMER RELATIONSHIP MANAGEMENT WITH TECHNOLOGY

COMMUNICATING THROUGH CRM

Customer relationship management (CRM) software can be used to enhance the quality of your relationships. A good example is the software's ability to improve communications between you and your contacts. With the ACT! software, for example, you can quickly prepare and send a letter, a fax, or an e-mail to one or more people with records in the database. Recipients of your appointment confirmations, information verifications, company or product news, or brief personal notes, recognize and appreciate your effort to keep them informed. The written word conveys consideration and helps avoid misunderstandings and miscommunications. CRM empowers you to easily use the written word to advance your relationship building. (See the exercise, Preparing Letters with CRM, at p. 68 for more information.)

Relationship Strategies Focus on Four Key Groups

Establishing and maintaining a partnering-type relationship internally as well as one with the customers is a vital aspect of selling. High-performance sales personnel build strong relationships with four groups (Fig. 3.2):

1. *Customers.* As noted previously, a major key to success in selling is the ability to establish working relationships with customers in which mutual support, trust, and goals are nurtured over time. Salespeople who maintain regular contact with their customers and develop sound business relationships based on mutual trust are able to drive up sales productivity according to research conducted by the American Productivity and Quality Center.[11]

   John Franco, former president of Learning International, says that in some cases the salesperson must move beyond the role of trusted consultant to gain full acceptance by the customer. He further states that in today's highly competitive business climate the salesperson needs to be perceived as someone who is working on the customer's team as a member of the customer's organization.[12]

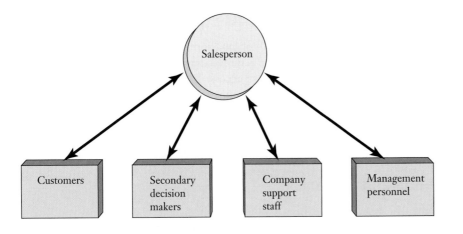

Figure **3.2**
An effective relationship strategy helps high-performing salespeople to build and maintain win–win relationships with a wide range of key groups.

▸▸ A Selling Partner

P PREPARES STRATEGICALLY for a long-term, high-quality relationship that solves customer's problems

A ASKS QUESTIONS to get on the customer's agenda

R RESTATES CUSTOMER NEEDS with confirmation questions

T TEAMS with support people to custom-fit solutions

N NEGOTIATES DOUBLE-WIN SOLUTIONS with joint decision making

E EXCEEDS CUSTOMER EXPECTATIONS whenever possible

R REEXAMINES the ongoing quality of the relationship frequently

2. *Secondary decision makers.* High-performance salespeople understand the importance of building relationships with the people who work with customers. In many selling situations the first person the salesperson meets is a receptionist, a secretary, or an assistant to the primary decision maker. These persons often can facilitate a meeting with the prospect. Also, the prospect may involve other people in making the buying decision. For example, the decision to buy a new copy machine may be made by a team of persons including the buyer and persons who will actually use the machine.

3. *Company support staff.* The maintenance of relationships internally is a vital aspect of selling. Support staff may include persons working in the areas of market research, product service, credit, training, or shipping. Influencing these people to change their priorities, interrupt their schedules, accept new responsibilities, or fulfill any other request for special attention is a major part of the salesperson's job. Most sales personnel readily admit that their productivity depends on the contributions of these people.

4. *Management personnel.* Sales personnel usually work under the direct supervision of a sales manager, a department head, or some other member of the firm's management team. Maintaining a good relationship with this person is important.

DEVELOPING THOUGHT PROCESSES THAT ENHANCE YOUR RELATIONSHIP STRATEGY

Industrial age folklore created the myth of the "born" salesperson—a dynamic, outgoing, highly assertive individual. Experience acquired during the information age has taught us that many other factors determine sales success. Key among these factors are a positive self-image and the ability to relate to others in effective and productive ways. With the aid of knowledge drawn from the behavioral sciences, we can develop the relationship strategies needed in a wide range of selling situations.

Self-Image—An Important Dimension of the Relationship Strategy

Self-image is shaped by the ideas, attitudes, feelings, and other thoughts you have about yourself that influence the way you relate to others. Psychologists have found that once we form a thought process about ourselves, it serves to edit all incoming information and influence our actions. Let us consider a salesperson who has come to believe that he cannot build strong relationships with high-level decision makers. Once this mental picture, or self-image, has been formed, it is unlikely that this salesperson can influence high-level executives in a sales situation. Essentially, this person is programmed to fail in attempts to build relationships at this level. There is no anticipation of improvement, so the negative self-image becomes a self-fulfilling prophecy. You simply cannot succeed at something unless you think you are going to succeed at it.

Self-Image and Success

Self-image is a powerful thought process influencing the direction of our lives. This process can set the limits of our accomplishments, defining what we can and cannot do. Realizing the power of self-image is an important breakthrough in our understanding of the factors that influence us.

A pioneer in the area of self-image psychology was the late Dr. Maxwell Maltz, author of *Psycho-Cybernetics* and other books devoted to this topic. We are indebted to him for two important discoveries that help us understand better the "why" of human behavior:

1. *Feelings and behavior are consistent with the self-image.* The individual who feels like a "failure" is likely to find some way to fail. There is a definite relationship between self-image and accomplishments at work. Generally speaking, the more positive your self-image, the greater your prospects for achieving success, because a positive self-image helps generate the energy needed to get things done.
2. *The self-image can be changed.* Numerous case histories show that you are never too young or too old to change your self-image and thereby achieve new accomplishments.[13]

A positive self-image (high self-esteem) is an important prerequisite to success in selling. According to a study conducted by Sentry Insurance, high self-esteem mixed with candor are the vital ingredients in the make up of top salespeople.[14] Low self-esteem, according to Nathaniel Branden, author of *Self-Esteem at Work*, correlates with resistance to change and with clinging to the known and familiar. He notes that low self-esteem is economically disadvantageous in an information economy where knowledge and new ideas count for almost everything.[15]

How can you develop a more positive self-image? How can you get rid of self-destructive ways of thinking? Bringing your present self-image out into the open is the first step in understanding who you are, what you can do, and where you are going. Improving your self-image does not happen overnight, but it can happen. A few practical approaches are summarized as follows:

1. *Focus on the future and stop being overly concerned with past mistakes or failures.* We should learn from past errors, but we should not be immobilized by them.
2. *Develop expertise in selected areas.* By developing "expert power" you not only improve your self-image but also increase the value of your contributions to your employer and your customers.
3. *Learn to develop a positive mental attitude.* To develop a more positive outlook, read books and listen to audio tapes that describe ways to develop a positive mental attitude. Consider materials developed by Denis Waitley, Stephen Covey, Brian Tracy, Dale Carnegie, and Zig Ziglar.

Later in this chapter you will learn how to develop and initiate a plan for self-improvement. If you want to improve your self-image, consider adopting this plan.

►► *Building Relationships in a Diverse World*

BUSINESS ETIQUETTE FOSTERS QUALITY RELATIONSHIPS

A diverse workforce often creates new challenges for those who want to practice good manners. To illustrate, what do you do if a client comes into your office in a wheelchair? Do you rise? A man and a woman of equal corporate status walk down an office corridor and arrive at a door. If the woman reaches the door first, should the man move ahead to open it for her?

Changing technology also creates questions in the mind of the person who wants to avoid a violation of the rules of good etiquette. Should you switch on speaker phones without letting the caller know that others are present in the room and listening? Should you leave personal messages on voice mail if several others have access to the messages?

The growth of multinational companies has created the need to understand international business etiquette. Many companies realize that their employees need to prepare for assignments that take them to foreign countries. If your travels take you to Japan, it's helpful to know that prolonged eye contact is considered offensive. In cultures where handshakes tend to linger longer than typical American handshakes, pulling your hand away too soon is interpreted as a rejection. Dorthea Johnson, director of The Protocal School of Washington, says, "If you have good manners, people notice. And if you have bad manners, people notice that too, especially in the international arena." Quality is a central concept in most organizations, and good manners are a central part of delivering on the quality mission.

If you are not able to complete a business etiquette training course, consider books such as *Letitia Baldrige's Complete Guide to Executive Manners* by Letitia Baldrige, *Miss Manners' Guide for the Turn-of-the-Millennium* by Judith Martin, *Business Etiquette in Brief* by Ann Marie Sabath, and *Complete Business Etiquette Handbook* by Barbara Pachter and Marjorie Brody.[a]

Double-Win

When the double-win approach is used, both the customer and the salesperson feel a sense of satisfaction.

Denis Waitley—consultant, national speaker, and author of several books—provides us with a brief and simple definition of the term **double-win**: "If I help you win, I win, too."[16] Both the customer and the salesperson leave the sale feeling a sense of satisfaction. The salesperson not only obtains the order but also sets the stage for a long-term relationship, repeat business, and future referrals. One author described this "win–win" approach as follows:

> You both come out of the sale feeling satisfied, knowing that neither of you has taken advantage of the other and that both of you have profited, personally and professionally, from the transaction. In the simplest terms, you know you have a win–win sales encounter when both you and the buyer come out of it feeling positive.[17]

The double-win strategy is based on such irrefutable logic that it is difficult to understand why any other approach would be used. However, some salespeople still have not accepted the merits of the win–win approach. They have adopted a win–lose approach, which means that the salesperson wins at the buyer's expense. When a salesperson sells a product that is not the best solution to the buyer's problem, the win–lose strategy has been used.

We can adopt the win–win attitude that is one of the principles of partnering-style selling. The starting point to development of a double-win philosophy is to compare the behaviors of persons who have adopted the win–lose approach with the behaviors of persons who have adopted the win–win approach (Fig. 3.3).

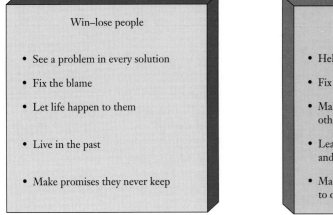

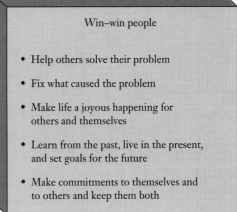

Figure **3.3**

The starting point to developing a double-win philosophy is to compare behaviors of win–lose salespeople with those of salespeople who have adopted the win–win approach.

(Adapted from a list of losers, winners, and double winners in *The Double Win* by Denis Waitley.)

Character and Integrity

Your character and integrity strongly influence your relationships with others. **Character** is composed of your personal standards of behavior, including your honesty, integrity, and moral fiber.[18] Your character is based on your internal values and the resulting judgments you make about what is right and what is wrong. When your behavior is in tune with your professed standards and values—when you practice what you believe in—you have integrity. In a world of uncertainty and rapid change, integrity has become a valuable character trait. Salespeople with integrity can be trusted to do what they say they will do. One way to achieve trustworthiness in personal selling is to avoid deceiving or misleading the customer. More is said about this topic in Chapter 4, which examines the ethical conduct of salespeople.

NONVERBAL STRATEGIES THAT IMPROVE RELATIONSHIPS

The first contact between a salesperson and a prospect is very important. During the first few minutes—or seconds in some cases—the prospect and the salesperson form impressions of each other that either facilitate or distract from the sales call.[19] It is very difficult to rebound from a poor first impression.

Every salesperson projects an image to prospective customers, and this image influences how a customer feels about the sales representative. The image you project is the sum total of many verbal and nonverbal factors. The quality of your voice, the clothing you wear, your posture, your manners, and your communication style represent some of the factors that contribute to the formation of your image. We discuss body language, surface language, voice quality, and manners in this chapter. Communication style is examined in Chapter 16.

A pleasant smile sends a positive nonverbal message to the customer.

Effect of Body Language on Relationships

Body language is a form of nonverbal communication that has been defined as *messages without words* and *silent messages.* For example, a purchasing agent who continually glances at his watch is communicating a concern for time without using the spoken word. A salesperson who leans forward in her chair while talking to a customer (as opposed to slouching) is more likely to communicate a feeling of concern to this person.

Research indicates that when two people communicate, nonverbal messages convey much more impact than verbal messages. Words play a surprisingly small part in the communication process. Studies indicate that in a typical two-person conversation, only about 7 percent of our understanding comes from words spoken by the other person. About 38 percent of our understanding comes from what we hear. Does the other person sound sincere, credible, and knowledgeable? Every spoken message has a vocal element, coming not from *what* we say, but from *how* we say it. The voice communicates in many ways: through its tone, volume, and speed of delivery. A salesperson wishing to communicate enthusiasm needs to use a voice that is charged with energy.

About 55 percent of the meaning we attach to communication efforts by others is based on what we see or feel (Fig. 3.4). A positive message can be communicated to a customer with a smile, a firm handshake, good eye contact, and a professional appearance.[20]

Nonverbal messages can reinforce or contradict the spoken word. When your verbal message and body language are consistent, they give others the impression that you can be trusted and that what you say reflects what you truly believe. When there is a discrepancy between your verbal and nonverbal messages, you are less apt to be trusted.[21]

Figure **3.4**
When someone else is speaking, your understanding of what is said depends heavily on what you see or feel.

(Source: Moravian Study of Nonverbal Communication.)

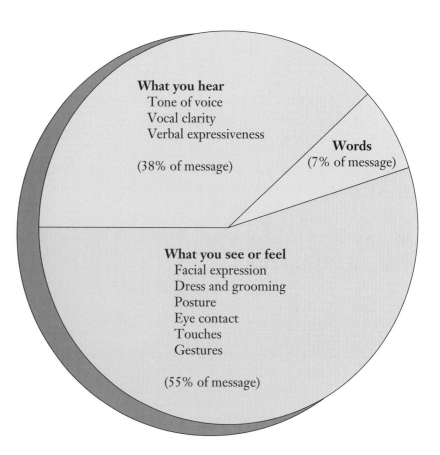

What you hear
Tone of voice
Vocal clarity
Verbal expressiveness

(38% of message)

Words
(7% of message)

What you see or feel
Facial expression
Dress and grooming
Posture
Eye contact
Touches
Gestures

(55% of message)

ENTRANCE AND CARRIAGE

As noted earlier, the first impression we make is very important. The moment a salesperson walks into a client's office, the client begins making judgments. Susan Bixler, author of *The Professional Image* and *Professional Presence*, makes this comment:

> All of us make entrances throughout our business day as we enter offices, conference rooms, or meeting halls. And every time we do, someone is watching us, appraising us, sizing us up, and gauging our appearance, even our intelligence, often within the space of a few seconds.[22]

Bixler says that the key to making a successful entrance is simply believing—and projecting—that you have a reason to be there and have something important to offer the client. You can communicate confidence with a strong stride, a good posture, and a friendly smile. A confident manner communicates to the client the message, "This meeting will be beneficial to you."

SHAKING HANDS

An inadequate handshake is like dandruff: no one mentions it, but everyone notices it. Today, the handshake is an important symbol of respect and in most business settings it is the proper greeting.[23]

In the field of selling the handshake is usually the *first* and frequently the *only* physical contact one makes during a sales call. The handshake can communicate warmth, genuine concern for the prospect, and an image of strength. It also can communicate aloofness, indifference, and weakness to the customer. The message we communicate with a handshake is determined by a combination of five factors:

1. *Eye contact during handshake.* Eyes transmit more information than any other part of the body, so maintaining eye contact throughout the handshaking process is important when two people greet each other.
2. *Degree of firmness.* Generally speaking, a firm handshake communicates a caring attitude, while a weak grip (the dead-fish handshake) communicates indifference.
3. *Depth of interlock.* A full, deep grip communicates friendship to the other person.
4. *Duration of grip.* There are no specific guidelines to tell us what the ideal duration of a grip should be. However, by extending the duration of the handshake we can often communicate a greater degree of interest and concern for the other person. Do not pump up and down more than once or twice.
5. *Degree of dryness of hands.* A moist palm not only is uncomfortable to handle but also can communicate the impression that you are quite nervous. Some people have a physiological problem that causes clammy hands and should keep a handkerchief within reach to remove excess moisture. A clammy hand is likely to repel most customers.[24]

The best time to present your name is when you extend your hand. When you introduce yourself, state your name clearly and then listen carefully to be certain you hear the customer's name. To ensure that you remember the customer's name, repeat it. In some cases you need to check to be sure you are pronouncing it properly.[25]

FACIAL EXPRESSIONS

If you want to identify the inner feelings of another person, watch facial expressions closely. The face is a remarkable communicator, capable of accurately signaling emotion in a split second and capable of concealing emotion equally well. We can tell in a blink of

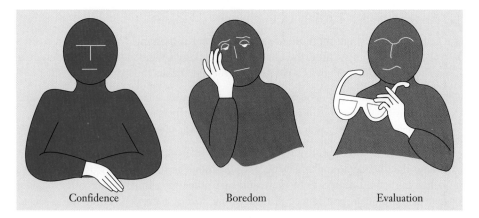

Confidence   Boredom   Evaluation

an eye if the customer's face is registering surprise, pleasure, or skepticism (Fig. 3.5). Facial expressions are largely universal so people around the world tend to "read" faces in a similar way. It is worth noting that the smile is the most recognized facial signal in the world and it can have a great deal of influence on others. George Rotter, professor of psychology at Montclair University, says, "Smiles are an enormous controller of how people perceive you." People tend to trust a smiling face.[26] Get in the habit of offering a sincere smile each time you meet with a prospect.

Effect of Appearance on Relationships

We form opinions about people based on a pattern of immediate impressions conveyed by appearance. The clothing we wear, the length and style of our hair, the fragrances we use, and the jewelry we display all combine to make a statement about us to others—a statement of primary importance to anyone involved in selling.

According to many of the top image consultants, clothing is particularly important. John T. Molloy, author of *Dress for Success, New Dress for Success*, and other books, was one of the first to acknowledge publicly the link between dress and the image we project to others. He is credited with introducing the term *wardrobe engineering*, a concept that was later refined by William Thourlby, Jacqueline Thompson, Emily Cho, Susan Bixler, and other noted image consultants. **Wardrobe engineering** combines the elements of psychology, fashion, sociology, and art into clothing selection. The position taken by Molloy and others is that clothing can evoke a predictable response.[27]

We all have certain views, or **unconscious expectations**, concerning appropriate dress. In sales work we should try to anticipate the expectations of our clientele. The clothing worn by salespeople does make a difference in terms of customer acceptance because it communicates powerful messages. The clothing we wear can influence our credibility and likability. Martin Siewert, a member of the business development team for Axiom Management Consulting, has adopted a flexible approach to dress. His company's policy favors an informal dress code, so he usually wears casual clothing at work unless he is meeting with a client. When he calls on customers, most of whom are Fortune 500 companies, he wears a suit and tie. "I want to show that I respect their culture," he says.[28]

Most image consultants agree that there is no single "dress for success" look. The appropriate wardrobe varies from one city or region to another and from company to company. However, there are some general guidelines that we should follow in selecting clothing for sales work. Three key words should govern our decisions: simplicity, appropriateness, and quality.

SIMPLICITY

The color of clothing, as well as design, communicates a message to the customer. Some colors are showy and convey an air of casualness. In a business setting we want to be taken seriously, so flashy colors should usually be avoided.

APPROPRIATENESS

Selecting appropriate clothing for sales work can be a challenge. We must carefully consider the clients we serve and decide what may be acceptable to them. Many salespeople are guided by the type of products they sell and the desired image projected by their employers.

QUALITY

The quality of our wardrobe also influences the image we project to customers. A salesperson's wardrobe should be regarded as an investment, with each item carefully selected to look and fit well. Susan Bixler says, "If you want respect, you have to dress as well as or better than your industry standards."[29]

VISUAL INTEGRITY

Visual presence must have a certain amount of integrity and consistency. The images you project are made up of many factors, and lack of attention to important details can negate your effort to create a good impression. Too much jewelry, a shirt that does not fit well, or unshined shoes can detract from the professional look you want to project. People often are extra alert when meeting someone new and this heightened consciousness makes every detail count.[30]

The image you project is made up of many factors, and lack of attention to important details can negate your efforts to create a good impression.

Effect of Voice Quality on Relationships

As noted previously, voice quality contributes about 38 percent of the meaning attached to spoken messages. On the telephone, voice quality is even more important because the other person cannot see your facial expressions, hand gestures, and other body movements. You cannot trade in your current voice for a new one. However, you can make your voice more pleasing to others. How?

Two suggestions are

1. *Do not talk too fast or too slowly.* Rapid speech often causes customers to become defensive. They raise psychological barriers because a "rapid-fire monologue" is associated with high-pressure sales methods. Many salespeople could improve their verbal presentation by talking more slowly. The slower presentation allows others to follow, and it allows the speaker time to think ahead—to consider the situation and make judgments. Another good tip is to vary the speed of your speech, leaving spaces between thoughts. Crowding too many thoughts together may confuse the listener.[31]

2. *Avoid a speech pattern that is dull and colorless.* The worst kind of voice has no color and no feeling. Enthusiasm is a critical element of an effective sales presentation. It also is contagious. Your enthusiasm for the product is transmitted to the customer. Your tone of voice mirrors your emotional state and physical well-being. When you are feeling good and enjoying a positive mental state, your voice naturally sounds upbeat, energetic, and enthusiastic. However, the normal stresses and strains of life can be reflected in your voice. Sometimes you have to manipulate your tone of voice to communicate greater warmth and enthusiasm. Before you make that important phone call or meet with a prospect, reflect on your state of mind. To drain tension from your voice, inhale and tense every muscle. Hold for a count of 5, and then exhale for a count of 10. If you want to sound warm and friendly, smile while speaking.[32]

Effect of Manners on Your Relationships

The study of manners (sometimes called etiquette) reveals a number of ways to enhance your relationship strategy. Salespeople who possess knowledge of the rules of etiquette can perform their daily work with greater poise and confidence. Think of manners as a universal passport to positive relationships and respect.[33]

With practice, anyone can have good manners without appearing to be "stiff" and at the same time win the respect and admiration of others. Space does not permit a complete review of this topic, but we cover some of the rules of etiquette that are especially important to salespeople.

1. *Avoid the temptation to address a new prospect by first name.* In a business setting, too much familiarity too quickly can cause irritation.

2. *Avoid offensive comments or stories.* Never assume that the customer's value system is the same as your own. Rough language and off-color stories can do irreparable damage to your image.

3. *Do not express personal views on political or religious issues.* There is seldom a "safe" position to take in these areas, so it is better to avoid these topics altogether.

4. *When you invite a customer to lunch, do not discuss business before the meal is ordered unless the client initiates the subject.* Also, avoid ordering food that is not easily controlled, such as ribs, chicken, or lobster.

5. *When you use voice mail, leave a clear, concise message.* Do not speak too fast or mumble your name and number.

It has been said that good manners make other people feel better. This is true because good manners require that we place the other person's comfort ahead of our own. One of the best ways to develop rapport with a customer is to avoid behavior that might be offensive to that person.

CONVERSATIONAL STRATEGIES THAT ENHANCE RELATIONSHIPS

The foundation for a long-term relationship with the customer is frequently a "get acquainted" type of conversation that takes place before any discussion of business matters. Within a few minutes it is possible to reduce the relationship tension that is so common when two people meet for the first time. This informal visit with the customer provides the salesperson with an opportunity to apply three of Dale Carnegie's guidelines for building strong relationships:

▶ Become genuinely interested in other people.

▶ Be a good listener. Encourage others to talk about themselves.

▶ Talk in terms of the other person's interest.[34]

In a relaxed and friendly atmosphere, the customer is more apt to open up and share information that helps the salesperson determine customer needs. A casual conversation is frequently the first step in developing a trusting relationship.

The length of this conversation depends on your sense of the prospect's reaction to your greeting, how busy the prospect appears to be, and your awareness of topics of mutual interest. In developing conversation the following three areas should be considered.

In a relaxed and friendly atmosphere, the customer is more apt to open up and share information.

►► Selling in Action

BUILDING RELATIONSHIPS WITH FREQUENT DEPOSITS

Building relationships in sales can be compared with making deposits in the bank. Regular bank deposits have a compounding effect, so over time you see steady growth in your account. Each of the following contacts with a customer or prospect is a deposit that can build the relationship:

- Send articles or reports of interest to your contacts. Be sure they are accompanied by a personal note.
- Send cards to celebrate an event such as a birthday or an anniversary.
- Contact customers after the sale to check on their level of satisfaction with the product.
- Express appreciation for purchases with a card, a letter, or a phone call.

Don't forget to make contact with secondary decision makers, support staff, and appropriate management personnel.[b]

Comments on Here and Now Observations

Observant salespeople are aware of the things going on around them. These observations can be as general as unusual developments in the weather or as specific as noticing unique artifacts in the prospect's office.

Compliments

When you offer a *sincere* compliment to your prospect, you are saying, "Something about you is special." Most people react positively to compliments because they appeal to the need for self-esteem. Your admiration should not be expressed, however, in phony superlatives that seem transparent. The prospect may suspect ulterior motives, which are unwelcome.

Search for Mutual Acquaintances or Interests

A frequent mode for establishing rapport with a new prospect is to find friends or interests you have in common. If you know someone with the same last name as your prospect, it may be appropriate to ask whether your friend is any relation. Anything you observe in the prospect's office or home might suggest an interest that you and your prospect share. Such topics of conversation appeal to your prospect's social needs.

STRATEGIES FOR SELF-IMPROVEMENT

Orson Welles, one of the most highly respected actors in this country, once said, "Every actor is very busy getting better or getting worse." To a large extent, salespeople are also "very busy getting better or getting worse." To improve, salespeople must develop an ongoing program for self-improvement. It is important to keep in mind that all improvement is self-initiated. Each of us controls the switch that allows personal growth and development to take place.

In the age of information, companies also need to build their websites around the concept of "a relationship strategy".

At the beginning of this chapter we introduce the concept of emotional intelligence. We note that this form of intelligence can be increased with the aid of self-development activities. Would you like to develop a more positive self-image? Improve your ability to develop double-win relationships? Develop effective nonverbal communication skills? Improve your speaking voice? These relationship-building strategies can be achieved if you are willing to follow these steps:

Step one: set goals. Goal setting, as noted previously, is an important element of any self-improvement plan. The goal-setting process requires that you be clear about what you want to accomplish. If your goal is too general or vague, progress toward achieving that goal is difficult to observe. An important step in the goal-setting process is to put the goal in writing.

This salesperson has set a fitness goal. Physical fitness can be an important part of a self improvement program.

Step two: use visualization. To make your goals a reality, engage in visualization. Forming a mental picture of yourself succeeding in goal attainment actually affects your behavior. Mary Lou Retton and many other Olympic stars have used visualization. She described her preparation for the gymnastics event this way:

> When I visualized myself going through a beam routine, I didn't imagine myself falling. I visualized myself on the beam—perfect. Always picture it perfect.[35]

You can work the same "mental magic" in goal setting by visualizing yourself as the person you want to be. For example, spend time developing mental pictures of successful experiences with prospective or established customers.

Step three: monitor your self-talk. Shad Helmstetter, author of *What You Say When You Talk to Yourself*, defines **self-talk** as "a way to override our past negative programming by erasing or replacing it with conscious, positive new directions."[36] Self-talk is an effective way to get rid of barriers to goal achievement. Helmstetter suggests that we develop specific positive self-talk statements and repeat them often to keep ourselves on target in terms of goal attainment.

Step four: recognize your progress. When you see yourself making progress toward a goal, or achieving a goal, reward yourself. This type of reinforcement is vital when you are trying to change a behavior. There is nothing wrong with taking pride in your accomplishments.

Self-improvement efforts can result in new abilities or powers, and they give us the motivation to utilize more fully the talents we already have. As a result, our potential for success is greater.

Summary

The manner in which salespeople establish, build, and maintain relationships is a major key to success in personal selling. The key relationships in selling include management personnel, company support staff, secondary decision makers, and customers.

The concept of *partnering* is defined and discussed in detail. Partnering emphasizes building a strong relationship during every aspect of the sale and working hard to maintain a quality relationship with the customer after the sale.

An understanding of the psychology of human behavior provides a foundation for developing relationship strategies. In this chapter we discuss the link between *self-image* and success in selling. Self-imposed fears can prevent salespeople from achieving success.

We describe several factors that influence the image you project to customers. The image others have of us is shaped to a great extent by nonverbal communication. We may choose the right words to persuade a customer to place an order, but aversive factors communicated by our clothing, handshake, facial expression, tone of voice, and general manner may prejudice the customer against us and our product or service.

There are few absolute standards for defining aversive factors. Beyond obvious matters such as slovenly dress and rude manners you must develop your own awareness of geographic and social factors, as well as your knowledge of particular customers, to know what might be considered aversive.

We also discuss the importance of self-improvement. A four-step, self-improvement plan is described.

KEY TERMS

Emotional Intelligence
Partnering
Self-Image
Double-Win
Character

Body Language
Wardrobe Engineering
Unconscious Expectations
Self-Talk

REVIEW QUESTIONS

1. List the three prescriptions that serve as the foundation for development of a relationship strategy.
2. How important are establishing, building, and maintaining relationships in the selling process? List the four groups of people with whom sales personnel must be able to work effectively.
3. Define the term *partnering*. Why has the building of partnerships become more important today?
4. Defend the statement, "Successful relationships depend on a positive self-image."
5. Describe the double-win or win–win approach to selling.
6. How is our self-image formed? Why is a positive self-image so important in personal selling?
7. Describe the meaning of the term **emotional intelligence**.
8. Identify three conversational methods that can be used to establish relationships.
9. Describe the meaning of the term **body language**.
10. List and describe each step in the four-step, self-improvement plan.

APPLICATION EXERCISES

1. Select four salespeople you know and ask them if they have a relationship strategy for working with customers, management personnel, secondary decision makers, and company support staff.
2. The partnering style of selling is emphasized in Chapters 1 and 3. To gain more insight into the popularity of this concept, use one of your Internet search engines to key in the words "partnering + selling." Notice the large number of documents related to this query. Click on and examine several of these documents to learn more about this approach to selling.
3. Complete the following etiquette quiz. Your instructor will provide you with answers so you can check your responses.
   a. On what side should you wear your name tag?
   b. Is it appropriate to drink beer from a bottle at a reception?
   c. When introducing a female salesperson to a male prospect, whose name should be spoken first?
   d. At the table, when should you place your napkin in your lap?
   e. Is it ever proper to comb, smooth, or touch your hair while seated at a restaurant table?
4. Move quickly through the following list of traits. Use a check mark beside those that fit your self-image. Use an *X* to mark those that do not fit. If you are unsure, indicate with a question mark.

_____ I like myself.   _____ I trust myself.
_____ People trust me.   _____ I often do the wrong thing.
_____ I usually say the right thing.   _____ People avoid me.
_____ I dislike myself.   _____ I enjoy work.
_____ I waste time.   _____ I control myself.
_____ I put up a good front.   _____ I enjoy nature.
_____ I use my talents.   _____ I am dependent on others for
_____ I feel hemmed in.   ideas.
_____ I use time well.   _____ I am involved in solving
_____ I enjoy people.   community problems.
_____ I usually say the wrong thing.   _____ I do not use my talents fully.
_____ I am discouraged about life.   _____ I do not like myself.
_____ I have not developed my talents. _____ I do not like to be around people.
_____ People like to be around me.

Now look at the pattern of your self-assessment.

a. Is there a pattern?
b. Is there a winner or loser pattern?
c. What traits would you like to change? (List them.)
d. Pick the trait you would like to change the most, and prepare a plan to achieve this change.

5. It is pointed out in this chapter that clothing communicates strong messages. In this exercise you become more aware of whether or not your clothes communicate the messages you want them to communicate.

a. Make a chart like the one that follows:

ITEM OF CLOTHING BEING ANALYZED	WHAT I WANT MY CLOTHES TO SAY ABOUT ME TO OTHERS	WHAT OTHERS THINK MY CLOTHING SAYS

b. In the first column, list the clothing you are now wearing, for example, dress slacks, dress shoes, and sweater; athletic shoes, jeans, and T-shirt; or suit, tie, and dress shoes.
c. In the middle column, describe the message you would like the clothes you have chosen to say. For example, "I want to be comfortable," "I want people to notice me," or "I want people to understand how proper and organized I am."
d. Have somebody else fill in the third column by describing what your clothes do say about you.
e. Compare the two columns. Do your clothes communicate what you want them to? Do the same exercise for social dress, casual dress, business attire, and hairstyle.

CRM APPLICATION EXERCISE

Preparing Letters with CRM

Load the ACT! software and look up (Lookup) My Record. This screen identifies the person using the database which, in this case, was Pat Silva and now will be you. Replace Pat Silva's name with your own.

The ACT! software demonstrates how customer relationship management (CRM) programs are designed to be used by people in a hurry or without extensive typing skills. Menu choices can be made with the mouse, by typing simple key combinations, or by selecting an icon. This means that a procedure, such as preparing and printing correspondence, can be started by (1) selecting with a mouse the word <u>W</u>rite, then the word <u>L</u>etter, from the menus; (2) pressing the Alt key and the W (<u>W</u>rite) keys at the same time (Alt+W), and then the L (<u>L</u>etter) key; or (3) picking the Letter icon with the mouse.

A blank letter with the date, inside address, salutation, closing line, your name, and your title will appear on your screen. All you need to do is begin typing the letter. With your printer connected you can print this same letter by selecting <u>P</u>rint from the <u>F</u>ile menu. With the File menu open, note that the right column displays key combinations, such as Ctrl+P to print.

Find the record for Brad Able by choosing <u>L</u>ookup, <u>L</u>ast Name; type in the name "Able"; and press Enter. With Brad Able's record on the screen, choose the letter icon or <u>W</u>rite and <u>L</u>etter from the menus. Prepare and then print a brief letter to Brad Able confirming an appointment to meet at his office next Thursday at 9:00 A.M. to discuss his training needs. Your letter should feature the double-win approach discussed in Chapter 3.

CASE PROBLEM

When people buy or sell a home, they hold their realtor to high standards. After all, for most people the home purchase represents the largest single investment they will make throughout their lifetime. The salespeople employed by Fred Sands Realtors (fredsands.com) introduced at the beginning of this chapter, understand the magnitude of the home purchase or home sale experience. They know that the customers are anxious to partner with someone who can be trusted to look after their best interests.

When new salespeople join the Fred Sands Realtors sales force, they usually come under the tutelage of Sandra Khadra, vice president of marketing. She helps salespeople form a professional image that appeals to the type of clientele served by the company. She knows that there is a direct link between the image projected by the salespeople and the success of the company. When working with salespeople, she emphasizes the following points:

▶ Customers notice even the little details such as the quality of stationery, note paper, and business cards. If the business card features a photo of the salesperson, the person should be looking straight ahead, not away from the camera. This pose permits the salesperson to make eye contact with the customer.

▶ Salespeople at Fred Sands Realtors must be able to build rapport with a variety of personality types. Some customers are quiet, reserved, and somewhat guarded when expressing their views. Others are more impulsive and express their views openly. Salespeople are encouraged to alter their communication style to increase the comfort level of the customer. Sandra Khadra encourages salespeople to mirror the behavior of the prospect to the greatest extent possible. She says that it is always important to gauge how your communication style impacts on the prospect. A positive attitude is another important aspect of the relationship-building process at Fred Sands Realtors.

▶ In some cases salespeople at Fred Sands Realtors must communicate across language and cultural barriers. Foreign-born clients are becoming more common, and this means that salespeople must gain a greater understanding and respect for cultural diversity. To impose our way of doing business on every prospect is short-sighted.

▶ Sandra Khadra suggests that salespeople should find out what customers value. What is the most important aspect of the home purchase or home sale? Most customers do not open up and share important information until they trust the salesperson. (See chapter opener on p. 49 for more information.)

Questions

1. Does it appear that Fred Sands Realtors supports the three prescriptions that serve as a foundation of the relationship strategy? (See Strategic/Consultative Selling Model.) Explain your answer.

2. Why should real estate salespeople spend time developing a relationship strategy? What might be some long-term benefits of this strategy?

3. Is it ever appropriate to touch your client other than a handshake? Explain your answer.

4. What are some benefits to the salesperson who can mirror the behavior of the prospect?

5. What are some precautions to take when preparing a meeting with a foreign-born prospect?

Ethics: The Foundation for Relationships in Selling

When you finish reading
this chapter, you should
be able to

1. Discuss the influence
   of ethical decisions on
   relationships in selling

2. Describe the factors
   that influence the ethical conduct of sales
   personnel

3. Compare legal versus
   ethical standards

4. Explain how role mod-
   els influence the ethical conduct of sales
   personnel

5. Discuss the influence
   of company policies
   and practices on the
   ethical conduct of
   salespeople

6. Explain how values
   influence behavior

7. Discuss guidelines for
   developing a personal
   code of ethics

*H*erbert Schulte, a veteran Prudential Insurance (www.prudential.com) sales representative serving a small Illinois community, was forced to make a difficult ethical decision. His sales manager gave him a list of his middle-aged customers and sales literature
that described a Prudential life insurance policy as nursing home coverage. He contends
that his manager was implicitly recommending an insurance-industry practice called
"churning." With this practice, agents pressure customers to use built-up cash value in an
old policy to buy a new, more expensive one. In some cases information is withheld so customers fail to understand the negative aspects of the buying decision. Mr. Schulte realized
that the sales approach recommended by his sales manager would require that he mislead
his established customers. He refused to go along with the plan.[1] Mr. Schulte was one of
hundreds of Prudential sales representatives encouraged to use misleading sales practices.
Soon after the Prudential problems made headlines, the company began to reform its sales
practices and meet its legal obligations. Over 1,000 agents and managers were fired and a
fine of $35 million was paid. The company purchased full-page newspaper ads to apolo-
gize for "intolerable" deceptive sales practices. Later, Prudential agreed to a $2 billion
class-action settlement that involved 650,000 policyholders. The Prudential scandal provides a powerful example of a sales culture gone bad.[2]

MAKING ETHICAL DECISIONS

Making ethical decisions is a daily reality in the field of personal selling. In every selling situation, salespeople must judge the rightness or wrongness of their actions. As in any other professional field there is the constant temptation to compromise personal standards of conduct to achieve economic goals.

Ethics are the rules that direct your conduct and moral judgments.[3] They help translate your values into appropriate and effective behaviors in your day-to-day life. Ethics reflect the moral principles and standards of the community. Kickbacks and payoffs may be acceptable practices in one part of the world, yet may be viewed as unethical practices elsewhere. Exaggerated or inaccurate sales claims may be acceptable at one company, but forbidden at another company.

There is no one uniform code of ethics for all salespeople. However, a large number of business organizations, professional associations, and certification agencies have established written codes. For example, Certified Marketing Services International (CMSI), introduced in Chapter 2, requires all persons seeking certification to sign the CMSI Code of Ethics (Fig. 4.1).

Today, we recognize that character and integrity strongly influence relationships in personal selling. As noted in the previous chapter, character is composed of your personal standards of behavior, including your honesty and integrity. Your character is based on your internal values and the resulting judgments you make about what is right and what is wrong. The ethical decisions you make reflect your character strength.

We are indebted to Stephen Covey, author of *The Seven Habits of Highly Effective People*, for helping us better understand the relationship between character strength and success in personal selling. In his best selling book, Covey says that there are basic principles that must be integrated into our character.[4] One example is to always do what you say

Figure 4.1
CMSI CODE OF ETHICS FOR SALES PROFESSIONALS

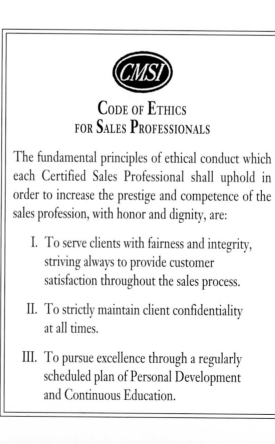

CMSI

CODE OF ETHICS
FOR SALES PROFESSIONALS

The fundamental principles of ethical conduct which each Certified Sales Professional shall uphold in order to increase the prestige and competence of the sales profession, with honor and dignity, are:

   I. To serve clients with fairness and integrity, striving always to provide customer satisfaction throughout the sales process.

  II. To strictly maintain client confidentiality at all times.

 III. To pursue excellence through a regularly scheduled plan of Personal Development and Continuous Education.

you are going to do. Fulfilling your commitments builds trust, and trust is the most important precondition of partnering.

Character Strength

Despite growing interest in business ethics throughout the past decade, unethical behavior has become all too common. One survey indicates that nearly half of the workers surveyed engaged in unethical or illegal acts during the year preceding the study. Many of the workers who had transgressed reported that they were under pressure to act unethically or illegally on the job.[5] Richard Sennett, author of *The Corrosion of Character*, says that the decline of character strength can be traced to conditions that have grown out of our fast-paced, high-stress, information-driven economy. He states that character strength builds as we display loyalty, mutual commitment, and the pursuit of long-term goals.[6] These are the very qualities needed to build strong buyer–seller relationships. Later in this chapter we discuss how salespeople can develop a personal code of ethics.

Ethics — An Historical Perspective

For centuries the principal guideline for dealing with merchants was **caveat emptor**, which means, "Let the buyer beware." This meant that a buyer was expected to look the product over carefully. Once the transaction was concluded, the business relationship ended for all practical purposes. The buyer could not make any claims against the seller at some later date.

With the evolution of the marketing era the caveat emptor philosophy of doing business fell into disfavor. This change resulted from two major forces. First, business leaders discovered that honest business dealings established a foundation for a long-term relationship with customers. The second force is consumer activism. Buyers have become more knowledgeable and more politically active. They demand high-quality products and honest business dealings. Consumer activists often lobby for new laws that restrict certain types of business practices.

A close examination of the history of ethics and ethical behavior reveals two interesting facts. The first is that it is difficult to define fundamental ethical principles to cover every business practice. What is considered wrong by one person or firm may be consid-

➤➤ Selling in Action

HONESTY FROM A QUARTERBACK'S PERSPECTIVE

Jeff Kemp, former National Football League quarterback, believes that sports can teach important moral lessons. Some of these lessons can be applied in personal selling. This is what he says about honesty:

> The importance of honesty colors all the rest of life. Why is truth so important? It is because respect, relationships, and unity all depend on truth. If you cannot be honest with people, you cannot have healthy relationships.

Kemp found that honesty was the foundation for harmony among team members. He says, "Without truth, I couldn't trust my teammates and they couldn't trust me."[a]

Character strength builds as we display loyalty, mutual commitment, and the pursuit of long term goals. These are the qualities needed to build strong buyer-seller relationships.

ered right by another. In the final analysis, each business firm must establish its own ethical standards. The second finding is that people are continually in the process of negotiating ethical norms. Situations keep changing, and we find it necessary to establish new standards. If a good customer is sexually harassing a salesperson, and this behavior is reported to the sales manager, what action should the manager take? The issue of third-party harassment often is not covered in written policies on sexual harassment.[7] You supervise salespeople who travel a great deal. You discover that it is possible to obtain major airfare price reductions by requiring salespeople to stay over on Saturday. Should you require them to spend weekends away from family members? Many business firms are struggling to align their values, ethics, and principles with the expectations of their salespeople and their customers.

FACTORS INFLUENCING THE ETHICS OF SALESPEOPLE

In the field of personal selling the temptation to maximize short-term gains by some type of unethical conduct is always present. Salespeople are especially vulnerable to moral corruption because they are subject to many temptations. A few examples follow:

> The competition is using exaggerated claims to increase the sale of its product. Should you counteract this action by using exaggerated claims of your own to build a stronger case for your product?

You have visited the buyer twice, and each time the person displayed a great deal of interest in your product. During the last visit the buyer hinted that the order might be signed if you could provide a small gift. Your company has a long-standing policy that gifts are not to be given under any circumstances. What do you do?

Your sales manager is under great pressure to increase sales. At a recent meeting of the entire sales staff this person said, "We have to beat the competition no matter what it takes!" Does this emotional appeal change your way of dealing with customers?

During a recent business trip you met an old friend and decided to have dinner together. At the end of the meal you paid for the entire bill and left a generous tip. Do you now put these non-business-related expenses on your expense account?

You are selling financial services for a bank and have developed a long list of satisfied customers. You are offered a similar position with a competing bank. If you accept the position, should you attempt to take your good customers with you?

These ethical dilemmas arise frequently in the field of selling. How do salespeople respond? Some ignore company policy, cast aside personal standards of conduct, and yield to the pressure. However, a surprising number of salespeople are able to resist. They are aided by a series of factors that help them distinguish right from wrong. Figure 4.2 outlines the positive forces that help them deal honestly and openly with prospects at all times. Next we discuss each of these factors.

Local, State, and Federal Laws

In the field of selling there are both legal standards and ethical standards. An ethical standard is an outgrowth of society's customs and attitudes. A legal standard is enforced by statute. Throughout the past decade there has been a noticeable increase in government

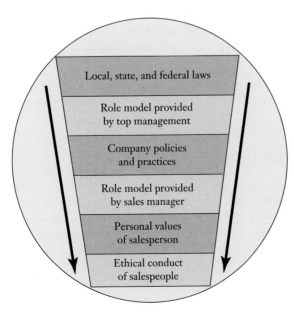

Figure 4.2
FACTORS DETERMINING
ETHICAL BEHAVIOR OF
SALESPEOPLE

Local, state, and federal laws

Role model provided
by top management

Company policies
and practices

Role model provided
by sales manager

Personal values
of salesperson

Ethical conduct
of salespeople

controls and penalties for wrongdoings. Business ethics got the attention of top management in the early 1990s when new federal sentencing guidelines went into effect. They provided increased fines for corporations that commit illegal acts and jail sentences for officers found to be responsible for the unlawful practice.

Today, nearly all sales activities are subject to regulation. Some of the most common federal laws deal with price competition, credit reporting, debt collection practices, motor vehicle safety, and land sales disclosure. Of course, there also are numerous state and local laws that affect personal selling.

Many companies are learning that resolving legal disputes in the courts can be costly and very time consuming. The normal time from filing to resolution of a civil case in the federal court system is three years.[8] A serious effort to prevent unethical activities can prevent costly litigation.

THE UNIFORM COMMERCIAL CODE

The Uniform Commercial Code (UCC) and its predecessor, the Uniform Sales Act, are the major laws influencing sales throughout the United States. Several areas featured in the UCC focus directly on the seller–buyer relationship. Some of the primary areas follow:

1. *Definition of a sale.* The code defines the legal dimensions of a sale. It clearly states that salespeople have the authority to legally obligate the company they represent.
2. *Warranties and guarantees.* The code distinguishes between express warranties and implied warranties. Express warranties are those that are described by the express language of the seller. Implied warranties are the obligations imposed by law on the seller that are not assumed in express language.
3. *Salesperson and reseller.* In many cases the salesperson has resellers as customers or prospects. Salespeople must be aware of their employer's obligations to the reseller.
4. *Financing of sales.* Often salespeople work for firms that are directly involved in financing products or services, or in arranging such financing from outside sources. A salesperson needs to be familiar with the legal aspects of these credit arrangements.
5. *Product consignment.* In some cases, goods are delivered to the buyer, but the title remains with the seller. This type of transaction can become complicated if the goods have a limited life span. Depreciation may occur with the passing of time. Salespeople should be familiar with the company's rights in cases where goods are sold on consignment.

The UCC is a legal guide to a wide range of transactions between the seller and the buyer. This law has been adopted throughout the United States and therefore has implications for most salespeople.

COOLING-OFF LAWS

A majority of the states have passed legislation that establishes a cooling-off period during which the consumer may void a contract to purchase goods or services. Although the provisions of these laws vary from state to state, their primary purpose is to give customers an opportunity to reconsider a buying decision made under a salesperson's persuasive influence. Many laws are designed to deal specifically with sales made in the consumer's home. In addition to state laws, the Federal Trade Commission (FTC) has adopted a trade regulation rule, which deals directly with sales practices. A cooling-off period for door-to-door sales is part of this legislation.

➤➤ *Doing Business in a Diverse World*

BRIBES SOMETIMES INFLUENCE FOREIGN DEALS

The Salt Lake City Organizing Committee has been busy polishing the image of the scandal-tainted 2002 Olympic Winter Games. The committee has been accused of giving International Olympic Committee (IOC) members thousands of dollars in gifts and cash to win their support for holding the games in Salt Lake City. People familiar with the location selection process say that bribes and kickbacks have been used frequently over the years. The Olympics are similar to a big international business. The host city typically wins millions of dollars in infrastructure improvements and millions more are spent after the games begin.

Companies that are involved in international trade often receive requests for bribes or kickbacks. In many cases these demands have come from foreign government officials. The United States outlawed foreign bribery in 1977 with the Foreign Corrupt Practices Act. In addition, most companies have their own ethics codes that prohibit the payment of bribes. In some cases international contract competitions are influenced by bribes. Winning a contract by paying a bribe, unfortunately, is still a common occurrence in some parts of the world.[b]

ETHICS BEYOND THE LETTER OF THE LAW

Too often people confuse ethical standards with legal standards. They believe that if you are not breaking the law, then you are acting in an ethical manner.[9] A salesperson's ethical sense must extend beyond the legal definition of what is right and wrong. To view ethics only in terms of what is legally proper encourages the question, "What can I get by with?" A salesperson must develop a personal code of ethics that extends beyond the letter of the law.

Top Management as Role Model

Ethical standards tend to filter down from the top of an organization. Employees look to company leaders for guidance. Chester Barnard, former president of New Jersey Bell, has stated that a leader's role is to harness the social forces in the organization, to shape and guide values. He describes good managers as value shapers concerned with the organization's informal social properties.[10] The organization's moral tone, as established by management personnel, is the most important single determinant of employee ethics. Today, top management must provide the best possible role model in the area of ethical behavior. People at the top must realize that actions speak louder than words. They are judged by what they do, not by what they say.

Minnesota Mutual Life Insurance Company has been able to steer clear of scandal for more than 100 years by adopting a values-based management philosophy that rewards integrity and honesty. Success at the management level requires commitment to the company's core values. Managers must demonstrate their ability to infuse ethical values in their subordinates.[11]

Personal selling, by its nature, promotes close working relationships. It is important that salespeople preserve the confidentiality of information they receive.

Company Policies and Practices

Company policies and practices can have a major impact on the ethical conduct of salespeople. Two researchers at the University of Pennsylvania surveyed over 400 industrial salespeople who were asked to make decisions concerning fourteen scenarios that posed ethical dilemmas. The findings indicate that company policies can have a significant influence on employees who are faced with ethical conflicts.[12]

Developing policy statements forces a firm to "take a stand" on various business practices. Distinguishing right from wrong can be a healthy activity for any organization. The outcome is a more clear-cut philosophy of how to conduct business transactions. Research conducted at the University of Chicago revealed that companies with a defined corporate commitment to ethical practices did better financially than firms that didn't make ethics a key management component.[13]

Sears, Roebuck and Company provides its employees with a booklet entitled *Code of Business Conduct.* It outlines the company position on a wide range of issues such as receiving gifts, employee discounts, care of company assets, and foreign business dealings. The booklet also includes guidelines for making ethical decisions (Table 4.1). Most marketing companies provide salespeople with guidelines in such areas as sharing confidential information, reciprocity, bribery, gift giving, entertainment, and business defamation.

SHARING CONFIDENTIAL INFORMATION

Personal selling, by its very nature, promotes close working relationships. Customers often turn to salespeople for advice. They disclose confidential information freely to someone they trust. It is important that salespeople preserve the confidentiality of information they receive.

It is not unusual for a customer to disclose information that may be of great value to a competitor. This might include development of new products, plans to expand into new

Table 4.1	**SEARS'S GUIDELINES FOR ETHICAL DECISION MAKING**

GUIDELINES FOR MAKING ETHICAL DECISIONS

1. Is it legal?
2. Is it within Sears shared beliefs and policies?
3. Is it right/fair/appropriate?
4. Would I want everyone to know about this?
5. How will I feel about myself?

Source: *Code of Business Conduct*, Sears, Roebuck and Company, 3333 Beverly Road, Hoffman Estates, IL 60179. Courtesy of Sears, Roebuck and Company.

markets, or anticipated changes in personnel. A salesperson may be tempted to share confidential information with a representative of a competing firm. This breach of confidence might be seen as a means of gaining favor. In most cases this action backfires. The person who receives the confidential information quickly loses respect for the salesperson. A gossipy salesperson seldom develops a trusting relationship with another business associate.

RECIPROCITY

Reciprocity is a mutual exchange of benefits, as when a firm buys products from its own customers. Some business firms actually maintain a policy of reciprocity. For example, the manufacturer of commercial sheets and blankets may purchase hotel services from firms that use its products.

Is there anything wrong with the "you scratch my back and I'll scratch yours" approach to doing business? The answer is sometimes yes. In some cases the use of reciprocity borders on commercial blackmail. Salespeople have been known to approach firms that supply their company and encourage them to buy out of obligation. The firm may be forced to buy products of questionable quality at excessive prices.

A business relationship based on reciprocity often has drawbacks. There is the ever-present temptation to take such customers for granted. A customer who buys out of obligation may take a backseat to customers who were won in the open market.

BRIBERY

The book *Arrogance and Accords: The Inside Story of the Honda Scandal* describes one of the largest commercial corruption cases in U. S. history. Over a 15-year period Honda officials received more than $50 million in cash and gifts from dealers anxious to obtain fast selling Honda cars and profitable franchises. Eighteen former Honda executives were convicted of obtaining kickbacks; most went to prison.[14]

In some cases a bribe is wrong from a legal standpoint. In almost all cases the bribe is wrong from an ethical point of view. However, bribery does exist, and a salesperson must be prepared to cope with it. It helps to have a well-established company policy to use as a reference point.

DILBERT

Reprinted by permission of United Feature Syndicate, Inc.

GIFT GIVING

Gift giving is a widespread practice in America. However, some companies do maintain a "no gift" policy. Many companies report that their policy is either no gifts or nothing of real value. At Hewlett Packard, advertising novelties, favors, or entertainment may be given to customers and suppliers under certain conditions: They are consistent with accepted business practice; they are of limited value and cannot be construed as a bribe or payoff; they do not violate any law, government regulation, or generally accepted ethical standards; and public disclosure of the facts should not embarrass the company.[15]

There are some gray areas that separate a gift from a bribe. Most people agree that a token of insignificant price, such as a pen imprinted with a company logo or a desk calendar, is appropriate. These types of gifts are meant to foster goodwill. A bribe, on the other hand, is an attempt to influence the person receiving the gift.[16]

Are there right and wrong ways to handle gift giving? The answer is yes. The following guidelines are helpful to any salesperson who is considering giving gifts to customers:

1. Do not give gifts before doing business with a customer. Do not use the gift as a substitute for effective selling methods.
2. Never convey the impression you are "buying" the customer's business with gifts. When this happens, the gift becomes nothing more than a bribe.
3. When gift giving is done correctly, the customer clearly views it as symbolic of your appreciation—a "no strings attached" goodwill gesture.
4. Be sure the gift is not a violation of the policies of your firm or of your customer's firm. Some firms do not allow employees to accept gifts at all. Other firms place a dollar limit on a gift's value.

In summary, if you have second thoughts about giving a gift, do not do it. When you are sure some token is appropriate, keep it simple and thoughtful.[17]

ENTERTAINMENT

Entertainment is a widespread practice in the field of selling and may be viewed as a bribe by some people. The line dividing gifts, bribes, and entertainment is often quite arbitrary.

Salespeople must frequently decide how to handle entertaining. A few industries see entertainment as part of the approach used to obtain new accounts. This is especially true when competing products are nearly identical. A good example is the cardboard box industry. These products vary little in price and quality. To win an account may involve knowing whom to entertain and how to entertain.

Gift giving is a widespread practice in America. Giving a customer an expensive watch would not be permitted at Hewlett Packard.

Entertainment is a highly individualized process. One prospect might enjoy a professional football game, while another would be impressed most by a quiet meal at a good restaurant. The key is to get to know your prospect's preferences. How does the person spend leisure time? How much time can the person spare for entertainment? You need to answer these and other questions before you invest time and money on entertainment.

BUSINESS DEFAMATION

Salespeople frequently compare their product's qualities and characteristics with those of a competitor during the sales presentation. If such comparisons are inaccurate, are misleading, or slander a company's business reputation, such conduct is illegal.[18] Competitors have sued hundreds of companies and manufacturer's representatives for making slanderous statements while selling.

What constitutes business defamation? Steven M. Sack, coauthor of *The Salesperson's Legal Guide*, provides the following examples:

1. *Business slander.* This arises when an unfair and untrue oral statement is made about a competitor. The statement becomes actionable when it is communicated to a third party and can be interpreted as damaging the competitor's business reputation or the personal reputation of an individual in that business.
2. *Business libel.* This may be incurred when an unfair and untrue statement is made about a competitor in writing. The statement becomes actionable when it is communicated to a third party and can be interpreted as damaging the company.
3. *Product disparagement.* This occurs when false or deceptive comparisons or distorted claims are made concerning a competitor's product, services, or property.[19]

The effectiveness of company policies as a deterrent to unethical behavior depends on two factors. The first is the firm's attitude toward employees who violate these policies. If violations are routinely ignored, the policy's effect soon erodes. Second, policies that influence personal selling need the support of the entire sales staff. Salespeople should have some voice in policy decisions; they are more apt to support policies they have helped develop.

Sales Manager as Role Model

The salesperson's actions often mirror the sales manager's behavior and expectations. This is not surprising when you consider the relationship between salespeople and their supervisors. They look to their supervisors for guidance and direction. The sales manager is generally the company's closest point of contact with the sales staff. This person is usually viewed as the chief spokesman for top management.

Sales managers generally provide new salespeople with their first orientation to company operations. They are responsible for interpreting company policy. On a continuing basis the sales manager monitors the salesperson's work and provides important feedback concerning conduct. If a salesperson violates company policy, it is usually the sales manager who is responsible for administering reprimands. If the moral fiber of a sales force begins to break down, the sales manager must shoulder a great deal of responsibility.

Sales managers influence the ethical behavior of salespeople by virtue of what they say and what they do. From time to time, managers must review their expectations of ethical behavior. Salespeople are under continuous pressure to abandon their personal ethical standards to achieve sales goals. Values such as integrity and honesty must receive ongoing support from the sales manager.

The sales manager's behavior must be consistent with a stated philosophy. Actions do speak louder than words; any inconsistency between words and deeds is likely to have a negative influence on the attitude of the sales staff.

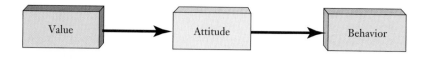

Figure 4.3
THE RELATIONSHIP OF VALUES, ATTITUDES, AND BEHAVIOR

Value → Attitude → Behavior

Salesperson's Personal Values

Ann Kilpatrick, a sales representative in the transportation industry, encountered an unexpected experience when entertaining a potential client. The client said, "Let's go to Johnny's." She was not familiar with Johnny's, but on arrival discovered it was a raunchy bar. Kilpatrick related that she sat there for five minutes and then said, "This is not what I was expecting. This is a sleazy place. Let's go somewhere else where we can talk." She was not willing to compromise her personal values to win a new account.[20]

Values represent the ultimate reasons people have for acting as they do. **Values** are your deep personal beliefs and preferences that influence your behavior. To discover what really motivates you, carefully examine what you value.[21] Sidney Simon, noted author in the field of values clarification, has said, "There's no place to hide from your values. Everything you do reflects them." Values serve as a foundation for our attitudes, and our attitudes serve as a foundation for our behavior (Fig. 4.3). We do not adopt or discard values quickly. In fact, the development of values is a lifelong process.

►► CUSTOMER RELATIONSHIP MANAGEMENT WITH TECHNOLOGY

EXERCISING CARE WITH CRM DATA

Customer relationship management systems enable you to collect information about people with whom you maintain relationships, including the taking of notes. It is a good practice to record more than basic transaction information, such as personal details about your customers. Reviewing your observations about the customers' behavior and your recording of their statements can help you understand them and their needs. Rereading their comments about ethical issues can assist you in assessing the value of maintaining a business relationship with them.

To be fair, it is important to record only the facts concerning your observations, not necessarily your conclusions. Information in an electronic database can last a long time and, for reasons such as litigation or company acquisitions, can be "mobile." This means that others may form an opinion about your customer, based on your recorded observations, with potential detrimental consequences for your customer. Because the customer may not be aware of the existence of the information in your database, that person does not have a fair opportunity to correct any erroneous conclusions. Another reason to carefully record only facts is the possibility that the information may be read by the customer. For example, there are instances in which a customer later joined the sales organization and gained access to the customer relationship management (CRM) system.

Most CRM systems contain scheduling functions, which means that you can set aside time on your calendar to attend meetings, make phone calls, and perform tasks. The scheduling tools usually include alarms, which remind you that a deadline is approaching. The disciplined use of these features can help you get tasks done on time. Taking advantage of the system's reminder tools can be especially important when it involves fulfilling your commitments. The system can help you build trust by reminding you to always do what you said you would do. (See the exercise, Preparing Mailing Labels with CRM, on p. 86 for more information.)

Although we live by a value system, this system is not always clear to us. One outcome of education and training is frequently the clarification of one's values. Life experiences also help people clarify their values.

Values can serve as a deterrent to unethical behavior in a selling situation. They help to establish our own personal standards concerning what is right and what is wrong. Ron Willingham, author of *Integrity Selling*®, says, "A salesperson's ethics and values contribute more to sales success than do techniques or strategies."[22] Some salespeople discover a values conflict between themselves and the employer. Some of the salespeople at Prudential Insurance Company of America were asked to engage in deceptive sales practices, and they rebelled. If you view your employer's instructions or influence as improper, you have three choices:

1. Ignore the influence of your values, and engage in unethical behavior. The end result is likely to be a loss of self-respect and a feeling of guilt. When salespeople experience conflicts between their actions and values, they also feel a loss of confidence and energy.[23] Positive energy is the result of creating value for the customer. Negative energy is experienced when salespeople fail to honor and embrace their ethical values.

2. Voice strong opposition to the practice that is in conflict with your value system. Take a stand, and state your beliefs. An anonymous author once said, "Following the path of least resistance is what makes men and rivers crooked." Your objective is to influence decisions made by your superiors.

3. Refuse to compromise your values, and be prepared to deal with the consequences. This may mean leaving the job. It also may mean that you will be fired.

Salespeople face ethical problems and decisions every day. In this respect they are no different from the doctor, the lawyer, the teacher, or any other professional. Ideally, they make decisions on the basis of the values they hold.

TOWARD A PERSONAL CODE OF ETHICS

Many people considering a career in selling are troubled by the thought that they may be pressured into compromising their personal standards of right and wrong. These fears may be justified. The authors of *The Ethical Edge*, a book that examines organizations that have faced moral crises, contend that business firms have given too little thought to the issue of helping employees to function ethically within organizations.[24] Many salespeople wonder if their own ethical philosophy can survive in the business world. These are some of their questions:

"Can good business and good ethics coexist?"

"Are there still business firms that value adherence to high ethical standards?"

"Is honesty still a valued personal trait in the business community?"

It is becoming more difficult to provide a concise yes or no answer to these questions. Times are changing, and it is getting harder and harder to tell the "good guys" from the "bad guys." We read about the unethical use of gifts and bribes by corporate officials. Investigations of the Medicaid program turn up overbilling and other unethical behaviors by doctors, pharmacists, and nursing home operators. Reports from colleges and universities indicate that cheating is becoming more common. Even some of our most respected political leaders have been guilty of tax fraud, accepting illegal campaign contributions, and accepting payments for questionable favors. We are tempted to ask, "Is everybody doing it?"

Our society currently is doing a great deal of soul-searching. Many people want to see a firming of ethical standards. Many leaders are keenly aware that unethical behavior

Personal selling must be viewed as an exchange of value. Salespeople who accept this ethical guideline view personal selling as something you do for customers, not something you do to customers.

threatens the moral fabric of our free enterprise system. If the business community cannot police itself, more and more people will be looking to government for solutions to the problem. One fact we have learned from history is that we cannot legislate morality.

In the field of athletic competition the participants rely heavily on a written set of rules. The referee or umpire is ever present to detect rule violations and assess a penalty. In the field of personal selling there is no universal code of ethics. However, some general guidelines can serve as a foundation for a personal code of business ethics.

1. *Personal selling must be viewed as an exchange of value.* Salespeople who maintain a value focus are searching for ways to create value for their prospects or customers. This value may take the form of increased productivity, greater profit, enjoyment, or security. The value focus motivates the salesperson to carefully identify the prospects' wants and needs.[25] Salespeople who accept this ethical guideline view personal selling as something you do *for* customers, not something you do *to* customers. The role of the salesperson is to diagnose buyer needs and determine if value can be created. Understanding the prospects' wants and needs should always precede any attempt to sell.[26]

2. *Relationship comes first, task second.* Sharon Drew Morgan, author of *Selling with Integrity,* says that you can't sell a product unless there is a level of comfort between you and the prospect. She encourages salespeople to take the time to create a level of comfort, rapport, and collaboration that encourages open communication.[27] Placing task before relationship is based on the belief that the salesperson knows more than the customer. Morgan reminds us, "The buyer has the answers, the seller has the questions."[28] These answers surface only when the buyer–seller relationship is characterized by rapport and trust.

3. *Be honest with yourself and with others.* To achieve excellence in terms of ethical practices, you have to believe that everything you do counts. Tom Peters in *Thriving on Chaos* said, "Integrity may be about little things as much as or more than big ones."[29] Integrity is about accuracy in completing your expense account. There is always the temptation to inflate the expense report for personal gain. Integrity is also about avoiding the temptation to stretch the truth, to exaggerate,

or to withhold information. Paul Ekman, author of *Telling Lies,* says that withholding important information is one of the primary ways of lying.[30] A complete and informative sales presentation may include information concerning the product's limitations. If you let your character and integrity be revealed in the little things, others can see you as one who acts ethically in all things. Any violation of honesty, however small, dilutes your ethical strength, leaving you weaker for the big challenges you will face sooner or later.[31]

Every day salespeople make decisions that have ethical ramifications. In some cases doing the right thing may not be popular with others. Price Pritchette, author of *The Ethics of Excellence* says:

> When you hold out for high standards, people are impressed—but they don't always like you for it. Not everybody will be on your side in your struggle to do the right thing.[32]

As you make ethical decisions, think long term, not short term. A serious ethical violation can be costly in terms of damage to your reputation.

Summary

At the beginning of this chapter we define *ethics* as the rules that direct your conduct and moral judgments. Ethics help us establish standards of honesty, loyalty, and fairness. We note that ethics are not legally constituted guidelines. To consider only what is legally right and wrong limits our perception of morality. Laws alone do not bring a halt to unethical selling practices.

Salespeople can benefit from the stabilizing influence of good role models. Although top management personnel are usually far removed from day-to-day selling activities, they can have a major impact on salespeople's conduct. Dishonesty at the top of an organization causes an erosion of ethical standards at the lower echelons. Sales managers provide another important role model. They interpret company policies and help establish guidelines for acceptable and unacceptable selling practices.

Company policies and practices can have a strong influence on the ethical conduct of salespeople. These policies often help salespeople cope with ethical conflicts.

Finally, salespeople must establish their own standards of personal conduct. They must decide how best to serve their company and build strong partnerships with their customers. The pressure to compromise one's ethical standards surfaces almost daily. The temptation to take the easy road to achieve short-term gains is always present. The primary deterrent is a strong sense of right and wrong. Three general guidelines that can serve as a foundation for a personal code of ethics are presented.

We strongly support the premise, "Bad ethics is bad business and unethical sales practices will ultimately destroy relationships with customers." Anyone who relies on unethical sales practices cannot survive in the selling field very long. These practices undermine the company's reputation and ultimately reduce profits.

KEY TERMS

Ethics	Reciprocity
Caveat Emptor	Values

Review Questions

1. What is the definition of *ethics*? Why is this topic receiving so much attention today?
2. What does *caveat emptor* mean? What are the two forces that have lessened the impact of this philosophy?
3. A close examination of the history of ethics and ethical behavior reveals two interesting facts. What are they?
4. What five factors help influence salespeople's ethical conduct?
5. What is the Uniform Commercial Code? Why is it needed?
6. What five primary areas in the Uniform Commercial Code focus directly on the relationship between the salesperson and the buyer?
7. Explain why the sales manager plays such an important role in influencing the ethical behavior of salespeople.
8. A company policy on ethics usually covers six major areas. What are they?
9. Is it ever appropriate to give gifts to customers? Explain.
10. List and describe three guidelines used as a foundation of a self-imposed code of business ethics.

Application Exercises

1. You find that you have significantly overcharged one of your clients. The error was discovered when you received his check. It is unlikely that the customer or your company will become aware of the overcharge. Because of this error, the company realized a high net profit on the sale. Your commissions are based on this profit. What, if anything, will you do about the overcharge?

2. Members of the National Candy Brokers Association are sales representatives for producers and importers of candy. These members have adopted a code of ethics to guide the development of marketing relationships with both their suppliers and their customers. Examine their code of ethics by accessing their Web address at www.candynet.com/.

3. You work for a supplier of medical equipment. Your sales manager informs you that he wants you to capture a certain hospital account. He also tells you to put on your expense account anything it costs to secure the firm as a client. When you ask him to be more specific, he tells you to use your own judgment. Up to this time you have never questioned your sales manager's personal code of ethics. Make a list of the items you believe can be legitimately charged to the company on your expense account.

4. For some time your strongest competitor has been making untrue derogatory statements about your product and about you as a salesperson. You know for a fact that her product is not as good as yours. Yet hers has a higher price. Several of your best customers have confronted you with these charges. Describe how you plan to answer them.

CRM Application Exercise

Preparing Mailing Labels with CRM

Load the ACT! software and select Report, Other. From the list of mailing label formats, choose avry5160, and press OK. In the Prepare Report window, pick Active Group and

Document and press OK. The mailing information for each contact will be displayed on the screen. Select File, Print and print this list.

A friend of yours is a salesperson with a firm that installs the cables used to connect network components, a service that your company does not offer. Your friend wants to know if you will share the customer list that you printed. What should be your response?

CASE PROBLEM

Don Davis dropped into the stores receiving department of Regina Steel Fabricators, one of his company's oldest and best accounts. He had been called by Bruce Hensman, their senior purchasing person, to inspect the last shipment of structural tubing that Don had sold them. According to Bruce, when the tubing was sheared to the lengths required, the shear had dimpled the ends of the tubes, and the dimples had not been removed as requested. The tubes were therefore not perfectly round, and the casters that were to fit into the ends would not do so without considerable effort.

Don arrived just after lunch, and while waiting for Gary Anderson, the stores supervisor, he noticed that there was a large shipment of stainless steel bolts and nuts sitting in the stores receiving area. They were marked type 304 stainless steel, one of the cheaper grades. He was curious, because he had given Bruce Hensman a price quotation the previous week on the same material in type 316 stainless steel, a much more expensive grade.

Don Davis approached a young clerk who was working in the receiving area. "Where did that shipment come from?" he asked.

"Quality Distribution," the young man replied, without looking directly at Don.

"What was the cost of the material?" Don inquired.

"Don't know. My copy of the order doesn't show a cost, nor does the packing slip that came in with the shipment," the young man said as he shrugged his shoulders.

"Is it supposed to be type 304 or type 316?" Don persisted.

"It just says stainless steel bolts and nuts on my copy of the purchase order," replied the clerk. "And the packing slip just says stainless steel as well. There's no mention of type of stainless. If you want to find out more, you'll have to contact Bruce Hensman in our purchasing department. This order was placed by him."

Don Davis was getting more curious as he thought about the shipment he had seen. When he returned to his office, he called Bruce Hensman, but he didn't mention what he had seen. "Bruce, I'm calling about that price quotation I gave you last week for type 316 stainless steel bolts and nuts. Will you give us an order?"

"Sorry. I placed the order with Quality Distribution last week because their price was better," Bruce replied. "You'll have to sharpen your pencil if you want our business."

Don Davis knew there was no way that Quality Distribution could compete on price because they were basically a small jobber account that really wasn't in the stainless steel business. But he didn't want to say that to Bruce Hensman, so he asked, "How much sharper?"

"Just a bit, but you know it wouldn't be honest for me to tell you," Bruce laughed.

After they talked for a few more minutes, Don Davis promised to try to be more competitive. When he hung up, he sat at his desk and stared at the wall. Don Davis knew he had to be careful. There was something wrong. He was not sure what it was, but he knew he had to get to the bottom of it fast. This was an important long-term account for his company, and as a relatively new salesperson Don Davis knew he couldn't afford to lose it.

Questions

1. Has Don Davis's behavior been ethical? Why or why not?
2. Has Bruce Hensman's behavior been ethical? Why or why not?
3. What should Don Davis do?

DEVELOPING A PRODUCT STRATEGY

➤ Part III examines the important role of complete and accurate product, company, and competitive knowledge in personal selling. Lack of knowledge in these areas impairs the salesperson's ability to configure value-added solutions. Part III also describes several value-added selling strategies.

Service is not a competitive edge, it is the competitive edge. People do not buy just products; they also buy expectations. One expectation is that the item they buy will produce the benefits the seller promised. Another is that if it doesn't, the seller will make good on the promise.

KARL ALBRECHT AND RON ZEMKE, SERVICE AMERICA: DOING BUSINESS IN THE NEW ECONOMY

Creating Product Solutions

When you finish this chapter, you should be able to

1. Explain the importance of developing a product strategy

2. Describe product configuration

3. Identify reasons why salespeople and customers benefit from thorough product knowledge

4. Discuss the most important kinds of product and company information that salespeople use in creating product solutions

5. Describe how knowledge of competition improves personal selling

6. List major sources of product information

7. Explain the difference between product features and buyer benefits

8. Demonstrate how to translate product features into buyer benefits

*B*obbi Meredith has a lot in common with many members of today's sales force. First, she is selling a service, not a tangible product. She works with corporate clients who use some form of telecommunications to market their goods and services. Second, she is working for a small business firm. After 14 years with AT&T, a giant in the communications field, she took a sales position with Lo/Ad Communications, a small telecommunications service bureau. Most of the prospects Bobbi calls on know that the telephone can be used to enhance sales and customer service, but they need help understanding the specific applications of technology to sales and marketing. Bobbi is viewed by most clients as a consultant who can configure a customized product solution to enhance their marketing efforts. Her biggest challenge is researching the customer's marketing goals and specific promotional needs, and then preparing a product solution tailored to the customer's needs. The key to success for Bobbi Meredith, and many other salespeople, is the development of a successful product strategy.[1]

DEVELOPING A PRODUCT SOLUTION

Creating the right product solution with the right price for the customer is the most important part of the salesperson's job. The task has become more difficult because of changing customer expectations. A growing number of customers are seeking a customized product solution. The Industrial Age model of making products cheaper by making them the same is no longer acceptable in many markets. The customized product solution appeals to the customer's desire for choices. Regis McKenna says that choice has become a higher value than brand.[2]

As noted in Chapter 1, a product strategy helps salespeople make correct decisions concerning the selection and positioning of products to meet identified customer needs. The **product strategy** is a well-conceived plan that emphasizes becoming a product expert, selling benefits, and configuring value added solutions (Fig. 5.1). Configuring value added solutions is discussed in detail in Chapter 6.

Figure **5.1**
Developing a product strategy enables the salesperson to custom fit products or services to the customer's needs.

Strategic/Consultative Selling Model	
Strategic step	Prescription
DEVELOP A PERSONAL SELLING PHILOSOPHY	☑ ADOPT MARKETING CONCEPT ☑ VALUE PERSONAL SELLING ☑ BECOME A PROBLEM SOLVER/PARTNER
DEVELOP A RELATIONSHIP STRATEGY	☑ ADOPT DOUBLE-WIN PHILOSOPHY ☑ PROJECT PROFESSIONAL IMAGE ☑ MAINTAIN HIGH ETHICAL STANDARDS
DEVELOP A PRODUCT STRATEGY	☐ BECOME A PRODUCT EXPERT ☐ SELL BENEFITS ☐ CONFIGURE VALUE-ADDED SOLUTIONS

Explosion of Product Options

The domestic and global markets are overflowing with a vast array of goods and services. In some industries the number of new products introduced each year is mind-boggling. Consider these examples:

▶ Each year grocery stores introduce more than 10,000 new items. If you are a salesperson employed by a major food wholesaler such as Fleming Companies, Inc. or Super Value Stores, Inc., you face a real challenge when introducing a new product.

▶ Many companies develop and introduce new products to generate additional revenues. A good example is U.S. West Direct, a publisher of yellow page directories. The company has about a million business–customer prospects who can be segmented according to specific needs. Sales representatives use a series of questions to determine the client's unique circumstances, and then create the best product solution.[3]

▶ We have seen an explosion of new products in the securities and financial services field. In one segment, mutual funds, customers can choose from over 7,600 products.[4]

For the customer, this much variety creates a "good news—bad news" situation. The good news is that almost all buyers have a choice when it comes to purchasing a product or service. People like to compare various options. The bad news is that so many choices often complicate the buying process.

As we note in previous chapters, the new economy is about the growing value of knowledge. However, salespeople must do more than supply the customer with large amounts of information. They must provide the buyer with the specific knowledge needed to make the best possible buying decision. One of the most important roles of the salesperson is to simplify the customer's study of the product choices. Later in this chapter we discuss how product features (information) can add value when converted into specific benefits (knowledge) that can help the buyer make an intelligent buying decision.

Creating Solutions with Product Configuration

The challenge facing both customers and salespeople in this era of information overload is deciding which product applications, or combination of applications, can solve the buying problem. If the customer has complex buying needs, then the salesperson may have to bring together many parts of the company's product mix to develop a custom-fitted solution. The product selection process is often referred to as **product configuration**. Salespeople representing Cadalyst Resources, a Des Moines-based computer supplier, develop customer solutions that combine computer hardware, software, installation, and training. After a careful needs assessment, the Cadalyst sales representative prepares a proposal that illustrates how the different parts of the company's product mix come together to solve the customer's problem.

Product configuration is no less important in retail situations where the salesperson is selling a complex product. Assembling a professional wardrobe, preparing an interior design for a home or office, or putting together an automobile lease plan involves product configuration.

Many companies are using product configuration software to develop customized product solutions quickly and accurately. Product configuration software incorporates product selection criteria and associates them directly with customer requirements. Members of the sales force can use the sales configurator to identify product options, prices, delivery schedules, and other parts of the product mix while working interactively with the customer. Most of today's product configuration software can be integrated with contact management software programs such as ACT!, Goldmine, and Siebel. In addition to improving the quality of the sales proposal, this software reduces the time-consuming process of manually preparing written proposals.

Preparing Written Proposals

Written proposals are frequently part of the salesperson's product strategy. It is only natural that some buyers want the proposed solution put in writing. *Written proposals* can be

The challenge facing both the customer and the salesperson in this age of information is deciding which applications can solve the customer's long-term buying problem.

defined as a specific plan of action based on the facts, assumptions, and supporting documentation included in the sales presentation.[5] A well-written proposal adds value to the product solution and can set you apart from the competition. It offers the buyer reassurance that you will deliver what has been promised. Written proposals, which are often accompanied by a sales letter, vary in terms of format and content. Many government agencies, and some large companies, issue a request for proposal (RFP) that specifies the format of the proposal. Most proposals include the following parts:

Budget and overview. Tell the prospect the cost of the solution you have prescribed. Be specific as you describe the product or service features to be provided and specify the price.

Objective. The objective should be expressed in terms of benefits. A tangible objective might be to "reduce payroll expense by 10 percent." An intangible objective might be stated as "increased business security offered by a company with a reputation for dependability." Focus on benefits that relate directly to the customer's need.

Strategy. Briefly describe how you will meet your objective. How will you fulfill the obligations you have described in your proposal? In some cases this section of your proposal includes specific language: "Your account will be assigned to Susan Murray, our senior lease representative."

Schedule. Establish a time frame for meeting your objective. This might involve the confirmation of dates with regard to acquisition, shipping, or installation.

Rationale. With a mixture of logic and emotion present your rationale for taking action now. Once again, the emphasis should be on benefits, not features.[6]

Some written proposals follow a specific format developed by the company. The length of a proposal can vary from a single page to dozens of pages for a complex product.

The proposal should be printed on quality paper and free of any errors in spelling, grammar, or punctuation. Before completing the proposal, review the content one more time to be sure you have addressed all the customer's concerns. Also, determine if you have incorporated enough persuasion into the proposal. Did you use words and sentences that get the prospect's attention and build interest in your product solution?[7] Tips on how to develop a persuasive presentation are presented in Chapter 10.

Product Knowledge Adds Value

Company-sponsored sales training programs are giving increased emphasis to product knowledge because it can give a sales force a competitive advantage. Salespeople who can add value are in a strong position to close sales even when they do not have a price advantage. John Cady, account manager with Revere Electric Supply Company, continually monitors orders placed by his customers to identify alternative products or technologies. While working with the purchasing agent at Abbott Laboratories, he was able to recommend a new technology that was lower in price and more efficient. The estimated cost savings amounted to $122,000 for a one-year period. This is the type of assistance that builds strong partnerships.[8]

The remainder of this chapter is divided into five major sections. The first two sections examine the kinds of product information and company information required by the salesperson. The third section describes the type of information about the competition that is helpful to salespeople. Sources of information are covered in the fourth section, and the fifth section describes how product features can be translated into buyer benefits.

➤➤ BUILDING QUALITY PARTNERSHIPS

WRITING EFFECTIVE SALES LETTERS

Sales letters are increasingly being used by salespeople to describe features and benefits, position products, build relationships, and provide assurances to customers. Sales letters also are used in conjunction with prospecting plans. There are several standard rules that apply to all written sales letters. These include

1. Sales letters should follow the standard visual format of a business letter. They should contain in the following order: either a letterhead or the sender's address, date, inside address (the same as on the outside of the envelope), salutation, body of letter, complimentary close, typed name and handwritten signature of sender, and a notation of enclosures (if there are any).

2. Placement of the letter on paper should provide a balanced white space border area surrounding the entire letter. Three to five blank lines should separate the date and inside address; a single blank line should separate the inside address and the salutation, salutation and opening paragraph of the letter, and each paragraph. A single blank line should separate the last paragraph and the complimentary close. Single spacing should generally be used within the paragraphs.

3. Proper business punctuation includes a colon after the salutation and comma after the complimentary close.

4. Most sales letters include at least three paragraphs. The first paragraph should indicate why you are writing the letter; the second should be a summary of the benefits proposed; and the third paragraph should state what the next action step will be for the sales person, the customer, or both.

5. Proper grammar and spelling must be used throughout the entire letter. Business letters provide an opportunity to build a stronger relationship with the customer and close the sale. Improper placement, punctuation, spelling errors, or weak content conveys a negative impression to the reader and may result in a lost sale.

6. The use of the personal pronoun "I" should be minimized in a sales letter. To keep the letter focused on the customers needs, the pronoun "you" and "your" should appear throughout the body of the letter.

BECOMING A PRODUCT EXPERT

Steve Hawelli, president of Wordhampton Incorporated, an Easthampton, New York firm, believes that a good salesperson is a product expert. He gives this advice to his staff: "Constantly increase your product knowledge. Educate and train yourself to be a professional resource and not just a salesperson."[9] Ideally, a salesperson possesses product knowledge that meets and exceeds customer expectations. This section reviews some of the most common product information categories: (1) product development and quality improvement processes, (2) performance data and specifications, (3) maintenance and service contracts, and (4) price and delivery. Each is important as a potential source of knowledge concerning the product or service.

Product Development and Quality Improvement Processes

Companies spend large amounts of money in the development of their products. In **product development** the original idea for a product or service is tested, modified, and retested several times before it is offered to the customer. Each of the modifications is made with the thought of improving the product. Salespeople should be familiar with product development history. Often this information sets the stage for stronger sales appeals.

Patagonia, a company that makes high-quality sports and outdoor equipment and clothing, uses a unique product development process. Patagonia hires many expert kayakers, skiers, climbers, and fishermen who under actual conditions help develop and test the company's products. In the outdoor recreation market Patagonia wins high praise for its many product innovations.[10]

Quality improvement continues to be an important long-term business strategy for most successful companies. Salespeople need to identify quality improvement processes that provide a competitive advantage and to be prepared to discuss this information during the sales presentation. Motorola, Ritz-Carlton Hotels, and Xerox provide examples of companies that have won awards for implementing important quality controls. **Quality control**, which involves measuring products and services against established standards, is one dimension of the typical quality improvement process. At Pfizer's U.S. Pharmaceutical

CERTIFICATE OF APPROVAL

This is to Certify that the Quality Management System of:

RYKO Manufacturing Co. Inc.

11600 N.W. 54th Avenue, Grimes, IA
has been assessed and approved by INTERTEK Services Corporation
against the following quality assurance standards:

ISO 9001, BS EN 9001, and ANSI/ASQC Q9001-1994

The Quality Management System is applicable to:

The design, development, manufacture, installation and servicing of equipment and systems for the motor vehicle washing industry.

The approval is subject to the company maintaining its system to the required standards, which will be monitored by INTERTEK Services Corporation.

Approval Certificate No. *97-747*
Intitial Certification Date: *February 28, 1997*
Issue Date: *February 28, 1997*
Expiration Date: *February 28, 2000*

Director, Systems Registration

Accredited by the Dutch Council
for Accreditation for certification
and registration activities.

Figure **5.2**
Many international and some domestic companies do not purchase a company's *products* unless they have this highly respected ISO certification. As noted in Chapter 2, new ISO certification is now available for sales and marketing personnel.

Group, extensive training for salespeople represents an important quality control. Sales representatives must demonstrate their ability to present product information to physicians accurately and effectively.[11]

Many companies are investing a great deal of time and money to achieve International Organization for Standardization (ISO) 9000 certification. ISO is an internationally recognized quality standard that certifies the process a company uses to develop a product or service. Independent auditors are used to verify that a company is in compliance with the standards. Purchasers recognize that ISO 9000 certification assures a level of quality.[12] RYKO Manufacturing Company provides an example of a company that has met ISO quality assurance standards (Fig. 5.2).

Performance Data and Specifications

Most potential buyers are interested in performance data and specifications. Some typical questions that might be raised by prospects are

"What is the frequency response for this stereo loudspeaker?"

"What is the anticipated rate of return on this mutual fund?"

"What is the energy consumption rating for this appliance?"

"Are all your hotel and conference center rooms accessible to persons with physical disabilities?"

A salesperson must be prepared to address these types of questions in the written sales proposal and the sales presentation. Performance data are especially critical in cases in which the customer is attempting to compare the merits of one product with another.

In many fields today there are testing programs that provide comparative data concerning various products. For example, the Association of Home Appliance Manufacturers (AHAM) sponsors a program to verify the performance of household refrigerators and freezers. An independent testing laboratory verifies the total refrigerated volume and total shelf area of household refrigerators and freezers. The AHAM certification seal is affixed to each model of a product certified under this program.

Maintenance and Service Contracts

Prospects often want information concerning maintenance and care requirements for the products they purchase. The salesperson who can quickly and accurately provide this information has the edge. Proper maintenance usually extends the life of the product, so this information should be provided at the time of the sale.

Today, many salespeople are developing customized service agreements that incorporate the customer's special priorities, feelings, and needs. They work hard to acquire a real understanding of the customer's specific service criteria. If call return expectations are very important to the customer, the frequency and quantity of product-related visits per week or month can be included in the service contract. Customized service agreements add value to the sale and help protect your business from the competition.[13]

Price and Delivery

Potential buyers expect salespeople to be well versed in price and delivery policies on their products. This information is needed to develop a written sales proposal and the verbal sales presentation. The professional salesperson also should have similar information for competing products. Price objections represent one of the most common barriers to closing the sale.

In most situations the price quotation should be accompanied by information that creates value in the mind of the customer. The process of determining whether or not the proposal adds value is often called **quantifying the solution**. When the purchase represents a major buying decision, such as the purchase of a new computer system, quantifying the solution is important. One way to quantify the solution is to conduct a cost-benefit analysis to determine the actual cost of the purchase and savings the buyer can anticipate from the investment (Table 5.1).

Table **5.1**

Quantifying the solution often involves a carefully prepared cost-benefit analysis. This example compares the higher priced Phoenix semitruck trailer with the lower priced FB model, which is a competing product.

COST SAVINGS OF THE PHOENIX VERSUS FB MODEL FOR A 10-YEAR PERIOD
(ALL PRICES ARE APPROXIMATE)

	Cost Savings
• Stainless steel bulkhead (savings on sandblasting and painting)	$ 425.00
• Stainless steel rear door frame (savings on painting)	425.00
• Air ride suspension (better fuel mileage, longer tire life, longer brake life)	3,750.00
• Hardwood or aluminum scuff (savings from freight damages and replacement of scuff)	1,000.00
• LED lights (lasts longer; approximate savings: $50 per year × 10 years)	500.00
• Light protectors (save $50 per year on replacement × 10 years)	500.00
• Threshold plate (saves damage to entry of trailer)	200.00
• Internal rail reinforcement (saves damage to lower rail and back panels)	500.00
• Stainless steel screws for light attachment (savings on replacement cost)	200.00
• Domestic oak premium floor—$1\frac{3}{8}$ (should last 10 years under normal conditions)	1,000.00
• Doors—aluminum inner and outer skin, outside white finish, inside mill finish, fastened by five aluminum hinges (savings over life of trailer)	750.00
• Five-year warranty in addition to standard warranty covers bulkhead rust, LED lights, floor, scuff liner, glad hands, rear frame, mud flap assembly, and threshold plate (Phoenix provides a higher trade-in value)	1,500.00
Total approximate savings of Phoenix over 10-year period (all the preceding is standard equipment on a Phoenix; this trailer will sell for $23,500; an FB standard trailer would sell for $19,500)	$10,750.00
Less additional initial cost of Phoenix over FB standard	4,000.00
Overall cost savings of Phoenix over FB trailer	$ 6,750.00

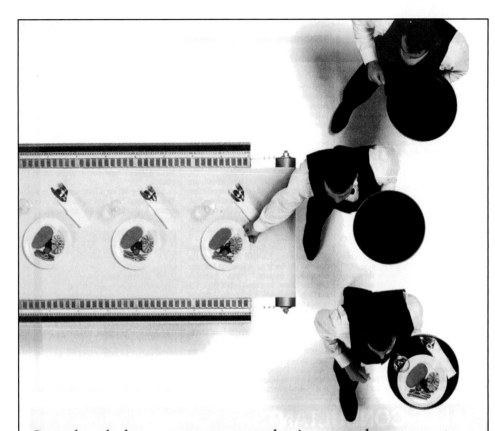

Some hotels do so many meetings, they've got it down to a science. Watch Guest Quarters raise it to an art.

It's sad, really, that doing the same thing over and over again doesn't often produce excellence, but merely predictability.

You might arrange your meeting through a big convention hotel, and settle for their routine best. Or, you can insist on something special, like Guest Quarters®.

At Guest Quarters, we pride ourselves in hosting only smaller business meetings. And we treat each one like it was the most important event we've ever held. Because we believe that every event, and every client that we serve, is one of a kind.

Every Guest Quarters Suite Hotel has conference rooms to handle your small meeting, with all the necessary equipment. Plus executive suites for more private conferences of up to ten people.

Your guests stay in spacious suites, with all the amenities and business services you expect in a first-class hotel.

Call for our FREE video.

Watch us raise meetings to an art on our video, "Small Business Meetings The Guest Quarters Way". We think it conveys what makes us, and our guests, special. Call today to speak to a meeting coordinator and order your free

copy. And watch us make your next small business meeting perfect the first time.

GUEST QUARTERS®
SUITE HOTELS

1-800-437-0651

Alexandria, VA • Austin, TX • Baltimore/Washington Int'l Airport, MD • Boston/Cambridge, MA • Boston/Waltham, MA • Charlotte, NC • Chicago, IL Cincinnati, OH • Columbus, OH • Dayton, OH • Fort Lauderdale, FL • Houston, TX • Indianapolis, IN • Mount Laurel, NJ • Nashville, TN • Orlando Int'l Airport, FL Philadelphia Int'l Airport, PA • Plymouth Meeting, PA • Raleigh/Durham, NC • Santa Monica, CA • Tampa Bay, FL • Troy, MI • Valley Forge, PA • Vero Beach, FL Walt Disney World® Village, FL • New Hampshire Ave., Washington, D.C. • Pennsylvania Ave., Washington, D.C.

Circle No. 118 on Reader Service Card

Guest Quarters adds value to its business meeting facilities with personalized service and attention to every detail.

The complexity of price information varies from one selling situation to another. In some cases the price is the same for all suppliers, and discounting is not a common practice. In other situations the price depends on the size of the purchase, payment plan, delivery method, and other factors. The salesperson must be able to price each part of the product configuration. Some salespeople also must be prepared to discuss leasing options. The salesperson who cannot compute and supply price information quickly and accurately is at a serious disadvantage. In Chapter 6 we discuss how to position products according to price.

KNOW YOUR COMPANY

A growing number of companies are recognizing that sales personnel are often the firm's closest point of contact with the customer, and therefore they need to be well informed. Often the customer's mental image of the organization is formed entirely through contact with a sales representative. In the eyes of the customer the salesperson is the company.

The decision to purchase a product or service often depends on the prospect's feeling about the company. We should never underestimate information about the company itself as a strong appeal that can be used during the sales presentation. This is especially true in situations in which products are similar. Life insurance, for example, can be purchased from a large number of firms at nearly identical rates.

Some companies such as Campbell Soup, AT&T, and American Express have what might be called "brand power." These companies, and the products offered to consumers, are quite well known. However, if you are selling loudspeakers made by Klipsch or financial services offered by Van Kampen Equity, you may find it necessary to spend considerable time providing information about the company.

Acquiring knowledge about your company is an important step toward developing complete product knowledge. In this section we examine the types of information needed in most selling situations.

Company Culture and Organization

Many salespeople take special pride in the history of the company they work for. At Proctor & Gamble (P & G), a company founded in 1837, employees note with pride that the hallmark of this highly successful firm is brands that enjoy market dominance. The authors of *The 100 Best Companies to Work for in America* note, "If a P & G brand does not hold down first place in its market, it's close to the top."[14] Pride can also develop in much younger companies such as Patagonia.

Every organization has its own unique culture. **Organizational culture** is a collection of beliefs, behaviors, and work patterns held in common by people employed by a specific firm. Most organizations over a period of time tend to take on distinct norms and practices. At Gear for Sports, employees are guided by a statement of values that communicates what is held important by the company (Fig. 5.3). Research indicates that the customer orientation of a firm's salespeople is influenced by the organization's culture. A supportive culture that encourages salespeople to offer tailor-made solutions to buyer problems sets the stage for long-term partnerships.[15]

Many prospects use the past performance of a company to evaluate the quality of the current product offering. If the company has enjoyed success in the past, there is good rea-

GEAR For Sports® Vision

*Guided by our GEAR values, we strive to be the
leader in quality and delivery of our
customer's image through marketing innovative
sportswear, accessories and services.*

GEAR Values

*GEAR For Sports' business is predicated on
respect for, and attention to, all of our customers,
business partners, employees, government
and community. We value:*

Customers
by exceeding their expectations.

Excellence
by taking pride and responsibility in everything we do.

Employees
by demonstrating respect and consideration for each other.

Teamwork
*by fostering trust and recognition
among all stakeholders.*

Professionalism
by exhibiting integrity and proficiency.

Innovation
by embracing creativity and change.

Social Responsibility
*by caring for and sharing with each other
and our community.*

GEAR   TANDEM   Event 1

Figure 5.3
At GEAR for Sports, the
employees are guided by a
statement of values that
communicates what is held
important by the company.

son to believe that the future will be bright. At least, this is the way most prospects view an organization.

Company Support for Product

"Service after the sale" is the theme of many marketing programs. Companies with this philosophy keep in touch with customers to determine if they are satisfied. For example, Olin Mathieson, a major chemical corporation, regularly checks with customers to get their reaction to services and keep real needs in perspective. Jagemann Stamping Company, a tool-and-die firm in Manitowoc, Wisconsin, often uses a sales team made up of a salesperson, an engineer, and line workers. Line workers can often answer the technical questions raised by a customer. Whenever there is a problem or defect, a small group of line workers is sent out with either a salesperson or an engineer to investigate. This involvement raises the worker's commitment to the customer.[16]

This salesperson uses a cellular phone to communicate effectively with the company and the customer.

►► *Building Relationships in a Diverse World*

WORLD-CLASS QUALITY AT RITZ-CARLTON

A small minority of American travelers find the $150 to $250 per night room rate at a Ritz-Carlton hotel to be a real bargain. They know that most luxury hotels of Ritz-Carlton's caliber charge much more. The 27 Ritz-Carlton hotels are world renowned for service and quality. The company operates 25 business and resort hotels in the United States, 2 in Australia, and 1 in Mexico. It also has nine international sales offices and employs 11,500 people. The company received the Malcolm Baldrige National Quality Award, the first given to a hospitality organization.

Ritz-Carlton hotels are characterized by distinctive facilities, highly personalized services, and exceptional food and beverages. The company credits its success to innovative human resource strategies and a high level of professionalism in dealing with customers. Although many hotel companies have rigorous training programs, the Ritz-Carlton Company is in a class by itself according to M. L. Smith, professor of hospitality marketing at the University of Nevada's College of Hotel Administration. He says, "They have figured out what guests want in a hotel, and they have learned how to exceed their expectations."

Carefully selected employees (many complete three interviews) start their career with a two-day orientation. During this period the new employees get acquainted with the company motto: "Ladies and gentlemen serving ladies and gentlemen." The two-day orientation is followed by 100 additional hours of training. At each level of the company—from corporate leaders to the sales staff and employees in individual work areas—teams are charged with setting objectives and devising action plans.

The salespeople who represent Ritz-Carlton convention and meeting services know they are selling a first-class service. They also know that the product they sell is likely to become even better.[a]

KNOW YOUR COMPETITION

Acquiring knowledge of your competition is another important step toward developing complete product knowledge. Salespeople who have knowledge of their competitor's strengths and weaknesses are better able to understand their own position, and adjust their selling strategy accordingly.[17] Prospects often raise specific questions concerning competing firms. If we cannot provide answers or if our answers are vague, the sale may be lost.

Your Attitude Toward Your Competition

Regardless of how impressive your product is, the customer naturally seeks information about similar products sold by other companies. Therefore, you must acquire facts about competing products before the sales presentation. Once armed with this information, you are more confident in your ability to handle questions about the competition.

The attitude you display toward your competition is of the utmost importance. Every salesperson should develop a set of basic beliefs about the best way of dealing with competing products. A few helpful guidelines follow:

1. *In most cases, do not refer to the competition during the sales presentation.* This shifts the focus of attention to competing products, which is usually not desirable. Always respond to direct questions, but do not initiate the topic.
2. *Never discuss the competition unless you have all your facts straight.* Your credibility suffers if you make inaccurate statements. If you do not know the answer to a specific question, simply say, "I do not know." It is also best to avoid generalizations about the competition.
3. *Avoid criticizing the competition.* You may be called on to make direct comparisons between your product and competing products. In these situations, stick to the facts and avoid emotional comments about apparent or real weaknesses. Prospects tend to become suspicious of salespeople who initiate strong criticism of the competition.

Customers appreciate an accurate, a fair, and an honest presentation of the facts. They generally resent highly critical remarks about the competition. Avoid mudslinging at all costs. Fairness is a virtue that people greatly admire.

Become an Industry Expert

Lee Boyan, sales consultant, suggests that salespeople become experts in an appropriate niche of an industry or a group of industries.[18] If the sales force includes several persons, each might assume responsibility for a specific area. One member of an office equipment sales team might, for example, concentrate on the banking industry. This person would read the appropriate trade journals and become active in professional associations that serve bankers' needs.

Xerox Corporation believes that education contributes to the success of its customers. Many of the Xerox courses are offered at the International Center for Training and Management Development pictured here.

Salespeople should closely examine the sources of information about their products and the industries where these products are used.

SOURCES OF PRODUCT INFORMATION

There are several sources of product information available to salespeople. Some of the most common include (1) product literature developed by the company, (2) sales training meetings, (3) plant tours, (4) internal sales and sales support team members, (5) customers, (6) product, (7) Internet, and (8) publications.

Product Literature

Most companies prepare materials that provide a detailed description of their product. This information is usually quite instructional, and salespeople should review it carefully. If the company markets a number of products, a sales catalog is usually developed. To save salespeople time, many companies give them computer software that provides a constantly updated, on-line product catalog. Advertisements, promotional brochures, and audio cassettes also can be a valuable source of product information.

Some salespeople develop their own product literature with the aid of electronic marketing encyclopedias. These libraries put a wide range of sales and marketing information at your fingertips. EnCyc Incorporated, a Holland, Michigan firm, has developed an encyclopedia that allows salespeople to create Power Point presentations automatically by pulling the right slides from an organized database.[19]

➤➤ CUSTOMER RELATIONSHIP MANAGEMENT WITH TECHNOLOGY

STARTING FAST WITH CRM

New salespeople can be over-whelmed by the amount of information they need to master. This includes information about the company and its processes, products, and customers. Companies can now make learning easier with information technology. Information about the company and its processes can be stored on the company's network, on its virtual private network (VPN), or on CD-ROM disks. Computer-based training (CBT) permits new employees to learn at their own pace about products—specifications, features, benefits, uses, and selling points.

Companies can now provide salespeople with software that they can use to accurately and effectively create product solutions. Electronic configuration software allows sales-people to select the components necessary to assemble a custom-tailored solution to meet their prospects' needs. This software guides users through the product selection process while assuring that the components are compatible with one another.

Companies can deliver to new salespeople a rich body of customer information through the strong commitment to the use of customer relationship management software. The salesperson who carefully records her business and relationship contacts with customers and prospects over time accumulates a valuable store of information. A new salesperson taking over these accounts can quickly "come up to speed" with these people and their needs. (See the exercise, Finding Product Information in CRM, on p. 113 for more information.)

Sales Training Meetings

As noted previously, company sponsored sales training programs frequently focus on product knowledge. Sales and marketing executives tend to view product knowledge training as a basic element of any sales training program.

New technology is providing long-distance learning opportunities for many salespeople. Ford Motor Company has developed a national interactive distance learning network called Fordstar. Salespeople can sit in a room at their home dealerships and learn via satellite from headquarters in Dearborn, Michigan.[20]

Plant Tours

Many companies believe that salespeople should visit the manufacturing plant and see the production process firsthand. Such tours not only provide valuable product information but also increase the salesperson's enthusiasm for the product. A new salesperson may spend several days at the plant getting acquainted with the production process. Experienced personnel within the organization also can benefit from plant tours.

Internal Sales and Sales Support Team Members

Amir Moussavian, senior vice president of sales at Giga Trend, Incorporated, believes professional salespeople learn from each other. He credits the success of his company to building a team knowledgeable about computer technology. Giga Trend's salespeople are

Distributor salespeople for Rich's Bakery are provided a free audio cassette that features tips on how to sell their product.

not reluctant to communicate their interests and share talents because commissions are pooled. The pooled commissions provide an incentive to help each other and learn from each other.[21] Team selling has become more popular, in part, because many complex sales require the expertise of several sales and sales support personnel.

Customers

Persons who actually use the product can be an important source of information. They have observed its performance under actual working conditions and can provide an objective assessment of the product's strengths and weaknesses. Some companies collect testimonials from satisfied customers and make this persuasive information available to the sales staff.

Surveys indicate that product knowledge training should be a basic element of any sales training program.

Product

The product itself should not be overlooked as a source of valuable information. Salespeople should closely examine and, if possible, use each item they sell to become familiar with its features. Investigation, use, and careful evaluation of the product provide a salesperson with additional confidence.

Internet

Many companies are using the Internet to showcase the features and benefits of their products. The Internet is also an excellent source of technical reports on various products. Some salespeople turn to the Internet to access information concerning competing products.

Publications

Trade and technical publications such as *Supermarket Business* and *Advertising Age* provide valuable product information. Popular magazines and the business section of the newspaper also offer salespeople considerable information about their products and their competition. A number of publications such as *Consumer Reports* test products extensively and report the findings in nontechnical language for the benefit of consumers. These reports are a valuable source of information.

Word of Caution

Is it possible to be overly prepared? Can salespeople know too much about the products and services they sell? The answer to both questions is generally no. Communication problems can arise, however, if the salesperson does not accurately gauge the prospect's level of understanding. There is always the danger that a knowledgeable salesperson can over-whelm the potential buyer with facts and figures. This problem can be avoided when sales-people adopt the feature–benefit strategy.

ADDING VALUE WITH A FEATURE – BENEFIT STRATEGY

Charles Revson, founder of the Revlon Company, once said, "In the factory we make cos-metics. In the store we sell hope." Throughout this chapter we stress the importance of acquiring information on the features of your product, company, and competition. Now it is important to point out that all successful sales presentations translate product features into buyer benefits. The "hope" that Charles Revson mentioned is a good example of a buyer benefit. Only when a product feature is converted to a buyer benefit does it make an impact on the customer. People do not buy features; they buy benefits.[22]

Distinguish Between Features and Benefits

To be sure we understand the difference between a product feature and a benefit, let us define these two terms.

A **product feature** is anything that can be felt, seen, or measured. A feature answers the question, "What is it?" Features include, for example, craftsmanship, durability, design, and economy of operation. In most cases these are technical facts about the prod-uct. They reveal how the product was developed and manufactured. Product features often are described in the technical section of the written sales proposal and in the literature pro-vided by the manufacturer.

A **product benefit** is whatever provides the customer with personal advantage or gain. It answers the question, "How will I benefit from owning or using the product?" If you mention to a prospect that a certain tire has a four-ply rating, you are talking about a product feature. If you go on to point out that this tire provides greater safety, lasts longer, and improves gas mileage, you are pointing out benefits.

Syscom Incorporated, based in Catonville, Maryland, sells training administration systems for use by training department administrators. One of its software products, TMS/WIN, can be used to manage a wide range of training department functions. One fea-

DOONESBURY   **by Garry Trudeau**

ture is self-service registration for employees who want to enroll in workshops or seminars. The benefit is a flexible registration procedure that does not require the involvement of a department staff member. The TMS/WIN program also provides e-mail interface with trainees. The benefit is improved communication with trainees before and after the scheduled training program. These and other features of TMS/WIN software become more appealing once they are converted to benefits the customer can fully appreciate.

Jerry Vass, consultant and sales trainer, says that the buyer has three questions about the product you sell: So what, what's in it for me, and can you prove it? He cautions salespeople to avoid burying the prospect with features that, by themselves, would not answer any of these questions. Vass also believes that very few salespeople have the ability to sell benefits instead of features.[23]

Use Bridge Statements

We know that people buy benefits, not features. One of the best ways to present benefits is to use a bridge statement. A **bridge statement** is a transitional phrase that connects a statement of features with a statement of benefits. This method permits customers to connect the features of your product to the benefits they receive. A sales representative of Fleming Companies, Inc. might use bridge statements to introduce a new snack food.

> "This product is nationally advertised, *which means* you will benefit from more presold customers."

> "You will experience faster turnover and increased profits *because* the first order includes an attractive display rack."

Some companies prefer to state the benefit first and the feature second. When this occurs, the bridge statement may be a word such as "because."

Identify Features and Benefits

A careful analysis of the product helps identify both product features and buyer benefits. Once all the important features are identified, arrange them in logical order. Then write beside each feature the most important benefit the customer can derive from that feature. Finally, prepare a series of bridge statements to connect the appropriate features and benefits. By using this three-step approach, a hotel selling conference and convention services,

Table 5.2

Salespeople employed by a hotel can enhance the sales presentation by converting features to benefits.

FEATURE	BENEFIT
Facilities	
The hotel conference rooms were recently redecorated.	This means all your meetings will be held in rooms that are attractive as well as comfortable.
All our guest rooms were completely redecorated during the past six months and many were designated as nonsmoking rooms.	This means your people will find the rooms clean and attractive. In addition, they can select a smoking or nonsmoking room.
Food Services	
We offer four different banquet entrees prepared by Ricardo Guido who was recently selected Executive Chef-of-the-Year by the National Restaurant Association.	This means your conference will be enhanced by delicious meals served by a well-trained staff.
Our hotel offers 24-hour room service.	This means your people can order food or beverage at their convenience.

Table **5.3**

Here we see company features translated into customer benefits.

FEATURE	BENEFIT
Our company has . . .	*This means for you* . . .
1. The best selection of motors in the area	• Choice of the best models to interface with your current equipment
	• Equipment operates more efficiently
2. Certified service technicians	• Well-qualified service personnel keep your equipment in top running condition
	• Less downtime and higher profits

and a manufacturer selling electric motors used to power mining equipment developed feature–benefit worksheets (Tables 5.2 and 5.3). Notice how each feature is translated into a benefit that would be important to someone purchasing these products and services. Table 5.3 reminds us that company features can be converted to benefits. Product analysis helps you decide what information might be included in the sales presentation. Research indicates that high-performance salespeople present recommendations more in terms of customer benefits than in terms of product features.[24]

Feature–Benefit Approach Complements Consultative Selling

Identifying product features and then converting these features to buyer benefits are integral parts of consultative selling. The salesperson should approach the customer with complete knowledge of the product or service. With the aid of questions the customer's buying needs are identified. Once the needs are known, the salesperson should discuss the features and benefits that specifically apply to that person. In this way the sales presentation is individualized for each customer. Everyone likes to be treated as an individual. A sales presentation tailored to individual customers communicates the message, "You are important and I want you to be a satisfied customer."

Summary

A salesperson whose product knowledge is complete and accurate is better able to satisfy customers. This is without doubt the most important justification for becoming totally familiar with the products you sell. It is simply not possible to provide maximum assistance to potential customers without this information. Additional advantages to be gained from knowing your product include greater self-confidence, increased enthusiasm, improved ability to overcome objections, development of stronger selling appeals, and the preparation of more effective *written sales proposals.*

A complete understanding of your company also yields many personal and professional benefits. The most important benefit, of course, is your ability to serve your customer most effectively. In many selling situations, customers inquire about the company's business practices. They want to know details about support personnel, product development, credit procedures, warranty plans, and product service after the sale. When salespeople are able to provide the necessary company information, they gain respect. They also close more sales.

This chapter also stresses knowing your competition. It pays to study other companies that sell similar products to determine whether they have competitive advantages or disadvantages.

Salespeople gather information from many sources. Company literature and sales training meetings are among the most important. Other sources include factory tours, customers, competition, publications, and actual experience with the product itself.

In the sales presentation and in preparing the written sales proposal, your knowledge of the product's features and your company's strengths must be presented in terms of the resulting benefits to the buyer. The information and benefits you emphasize depend on your assessment of the prospect's needs and motivation.

KEY TERMS

Product Strategy	Quantifying the Solution
Written Proposals	Organizational Culture
Product Development	Product Feature
Quality Control	Product Benefit
Product Configuration	Bridge Statement

REVIEW QUESTIONS

1. Provide a brief description of the term *product strategy.*
2. Some sales managers state, "Training given to sales personnel should stress product knowledge over any other area." List three reasons that support this view.
3. What is *product configuration*? Provide an example of how this practice is used in the sale of commercial stereo equipment.
4. Review the Gear for Sports statement of values and then identify the two items that you believe contribute the most to a salesperson's career success.
5. Define the term *organizational culture.* How might this company information enhance a sales presentation?
6. Basic beliefs underlie the salesperson's method of handling competition. What are three guidelines a salesperson should follow in developing basic beliefs in this area?
7. Explain what the customer's expectations are concerning the salesperson's attitude toward competition.
8. List and briefly describe the five parts included in most written sales proposals.
9. What are the most common sources of product information?
10. Distinguish between *product features* and *buyer benefits.*

APPLICATION EXERCISES

1. Secure, if possible, a copy of a customer-oriented product sales brochure or news release that has been prepared by a marketer. Many salespeople receive such selling tools. Study this information carefully; then develop a features–benefits analysis sheet.

2. Today many companies are automating their product configuration and proposal writing activities. Go to the Internet and find these providers of this software: *www.qwikquote.com* (for simple sales configuration); *www.results-online.com* (for moderately complex sales configuration); and *www.exactium.com* (for complex sales configuration). Click on each company's demonstration software and study the design of each product.

3. Select a product you are familiar with and know a great deal about. (This may be an item you have shopped for and purchased, such as a compact disc player or an automobile.) Under each of the categories listed, fill in the required information about the product.

   a. Where did you buy the product? Why?
   b. Did product design influence your decision?
   c. How and where was the product manufactured?
   d. What different applications or uses are there for the product?
   e. How does the product perform? Are there any data on the product's performance? What are they?
   f. What kinds of maintenance and care does the product require? How often?
   g. Could you sell the product you have written about in terms *a* through *f*? Why or why not?

CRM APPLICATION EXERCISE

Finding Product Information in CRM

Providing immediate access to product information can increase a salesperson's efficiency and responsiveness to customer requests. Computers excel at the task of quickly providing information. An example can be found in the ACT! CRM case study software. Basic information about networks is available in the Reference Library, a feature of this version of ACT!. After loading the software, select <u>V</u>iew, <u>R</u>eference Library, to view the networking information. Print this information by selecting <u>F</u>ile, <u>P</u>rint. While in the Reference Library, other library documents can be opened by selecting <u>F</u>ile, <u>O</u>pen, and double-clicking on one of the files that ends with "wpd." When finished, these ACT! word processing files can be closed by selecting <u>F</u>ile, <u>C</u>lose (Alt+F C).

CASE PROBLEM

Bobbi Meredith, introduced at the beginning of this chapter, recently identified a company that seems to be an excellent prospect for the telecommunications services offered by Lo/Ad Communications. The Cart Works manages several freestanding retail booths (often called kiosks) that operate in shopping malls. Many of the newer malls have incorporated kiosks to create the busy and happy atmosphere of an open marketplace. The design of the kiosk varies from a stationary booth to a movable cart. A typical kiosk offers a specialized product line such as greeting cards, inexpensive jewelry, T-shirts, sunglasses, candy, or snacks. A small number of kiosks can add a new dimension to the shopping atmosphere.

The Cart Works is currently seeking new entrepreneurs who want to operate a kiosk in a shopping mall. The company offers training and help in selecting a high-traffic location in the mall. Once a location is selected, members of The Cart Works staff decide what products are most likely to be popular at that location.

During the first call Bobbi learned that The Cart Works wants to expand its business to include several western states. The company is searching for an effective way to reach well-qualified entrepreneurs who are interested in operating a small business. The prospective entrepreneur is given a package of material that explains the advantages of operating a kiosk. When Bobbi makes her second call on The Cart Works, she needs to configure a product solution and make a specific proposal. She is considering two options:

Option one. Publicize a toll-free 800 number that is used to receive incoming calls generated by newspaper advertisements and direct mail. Callers will be given a brief introduction to The Cart Works' business opportunity and sent a package of materials.

Option two. Publicize a 900 number to encourage incoming calls. The caller will pay a small fee (50 cents per minute) for the call. The 900 number will be publicized in newspaper advertisements and direct mail. Callers will be given an introduction to The Cart Works concept and sent a package of materials.

A competing firm, Triangle Communications, also has called on The Cart Works and is preparing a proposal. The Triangle proposal involves the use of radio announcements to generate interest in this business opportunity. The radio commercials will encourage interested persons to attend an information meeting at a local hotel. A representative of The Cart Works will conduct the meeting. Persons who attend the meeting will be given a package of materials that explain this business opportunity. (See chapter opener on p. 91 for more information.)

Questions

1. Explain how Bobbi can use the three prescriptions for a product selling strategy in preparing and presenting her product solutions.

2. What are the major customer benefits of option one that was developed by Bobbi Meredith? Option two?

3. What are the major customer benefits of the proposal developed by Triangle Communications?

4. In addition to the actual product strategy developed by Bobbi Meredith, how important will company information (history, mission, past performance, product support, etc.) be in closing the sale?

5. Should Bobbi Meredith spend time learning about the competition? Explain. What should be her attitude toward the competition?

6. Is Bobbi Meredith's sales career one where becoming an industry expert would be important? Explain.

PARTNERSHIP-SELLING: A ROLE PLAY/SIMULATION
(see Appendix 3, p. 406)

PART I: DEVELOPING A PRODUCT STRATEGY

Read Employment Memorandum 1 on p. 411, which introduces you to your new training position with the Hotel Convention Center. You also should study the product strategy materials that follow the memo to become familiar with the company, product, and competitive knowledge you need in your new position.

Read the Customer Service/Sales Memorandum, on p. 447 and complete the two-part customer/service assignment provided by your sales manager. In item 1, you are to configure a price/product sales proposal; and in item 2 you are to write a sales cover letter for the sales proposal. Note that the information presented in the price/product sales proposal consists of product facts/features, and the information presented in your sales cover letter should present specific benefit statements. These forms should be custom fitted to meet your customer—B. H. Rivera's—specific needs. All the product information you need is in the product strategy materials provided as enclosures and attachments to Employment Memorandum 1, on p. 411.

Product-Selling Strategies That Add Value

*A*fter nearly a decade of market leadership, Sherpa Corporation (www.sherpa.com) was challenged by new competitors with fresher products. The Milpitas, California, maker of product data management manufacturing software needed a new marketing strategy. The company had not targeted any specific market and was attempting to be all things to all people. After a great deal of study, Sherpa decided to concentrate on dominating one market segment, aerospace and defense, and then use that success to dominate additional markets. Once the marketing plan was in place, Sherpa's next step was to create a sales strategy to support its marketing plan. In the past, the company's 20 sales representatives had been selling the software to technical buyers. New competitors with fresher products were getting the attention of these buyers. Sherpa's new strategy was to position its mature, time-proven technology as a profitable, low-risk alternative to new products that were unproven. A decision was made to target top executives who tend to be economic buyers interested in profit and revenue. These buyers tend to favor proven technologies from a company that is able to demonstrate the product's effectiveness with real examples of other customers. Sherpa's new competitors were not in a strong position to prove business benefits. Today, an expanded Sherpa sales force is confidently selling to new market segments.[1]

PRODUCT POSITIONING—A PERSONAL SELLING STRATEGY

Long-term success in today's dynamic global economy requires the continuous positioning and repositioning of products. **Product positioning** involves those decisions and activities intended to create and maintain a certain concept of the firm's product in the customer's mind. A product's "position" is the customer's concept of the product's attributes relative to the concept of competing products.[2] In a market that has been flooded with various types of sport-utility vehicles (SUVs), Land Rover has been positioned as a dependable vehicle that can climb a steep, rock-covered hillside with ease. Every effort has been made to create the perception of safety, durability, and security. To give sales representatives increased confidence in the Land Rover, the company has arranged plant tours and the opportunity to observe actual testing of the Land Rover vehicles under extremely demanding conditions.

Good positioning means that the product's name, reputation, and niche are well recognized. However, a good positioning strategy does not last forever. The positioning process must be continually modified to match the customer's changing wants and needs.[3]

Essentials of Product Positioning

Salespeople make important contributions to the process of product positioning. Most companies use a combination of marketing and sales strategies to give their products a unique position in the marketplace. Every salesperson needs a good understanding of the fundamental practices that contribute to product positioning. The chapter begins with a brief introduction to the concept of product differentiation. This is followed by an explanation of how products have been redefined in the age of information. The remainder of the chapter is devoted to three product-selling strategies that can be used to position a product. Emphasis is placed on positioning your product with a value-added strategy. In the age of information, salespeople who cannot add value to the products they sell will diminish in number and influence.

ACHIEVING PRODUCT DIFFERENTIATION IN PERSONAL SELLING

One of the basic tenets of sales and marketing is the principle of product differentiation. The competitors in virtually all industries are moving toward differentiating themselves on the basis of quality, price, convenience, economy, or some other factor. Salespeople, who are on the front line of many marketing efforts, assume an important role in the product differentiation process.

Many of the fastest-growing companies are creating strong positions in specific market segments. Three examples are described next:

Item: Cleveland-based Meridian Travel designed and initiated an education program that helps business customers learn how to spend their travel dollars efficiently. Cyndie Bender, founder and CEO of Meridian, explains that her accounts receive a detailed quarterly report that provides an analysis of their travel expenditures. These user-friendly reports make it easy for the customer to determine ways to reduce unnecessary travel expenses. Some of these reports spell out how a client can spend less with her company, and the result is sometimes lost sales. However, this service helps build customer loyalty, goodwill, and in some cases additional business for Meridian sales representatives.[4]

Item: Nordstrom, a department store chain based in Portland, Oregon, has achieved success by meeting the needs of consumers seeking upscale merchandise and a shopping experience that includes the personal touch. Nordstrom offers an in-depth selection of quality merchandise and outstanding customer service. Each store stocks fashion goods that reflect the lifestyles of customers in the surrounding area. Well-trained salespeople keep records on their customers'

Paul Farrow, founder of Walden Paddlers, created a niche market for his kayak by making it out of recycled plastic, designing it for ease of maneuverability, and giving it an attractive price. He used these product features to position this product in a competitive market.

sizes and preferences so that they can let customers know when an item that may be of interest to them arrives at the store. The result of this individualized approach is strong customer loyalty and repeat business.[5]

Item: Walden Paddlers, located in Acton, Massachusetts, is a successful new company with one product and one employee. Within one year the company was able to design, produce, and market a technically sophisticated kayak fashioned from recycled plastic. Paul Farrow, founder of the company, launched the new product by forming strategic partnerships with a designer, a manufacturer, a banker, an accountant, and other key persons. The decision to produce and sell a new type of kayak was made after a careful study of the market. Farrow decided that a kayak made of recycled plastic would have appeal in the water-sport market in which environmental awareness is important to buyers. As soon as the first kayaks were manufactured, Farrow started making sales calls to retail and wholesale firms that specialize in outdoor products. Within a few weeks he was able to line up several dealers for his product.[6]

Notice that all these businesses are selling their products and services in highly competitive markets. Also, each is attempting to achieve product and service differentiation. Personal selling has helped each company achieve success.

REDEFINING PRODUCTS IN THE AGE OF INFORMATION

Ted Levitt, former editor of the *Harvard Business Review*, says that products are problem-solving tools. People buy products if they fulfill a problem-solving need. Today's better-educated and more demanding customers are seeking a *cluster of satisfactions*. **Satisfactions** arise from the product itself, from the company that makes or distributes the product, and from the salesperson who sells and services the product.[7] Figure 6.1 provides a description of a three-dimensional *Product-Selling Model*.

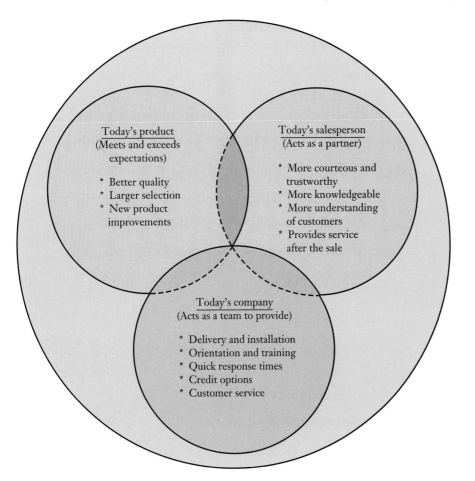

Figure 6.1
PRODUCT-SELLING MODEL
The product strategy should include a cluster of satisfactions that meet the needs of today's better educated and more demanding customers. Drawing from this cluster, the salesperson can custom fit presentations to meet a wide range of needs.

To illustrate how the cluster of satisfactions concept works in a business setting, let us examine a complex buying decision. King Soopers, a major grocery retailer in Colorado, maintains its own in-house, full-service advertising department. As part of a plan to update the department, the staff decided to purchase a computer system that could be used to develop high-quality, camera-ready copy and graphics for print ads.

The buying decisions at King Soopers were complex because the product, in various configurations, was available from several computer manufacturers. In addition, many distributors sold the same equipment. Of course, different distributors presented different proposals. Some of the questions the staff had to answer before making a buying decision follow:

Questions Related to the Product

What product is best for our type of operation?

Does the product have a good reputation for quality?

Given the cost of this product, will King Soopers receive a good return on investment?

Questions Related to the Company

Does this company provide the most advanced technology?

What is the company's reputation for manufacturing quality products?

What is the company's reputation for standing behind the products it sells?

Lexus, a company that emphasizes engineering sophistication, agrees to treat and refer to their customers as "guests".

WHAT IS LEXUS?

Lexus is... Engineering sophistication and manufacturing quality.

Lexus is... Luxury and performance.

Lexus is... An image and an expectation of excellence.

Lexus is... Valuing the customer as an important individual.

Lexus is... Treating customers the way THEY want to be treated.

Lexus is... A total experience that reflects professionalism and a sincere commitment to satisfaction.

Lexus is... "Doing it right the first time".

Lexus is... Caring on a personal level.

Lexus is... Exceeding customer expectations.

And... In the eyes of the customer I AM LEXUS !!!

00-LTT-034

Questions Related to the Salesperson

Does this salesperson possess the knowledge and experience needed to recommend the right product?

Can the salesperson clearly communicate product features and buyer benefits?

Can this salesperson be trusted?

Will this salesperson provide support services after the sale?

The purchase of a service may be no less complicated. Let us assume that you are planning a retirement banquet for the president of your company. The location of the banquet would likely depend on the type of food and beverage service available at hotels and restaurants in your community. This would be the *product* decision. The qualifications of the food and beverage salesperson or sales manager would also influence your buying decision because this is the person who describes the food, beverage, and meeting room options and works with you after the buying decision. You must be convinced that this person has the experience and skills necessary to do the job. In the final analysis you would make a buying decision based on your perception of the "whole product" that provides a cluster of satisfactions.

PRODUCT-POSITIONING OPTIONS

Product positioning is a concept that applies to both new and existing products. Given the dynamics of most markets, it may be necessary to reposition products several times in their lives because even solid, popular products can lose market position quickly. Salespeople

►► CUSTOMER RELATIONSHIP MANAGEMENT WITH TECHNOLOGY

MANAGING NEW PRODUCT INFORMATION WITH CRM

Today, salespeople are challenged to manage a steady stream of information about customers (needs) and products (solutions). From this stream of information, the sales professional must select product information that is relevant to a specific customer and deliver the information in a manner that can be understood by the customer. Customer relationship management (CRM) assists the busy salesperson by providing tools that can collect information and link it to those who need it. Most CRM systems can receive and organize information from e-mail, Web sites, and the files of reference material kept within the company's information system.

Sales professionals can add value to this information by summarizing, combining, and tailoring the information to meet a customer's needs.

When new product information is received, databases of customer data can be quickly searched to find those customers who might have an interest. The new product information can be merged into an e-mail, fax, or letter to that customer, along with other information (benefits) that can help the customer assess its value. Later, the CRM system can display a follow-up alert, reminding the sales professional of the information that was shared with the customer. (See the exercise, Informing Customers with CRM, at page 135 for more information.)

have assumed an important and expanding role in positioning products. To succeed in our overcommunicated society, marketers must use a more direct and personalized form of communication with customers. Advertising directed toward a mass market often fails to position a complex product.

Throughout the remainder of this chapter we discuss specific ways to use various product-positioning strategies. We explain how salespeople can (1) position new and emerging products versus well-established products, (2) position products with price strategies, and (3) position products with value-added strategies.

Positioning New and Emerging Products versus Mature and Well-Established Products

In many ways, products are like human beings. They are born, grow up, mature, and grow old. In marketing, this process is known as the **product life cycle**. The product life cycle includes the stages a product goes through from the time it is first introduced to the market until it is discontinued. As the product moves through its cycle, the strategies relating to competition, promotion, pricing, and other factors must be evaluated and possibly changed. The nature and extent of each stage in the product life cycle are determined by several factors, including:

1. The product's perceived advantage over available substitutes
2. The product's benefits and the importance of the needs it fulfills
3. Competitive activity, including pricing, substitute product development and improvement, and effectiveness of competing advertising and promotion.
4. Changes in technology, fashion, or demographics[8]

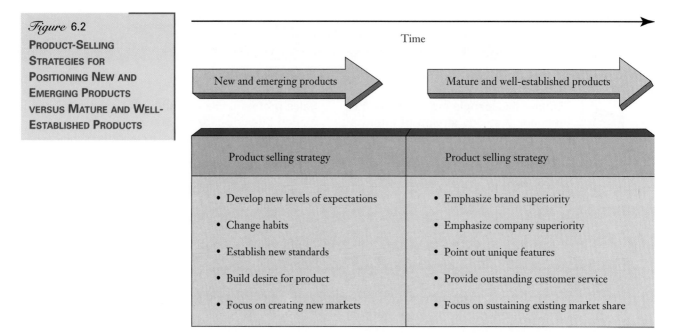

Figure 6.2

Product-Selling Strategies for Positioning New and Emerging Products versus Mature and Well-Established Products

As we attempt to develop a product-selling strategy, we must consider where the product is positioned in terms of the life cycle. The sales strategy used to sell a new and emerging product is much different from the strategy used to sell a mature, well-established product (Fig. 6.2).

SELLING NEW AND EMERGING PRODUCTS

Sometimes a promising new product enters the marketplace with high hopes, but initial sales are disappointing. This was the case when the Ricoh MV715 was first introduced. The MV715 was a multifunctional office product that gave users the capability to fax, copy, and print from one station. Potential customers were skeptical that a single product could take the place of several others. Ricoh Corporation decided to interview customers who had purchased the MV715 to determine how they used the product and if it had made their offices more efficient. After careful analysis of interviews with 200 buyers, the company discovered that salespeople had not adjusted their selling style to fit the new product. They had failed to position the product so that it appealed to buyers.[9]

Price is just one factor to consider when you are selling a new product such as the Ricoh MV715. A product that is both new and innovative often requires the efforts of a highly motivated salesperson who has received intensive sales and technical training.[10] Selling strategies used during the new and emerging stage (see Fig. 6.2) are designed to develop a new level of expectation, change habits, and in some cases establish a new standard of quality. The goal is to build desire for the product.

SELLING MATURE AND WELL-ESTABLISHED PRODUCTS

Mature and well-established products are usually characterized by intense competition as new brands enter the market. At this point, customers accept the products, and they are aware of competing products. With new and emerging products, salespeople may initially have little or no competition and may dominate the market; however, this condition may not last long.

Northwestern Mutual Life Insurance continuously provides its 6,000 independent sales agents with new products. Yet the company finds that its new products are quickly copied by competing insurance companies. When competing products enter the market, Northwestern sales agents must adopt new strategies. One positioning strategy is to emphasize the company's 130 years of superior service to policyholders. Agents often describe Northwestern as the "supportive" company that gives a high priority to service after the sale.[11] The objective is to create in the customer's mind the perception that Northwestern is a solid company with a long history of good service to policyholders.

The relationship strategy is often critical in selling mature and well-established products. To maintain market share and ward off competitors, many salespeople work hard to maintain a strong relationship with the customer. At Northwestern, salespeople have found that good service after the sale is one of the best selling strategies because it builds customer loyalty.

Positioning Products with a Price Strategy

Price, promotion, product, and place are the four elements that make up the marketing mix. Pricing decisions must be made at each stage of the product life cycle. Therefore, setting the price can be a complex process. The first step in establishing price is to determine the firm's pricing objectives. Some firms set their prices to maximize their profits. They aim for a price as high as possible without causing a disproportionate reduction in unit sales. Other firms set a market share objective. Management may decide that the strategic advantage of an increased market share outweighs a temporary reduction in profits. Many of the new companies doing business on the Internet have adopted this approach.

Pricing strategies often reflect the product's position in the product life cycle. When compact disc players were in the new and emerging stage, customers who wanted this innovative equipment were willing to accept the $1,000 per unit price tag.

TRANSACTIONAL SELLING TACTICS THAT EMPHASIZE LOW PRICE

Some marketers have established a positioning plan that emphasizes low price and the use of transactional selling tactics. These companies maintain a basic strategy that focuses on meeting competition. If the firm has meeting competition as its pricing goal, it makes every effort to charge prices that are identical or close to those of the competition. Once this positioning strategy has been adopted, the sales force is given several price tactics to use. Salespeople can alter (lower) the base price through the use of discounts and allowances. Discounts and allowances can take a variety of forms. A few of the more common ones follow:

Quantity discount. The quantity discount allows the buyer a lower price for purchasing in multiple units or above a specified dollar amount.

Time-period pricing. With time-period pricing, the salesperson adjusts the price up or down during specific times to spur or acknowledge changes in demand.[12] Off-season travel and lodging prices provide examples.

Promotional allowance. A promotional allowance is a price reduction given to a customer who participates in an advertising or a sales support program. Many salespeople give supermarkets promotional allowances for advertising or displaying a manufacturer's products.

Another option available to salespeople facing a buyer with a low price buying strategy is to "unbundled" product features. Let's assume that a price conscious customer wants to schedule a conference that will be accompanied by a banquet style meal. To achieve

▶▶ BUILDING QUALITY PARTNERSHIPS

HOW DO CUSTOMERS JUDGE SERVICE QUALITY?

In the growing service industry there is intense price competition. From a distance, one gets the impression that every buyer decision hinges on price alone. However, a closer examination of service purchases indicates that service quality is an important factor when it comes to developing a long-term relationship with customers.

How do customers judge service quality? Researchers at Texas A&M University have discovered valuable insights about customer perceptions of service quality. They surveyed hundreds of customers in a variety of service industries and discovered that five service-quality dimensions emerged:

1. *Tangibles:* These are details the customers can see, such as the appearance of personnel and equipment.

2. *Reliability:* This is the ability to perform the desired service dependably, accurately, and consistently.

3. *Responsiveness:* This is the willingness of sales and customer service personnel to provide prompt service and help customers.

4. *Assurance:* This includes the employees' knowledge, courtesy, and ability to convey trust and confidence.

5. *Empathy:* This means the provision of caring, individualized attention to customers.

Customers apparently judge the quality of each service transaction in terms of these five quality dimensions. Companies need to review these service-quality dimensions and make sure that each area measures up to the customers' expectations. Salespeople should recognize that these dimensions have the potential to add value to the services they sell.[a]

a lower price, the salesperson might suggest a cafeteria style meal, thereby eliminating the need for servers. This product configuration involves less cost to the seller, and cost savings can be passed on to the buyer. A salesperson representing a line of computer products might reduce the selling price by altering or eliminating certain assurances and/or warranties.

These examples represent only a small sample of the many discounts and allowances salespeople use to compete on the basis of price. Price discounting is a competitive tool available to large numbers of salespeople. Excessive focus on low prices and generous discounts, however, can have a negative impact on profits and sales commissions.

CONSEQUENCES OF USING LOW-PRICE TACTICS

Pricing is a critical factor in the sale of many products and services. In markets where competition is extremely strong, setting a product's price may be a firm's most complicated and important decision.

The authors of *The Discipline of Market Leaders* encourage business firms to pick one of three disciplines—best price, best product, or best service—and then do whatever is necessary to outdistance the competition. However, the authors caution us not to ignore the other two disciplines: "You design your business to excel in one direction, but you also have to strive to hit the minimum in the others."[13] Prior to using low-price tactics, everyone involved in sales and marketing should answer these questions:

▶ *Are you selling to high- or low-involvement buyers?* Some people are emotionally involved with respected brands such as BMW, Sony, and American Express. A part of their identity depends on buying the product they consider the best. Low-involvement buyers care mostly about price.[14]

▶ *How important is quality in the minds of buyers?* If buyers do not fully understand the price–quality relationship, they may judge the product by its price. For a growing number of customers, long-term value is more important than short-term savings that result from low prices. A broad-based desire for high quality and "value" as opposed to the lowest possible price suggests that price alone is an inadequate competitive tool.[15]

▶ *How important is service after the sale?* For many buyers, service after the sale is a critical factor. In some cases, low-price tactics mean less service. If low price results in fewer services after the sale or a reduction in the quality of service, some customers are less likely to buy the product.

INFLUENCE OF ELECTRONIC COMMERCE ON PRICING

Companies large and small are racing to discover new sales and marketing opportunities on the Internet. Products ranging from personal computers to term insurance can be purchased from various Web sites. Salespeople who are involved primarily in transactional

"WE HAVE QUALITY AND WE HAVE LOW PRICES...
WHICH DO YOU WANT?"

selling and add little or no value to the sales transaction often are not able to compete with on-line vendors. To illustrate, consider the purchase of insurance. At the present time it is possible to purchase basic term insurance on line from InsureMarket.com, AccuQuote.com, and other Web sites. A well-informed buyer, willing to visit several Web sites, can select a policy with a minimum amount of risk. In the case of long-term care insurance, which can pay for health care at home or in a nursing home, the buyer needs the help of a well-trained agent. These policies are complex and the premiums are high. GE Capital Assurance Company, one of several companies selling this type of insurance, has 1,100 agents devoted solely to selling long-term care insurance and about 7,500 independent agents who include this insurance among other offerings.[16]

Investors now have more choices than they have had in the past. Persons who need little or no assistance buying stocks can visit the Charles Schwab Web site, E*Trade, or a similar on-line vendor. The person who wants help selecting a stock can turn to a broker, such as Merrill Lynch or Paine Webber, that offers both full-service and on-line options. Full-service brokers can survive and may prosper as long as they can add value to the sales transaction. The new economy is reshaping the world of commerce and every buyer has more choices.

Positioning Your Product with a Value-Added Strategy

Many progressive marketers have adopted a market plan that emphasizes **value-added strategies**. Companies add value to their product with one or more intangibles such as better trained salespeople, increased levels of courtesy, more dependable product deliveries, better service after the sale, and innovations that truly improve the product's value in the eyes of the customer. In today's highly competitive marketplace these value-added benefits give the company a unique niche and a competitive edge.

When Raytheon Company began selling IBM computer clones, salespeople emphasized the lower price and similarities in the products. However, price discounting alone proved insufficient when competing with a well-established brand name. Once the salespeople began to emphasize the differences in the products, especially features that improved the efficiency of users, sales improved. In the buyer's mind, productivity, more than price, added value to the Raytheon computers.[17]

Customers who visit a Nordstrom department store are introduced to a value-added shopping experience. Each department offers a wide selection of top-quality products, and shoppers are waited on by well-trained salespeople who are courteous and knowledgeable. Flowers in the dressing rooms and music from a grand piano on the main floor enhance shopping at the store. Nordstrom spends heavily to "overstaff" the sales floor so customers do not have to wait for assistance.

VALUE ADDED—A NEW CHALLENGE FOR SALESPEOPLE

Salespeople are usually in the best position to explain the features and benefits that add value to a product or service. At Meridian Travel, introduced at the beginning of this chapter, the travel counselor can describe the benefits of the quarterly travel report given to customers. The salesperson can discover what adds value (in the mind of the customer) and then determine ways to add this value. Adding value starts with building a knowledge base. Dan Kosch, president of a Connecticut-based sales consulting and training company, says, "Show customers that you understand their business, their concerns, and what they hope to accomplish."[18] This knowledge helps you direct the customers attention from price to value.

In a business-to-business selling situation the most powerful value-added strategy is often one that enhances the customer's profitability. The salesperson describes features, programs, and services that affect the customer's profits by enhancing revenues, reducing costs, or helping deflect future costs.[19] Sales representatives employed by Airgas, North America's leading supplier of industrial, medical, and specialty gases and related equipment, emphasize to customers the value of doing business with a vendor that can meet all their primary needs: quality products that are delivered on time, orders that are complete,

If this Mercedes Benz Vision SLA concept car is brought to market, salespeople will assume an important role in positioning the features and benefits that add value.

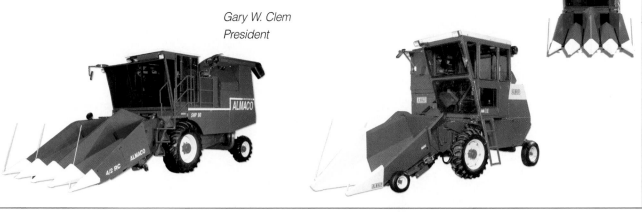

Dear Valued Customer:

ALMACO takes great pride in our long and successful history of working with the agricultural research industry. Our roots stretch back to the 1880s when we began as a blacksmith shop in the community of Ames, Iowa.

Over the last 25 years we have focused our efforts specifically toward meeting the needs of clients engaged in agricultural research. To this end, we have partnered with the life science experts throughout the world.

Our mission statement echoes our dedication to our customers:

ALMACO will form an alliance with clients to help them pursue their research goals. ALMACO will create, market, and support high quality, value added, information rich machinery, and technologies for use in the agricultural research industry.

This new catalog is a reflection of ALMACO's efforts to meet the continually changing needs of our customers. As you look through the products featured in these pages, please accept our thanks for your past business. We look forward to continuing to serve your needs in the future.

Sincerely,

Gary W. Clem
President

Salespeople representing Almaco use the mission statement as a sales tool to communicate a high quality, value added, information rich partnering strategy to their customers.

Value added can mean many things. It may be helping customers select a product that meets or exceeds their expectations. It can also mean having the product available and attractively wrapped upon short notice.

and bills that are accurate. They explain that doing business with a single vendor can reduce procurement costs. Once the customer needs are determined, salespeople identify the cost savings, put a dollar figure on those savings, and then support the numbers with documentation. Airgas does not attempt to be a low-price vendor. The strategy is to show the customer the difference between buying a product that's a one-time, low-price solution and developing a long-term relationship with a dependable and efficient full-service provider.[20]

In some cases the salesperson can add value by doing something extra for the customer. For example, the salesperson might offer to help a customer identify ways to make his business more efficient. Suggestions that result in improved cash flow, more effective use of equipment, or expansion of the customer base are certainly appreciated. This assistance adds value to the relationship between the salesperson and the customer.

Selling the Value-Added Product

To understand fully the importance of the value-added concept in selling, and how to apply it in a variety of selling situations, it helps to visualize every product as being four dimensional. The *total product* is made up of four "possible" products: the generic product, the expected product, the value-added product, and the potential product[21] (Fig. 6.3).

GENERIC PRODUCT

The **generic product** is the basic, substantive product you are selling. Generic product describes only the product category, for example, life insurance, rental cars, or personal computers. Every Ritz-Carlton hotel offers guest rooms, one or more full-service restaurants, meeting rooms, guest parking, and other basic services. For Mayflower Transit, a company that provides moving services, the generic product is the truck and trailer that move the customer's household items. At the generic level, Nordstrom provides categories

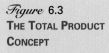

Figure **6.3**

THE TOTAL PRODUCT CONCEPT

An understanding of the four "possible" products is helpful when the salesperson develops a presentation for specific types of customers.

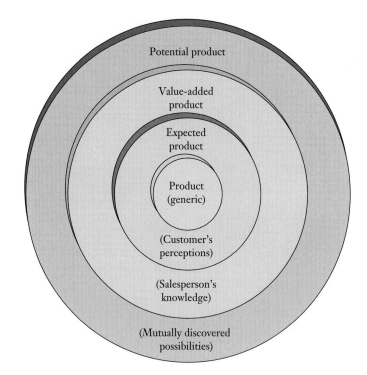

of goods traditional to an upscale specialty clothing retailer.[22] The generic products at a bank are money that can be loaned to customers and basic checking account services.

The capability of delivering a generic product simply gives the marketer the right to play in the game, to compete in the marketplace.[23] Generic products, even the lowest priced ones, often cannot compete with products that are "expected" by the customer.

EXPECTED PRODUCT

Every customer has minimal purchase expectations that exceed the generic product itself.[24] Ritz-Carlton must offer not only a comfortable guest room, but also a clean one. Some customers expect a "super" clean room. Mayflower must provide a clean, well-maintained moving van *and* a well-trained crew. The **expected product** is everything that represents the customer's minimal expectations. The customer at a Nordstrom store *expects* current fashions and well-informed salespeople.

The minimal purchase conditions vary among customers, so the salesperson must acquire information concerning the expected product that exists in the customer's mind. Every customer perceives the product in individualized terms, which a salesperson cannot anticipate. To say that every customer is unique might seem trite, but when salespeople fully accept this fundamental of personal selling, they are better prepared to apply the value-added concept.

When the customer expects more than the generic product, the generic product can be sold *only* if those expectations are met.[25] To determine each customer's expectations requires the salesperson to make observations, conduct background checks, ask questions, and listen to what the customer is saying. We are attempting to discover both feelings and facts.

Research reported in the *Harvard Business Review* indicates that it is very difficult to build customer loyalty if you are selling only the expected product. Customer satisfaction and loyalty do not always move in tandem. The customer who purchases the services of Ernst & Young Consulting may feel satisfied after the project is completed, but never do business with the company again. Customer loyalty is more likely to increase when the purchase involves a value-added product.[26]

VALUE-ADDED PRODUCT

The **value-added product** exists when salespeople offer customers more than they expect. When you make a reservation at one of the Ritz-Carlton hotels, and request a special amenity such as a tennis lesson, a record of this request is maintained in the computer system. If you make a reservation at another Ritz-Carlton at some future date, the agent informs you of the availability of a tennis court. The guest who buys chocolate chip cookies in the lobby gift shop in New Orleans may find a basket of them waiting in his room in Boston two weeks later. The hotel company uses modern technology to surprise and delight guests.[27] Nordstrom spends heavily to overstaff the sales floor by traditional standards. The company also overspends to ensure the availability of more sizes and colors than usual. This upscale retailer is attempting to add value by exceeding customer expectations.

As competition intensifies, and as products and prices become more similar, companies must work harder to distinguish themselves and their products from the competition. They must increase their efforts to find out what customers need and then satisfy those needs with added value. In most cases, the salesperson delivers the value-added product.[28]

How can a salesperson create a value-added product or service? Larry Wilson, noted author and sales consultant, says that adding value means *always* working outside your job description to exceed customer expectations.[29] Salespeople who have adopted the value-added philosophy routinely meet clients' expectations and then exceed those expectations.

The value-added product strategy varies from one situation to another. Eileen Tertocha, a sales representative with Skipper Morrison Realtors, has developed a unique value-added strategy for new home owners:

> I give my customers first-class treatment on moving day, including plenty to eat for both the family and the movers. Then, on a regular day-to-day basis, I check to see if everything is going okay or if they need any help from me or anyone else.[30]

Eileen Tertocha's goal is to make moving as easy as possible. She goes beyond the customer's expectations to take care of a variety of details.

One of the most powerful value-added strategies is personalized service. This **interpersonal value** is win–win relationship building with the customer (as described in Chapter 3) that results from keeping that person's best interests always at the forefront. Marilyn Carlson Nelson, CEO of Carlson Companies Inc., one of the largest privately held companies in the world, says that personal selling is really about proving you are a good match for your customer and then backing your claim with facts. She also views selling as a service:

> Selling is not about peddling a product. It's about wrapping that product in a service—and about selling both the product and the service as an experience. That approach to selling helps create a vital element of the process: a relationship.[31]

POTENTIAL PRODUCT

After the value-added product has been developed, the salesperson should begin to conceptualize the **potential product**. The potential product refers to what may remain to be done, that is, what is possible.[32] As the level of competition increases, especially

In the hotel and convention center market, if the initial "value added product" meets and exceeds the customers expectation, future sales revenue from the "potential product" could be several times the amount of the first sale.

in the case of mature products, salespeople must look to the future and explore new possibilities.

In the highly competitive food services industry, restaurant owners like to do business with a distribution sales representative (DSR) who wants to help make the business profitable. The DSR who assumes this role becomes a true partner and looks beyond the customer's immediate and basic needs. The potential product might consist of a careful study of the restaurant's current menu and appropriate recommendations to the owner. To deliver the potential product, a salesperson must discover and satisfy new customer needs, which requires imagination and creativity.

Steelcase Incorporated, a leading manufacturer of office furniture, has developed the Personal Harbor Workspaces. The product is designed to be clustered around common work areas that invite teamwork and collaboration. These circular workstations offer buyers a twenty-first century version of the traditional office cubicle. The podlike workstation is such a departure from conventional office design that customers were initially unable to comprehend its potential. Salespeople quickly learned that a traditional product-oriented presentation would not work. Meetings between Steelcase salespeople and customers involved discussions of concepts such as team building, organizational communication, and employee interaction. Steelcase developed "advanced solution teams" that adopted a true consultative role. These teams meet with people in the organization who are more interested in the potential of the Personal Harbor Workspaces than in its price.[33]

The potential product is more likely to be developed by salespeople who are close to their customers. Many high-performing salespeople explore product possibilities with

►► Selling in Action

PRICING YOUR PROFESSIONAL FEES

The age of information has created many career opportunities for people who want to sell professional services. Strong demand for professional services has surfaced in such diverse fields as telecommunications, banking, computer technology, training, and health care. Dana Martin spent 18 years working in the human resources division of Allstate Insurance Company. His specialty was the design and delivery of training programs. He decided to leave the corporate environment and start his own training firm. Martin, like thousands of other professional service providers, had to decide how much to charge for his service. Before he could sell the first training program, he had to decide how much to charge. Should he price his service on an hourly basis or on a project basis? Here are some points to consider when determining fees:

- *Experience:* In the case of Dana Martin, new clients benefit from what he has learned during many years at Allstate.

- *Exclusivity:* If you are one of only a small number of people with a particular capability, you may be able to charge more. Specialists often charge higher fees than generalists.
- *Target Market:* Some markets are very price sensitive. If you are selling your services to large corporations that are used to paying high fees, you may be able to set your fees higher. If you are providing your services to small business clients, expect resistance to high fees.
- *Value:* How important is your service to the client? In the late 1990s, many companies needed help preparing their computers for transition to the year 2000. This was known as the "Y2K" problem. These firms were willing to pay high fees for this assistance. Some service providers charge higher fees because they add value in one form or another.[b]

General Mills is emphasizing a value-added strategy by supplying independent distributor salespeople with training materials and programs.

their customers on a regular basis. Potential products are often mutually discovered during these exchanges.

Adding Value—A Future Perspective

Every indication points toward product-selling strategies that add value becoming more important in the future. New product life cycles have shrunk by half or more during the past decade. A life cycle of six months is not uncommon.[34] Value-added-selling strategies can be very effective during the new and emerging stage. Some companies that have experienced low profits with low-priced products may be reinventing their products. They may develop products that provide benefits people think are worth paying for. Maytag Corporation developed the environment-friendly Neptune washer that has been popular among well-off customers. The $1,100 price of the Neptune is twice as much as conventional washers.[35]

Products have always been characterized by their fixed and uniform design, whereas services are much easier to customize.[36] The new economy is primarily a service economy that very often gives buyers a customized solution to their problem. Many buyers are searching for a solution that includes the right combination of value-added attributes.

Summary

Success in today's dynamic global economy requires the continuous positioning and repositioning of products. Product positioning involves those decisions and activities intended to create and maintain a certain concept of the firm's product in the customer's mind. Salespeople can make an important contribution to the process of product positioning. In many cases they assume an important role in product differentiation.

We note that today's better educated customers are often seeking a cluster of satisfactions. They seek satisfactions that arise from the product itself, from the company that makes or distributes the product, and from the salesperson who sells and services the product.

We introduce the major product-positioning strategies available to salespeople: positioning new and emerging products versus mature and well-established products, positioning with a price strategy, and positioning with a value-added strategy.

Part of this chapter is devoted to the total product concept. The total product is made up of four possible products. This range of possibilities includes the generic product, the expected product, the value-added product, and the potential product.

KEY TERMS

Product Positioning	Value-Added Strategy
Satisfactions	Generic Product
Product Life Cycle	Expected Product
Quantity Discount	Value-Added Product
Time-Period Pricing	Interpersonal Value
Promotional Allowance	Potential Product

REVIEW QUESTIONS

1. Why has product differentiation become so important in sales and marketing?
2. According to Ted Levitt, what is the definition of a product? What satisfactions do customers want?
3. Explain what is meant by *positioning* as a product-selling strategy.
4. Why have salespeople assumed an important role in positioning products? What major economic developments have influenced product positioning?
5. Briefly describe the influence of electronic business on pricing. What types of products are likely to be sold on the Internet?
6. What are the possible consequences a salesperson might experience when using low-price tactics?
7. Read the Building Quality Partnerships insight titled "How Do Customers Judge Service Quality." How might this information help a salesperson who wants to adopt the value-added-selling strategy?
8. What are some of the common ways salespeople add value to the products they sell?
9. What are the four possible products that make up the *total product* concept?
10. Describe the difference between a generic product and a value-added product.

APPLICATION EXERCISES

1. Secure catalogs from two competing industrial supply firms or two competing direct mail catalog companies. Assume one of the represented businesses is your employer. After studying the catalogs, make a comparative analysis of your company's competitive advantages.
2. The Ritz-Carlton hotel chain illustrates the total product concept discussed in this chapter. Research value-added information on the Ritz-Carlton chain by accessing the www.ritzcarlton.com Web site. Choose a location and click on "Conference Facilities." Click on the fact sheet and print the information presented. Circle at least five features you consider value-added. Examine the room rates by clicking on accommodations. On the fact sheet you printed, record the room rate for a single and double occupancy room.
3. Interview the manager of a local supermarket that sells a large assortment of national brands such as Nabisco, Kellogg's, and Del Monte. Ask this person what kinds of appeals are used by sales representatives of national brand products when they request more shelf space. Determine how frequently they offer trade or advertising allowances.
4. Call a local financial services representative specializing in stock, bond, or equity fund transactions. Ask what percentage of clients rely on the information given to make complex decisions on their investments. Also ask this person if customers believe that advice in custom fitting investment programs adds value to their decision making. Find out whether financial products are getting more or less complex and what effect this will have on providing value-added service in the future.

CRM APPLICATION EXERCISE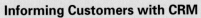

Informing Customers with CRM

The notes in the ACT! database software contain two references to Extranets, another system offered by SimNet Systems. One account is a prospective buyer of an Extranet who

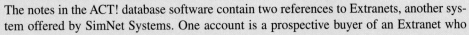

needs more information. The other account has an Extranet and is willing to show it to others. The Reference Library also contains information about private virtual networks, including Extranets. Find the two accounts by selecting Lookup, Keyword; type "Extranet," check Notes, uncheck Contact, and press Enter. After searching, ACT! displays two records. An examination of the notes shows the account with an Extranet and the one with an interest. Make a note of the name of the organization now using an Extranet. Close the notes screen (File, Close) and use the Page Up or Page Down key to display the account that needs information. Select View, Reference Library to display the information about networks. Page Down to the last paragraph of that document, titled VPN. Highlight the paragraph with your mouse and select Edit, Copy. Select File, Close to close the library. Select Write, Letter, and enter the following: "You might find this of interest." Press Enter twice to begin a new paragraph. Select Edit, Paste to add the information from the Reference Library. Press Enter twice again for a new paragraph, type "If you wish, I can arrange for you to look at the Extranet in use at," and then enter the name of the person and organization using the Extranet. Select File, Print (Ctrl+P) to print the letter and File, Close to close the letter window.

CASE PROBLEM

Many of the most profitable companies have discovered that there are "riches in market niches." They have developed products and services that meet the needs of a well-defined or newly created market. Steelcase Incorporated, a leading source of information and expertise on work effectiveness, has been working hard to develop products that meet the needs of people who do most of their work in an office environment. The company motto is, "The office environment company." One of its newest products is the Personal Harbor Workplaces, a self-contained, fully equipped, and totally private podlike workstation. Steelcase sales literature describes the product as ideal for companies that are tired of waiting for the future:

> They were developed to support the individual within a highly collaborative team environment, and they work best when clustered around common work areas equipped with mobile tables, carts, benches, screens, and other Steelcase Activity Products. These "commons" are meant to be flexible spaces that enhance communication and facilitate interaction.

Steelcase realized that selling this advanced product would not be easy, so a decision was made to develop an advanced sales team to presell the Personal Harbor before its major introduction. Once the team started making sales calls, it became evident that a traditional product-oriented sales presentation would not work. The Personal Harbor was a departure from conventional office design, so many customers were perplexed. Sue Sacks, a team member, said, "People acted like we had fallen from Mars." Team members soon realized that to explain the features and benefits of the product they had to begin studying new organizational developments such as team-oriented workforces and corporate reengineering. The advanced sales team was renamed advanced solutions team. Sales calls put more emphasis on learning about the customers' problems and identification of possible solutions. Members of the team viewed themselves as consultants who were in a position to discuss solutions to complex business problems.

The consultative approach soon began to pay off in sales. One customer, a hospital, was preparing to build a new office building and needed workstations for 400 employees. The hospital had formed a committee to make decisions concerning the purchase of office equipment. After an initial meeting between the Steelcase sales team and the hospital committee, a visit to the Steelcase headquarters in Grand Rapids, Michigan, was arranged. The hospital committee members were able to tour the plant and meet with selected Steelcase experts. With knowledge of the hospital's goals and directions, Sue Sacks was able to arrange meetings with Steelcase technical personnel who could answer specific questions. The hospital ultimately placed an order worth more than a million dollars.

Questions

1. To fulfill a problem-solving need, salespeople must often be prepared to communicate effectively with customers who are seeking a cluster of satisfactions (see Fig. 6.1). Is it likely that a customer who is considering the Personal Harbor Workspaces will seek information concerning all three dimensions of the Product-Selling Model? Explain your answer.

2. What product-selling strategies are most effective when selling a new and emerging product such as the Personal Harbor Workspaces?

3. Sue Sacks and other members of her sales team discovered that a traditional product-oriented presentation would not work when selling the Personal Harbor Workspaces. Success came only after the team adopted the consultative style of selling. Why was the product-oriented presentation ineffective?

4. Sue Sacks and other members of the advanced team found that the consultative approach resulted in meetings with people higher in the customer's organization. "We get to call on a higher level of buyer," she said. Also, the team was more likely to position the product with a value-added strategy instead of a price strategy. In what ways did the advanced solutions team members add value to their product? Why was less emphasis placed on price during meetings with the customer?

PART IV

DEVELOPING A CUSTOMER STRATEGY

➤ With increased knowledge of the customer the salesperson is in a better position to achieve sales goals. This part presents information on understanding buyer behavior, discovering individual customer needs, and developing a prospect base.

Personal Selling Philosophy

Customer Strategy

Relationship Strategy

Building Quality Partnerships

Presentation Strategy

Product Strategy

One of the two sustainable strategic advantages in the new global marketplace is an obsession with customers. Customers, not markets.

TOM PETERS
THRIVING ON CHAOS

Understanding Buyer Behavior

The final decade of the twentieth century was characterized by a major power shift in the direction of the customer. The new economy not only gives the customer more choices but also provides more information needed to make those choices. Granted, information overload often creates confusion in the marketplace, but we must not lose sight of the power shift.

We know that new products must satisfy the customer's needs, but identifying these needs can be very challenging. No one understands this challenge better then Kim Fernandez, director of natural food sales for Alta Dena Certified Dairy (www. altadenadairy.com). She sells a wide range of natural dairy foods to wholesalers and retailers. Almost all her products are displayed in the dairy department. In a typical supermarket, the dairy department accounts for about 9 percent of sales. Kim Fernandez is responsible for servicing existing accounts and obtaining new accounts. She also is responsible for introducing new products.[1] This is a challenging part of her work in view of the fact that 800–900 new dairy products are introduced each year. The proliferation of new items is an attempt to satisfy more consumer needs.

DEVELOPING A CUSTOMER STRATEGY

The greatest challenge to salespeople in the age of information is to improve responsiveness to customers. In fact, a growing number of sales professionals believe the customer has supplanted the product as the driving force in sales today. As noted by Larry Wilson, "The products of one company in an industry are becoming more and more similar to those of the competition."[2] The salesperson can distinguish between similar products and services and help the customer to perceive important differences.

Adding Value with a Customer Strategy

A **customer strategy** is a carefully conceived plan that results in maximum customer responsiveness. One major dimension of this strategy is to achieve a better understanding of the customer's buying needs and motives. When salespeople take time to discover these

Figure **7.1**
Today, the greatest challenge to salespeople is to improve responsiveness to customers. Understanding why and how customers buy and knowing who prospects are form the foundation blocks for the salesperson to develop a highly responsive customer strategy.

	Strategic/Consultative Selling Model	
Strategic step	Prescription	
DEVELOP A PERSONAL SELLING PHILOSOPHY	☑ ADOPT MARKETING CONCEPT ☑ VALUE PERSONAL SELLING ☑ BECOME A PROBLEM SOLVER/PARTNER	
DEVELOP A RELATIONSHIP STRATEGY	☑ ADOPT DOUBLE-WIN PHILOSOPHY ☑ PROJECT PROFESSIONAL IMAGE ☑ MAINTAIN HIGH ETHICAL STANDARDS	
DEVELOP A PRODUCT STRATEGY	☑ BECOME A PRODUCT EXPERT ☑ SELL BENEFITS ☑ CONFIGURE VALUE-ADDED SOLUTIONS	
DEVELOP A CUSTOMER STRATEGY	☐ UNDERSTAND BUYER BEHAVIOR ☐ DISCOVER CUSTOMER NEEDS ☐ DEVELOP PROSPECT BASE	

needs and motives, they are in a much better position to offer customers a value-added solution to their buying problem.

Every salesperson who wants to develop repeat business should figure out a way to collect and systematize customer information. As part of the customer strategy, many salespeople use some type of customer profile. The authors of *Reengineering the Corporation* discuss the importance of collecting information about the unique and particular needs of each customer:

> Customers—consumers and corporations alike—demand products and services designed for their unique and particular needs. There is no longer any such notion as *the* customer; there is only *this* customer, the one with who a seller is dealing at the moment and who now has the capacity to indulge his or her own personal tastes.[3]

The first prescription for developing a customer strategy focuses on buyer behavior (Fig. 7.1). Every salesperson needs a general understanding of why and how people buy, which is the topic of this chapter. The second prescription emphasizes the discovery of individual customer needs. The third prescription for developing a customer strategy emphasizes building a strong prospect base, which is discussed in Chapter 8.

COMPLEX NATURE OF CUSTOMER BEHAVIOR

The forces that motivate customers can be complex. Arch McGill, former vice president of IBM, reminds us that individual customers perceive the product in their own terms, and that these terms may be "unique, idiosyncratic, human, emotional, end-of-the-day, irrational, erratic terms."[4] Different people doing the same thing, for example, purchasing a personal computer (PC), may have different needs that motivate them; and each person may have several motives for a single action.

The proliferation of market research studies, public opinion polls, surveys, and reports of "averages" makes it easy to fall into the trap of thinking of the customer as a number. The customer is a person, not a statistic. Companies that fully accept this basic truth are likely to adopt a one-to-one marketing strategy. The one-to-one strategy is based on a bedrock concept: Treat different customers differently. The one-to-one marketer focuses on cultivating a long-term relationship with each customer in order to sell that customer many products over an entire lifetime of patronage. This is a concept that works not only for the retail customer but also for business-to-business transactions, distributors, and service providers both in the public and private sectors.[5]

FORCES INFLUENCING BUYING DECISIONS

Figure 7.2 illustrates the many forces that influence buying decisions. Notice that individual psychological and physiological needs, combined with group influences, shape customer perceptions and buying motives. As we explain each part of the model, a better understanding of buyer behavior emerges.

Individual Needs That Influence Buying Decisions

Basic human needs have changed little throughout our economic history. However, the ways in which needs are fulfilled has changed greatly during the age of information.[6] The starting point for developing an understanding of the forces influencing buying decisions is a review of the individual needs that shape the customer's behavior. To gain insights into customer behavior motivated by both physiological and psychological needs, it is helpful to study the popular hierarchy of needs developed by Abraham Maslow.

➤➤ Selling in Action

DEVELOPING A "SEGMENT BUSTER"

The Chrysler PT Cruiser has been described as a wacky-looking cross between a 1937 Ford and a London Taxicab. Some view it as part 1920s gangster car and part 1950s hot rod. DaimlerChrysler AG describes the car as a sure-fire "segment buster" that combines the room of a minivan with the flair of a sport-utility vehicle and the utility of a small car. The car is built in Mexico and sold in North America and in about 40 foreign markets.

DaimlerChrysler knows that some people will love the car and some will hate it. The PT (which stands for personal transportation) Cruiser is the company's first vehicle designed entirely through an unconventional market-research process known as "archetype research." This research was conducted by a French-born medical anthropologist named G. Clotaire Rapaille. The process began with a series of free-wheeling, three-hour focus group sessions in Great Britain, France, Germany, Italy, and North America. With lights dimmed and mood music playing, participants were asked to drift back to their childhoods and jot down the memories invoked by the prototype PT Cruiser parked in the room. After the sessions, Dr. Rapaille and members of the research team pored over the stories looking for emotions sparked by the vehicle. This research led to major design changes that made the car look even more outlandish. The final design is one that thrills some and puts off others, just what the research team hoped to accomplish.[a]

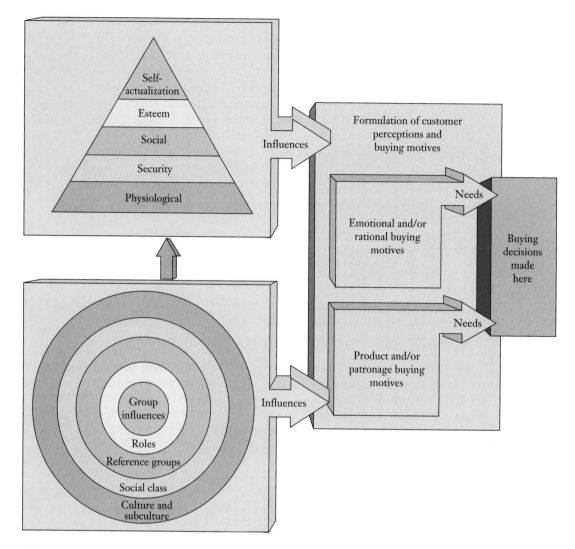

Figure 7.2

The forces that motivate customers to make specific buying decisions are complex. This model illustrates the many factors that influence buyer behavior. It can serve the salesperson as a guide for developing a highly responsive customer strategy.

MASLOW'S HIERARCHY OF NEEDS

According to Abraham Maslow, basic human needs are arranged in a hierarchy according to their strength. His theory rests on the assumption that as each lower level need is satisfied, the need at the next level demands attention.

Physiological Needs Sometimes called primary needs, **physiological needs** include the needs of food, water, sleep, and shelter. Maslow placed our physiological needs at the bottom of the pyramid. He believed that these basic needs tend to be strong in the minds of most people. As these more basic needs (hunger, thirst, shelter, etc.) are satisfied, a person seeks to satisfy the higher needs. Efforts to satisfy the higher needs must be postponed until the basic physical needs are met.

Maslow describes people as wanting animals who strive to satisfy higher needs after lower needs have been satisfied. People tend to satisfy their needs systematically, in most cases, starting with the most basic and moving up the ladder.

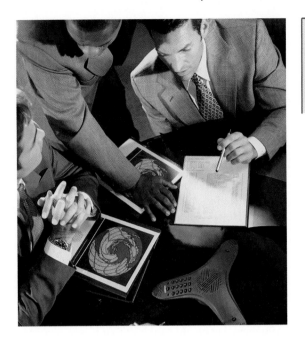

There is no longer any such notion as *THE* customer, there is only *this* customer, the one with whom a seller is dealing with at the moment.

Security Needs After physiological needs have been satisfied, the next need level that tends to dominate is safety and security. **Security needs** represent our desire to be free from danger and uncertainty. The desire to satisfy the need for safety and security often motivates people to purchase such items as medical and life insurance or a security alarm for the home or business. The buyer who voices a strong desire to have products delivered on time and undamaged may be motivated by security needs. For a banking customer the security need might surface as a desire for accessibility, timely hours of operation, or localized access to service.[7] Working with a competent, trusted salesperson gives the customer a feeling of security.

Social Needs The need to belong, or **social needs**, reflect our desire for identification with a group and approval from others. These needs help explain our continuing search for friendship, companionship, and long-term business relationships. This "need to belong" is more than just an urge—it is a fundamental human need.[8] This level of Maslow's hierarchy of needs helps us understand why many customers want to be treated as partners. They desire an accessible, two-way relationship.

Esteem Needs At the fourth level of Maslow's need priority model appear **esteem needs**. Esteem needs reflect our desire to feel worthy in the eyes of others. We seek a sense of personal worth and adequacy, a feeling of competence. In simple terms, we want to feel that we are important. When Debra Tarleton, a resident of Charlotte, North Carolina, turned her retirement savings over to a securities broker, she expected to be an involved partner in the investment process. When a year passed without her hearing from the broker, it became apparent he did not value her input. The broker could have easily granted Tarleton prestige and stature by giving her regular reports on her investment and opportunities for input.[9]

Self-Actualization Needs Maslow defined the term **self-actualization** as a need for self-fulfillment, a full tapping of one's potential. It is the need to "be all that you can be," to have mastery over what you are doing. One goal of consultative selling is to help the customer experience self-actualization in terms of the relationship with the salesperson. The self-actualized customer relationship is a true partnership. The salesperson is continuously updating customer information and providing value-added services. After a bad experience with her first broker, Debra Tarleton experienced a feeling of self-actualization when she turned her investment portfolio over to Lorraine Fiorillo, a Prudential Securities financial planner. Fiorillo helped her set up an individual retirement account and a self-employment pension plan for her business.[10]

The five-level need priority model developed by Maslow is somewhat artificial in certain instances. At times several of our needs are interacting together within us. One example is the business lunch. Not only are you conducting business with a client but also you are satisfying your needs for food and beverages, for engaging in social activities, and perhaps for feeling important in your own eyes and—you hope—in the eyes of your customer.[11] However, the model does provide salespeople with a practical way of understanding which need is most likely to dominate customer behavior in certain situations.

Group Influences That Influence Buying Decisions

As noted earlier, the people around us also influence our buying decisions. These **group influences** can be grouped into four major areas: (1) role influences, (2) reference groups, (3) social class, and (4) culture and subculture[12] (Fig. 7.3). Salespeople who understand these roles and influences can develop the type of insight customers view as being valuable.

Figure **7.3**

To gain additional insights into customers' motivations, it is helpful to study the group influences that affect buying decisions.

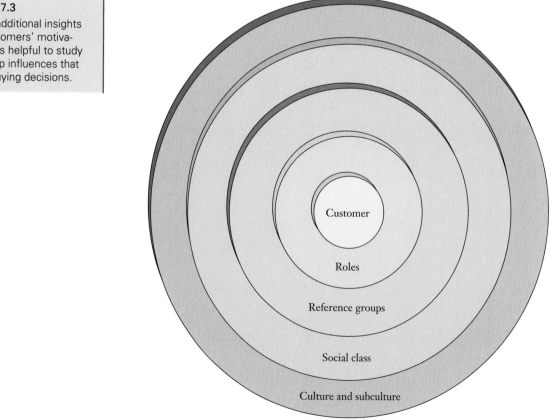

Customer

Roles

Reference groups

Social class

Culture and subculture

Role Influence

Throughout our lives we occupy positions within groups, organizations, and institutions. Closely associated with each position is a **role**: a set of characteristics and expected social behaviors based on the expectations of others. All the roles we assume (student, member of the school board, or position held at work) influence not only our general behavior but also our buying behavior. In today's society, for example, a woman may assume the role of mother at home and purchasing manager at work. In the manager's role she may feel the need to develop a conservative wardrobe or purchase a leadership training course.

Reference Group Influence

A **reference group** consists of the categories of people that you see yourself belonging to, and with which you habitually compare yourself. Members of a reference group tend to influence the values, attitudes, and behaviors of one another.[13] The reference group may act as a point of comparison and a source of information for the individual member. For example, Pi Sigma Epsilon, the national fraternity in marketing, sales management, and selling, may serve as a reference group for a college business major. In the business community, a chapter of the American Society for Training and Development, or Sales & Marketing Executives International may provide a reference group for its members. As members of a reference group we often observe other people in the group to establish our own norms, and these norms become a guide for our purchasing activity. Of course, the degree to which a reference group influences a buying decision depends on the strength of the individual's involvement with the group and the degree of susceptibility to reference group influence.

Social Class Influence

A **social class** consists of people who are similar in occupational prestige, values, lifestyles, interests, and behaviors.[14] The criteria used to rank people according to social class vary from one society to another. In some societies, land ownership allows entry into a higher social class. In other societies, education is a major key to achieving upper class status. The neighborhood we live in and the type, value, and condition of our home also represent class indicators. To some degree, individuals within social classes have similar attitudes, values, and possessions.

How many social classes are there? There is no clear answer to that question, but sociologists usually employ between three and six categories. At one extreme is the upper class, which usually consists of "old money" people who possess inherited wealth. They buy large homes, obtain degrees from prestigious institutions, travel extensively, and tend to buy quality products. At the other extreme is the lower class, which is characterized by persons with little formal education and considerably less income. Marketers often focus attention on a specific social class. Metropolitan Life Insurance Company, a large provider of life insurance to the middle class, announced it is targeting more affluent customers for new business. Metropolitan Life has assigned 300 salespeople to sell policies to individuals earning $150,000–$200,000 annually.[15]

Cultural Influence

Culture can be defined as the accumulation of values, rules of behavior, forms of expression, beliefs, transmitted behavior patterns, and the like for a group of people who share a common language and environment. Culture tends to encourage or discourage particular

Sales force automation. GoldMine Software Corporation offers an auto-mated system for quick access to information on why your customer buys.

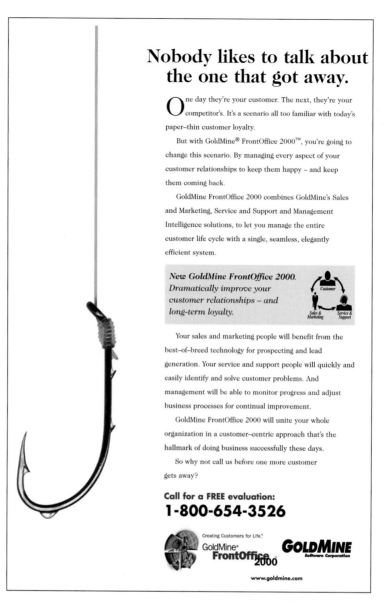

behaviors and mental processes.[16] We maintain and transmit our culture chiefly through language. Culture has considerable influence on buying behavior. Today, culture is getting more attention because of the rapid increases in immigrant groups. As cultural diversity increases, companies must reexamine their sales and marketing strategies.

Within many cultures there are groups whose members share ideals and beliefs that differ from those held by the wider society of which they are a part. We call such a group a **subculture**.[17] Among the many U.S. subcultures are the teenage, elderly, and Native American subcultures. Members of a subculture may have stronger preferences for certain types of foods, clothing, and housing.

A breakdown in communications, and even conflict, can arise from the differences between the culture of the sales representative and the culture of the customer. Consider the impact of culture on the daily work of pharmaceutical representatives. The culture of physicians is quite different than the culture of mainstream society. To complicate matters even further, there are microcultures within the physician group. For example, the religious

➤➤ CUSTOMER RELATIONSHIP MANAGEMENT WITH TECHNOLOGY

MANAGING MULTIPLE CONTACTS WITH CRM

Salespeople often find that groups of their contacts have common interests and buying motives. Customer and prospects may be segmented into groups by buying influences, by the products they purchase, by the industries they are involved in, or by their size. Customer relationship management (CRM) software can enable the salesperson to easily link contacts together as groups and "mass-produce" information that is custom-fitted to the needs of people in a specific group. For example, each owner of a specific product may receive a telephone call, personalized letter, or report that describes the benefits of a new accessory available from the salesperson. (See the exercise, Managing Multiple Contacts with CRM, at p. 163 for more information.)

convictions of one physician might keep him from prescribing a certain pharmaceutical product. A simple process of cultural awareness on the part of salespeople can prevent misunderstandings from happening.[18]

PERCEPTION—HOW CUSTOMER NEEDS ARE FORMED

Perception is the process of selecting, organizing, and interpreting information inputs to produce meaning. The information inputs are sensations received through sight, taste, hearing, smell, and touch.[19] Our perception is shaped by group influences as well as the psychological and physiological conditions within us (see Fig. 7.2). Perception determines what is seen and felt; therefore it influences our buying behavior. The importance of perception was emphasized by Al Ries, co-author of *Positions: The Battle for Your Mind*: "It's perception that determines whether you win or lose in the marketplace."[20]

We tend to screen out or modify stimuli, a process known as *selective perception*, for two reasons. First, we cannot possibly be conscious of all inputs at one time. Just the commercial messages we see and hear each day are enough to cause sensory overload. Second, we are conditioned by our social and cultural background, and our physical and psychological needs, to use selectivity.

Buyers may screen out or modify information presented by a salesperson if it conflicts with their previously learned attitudes or beliefs. The prospect who is convinced that "I will never be able to master the personal computer" is apt to use selective perception when the salesperson begins discussing user-friendly features. Salespeople who can anticipate this problem of selective perception should acquire as much background information as possible before meeting with the prospect. During the first meeting with the customer, the salesperson should make every effort to build a strong relationship so that the person opens up and freely discusses personal perceptions. Salespeople who do this have accepted one of the great truisms in sales and marketing: "Facts are negotiable. Perception is rock solid."

People involved in sales and marketing need to review their own perceptions periodically to see if they are accurate. For many years, marketers have mistakenly stereotyped older Americans as crotchety grandparents living on a modest fixed income. The truth is that many senior citizens are in the middle to high income bracket and see themselves much younger than their chronological years.

The image projected by Pentium, a processor from Intel, has considerable impact on buyer behavior.

BUYING MOTIVES

Every buying decision has a motive behind it. A **buying motive** can be thought of as an aroused need, drive, or desire. This motive acts as a force that stimulates behavior intended to satisfy the aroused need. Our perceptions influence or shape this behavior. An understanding of buying motives provides the salesperson with the reasons why customers buy.

As you might expect, some buying decisions are influenced by more than one buying motive. The buyer of catering services may want food of exceptional quality served quickly so all her guests can eat together. This customer also may be quite price conscious. In this situation the caterer should attempt to discover the *dominant buying motive* (DBM). The DBM may have the greatest influence on the buying decision.[21] If the customer is anxious to make a good impression on guests who have discriminating food tastes, then food quality may be the dominant buying motive.

Successful salespeople have adopted a product strategy that involves discovery of the buying motives that influence the purchase decision. In Chapter 10, we describe a need identification process that can be used to discover the customer's buying motives.

Emotional versus Rational Buying Motives

A careful study of buyer behavior reveals that people make buying decisions based on both emotional and rational buying motives. An **emotional buying motive** is one that prompts the prospect to act because of an appeal to some sentiment or passion. When customers buy expensive Harley-Davidson motorcycles, they are paying for much more than a high-flying hog. They are purchasing entry into a community of like-minded enthusiasts who share a passion for all things Harley.[22] Emotions can be powerful and often serve as the foundation of the dominant buying motive. A **rational buying motive** usually appeals to the prospect's reason or judgment based on objective thought processes. Some common rational buying motives include profit potential, quality of service, and availability of technical assistance.

Mapping software such as BusinessMAP PRO can help target customers and prospects.

EMOTIONAL BUYING MOTIVES

A surprising number of purchases are guided by emotional buying motives. This is why many firms use emotional appeals. Even technology firms sometimes rely on these appeals. Cascade Communications Corporation, maker of Internet traffic switches, promises, "Technology that reaches right into our lives." GTE, the giant telecommunications firm, says, "We're working to help make your life easier." Ads for Gulfstream business jets explain how the planes can save executives time and also describe the roomy interiors that offer comfort to the passengers.

Doing business in America, or anyplace else in the world, is never purely a rational or logical process. To inspire people and move them in the right direction, you have to engage them emotionally.[23] In a world filled with look-alike products, emotional factors can have considerable influence. If two vendors have nearly identical products, then the influence of the vendors' salespeople becomes more important. The salesperson who is able to connect at a personal level has the advantage.

Salespeople should make every effort to discover the emotions that influence buying decisions. Emotions help explain the "why" behind buying decisions. The salesperson who is able to identify and satisfy the customer's emotional buying motives is performing an important service.

RATIONAL BUYING MOTIVES

A purchase based on rational buying motives is generally the result of an objective review of available information. The buyer closely examines product or service information with an attitude that is relatively free of emotion. Professional buyers or purchasing agents are most likely to be motivated by rational buying motives such as on-time delivery, financial gain, competent installation, saving of time, increased profits, or durability.

The buyers who work for Wal-Mart, the largest and most profitable retailer in the world, are tough, aggressive, and focused. They want to do business with salespeople who are well prepared and know how their product can complement the product mix in Wal-Mart stores. Bob Gehm, a vice president for West Point Stevens, makes frequent calls on Wal-Mart buyers. He says, "They expect you to give them the best price, the best value, and the best service."[24]

In the face of increased competition, professional buyers such as those employed by Wal-Mart want to partner with salespeople who can respond to their rational buying motives. This is especially true in the fields of manufacturing and processing, where salespeople are expected to offer powerful insights into helping firms make products better, faster, and cheaper.

Patronage versus Product Buying Motives

Another way to help explain buyer behavior is to distinguish between patronage and product buying motives. Patronage buying motives and product buying motives are learned reasons for buying. These buying motives are important because they can stimulate repeat business and referrals.

Rational buying motives usually influence the purchase decisions of the professional buyer.

PATRONAGE BUYING MOTIVES

A **patronage buying motive** is one that causes the prospect to buy products from one particular business. The prospect usually has had prior direct or indirect contact with the business and has judged this contact to be beneficial. In those situations where there is little or no appreciable difference between two products, patronage motives can be highly important. At a time when look-alike products are very common, these motives take on a new degree of importance. Some typical patronage buying motives are described as follows:

Superior Service As noted earlier in this text, superior service adds value to the product. In many cases the value-added product builds customer loyalty.

Selection Some firms make every effort to carry a complete selection of products. The prospect is usually quite certain that the item needed is available.

Quality. Value. Excellence.
Why not have it all?

Ever hear this, *"You can't please everybody?"*

That might be true—unless you serve luscious, Driscoll's berries to your customers.

The deep, sweet flavor and superb quality of Driscoll's berries win customer acclaim with every presentation and with every bite.

Foodservice operators count on Driscoll's for consistent quality and flavor of a full line of berries.

They know, too, that they can trust Driscoll's for a meticulous food safety program all the way from growing to harvest to packing.

From fantastic flavor and menu versatility to consumer satisfaction, superb Driscoll's berries really do please everybody.

When you offer the added value of the finest berries in the world, that attention to quality is a positive reflection of your menu and your operation.

Driscoll's
The Finest Berries in the World

©1999 Driscoll Strawberry Associates, Inc., P.O. Box 50045, Watsonville, CA 95077 (831) 763-5000 www.driscollsberries.com

Salespeople who stress product attributes such as the ones in this Driscoll ad, are positioning their product to meet the customer's "product buying motives".

In many business to business buying situations the competence of the sales representative can be the Dominant Buying Motive (DBM).

Competence of Sales Representatives   There is no doubt that the salesperson is in a unique position to develop a loyal customer following. A salesperson who knows the product and is willing to give "something extra" to the customer is an asset to any firm.

PRODUCT BUYING MOTIVES

A **product buying motive** is one that leads a prospect to purchase one product in preference to another. Interestingly enough, this decision is sometimes made without direct comparison between competing products. The buyer simply believes that one product is superior to another.

There are numerous buying motives that trigger prospects to select one product over another.

Brand Preference   Many marketers seek to develop brand loyalty. Maytag, Mercedes-Benz, and United Van Lines serve as examples of companies that have developed a strong brand preference.

Quality Preference   J. D. Power, founder of J. D. Power and Associates, says, "We define quality as what the customer wants."[25] Today's customer is likely to have high-quality standards.

Price Preference   Most prospects are price conscious to some degree. If a product has a price advantage over the competition and quality has not been sacrificed, it probably enjoys success in the marketplace. The forces of globalization and deregulation, and the growth of electronic commerce, has resulted in the expansion of low price options available to today's customer.

"I can't decide. I'm having a brand identity crisis."

Source: *The New Yorker,* April 13, 1998, p. 60.

Design or Engineering Preference Many companies are betting that superior product design will be the key to winning customers in the twenty-first century. One of these companies is Deere & Company, maker of farm implements. The powerful 8000 model John Deere tractor, priced from $110,000 to $138,000, offers farmers design features such as an air-conditioned cabin with excellent forward and rearward visibility and a four-wheel drive system that offers a tight turning radius.[26]

HOW CUSTOMERS MAKE BUYING DECISIONS

Several commonly accepted theories explain how people arrive at a buying decision. Three of the most popular theories are described in this section. One traditional point of view holds that the salesperson closes the sale by guiding the prospect through five mental processes. We refer to this approach as the **buyer action theory**. A second traditional theory is based on the assumption that a final buying decision is possible only after the prospect has answered five logical questions. This is called the **buyer resolution theory**. Both of these theories thrived during the past 40 years when the main focus was on the product. The third explanation of how people buy is "prospect" oriented and is called the **need–satisfaction theory**. This approach to the selling–buying process gives maximum attention to a highly responsive customer strategy that ensures satisfaction of prospect needs. It has been adopted by successful marketers who realize the benefits associated with long-term partnerships.

Buyer Action Theory

From a traditional point of view there are five mental steps that lead to a buying decision: (1) attention, (2) interest, (3) desire, (4) conviction, and (5) action. The salesperson's role is to guide the prospect through each step. These five steps have application in advertising, public relations, publicity, and sales promotion as well as personal selling.

ATTENTION

There is no hope of selling a product unless you first get the prospect's attention. In some cases this is not an easy task. A potential buyer may be preoccupied with a variety of concerns and may view your presence as an intrusion. The salesperson can take a number of steps to attract and hold a potential buyer's attention. These are discussed in a later chapter.

INTEREST

The second step in the buying process is development of interest in the product. A salesperson must determine the best way to convert attention to interest. The manner in which this is done varies, of course. In some selling situations the prospect's interest might be sparked by a product demonstration. In another situation the salesperson may use a series of stimulating questions to create interest.

DESIRE

Desire moves us to possess an object or to participate in an experience that we perceive as enjoyable or satisfying. It can be a compelling factor in life. We can all recall instances when the desire within us became almost overwhelming. This desire may have been kindled by the sounds of a high-quality stereo system or by knowledge that a new computer can improve your productivity.

CONVICTION

At the conviction stage the prospect has decided the product is a genuine value, with features that justify its price. Competing products have been ruled out. The salesperson has removed doubt from the buyer's mind. At this stage, the prospect can rationalize the purchase to himself and others.

ACTION

Once the buyer makes the first four decisions, the stage is set to close the sale. Sometimes the fifth decision is made quickly and effortlessly. In other cases the prospect shows signs of procrastination. In some cases a small amount of pressure applied at the right time motivates buyer action. Several persuasive techniques available to the salesperson are discussed later in this textbook.

PROS AND CONS OF THE BUYER ACTION THEORY

This approach to selling is most common in situations where product features and benefits are easily understood by the prospect, the product is not expensive, and the purchase does not require multiple decision makers. It is frequently used to sell clothing, jewelry, household appliances, and other consumer goods. This approach usually is not effective in those selling situations that involve complex products and multiple decision makers.

Buyer Resolution Theory

The buyer resolution theory (sometimes referred to as the 5-Ws theory) also recognizes that selling is a mental process. This view of the selling–buying process recognizes that a purchase is made only after the prospect has made five buying decisions involving specific, affirmative responses to the following questions:

1. Why should I buy? (need)
2. What should I buy? (product)
3. Where should I buy? (source)
4. What is a fair price? (price)
5. When should I buy? (time)

WHY SHOULD I BUY?

Realistically, it is sometimes difficult to provide prospects with an answer to this question. In many cases salespeople fail in their attempt to help customers become aware of a need. Thus large numbers of potential customers are not sufficiently persuaded to purchase products that provide them with genuine buyer benefits. Many businesses are operating with inefficient and outdated equipment. A majority of Americans classified as "head of household" have too little insurance.

WHAT SHOULD I BUY?

If a prospect agrees that a need does exist, then you are ready to address the second buying decision. You must convince the prospect that the product being offered can satisfy the need. In most cases the buyer can choose from several competing products.

WHERE SHOULD I BUY?

As products become more complex, consumers are giving more attention to "source" decisions. In a major metropolitan area the person who wants to buy a Laserjet 3100 or a competing product can choose from several sources. As we noted in Chapter 5, company features such as certified service technicians or complete parts inventory may permit a company to enjoy a competitive advantage.

WHAT IS A FAIR PRICE?

Today's better educated and better informed consumers are searching for the right balance between price and value (benefits). They are better able to detect prices that are not competitive or do not correspond in their minds with the product's value. Salespeople who represent higher priced products and services such as Patek Philippe watches (prices start at $6,000), Oxford suits (prices start at $1,000), or meeting and banquet space at Loews Resort (upscale facility near Tucson) must be prepared to explain the product features that justify the higher price.

WHEN SHOULD I BUY?

A sale cannot be closed until a customer has decided when to buy. In some selling situations the customer may want to postpone the purchase because of reluctance to part with the money. The desire to postpone the purchase also might exist because the customer cannot see any immediate advantage to purchasing the product now.

PROS AND CONS OF THE BUYER RESOLUTION THEORY

The buyer resolution theory recognizes that a purchase is made only after the prospect has made all five buying decisions. The omission of any of these decisions results in no sale. One strength of this sales approach is that it focuses the salesperson's attention on five important factors that the customer is likely to consider before making a purchase. This approach helps structure the information-gathering process. Answers to these five questions provide valuable insights about the customer's buying strategy. One important limitation of this theory is that it often is not possible to anticipate which of the five buying decisions might be most difficult for the prospect to make. Customers often have an established buying process or cycle; and when the selling process does not mesh with the buying process, a sale is not likely.[27] Therefore, a "canned" or highly inflexible sales presentation would not be appropriate. Also, there is no established sequence in which prospects make these decisions. A decision concerning price may be made before the source decision is made. These limitations remind us that a sales presentation must be flexible enough to accommodate a variety of selling situations.

Need – Satisfaction Theory

The need–satisfaction theory is the foundation of consultative selling, which is described in Chapter 1. This buying process theory is based on the assumption that buying decisions are made to satisfy needs. The role of the professional salesperson is to identify these needs and then recommend a product or service that satisfies them.

The consultative selling approach, coupled with strategic planning, sets the stage for long-term partnerships that result in repeat business and referrals. Put another way, strate-

➤➤ *Building Relationships in a Diverse World*

KEEPING PACE WITH A CHANGING CUSTOMER BASE

No other country on earth is as multiracial and multicultural as the United States of America. This diversity presents marketers with major opportunities and major challenges. Marlene L. Rossman, author of *Multicultural Marketing*, says, "While many companies have fought over slices of the tiny yuppie market, the mature market, the senior market, the woman's market, and the other slow-growth markets, they have ignored the ethnic market, the fastest-growing and most profitable market of them all." Several demographic trends indicate that America will be characterized by even more diversity in the years ahead. In the 1980s, 8.7 million people immigrated to America. The U.S. Census Bureau indicates that even more immigrants entered America in the 1990s. Minority populations now make up one quarter of our total population. Marketers must recognize that members of ethnic groups are today less inclined to transform their ethnic identity into an American identity. Hispanics, for example, have fueled the rapid growth of Latin music. In California, builders are taking time to study the traditions, beliefs, and customs of the growing Asian population; and home builders in the Atlanta area are attempting to learn more about the African American home buyers. As we begin the twenty-first century, it is important to learn how to sell to the new demographics.[b]

gic planning gives us the opportunity to maximize the benefits of consultative selling. As noted earlier, salespeople who develop correct strategies are more likely to make sales presentations to the right person, at the right time, and in a manner most likely to achieve positive results.

The need–satisfaction theory encompasses the concept that salespeople should conduct a systematic assessment of the prospect's situation. This usually involves collecting as much information as possible prior to the sales call and using a series of carefully worded questions to obtain the customer's point of view during the sales call. These questions lead the customer to talk more freely and help the salesperson pinpoint the customer's needs. Each customer should be thought of as a separate target market, with the salesperson trying to adapt to each one's needs.

The need–satisfaction approach to selling is based on a series of basic beliefs about the professional salesperson's role. These beliefs help us develop our own personal philosophy of selling, which serves as our "conscience" in selling situations. The key basic beliefs that serve as foundation stones for the need–satisfaction theory follow:

1. Effective communication exists between the buyer and the seller. *Two-way communication will provide for a mutual exchange of ideas, feelings, and perceptions.*
2. Systematic inquiry is necessary to establish the individual needs of unique customers. A lengthy discussion of the product or service is postponed until the salesperson becomes well acquainted with the prospect. In almost every selling situation, information supplied by the customer is essential. We must keep in mind the importance of treating diverse customers differently. The mass market is disappearing because a growing number of customers need custom solutions.
3. Salespersons take a *two-way advocacy* position, representing the interests of their company and of their clients with equal dignity and skill. High-performance salespeople bring to the sales task a genuine sensitivity for the customer's needs.
4. In some selling situations the salesperson reaches the conclusion that the product does not provide the best solution (or the entire solution) to the customer's problem. For instance, people who sell elaborate computer systems sometimes help shape a client's entire strategic business plan. These salespeople may naturally use some of their own "solutions" (their companies' products). However, they may incorporate other people's solutions as well, including their competitors' products.
5. Every effort should be made to develop a *long-term relationship with the customer.* Today, customers want a partner, someone who shares the same goals. Salespeople who can suggest ways to improve productivity, increase profits, and improve service, for example, are more likely to become valued partners.

Most customers feel less stress in the presence of a salesperson who has adopted the need–satisfaction philosophy of selling. The buying process is more relaxed and less threatening. They become genuine participants in the selling–buying process and begin to view the salesperson as a partner.

A growing number of firms such as Nordstrom, Xerox, and Marriott use some variation of consultative selling. This approach works effectively in all types of selling situations. It does not matter whether you are selling financial securities, computer systems, or training programs. It does not matter whether you are focusing on the needs of an individual or working on a strategic plan with the divisional vice president of a corporation. You still can apply consultative selling skills. You are engaging in progressive levels of complexity, not a fundamentally different approach.[28]

Figure 7.4 provides a comparison of the need–satisfaction theory with the buyer action and buyer resolution theories. The benefits of the need–satisfaction theory to the buyer and the seller are obvious.

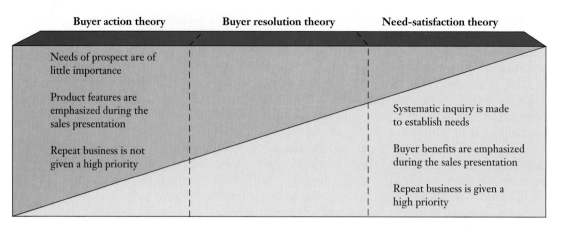

Figure 7.4

The need–satisfaction theory provides salespeople with the strongest foundation for developing a highly responsive customer strategy.

DISCOVERING INDIVIDUAL CUSTOMER BUYING MOTIVES

Buyer behavior changes as people assume new roles, adopt new reference groups, and experience an increase or decrease in income. This is the reason salespeople need to develop a "customer" orientation instead of a "market" orientation. What is the difference? In the words of Tom Peters and Nancy Austin, "Markets do not buy products, customers do."[29]

A customer orientation can give a salesperson a tremendous competitive advantage in the marketplace. All it takes is the right mind-set. It means recognizing that customer A may buy or not buy your product for different reasons from those of customer B. It means that we must understand customers better than they understand themselves. It means appreciating your customers unstated and unmet needs. It means knowing their businesses or lifestyles in ways that extend beyond their use of your current product or service.[30] When we ask appropriate questions, listen to the responses, and make observations, we often can discover the customer's unique buying motives.

Questions

Salespeople should think of themselves as nondirective counselors. They should use questions to get prospects talking about themselves and their buying needs. As prospects open up, the salesperson is given a golden opportunity to discover their wants, needs, and perceptions. In business-to-business selling situations the questions are often specific and direct: "When will you begin shipping the new product line," or "when will the plans for the plant expansion be finalized?" Salespeople need to recheck and verify facts constantly.[31] The questioning process is examined in detail in Chapter 10.

Listening

It has been said, "We cannot learn when we are talking." This point seems of particular importance as we attempt to get acquainted with prospects. By asking questions and then pausing to let the prospect talk, we can obtain a better understanding of the forces that are shaping buyer behavior. If you let people talk and listen carefully, they actually tell you how to sell to them.

Observation

As noted in Chapter 3, we should be as observant as possible before and during the sales presentation. Before meeting with a prospect, look at the physical surroundings and try to identify clues that may tell you more about the prospect. Read the customer's trade journals. During the presentation, observe the prospect's facial expression and body movements. Emotions are often communicated by nonverbal behavior.

In an ideal situation the information collected with questions, listening, and observations can be entered into a database that is easily accessible to people throughout the organization. As noted by one expert on buyer behavior, "A business that doesn't equip itself with the capability to remember what makes each of its customers different probably won't be in business for long."[32]

As buyers become better educated and more sophisticated, it becomes more critical than ever to gain an understanding of why people buy. Sales personnel must individualize each sales presentation to discover the most dominant buying motives. The most effective ways to discover individual customer buying motives and needs are discussed in Chapter 10.

Summary

The importance of developing a *customer strategy* is introduced in this chapter. This type of planning is necessary to ensure maximum customer responsiveness. The complex nature of customer behavior also is discussed. We note that buyer behavior is influenced in part by individual (physical and psychological) needs. Maslow's popular model ranks these needs. There are also a number of group influences that shape our psychological needs to various degrees. Buyer behavior is influenced by the roles we assume, reference groups, social class, and culture.

Perception was defined as the process of selecting, organizing, and interpreting information inputs to produce meaning. We use our five senses to assign meaning to these inputs. Our perception is shaped by social influences as well as the psychological and physiological conditions within us.

We discuss *emotional and rational buying motives*. Emotional buying motives prompt the prospect to act because of an appeal to some sentiment or passion. Rational buying motives tend to appeal to the prospect's reasoning power or judgment.

We also compare patronage and product *buying motives*. Patronage buying motives grow out of a strong relationship that has developed between the customer and the supplier. When competing products are quite similar, patronage motives can be very important. Product buying motives are usually in evidence when a prospect purchases one product in preference to another.

This chapter also presents several theories that explain the buying process. Three of the most popular theories are the *buyer action theory,* the *buyer resolution theory,* and the *need–satisfaction theory.* The discovery of *buying motives* also is discussed.

KEY TERMS

Customer Strategy
Physiological Needs
Security Needs
Social Needs
Esteem Needs
Self-Actualization
Group Influences
Role
Reference Group
Social Class
Culture

Subculture
Perception
Dominant Buying Motive
Buying Motive
Emotional Buying Motive
Rational Buying Motive
Patronage Buying Motive
Product Buying Motive
Buyer Action Theory
Buyer Resolution Theory
Need–Satisfaction Theory

REVIEW QUESTIONS

1. According to the Strategic/Consultative Selling Model, what are the three prescriptions for the development of a successful customer strategy?
2. Explain how Maslow's hierarchy of needs affects buyer behavior.
3. Describe the four group influences that affect buyer behavior.
4. What is meant by the term *perception*?
5. Distinguish between emotional and rational buying motives.
6. List three commonly accepted theories that explain how people arrive at a buying decision.
7. What are the steps in the buyer action theory? To what other sales promotion methods does this theory apply?
8. List the five basic beliefs that serve as a foundation for the need–satisfaction theory.
9. List and describe three methods salespeople use to discover buying motives.
10. J. D. Power, founder of J. D. Power and Associates, says, "We define quality as what the customer wants." Do you agree or disagree with his observations? Explain your answer.

APPLICATION EXERCISES

1. Select several advertisements from a trade magazine. Analyze each one, and determine what rational buying motives the advertiser is appealing to. Do any of these advertisements appeal to emotional buying motives?
2. Select a magazine that is aimed at a particular consumer group, for example, *Architectural Digest*, *Redbook*, or *Better Homes and Gardens*. Study the advertisements and determine what buying motives they appeal to.

3. The J. D. Power and Associates company is referenced in the product buying motives section of this chapter. This company is now providing information on customer buying satisfaction and buying habits on the Internet. Locate them at www.jdpower.com. Click on "Hot off the press" and examine their customer satisfaction reports and buying habits.

CRM APPLICATION EXERCISE

Managing Multiple Contacts with CRM

The ACT! database software identifies four firms involved with architecture. You can look up these firms and arrange to make contact with them. Start by selecting Lookup, Other, and, on the blank record, enter "architectural" in the Account Code field and click OK. ACT! then displays four records with architectural in that field.

For scheduling multiple telephone calls, start with the first record, Bryan Enterprises, and select the schedule call icon or select the following menu choices: Schedule, Calls. Use your mouse to select the following Monday, pick OK, select 9:00 A.M., pick OK, choose Follow up on the menu, and pick OK. On the next window, called Schedule an Activity, select the box labeled "Contact . . ." that displays another window called Select a Contact. On the Select a Contact window, pick the box labeled Lookup. This returns you to the Schedule an Activity window, where you can pick OK.

To confirm that a phone call was scheduled with each person in these architectural firms, select View, Task List. When the task list window appears, choose the Time Period, Future. Pick OK when finished.

For creating form letters to send to each of the four people in the four architectural firms, select Write, Edit Template, type the word "letter," and press Enter. A template with codes is displayed. Type the words, "I'll call Monday"; next select File, Save As, and type "Form"; then press Enter. Select File, Close. To prepare the four letters, select Write, Form Letter, type "Form," and press Enter. On the next window—labeled Prepare Form Letter—choose Active Lookup and Document, and then pick OK. The first form letter is displayed on your screen. By pressing the PageDown key, you can review all four letters. Select Print (Ctrl+P) to print the four letters and File, Close to close the letter window.

CASE PROBLEM

Kim Fernandez, director of natural food sales for Alta Dena Certified Dairy (www. altadenadairy.com), takes a great deal of pride in her efforts to win new customers for her line of natural dairy foods. As a sales representative for this national company (introduced at the beginning of this chapter), she is in a key position to meet the needs of a growing number of health conscious consumers.

Like most professional salespeople, Kim Fernandez is continuously developing new accounts, servicing existing accounts, and introducing new products. When she calls on a large regional grocery wholesaler, such as Fleming Companies, closing the sale can be challenging. Wholesalers do not want to inventory products that do not appeal to the retail supermarkets they serve. Wholesalers want to buy products from companies that maintain the highest quality production standards and provide outstanding service after the sale. Wholesalers also want to buy products at the lowest possible prices. The retail supermarkets (chain operated and independent) that Kim Fernandez calls on are no less demanding. They operate in a competitive environment and must offer products at the lowest possible price.

The motto, "Give the consumers what they want," could easily be adopted by the typical American supermarket. A typical store features from 10,000 to 12,000 items. Some large supermarkets feature over 20,000 different items. Thousands of new products are introduced each year, so buyers must make many difficult purchase decisions. Supermarket dairy departments have been revitalized in recent years by the growth of new items. Each year from 800 to 900 new dairy products are introduced. When Alta Dena Certified Dairy introduces a new product, the sales force must work hard to win acceptance.

Kim's product line includes yogurt, butter, cottage cheese, milk, ice cream, cheese, and many other dairy products. The company makes every effort to offer only products that are of the highest quality and made with all natural ingredients. The Alta Dena research and development (R&D) laboratory is constantly searching for ways to improve existing products and develop new ones. Customers often are involved in the product development process. They are given samples and encouraged to give their impressions. The Alta Dena product development staff, along with the sales staff, work hard to determine the customer's wants and needs. Kim often takes samples of new products to supermarkets and involves the dairy department staff in a taste test. When Kim meets with a prospect, she asks several questions to determine the person's needs and buying motives. She realizes that in some cases several motives may influence the purchase decision. She also knows that buying behavior is influenced by perception, so she must probe to find out what prospects are really thinking. The prospect who believes that natural dairy products have a short shelf life may be reluctant to carry her line of products. If this perception is uncovered, then Kim knows how to respond to it.

Kim views education as a major sales tool. She often explains the quality controls used at Alta Dena plants and even invites customers to participate in plant tours. She talks about the "contented cows" that make up the Alta Dena dairy herd. She knows that education can add value to her products. Kim also knows that a long-term partnership with the customer is based on attention to details. She checks on deliveries and makes sure all complaints are handled quickly and courteously. (For more information see chapter opener on p. 141.)

Questions

1. Does it appear that Kim Fernandez has built her customer strategy on the three prescriptions featured in the Strategic/Consultative Selling Model? Explain.

2. What aspects of the need–satisfaction theory has Kim Fernandez incorporated into her approach to customers? Explain.

3. As a buyer for a large supermarket chain, would you be most influenced by rational or emotional buying motives? Explain.

4. What steps has Kim Fernandez taken to build a long-term partnership with her customers?

Developing a Prospect Base

When you finish reading this chapter, you should be able to

1. Discuss the importance of developing a prospect base

2. Identify and assess important sources of prospects

3. Describe criteria for qualifying prospects

4. Explain common methods of organizing prospect information

5. Name some characteristics that are important to learn about customers as individuals and business representatives

6. Describe the steps in developing a prospecting and sales forecasting plan

Craig Phillips, a sales representative for International Dehydrated Foods, has found a "no hassle" method of maintaining contact with over 500 people with whom he works. He is using ACT! contact software developed by SalesLogix (www.interact.com). He now can maintain a detailed profile of every customer and customer support personnel. With a single key stroke on his lap-top computer he can bring up detailed information on each contact. Customer service has been improved because the ACT! software reminds him when it is time to make a follow-up call. The ACT! software also makes it easy to network with other members of the sales force and his sales manager.[1]

ACT! and other software vendors such as Epicor and Siebel Systems are helping companies develop effective customer relationship management (CRM) systems. These systems are at the heart of every successful one-to-one marketing initiative. Success in selling depends on one's ability to identify prospects, gain insight into the prospect's needs, and develop an accurate picture of the prospect's value.[2]

PROSPECTING—AN INTRODUCTION

Gerhard Gschwandtner, editor of *Selling Power*, says, "The main purpose of a salesperson is not to make sales, but to create customers."[3] Identifying potential customers is an important aspect of the customer strategy. In the terminology of personal selling this process is called **prospecting**. A potential customer, or **prospect**, is someone who has three basic qualifications. First, the person must have a need for the product or service. Many companies attempt to identify a target market that includes those prospects who qualify on the basis of need. Second, the individual must be able to pay for the purchase. An important fundamental of consultative selling is that prospects should not be persuaded to buy products they cannot afford. Third, the prospect must be authorized to purchase the product. Finding prospects who can make the purchase is not as easy as it sounds. In many situations the salesperson must make the sales presentation to multiple decision makers. One of these decision makers might be the technical expert who wants an answer to the question: "Does the product meet the company's specifications?" Another decision maker may be the person who will actually use the product. The employee who will use the forklift truck

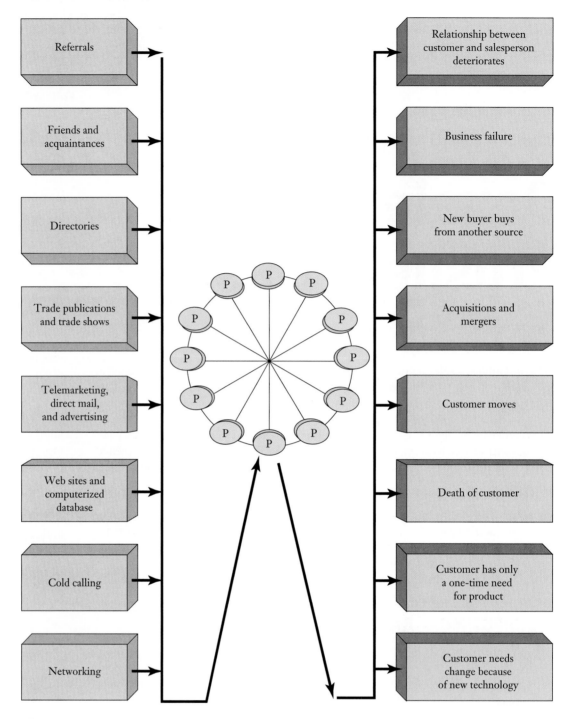

Figure 8.1

The "Ferris Wheel" concept, which is aimed at supplying an ongoing list of prospects, is part of world sales record holder Joe Girard's customer strategy.

you are selling may be involved in the purchase decision. Of course, there is often a "purse-string" decision maker who has the ultimate authority to release funds for the purchase.[4]

The goal of prospecting is to build a **prospect base** made up of current customers and potential customers. Many successful companies find that current customers account for a large percentage of their sales. Every effort is made to keep these clients satisfied because they provide the repeat business that is necessary to maintain profitability.

Importance of Prospecting

Every salesperson must cope with customer attrition, that is, the inevitable loss of customers over a period of time, which can be attributed to a variety of causes. Unless new prospects are found to replace lost customers, a salesperson eventually faces a reduction in income and possible loss of employment.

To better understand the significance of prospecting, let us examine a few common causes of customer attrition.

The customer may move to a new location outside the salesperson's territory. The American population is very mobile. This cause of attrition is especially common in the retail and service areas.

A firm may go out of business or merge with another company. In some areas of business the failure rate is quite high. In recent years, we have witnessed a record number of mergers that have caused massive changes in purchasing plans.

A loyal buyer or purchasing agent may leave the position because of promotion, retirement, resignation, or serious illness. The replacement may prefer to buy from someone else.

Some studies reveal that the average company loses 15–20 percent of its customers every year. Depending on the type of selling, this figure might be higher or lower. It becomes clear that many customers are lost for reasons beyond the salesperson's control. If salespeople want to keep their earnings at a stable level, they need to develop new customers.

Joe Girard, popular sales trainer, uses the "Ferris wheel" concept to illustrate the relationship between prospecting and loss of customers due to the attrition factors described earlier. As people get off the Ferris wheel, the operator fills their seats one at a time, moves the wheel a little, and continues this process until all the original riders have left the wheel and new ones come aboard (Fig. 8.1). In reality, of course, established customers do not come and go this fast. With the passing of time, however, many customers are replaced.

PROSPECTING REQUIRES PLANNING

Prospecting should be viewed as a systematic process of locating potential customers. Some prospecting efforts can be integrated easily into a regular sales call. Progressive marketers are doing three things to improve the quality of the prospecting effort:

1. *Increase the number of people who board the Ferris wheel.* You want to see a continuous number of potential prospects board the Ferris wheel because they are the source of sales opportunities. If the number of potential prospects declines sharply, the number of sales closed also declines.
2. *Improve the quality of the prospects who board the Ferris wheel.* Companies that have adopted the quality improvement process concept view this phase of prospecting as critical. They have established quality standards that ensure a steady supply of prospects with high profit potential.[5] In the absence of such quality standards it may be necessary to "fire" an unproductive customer at a later date. This becomes necessary when customers demand more sales and service resources than their purchase volume justifies.[6]
3. *Shorten the sales cycle by quickly determining which of the new prospects are qualified prospects—qualified as to need, ability to pay, and authority to*

purchase the product. Gerhard Gschwandtner says, "Time is the ultimate score-keeper in the game of selling." He points out that many salespeople do not meet their sales goals because they do not quickly qualify new prospects.[7] Later in this chapter we examine qualifying practices and discuss how to shorten the sales cycle with sales automation methods.

In most selling situations, prospecting begins with a study of the market for your product or service. When Pitney Bowes first developed the desktop postage meter, the company conducted a careful study of the market. At first glance, equipment of this nature seemed well suited only to a large business firm. With additional market analysis the company identified many additional customers who could benefit from purchasing the product. Many small business firms use this product today.

Prospecting Attitude

As noted in Chapter 4, attitudes serve as a foundation for our behavior. Salespeople who view prospecting as an important key to success spend time every day on this activity. Prospecting is not thought of as a chore, but an opportunity to identify persons who can benefit from owning your product. Prospecting is viewed as a process that can take place in virtually any environment—in social situations, on an airplane, during a professional meeting, or in any situation where people are present.[8]

Prospecting requires self-discipline. Paul S. Goldner, author and sales trainer, suggests that you make an appointment with yourself for one hour of prospecting each day. He says that the time to prospect will never be exactly right, so use the appointment to ensure that this important sales activity does not get postponed.[9]

▶▶ CUSTOMER RELATIONSHIP MANAGEMENT WITH TECHNOLOGY

USING THE SAME CRM SOFTWARE AS AT&T

AT&T implemented a CRM program that resulted in major increases in productivity and improved customer service. The first stage of the automation project involved 11,000 desktop computers and the popular ACT! software. This combination of hardware and software resulted in a reported 15–20 percent improvement in productivity. AT&T salespeople gained easier and quicker access to account information such as the prospect's name, title, company, assistant's name, and notes concerning the account. Placing the database on a server gives all network users access to this important information.

Information in a CRM database can be reviewed prior to calling or visiting a prospect, thus ensuring a more personalized contact. Through CRM, salespeople gain a competitive edge in relating to their prospects' needs and interests.

You have the opportunity to use a demonstration version of the same software (ACT!) used by AT&T. Just as an AT&T salesperson, you are assigned a number (20) of prospect accounts and given individual and company information about each account's contact person in the database software. Your participation in the CRM case study and exercises will give you hands-on experience with the strategic development of a prospect base, using modern sales technology. You not only will be using the same software being used by thousands of salespeople but also will be working with data that are derived from authentic selling challenges. (See the CRM Case Study, Reviewing the Prospect Database, at p. 185 for more information.)

SOURCES OF PROSPECTS

Every salesperson must develop a prospecting system suited to a particular selling situation. Some of the several sources of prospects follow, and each should be carefully examined:

Referrals

Friends, family members, and centers of influence

Directories

Trade publications

Trade shows

Telemarketing

Direct response advertising and sales letters

Web site

Computerized database

Cold calling

Networking

Educational seminars

Prospecting by nonsales employees

The DMI marketing information system

1. Description of the horizontal display
2. Range of the horizontal display
3. Horizontal row totals
4. Vertical column totals
5. State totals
6. SIC Code numbers
7. Description of SIC Code industries

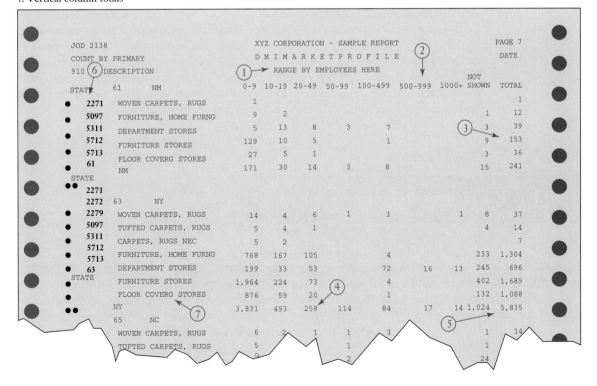

Figure 8.2

Computerized product analysis reports such as this one from Dun & Bradstreet help salespeople to locate prospects as part of a customer strategy.

Referrals

The use of referrals as a prospecting approach has been used successfully in a wide range of selling situations. In most cases referral leads result in higher close rates, larger sales, and shorter sales cycles. A **referral** is a prospect who has been recommended by a current customer or by someone who is familiar with the product. Satisfied customers, business acquaintances, and even prospects who do not buy, often can recommend the names of persons who might benefit from owning the product. Research in the field of personal selling indicates that it takes much less time to sell a qualified, referred lead than it does to sell a nonqualified, nonreferred lead.[10] Endless chain referrals, and referral letters and cards represent two variations of this prospecting tactic.

ENDLESS CHAIN REFERRALS

The endless chain approach to obtaining referrals is easy to use because it fits naturally into most sales presentations. A salesperson selling long-term health care insurance might say, "Miss Remano, whom do you know who might be interested in our insurance plan?" This open-ended question gives the person the freedom to recommend several prospects and is less likely to be answered with a no response. Be sure to use your reference's name when you contact the new prospect—"Mary Remano suggested that I call you. . . ."

REFERRAL LETTERS AND CARDS

The referral letter method is a variation of the endless chain technique. In addition to requesting the names of prospects, the salesperson asks the customer to prepare a note or letter of introduction that can be delivered to the potential customer. The correspondence is an actual testimonial prepared by a satisfied customer. Some companies use a referral card to introduce the salesperson. The preprinted card features a place for your customer to sign the new prospect's name and his own name, and can be used as part of the sales presentation.

Using an existing customer as an intermediary has several advantages. The amount of time spent on prospecting can be reduced, and the referral can make it easier to get an appointment. In addition, the views of a satisfied customer often have a great deal of

---

▶▶ BUILDING QUALITY PARTNERSHIPS

PROSPECTING WITH YOUR PARTNERS

When Megan Michael sees a new office building going up, she stops her car and makes inquiries about who is to occupy the building. As a sales representative for BKM Total Office, an office furniture supplier in San Diego, she needs to be aware of new office space. However, this approach is not her most important prospecting method. She has found the telephone to be her most effective prospecting tool. Michael speaks regularly with her customers to find out if they know companies that might need BKM's products. Architects, designers, and builders who have previously worked with Michael have proved to be good sources of referrals. The key to her prospecting success is maintaining a strong relationship with her customers. She realizes that you must be an effective partner before you can ask for help.[a]

impact on the prospect. Salespeople who are viewed as product experts and are recognized as problem solvers and partners, are more likely to be the beneficiaries of referrals.

Friends, Family Members, and Centers of Influence

A person who is new in the field of selling often uses friends and family members as sources of information about potential customers. It is only natural to contact people we know. In many cases these people have contacts with a wide range of potential buyers.

The center-of-influence method involves establishing a relationship with a well-connected, influential person who is willing to provide prospecting information. This person may not make buying decisions, but has influence on other people who do. To illustrate, consider the challenge facing Gary Schneider, creator of a powerful software product that would help small farmers optimize their crop selection. After spending several years developing the product, Schneider and his wife began selling the product one copy at a time. During one cold call on a major crop insurer, American Agrisurance, he met a senior researcher who immediately saw the benefits of the software product. This respected researcher is in a position to influence buying decisions at his company and to provide prospect information for other crop insurers.[11]

Directories

Directories can help salespeople search out new prospects and determine their buying potential. A list of some of the more popular national directories is provided next:

Middle Market Directory lists 14,000 firms worth between $500,000 and $1 million (available from Dun & Bradstreet).

Directory of Corporate Affiliations profiles about 4,000 leading U.S. companies along with their subsidiaries, divisions, and affiliates (available from Macmillan Directory Division).

Standard & Poor's Corporation Records Service provides details on more than 11,000 companies (available from Standard and Poor's).

Thomas Register of American Manufacturers provides a listing of 60,000 manufacturers by product classifications, addresses, and capital ratings (available from Thomas Publishing Company).

Polk City Directory provides detailed information on the citizens of a specific community. Polk, in business for over 125 years, publishes about 1,100 directories covering 6,500 communities in the United States and Canada. It usually can be obtained from the city government or chamber of commerce.

These are just a few of the better known directories. There are hundreds of additional directories covering business and industrial firms on the regional, state, and local levels. Some directories are free, while others must be purchased at a nominal fee. One of the most useful free sources of information is the telephone directory. Most telephone directories have a classified (yellow pages) section that groups businesses and professions by category.

If you are involved in the sale of products in the international market, a valuable resource is the world traders data reports published by U.S. and Foreign Commercial Service (US & FCS), which has district offices located in several cities throughout the nation. If you want to know more about a prospective customer or agent in a foreign country, US & FCS can provide a complete profile, including background information within the local business community, payment history, creditworthiness, and overall reliability and suitability as a trade contact.

Trade Publications

Trade publications provide a status report on every major industry. If you are a sales representative employed by Super Valu Stores, Fleming Companies Inc., Sysco Corporation, or one of the other huge food wholesaling houses that supplies supermarkets, then you can benefit from a monthly review of *Progressive Grocer* magazine. Each month this trade publication reports on trends in the retail food industry, new products, problems, innovations, and related information. Trade journals such as *Women's Wear Daily*, *Home Furnishings*, *Hardware Retailer*, *Modern Tire Dealer*, and *Progressive Architecture* are examples of publications that might help salespeople identify prospects.

Trade Shows

A trade show is a large exhibit of products that are, in most cases, common to one industry, such as electronics or office equipment. The prospects walk into the booth or exhibit and talk with those who represent the exhibitor. In some cases, sales personnel invite existing customers and prospects to attend trade shows so they can have an opportunity to demonstrate their newest products.

The *Thomas Register of American Manufacturers* is one source of prospects for salespeople.

Thomas Register of American Manufacturers
Order Now And Get All Of This...

The most complete listings of North American manufacturers available with 1.5 million listings...
- 149,000 companies
- 50,000 product and service headings
- 1,700 company catalogs
- 105,000 brand and trade names
- 98,000 supplier ads for vendor comparisons

Over 50,000 pages of facts and figures organized to help you find the information you need in seconds. Who makes it? ...Who's closest? ...Who do I contact to order? ...Who do I contact to sell? ...What's their phone number and address? *You'll find the answers you need in Thomas Register — fast.*

To Order Call 212–290–7277 or Fax 212–290–7365

Research studies indicate that it is much easier to identify good prospects and actually close sales at a trade show. In most cases, fewer sales calls are needed to close a sale if the prospect was qualified at a trade show. Some marketers use special qualifying methods at trade shows. Brian Jeffrey, president of Jeffrey & Jeffrey Associates in Ontario, Canada, prepares a list of seven questions that can quickly qualify or disqualify prospects at a trade show.[12]

Telemarketing

Telemarketing is the practice of marketing goods and services through telephone contact. It has become an integral part of many modern sales and marketing campaigns. One use of telemarketing is to identify prospects. A financial services company used telemarketing to identify prospects for its customized equipment leasing packages. Leads were given to salespeople for consideration. Telemarketing also can be used to quickly and inexpensively qualify prospects for follow-up. Some marketers use the telephone to verify sales leads generated by direct mail, advertisements, or some other method.

Direct Response Advertising and Sales Letters

Many advertisements invite the reader to send for a free booklet or brochure that provides detailed information about the product or service. In the category of business-to-business marketing, advertising has the greatest inquiry-generating power.[13] Some firms distribute postage-free response cards (also known as bingo cards) to potential buyers. Recipients are encouraged to complete and mail the cards if they desire additional information. In some cases the name of the person making the inquiry is given to a local sales representative for further action.

Sales letters can be incorporated easily into a prospecting plan. The prospecting sales letter is sent to persons who are in a position to make a buying decision. Shortly after mailing the letter (three or four days) the prospect is called and asked for an appointment. The call begins with a reference to the sales letter. To make the letter stand out, some salespeople include a promotional item. As noted in Chapter 5, all sales letters must be written with care. To get results, sales letters must quickly get the reader's attention.

Web Site

Thousands of companies and business people who understand the impact of the age of information have established Web sites on the World Wide Web. A **Web site** is a collection of Web pages maintained by a single person or organization. It is accessible to anyone with a computer and a modem. Harris Simkovitz, an independent financial-products broker in Cherry Hill, New Jersey, decided to use a Web site to reach prospects. He designed a single Web page that features his picture, his biographical information, and his financial-planning philosophy. If this modest effort proves to be successful, he can later change the Web page content or add additional Web pages.[14] By contrast, large firms, such as Century 21, maintain Web sites that feature 20–30 Web pages. Web sites are frequently used for lead generation.

Computerized Database

With the aid of electronic data processing it is often possible to match product features with the needs of potential customers quickly and accurately. In many situations a firm can develop its own computerized database. In other cases it is more economical to purchase

With computers salespeople can accumulate a great deal of information about individual customers and use this information to personalize the selling process.

the database from a company that specializes in collection of such information. One example is the D&B MarketPlace, a CD-ROM database (also available on line) with extensive information about 10 million businesses nationwide. This database is updated quarterly.[15] Some databases focus on a specific prospect category. For example, lists are available for boat enthusiasts, computer industry professionals, and subscribers to many of the nation's magazines.

With the aid of a personal computer (PC), salespeople can develop their own detailed customer files. The newer PCs provide expanded storage capacity at a lower price than in the past. This means that salespeople can accumulate a great deal of information about individual customers and use this information to personalize the selling process. For example, a PC can help an independent insurance agent maintain a comprehensive record of each policyholder. As the status of each client changes (marriage, birth of children, etc.), the record can be easily updated. With the aid of an up-to-date database the agent can quickly identify prospects for the various existing and new policy options.

Cold Calling

With some products, cold call prospecting is an effective approach to prospect identification. In **cold calling** the salesperson selects a group of people who may or may not be actual prospects and then calls (phone or personal visit) on each one. For example, the sales representative for a wholesale medical supply firm might call on every hospital in a given community, assuming that each one is a potential customer. Many new salespeople must rely on the cold call method because they are less likely to get appointments through referrals.[16] It takes time to develop a group of established customers who are willing to give referrals.

Successful cold calls do not happen spontaneously. Some strategic thinking and planning must precede personal visits and telephone calls. Who do you contact? What do you say during the first few seconds? What message should you leave on voice mail? These and other questions are answered in Chapter 9.

Networking

One of the most complete books on networking is *Dig Your Well Before You're Thirsty* by Harvey Mackay. He says, "If I had to name the single characteristic shared by all the truly successful people I've met over a lifetime, I'd say it's the ability to create and nurture a network of contacts."[17] Networking skills are of special importance to new salespeople who cannot turn to a large group of satisfied customers for referrals and leads. Professionals (accountants, lawyers, consultants, etc.), entrepreneurs, managerial personnel, and customer service representatives also must develop networking skills.

In simple terms, **networking** is the art of making and using contacts, or people meeting people and profiting from the connections.[18] A growing number of consultants in the field of personal selling are recommending networking as an important source of prospects. Although networking has become one of the premier prospecting methods of

Increasingly, lists of prospects are becoming available on the Internet. These lists can be used as a "combination approach" with direct mail, telemarketing, or cold calling.

the past decade, many salespeople are reluctant to seek referrals in this manner. In addition, many salespeople do not use effective networking practices. Skilled networkers suggest the following guidelines for identifying good referrals:

1. *Meet as many people as you can.* Networking can take place on an airplane, at a Rotary Club meeting, at a trade show, or at a reception.
2. *When you meet someone, tell the person what you do.* Give your name and describe your position in a way that explains what you do and invites conversations. Instead of saying, "I am in stocks and bonds," say, "I am a financial counselor who helps people make investment decisions."
3. *Do not do business while networking.* It usually is not practical to conduct business while networking. Make a date to call or meet with the new contact later.
4. *Offer your business card.* The business card is especially useful when the contact attempts to tell others about your products or services.
5. *Edit your contacts and follow-up.* You cannot be involved with all your contacts, so separate the productive from the nonproductive. Send a short letter to contacts you deem productive and include business cards, brochures—anything that increases visibility.[19]

There are three types of networks salespeople should grow and nurture. Every salesperson can be well served by networking within their own organization. You never know when someone in finance or shipping may be needed to help solve a problem or provide you with important information. A second form of networking involves establishing contacts inside your industry. Make contact with experts in your field, top performers, leaders, successful company representatives, and even competitors. The third form of networking involves business contacts with people outside of your industry such as bankers, government officials, developers, and other people in your community. The local golf course is frequently a good place to make these contacts.[20]

Educational Seminars

Many salespeople are using educational seminars as a method of identifying prospects. Seminars provide an opportunity to showcase your product without pressuring prospects to buy. The owners of Source Digital Systems, a McLean, Virginia firm that sells video-editing systems, attracted 128 corporate prospects to an educational seminar held next door to the Baltimore Orioles baseball field. While the guests enjoyed lunch, the staff demonstrated the newest video-editing technology. The group was given an opportunity to ask questions and complete a survey form. Afterward, everyone attended an Orioles–Red Sox game. Within two months the company closed six sales worth $420,000.[21] Many banks, investment firms, accounting firms, wine merchants, and consulting companies use seminars to generate new prospects. When inviting prospects, be clear about the seminar's content and always deliver what you promise.[22]

Prospecting by Nonsales Employees

Should service technicians, receptionists, bank tellers, and other nonsales personnel be involved in prospecting? In a growing number of organizations the answer is yes. Prospecting does not need to be the exclusive responsibility of the sales force.

Employees do not have to work in sales to identify potential customers. However, they may not be alert to opportunities unless they are given an orientation to this role. Nonsales personnel need special training to function effectively in this role. Also, an incentive program can keep them focused on new business opportunities for the organization.

➤➤ Selling in Action

SEMINAR SELLING

The use of educational seminars has become an important prospecting method. You can educate prospective customers with brochures, news releases, catalogs, or your Web site, but educational seminars offer the advantage of face-to-face contact. Barbara Siskind, in her book *Seminars to Build Your Business*, identifies 15 objectives for hosting seminars. A few of the most important ones follow:

Obtain sales leads. This is one of the most common objectives for seminars. You can obtain the names of attendees and arrange appointments for future sales calls. Seminars also may help identify actual product users, technical support people, or engineers who, although they may not be the decision maker, may influence the purchase decision.

Promote your place of business. Your place of business can become a destination for people who might otherwise not consider visiting it. You have an opportunity to create awareness of your company and develop a positive image for your entire operation and its capabilities.

Showcase and demonstrate your expertise. Seminars allow you to show a carefully targeted group of people that you really know your stuff. Salespeople can be supported by technical experts and others in the organization who can address clients' specific concerns.

Polaroid Canada advertised educational seminars across Canada where imaging specialists assisted prospective clients in exploring imaging solutions. Toronto-based Charon Systems, Incorporated, a systems integrator that deploys networks for organizations, regularly organizes seminars for 80–100 technology people from midsized firms. President David Fung estimates that 25 percent of prospects become clients.[b]

Combination Approaches

In recent years we have seen an increase in the number of prospecting approaches used by salespeople. In many cases, success in selling depends on your ability to use a combination of the methods described in this chapter. For example, the large number of prospects identified at a trade show might be used to develop an effective telemarketing program. Prospects are called and an effort is made to set up a personal call. Prospects identified at a trade show or educational seminar also might be sent a sales-oriented newsletter or a sales letter.

QUALIFYING THE PROSPECT

Through prospecting a large number of people or organizations that appear to need the product can be found. This list should be examined to target the most promising prospects. A **target market** is a well-defined set of present and potential customers that an organization attempts to serve.[23] Refining the prospect list is essential for two reasons. First, a salesperson cannot afford to spend time calling on persons who are not real prospects. Time conservation should be a primary concern. Second, a salesperson may sometimes identify prospects who cannot place an order large enough to cover the cost of the sales call. Many companies have established ratios of sales volume to sales expense that must be taken into consideration when prospecting. The average sales call costs more than $200, so salespeople must try to avoid calls on customers who have limited buying potential.

It is important to keep in mind that calling on potential customers is much more time consuming than calling on established customers. In terms of sales closings, a new customer can require about three times the number of contacts compared with closing a sale with an established customer.[24]

Not all prospects are equal. A salesperson might begin with a list of 25 potential customers. After careful study, 10 of the names are eliminated because they do not appear to need the product. Then the salesperson estimates the potential sales that might be generated from the remaining prospects. By using this approach, the salesperson eliminates another five persons because the potential order would not be large enough to cover sales call expenses. The remaining names in this hypothetical situation might be ranked according to anticipated sales volume. The process of identifying prospects who should be contacted is called **qualifying**.

In many selling situations it is possible to establish criteria that can be used to qualify prospects. To rate the names that appear on the prospect list, it is sometimes helpful to ask yourself several basic questions:

1. Does the name represent a customer who already is buying from you? If so, is there a chance you can obtain additional business?
2. Is the name a former customer? If so, do you know why the person stopped buying from you? Should you make another contact with this person?
3. Does the name represent a user of your type of product? Is this person currently buying from one of your competitors?
4. What is the amount of potential sales that can be generated from the prospect? As noted before, not all prospects are equal.
5. What is the prospect's credit rating? (Note: The *Dun & Bradstreet Reference Book* is one excellent source of credit information.)

This list of questions can be revised to meet the needs of many different types of salespeople. A sales representative for an industrial equipment dealer may see the qualifying process differently from the person who sells commercial real estate. The main consideration is providing accurate answers to each question.

ORGANIZING YOUR PROSPECT INFORMATION

When it comes to organizing prospect information, the salesperson has two choices. Some salespeople record prospect information on blank file cards (4 × 6 is the most popular), on preprinted file cards that have space for specific kinds of information, or in loose-leaf notebooks. At Nordstrom and some other department stores, salespeople record information about each customer in a "personal book." Successful salespeople often have three or four bulging books that help them provide more personalized service to each customer. Salespeople at Nordstrom have recently moved a great deal of the customer information to a centralized computer data base. In addition to the customer's name, address, and account number, they record the person's sizes, style preferences, hobbies and interests, birthday, previous items purchased, and any other appropriate information. With this information available, each customer becomes a "prospect" for future purchases. Sales personnel often call their customers when new products arrive.

Harvey Mackay instructs his salespeople to develop a 66-question customer profile. The form is divided into categories such as education, family, business background, special interests, and lifestyle. In the process of collecting and analyzing this information, the salesperson gets to know the customer better than competing salespeople do. Harvey Mackay describes the benefits of developing a customer profile:

> If selling were just a matter of determining who's got the low bid, then the world wouldn't need salespeople. It could all be done on computers. The "Mackay 66" is designed to convert you from an adversary to a colleague of the people you're dealing with and to help you make sales.[25]

Mackay says that the 66-item customer profile helps the salesperson systematize information in a way that makes it more useful and accessible.

The use of file cards and notebooks are adequate for salespeople who deal with a small number of prospects and do not get involved in complex sales. The use of some type of computerized system is more appropriate for salespeople who deal with large numbers of prospects, frequently get involved in complex sales, and must continually network with management and members of the sales support team. In a study conducted by *Sales & Marketing Management* it was found that more than one third of the companies surveyed use an automated lead management system.[26] With the aid of modern technology, salespeople can retrieve data from various sources no matter where they are. Regardless of the system used, most salespeople need to collect and organize two kinds of prospect information: information about the prospect as an individual and information about the prospect as a business representative.

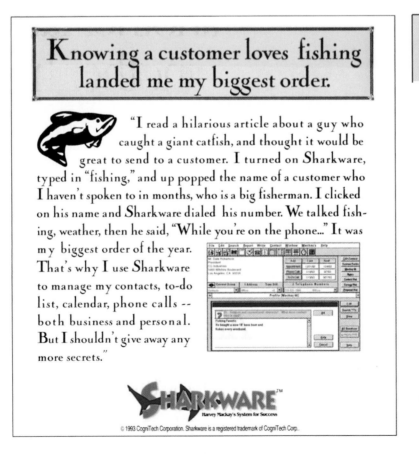

This ad reminds us that it is important to be able to recall personal information about the customer.

Prospect as an Individual

The foundation for a sales philosophy that emphasizes the building of partnerships is the belief that we should always treat the other person as an individual. Each prospect is a one-of-a-kind person with a number of unique characteristics. The only possible way we can treat the prospect as an individual is to learn as much as possible about the person. The starting point is to learn the correct spelling and pronunciation of the prospect's name. Then acquire information about the person's educational background, work experience, special interests, hobbies, and family status. Interview industry people or employees at the company to acquire personal information.[27]

In Chapter 16 you are introduced to the concept of communication-style bias and the benefits derived from an understanding of communication styles. You will also learn how to overcome communication-style bias and build strong selling relationships with style flexing. If at all possible, acquire information concerning the prospect's communication style before the sales call. Business associates or close friends of the prospect can supply this helpful information. (Communication styles are identified for each prospect in the sales automation case study.)

A lasting business partnership is based in large part on a strong personal relationship. Dale Carnegie, a pioneer in the field of human relations training and author of *How to Win Friends and Influence People*, recognized the importance of taking a personal interest in others. He said, "You can make more friends in two months by becoming inter-

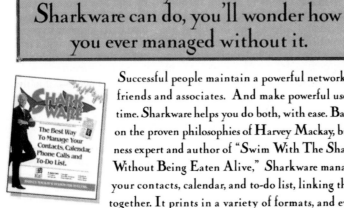

Most salespeople who are now using contact management software wonder how they ever got along without it.

ested in other people than you can in two years by trying to get other people interested in you."

Prospect as a Business Representative

In addition to personal information about the prospect, it is important to collect certain business-related facts. This is especially important when the prospect is associated with a business. At the outset determine if the prospect is authorized to purchase your product or service. Salespeople also must be concerned about the prospect's ability to buy. A potential buyer's credit rating is easy to check in most cases.

Before calling on the prospect it pays to review various aspects of the company operation. Research starts with a document search for information about the company and industry.[28] What does the company manufacture or sell? How long has the firm been in business? Is the firm a leader in the field? Does the firm have expansion plans?

Most established firms have been doing business with one or more other suppliers. When possible, find out who the company buys from and why. It always helps to know in advance who the competition is. Salespeople who take time to study personal and business facts are in a stronger position to meet the prospect's needs. They also close more sales.

In most cases, an appointment saves time and money.

DEVELOPING A PROSPECTING AND SALES FORECASTING PLAN

A major barrier to prospecting is time. There never seems to be enough time for a salesperson to do everything that needs to be done. In many situations, less than half of the work week is devoted to actual sales calls. The remainder of the time is spent identifying and screening prospects, travel, paperwork, planning, sales meetings, and servicing accounts. Time devoted to prospecting often means that less time is available for actual selling. Given a choice, salespeople would rather spend their time with established customers. Attrition, of course, gradually reduces the number of persons in this category, and prospecting may be necessary for survival.

Prospecting activities can be approached in a more orderly fashion with the aid of a plan. It is difficult to prescribe one plan that fits all selling situations; however, most situations require the following similar types of decisions:

1. *Prepare a list of prospects.* You may recall that the prospect base includes current customers and potential customers. The process of enlarging the prospect base to include potential customers varies from one industry to another. In the food service distribution industry, salespeople often start with a territorial audit.[29] This involves the collection and analysis of information about every food service operator (restaurants, hotels, colleges, etc.) in a given territory. Important information such as the name of the operation, name of owner or manager, type of menu, and so forth is recorded on a card or entered into a PC. Some salespeople in this industry pinpoint each operator on a map of the territory. When the audit is complete, the salesperson analyzes the information on each food service operator and selects those who should be contacted.

    A salesperson who sells hotel and convention services could use a variation of the territorial audit. The list of prospects might include local businesses, educational institutions, civic groups, and other organizations who need banquet or conference services.

2. *Forecast the potential sales volume that might be generated by each new account for each product.* A **sales forecast** outlines expected sales for a specific product or service to a specific target group over a specific period of time. With a sales forecast the salesperson is able to set goals, establish a sales budget, and allocate resources with greater accuracy.

    Preparing an accurate sales forecast can be a real challenge. Jack Stack, CEO of Springfield Remanufacturing Corporation and author of *The Great Game of Business*, says that sales forecasts are based too often on gut feelings and wishful thinking. Salespeople need to begin the forecasting process with a careful estimate of sales volume to current customers. This is followed by an assessment of new sales to prospects that can be identified during the sales forecast period.[30]

3. *Anticipate prospect calls when planning the sales route; a systematic routing plan saves time and reduces travel expenses.* The procedure used to determine which customers and prospects are to be visited during a certain period of time is called **routing**. Consider calls on prospective customers in developing your route plan. This approach helps minimize the cost of developing new accounts.

A plan helps give prospect identification greater purpose and direction. It also helps reduce the cost of developing new customers. Without a plan, salespeople tend to give prospecting too little attention.

Summary

Prospect identification has been called the lifeblood of selling. A continuous supply of new customers must be found to replace those lost for various reasons. *Prospecting* is the systematic process of locating potential customers.

Analysis of both your product and your existing customers can help to identify, locate, and even profile your prospects. Important sources of new customers include *referrals* (both endless chain referrals, and referral letters and cards); friends, family members, and centers of influence; directories; trade publications; trade shows; telemarketing; direct response advertising and sales letters; *Web sites*; computer databases; cold calling; educational seminars; networking; and prospecting by nonsale employees.

These prospecting techniques produce a list of names that must be evaluated using criteria developed by each salesperson. The process of prospect evaluation is called *qualifying*. Basic questions that can be used to qualify a prospect include, is the person already buying from you, is the person a former customer, is the person a user of your product, and is the person currently buying from a competitor? An estimate of the amount of sales that could be generated from this prospect, and the prospect's credit rating also should be determined.

Information about both customers and prospects should be recorded systematically, whether on a special form, in a notebook, on cards, or in a computerized database. Information that is important to include about customers as individuals includes the correct name, age and experience, education, family status, special interests and hobbies, and communication style. Information that is important to include about customers as representatives of their business include the authority to buy, the business's ability to pay, the company operations, and the company buying practices.

Development of a prospecting and sales forecasting plan requires preparing a list of prospects, creating a forecast of potential sales volume from each new account, and anticipating prospect calls when planning a sales route.

KEY TERMS

Prospecting	Cold Calling
Prospect	Networking
Prospect Base	Target Market
Referral	Qualifying
Telemarketing	Sales Forecast
Web Site	Routing

REVIEW QUESTIONS

1. What three qualifications must an individual have to become a prospect?
2. Why is an understanding of customer attrition important to salespeople? What percentage of a firm's customers are lost each year?
3. Describe three steps progressive marketers are taking to improve the quality of the prospecting effort.
4. List the major sources of prospects.
5. Explain how the endless chain referral prospecting method works.

6. Discuss how direct response advertising and sales letters can be used to identify prospects.

7. What are the two most common methods of organizing prospect information?

8. What is *networking*? How might a real estate salesperson use networking to identify prospects?

9. What does the term *qualifying* mean? Why is this step in prospecting important?

10. What is *routing*? How does this relate to the prospecting plan?

Application Exercises

1. You are a sales representative for the Xerox Corporation. Assuming Xerox has just designed a new, less expensive, and better quality copying machine, make a list of 15 prospects you would plan to call. From the material in this chapter, identify the sources you would use in developing your prospect list.

2. You are in the process of interviewing for a sales position with the Connecticut General Insurance Company. In addition to filling out an application form and taking an aptitude test, one of the items the agency manager requests of you is to develop a list of prospects with whom you are acquainted. He informs you that this list includes the prospects you will be working with during the first few weeks of employment. The agency manager recommends that you list at least 50 names. Prepare a list of 10 acquaintances you have that would qualify as prospects.

3. Sales automation software is most commonly used in the prospecting phase of selling. New product releases are continually being developed that provide additional features and benefits to salespeople. The software used in this book is marketed by SalesLogix, a leader in the field. Access the SalesLogix (www.interact.com) Web page and research the latest version of ACT! Click on and examine the latest demonstration copy of this popular sales automation software.

4. Locating companies to work for is a form of prospecting. Assuming you are interested in changing careers, develop a list of 10 companies for which you would like to work. Assign each company a priority according to your interest, from the most desirable (1) to the least (10). Organize your list in six columns showing the company name, telephone number, address, person in charge of hiring, prospect information, and priority. What sources did you use to get this information?

Case Problem

Bill Coleman, general manager for ACT! contact software from SalesLogix (www. interact.com), says, "Once you have a customer, maintaining the relationship is a lot cheaper than finding a new customer." A growing number of salespeople are using ACT! software or one of its competitors to improve service to customers. Shannon O'Connell, sales representative for 800-SOFTWARE Incorporated (one of the nation's largest resellers of microcomputer products), is giving her customers added value with ACT! contact software. Like most other salespeople, she is trying to cope with expanded duties, faster work pace, and customers with high expectations. ACT! software helps her in the following ways:

Customer profile. Complete information on each customer is available on screen at the touch of a key. In addition to name, phone number, and address, she has a complete record of all past contacts. The profile also includes important personal as well as business information about the customer.

Organization and planning. It is no longer necessary for Shannon to prepare a written "to do" list or a planning calendar. All this information can be entered easily into her portable computer. In the morning she simply clicks her Day At A Glance command where she is reminded of scheduled appointments, follow-up phone calls that need to be made, and other activities. If she needs to make a call at 2:00 P.M., she can press the Set Alarm button, which serves the same purpose as an alarm clock.

Correspondence. ACT! software features a built-in word processor that makes it easy to prepare memos, letters, and reports. To send a standard follow-up letter to a customer, she simply brings up the letter from storage, enters the customer's name, and presses the appropriate key. The word processor automatically prints the inside address and mailing label. With ACT! software you can even send and receive e-mail. Most salespeople are responsible for numerous reports. The ACT! software can be used to generate a wide range of reports with a minimum of effort. It features 30 predefined reports for use in a wide range of sales and sales support areas.

David Florence, a sales representative with Motorola-EMBARC, makes over 100 phone calls each day. He appreciates the ACT! feature that permits automatic telephone dialing. He simply identifies the customer's name and presses a key.

Questions

1. If your goal is to maintain long-term partnerships with each of your customers, what features of the ACT! contact software are most helpful?

2. Let us assume you are selling copy machines in a city with a population of 100,000 people. Your territory includes the entire city. What features of the ACT! software would you use most frequently?

3. Some salespeople who could benefit from use of ACT! software or a competing product continue to use a Rolodex or note cards to keep a record of the customers they call on. What are some barriers to adoption of this type of technology?

4. Examine the first ACT! Contact Screen presented in Appendix 2.
   a. What is Bradley Able's position within the company?
   b. What is the "date expected" for the sale to close?
   c. What is the forecasted dollar amount of this potential sale?

CRM CASE STUDY

Reviewing the Prospect Database

Becky Kemley is the sales manager in the Dallas, Texas office of SimNet Systems, which sells network products and services. The productivity and the critical mission of Becky's customers can be considerably enhanced by selecting and using the correct LAN (local area network), WAN (wide area network), or VPN (virtual private network) systems. Becky's company is called a value-added reseller (VAR) because its people help customers maximize the value of the products bought through SimNet.

Becky's sales and technical support people may spend several months in the sales process (sales cycle). Salespeople telephone and call on prospects to determine if they qualify for SimNet's attention. Time is taken to study the customer's needs (needs discovery). The expert opinion of SimNet's technical people is incorporated into a sales proposal that is presented to the prospective customer. The presentation may be made to a number of decision makers in the prospect's firm. The final decision to purchase may follow weeks of consideration within the firm and negotiations with SimNet.

Once a decision is made by a customer to buy from SimNet, Becky's people begin the process of acquiring, assembling, and installing the network system; and then follow through with appropriate training, integration, and support services.

Becky's company must carefully prospect for customers. SimNet may invest a significant amount of time helping a potential customer configure the right combination of products and services. This means that only the most serious prospects should be cultivated. Further, Becky's people must ascertain that if the investment of time is made in a prospective customer, the prospect will follow through with purchases from SimNet.

Becky is responsible for assuring that prospect information is collected and used effectively. The network salespeople use the ACT! CRM software to manage their prospect information. The system, which is the same as the software available for download, allows salespeople to document and manage their sales efforts with each prospect.

Becky has just hired you to sell for SimNet beginning December 1. Becky has given you the files of Pat Silva, a salesperson who just has been promoted to SimNet's corporate headquarters. Becky has asked you to review the status of Pat's 20 prospect accounts. Pat's customers have been notified that Pat is leaving and that a new salesperson, you, will be contacting them. Becky wants you to review each prospect's record. You are to meet with Becky next Monday and be prepared to answer the following questions.

Questions

1. Which contact can you ignore immediately *as a prospect* for making a potential purchase?

2. Referring only to the *date close* category, which four prospects would you call immediately?

3. Referring only to the *dollar amount* of sales forecasted category, which four accounts would you call first? Does the likelihood of closing percentage category have any influence on decisions concerning which prospects to call first? Why?

4. According to information on the records and Notes (View Notes) windows, which prospecting method did Pat Silva appear to use the most? Give examples.

DEVELOPING A PRESENTATION STRATEGY

➤ The chapters included in Part V review the basic principles used in the strategic/consultative sales presentation. This information is used as you prepare presentation objectives, develop a presentation plan, and identify ways to provide outstanding service after the sale.

To play any game well, you first have to learn the rules, or principles of the game. And second, you have to forget about them. That is, you have to learn to play without thinking about the rules. This is true whether the game is chess or golf or selling. Shortcuts won't work.

AL RIES AND JACK TROUT

MARKETING WARFARE

Approaching the Customer

A pharmaceutical company that manufactures and distributes "miracle" drugs to health professionals really does not need a sales force, right? After all, if you are selling life-saving medical products you do not need to worry about sales efforts, right? The truth is, salespeople have played a key role in the success of Amgen (www.amgen.com), a relatively new pharmaceutical company that at one time had nothing to sell. Only after the Federal Drug Administration (FDA) approved a small number of drugs did Amgen evolve from a research and development (R&D) laboratory to a manufacturer to a marketer. A breakthrough by the Amgen R&D laboratory set the stage for the new company direction. The new drugs had to be manufactured and sold to the medical community.

One of the first salespeople hired was Deborah Karish. She soon found that one of her greatest challenges was winning acceptance of her company, which was new to members of the medical community. Prospects were accustomed to buying products from well-established pharmaceutical companies. During a typical sales call Deborah is selling her company, her products, and herself. Health care professionals need ample assurances that she is well qualified to give sound professional advice concerning the use of complex medical products.[1]

As noted in Chapter 2, there are a wide range of career options in the field of personal selling. How do you know if you have selected the most suitable sales position? If the position provides you with the new energy needed each day to be a true consultant to your customers, then you have probably made the right choice. Shelly Jones, a partner with the consulting firm Korn/Ferry International, says that sales positions in the age of information require the ". . . sophisticated skills of a business consultant, including the ability to spot opportunities in a changing marketplace." He also says, "The selling function will be less pitching product and more integrating your product into the business equation of your client, understanding the business environment in which your client operates."[2] This chapter provides you with the information needed to assume the role of consultant when approaching the customer.

DEVELOPING THE PRESENTATION STRATEGY

The presentation strategy combines elements of the relationship, product, and customer strategies. Each of the other three strategies must be developed before a salesperson can develop an effective presentation strategy.

The **presentation strategy** is a well-conceived plan that includes three prescriptions: (1) establishing objectives for the sales presentation, (2) developing the presale presentation plan needed to meet these objectives, and (3) renewing one's commitment to providing outstanding customer service (Fig. 9.1, Strategic/Consultative Selling Model).

The first prescription reminds us that we need to establish one or more objectives for each sales call. High-performance salespeople like Deborah Karish understand that it is often possible to accomplish several goals during a single call. A common objective of sales calls is to collect information about the prospect's needs. Another common objective is to build relationships with those who make the buying decision.

A carefully prepared presentation plan ensures that salespeople are well organized during the sales presentation and prepared to achieve their objectives. A six-step presentation plan is introduced later in this chapter.

Establishment of objectives for the sales presentation and preparation of the presale presentation plan must be guided by a strong desire to offer outstanding customer service. Achieving excellence is the result of careful needs analysis, correct product selection, clear

Figure **9.1**
The Strategic/Consultative Selling Model provides the foundation for a successful consultative presentation strategy.

Strategic/Consultative Selling Model*	
Strategic step	Prescription
DEVELOP A PERSONAL SELLING PHILOSOPHY	☑ ADOPT MARKETING CONCEPT ☑ VALUE PERSONAL SELLING ☑ BECOME A PROBLEM SOLVER/PARTNER
DEVELOP A RELATIONSHIP STRATEGY	☑ ADOPT DOUBLE–WIN PHILOSOPHY ☑ PROJECT PROFESSIONAL IMAGE ☑ MAINTAIN HIGH ETHICAL STANDARDS
DEVELOP A PRODUCT STRATEGY	☑ BECOME A PRODUCT EXPERT ☑ SELL BENEFITS ☑ CONFIGURE VALUE-ADDED SOLUTIONS
DEVELOP A CUSTOMER STRATEGY	☑ UNDERSTAND BUYER BEHAVIOR ☑ DISCOVER CUSTOMER NEEDS ☑ DEVELOP PROSPECT BASE
DEVELOP A PRESENTATION STRATEGY	☑ PREPARE OBJECTIVES ☑ DEVELOP PRESENTATION PLAN ☑ PROVIDE OUTSTANDING SERVICE
* Strategic/consultative selling evolved in response to increased competition, more complex products, increased emphasis on customer needs, and growing importance of long-term relationships.	

presentations, informative demonstrations, win–win negotiations, and flawless service after the sale. Salespeople who are committed to doing their best in each of these areas are richly rewarded.

Presentation Strategy Adds Value

The importance of planning and preparation was recognized in a national survey of 1,500 sales managers and sales representatives. When they were asked to rank 14 personal selling skills in order of importance to their *long-term success,* precall planning was ranked as most important.[3]

How does precall planning add value? Value is added when you position yourself as a resource—not just a vendor. You must prove that you have important ideas and advice to offer.[4] A well-planned presentation adds value when it is based on carefully developed sales call objectives and a presentation plan needed to meet these objectives. Good planning ensures that the presentation is customized to meet the needs of the prospect.

PLANNING THE PREAPPROACH

Preparation for the actual sales presentation is a two-part process. Part one is referred to as the **preapproach**. The preapproach involves preparing presale objectives and developing a presale presentation plan. Part two is called the **approach** and involves making a favorable first impression, securing the prospect's attention, and developing the prospect's interest in the product (Fig. 9.2). The preapproach and approach, when handled correctly, establish a foundation for an effective sales presentation.

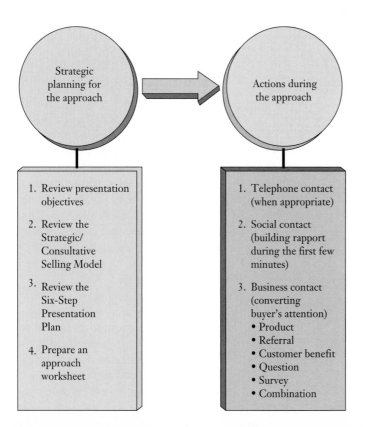

Figure **9.2**
Preparing for the presentation involves planning for the activities that occur before meeting the prospect and for the first few minutes of actual contact with the prospect.

Strategic planning for the approach

Actions during the approach

1. Review presentation objectives

2. Review the Strategic/ Consultative Selling Model

3. Review the Six-Step Presentation Plan

4. Prepare an approach worksheet

1. Telephone contact (when appropriate)

2. Social contact (building rapport during the first few minutes)

3. Business contact (converting buyer's attention)
   • Product
   • Referral
   • Customer benefit
   • Question
   • Survey
   • Combination

The preapproach should be viewed as a key step in preparing for each sales presentation. Professional salespeople complete the preapproach for every presentation whether it involves a new account or an established customer. The preapproach includes the first two prescriptions for developing a presentation strategy: establishing objectives and creating a presale presentation plan.

Establishing Presentation Objectives

Sales representatives employed by Nalco Chemical Company prepare for each sales call by filling out a 13-point precall planner. One section of this form requires the salesperson to identify the objectives of the call. Nalco is a company that emphasizes professionalism, long-term partnerships, and staying focused on customer needs.[5]

We know that most sales are not closed during the first contact with the customer, so why not establish other objectives? Here are some additional objectives that might be considered during the preapproach:

1. Obtain personal and business information to update the customer's file.
2. Conduct a needs assessment to determine if your product is suitable. (A second call may not be necessary.)
3. Involve prospect in a product demonstration.
4. Make an appointment with the prospect's boss who is the decision maker.
5. Secure a list of referrals.
6. Provide postsale service.

Setting multiple objectives helps reduce the fear of failure that salespeople often feel during the preapproach stage. It can be a confidence-raising experience. Achieving one or more objectives engenders a feeling of accomplishment. Once you have an appointment with the prospect and the presentation objectives have been established, consider sending a fax or e-mail message that outlines the agenda for the meeting. This will confirm the appointment and clarify the topics to be discussed.[6]

FACTORS INFLUENCING PRESENTATION OBJECTIVES

There are a number of factors affecting the objectives that you select for a sales presentation. Will the presentation be made to one person or a group? How familiar is the prospect with the product? How much time do you need to spend with the prospect? Answers to these and other questions help the salesperson establish appropriate objectives.

Multicall Sales Presentations   The use of **multicall sales presentations** also affects the objectives that are established. Many companies that have adopted the need–satisfaction approach to personal selling use multiple sales calls. The purpose of the first call is to collect and analyze certain basic information that is used to develop a specific proposal. Once the proposal is prepared, the salesperson makes a second appointment to present it. In many cases additional calls are needed to close the sale. The complexity of products has led to longer sales cycles in many industries.

Multicall sales presentations have become more common in the retail field. The sale of expensive recreational vehicles, leased automobiles, boats, and quality sound systems for the home or business often require more than one sales call. Sales personnel employed by Tom James Company, a firm that sells individually tailored suits, use a three-call plan. During the first home or office visit, the client reviews designs, picks out the fabric from a sample board of one-inch swatches, and gets measured. The suit is fitted during a second call and delivered during the third call.[7] Each of these calls may require different objectives.

Proxima® brings the power of your computer to the meeting room.

Proxima LCD projection products extend the reach of your desktop computer into the meeting room. And that means fewer, more productive meetings! Using the tools and data you already have at your desk, you can project precisely the same images you see on your computer screen. In brilliant color. For all to see.

Desktop Projection™

Think of it as "Desktop Projection"—the link between your computer and the workgroup. Desktop Projection lets you focus everyone's attention on the large screen. A Desktop Projection solution allows the entire group to explore "what-if" scenarios, perform on-the-spot problem solving, or fine tune ideas in brainstorming sessions.

And once you have formulated your concepts in the workgroup, you can present them at meetings, training sessions, or boardroom presentations. You can even augment presentations with video by connecting a video source, such as a VCR or laserdisc, to a Proxima projection system.

DESKTOP PROJECTION

It's all so easy!
Just plug the Proxima LCD projection product into the video port of your IBM® PC or compatible or Apple® Macintosh®. Your presentation, project management, spreadsheet, or multimedia software is now on-line—without the need for flip charts, 35-mm slides, or overhead transparencies.

Just set the panel on an overhead projector.

And with Proxima's unique Cyclops™ pointer system, you get all the capabilities of a cordless mouse—and more. Simply touch the wand to your projection screen, point and click to control your computer right at the projected image. With Cyclops, you will add an element of magic and excitement that will captivate your audience!

Whether your meeting is in a conference room, classroom, or auditorium, Proxima has a Desktop Projection solution to meet your needs. To find out more about Desktop Projection and how to run more effective meetings, call our toll free number today.

(800) 447-7694

PROXIMA®

Proxima Corporation 6610 Nancy Ridge Drive • San Diego, CA 92121-3297 • (619) 457-5500. In Europe: Horsterweg 24 • 6191 RX Beek • The Netherlands • +31 43 65 02 48 Proxima is a registered trademark and Cyclops and Desktop Projection are trademarks of Proxima Corporation. Other trademarks are the property of their respective owners.

Team versus One-Person Presentation Objectives

In today's ever-changing business environment, teamwork has surfaced as a major development. A survey of 19,000 salespeople and sales managers has found that about one quarter of the people contacted use sales teams.[8] Presale planning and the actual sales presentation often require two or more people.[9] Team selling is ideally suited to organizations that sell complex, or customized products and services that require direct communication between customers and technical experts. In some situations the involvement of technical experts can shorten the selling cycle. The team approach often results in more precise need identification, improved selection of the product, and more informative sales presentations. To achieve greater customization, Burlington Menswear, a New York-based clothing manufacturer, uses teams on most sales calls. Salespeople are teamed with a representative from a support area such as R&D, operations planning, or styling. These specialists often improve the need identification process and the identification of solutions to the customer's buying problem.[10] Complex problems often require pooled expertise.

Some presentation strategies involve a team approach. The sales team might include a technical specialist or a senior company executive.

As noted in Chapter 1, we are seeing the growth of strategic alliances. These long-term partnerships are especially common in business-to-business sales. Teams often are involved in forming the alliance and making purchase decisions after the alliance is established. When a customer's decision-making process is guided by a team, the seller is likely to use a team-selling approach.[11]

A variation of the team approach to selling is used by some marketers. Salespeople are trained to seek the assistance of another salesperson or actually turn the customer over to another salesperson when problems surface. The other salesperson may bring to the selling situation greater ability to identify the customer's needs or select the appropriate product. Salespeople who have well-prepared presale objectives know when to seek assistance from another professional.

Selling to a Buying Team

In some cases salespeople must address and satisfy both the individual and collective concerns of each participant in a multibuyer situation. The decision makers may be members of a well-trained buying team, a buying committee assembled for a one-time purchase, or a board of directors.

As in any type of selling situation, the salesperson should attempt to determine the various buying influences. When possible, the role of each decision maker, the amount of influence he exerts, and each decision maker's needs should be determined before or during the presentation. Careful observation during the presentation can reveal who may use the product, who controls the finances, and who can provide the expertise necessary to make the correct buying decision.

When you make a group selling presentation, make sure all parties feel involved. Any member of the group who feels ignored could prevent you from closing the sale. Be sure to direct questions and comments to all potential decision makers in the group.

Find out if there are any silent team or committee members. A silent member is one who can influence the buying decision but does not attend the presentation. Silent members are usually senior managers who have a major influence on the buying decision. If a silent member does exist, you must find a way to communicate, directly or indirectly, with this person.[12]

>> Selling in Action

NO TECH TO HIGH TECH

Account planning by the 70 sales representatives at Sebastiani Winery used to be a time-consuming process. Without the aid of modern technology, salespeople were forced to manually analyze two monthly reports that were inches thick. Preparing for a sales call was burdensome. Some salespeople said that they spent almost half their time analyzing reports. A major sales force automation (SFA) initiative was started in the late 1990s. The project had these four objectives:

• Improve communication through the use of e-mail, file sharing, and intranet technology

• Support needed to develop multimedia presentations
• Provide data analysis capabilities
• Ease the administrative burden

Each member of the Sebastiani sales force received a laptop loaded with Windows, PowerPoint, e-mail, and Business Objects—the software needed for analyzing data. The new technology was introduced during a three-day training program. Today, salespeople have the ability to do account planning that is much more effective than in the past.

Informative, Persuasive, and Reminder Presentation Objectives

When preparing presale presentation objectives, it is important to make a decision concerning the overall purpose of the presentation. The major purpose may be to inform, persuade, or remind. The sale of highly technical products and services often begins with an informative sales presentation. The customer needs to be familiar with the product before making a buying decision. In another situation, where the customer's needs have been carefully identified and your product is obviously suited to these needs, a persuasive presentation would be appropriate. In the case of repeat customers, it is often necessary to remind them of the products and services you offer.

INFORMATIVE PRESENTATION

The objective of a presentation that involves a new or unique product is generally to inform customers of its features and explain how these features can benefit the customer. Typically, people do not purchase a product or service until they become familiar with its application. Informative presentations are usually more prevalent when the product is being first introduced to the market. A **detail salesperson** (introduced in Chapter 2) usually spends a great deal of time informing customers of new products and changes in existing products.

Careful observation during the presentation can reveal who may use the product, who controls the finances, and who can provide the expertise necessary to make the correct buying decision.

PERSUASIVE PRESENTATION

Some degree of persuasion is common to nearly all sales presentations. **Persuasion**—the act of presenting product appeals so as to influence the prospect's beliefs, attitudes, or behavior—is a strategy designed to encourage the buyer to make a buying decision. Persuasion can be integrated into every phase of the sales presentation. A friendly greeting and a firm handshake at the time of initial customer contact represents a relationship-oriented form of persuasion. An enthusiastic sales demonstration is another type of persuasion common in sales. Additional forms of persuasion include converting features to buyer benefits, repeating feature–benefit statements, and asking for the sale. Persuasive strategies are designed to elicit a positive response from the prospect. It is never a good idea, however, to apply too much persuasion in an attempt to sell a product or service. These actions can perpetuate the stereotype of the pushy, unprofessional salesperson.

REMINDER PRESENTATION

In some selling situations, the primary objective of the sales call is to remind the prospect of products and services offered by the company. Without this occasional reminder the prospect may forget information that is beneficial. Computer salespeople might periodically remind customers about special services—training classes, service contracts, and customized programming, for example—available from the company they represent. An occasional reminder can prevent the competition from capturing the business.

Consideration of whether the overall presentation objective should be to inform, persuade, or remind can have a significant influence on your presale presentation plan and your efforts to provide outstanding service.

The time available to prepare presale objectives and create presale presentations varies depending on the complexity of the product, the customer's knowledge of the product, and other factors. The successful outcome of a complex sale is usually dependent on the time and effort invested in preparation.

In some selling situations, the saleperson is given little time to prepare for the sales presentation. This is the case in some retail and service situations where customers arrive unannounced.

DEVELOPING THE SIX-STEP PRESENTATION PLAN

Once you have established objectives for the sales presentation, the next step (prescription) involves developing the presentation plan. This plan helps you achieve your objectives.

Today, with increased time constraints, fierce competition, and rising travel costs, the opportunity for a face-to-face meeting with customers may occur less frequently. The few minutes you have with your customers may be your only opportunity to win their business, so that careful planning is more critical than ever. Ken Daniels, team leader at AT&T Global Information Solutions, says, "Plan each sales call before you make it so you don't get sidetracked."[13]

In preparation for development of the presentation strategy, it is helpful to review the three broad strategic areas that have been described in previous chapters: relationship strategy, product strategy, and customer strategy. Why is this review so critical? It is because today's dynamic sales presentations require consideration of the simultaneous influences of the relationship, product, and customer strategies. A careful review of these three areas sets the stage for flexible presentations that meet the needs of the customer.

Planning the Presentation

Once you have sufficient background information, you are ready to develop a "customized" presale presentation plan. The plan is developed after a careful review of the **six-step presentation plan** (Fig. 9.3). This planning aid is a tentative list of activities that can take place during the sales presentation. These presale activities can further strengthen your self-confidence and help avoid confusion in the presence of the prospect.

The Six-Step Presentation Plan	
Step One: APPROACH	☐ Review Strategic/Consultative Selling Model ☐ Initiate customer contact
Step Two: PRESENTATION	☐ Determine prospect needs ☐ Select product or service ☐ Initiate sales presentation
Step Three: DEMONSTRATION	☐ Decide what to demonstrate ☐ Select selling tools ☐ Initiate demonstration
Step Four: NEGOTIATION	☐ Anticipate buyer concerns ☐ Plan negotiating methods ☐ Initiate double-win negotiations
Step Five: CLOSE	☐ Plan appropriate closing methods ☐ Recognize closing clues ☐ Initiate closing methods
Step Six: SERVICING THE SALE	☐ Suggestion selling ☐ Follow through ☐ Follow-up calls
Service, retail, wholesale, and manufacturer selling	

Figure 9.3
**THE SIX-STEP
PRESENTATION PLAN**
A presale plan is a logical
and an orderly outline that
features a salesperson's
thoughts from one step to
the next in the presentation.
Each step in this plan is
explained in Chapters 9–14.

Customizing the Presentation

Preparing a customized sales presentation can take a great deal of time and energy. Nevertheless, this attention to detail gives you added confidence and helps you avoid delivering unconvincing hit-or-miss sales talks.

A well-planned sales presentation is a logical and orderly outline that features the salesperson's own thoughts from one step to the next. The presentation is usually divided into six main parts (see Fig. 9.3).

1. *Approach.* Preparation for the approach involves making decisions concerning effective ways to make a favorable first impression during the initial contact, securing the prospect's attention, and developing the prospect's interest in the product. The approach should set the stage for an effective sales presentation.
2. *Presentation.* The presentation is one of the most critical parts of the selling process. If the salesperson is unable to discover the prospect's buying needs, select a product solution, and present the product in a convincing manner, the sale may be lost. Chapter 10 covers all aspects of the sales presentation.
3. *Demonstration.* An effective sales demonstration helps verify parts of the sales presentation. Demonstrations are important because they provide the customer with a better understanding of product benefits. The demonstration, like all other phases of the presentation, must be carefully planned. Chapter 11 is devoted exclusively to this topic.

The sales presentation should be a model of good two-way communication.

4. *Negotiation.* Buyer resistance is a natural part of the selling/buying process. An objection, however, does present a barrier to closing the sale. For this reason, all salespeople should become skillful at negotiating resistance. Chapter 12 covers this topic.
5. *Close.* As the sales presentation progresses, there may be several opportunities to close the sale. Salespeople must learn to spot closing clues. Chapter 13 provides suggestions on how to close sales.
6. *Servicing the sale.* The importance of developing a long-term relationship with the prospect is noted earlier in this chapter. This rapport is often the outgrowth of postsale service. Learning to service the sale is an important aspect of selling. Chapter 14 deals with this topic.

In some cases you can assess the value of a concept by determining how long it has existed. A truly valuable idea or concept is timeless. The six parts of the presale presentation plan checklist have been discussed in the sales training literature for several decades; therefore, they might be described as fundamentals of personal selling. These steps are basic elements of almost every sale and frequently occur in the same sequence. Of course, some sales are made without an objection, and some customers buy before the salesperson attempts to close.

Although these six selling *basics* are part of nearly every seminar, workshop, and course devoted to sales training, the emphasis given each varies depending on the nature of the selling situation.

THE APPROACH

After a great deal of preparation it is time to communicate with the prospect, either by face-to-face contact or by telephone. We refer to the initial contact with the customer as the *approach.* All the effort you have put into developing relationship, product, and customer strategies can now be applied to the presentation strategy. If the approach is effective, you may be given the opportunity to make the sales presentation. If, however, the approach is not effective, the chance to present your sales story may be lost. You can be the best pre-

➤➤ *Building Relationships in a Diverse World*

SELLING ACROSS CULTURES

The growth of international trade is creating some communication problems for salespeople. More firms are opening branch offices abroad or entering into joint ventures with foreign corporations than ever before. Yet all too often Americans going overseas have little knowledge of the language and culture of the host country.

There are many subtle communication traps awaiting the unwary. For example, if you are visiting with a prospect in Mexico, you should always inquire about the person's spouse and family. In Saudi Arabia, you should not inquire about a client's family. In Latin America, people are often late for scheduled meetings. In Sweden, you should try to be prompt to the second.

A buyer for Marks & Spencer's, one of England's major department store chains, reminds us that communication style may be an issue in some cultures. He says, "If you want to sell to the British, write a nice, clear, nonexaggerating letter explaining the simple facts of your business, and ask for an appointment to come over and see me. I will be busy, but British buyers, unlike American buyers, will see you. I will give you half an hour to persuade me, and if you are flamboyant, I will reject most of what you say."

Many organizations are beginning to realize they must prepare their foreign-based employees for the diverse aspects of the new culture in which they will be living and working. For example, American females should be prepared to cope with far more male chauvinism than they would encounter back home. Men and women alike learn that aggressiveness may be counterproductive in some countries. In Japan, for example, people who wait and listen in a conversation earn respect.

How about business cards? Business cards are very important in most foreign countries, and it is common courtesy to have your card printed in English as well as in the local language.[a]

pared salesperson in the business, but without a good approach there may be little chance for a sale.

The approach has three important objectives. First, you want to build rapport with the prospect. Second, you want to capture the person's full attention. Never begin your sales story if the prospect seems preoccupied and is not paying attention. Third, you want to generate interest in the product you are selling.

In some selling situations the first contact with the customer is a telephone call. The call is made to schedule a meeting or in some cases conduct the sales presentation. The face-to-face sales call starts with the social contact and is followed by the business contact. The telephone contact, social contact, and business contact are discussed in this section.

Attention—Today's Scarce Resource

We live in a world that is threatened by an information glut. Technological advancements that have surfaced in the age of information have so dramatically advanced the communication process that people are often overwhelmed with too much information. Key decision makers complain that they must cope daily with message overload created by e-mail, voice mail, faxes, memos, phone calls, and letters. Many say that the communications barrage interrupts them three or more times every hour.[14]

Attention has become one of today's scarcest resources. Many of the people we need to communicate with are distracted and unable to concentrate.[15] Salespeople must learn how to connect with prospects and then figure out how to get their attention. Keeping in touch with established customers is no less important.

The Telephone Contact

A telephone call provides a quick and inexpensive method of scheduling an appointment. Appointments are important because many busy prospects may not meet with a salesperson who drops in unannounced. An appointment provides benefits to both the prospect and the salesperson. The prospect knows about the sales call in advance and can therefore make the necessary advance preparation. The buyer then is in a better position to give attention to the sales presentation.

Some salespeople use the telephone exclusively to establish and maintain contact with the customer. As noted in Chapter 2, inside salespeople rely almost totally on the telephone for sales. **Telesales**, not to be confused with telemarketing, include many of the same elements as traditional sales: gathering customer information, determining needs, prescribing solutions, negotiating objections, and closing sales. Telesales usually are not scripted, a practice widely used in telemarketing. In some situations, telesales are as freewheeling and unpredictable as a face-to-face sales call. IBM is one of several companies that is expanding the telesales concept to sell to customers in North America and throughout the world.[16]

In Chapter 3 we examined some of the factors that influence the meaning we attach to an oral message from another person. With the aid of this information we can see that communication via telephone is challenging. The person who receives the call cannot see our facial expression, gestures, or posture, and therefore must rely totally on the sound of our voice and the words used. The telephone caller has a definite handicap.

The telephone has some additional limitations. A salesperson accustomed to meeting prospects in person may find telephone contact impersonal. Some salespeople try to avoid using the telephone because they believe it is too easy for the prospect to say no. It should be noted that these drawbacks are more imagined than real. With proper training a salesperson can use the telephone effectively to schedule appointments. When you make an appointment by telephone, use the following practices:

Plan in advance what you will say. It helps to prepare written notes to use as a guide during the first few seconds of the conversation. What you say is determined by the objectives of the sales call. Have a calendar available to suggest and confirm a date, time, and place for the appointment. Be sure to write it down.

Politely identify yourself and the company you represent. Set yourself apart from other callers by using a friendly tone and impeccable phone manners. This approach helps you avoid being shut out by a wary gatekeeper (secretary or receptionist).

State the purpose of your call and explain how the prospect can benefit from a meeting. In some cases it is helpful to use a powerful benefits statement that gets the prospect's attention and whets the person's appetite for more information. Present only enough information to stimulate interest.

Show respect for the prospect's time by telling the person how much time the appointment may take. Emphasize that you know her time is valuable.

Confirm the appointment with a brief note or letter with the date, time, and place of your appointment. Enclose your business card and any printed information that can be of interest to the prospect.[17]

"I don't think of myself as the Jenkins Doolittle & Bloom gatekeeper. I rather prefer lead blocker."

In some cases a secretary, assistant, or receptionist may screen incoming telephone calls. Be prepared to convince this person that your call is important. Always treat the gatekeeper with respect and courtesy.

Source: *Wall Street Journal*, March 10, 1999, p. A-23

You should anticipate resistance from some prospects. After all, most decision makers are very busy. Be persistent and persuasive if you genuinely believe a meeting with the prospect can be mutually beneficial.

EFFECTIVE USE OF VOICE MAIL

The growing popularity of voice mail presents a challenge to salespeople. What type of message sets the stage for a second call or stimulates a return call? It's important to anticipate voice mail and know exactly what to say if you reach a recording. The prospect's perception of you is based on what you say and voice quality. The following message almost guarantees that you will be ignored:

Ms. Simpson, I am Paul Watson and I am with Elliott Property Management Services. I would like to visit with you about our services. Please call me at 862-1500.[18]

The telephone contact can set the stage for the social and business contact. The first few seconds of the call are crucial to the image you project.

➤➤ CUSTOMER RELATIONSHIP MANAGEMENT WITH TECHNOLOGY

PLANNING PERSONAL VISITS

Personally visiting prospects and customers helps build strong relationships, yet traveling is expensive and time consuming. A salesperson is challenged to plan visits that optimize the investment represented by each trip. Access to customer relationship management (CRM) prospect records helps salespeople quickly identify all the accounts in a given geographic area.

CRM empowers salespeople to rapidly review and compare an area's prospects on the basis of position in sales cycle, potential size of account or purchase, likelihood of sale, and contribution that the visit could make to information gathering and relationship building. A well-managed CRM database provides salespeople with appropriate business and social topics to discuss when calling selected prospects for an appointment. (See the exercise, Planning Personal Visits, at page 209 for more information.)

Note that this message provides no compelling reason for the prospect to call back. It offers no valid item that would stimulate interest. The voice mail message should be similar to the opening statement you would make if you had a face-to-face contact with the prospect:

> Miss Simpson, my name is Paul Watson and I represent Elliott Property Management Services. We specialize in working with property managers. We can help you reduce the paperwork associated with maintenance jobs and provide an easy way to track the progress of each job. I would like the opportunity to visit with you and will call back in the morning.[19]

Note that this message is brief and describes results that customers can receive. If Paul Watson wants a callback, then he needs to give the best time to reach him. He should give his phone number slowly and completely. It's usually best to repeat the number.

The Social Contact

According to many image consultants, "First impressions are lasting impressions." This statement is essentially true, and some profitable business relationships never crystallize because some trait or characteristic of the salesperson repels the prospective customer. Sales personnel have only a few minutes to create a positive first impression. Dr. Leonard Zunin, coauthor of *Contact: The First Four Minutes*, describes what he calls the "four-minute barrier." In this short period of time a relationship can be established or denied. Susan Bixler, author of *The New Professional Image*, describes the importance of the first impression this way:

> Books are judged by their covers, houses are appraised by their curb appeal, and people are initially evaluated on how they choose to dress and behave. In a perfect world this is not fair, moral, or just. What's inside should count a great deal more. And eventually it usually does, but not right away. In the meantime, a lot of opportunities can be lost.[20]

To be certain your first impression is appropriate, review the material in Chapter 3. The information in this chapter is timeless and can serve you well today and in the future.

DEVELOPING CONVERSATION

The brief, general conversation during the social contact should hold the prospect's attention and establish a relaxed and friendly atmosphere for the business contact that is to follow. As mentioned in Chapter 3, there are three areas of conversation that should be considered in developing a social contact:

1. *Comments on here and now observations.* These comments may include general observations about an article in the *Wall Street Journal*, the victory of a local athletic team, or specific comments about awards on display in the prospect's office.
2. *Compliments.* Most customers react positively to sincere compliments. Personal items in the prospect's office, achievements, or efficient operation of the prospect's business provide examples of what can be praised.
3. *Search for mutual acquaintances or interests.* The discovering of mutual friends or interests can serve as the foundation for a strong social contact.

Communication on a personal basis is often the first step in discovering a common language that can improve communication between the salesperson and the prospect. How much time should be devoted to the social contact? There is no easy answer to this question. The length of the conversation depends on the type of product or service sold, how busy the prospect appears to be, and your awareness of topics of mutual interest.

The Business Contact

Converting the prospect's attention from the social contact to the business proposal is an important part of the approach. When you convert and hold your prospect's attention, you have fulfilled an important step in the selling process. Furthermore, without success in the beginning, the door has been closed on completing the remaining steps of the sale.

Some salespeople use a carefully planned opening statement or a question to convert the customer's attention to the sales presentation. A statement or question that focuses on the prospect's dominant buying motive is, of course, more likely to achieve the desired results. Buyers must like what they see and hear and must be made to feel that it is worthwhile to hear more.

Throughout the years, salespeople have identified and used a number of effective ways to capture the prospect's attention and arouse interest in the presentation. Five of the most common are explained in the following material:

Product demonstration approach

Referral approach

Customer benefit approach

Question approach

Survey approach

We also discuss combining two or more of these approaches.

PRODUCT DEMONSTRATION APPROACH

This straightforward method of getting the prospect's attention is used by sales representatives who sell copy machines, photographic equipment, automobiles, construction equipment, office furniture, and many other products. If the actual product cannot be demonstrated, salespeople can use appropriate audiovisual technology such as computer-generated graphics, slides, and videotapes. Trish Ormsby, a sales representative for Wells

►► BUILDING QUALITY PARTNERSHIPS

THE SOCIAL CONTACT

The social contact should be viewed as effective communication on a personal basis. This brief conversation establishes the foundation for the business contact, so it should never be viewed as an insignificant part of the presentation strategy. The following guidelines can help you develop the skills needed to make a good social contact.

1. *Prepare for the social contact.* Conduct a background check on topics of interest to the person you are contacting. This includes reviewing information in the prospect data base, reading industry reports, and searching the Internet. Once you arrive at the customer's office, you will discover additional information about the person's interests. Most people communicate what is important to them in the way they personalize their work environment.

2. *Initiate social contact.* The most effective opening comments should be expressed in the form of an open-ended question, such as "I understand you have just been elected President of the United Way?" You can improve the possibility of a good response to your verbal question by applying nonverbal communication skills.

Appropriate eye contact, voice inflections that communicate enthusiasm, and a warm smile will increase the customer's receptivity to your opening comments.

3. *Respond to the customer's conversations.* When the customer responds, it is imperative that you acknowledge the message both verbally and nonverbally. The verbal response might be "That is really interesting" or any other appropriate comment. Let the customer know you are listening and you want her to continue talking.

4. *Keep the social contact focused on the customer.* Because you cannot control where a conversation might go, you may be tempted to focus the conversation on topics with which you are familiar. A response such as "Several years ago I was in charge of our company's United Way Campaign and we had a difficult time meeting our goal" shifts the focus of the conversation back to you. Continue to focus the conversation on topics that are of interest to the customer. Dale Carnegie said that one of the best ways to build a relationship is to encourage others to talk about themselves.

Fargo Alarm Services, uses her portable computer to create a visual image of security systems that meet the customer's security needs.[21]

REFERRAL APPROACH

Research indicates that another person is far more impressed with your good points if these points are presented by a third party rather than by you. The referral approach is quite effective because a third party (a satisfied customer) believes the prospect can benefit from your product. This type of opening statement has universal appeal among salespeople from nearly every field.

When you use the referral approach, your opening statement should include a direct reference to the third party. Here is an example: "Mrs. Follett, my name is Kurt Wheeler, and I represent the Cross Printing Company. We specialize in printing all types of business forms. Mr. Ameno—buyer for Raybale Products, Incorporated—is a regular customer of ours, and he suggested I mention his name to you."

CUSTOMER BENEFIT APPROACH

One of the most effective ways to gain a prospect's attention is to immediately point out one benefit of purchasing your product. Start with the most important issue (or problem) facing the client.[22] When using this approach, the most important buyer benefit is included in the initial statement. For example, the salesperson selling a Minolta Maxxum 5000i camera might open with this statement:

> The Maxxum 5000i's autofocus system gives you the flexibility to shoot panoramic landscapes, striking portraits, and fast-moving sports action. With this system, your pictures always come out in precise focus.

Another example taken from the office copy machine field is

> This new office copy machine can save your office staff valuable time each day. It will copy work nearly twice as fast as any other machine on the market.

The key to achieving success with the customer benefit approach is advance preparation. You must know a great deal about your prospect to pinpoint the buyer benefit that should be emphasized in your opening statement.

The survey approach offers many advantages. It is generally a nonthreatening way to open a sales call. You simply are asking permission to acquire information that can be used to determine the buyer's need for the product.

QUESTION APPROACH

The question approach has two positive features. First, a question almost always triggers prospect involvement. Very few people avoid answering a direct question. Second, a question gets the prospect thinking about a problem that the salesperson is prepared to solve.

Molly Hoover, a sales training consultant, conducts training classes for sales managers and car dealers who want to better understand the subtleties of selling to the new woman car buyer. She suggests an approach that includes a few basic questions such as:

> "Is the vehicle for business or pleasure?"
> "Will you be buying within the next week or so?"[23]

These opening questions are not difficult to answer, yet they get the customer mentally involved. Some of the best opening questions are carefully phrased to arouse attention. The authors of *The Sales Question Book* offer some good examples:

> "Are you aware that we just added three new services to our payroll and accounting package? Could I tell you about them?"
> "We are now offering all our customers a special service that used to be reserved for our largest accounts. Would you be interested in hearing about it?"[24]

Once you ask the question, listen carefully to the response. If the answer is yes, proceed with an enthusiastic presentation of your product. If the answer is no, then you may have to gracefully try another approach or thank the prospect for her time and depart.

SURVEY APPROACH

Robert Hewitt, a Monterey, California, financial planner, has new clients fill out a detailed questionnaire before the first appointment. This procedure is part of his customer strategy. He studies the completed questionnaire and other documents before making any effort to find a solution to any of the customer's financial planning needs. The survey (data collection) is an important part of the problem-solving philosophy of selling. It often is used in selling office machines, business security systems, insurance, and other products where the need cannot be established without careful study.

The survey approach offers many advantages. It is generally a nonthreatening way to open a sales call. You simply are asking permission to acquire information that can be used to determine the buyer's need for your product. Because the survey is tailor-made for a specific business, the buyer is given individual treatment. Finally, the survey approach helps avoid an early discussion of price. Price cannot be discussed until the survey is completed.

The product, referral, customer benefit, question, and survey approaches offer the salesperson a variety of ways to set the stage for the presentation strategy. With experience, salespeople learn to select the most effective approach for each selling situation. Table 9.1 provides examples of how these approaches can be applied in real-world situations.

COMBINATION APPROACHES

A hallmark of consultative selling is flexibility. Therefore, a combination of approaches sometimes provides the best avenue to need identification. Sales personnel who have

---

Table 9.1   **BUSINESS CONTACT WORKSHEET**

This illustrates how to prepare effective real-world approaches that capture the customer's attention.

METHOD OF APPROACH	WHAT WILL YOU SAY?
1. Product	1a. *(Retail clothing)* "*We have just received a shipment of new fall sweaters from Braemar International.*"
	1b. *(Business forms manufacturer)* "*Our plant has just purchased a $300,000 Harris Graphics composer, Mr. Reichart; I would like to show you a copy of your sales invoice with your logo printed on it.*"
2. Customer benefit	2. *(Real estate)* "*Mr. and Mrs. Stuart, my company lists and sells more homes than any other company in the area where your home is located. Our past performance would lead me to believe we can sell your home within two weeks.*"
3. Referral	3. *(Food wholesaler)* "*Paula Doeman, procurement manager for Mercy Medical Center, suggested that I provide you with information about our computerized 'Order It' system.*"
4. Question	4. *(Hotel convention services)* "*Mrs. McClaughin, will your Annual Franchisee Meeting be held in April?*"
5. Survey	5a. *(Custom-designed computer software)* "*Mr. Vasquez, I would like the opportunity to learn about your accounts receivable and accounts payable procedures. We may be able to develop a customized program that will significantly improve your cash flow.*"
	5b. *(Retail menswear)* "*May I ask you a few questions about your wardrobe? The information will help me better understand your clothing needs.*"

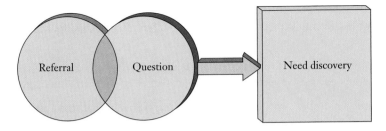

Figure **9.4**
Combination approaches provide a smooth transition to the need discovery part of the consultative presentation.

adopted the consultative style, of course, use the question and survey approaches most frequently. Some selling situations, however, require that one of the other approaches be used, either alone or in combination with the question and survey approaches (Fig. 9.4). An example of how a salesperson might use a referral and question approach combination follows:

Salesperson: Carl Hamilton at Simmons Modern Furniture suggested that I visit with you about our new line of compact furniture designed for today's smaller homes. He believes this line might complement the furniture you currently feature.

Customer: Yes, Carl called me yesterday and mentioned your name and company.

Salesperson: Before showing you our product lines, I would like to ask you some questions about your current product mix. First, what do you currently carry in the area of bedroom furniture?

DEALING WITH THE "BAD-TIMING" RESPONSE

If the approach is effective, you usually are given an opportunity to make the sales presentation. However, the prospect may attempt to delay the presentation with a statement such as, "The time just isn't right, call me back later." Before you agree to a follow-up call, try to determine if the prospect is really interested in your product and willing to take action in the future. Your response might sound like this, "I certainly do not mind scheduling another call, but first, do you agree that my product is one you see yourself using?" You do not want to waste time on a follow-up call if the person is not a prospect. If the timing of your call is truly a problem, find out why. A real prospect has a reason and is likely to explain it. This information helps you schedule your sales call at the right time.[25]

Coping with Sales Call Reluctance

The transition from the preapproach to the approach is sometimes blocked by sales call reluctance. Fear of making the initial contact with the prospect is a problem for rookies and veterans, and people in every selling field. Research conducted by Behavioral Sciences Research Press, Incorporated, reveals that about 40 percent of all salespeople, at some point, experience call reluctance. For new salespeople, the problem can be career threatening.[26] Sales call reluctance may stem from concern about interrupting or intruding on the prospect, saying the wrong thing, or not being able to respond effectively to the person who quickly begins asking questions. Sales call reluctance may surface because the salesperson fears rejection. Regardless of the reasons for sales call reluctance, you can learn to deal with it. These are some suggestions:

▶ *Be optimistic about the outcome of the initial contact.* It is better to anticipate success than to anticipate failure. Martin Seligman, professor of psychology at the University of Pennsylvania and author of the best-selling book *Learned Optimism*, says that success in selling requires a healthy dose of optimism.[27] The anticipation of failure is a major barrier to making the initial contact.

▶ *Practice your approach before making the initial contact.* A well-rehearsed effort to make the initial contact increases your self-confidence and reduces the possibility that you may handle the situation badly.

▶ *Recognize that it is normal to feel anxious about the initial contact.* Even the most experienced salespeople experience some degree of sales call reluctance.

▶ *Develop a deeper commitment to your goals.* Abraham Zaleznik, professor emeritus at Harvard Business School, says, "If your commitment is only in your mind, then you'll lose it when you encounter a big obstacle. If your commitment is in your heart *and* your mind, you'll create the power to break through the toughest obstacles."[28]

Summary

As one sales consultant noted, "Organization multiplies the value of anything to which it is applied." This is especially true of precall planning. The well-prepared salesperson approaches the sales call with an attitude of confidence and expectancy.

Developing a presentation strategy involves preparing presale objectives, developing a *presale presentation* plan, and providing outstanding customer service. The presentation strategy combines elements of the relationship, product, and customer strategies.

Preparation for the sales presentation is a two-part process. Part one is referred to as the *preapproach* and involves preparing presale objectives and developing a presale presentation plan. Part two is called the *approach* and involves making a good first impression, securing the prospect's attention, and developing the prospect's interest in the product.

Over the years, salespeople have identified several ways to convert the prospect's attention and arouse interest in the presentation. Some of the most common ways include the product demonstration approach, referral approach, customer benefit approach, question approach, and survey approach. This chapter also includes information on the social contact, the business contact, and how to cope with sales call reluctance.

Key Terms

Presentation Strategy	Detail Salesperson
Preapproach	Persuasion
Approach	Six-Step Presentation Plan
Multicall Sales Presentations	Telesales

Review Questions

1. What is the purpose of the preapproach? What are the two prescriptions included in the preapproach?

2. Explain the role of objectives in developing the presale presentation plan.

3. Why should salespeople establish multiple-objective sales presentations? List four possible objectives that could be achieved during a sales presentation.

4. Describe some common applications of telesales.

5. Describe the major purpose of the informative, persuasive, and reminder sales presentations.

6. What are the major objectives of the approach?

7. Review the Building Quality Partnerships box on p. 204. Briefly describe the four guidelines that can help you make a good social contact.

8. What are some rules to follow when leaving a message on voice mail?

9. What methods can the salesperson use to convert the prospect's attention to the sales presentation?

10. Discuss why combination approaches are considered an important consultative-selling practice. Provide one example of a combination approach.

APPLICATION EXERCISES

1. Assume that you are a salesperson who calls on retailers. For some time you have been attempting to get an appointment with one of the best retailers in the city to carry your line. You have an appointment to see the head buyer in one and one half hours. You are sitting in your office. It will take you about 30 minutes to drive to your appointment. Outline what you should be doing between now and the time you leave to meet your prospect.

2. Tom Nelson has just graduated from Aspen College with a major in marketing. He has three years of experience in the retail grocery business and has decided he would like to go to work as a salesperson for the district office of Procter & Gamble. Tom has decided to telephone and set up an appointment for an interview. Write out exactly what Tom should *plan* to say during his telephone call.

3. Concepts from Dale Carnegie's *How to Win Friends and Influence People* can help you prepare for the social contact. Access the Dale Carnegie Training home page (www.dalecarnegie.com) on the Internet and examine the courses offered. Click on the "Sales Advantage Course" and read the description. Note the books that are used with this course. Are enthusiasm and remembering names important parts of the approach?

CRM APPLICATION EXERCISE

Planning Personal Visits

CRM software allows trip planners to examine the status of prospects in the geographic area to be visited. Access your ACT! database. Assume that using the ACT! software you wish to visit prospects in the city of Bedford, Texas. The software permits a fast field search capability of selecting and sorting the records of prospects in that city: Lookup, City, type "Bedford," and press Enter. After arranging by phone to visit these people, the salesperson can print the information contained in these records and take them along: Report, Contact Report, Active Lookup, Printer, and Enter. You should now have printed information about all customers in Bedford. Salespeople today use the Internet to schedule trip transportation and lodging, and to check the weather forecast.

CASE PROBLEM

When Deborah Karish wakes up in the morning, she does not have to worry about a long commute to work. Her office is in her home. As an Amgen (www.amgen.com) pharmaceutical sales representative, Deborah spends most of her day visiting hospitals, medical clinics, and doctors' offices. She spends a large part of each day serving as a consultant to doctors, head nurses, pharmacists, and others who need information and advice about the complex medical products available from her company. As might be expected, she also spends a considerable amount of time conducting informative presentations designed to achieve a variety of objectives. In some situations she is introducing a new product and in other cases she is providing up-to-date information on an existing product. Some of her presentations are given to individual health care professionals, and others are given to a group. Each of these presentations must be carefully planned.

Amgen began as a research and development laboratory. After developing a few breakthrough drugs and getting approval from the FDA to sell them, a decision was made to create a manufacturing facility and initiate a nationwide marketing program. Although Amgen had discovered what might be described as "miracle" drugs, management knew that a sales force would be needed to win acceptance of the new products. Doctors are very cautious when it comes to prescribing a new drug to their patients. They demand accurate information concerning principal uses of the drug, dosage forms and strengths, dose instructions, and possible side effects.

Deborah uses informative and reminder presentations almost daily in her work. Informative presentations are given to doctors who are in a position to prescribe her products. The verbal presentation often is supplemented with audiovisual aids and printed materials. Reprints of articles from leading medical journals are often used to explain the success of her products in treating patients. These articles give added credibility to her presentations. Some of her informative presentations are designed to give customers updates on the prescription drugs she sells. Reminder presentations are frequently given to pharmacists who must maintain an inventory of her products. She has found that it is necessary to periodically remind pharmacists of product delivery procedures and policies, and special services available from Amgen. She knows that without an occasional reminder, a customer can forget information that is beneficial.

In some cases a careful needs analysis is needed to determine if her products can solve a specific medical problem. Every patient is different, so generalizations concerning the use of her products can be dangerous. When doctors talk about their patients, Deborah must listen carefully and take good notes. In some cases she must get additional information from company support staff. If a customer needs immediate help with a problem, she gives the person a toll-free 800 number to call for expert advice. This line is an important part of the Amgen customer service program.

Deborah's career in pharmaceutical sales has required continuous learning. In the beginning she had to learn the meaning of dozens of medical terms and become familiar with a large number of medical problems. If a doctor asks, "What is the bioavailability of Neutogen?" she must know the meaning of the medical term and be knowledgeable about this Amgen product.

Deborah also spends time learning about the people with whom she works. She recently said, "If I get along with the people I work with it makes my job a lot easier." When meeting someone for the first time, she takes time to assess his communication style and then adjusts her own style to meet his needs. She points out that in some cases the competition offers a similar product at a similar price. In these situations a good relationship with the customer can influence the purchase decision. (For more information refer to the opening paragraph on page 189.)

Questions

1. If you become a pharmaceutical sales representative, how important is it to adopt the three prescriptions for a presentation strategy? Explain.

2. Deborah Karish spends a great deal of time giving individual and group presentations. Why is it essential that she be well prepared for each presentation? Why would a "canned" presentation, one that is memorized and delivered almost word for word, be inappropriate in her type of selling?

3. Salespeople are encouraged to establish multiple-objective sales presentations. What are some objectives that Deborah Karish might achieve during a sales presentation to doctors who are not currently using her products?

4. What are some special challenges faced by Deborah Karish when she makes a group presentation? How might she enhance her group presentations?

5. Put yourself in the position of a pharmaceutical sales representative. Can you envision a situation when you might combine the elements of an informative, persuasive, and reminder presentation? Explain.

CRM CASE STUDY

Establishing Your Approach

Becky Kemley, your sales manager at SimNet Systems, has notified Pat Silva's former prospects, by letter, that you will be calling on them soon. She wants to meet with you tomorrow to discuss your preapproach to your new prospects. Please review the records in the ACT! database.

Questions

1. Becky wants you to call on Robert Kelly. Describe what your call objectives would be with Mr. Kelly.

2. Describe a possible topic of your social contact with Mr. Kelly and how you would convert that to a buying contact.

3. Becky has given you a reprint of a new article about using networks for warehouse applications. Which of your prospects might have a strong interest in this kind of article? How would you use this article to make an approach to that prospect?

PARTNERSHIP SELLING: A ROLE PLAY/SIMULATION
(see Appendix 3, p. 406)

DEVELOPING A RELATIONSHIP STRATEGY

Read *employment memorandum 2*, which announces your promotion to account executive. In your new position, you will be assigned by your instructor to one of the two major account categories in the convention center market. You will be assigned to either the *association accounts market* or the *corporate accounts market.* Association accounts includes customers who have the responsibility for planning meetings for the association or group they are a member of, or are employed by. Corporate accounts includes customers who have responsibility for planning meetings for the company they represent. (You will remain in the account category for the rest of the role plays.)

Note the challenges you may have in your new position. Each of these challenges are represented in the future *sales memoranda* you receive from your sales manager.

Read *sales memorandum 1* for the account category you are assigned. (Note that the "A" means association and your customer is Erin Adkins, and "B" means corporate and your customer is Leigh Combs.) Follow the instructions in the sales memorandum and strategically prepare to approach your new customer. Your call objectives are to establish a relationship (social contact), share an appealing benefit, and find out if your customer is planning any future conventions (business contact).

You may be asked to assume the role of a customer in the account category that you are not assigned as a salesperson. Your instructor will provide you with detailed instructions for correctly assuming this role.

CHAPTER 10

Creating the Consultative Sales Presentation

When you finish reading this chapter, you should be able to

1. Describe the characteristics of the consultative sales presentation

2. Explain how to determine the prospect's needs

3. Discuss the use of questions to determine needs

4. Select products that match customer needs

5. List and describe three types of need–satisfaction presentation strategies

6. Present general guidelines for developing effective presentations

*W*hen Dave Tripp, sales representative for Harper Collins Publishers, won the "Sales Rep of the Year" award, his loyal customers were not surprised. To maximize service to his 30 retail and wholesale accounts in the Wisconsin and Minnesota area, he uses the consultative-selling approach exclusively. He takes pride in his ability to look through the bookseller's eyes and answer the question, "What can I do to bring more customers into this store?" Carol Erdahl, co-owner of The Red Balloon Bookshop, says, "It's his job to present what's new, but he's always looking out for us, suggesting ways to promote the books."[1]

Tripp sees himself as a partner in the management of each bookstore. Drawing on his knowledge of what types of books sell well at each store, he works with buyers to predict demand for new releases. He also understands the value of building a relationship with store employees. He is on a first-name basis with salespeople at each store. He gets acquainted with their reading preferences and makes sure they get advanced copies of books in their favorite genres (science fiction, how-to, poetry, etc.).

Tripp's service to his customers is really the manifestation of such qualities as product knowledge (he needs to keep on top of a list of more than 16,000 books), dependability, and service after the sale.[2]

A growing number of salespeople, like David Tripp, have adopted the consultative sales presentation (Fig. 10.1). They support the selling philosophy expressed by Suzanne Vilardi, area sales manager of Swift Transportation:

Be a consultant, a partner, an extension of your client's business. Be a friend, a problem solver. Balance your client's best interests with those of your own and your company.[3]

Figure 10.1
CREATING THE SALES
PRESENTATION

The Six–Step Presentation Plan	
Step One: APPROACH	☑ Review Strategic/Consultative Selling Model ☑ Initiate customer contact
Step Two: PRESENTATION	☐ Determine prospect needs ☐ Select product or service ☐ Initiate sales presentation
Step Three: DEMONSTRATION	☐ Decide what to demonstrate ☐ Select selling tools ☐ Initiate demonstration
Step Four: NEGOTIATION	☐ Anticipate buyer concerns ☐ Plan negotiating methods ☐ Initiate double–win negotiations
Step Five: CLOSE	☐ Plan appropriate closing methods ☐ Recognize closing clues ☐ Initiate closing methods
Step Six: SERVICING THE SALE	☐ Suggestion selling ☐ Follow through ☐ Follow-up calls
Service, retail, wholesale, and manufacturer selling	

Figure 10.2 features key concepts related to creating the consultative sales presentation. This approach can be used effectively in the four major employment settings: service, retail, wholesale, and manufacturing. It results in increased customer satisfaction, more sales, fewer cancellations and returns, more repeat business, and more referrals.

CONSULTATIVE SALES PRESENTATION

As we note in Chapter 9, an effective approach sets the stage for the sales presentation. Once you have established rapport with the prospect, captured the prospect's full attention, and generated interest in your product, you can begin the sales presentation with confidence. To be most effective, the salesperson should think of the presentation as a four-part process. The Consultative Sales Presentation Guide (Fig. 10.3) features these four parts.

Part One — Need Discovery

A review of the behaviors displayed by high-performance salespeople helps us understand the importance of precise need discovery. They have learned how to skillfully diagnose and solve the customer's problems better than their competitors. This problem-solving capability translates into more repeat business and referrals, and fewer order cancellations and returns.

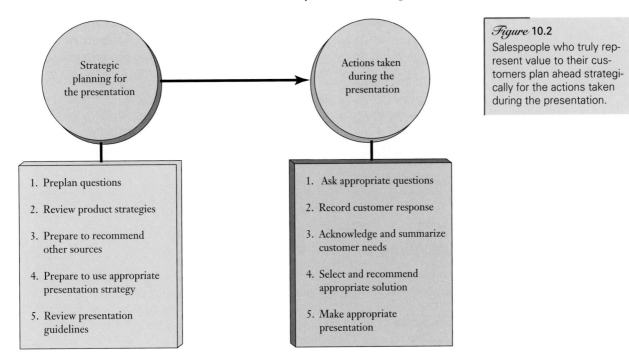

Figure **10.2**
Salespeople who truly represent value to their customers plan ahead strategically for the actions taken during the presentation.

Unless the selling situation requires mere order taking (customers know exactly what they want), need discovery is a standard part of the sales presentation. It may begin during the approach, if the salesperson uses questions or a survey during the initial contact with the customer. If neither of these two methods is used during the approach, need discovery begins immediately after the approach.

The pace, scope, depth, and time allocated to inquiry depend on a variety of factors. Some of these include the sophistication of the product, the selling price, the customer's knowledge of the product, the product applications, and, of course, the time available for dialogue between the salesperson and the prospect. Each selling situation is different, so a standard set of guidelines for need discovery is not practical. Additional information on need discovery is presented later in the chapter.

Part Two — Selection of the Product

The emphasis in sales and marketing in the age of information is on determining customer needs and then selecting or configuring custom-fitted solutions to satisfy these needs. Therefore, an important function of the salesperson is product selection and recommen-

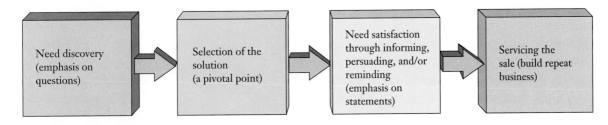

Figure **10.3**
THE CONSULTATIVE SALES PRESENTATION GUIDE
To be most successful, the salesperson should think of the sales presentation as a four-part process.

dation. The salesperson must choose the product or service that can provide maximum satisfaction. When making this decision, the salesperson must be aware of all product options, including those offered by the competition. A John Deere farm equipment salesperson can, for example, offer a farmer a seed planter that features an almost endless combination of features. Some farmers want 4-row planters; others want a 24-row planter. Some use the planter to apply liquid fertilizer; others want a planter to apply dry fertilizer. A farmer can order a planter from Deere according to more than a million permutations.[4]

Salespeople who have the ability to diagnose a need accurately and select the correct product to fill this need deliver more value to the customer and achieve the status of trusted adviser.[5] They face less buyer resistance and close more sales.

Part Three—Need Satisfaction through Informing, Persuading, or Reminding

The third part of the consultative sales presentation consists of communicating to the customer, both verbally and nonverbally, the satisfaction that the product or service can provide. The salesperson places less emphasis on the use of questions and begins making statements. These statements are organized into a presentation that informs, persuades, or reminds the customer of the most suitable product or service. Later in this chapter, and in several of the remaining chapters, we discuss specific strategies used in conjunction with the demonstration, negotiating buyer resistance, and closing the sale.

Part Four—Servicing the Sale

Servicing the sale is a major dimension of the selling process. These activities, which occur after closing the sale, ensure maximum customer satisfaction and set the stage for a long-term relationship with the customer. Service activities include suggestion selling, making credit arrangements, following through on assurances and promises, and dealing effectively with complaints. This topic is covered in detail in Chapter 14.

The sales presentation can inform, remind, or persuade.

In those cases where a sale is normally closed during a single sales call, the salesperson should be prepared to go through all four parts of the Consultative Sales Presentation Guide. However, when a salesperson uses a multicall approach, preparation for all the parts is usually not practical. The person selling computer systems or investments, for example, almost always uses a multicall sales presentation. Need discovery (part one) is the focus of the first call.

NEED DISCOVERY

A lawyer does not give the client advice until the legal problem has been carefully studied and confirmed. A doctor does not prescribe medication until the patient's symptoms have been identified. In like manner, the salesperson should not recommend purchase of a product without a thorough need identification.

Your best bet is to adopt the style used so successfully by most counselors. You start with the assumption that the client's problem is not known. The only way to determine and confirm the problem is to get the other person talking. You must obtain information to properly clarify the need. The counselor style requires that you be more concerned about the customer's welfare than closing the sale. This is consistent with the trend we discussed previously. The emphasis in selling has shifted from the product to the customer.

The counselor style often creates need awareness. Many customers do not realize that they actually have a need for your product or service. Even when they are aware of their need, they may not realize that an actual solution to their problem exists.

Need discovery begins with precall preparation when the salesperson is acquiring background information on the prospect. It continues once the salesperson and the customer are engaged in a real dialogue. Through the process of need discovery the salesperson establishes two-way communication by asking appropriate questions and listening carefully to the customer's responses. These responses usually provide clues concerning the customer's dominant buying motive (Fig. 10.4).

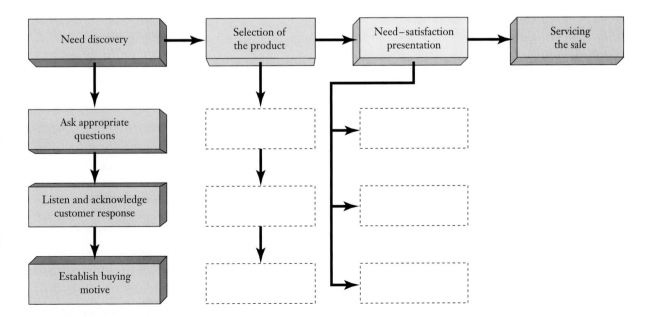

Figure **10.4**
THREE DIMENSIONS OF NEED DISCOVERY

Asking Questions

Questions provide one of the most effective ways to involve the prospect. Appropriate questions reduce tension and build trust in a selling situation because they communicate interest in the other person's welfare. A sales presentation devoid of questions closes the door on meaningful two-way communication.

The art and science of using questions were discussed by Socrates more than 2,300 years ago. He noted, among other things, that questions tend to make people think. Kevin Daley, CEO of Communispond, describes the benefits of the Socratic approach: "The customer opens up and gives lots of useful information. A high level of trust is established, and the customer owns the decisions made."[6] In any selling situation we want the prospect to be actively thinking, sharing thoughts, and asking questions. Until the person begins to talk freely, the salesperson can have difficulty discovering dominant buying motives and perceptions. A well-planned sales presentation includes a variety of preplanned questions (Table 10.1). We describe the four most common types of questions used in the field of personal selling.

INFORMATION-GATHERING QUESTIONS

Linda Richardson, an adjunct personal selling professor at the Wharton Graduate School, has developed a corporate sales training program called Dialogue Selling. She says that the first step in the partnership-building process is to ask general questions that help you acquire important information about the prospect.[7] At the beginning of most sales presen-

Table 10.1   TYPES OF QUESTIONS USED IN CONJUNCTION WITH CONSULTATIVE SELLING

TYPE OF QUESTION	DEFINITION	WHEN USED	EXAMPLES
Information-gathering questions	General questions designed to get the prospect to disclose certain types of basic information	Usually at the beginning of a sale	"Can you describe the type of leasing plan you envision?" (auto leasing)
Probing questions	More specific questions designed to uncover and clarify the prospect's perceptions and opinions	When you feel the need to obtain more specific information that is needed to fully understand the problem and prescribe a solution	"What type of image do you want your advertising to project to current and potential customers?" (newspaper advertising)
Confirmation questions	Designed to find whether or not your message is understood by the prospect	After each important item of information is presented	"Do you see the merits of purchasing a copy machine with the document enlargement feature?" (office copy machine)
Summary confirmation questions	Designed to clarify your understanding of the prospect's needs and buying conditions	Usually used after several items of information have been presented	"I would like to summarize what you have told me thus far. You want a four-bedroom home with a basement and a two-car garage." (real estate)

Table 10.2	**NEED DISCOVERY WORKSHEET**

Preplanned questions (sometimes used with preprinted forms) are increasingly being used in service, retail, wholesale, and manufacturer selling. Salespeople who use the consultative approach frequently record answers to their questions and use this information to correctly select and recommend solutions that build repeat business and referrals. (Questions taken from *Shearson Lehman Brothers Selling Skills Training Program*.)

PREPLANNED QUESTIONS TO DISCOVER BUYING MOTIVES	CUSTOMER RESPONSE
1. *"Tell me a little bit about your investment portfolio."*	
2. *"What is the history of your family income?"*	
3. *"What are your major concerns when managing your financial affairs?"*	
4. *"What are your current investment objectives?"*	
5. *"What do you expect from your financial services consultants?"*	
6.	
7.	
8.	
9.	
10.	

tations, there is a need to collect certain basic information. **Information-gathering questions** are designed to elicit such information (see Table 10.1).

In most cases information-gathering questions are easy to answer. These questions help us acquire facts about the prospect that may reveal the person's need for the product or service. Questions of this type also help build rapport with the customer. Here are some general information-gathering questions that can be used in selected selling fields.

> "This call is not about selling, but about learning. I'd like to learn more about your situation and your needs. Could you help me with that?"

> "Can you give me a close estimate of how many people will attend your meeting? I need this information to develop a facilities plan that will meet your needs?"[8]

Many salespeople use preplanned information-gathering questions. These questions are sometimes listed on a form or checklist. If the company does not provide a preprinted form or checklist, a worksheet (Table 10.2) can be easily developed. It is common practice to get the customer's permission before asking the first question. You might simply ask, "Do you mind if I get your answers to a few questions?"

the small society   **by Brickman**

A GOOD SALESPERSON AND A GOOD DOCTOR HAVE ONE THING IN COMMON. THEY ENCOURAGE QUESTIONS.

(Reprinted with special permission of King Features Syndicate.)

In some cases the use of certain types of information-gathering questions can have negative consequences. Prospects often expect salespeople to do their homework and acquire certain basic information from other sources prior to the sales presentation. In the eyes of a busy prospect, the salesperson who seems to be poorly prepared for the sales presentation may appear unprofessional.

PROBING QUESTIONS

Throughout the sales presentation the salesperson should make every effort to clarify the prospect's perceptions and opinions. Some may have a limited vocabulary for describing their problems; they know a problem exists but have difficulty expressing their views. High-performance salespeople realize that there is a common tendency for people to speak in generalities.[9]

Probing questions help you to uncover and clarify the prospect's perceptions and opinions (see Table 10.1). These questions encourage customers to give you more details about their problems. The more time customers invest in talking to you about their problems, the greater your chance of seeing the total picture.

Although probing techniques vary from one selling situation to another, there is a general format you should observe. Your probing should begin on a general basis and gradually narrow to the specifics that ultimately give you the information needed to fully understand the problem and prescribe a solution.[10] Two examples of general probing questions are

"How do you feel about using a computer to keep your expense records?"

"What kinds of solutions have you already considered?"

These general probing questions are not threatening, and they give prospects a chance to talk about a problem or issue from their point of view. These questions also keep the focus of the sales presentation on the customer's agenda. General probing questions establish a rapport that is hard to achieve in any other way.

As the sales presentation progresses, you need to use more specific probing questions that uncover the clues you need to custom fit your product or service to the prospect's needs. The following probing questions are more specific and more focused:

This real estate salesperson, with the help of a computerized database of homes, is using probing and confirmation questions to clarify the needs of the customer.

"What would be the consequences if you choose to do nothing about your current record-keeping problems?"

"Would a 20 percent reduction in turnaround time improve your profit picture?"

The best sales presentations are characterized by active dialogue. As the presentation progresses, the customer becomes more open and shares perceptions, ideas, and feelings freely. A series of good probing questions stimulate the prospect to discover things that he had not considered before. Too many rapid-fire probing questions may be threatening to your customer and should be avoided.

CONFIRMATION QUESTIONS

As a ship moves from one port to another, the captain and crew must continuously check instruments to be certain they stay on course. In a selling situation you must, from time to time, use confirmation questions to avoid the same problem. Is your language too technical? Is the prospect listening to you? Are you on target in terms of the person's needs and interests? Does the prospect agree with what you are saying? **Confirmation questions** are

> ## ►► BUILDING QUALITY PARTNERSHIPS
>
> ### SOLVING CUSTOMER PROBLEMS USING A MULTIPLE QUESTION APPROACH
>
> Neil Rackham conducted studies of 35,000 sales calls and from this research developed the material for his book titled *Spin Selling*. The book describes strategies for making large-ticket sales and is based on a close examination of successful salespeople. SPIN is an acronym for situation, problem, implication, and need–payoff. Rackham recommends the multiple question approach that involves using four types of questions in a specific sequence.
>
> *Situation questions.* These questions are used to collect facts and background information about the customer's existing situation. Some examples of situation questions include: How long have you held this position? How many people do you currently employ? Do you usually purchase or lease your equipment? These questions help you acquire information that may be needed later in the sales presentation.
>
> *Problem questions.* These questions help the salesperson uncover specific problems, difficulties, or dissatisfactions. The salesperson is searching for areas where her product or service can solve existing problems. Examples of problem questions follow: Does your Canon copy machine make copies fast enough for you? Are you happy with your current lease plan? If the
>
> salesperson discovers a problem area, he uses implication questions.
>
> *Implication questions.* These questions encourage the customer to think about the consequences of the problem. The objective of implication questions is to get the customer to understand the true dimensions of the problem area. If the customer who owns the Canon copy machine complains about delays caused by slow operation of the machine, the salesperson might ask this implication question: "Does the slow operation of the machine have a negative impact on office productivity? How do you think a faster copy machine would improve office productivity?"
>
> *Need–payoff questions.* These questions build up the value or usefulness of a proposed solution in the customer's mind. Need–payoff questions focus on the solution instead of the problem. Here is an example: "Would restricted phone lines provide the cost savings you desire?"
>
> UPS is one of several companies that prepares its salespeople to apply the principles of SPIN selling. Sales representatives complete a training program that prepares them to use the four types of questions at appropriate points during the sales presentation.[a]

used throughout the presentation to determine if the message is correctly understood by the prospect (see Table 10.1). Many confirmation questions are simple and to the point.

"If I understand you correctly, you want the Dolby 'C' noise reduction feature. Is that correct?"

"Will this location appeal to your business partner?"

"Would you like me to explain how the security system is activated?"

Confirmation questions not only maintain the prospect's attention but also clear up misunderstandings. In an ideal situation, the salesperson is getting feedback from the prospect throughout the presentation.

SUMMARY CONFIRMATION QUESTIONS

The length of a sales presentation can vary from a few minutes to an hour or more, depending on the nature of the product, the customer's knowledge of the product, and other factors. As the sales call progresses, the amount of information available to the salesperson and the customer increases. In most cases, the customer's buying conditions surface. **Buying conditions** are those qualifications that must be available or fulfilled before the sale can be closed. The customer may buy only if the product is available in a certain color or can be delivered by a certain date. In some selling situations, product installation or service after the sale are considered important buying conditions by the customer. In a complex sale, several buying conditions may surface. The salesperson has the responsibility of clarifying and confirming each condition.

One of the best ways to clarify and confirm buying conditions is with **summary–confirmation questions** (see Table 10.1). To illustrate, let us consider a situation where Tammy Harris, sales manager at a major hotel, has interviewed a prospect who wants to schedule a large awards banquet. After a series of information-gathering, probing, and confirmation questions, Tammy feels confident she has collected enough information to prepare a proposal. However, to be sure that she has all the facts and has clarified all important buying conditions, she asks the following summary confirmation questions:

"Let me summarize the major items you have mentioned. You need a room that will comfortably seat 60 persons and 10 of these persons will be seated at the head table?"

If the customer responds in the affirmative, Tammy continues with another summary confirmation question:

"You want chicken served as the main course, and the price per person for the entire meal cannot exceed $15?"

Once all the buying conditions are confirmed, Tammy can prepare a proposal that reflects the specific needs of the customer, which results in a win–win situation. The salesperson wins because the proposal is custom fitted to meet the customer's requirements. The chances of closing the sale improve. Also, the customer wins because she had the opportunity to clarify buying conditions and now is able to review a specific proposal.

Eliminate Unnecessary Questions

It is important to avoid the use of unnecessary questions during a sales call. As noted previously, salespeople need to acquire as much information as possible about the prospect before the first meeting. This preapproach information gathering is especially important when the prospect is a corporate buyer. These buyers expect the salesperson to be well

▶▶ CUSTOMER RELATIONSHIP MANAGEMENT WITH TECHNOLOGY

REVIEWING ACCOUNT STATUS

Salespeople regularly review the status of their prospects' records in their customer relationship management (CRM) databases. In some cases, this is done on the computer screen. In other situations, a printed copy of the records can enhance the process.

Salespeople review their files to ascertain at what phase in the Consultative Sales Presentation Guide each prospect is in the sales cycle. Then they decide which action to take to help move the prospect to the next phase. Sales managers can be helpful with this process, especially for new salespeople. Managers can help salespeople evaluate the available information and suggest strategies designed to move to the next phase.

Even experienced salespeople count on their sales managers to help plan presentations. Managers can help salespeople evaluate their prospects' needs, select the best solution, and plan a presentation most likely to succeed. (See the exercise, Printing the Customer Database, at p. 238 for more information.)

informed about their operation and not waste time asking a large number of basic information-gathering questions. A growing number of corporate buyers want to establish a long-term partnership with suppliers. They assume that potential partners will conduct a careful study of their company before the first sales call.

Listening, and Acknowledging the Customer's Response

Stephen Covey, the noted author and consultant, says that most salespeople sell products, not solutions. To correct this situation he encourages us, "Seek first to understand, then to be understood."[11] To understand the customer, we must listen closely and acknowledge every response.

The listening efficiency rate for most people is about 25 percent. This means they miss about 75 percent of the messages spoken by other people. Why has the skill of listening fallen on hard times? Good listening takes time and time has become a scarce commodity in our fast-paced world. Also, watching television encourages passive instead of active listening. Many people spend from four to six hours a day watching television and in the process acquire passive instead of active listening skills.[12]

DEVELOPING ACTIVE LISTENING SKILLS

What does listening really mean? Listening is an active process that requires your participation. Too frequently, hearing is confused with listening.

The late Carl Rogers stated that through active listening we can understand what people mean when they speak and what they are feeling. **Active listening** is the process of sending back to the person what you as a listener think the individual meant, both in terms of content and in terms of feelings. It involves taking into consideration both verbal and nonverbal signals.[13] This approach to listening enables the salesperson to check on the accuracy of what the customer said and what the customer meant. Active listening involves three practices that can be learned easily.

In many selling situations note taking will demonstrate a high level of professionalism.

Focus Your Full Attention This is not easy because the delivery of the messages we hear is often much slower than our capacity to listen. Thus we have plenty of time to let our minds roam, to think ahead, and to plan what we are going to say next. Our senses are constantly feeding us new information while someone is trying to tell us something. Staying focused is often difficult and involves maintaining eye contact with the speaker and not letting distractions interfere.[14]

Paraphrase the Customer's Meaning This involves stating in your own words what you think the person meant. This technique not only helps ensure understanding but also is an effective customer relations strategy. The customer feels good knowing that not only are you listening to what has been said but also you are making an effort to ensure accuracy. Paraphrasing also helps you remember what was said.[15]

In addition to paraphrasing the content, echo the feelings you felt were expressed or implied. It is important that we check on our perception of the customer's feelings. This step is especially helpful if the person is experiencing negative emotions such as doubt or frustration.

Take Notes Although note taking is not necessary in every sales presentation, it is important in complex sales where the information obtained from the customer is critical to the development of a good proposal. It is important that you capture your customer's major points. Make sure your notes are brief and to the point.[16] Lauren Arethas, eastern regional manager for *Interiors* magazine, says that a note pad and pen represent her most important sales tools. She states that when customers see her taking notes, their posture changes from a defensive, "Here comes the sales pitch," to a welcoming, "My needs are important."[17] A.T. Cross pen company has developed an electronic pen-and-notepad combination that enables the user to quickly convert handwritten notes to text.

Active listening is not easy. Gerry Mitchell, chairman of the Dana Corporation, described listening as "tough and grinding work." Like learning to give a speech, learning

to listen takes practice. Many salespeople are enrolling in seminars and workshops designed to develop listening skills.

Establishing Buying Motives

The primary goal of questioning, listening, and acknowledging is to uncover prospect needs and establish buying motives. Our efforts to discover prospect needs can be more effective if we focus our questioning on determining the prospect's primary reasons for buying. When a customer has a definite need, it is usually supported by specific buying motives.

Vicki Lynn Cusick attempts to custom-fit her product solutions to meet the unique needs of each customer. Her average sale includes 31 items selected from the 5,000 products she represents.

SELECTION OF THE PRODUCT

The second part of the consultative sales presentation consists of selecting or creating a solution that satisfies the prospect's buying motives. After identifying the buying motives the salesperson carefully reviews the available product options. At this point the salesperson is searching for a specific solution to satisfy the prospect's buying motives. Once the solution has been selected, the salesperson makes a recommendation to the prospect (Fig. 10.5).

If the sale involves several needs and the satisfaction of multiple buying motives, selection of the solution may take several days or even weeks, and may involve the preparation of a detailed sales proposal. A company considering the purchase of automated office equipment would likely present this type of challenge to the salesperson. The problem needs careful analysis before a solution can be identified.

Match Specific Benefits with Buying Motives

As we note in Chapter 6, products and services represent problem-solving tools. People buy products when they perceive that they fulfill a need. We also note that today's more demanding customers seek a cluster of satisfactions that arise from the product itself, from the company that makes or distributes the product, and from the salesperson who sells and services the product (see Fig. 6.1). Each of these clusters may add value to the sale. Once the customer's needs and buying motives are firmly established, the salesperson can determine which specific benefits to emphasize. The emphasis here is on *specific* instead of *general* benefits. Research indicates that the success of a sales call is related to the number of different needs discovered and the specific benefits highlighted in response to those needs.

Configure a Solution

Most salespeople bring to the sale a variety of products or services. Salespeople who represent food distributors can offer customers a mix of several hundred items. Most pharmaceutical sales representatives can offer the medical community a wide range

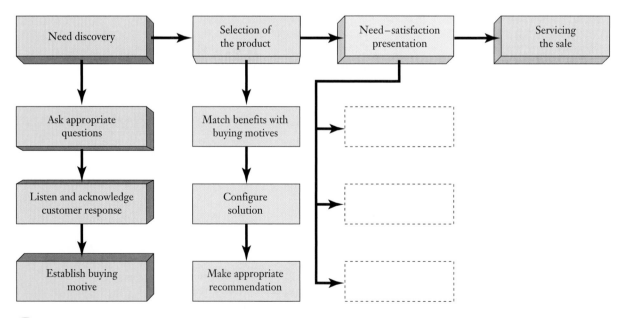

Figure 10.5
THREE DIMENSIONS OF PRODUCT SELECTION

CATHY © CATHY GUISEWITE
(Reprinted with permission of UNIVERSAL PRESS SYNDICATE. All rights reserved.)

of products. Circuit City, a large retailer of electronics, offers customers a wide range of audio and visual entertainment options. The customer who wants to purchase a sound system, for example, can choose from many combinations of receivers, speakers, and so on.

Make Appropriate Recommendations

The recommendation strategies available to salespeople are similar to those used by a doctor who must recommend a solution to a patient's medical problem. In the medical field, three possibilities for providing patient satisfaction exist. In situations in which the patient easily understands the medical problem and the appropriate treatment, the doctor can make a recommendation, and the patient can proceed immediately toward a cure. If the patient does not easily understand the medical problem or solution, the doctor may need to discuss thoroughly with the patient the benefits of the recommended treatment. If the medical problem is not within his medical specialty, the doctor may recommend a specialist to provide the treatment. In consultative selling the salesperson has these same three counseling alternatives.

RECOMMEND PRODUCT — CUSTOMER BUYS IMMEDIATELY

The selection and recommendation of products to meet customer needs may occur at the beginning of the sales interview, such as in the product approach; during the interview, just after the need discovery; or near the end, when minor resistance has been handled. At any of these three times, the presentation of products that are well matched to the prospect's needs may result in an immediate purchase.

RECOMMEND PRODUCT — SALESPERSON MAKES NEED — SATISFACTION PRESENTATION

This alternative requires a full presentation of product benefits including demonstrations and handling of any objections before the sale is closed. In this situation the customer may not be totally aware of a buying problem, and the solution may not be easily understood or apparent. Because of this, the salesperson needs to make an in-depth presentation to define the problem and communicate a solution to the customer.

RECOMMEND ANOTHER SOURCE

Earlier in this book we indicated that professional salespeople may recommend that a prospect buy a product or service from another source, maybe even a competitor. If, after a careful needs assessment, the salesperson concludes that the products represented do not satisfy the customer's needs, the consultative salesperson should recommend another source.

NEED SATISFACTION — SELECTING A PRESENTATION STRATEGY

Decisions concerning which presentation strategy to emphasize have become more complex. This is due to several factors discussed in previous chapters: longer sales cycles, multiple buying influences, emphasis on repeat sales and referrals, greater emphasis on custom fitting of products, and building of long-term partnerships.

Conducting business in the new economy, which is based on the assets of knowledge and information, requires that we think about ways to improve the sales presentation. This is how one author described this challenge:[18]

> As we move from the rutted byways of the Industrial Age to the electronic thoroughfares of the Information Age, business presentations become a measure of our ability to adapt to new surroundings. The most successful and forward-thinking companies already have assigned presentations a new, fundamental, and strategic importance.

Today, we need a broader range of presentation strategies. The need–satisfaction strategy involves assessing the customer's needs; selecting the product; and deciding whether to use an informative, persuasive, or reminder presentation (Fig. 10.6).

Informative Presentation Strategy

To be informative, a message must be clearly understood by the customer. Of course, clarity is important in any presentation, but it needs special attention in a presentation whose primary purpose is to inform. The **informative presentation** emphasizes factual informa-

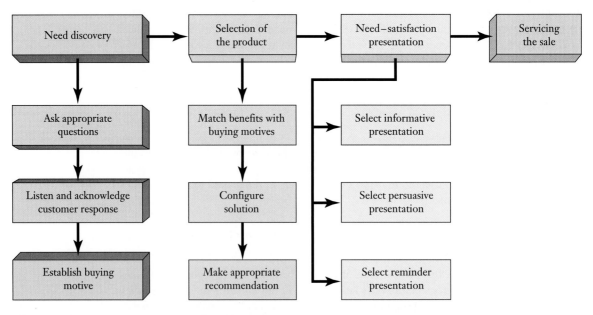

Figure 10.6
THE THREE STRATEGIES TO USE IN DEVELOPING AN EFFECTIVE NEED–SATISFACTION PRESENTATION

tion often taken from technical reports, company-prepared sales literature, or written testimonials from persons who have used the product. This type of presentation is commonly used to introduce new products and services. This strategy emphasizes clarity, simplicity, and directness.

A variety of factors motivate sales personnel to adopt the informative presentation. Some have discovered that this strategy works best when you sell highly complex products that have to be custom fitted to unique needs. In addition, if the product's price is quite high, a factual presentation, devoid of emotion, may be the best approach. Some salespeople simply think that it is not appropriate to use persuasion during the sales presentation. They believe that a product should stand on its own merits and persuasion should not be necessary to sell it.

Within most major industries new products are appearing at a rapid rate. Many of these products are introduced through informative sales presentations.

Persuasive Presentation Strategy

Many salespeople believe that when a real need for their product exists, the stage is set for a persuasive presentation. The major goal of the **persuasive presentation** strategy is to influence the prospect's beliefs, attitudes, or behavior and to encourage buyer action. Persuasive sales presentations include a subtle transition stage where the dialogue shifts from an intellectual emphasis to an emotional appeal.

Persuasion is commonly used in all professions. Medical doctors routinely use persuasion to influence patient behavior. In fact, doctors involved in the growing field of preventive medicine rely heavily on persuasion to encourage patients to adopt certain health practices. Teachers use persuasion to encourage students to complete assignments. Lawyers use persuasion to influence clients' feelings and opinions.

In the field of personal selling, persuasion is an acceptable strategy once a need has been identified and a suitable product has been selected. When it is clear that the buyer can benefit from ownership of the product or service, an enthusiastic and persuasive sales presentation is usually appropriate.

The persuasive presentation strategy requires a high level of training and experience to be effective, because a poorly planned and delivered persuasive presentation may raise the prospect's anxiety level. The persuasive presentation, when handled properly, does not trigger fear or distrust.

Reminder Presentation Strategy

Studies show that awareness of a company's products and services declines as promotion is stopped. This problem represents one of the reasons many companies employ missionary salespeople to maintain an ongoing awareness and familiarity with their product lines. Other types of salespeople also use this presentation strategy. Route salespeople rely heavily on **reminder presentations** (sometimes called *reinforcement presentations*) to maintain their market share. They know that if they do not make frequent calls and remind customers of their products, the competition is likely to capture some customers. The 12,800 Frito-Lay salespeople are in a strong position to use the reminder presentation strategy because they use handheld computers to manage orders. It only takes a minute or two to review a programmed product list in the presence of a customer.[19]

The reminder presentation also has many applications at the retail level. Sales personnel working with repeat customers are in a good position to remind them of products or services offered in their own department or another department located in some other area of the business.

Reminder presentations assume that in most cases the prospect understands at least the basic product features and buyer benefits. Salespeople using this strategy understand the value of repetition. They know that many of their recommendations may not be accepted until the second, third, or fourth time.

In some cases the reminder presentation focuses on factors other than a specific product or service. The presentation may include information that indirectly influences the sale. For example, a salesperson might describe a new automated package and delivery system that can improve service to customers.

GUIDELINES FOR DEVELOPING A PERSUASIVE PRESENTATION STRATEGY

There are many ways to incorporate persuasion into a sales presentation. In this section we review a series of guidelines that should be followed during preparation of a persuasive presentation.

Place Special Emphasis on the Relationship

Throughout this book we emphasize the importance of the relationship strategy in selling. Good rapport between the salesperson and the prospect is a necessary foundation for the use of a persuasive sales presentation. Robert Cialdini, an Arizona State University faculty member who specializes in persuasion research, says that people prefer to comply with requests or suggestions from people they know and like.[20] People seldom purchase products from salespeople they dislike or distrust.

When you are speaking to a group, you want members to feel as if you're talking directly to them individually. Throughout the presentation make eye contact with various group members and involve them when appropriate. Eye contact tends to bond you to your audience.[21] Also, you should stand during most presentations. Standing tends to add energy to your presentation because you have more options in terms of body language.

Sell Benefits and Obtain Customer Reactions

People do not buy things, they buy what the things can do for them. They do not buy an auto battery, they buy a sure start on a cold morning. Office managers do not buy laser printers, they buy better looking letters and reports. Every product or service offers the customer certain benefits. The benefit might be greater comfort, security, feeling of confidence, or economy.

Some salespeople make the mistake of emphasizing only product features. They fail to translate these features into buyer benefits. If you are selling Allstate insurance, for example, you should become familiar with the service features. One feature is well-trained employees and the convenient location of Allstate offices across the nation. The benefit to customers is greater peace of mind in knowing that they can receive good service at a nearby location.

After you state the feature and convert it into a buyer benefit, obtain a reaction from the customer. You should always check to see if you are on the right track and your prospect is following the logic of your presentation. The reactions can be triggered by a simple confirming question. Some examples follow:

FEATURE	BENEFIT	CONFIRMING QUESTION
Commercial-size package	Money saved	"You are interested in saving money, are you not?"
Automatic climate control system for automobile	Temperature in car not varying after initial setting	"Would you like the luxury of setting the temperature and then not worrying about it?"

The feature–benefit–reaction (FBR) approach is used by many high-performance sales-people. Involving the customer with a confirmation question helps you maintain two-way communication with the customer.

Minimize the Negative Impact of Change

As we noted earlier, salespeople are constantly threatening the status quo. They sell people the new, the different, and the untried. In nearly all selling situations the customer is being asked to consider change of some sort, and in some cases it is only natural for the person to resist change.

Whenever possible, we should try to help the customer view change in a positive and realistic way. Change is more acceptable to people who understand the benefits of it and do not see it as a threat to their security. The prospect must be given realistic expectations about the products they are buying.[22] If the salesperson creates unrealistic expectations by exaggerating buyer benefits, long-term problems are likely to surface. The credibility of the salesperson and the company she represents may suffer.

Place the Strongest Appeal at the Beginning or End

Research indicates that appeals made at the beginning or end of a presentation are more effective than those given in the middle. A strong appeal at the beginning of a presentation, of course, gets the prospect's attention and possibly develops interest. Made near the end of the presentation, the appeal sets the stage for closing the sale.

Target Emotional Links

An important key to successful persuasion is a good understanding of your prospect so that you know which emotion links to target. **Emotional links** are the connectors between your messages and the internal emotions of the prospect.[23] Some common emotional links in the business community are quality improvement, on-time delivery, increased market share, innovation, customer service, and reduction of operating expenses. Targeting just a few emotional links can increase your chances of closing the sale. When you target emotional links, use persuasive words such as proven, efficient, save, convenient, world-class, new, and improved. Also, use the language that your prospect is most tuned to.

Use Metaphors, Stories, and Testimonials

Metaphors, sometimes referred to as *figurative language*, are highly persuasive sales tools. Metaphors are words or phrases that suggest pictorial relationships between objects or ideas. With the aid of metaphors you can paint vivid, visual pictures for prospects that command their attention and keep their interest. The success of the metaphor rests on finding common ground (shared or well-known experiences) so that your message gets a free boost from a fact already known or believed to be true. A salesperson presenting a new computer system that has a very fast data analysis capability might say, "The speed of our system, compared to what you are used to, would be like comparing an Olympic sprinter to a toddler just learning to walk."[24]

Donald J. Moine, noted speaker and sales trainer, says that stories not only help you sell more products but also help you enrich relationships with your customers. A good story focuses the customer's attention and can effectively communicate the value of a product or a service as well. Xerox and IBM represent just two examples of companies that use stories to inspire the selling effort.[25]

Many salespeople find it beneficial to quote a specific third party. Third-party testimonials from satisfied clients can help a prospect feel confident about using your product.

GENERAL GUIDELINES FOR CREATING EFFECTIVE PRESENTATIONS

There are many ways to make all three need–satisfaction presentation strategies more interesting and more valuable. A more effective presentation can be developed using the following general guidelines. Each of these guidelines are discussed in more detail in Chapters 11–14.

Strengthen the Presentation Strategy with an Effective Demonstration

The need–satisfaction presentation can be strengthened if the salesperson preplans effective demonstrations that clarify the product features and benefits. Many salespeople encounter doubt or skepticism during the sales presentation. The prospect often wants some kind of assurance or proof. We must be prepared to substantiate our claims with fac-

tual information. This information can be provided in several ways. The following list of proof strategies is explained in detail in Chapter 11.

Product itself	Portfolios
Models	Graphs, charts, and test results
Photos and illustrations	Laptop computers and demonstration software
Testimonials and case histories	Audiovisual technology
Reprints	Bound paper presentations

Preplan Methods for Negotiating and Closing the Sale

It is a good idea to assume that customers want to make the most efficient use of the time they spend purchasing goods and services. To make your presentation as concise and to the point as possible, you should preplan methods for negotiating misunderstandings or resistance that often surfaces during the presentation. You need to bring some degree of urgency to the selling environment by presenting focused solutions.[26] In most cases the focus of the negotiation is on one of the following areas:

- *Need* awareness is vague or nonexistent.

- *Price* does not equal perceived value.

- The buyer is satisfied with present *source.*

- The *product* does not meet the buyer's perceived requirement.

Methods used to negotiate buyer resistance in each of these areas are introduced in Chapter 12.

It also is important to preplan closing and confirming the sale. This planning should include a review of closing clues that may surface during the sales presentation and methods of closing the sale. These and other topics are discussed in Chapter 13.

The dynamic nature of selling requires that the salesperson be prepared to respond to a wide variety of questions from the customer.

Plan for the Dynamic Nature of Selling

The sales presentation is a dynamic activity. From the moment the salesperson and the customer meet, the sales presentation is being altered and fine-tuned to reflect the new information available. During a typical presentation the salesperson asks numerous questions, discusses several product features, and describes the appropriate product benefits. The customer also is asking questions and, in many cases, voicing concerns. The successful sales presenta-

Consultative selling skills	Parts of the Sales Presentation			
	Need discovery	Selecting solution	Need–satisfaction presentation	Servicing the sale
Questioning skills	• As a question approach • To find needs and buying motives • To probe for buying motives • To confirm needs and buying motives	• To confirm selection	• To confirm benefits • To confirm mutual understanding	• To make suggestions • To confirm delivery and installations • To handle complaints • To build goodwill • To secure credit arrangements
Presenting benefits	• As a benefit approach • To discover potential benefits	• To match up with buying motives	• To present and summarize features effectively	• To make suggestions • To use credit as a close
Demonstrating skills	• As a product approach • To clarify need	• To clarify selection	• To strengthen product claims	• When making effective suggestions
Negotiating skills	• To overcome initial resistance to sales interview • To overcome need objection	• To overcome product objection	• To overcome source, price, and time objection	• In handling complaints • To overcome financing objection
Closing skills	• When customer has made buying decision	• When buyer immediately recognizes solutions	• Whenever buyer presents closing signals	• After suggestion • To secure repeats and referrals

Figure **10.7**
THE SELLING DYNAMICS MATRIX
Salespeople can select from a variety of skills throughout the sales presentation.

tion is a good model of two-way communication. Because of the dynamic nature of the sales presentation, the salesperson must be prepared to apply several different selling skills to meet the variety of buyer responses. Figure 10.7 illustrates how the various selling skills can be applied during all parts of the sales presentation. In creating effective presentations the salesperson should be prepared to meet a wide range of buyer responses with effective questions, benefit statements, demonstrations, negotiating methods, and closing methods.

Keep Your Presentation Simple and Concise

Numerous surveys indicate that customers like sales presentations that are concise and free of unnecessary complexity. When the salesperson gives clients too much information or discusses topics that do not deal with their individual needs, they simply stop paying attention.[27]

The best way to achieve conciseness is to preplan your sales call. Think ahead of time about what you are going to say and do. Anticipate questions and objections the prospect may voice, and be prepared with accurate information and concise answers.

In many selling situations there is a certain amount of time pressure. Rarely does a salesperson have an unlimited amount of time to spend with the customer. Figure 10.8 illustrates an ideal breakdown of time allocation between the salesperson and the prospect during all three parts of the sales presentation. In terms of involvement the prospect assumes a greater role during the need–discovery stage. As the salesperson begins the product selection process, the prospect's involvement decreases. During the need–satisfaction stage the salesperson is doing most of the talking, but note that the prospect is never excluded totally.

In addition to preplanning the sales presentation, consider a "dress rehearsal" in front of your colleagues. A less threatening approach might be to practice in front of your spouse or a close friend. Videotaping the rehearsal can help you see how you really look.

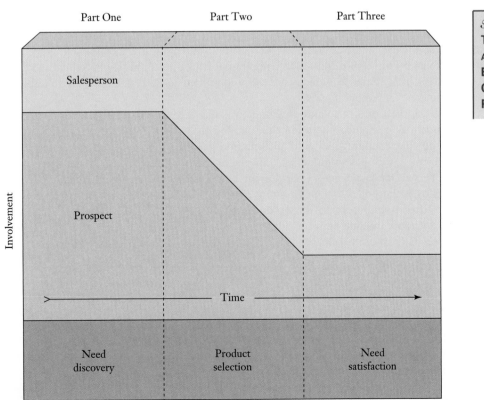

Figure 10.8
TIME USED BY SALESPERSON AND CUSTOMER DURING EACH PART OF THE CONSULTATIVE SALES PRESENTATION

Do you appear too stiff and motionless? Do you talk too fast or too slow? It's a good idea to practice presentations with specific customers in mind.[28]

The Consultative Sales Presentation and the Transactional Buyer

Throughout this chapter you have been given a comprehensive introduction to the consultative sales presentation. It is important to keep in mind that the fundamentals of consultative selling must be customized to meet the individual needs of the customer. For example, some of the guidelines for developing an effective presentation must be abandoned or greatly altered when you are working with a transactional buyer. In Chapter 1 we described transactional selling as a process that most effectively matches the needs of the buyer who is primarily interested in price and convenience. In most cases the transactional buyer understands what product they need and when they need it. In many situations they are interested only in the product itself and not in what the company or the salesperson can do to create additional value. The customer may even resent time spent with the salesperson, especially time spent on need discovery. The Internet has armed many transactional buyers with a great deal of information, so the salesperson that spends time asking information-gathering questions or making a detailed informative presentation may be wasting the customers time. Most of these buyers want the salesperson to configure a product solution that focuses on pricing and delivery issues.[29]

Summary

A well-planned and well-executed presentation strategy is an important key to success in personal selling. To be most effective, the presentation should be viewed as a three-part process: *need discovery*; selection of the product; and need satisfaction through informing, persuading, or reminding.

The most effective sales presentation is characterized by two-way communication. It should be a dialogue between the salesperson and the prospect, whose involvement should be encouraged with information-gathering, probing, confirmation, and *summary–confirmation questions*. Beware of assuming information about the prospect, and be sure the language of your presentation is clearly understood. Listen attentively as the prospect responds to your questions or volunteers information.

After making a good first impression during the approach and getting the customer's full attention, the salesperson begins the presentation. The salesperson's ability is tested during this part of the sale, because this is where the prospect's buying motives are established. The salesperson's ability to verbalize product benefits also are being tested during this part of the sale.

Once you have selected a product or service that matches the customer's needs, you must decide which presentation strategy to emphasize. Need satisfaction can be achieved through informing, persuading, or reminding. The salesperson can, of course, use a combination of these presentation strategies in some cases. An effective presentation is an important part of the sales call and often determines the ease or difficulty of proceeding through the rest of the steps to a successful sale.

KEY TERMS

Need Discovery
Information-Gathering Questions
Probing Questions
Confirmation Questions
Buying Conditions
Summary–Confirmation Questions

Active Listening
Informative Presentation
Persuasive Presentation
Reminder Presentation
Emotional Links

REVIEW QUESTIONS

1. List and describe the four parts of the Consultative Sales Presentation Guide.
2. List and describe the four types of questions commonly used in the selling field.
3. Define the term *buying conditions*. What are some common buying conditions?
4. What is the listening efficiency rate of most people? Describe the process of active listening, and explain how it can improve the listening efficiency rate.
5. Discuss the major factors that should be considered during the product selection phase of the consultative sales presentation.
6. Distinguish between the three types of need–satisfaction presentations: informative, persuasive, and reminder.
7. What are the guidelines to be followed when developing a persuasive sales presentation?
8. What are some advantages of using the feature–benefit–reaction (FBR) approach?
9. Discuss those factors that contribute to the dynamic nature of selling. What skills are used by salespeople to cope with the dynamic nature of personal selling?
10. Read the introduction that begins on p. 213 and then evaluate Dave Tripp's practice of building a close relationship with salespeople who work in the bookstores he visits. Does this practice represent appropriate use of Tripp's limited time? Explain.

APPLICATION EXERCISES

1. Assume that you are a salesperson working in each of the following kinds of selling careers, and assume further that the prospect has given you no indication of what she is looking for. Identify the kinds of questions you can use to find your prospect's specific needs.
   a. Personal computer
   b. Carpet
   c. Financial planning
2. You are a department manager and have called a meeting with the five staff members in your department. The purpose of your meeting is to inform your staff of a new procedure your company has adopted. It is important that you develop understanding and support. What steps can you take to enhance communication with the group?
3. Pick a job that you would really like to have and for which you are qualified. Assume you are going to be interviewed for this job tomorrow afternoon. You really want this position and therefore want to be persuasive in presenting your qualifications. List facts about your qualifications concerning where you have worked previously, how much education you have, and what involvement in hobbies and activities

you have. Use the feature–benefits worksheet in Chapter 5 (Table 5.1) as a guide to convert these employee facts to employer benefits in the form of selling statements.

4. The book *Spin Selling* was introduced in this chapter. Visit the www.amazon.com Web site and access this book. Examine the reviews provided by customers who have read the book.

CRM APPLICATION EXERCISE

Printing the Customer Database

Sales managers regularly help salespeople review the status of their accounts. These strategic account review meetings often involve examining all the information available on the salespeople's most promising prospects. Both the sales manager and the salesperson have a copy of all information currently available for the accounts either on their computer screens or on paper. To produce a paper record of the information contained in the ACT! database, select: Lookup, Everyone, Report, Contact Report, Active Group, Printer, and Enter. Approximately 40 pages of information will be printed.

CASE PROBLEM

Annette Peterson is a real estate salesperson for Modern Homes, Incorporated. A young couple, John and Beth Reems, was referred to Annette by the sales manager. John and Beth are being transferred into the city due to John's job as manager of a local men's clothing store. Beth had been a computer systems analyst in a department store and will be looking for a similar position after the move.

Annette had no opportunity to visit with John and Beth until they arrived in the city today. The sales manager set up an appointment for them to meet at the office at 1:00 P.M. After their arrival the following sales presentation occurred:

Annette: Good afternoon, Mr. and Mrs. Reems. My name is Annette Peterson.

John: Good afternoon. I am John Reems and this is my wife, Beth.

Beth: Good afternoon, Mrs. Peterson, we were looking forward to meeting you.

Annette: Please call me Annette. And how was your flight?

John: Oh, we had a lovely flight and got a wonderful view of the city as we circled for landing.

Beth: I enjoyed the flight also, and am looking forward to seeing the city and driving around to view the homes for sale. Our flight back leaves at 8:30 P.M. so we are not going to have a lot of time. Our looking is going to have to move rather quickly.

Annette: My sales manager told me you would have a limited time, so I've prepared an agenda for us to follow this afternoon. I have four homes that I selected from our computerized database. I picked up the keys for all four of them so we can drive out and take a look. Before we get going, though, I would like to show you each home and tell you a little about it. With the aid of my laptop computer I can show you interior and exterior pictures of each home.

John and Beth: Oh!

Annette: Here is the first one. It is priced at $146,000, has 2,000 square feet, and is a two-story. This house has two bathrooms and is located on a 65 by 135 foot lot. It was built in 1975 and has Andersen windows.

John and Beth: Uh-huh! (Beth looks for a pencil in her purse.)

Annette: Now here is a picture of the second house. I do not like this one as well as the first, but I thought maybe you would like to see it. This home was built in 1987 and is priced at $140,000. The taxes are $3,000 a year. It has 1,600 square feet and has U.S. Steel siding on it. It also has an attached 22 by 24 foot garage. The lot is 80 by 140 feet. It is a ranch-style home.

John and Beth: We do like ranch-style homes.

Annette: This picture is the third home that I chose. I really like this one. It is a split-level, priced at $138,900. The taxes are—oh, I'm sorry, the taxes do not seem to be listed for this one. I am sure we can find out what they are, however, if you are interested.

John: Well, we really are not interested in split-level homes. There are too many stairs to climb. By the way, how far are these homes from the store?

Annette: Well, most customers I have worked with do not concern themselves with how far, but rather how long it will take them to get to work. You will find that the city has an excellent system of streets with rapid uncongested traveling. The homes I am going to show you are all located in a suburb called Arbor Oaks. It would take you about 20 minutes to get from there to your store.

John: I see. (John looks at his watch to see what time it is.)

Annette: Here is the fourth home I picked out (showing pictures of the fourth home). This one is also a two-story and has a 24 by 24 foot garage. The price is $139,000 and it has an assumable mortgage of $80,500 with a 10 percent loan. The home is located on a cul-de-sac, with a 90 by 160 foot lot. I went through this house last week and remember that it has oak wainscoting in the family room and also vinyl siding. It has a high-efficiency furnace, air conditioner, and Maytag appliances.

Questions

1. Describe what you think John and Beth's impressions are of Annette.

2. Evaluate the strengths of Annette Peterson's presentation strategy.

3. Evaluate the weaknesses of this presentation strategy.

4. Assume you are the real estate salesperson in this case problem; then write out an outline that you would follow in giving your sales presentation.

5. Assuming that Annette Peterson follows the same pattern in the demonstration and close that she already has established in the presentation thus far, is she likely to close the sale? Why or why not?

6. Select five features brought out by Annette and convert them to buyer benefits. Use the forms presented in Chapter 5 (Tables 5.1 and 5.2).

CRM CASE STUDY

Planning Presentations

Becky Kemley, your sales manager at SimNet Systems, wants to meet with you this afternoon to discuss the status of your accounts. It is common for prospects to have several contacts with SimNet before ordering a network system. These multicall contacts, or sales cycle phases, usually include getting acquainted and prequalifying, needs discovery, proposal presentation, closing, and account maintenance. Becky wants to know what phase each account is in and, particularly, which accounts may be ready for a presentation.

Questions

1. Which five accounts already have had a needs discovery? Which two accounts are scheduled for a needs discovery? Which six accounts are likely to buy but have not yet had a needs discovery?

2. Which two accounts have had a needs discovery and now need a product solution configured?

3. Which three accounts do not now have a network and appear to be ready for your sales presentation?

4. For those accounts listed next that are ready for your sales presentation, which strategy would you use for each: informative, persuasive, or reminder?
   a. Able Profit Machines
   b. Big Tex Auto Sales
   c. International Studios
   d. Lakeside Clinic

5. Which accounts appear to be planning to buy without a needs discovery or product configuration/proposal? What risks does this pose?

PARTNERSHIP SELLING: ROLE PLAY/SIMULATION
(see Appendix 3, p. 406)

UNDERSTANDING YOUR CUSTOMER'S BUYING STRATEGY

Read *sales memorandum 2* ("A" or "B" depending on the account category you were assigned in Chapter 9). Your customer has called you back because you made such a good approach in call 1 and wants to visit with you about a convention recently assigned. In this call you are to use the information gathered in sales call 1 to reestablish a good relationship, discover your customer's convention needs, and set an appointment to return and make a presentation.

Follow the instructions carefully and prepare information-gathering questions prior to your appointment. Keep your information-gathering questions general and attempt to get your customer to openly share information. Use probing questions later during the appointment to gain more insight. Be careful about doing too much of the talking. In the need discovery, your customer should do most of the talking, with you taking notes and using them to ask confirmation and summary–confirmation questions to check the accuracy of your perceptions concerning what the customer wants. After this meeting you will be asked to prepare a sales proposal from the information you have gathered.

Your instructor may again ask you to assume the role of a customer in the account category that you are not assigned to as a salesperson. If so, you will receive detailed customer instructions that you should follow closely. This will provide you with an opportunity to experience the strategic/consultative/partnering style of selling from a customer's perspective.

Custom Fitting the Sales Demonstration

When you finish reading this chapter, you should be able to

1. Discuss the important advantages of the sales demonstration

2. Explain the guidelines to be followed when planning a sales demonstration

3. Complete a demonstration worksheet

4. Develop selling tools that can strengthen your sales presentation

5. Discuss how to use audiovisual presentations effectively

LEARNING OBJECTIVES

*M*arcus Graham, founder of GM Voices, spends a great deal of time trying to determine the best way to demonstrate a product that prospects can hear, but cannot see. His company records telephone commands (voice prompts) for banks, retailers, airlines, and other companies that receive a large number of calls. He also creates professionally recorded voice mail prompts for use with voice mail systems and Web pages. To meet global demand for his services, Graham has engaged free-lance translators and voice talents from countries around the world.

As competition increases, GM Voices has turned to various forms of technology to enhance prospect demonstrations. The company invested $150,000 in a CD-ROM with high impact animation and 40 minutes of spoken text that presents voice samples and testimonials from customers. Advances in printing technology have provided GM Voices with an inexpensive demonstration option. For as little as $30 a customized printed presentation can be prepared for the prospect.[1] Presentation technology is advancing at a rapid rate, and most salespeople are using one or more technologies to improve the effectiveness of their sales performance.

IMPORTANCE OF THE SALES DEMONSTRATION

Trying to get a message through to an information-overloaded customer is one of the major challenges facing salespeople today. If the customer isn't paying attention, there is little chance of closing the sale.[2] The increase in look-alike products and greater competition present additional challenges. The sales demonstration has become a more important communication tool. A well-planned **demonstration** adds sensory appeal to the product

Figure 11.1
Conducting the Sales Demonstration

The Six–Step Presentation Plan	
Step One: APPROACH	☑ Review Strategic/Consultative Selling Model ☑ Initiate customer contact
Step Two: PRESENTATION	☑ Determine prospect needs ☑ Select product or service ☑ Initiate sales presentation
Step Three: DEMONSTRATION	☐ Decide what to demonstrate ☐ Select selling tools ☐ Initiate demonstration
Step Four: NEGOTIATION	☐ Anticipate buyer concerns ☐ Plan negotiating methods ☐ Initiate double–win negotiations
Step Five: CLOSE	☐ Plan appropriate closing methods ☐ Recognize closing clues ☐ Initiate closing methods
Step Six: SERVICING THE SALE	☐ Suggestion selling ☐ Follow through ☐ Follow-up calls
Service, retail, wholesale, and manufacturer selling	

(Fig. 11.1). It attracts the customer's attention, stimulates interest, and creates desire. It usually is not possible to make this type of impression with words alone.

A product demonstration contributes in a positive way to the selling/buying process. Both the customer and the salesperson benefit. The prospect can evaluate the product or service more effectively. The salesperson finds it easier to show what the product can do and how it can fit the customer's needs. Strategic planning, of course, sets the stage for an effective demonstration that adds value to the sale (Fig. 11.2). Some of the most important benefits of the sales demonstration are discussed next.

Improved Communication and Retention

In a previous chapter we note the limitation of the verbal presentation; words provide only part of the meaning attached to messages that flow between the salesperson and the prospect. When we try to explain a point with words alone, people frequently do not understand our messages.

Why is communication via the spoken word alone so difficult? One major reason is that we are visually oriented from birth. We grow up surrounded by the influence of movies, television, commercial advertising, road signs, and all kinds of visual stimulation. People are accustomed to learning new concepts through the sense of sight or through a combination of seeing and hearing.

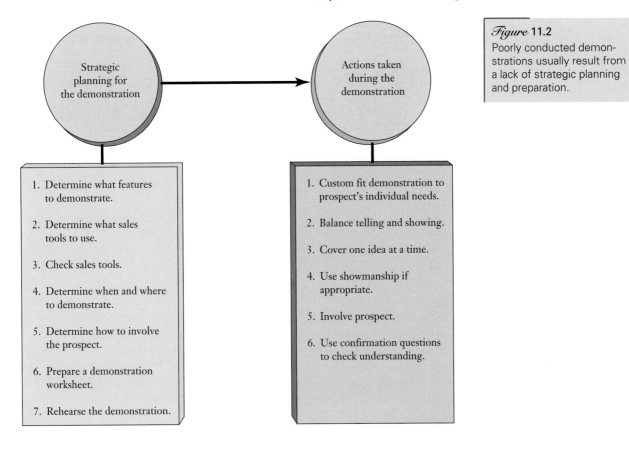

Strategic planning for the demonstration

1. Determine what features to demonstrate.

2. Determine what sales tools to use.

3. Check sales tools.

4. Determine when and where to demonstrate.

5. Determine how to involve the prospect.

6. Prepare a demonstration worksheet.

7. Rehearse the demonstration.

Actions taken during the demonstration

1. Custom fit demonstration to prospect's individual needs.

2. Balance telling and showing.

3. Cover one idea at a time.

4. Use showmanship if appropriate.

5. Involve prospect.

6. Use confirmation questions to check understanding.

Figure 11.2
Poorly conducted demonstrations usually result from a lack of strategic planning and preparation.

Many sales representatives recognize the limitations of the spoken word. When talking to prospects about the economic benefits of delivering training programs with a satellite system, a salesperson used a table (Table 11.1) to illustrate savings. With the aid of this table, prospects can visualize the economic benefits of the satellite delivery system compared with a competing system using high-bandwidth terrestrial lines.

Strategic selling today involves customizing a product demonstration to each customer's unique set of buying conditions.

Table 11.1	HOW MUCH CAN A SATELLITE SYSTEM SAVE YOU?			
TYPE OF SYSTEM	PER PERSON COST 20 SITES	PER PERSON COST 30 SITES	PER PERSON COST 40 SITES	PER PERSON COST 50 SITES
Satellite delivery system	$7.80	$7.20	$6.60	$6.00
High-bandwidth terrestrial lines	$7.10	$7.40	$7.70	$8.00

These cost estimates are based on current satellite broadcast rates and rates for use of terrestrial lines. The per person cost is based on an audience size of 25 trainees at each site.

In many selling situations the buyer does not make an immediate buying decision. The decision to buy may be made several days or weeks after the presentation. Therefore, retention of information is important.

When we rely on verbal messages alone to communicate, retention of information is minimal. A number of studies provide evidence to support this important point. Research conducted at Harvard and Columbia Universities found that retention increases from 14 to 38 percent when the spoken word is accompanied with effective visuals. In addition, the time needed to present a concept can be reduced by up to 40 percent with the use of appropriate visuals.[3]

Proof of Buyer Benefits

A well-planned and well-executed sales demonstration is one of the most convincing forms of proof. This is especially true if your product has dramatic points of superiority.

Salespeople representing Epson, Canon, Hewlett Packard, and other manufacturers can offer the customer a wide range of printers. What is the real difference between a $200 basic printer and a $700 laser printer? The laser equipment prints a neater and more attractive letter or report. The most effective way to provide proof of this buyer benefit is to show the customer material that has been printed on both printers. By letting the prospect compare the examples, the salesperson is converting product features to a buyer benefit. Be prepared to prove with tests, findings, and performance records every claim you make.

Feeling of Ownership

Many effective sales demonstrations give the prospect a temporary feeling of ownership. This pleasant feeling builds desire to own the product. Let us consider the person who enters a men's clothing store and tries on a Hart Shaffner and Marx suit. During the few moments the customer is wearing the suit a feeling of pride is apt to develop. If the suit fits well and looks good, desire to own it probably builds.

Successful automobile salespeople encourage prospects to go for a demonstration ride. The new car almost always seems superior to the buyer's older model. Without a demonstration ride, of course, the opportunity to build this desire would be lost.

Many firms offer prospects an opportunity to enjoy products on a trial basis. This is done to give people a chance to assess the merits of the product in their own home or business. Some firms that sell office equipment and office furniture use this sales strategy.

➤➤ *Building Relationships in a Diverse World*

DO YOU NEED A VOICE COACH?

African Americans, Hispanics, Asians, Native Americans, and recent immigrants to America often face special challenges in verbal communication. New arrivals may have a unique accent because the phonetic habits of the speaker's native language are carried over to the new language. Many people born and raised in America have a strong regional accent. Should this uniqueness be viewed as a problem? Kim Radford, vice president of marketing at Wachovia Trust Company, had to answer this question soon after graduating from college. He took a position as a stockbroker in Charleston, West Virginia. Radford, an African American, conducted most of his business on the telephone and seldom met clients face to face. Early on, someone said, "Kim, you need to get that black accent out of your voice if you're going to be successful in this business." Radford faced a real dilemma: He wanted to be successful, but he did not want to compromise his personal integrity. He talked to several people, black and white, and the advice he received boiled down to this guideline:

> Stay honest to yourself, but communicate and be understood. There's no need to clean up the fact that you sound black as long as you're articulate and your diction's good and people can understand you.

It is a fact of life that people in every community are certain that the way they talk is the "natural" way. So if you believe that your accent and dialect need to be changed, or you want to improve pronunciation, consider seeking help from a voice coach.[a]

Other Benefits

Most salespeople gain added self-confidence when they incorporate an effective demonstration into the sales presentation. This is especially true of new salespeople who have not polished their verbal sales story. It is reassuring to know that it is not necessary to rely completely on verbal skills.

PLANNING EFFECTIVE DEMONSTRATIONS

An effective sales demonstration is the result of both planning and practice. Planning gives the salesperson a chance to review all the important details that should be considered in advance of the actual demonstration. Practice (or rehearsal) provides an opportunity for a trial run to uncover areas that need additional polish. During the planning stage it helps to review a series of guidelines that have helped salespeople over the years to develop effective demonstrations.

Use Custom-Fitted Demonstrations

In nonmanipulative selling, each presentation is custom tailored because individual client problems and priorities are unique. In other words, every aspect of the sales presentation, including the demonstration, should relate to the needs or problems mutually identified by the prospect and the salesperson.

It is possible to develop a sales demonstration so structured and so mechanical that the prospect feels like a number. We must try to avoid what some veteran marketing

Bell's 18 member sales force, all of whom are licensed helicopter pilots, can introduce the Bell product line with a video presentation, and then follow up with a demonstration flight if necessary.

people refer to as the *depersonalization* of the selling/buying process. If the demonstration is overly structured, it cannot be personalized to meet specific customer wants and needs.

Bell Helicopter (www.bellhelicopter.com) sells a product with countless custom options, and each option changes its price and performance. One customer may want a helicopter for emergency medical care and another may want one for electronic news gathering. Bell's 18-member sales force, all of whom are licensed helicopter pilots, can introduce the Bell product line with a video presentation, and then follow up with a demonstration flight if necessary. Sales representatives also have access to a sales configuration system that supports the customization process. Price and performance data can be quickly determined for each accessory needed by the customer. The software automatically provides answers to the numerous questions that can surface during the sales presentation.[4]

Choose the Right Setting

The location of the sales demonstration can make a difference. Some companies routinely rent space at a hotel, motel, or conference center so that the demonstration can be conducted in a controlled environment free of noise and other interruptions.

TRACKING DOWN A SALE

Care Trak is a product designed to locate patients who suffer from the effects of brain injuries or Alzheimer's disease who may wander away from a care center and get lost. During a sales call at a New Jersey nursing home, a sales representative was explaining the benefits of Care Trak when a doubting staff member picked up the transmitter and asked the salesperson to wait 20 minutes and then try to find him. After a 20-minute wait, the salesperson began the search under the watchful eyes of the nursing home administrator and members of the nurs-ing staff. After tracking the staff member to a specific location, the locater signal became very strong in spite of the fact that they were stand-ing in the middle of an empty hallway. At that point the staff members began having doubts about the value of the equipment. Then the salesperson pointed the directional antenna straight up to the ceiling. He pushed aside a ceil-ing tile to reveal the nursing home employee in his hiding place. The nursing home placed an order for the product that day.[b]

A firm selling modern log homes frequently conducts an open house at the site of a newly completed house. Potential customers are invited by letter or personal contact to tour the home at appointed times. After touring the home, prospects view a 20-minute video that explains how the homes are constructed. Pictures of other homes built by the company also are shown.

Many salespeople visit the prospect's office and talk to the person across the desk. David Peoples, author of *Selling to the Top*, believes there is a better setting for the presen-tation. He suggests a one-on-one, stand-up presentation in a conference room that ensures privacy. This approach puts the customer on a pedestal and gives the person a feeling of being very special.[5]

Check Sales Tools

Be sure to check every item to be used in conjunction with the sales demonstration. If you are using audiovisual equipment, be certain that it is in good working condition. When using a projector, always carry an extension cord and a spare bulb. If you are selling real estate, the most critical aspect of preparing for the demonstration is becoming familiar with the property. Never show a home you have not seen.[6]

Cover One Idea at a Time

Pace the demonstration so that the customer does not become confused. Offer one idea at a time, and be sure the customer understands each point before moving on. This practice is especially important if the primary purpose of your sales presentation is to inform. When you neglect this practice, there is the danger that the customer's concentration may remain fixed on a previous point. Some demonstrations are ruined by a salesperson who moves too rapidly from one point to another. A good rule of thumb is to use a confirmation question to get agreement on each key point before moving on to the next. This approach makes closing easier because you have secured agreement on key points throughout the demon-stration. Make the customer a part of every step.

Appeal to All Senses

In conducting a sales demonstration it is a good idea to appeal to all appropriate senses. Each of the five senses—sight, hearing, smell, touch, and taste—represents an avenue by which the salesperson can attract the prospect's attention and build desire.

Although sight is considered the most powerful attention-attracting sense, it may not be the most important motivating force in every selling situation. When presenting a food product, the taste and aroma may be critical.

Gary Eberle, owner of Eberle Winery located in San Luis Obispo County, California, understands the importance of reaching the prospect through as many senses as possible. He spends several months each year selling his wines to retailers and restaurant owners. This hardworking entrepreneur says, "Ten months of the year I sell wine for a living, so I can play with my hobby for the other two months, which is making wine."[7] The sales presentation for a quality wine usually highlights four areas:

Consumer demand. The wine's sales potential is described in realistic terms.

Marketing strategies. Suggested ways to merchandise the wine are discussed.

Bouquet. The distinctive fragrance of the wine is introduced.

Taste. A sample of the wine is given to the prospect in a quality wineglass.

Note that a sales presentation featuring these appeals can reach the prospect through four of the five senses. Collectively, these appeals develop a strong motivating force. When you involve more than one sense, the sales presentation is more informative and more persuasive.

Comprehension and retention can be enhanced with visual images.

Balance Telling, Showing, and Involvement

Some of the most effective sales demonstrations combine telling, showing, and involvement of the prospect. To plan an effective demonstration, consider developing a demonstration worksheet. Simply divide a sheet of paper into three columns. Head the first column, "Feature to be demonstrated." Head the second column, "What I will say." Head the third column, "What I or the customer will do." List the major features you plan to demonstrate in proper sequence in the first column. In the second column, describe what you will say about the feature, converting the feature to a customer benefit. In the third column, describe what you (or the customer) will do at the time this benefit is discussed. A sample demonstration worksheet appears in Figure 11.3.

Prospects can be involved in many demonstrations. Two retail examples follow:

Furniture. To prove comfort or quality, have the buyer sit in a chair, lie on a mattress, or feel the highly polished finish of a coffee table.

Clothing. Have the customer try it on to highlight style, fit, and comfort features. This involvement is especially important in the sale of quality garments.

If it is not possible for the prospect to participate in the demonstration or handle the product, place sales literature, pictures, or brochures in the person's hands. After the sales call these items remind the prospect of not only who called but also why.

Some information age demonstrations involve the customer in some type of virtual reality. DaimlerChrysler AG is developing what it calls Virtual Vehicle, which uses virtual reality to let customers assess different combinations of colors, fabrics, and wheel designs on Mercedes-Benz (www.mbusa.com/models/index.html) cars. Holding a flat, color-touch screen, a customer can walk around a computer-generated image of a car and click on various options. Click on the seat and you can change the fabric at lightning speed. Click on the radio and you can alter the speaker configuration; you hear the sound immediately. Once all the decisions are made, the customer can get a binding delivery date straight from the factory.[8]

Demonstration Worksheet		
Feature to Be Demonstrated	**What I Will Say (Include Benefit)**	**What I or the Customer Will Do**
Special computer circuit board to accelerate drawing graphics on a color monitor screen.	"This monitor is large enough to display multiple windows. You can easily compare several graphics."	Have the customer bring up several windows using computer keyboard.
Meeting room setup at a hotel and conference center.	"This setup will provide three feet of elbow space for each participant. For long meetings, the added space provides more comfort."	Give the customer a tour of the room and invite her to sit in a chair at one of the conference tables.

Figure **11.3**

The demonstration worksheet enables the salesperson to strategically plan and then rehearse demonstrations that strengthen the presentation.

Presenting product features and buyer benefits in an interesting and appealing way requires some amount of creativity.

Develop Creative Demonstrations

Presenting product features and buyer benefits in an interesting and appealing way requires some amount of creativity. One study indicated that 90 percent of the salespeople who were surveyed agreed that creativity is critical in selling.[9] Creativity is needed to develop a sales demonstration that can gain attention and increase desire. The ability to come up with problem-solving answers or different ways of looking at situations is greatly valued in today's fast-changing business environment. Some of the creative skills we need to cultivate include capacity for divergent thinking, ability to break problem-solving habits (mental sets), persistence in problem solving, and willingness to take risks.[10] One way to

Source: Sales & Marketing Management, July 1998, p. 18.

The 5th Wave   By Rich Tennant

"GET READY, I THINK THEY'RE STARTING TO DRIFT."

develop a more creative approach to sales demonstrations is to ask "What if . . . ?" questions, and then to record your answers. This exercise is best done when you feel relaxed and rested. Relaxation enhances the creative process.[11]

Rehearse the Demonstration

While you are actually putting on the demonstration, you need to be concentrating on a variety of details. The movements you make and what you say and do should be so familiar to you that each response is nearly automatic. To achieve this level of skill, you need to rehearse the demonstration.

Rehearse both what you are going to say and what you are going to do. Merrie Spaeth, consultant and author of *Marketplace Communication*, says, ". . . if you don't rehearse, the best-conceived idea can go wrong."[12] Say the words aloud exactly as if the prospect were present. It is surprising how often a concept that seems quite clear as you think it over becomes hopelessly mixed up when you try to discuss it with a customer. Rehearsal is the best way to avoid this embarrassing situation. Whenever possible, have your presentation/demonstration videotaped before you give it. This is perhaps the best way to perfect what you say and do.

SALES TOOLS FOR EFFECTIVE DEMONSTRATIONS

Nearly every sales organization provides its staff with sales tools or proof devices of one kind or another. Many of these, when used correctly, augment the sales effort. If the company does not provide these items, the creative salesperson secures or develops sales tools independently. In addition to technology-based presentations, sales personnel can utilize a wide range of other selling aids. Creative sales people are continually developing new types of sales tools. The following section summarizes some of the most common tools used today.

Product Itself

Without a doubt the best-selling aid is often the product itself. As noted previously, Bell Helicopter uses an effective video to describe various products. However, some customers do not buy without a demonstration ride. In the growing market for ergonomic office chairs, ranging in price from $700 to $2,900, furniture makers know the best way to close the sale is to provide an opportunity for the customer to sit in the chair. With growing awareness of the hazards of poor sitting posture and bad ergonomics, more people are searching for a comfortable work chair.[13]

When demonstrating the actual product, be sure it is typical in terms of appearance and operation. Try to avoid a situation in which it becomes necessary to apologize for appearance, construction, or performance. Of course, you should be able to demonstrate the product skillfully.

Models

In some cases it is not practical to demonstrate the product itself because it is too big or immobile. It is easier to demonstrate a small-scale model or cross section of the original equipment. A working model, like the actual product, can give the prospect a clear picture of how a piece of equipment operates.

With the aid of modern technology it's possible to create a model in picture form. ClosetMaid (www.closetmaid.com), a manufacturer of ventilated wire for commercial closets and other storage products, uses desktop visualization software to create a three-dimensional presentation that allows customers to see exactly what the finished facility will look like. Sales representatives can print out a hard copy so the customer has a picture of the custom-designed model for future reference. With the aid of this visualization technology, ClosetMaid salespeople can modify closet layouts on screen and produce a detailed bill of materials for each project.[14]

Photos and Illustrations

The old proverb, "One picture is worth a thousand words," can be put into practical application by a creative salesperson. A great deal of information can be given to the prospect with the aid of photos and illustrations. Consider these creative uses of photos:

> The salespeople at Domain's home-furnishing stores know that people who shop for furniture usually visit several stores and compare products. Before potential customers leave the store, they are given a Polaroid snapshot of the furniture they are considering. The salesperson writes his name on the back of the photo.[15]

> Chris Roberts, area manager for Downing Displays, a manufacturer of trade show displays, says that the photo presentation book is the most important item he takes on a first sales call. He says, "Because what we sell is very visual, it's important for the client to *see* the displays."[16]

Some salespeople organize photographs in a presentation album or a portfolio. Either option provides the flexibility needed by salespeople.

Portfolio

A **portfolio** is a portable case or loose-leaf binder containing a wide variety of sales-supporting materials. The portfolio is used to add visual life to the sales message and to prove claims. A person who sells advertising might develop a portfolio including the following items:

> Successful advertisements used in conjunction with previous campaigns

> Selected illustrations that can be incorporated into advertisements

> A selection of testimonial letters

> One or more case histories of specific clients who have used the media with success

The portfolio has been used as a sales aid by people who sell interior design services, insurance, real estate, securities, and convention services. It is a flexible sales aid that can be revised at any time to meet the needs of each customer.

Reprints

Leading magazines and journals sometimes feature articles that directly or indirectly support the salesperson's product. A reprint of the article can be a forceful selling aid. It is also an inexpensive selling tool. Pharmaceutical and medical sales representatives often use reprints from journals that report on research in the field of medicine. A few years ago Closure Medical Corporation received approval to sell Dermabond (www.dermabond.com), a surgical glue used to close cuts. This innovative product received national attention when the prestigious *Journal of the American Medical Association* concluded that gluing a

Photos often can be used to clarify verbal messages.

wound could be just as effective as sewing it shut. Salespeople representing Dermabond used the article to help educate doctors on the product's merits and applications.[17]

In many cases prospects are far more impressed with the good points of your product if they are presented by a third party rather than you. A reprint from a respected journal can be very persuasive.

Graphs, Charts, and Test Results

Graphs and charts can be used to illustrate change of some variable such as payroll expense, fuel consumption, or return on investment. For example, a bar graph might be used to illustrate the increase in fuel costs over a 10-year period.

Although graphs are usually quite descriptive, the layperson may misunderstand them. It is best to interpret the graph for the prospect. Do not move too fast because the full impact of the message may be lost.

A variety of charts have been developed to be used in conjunction with the sales demonstration. One popular type of chart is the flip chart. It consists of illustrations or messages on individual sheets of paper. The salesperson can face the prospect while turning pages. A variety of illustrations and printed messages can be put on the various pages.

Test results from a reliable agency often can be convincing. This is especially true when the test results are published by a respected independent agency such as J. D. Powers and Associates.

Laptop Computers and Demonstration Software

As noted previously, a growing number of companies have started equipping salespeople with small, portable computers weighing only a few pounds. With the aid of these small computers a salesperson can compute financial options on the spot and close sales that might otherwise be lost. Salespeople using computers to send electronic messages or to get information from the corporate mainframe, spend less time in the office and more time on the road.

A growing number of salespeople are using portable computers in conjunction with sales presentations.

Thanks to modern computer technology it's possible to conduct impressive multiple, simultaneous product demonstrations without leaving your office. Let's assume you are presenting a new employee disability insurance plan to members of the DaimlerChrysler human resources staff. One key decision maker is based in Germany and the other in the United States. With the aid of Pixion PictureTalk software, or a similar product, you can use the Internet to conduct the demonstration for both persons in real time. Sales managers might use this same approach to train members of their sales team in remote offices.

Personal computers (PCs) have played an important role in increasing sales force productivity. Salespeople have instant access to customer data, so it is often easier to customize the sales presentation. Many salespeople report that PC-based presentations, using graphics software, are very effective. Today's PC can produce striking visuals and attractive printed material that can be given to the customer for future reference.

ENHANCING DEMONSTRATIONS WITH POWERPOINT

The PowerPoint software program from Microsoft is a popular presentation package that is included in the Microsoft Office Suite (www.microsoft.com/office/using.htm.) of software programs. PowerPoint is so common that many prospects find the standard presentation graphics very familiar. Salespeople who want their demonstration to look unique, and different from the competition, can create their own corporate template, animate their logo, or put video clips of their own company information into the PowerPoint presentation.[18] In the corner of the screen a video can be embedded, along with a picture of the salesperson, so that the electronic demonstration is more personalized. The help files that are available with PowerPoint, and with competing software such as LMSoft, offer salespeople many ways to enhance their demonstrations. Members of the 500-person

Presentation packages such as PowerPoint and Excel spreadsheets are available with the Microsoft Office Suite of software products.

Goodyear Tire and Rubber Company sales force can customize their PowerPoint presentations by using some of the 450 photo assets that can be obtained from the company intranet.[19]

CREATING ELECTRONIC SPREADSHEETS

For many years, salespeople have been using electronic spreadsheets to prepare sales proposals. The electronic spreadsheet is an excellent tool to organize the numbers involved in preparing quotes, such as quantities, costs, and prices. The electronic spreadsheet allows the user to answer "what if" questions about the effects of lowering costs or raising prices. Once the preparation work is finished, the electronic spreadsheet itself can be printed and used to serve as the proposal or to accompany the proposal.[20] The spreadsheet data can also be converted to a chart or graph that can enhance the proposal.

Many computers sold today include an electronic spreadsheet program. The leading electronic spreadsheet, Excel, is part of Microsoft's Office Suite of products. If you have access to Excel, or any other electronic spreadsheet software, you can explore the power of this tool for preparing proposals.

Audiovisual Technology

A large number of companies provide their salespeople with audiovisual aids such as videotapes, 35-mm slides, and computer-based presentations. There are several reasons audiovisual presentations have become more commonplace. First, there have been major

►► Building Quality Partnerships

Developing Professional Looking Printed Materials

The assistance needed to develop an attractive portfolio or bound paper presentation may be closer than you think. Major office products retailers such as Staples or Office Depot, and quick printers such as Kinko's, offer a variety of services needed by salespeople. They maintain a large inventory of presentation paper needed to make presentation materials attractive and professional looking. You can purchase high-quality plastic sheet protectors that can improve the effectiveness of your portfolio presentation. These service centers are equipped with the newest printers and copy machines, so quality materials can be prepared quickly.

advances in the development of hardware and software. The equipment is more reliable, more compact, and easier to operate.[21] Software is continuously improving. Many of today's videos, software packages, and transparencies feature professional actors, top-notch photography, and attractive graphics.

Many companies find that audiovisual presentations, although expensive to produce, can be a good investment. These presentations often reveal product uses, values, features, and benefits in an interesting manner that encourages the prospect to listen and ask questions. When GTE began selling its new digital Airfone system to various airlines, the sales staff used a multimedia program that included video, sound, animation, and other high-tech wizardry. The sales team needed a powerful visual presentation that would deliver a wealth of technical information in an entertaining manner.[22]

When an audiovisual presentation fails to live up to expectations, some companies find that salespeople are not using the materials correctly. Most salespeople are not audiovisual experts and need training. Next you are given some suggestions on how to use audiovisual presentations to achieve maximum impact.

1. Be sure the prospect knows the purpose of the presentation. Preview the material and describe a few highlights. Always try to build interest in advance of the audiovisual presentation.
2. Be prepared to stop the presentation to clarify a point or to allow the prospect to ask questions. Do not permit the audiovisual presentation to become a barrier to good two-way communication.
3. At the conclusion of the audiovisual presentation, review key points and allow the prospect an opportunity to ask questions.

Finally, realize that the audiovisual presentation cannot do the selling for you. Audiovisual technology provides support for the major points in your presentation. No matter how exotic the sales tool, you are still the central figure in the selling situation.

Bound Paper Presentations

Although many salespeople are using some type of presentation technology in conjunction with the sales demonstration, paper is still widely used. For many sales and marketing organizations, bound paper presentations continue to be the most popular medium.[23] With the aid of computer-generated graphics, it is easy to print attractive graphs, charts, and other proof information. Product guarantees and warranties are sometimes included in a bound paper presentation. Some marketers use guarantees and warranties to differentiate

their products from competing products. Customer testimonials represent another common element of bound paper presentations. A testimonial letter from a prominent satisfied customer provides persuasive evidence that the product has support in the industry. Proof letters describing tangible benefits of the product also can enhance credibility. Prospects like bound paper presentations because the document is readily available for future reference.

Summary

In selling, the prospect is moving from a known quantity (the money in hand or an obligation for future payment) to something of an unknown quantity (amount of satisfaction to be gained from the potential purchase). With most people this produces anxiety and insecurity. The professional salesperson reduces prospect anxiety and insecurity by supplying proof of product performance. The objective of the *demonstration* part of sales is to supply this proof.

People perceive impressions through the five senses. In the presentation the salesperson communicates verbally to the prospect primarily through the sense of sound. In the demonstration the salesperson broadens communication strategy to include as many of the other senses as possible. Generally, the more senses we appeal to, the more believable our sales appeal becomes.

In the demonstration the senses of sound and sight are combined when we tell the prospect about a product benefit and show the product, or a visual presentation of the product, at the same time. When we ask the prospect to personally operate the product or examine a sales tool, we simultaneously introduce a third sense—the sense of touch. If appropriate, the salesperson should appeal also to the senses of taste and smell.

Nearly every marketing-driven organization provides its salespeople with a variety of sales tools to use in the demonstration. A partial list of these tools includes the product itself, models, photos, reprints, *portfolios*, graphs, charts, test results, testimonials, case histories, audiovisual presentations, laptop computers, demonstration software, and bound paper presentations.

KEY TERMS

Demonstration   Portfolio

REVIEW QUESTIONS

1. List the benefits of using a sales demonstration during the presentation of a product or service.
2. What effect does showing (appealing to the sense of sight) have on retention when combined with an oral presentation?
3. Discuss the advantages of using the demonstration worksheet.
4. Explain why a salesperson should organize the sales presentation so that it appeals to as many of the five senses as possible.
5. List the guidelines to follow in planning an effective demonstration.
6. Develop a list of the sales tools that the salesperson should consider when planning a sales demonstration.
7. Describe the merits of a bound paper presentation. What can be done to strengthen the persuasive power of a bound paper presentation?
8. Explain how magazines and trade journals can be used to assist the salesperson in a persuasive sales presentation.
9. Explain why audiovisual presentations are becoming more popular as a means of support for sales demonstrations.
10. What are some of the common sales functions performed by small, laptop computers and demonstration software?

APPLICATION EXERCISES

1. In many selling situations it is difficult, if not impossible, to demonstrate the product itself. List means other than the product itself that can be used to demonstrate the product features and benefits.

2. Develop a list of sales tools you could use in a job interview situation. What tools could you use to demonstrate your skills and capabilities?

3. As noted in this chapter, demonstration software is becoming increasingly popular. Real estate salespeople are using this software to showcase homes to prospective buyers. Assume you are a salesperson for First Realty Better Homes and Gardens Real Estate, and you have a customer that wants a $250,000 to $300,000 home in the Des Moines' Suburb of Clive. Go to the www.firstrealtybhg.com web site and click on the "select a location" button. Next click on Des Moines and select the suburb "Clive". Input the data you have from your customer and request a search for homes in this category. From your search, select two homes and click on the "virtual tour" button. Examine the exterior and interior features of these two homes.

CASE PROBLEM

Jack Alber is a manufacturer's sales representative for the Mayflower Appliance Company. Jack recently graduated from college with a major in marketing and went to work for Mayflower shortly thereafter. Mayflower manufactures and markets a line of small home appliances. As a sales representative, Jack calls on wholesalers and retailers that distribute small electrical appliances. Recently, Mayflower introduced in limited test markets a new line of small food processors. The company selected the name Orkan Food Processor for its new product line. After careful analysis of consumer, retailer, and wholesaler reactions in the test markets, Mayflower made several product improvements. Mayflower planned a full-scale introduction of the improved Orkan food processor for autumn. The promotion was planned to coincide with the important gift-buying season from October to December.

To accomplish the sales goal of 1 million units during the first year, Mayflower began its distribution promotion in June. In a national sales meeting, all sales representatives, including Jack Alber, were introduced to the new product line. The sales representatives were informed that the sales promotion for the Orkan Food Processor would be the biggest in the company's history. The sales promotion program involved the following:

1. A million-dollar advertising campaign including the Oprah Winfrey Show
2. Sales banners and window stickers for retailers, to develop point-of-purchase promotions
3. A package that featured four-color printed pictures of the Orkan Food Processor and shelf signs
4. For each of the sales representatives a sales kit with these items: (a) the Orkan Food Processor itself; (b) the package; (c) the sales banners, newspaper advertising slicks, and catalog specification sheets; and (d) a notebook computer and CD-ROM presentation software

The CD-ROM presentation also contained a sales message from Mayflower's vice president of sales that outlined test market results, projected profit potential of the Orkan Food Processor, comments from consumers and retailers, and film clips of Oprah Winfrey making commercials for Orkan. The presentation was designed to be shown to retailers and wholesalers who were prospective dealers and distributors for the Orkan Food Processor.

This was the first time Jack had come into contact with CD-ROM technology. Jack was a persuasive communicator and felt his best presentation was based on one-to-one communication with the prospect. Jack felt reluctant about trying to integrate electronic media into his presentation, even though he felt it was well prepared. Jack thought that it would be awkward to carry in and set up, the equipment, and that he would lose the personal touch he had been so successful with in the past. As Jack flew home from the sales meeting, he decided he would try to introduce the new product line in his territory without using the CD-ROM presentation.

Questions

1. Based on Jack's strong personal selling skills, do you agree or disagree with his decision not to use the CD-ROM presentation. Why?

2. Describe how you would organize the presentation without the use of the media presentation. Indicate where you would use each of the sales tools.

3. Describe how you would organize the presentation with the use of the CD-ROM presentation.

4. Describe the benefits you would emphasize in selling the Orkan Food Processor to (a) the wholesaler, (b) the retailer, and (c) the ultimate consumer.

5. Describe the senses you could appeal to in demonstrating the Orkan Food Processor. Explain how you would make each of these appeals.

6. How could you involve the prospect in demonstrating the Orkan Food Processor?

CRM CASE STUDY

Custom Fitting the Demonstrations

Your SimNet Systems sales manager, Becky Kemley, has asked you to meet with her to discuss demonstrations. She wants you to tell her if any of your accounts need a demonstration and, if so, what type of demonstration.

Questions

1. Which two accounts need a demonstration of the speed and power capabilities of the recommended network?

2. Which account needs to be shown that the recommended network product configuration can meet the account's specifications?

3. Which account with many sites needs a demonstration of SimNet's ability to put together a complex solution?

4. Which account seeking a low price needs a testimonial of SimNet's value-added ability to help customers maximize the power of their network?

5. Which account needs a demonstration of SimNet's financial stability?

PARTNERSHIP SELLING: A ROLE PLAY/SIMULATION
(see Appendix 3, p. 406)

DEVELOPING A SALES PRESENTATION STRATEGY—
THE DEMONSTRATION

Read *sales memorandum 3* ("A" or "B" depending on the category you were assigned in sales call 1). In this role play your call objectives are to make a persuasive presentation, negotiate any customer concerns, and close and service the sale.

At this time you should complete item 1 of the presentation plan and prepare and price a product solution. This should include completing the sales proposal form. Also, you should obtain a three-ring binder with pockets in the front and back for the development of a portfolio presentation. In this binder you should prepare your presentation and demonstration, following the instructions in items 2a, 2b, 2c, and 2d under the presentation plan. The presentation and demonstration materials (use the product strategy materials, i.e., photos, price lists, menus, awards, etc., provided to you with employment memorandum 1) should be placed in the three-ring binder as a part of your portfolio presentation. Using PowerPoint software, you may want to produce computer generated presentation graphics to enhance your demonstrations. You should also consider using presentation paper and sheet protectors described on p. 256. You may want to select a person as your customer and rehearse the use of these materials.

CHAPTER 12

When you finish reading this chapter, you should be able to

1. Describe common types of buyer concerns

2. Outline general strategies for negotiating buyer concerns

3. Discuss specific methods of negotiating buyer concerns

4. Describe ways to deal effectively with buyers who are trained in negotiating

Negotiating Buyer Concerns

*T*he Stouffer Esmeralda Resort located in Palm Springs, California, is a world-class hotel that offers the guest almost every amenity except a view of the ocean. The resort is located in the desert. Business meeting planners, representing groups from 50 to 500 persons, frequently seek what is called a *water destination*, a meeting site near a lake or the ocean. Sherry Binger, sales manager at the Esmeralda Resort, has a ready response when customers raise concerns about a land-based location. She describes the exquisite swimming pools offered by the Esmeralda and the Oasis water park that can be used for water games. A wave machine is used at the water park to simulate ocean waves. She also describes the other recreation facilities that include a golf course, tennis courts, and a health spa. Of course, some types of buyer concerns are not communicated openly to Sherry and other members of the sales staff. She must often work hard to identify the resistance, clarify it, and then overcome it.[1]

NEGOTIATING BUYER CONCERNS AND PROBLEMS

Today, salespeople like Sherry Binger are more likely to anticipate buyer concerns and plan negotiating methods (Fig. 12.1). The person who makes the buying decision is not only better educated in most cases but also better prepared to make a decision.

Negotiation—Part of the Win–Win Relationship Strategy

Frank Acuff, negotiations trainer and author of *How to Negotiate Anything with Anyone, Anywhere around the Globe*, says, "Life is a negotiation."[2] Negotiating skills have application almost daily in our personal and professional lives.

Some of the traditional personal selling books discussed how we should "handle" buyer objections. The message communicated to the reader was that personal selling is a

The Six–Step Presentation Plan	
Step One: APPROACH	☑ Review Strategic/Consultative Selling Model. ☑ Initiate customer contact.
Step Two: PRESENTATION	☑ Determine prospect needs. ☑ Select product or service. ☑ Initiate sales presentation.
Step Three: DEMONSTRATION	☑ Decide what to demonstrate. ☑ Select selling tools. ☑ Initiate demonstration.
Step Four: NEGOTIATION	☐ Anticipate buyer concerns. ☐ Plan negotiating methods. ☐ Initiate double–win negotiations.
Step Five: CLOSE	☐ Plan appropriate closing methods. ☐ Recognize closing clues. ☐ Initiate closing methods.
Step Six: SERVICING THE SALE	☐ Suggestion selling. ☐ Follow through. ☐ Follow-up calls.
Service, retail, wholesale, and manufacturer selling.	

Figure 12.1
NEGOTIATING CUSTOMER CONCERNS AND PROBLEMS

"we versus they" process. Somebody wins, and somebody loses. The win–win solution, where both sides win, was not offered as an option.

Too often we were led to believe that buying problems or objections needed to be approached with some type of manipulation. Ron Willingham, author of *Integrity Selling*, notes the important difference between negotiation and manipulation:

> We don't view negotiation as manipulation. We don't see it as outtalking, outsmarting, or out-maneuvering people. We don't view it as combat or as an adversary relationship. Instead we view negotiating as a win–win activity—where seller and buyer sit down together and attempt to work out the best solution for both sides.[3]

In negotiations there are only two possible outcomes: win–win and lose–lose. The win–lose scenario is a deception. When the salesperson wins and the customer loses, it is a double loss. If the customer wins and the salesperson loses, it is also a double loss.[4] When the salesperson makes too many concessions and feels like a loser, service after the sale is likely to suffer. In fact, the salesperson may avoid dealing with the customer in the future. Win–win negotiations result in mutual respect, stronger relationships, and greater loyalty on the part of the salesperson and the customer.

What is **negotiation**? One definition is "working to reach an agreement that is mutually satisfactory to both buyer and seller." It involves building relationships instead of making one-time deals.[5] As we noted in Chapter 1, the salesperson increasingly serves as a

Negotiation is defined as "working to reach an agreement that is mutually satisfactory to both buyer and seller." It involves building relationships instead of making one-time deals.

consultant or resource and provides solutions to buyers' problems. The consultant seeks to establish and maintain long-term relationships with customers. The ability to negotiate problems or objections is a necessary skill for all salespeople who adopt the consultative approach to personal selling. Figure 12.2 outlines the steps a salesperson can take to anticipate and negotiate problems.

Figure 12.2
Today salespeople must be prepared to anticipate and negotiate buyer concerns and problems.

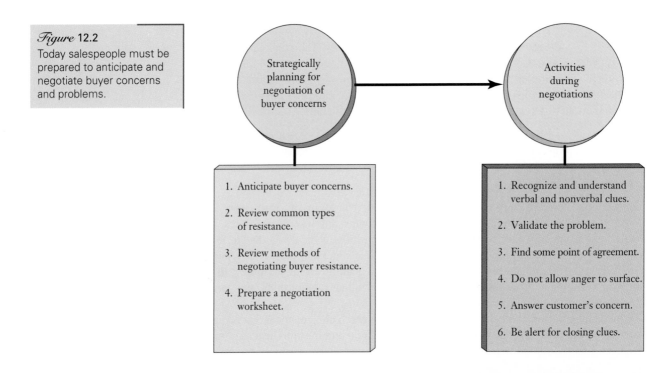

Strategically planning for negotiation of buyer concerns

1. Anticipate buyer concerns.

2. Review common types of resistance.

3. Review methods of negotiating buyer resistance.

4. Prepare a negotiation worksheet.

Activities during negotiations

1. Recognize and understand verbal and nonverbal clues.

2. Validate the problem.

3. Find some point of agreement.

4. Do not allow anger to surface.

5. Answer customer's concern.

6. Be alert for closing clues.

Negotiation Is a Process

It is important to keep in mind that negotiations often take place throughout the sales process—not just at the closing stage. Early negotiations may involve the meeting location, who will attend the sales presentation, or the amount of time available for the first meeting. Salespeople sometimes make early concessions to improve the relationship. This approach may set a costly precedent for later in the sale.[6] Some concessions can have a negative influence on the sales presentation. If, for example, you need 40 minutes for an effective product demonstration, do not agree to a 20-minute meeting.

Establishing a strategic alliance, described in Chapter 1 as the highest form of partnering, requires lengthy negotiations. These negotiations may extend over several months. Once the alliance is finalized, negotiations continue when concerns voiced by one party or the other surface.

COMMON TYPES OF BUYER CONCERNS

Salespeople learn that patterns of buyer resistance exist, and they therefore can anticipate that certain concerns may arise during the sales call. With this information it is possible to be better prepared for each meeting with a customer. The great majority of buyer concerns fall into five categories: need, product, source, price, and time.

Concerns Related to Need for the Product

If you have done your homework satisfactorily, then the prospect you call on probably has a need for your product or service. You still can expect, however, that the initial response may be, "I do not need your product." This might be a conditioned response that arises nearly every time the prospect meets with a sales representative. It also may be a cover-up for the real reason for not buying, which might be lack of funds, lack of time to examine your proposal carefully, or some other reason.

In some selling situations you can anticipate with great accuracy that concerns will surface. Take, for example, the person selling a new type of office telephone equipment. This equipment is very advanced and makes most existing equipment obsolete. Although the equipment offers the buyer many special features, resistance may still arise. Potential customers who already own reliable equipment are apt to say, "We are happy with our current system." Potential customers who own basic equipment may say, "We can get along well without this equipment." In both cases the salesperson has encountered indifference related to need.

Sincere need resistance is one of the great challenges that faces a salesperson. Think about it for a moment. Why would any customer want to purchase a product that does not seem to provide any real benefits? Unless we can create need awareness in the prospect's mind, there is no possible way to close the sale.

If you are calling on business prospects, the best way to overcome need resistance is to prove that your product is a good investment. Every privately owned business hopes to make a profit. Therefore, you must demonstrate how your product or service can contribute to that goal. Can your product increase sales volume? Can it reduce operating expenses? If the owner of a hardware store says, "I already carry a line of high-quality tools," point out how a second line of less expensive tools can appeal to another large segment of the buying public. With the addition of the new line the store can be in a better position to compete with other stores (discount merchandise stores and supermarkets) that sell inexpensive tools.

THE DESIRE TO BUY LOW IS QUITE COMMON. HOWEVER, WHEN BUYERS ARE FACED WITH INFORMATION OVERLOAD, THEIR DECISIONS BECOME MORE DIFFICULT. WHEN CONCERNS SURFACE, SALESPEOPLE NEED TO EXPLAIN THE BENEFITS THAT ADD VALUE AND USE SKILLFUL NEGOTIATIONS TO GAIN ACCEPTANCE OF THE SELLING PRICE. IF THE SELLING PRICE IS TOO LOW, PROFIT MARGINS MAY SUFFER.

Fast Company, December 1998.

In some selling situations you must help the prospect solve a problem before you have any chance of closing the sale. Suppose the prospect says, "I am already overstocked." If you call on wholesalers or retailers, expect to hear this objection quite frequently. Often the prospect is unwilling to buy additional merchandise until older stock is sold. If there is no demand for the older merchandise, then a real problem exists. In this situation your best bet is to offer the buyer one or more solutions to the problem. Some tactics are

1. Suggest that the prospect hold a special sale to dispose of the unsold merchandise. It even may be necessary to sell the stock at a loss to recover at least part of the original investment. Closeouts can be painful, but it may be the best option.
2. Ask the prospect to accept a trial offer on a guaranteed sale or consignment basis. This option allows the customer to acquire new merchandise without an initial cash investment and opens the door for your product.
3. If company policy permits, consider negotiating the purchase of the prospect's inventory. Give the customer a credit against a minimum opening order.

The key to negotiating buyer concerns in many cases is creative problem solving. Work closely with the prospect to overcome the barrier that prevents closing the sale.

Concerns about the Product

In some cases the product itself becomes the focal point of buyer resistance. When this happens, try to discover specific reasons why the prospect has doubts about your product. Often you may find that one of the following factors has influenced the buyer's attitude:

1. *The product is not well established.* This is a common buyer concern if you are selling a new or relatively new product. People do not like to take risks. They need plenty of assurance that the product is dependable. Use laboratory test results, third-party testimonials from satisfied users, or an effective demonstration to illustrate the product's strong points.
2. *The product will not be popular.* If the product is for resale, discuss sales results at other firms. Discuss the success other firms have had with your product. Also, dis-

cuss any efforts your company has taken to increase demand. For example, show the prospect sample advertisements that have appeared in the newspaper or commercials that have appeared on television.

3. *Friends or acquaintances did not like the product.* It is not easy to handle this buyer concern. After all, you cannot say, "Your friend is all wet—our product is the best on the market!" Move cautiously to acquire more information. Use questions to pinpoint the problem, and clarify any misinformation that the person may have concerning your product.

4. *The present product is satisfactory.* Change does not come easily to many people. Purchasing a new product may mean adopting new procedures or retraining employees. In the prospect's mind the advantages do not outweigh the disadvantages, so buyer resistance surfaces. To overcome this concern, we must build a greater amount of desire in the prospect's mind. Concentrate on superior benefits that give your product a major advantage over the existing product, or reconfigure the product to better meet the customer's needs.

Concerns Related to Source

One of the hardest problems for a salesperson to overcome is the source objection. This is especially true if prospects feel genuine loyalty to their present supplier. We should not be surprised to hear a prospect say, "I have been buying from the Ralston Company for years, and their people have always treated me right." After all, the Ralston Company sales staff has no doubt taken great care to develop close ties with this prospect.

When dealing with the loyalty problem, it is usually best to avoid direct criticism of the competing firm. Negative comments are apt to backfire because they damage your professional image. It is best to keep the sales presentation focused on the customer's problems and your solutions.

There are positive ways to cope with the loyalty objection. Some suggestions follow:

1. *Work harder to identify problems your company can solve with its products or services.* With the help of good questions, you may be able to understand the prospect's problems better than your competitors.[7]

2. *Point out that the business may profit from the addition of a second line.* You do not expect the person to drop the present supplier, but you do want the person to try your product.

3. *Point out the superior benefits of your product.* By doing this you hope the logic of your presentation can overcome the emotional ties that may exist between the prospect and the present supplier.

4. *Encourage the prospect to place a trial order, and then evaluate the merits of your product.* Again, you are not asking the person to quit the present supplier.

5. *Point out that the prospect's first obligation is to the business.* As owner or manager, the person should continually be searching for ways to maintain or increase profits.

6. *Try to stay visible and connected.* Every contact with the prospect is one more step in building a relationship. Anthony Tringale, owner of Insurance Consulting Group in Fairfax, Virginia, says that he is involved with many potential clients in social and charitable events.[8] One subtle way to keep in touch is with a newsletter.

Source concerns also can be directed toward your company. For reasons that may be difficult to uncover, the prospect simply may not want to do business with your firm. Try to get the person to be specific about problems with your company. You must deal decisively with perceptions that are not accurate.

➤➤ BUILDING QUALITY PARTNERSHIPS

APPLYING NEGOTIATION SKILLS IN THE JOB MARKET

Chester L. Karrass, creator of the Effective Negotiating seminar, says, "In business, you don't get what you deserve, you get what you negotiate." This is good advice for the job seeker. Most employers do not propose the highest wage possible at the beginning of the offer. If you want a higher starting wage, you must ask for it. Employers often have a predetermined range for each position and the highest salary is reserved for the applicant who brings something extra to the job. To prepare for a productive negotiation, you must know your own needs and you must know something about the worth of the position. Many employers tell you the salary range prior to the interview. The Internet can be a good source of salary information for certain types of jobs. In terms of your needs, try to determine what you care about the most: interesting work, future promotion, or flexible work schedule. If you are willing to negotiate, you can increase your pay by hundreds or even thousands of dollars. Be prepared to sell yourself, negotiate the salary you believe is appropriate, and achieve a win–win solution in the process.[a]

Concerns Related to Price

There are two important points to keep in mind concerning price resistance. It is one of the most *common* buyer concerns in the field of selling. Therefore, you must learn to negotiate skillfully in this problem area. The price objection also is one of the most common excuses. When people say, "Your price is too high," they probably mean, "You have not sold me yet." In the eyes of most customers, value is more important than price.

Although price may not be the real barrier to closing the sale, do not overlook its importance. It is a major concern for many people. The professional buyer has no other choice than to search for the best possible buy. The typical prospect also is value conscious. It is important to keep in mind that in almost every selling situation getting the order depends on the right combination of price and quality.[9]

COPING WITH BUYERS WHO ARE TRAINED IN NEGOTIATION

In recent years, we have seen an increase in the number of training programs developed for professional buyers. One such course is Fundamentals of Purchasing for the Newly Appointed Buyer, offered by the American Management Association. Enrollees learn how to negotiate with salespeople. Some salespeople also are returning to the classroom to learn negotiation skills. Acclivus Corporation (www.acclivus.com), a Dallas-based training company, offers the Acclivus Sales Negotiation System for salespeople who work in the business-to-business selling arena. Karrass Limited (www.karrass.com) offers the Effective Negotiating seminar.

Professional buyers often learn to use specific tactics in dealing with salespeople. Homer Smith, author of *Selling through Negotiation*, provides these examples.

Budget Limitation Tactic[10]   The buyer may say, "We like your proposal, but our budget for the convention is only $8,500." Is the buyer telling the truth, or is the person testing your price? The best approach in this instance is to take the budget limitation seriously and use appropriate negotiation strategies. One strategy is to reduce the price by eliminating some items. In the case of a fleet truck sale the salesperson might say, "We can deliver the trucks without radios and thus meet your budget figure. Would you be willing to purchase trucks without radios?"

Take-It-or-Leave-It Tactic[11] How do you respond to a buyer who says, "My final offer is $3,300, take it or leave it"? A price concession is, of course, one option. However, this is likely to reduce profits for the company and lower your commission. An alternative strategy is to confidently review the superior benefits of your product and make another closing attempt. Appealing to the other person's sense of fairness also may move the discussion forward. If the final offer is totally without merit, consider calling a halt to the negotiation to allow the other party to back down from his position without losing face.[12]

Let-Us-Split-the-Difference Tactic[13] In some cases the salesperson may find this price concession acceptable. If the buyer's suggestion is not acceptable, then the salesperson might make a counteroffer.

These tactics represent only a sample of those used by professional buyers. To prepare for these and other tactics, salespeople need to plan their negotiating strategies in advance and have clear goals. To avoid falling prey to negotiating tricks, study all relevant information related to the sale and decide in advance on the terms you can (and cannot) accept.[14]

NEGOTIATING PRICE WITH A LOW-PRICE STRATEGY

As noted in Chapter 6, some marketers have positioned their products with a price strategy. The goal is to earn a small profit margin on a large sales volume. Many of these companies have empowered their salespeople to use various low-price strategies such as quantity discounts, trade discounts, seasonal discounts, and promotional discounts. Some salespeople are given permission to match the price of any competitor. As noted in Chapter 6, one of the consequences of using low-price tactics may be lower commissions and lower profits.

HOW TO DEAL WITH PRICE CONCERNS

As we have noted, price resistance is common, so we must prepare for it. There are some important "do's and don'ts" to keep in mind when the price concern surfaces.

Do Add Value with a Cluster of Satisfactions As noted in Chapter 6, a growing number of customers are seeking a cluster of satisfactions that includes a good product, a salesperson who is truly a partner, and a company that stands behind its products (see Fig. 6.1). Many business firms are at a competitive disadvantage when the price alone is considered. When you look beyond price, however, it may become obvious that your company offers more value for the dollar.

Stephen Smith, senior account manager for Bell Atlantic, says that price is like the tip of the iceberg—it is often the only feature the customer sees. Salespeople need to direct the customer's attention to the value-added features that make up the bulk of the iceberg that is below the surface (Figure 12.3).[15] Do not forget to sell yourself as a high-value element of the sales proposal. Emphasize your commitment to customer service after the sale.

Do Not Make Price the Focal Point of Your Sales Presentation You may need to discuss price, but do not bring it up too early. The best time to deal with price is after you have reviewed product features and discussed buyer benefits. Unfortunately, many salespeople volunteer a price reduction without being asked. In most cases, this happens because the salesperson does not fully understand the benefits that add value to his product.[16]

You increase the chances for a win–win outcome by increasing the number of issues you can resolve. If you negotiate price along with delivery date, support services, or volume purchases, you increase the opportunities for a trade-off so you and the customer both win something of value.[17]

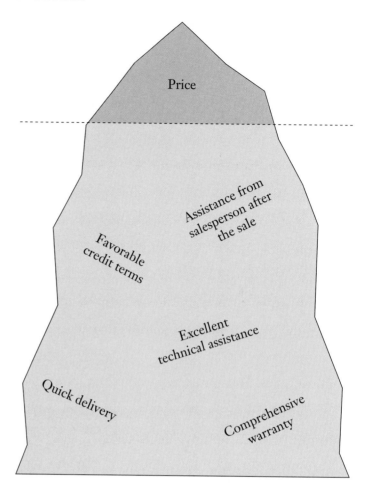

Do Not Apologize for the Price   When you do mention price, do so in a confident and straightforward manner. Do not have even a hint of apology in your voice. Convey to the prospect that you believe your price is fair and make every effort to relate price to value. Many people fear paying too much for a product or service. If your company has adopted a value-added strategy, point this fact out to the prospect. Then discuss how you and your company add value.

Do Point Out the Relationship between Price and Quality   In our highly competitive, free enterprise economy there are forces at work that tend to promote fair pricing. The highest quality can never be obtained at the lowest price. Quality comes from that Latin word *qualitas*, meaning, "What is the worth?" When you sell quality, price is more likely to be secondary in the prospect's mind. Always point out the value-added features that create the difference in price. Keep in mind that cheap products are built down to a price rather than up to a standard.[18] If you believe in your product and understand its unique features, price concerns do not bother you.

Do Explain the Difference between Price and Cost   Price represents the initial amount the buyer pays for the product. Cost represents the amount the buyer pays for a product as it is used over a period of time. The price–cost comparison is particularly relevant with a product or service that lasts a long time or is particularly reliable. If one product requires servicing once a year, and a lower priced competing product requires servicing three times a year, the extra service calls must be part of the price–cost equation. In this case the product with the lower initial cost may *cost* more because of the two extra service calls.[19]

> It's unwise to pay too much. But it's worse to pay too little.
>
> When you pay too much, you lose a little money, that is all.
>
> When you pay too little you sometimes lose everything, because the thing you bought was incapable of doing the thing it was bought to do.
>
> The common law of business balances prohibits paying a little and getting a lot. It can't be done.
>
> If you deal with the lowest bidder, it is well to add something for the risk you run.
>
> *John Ruskin*

Do Not Make Concessions too Quickly Give away concessions methodically and reluctantly, and always try to get something in return. A concession given too freely can diminish the value of your product. Also, giving a concession too easily may send the signal you are negotiating from a position of weakness.[20]

When the pressure to make price concessions builds, consider unbundling product features in order to achieve a more competitive price. As we have noted in previous chapters, many transactional buyers are primarily interested in price and convenience, so consider eliminating features that contribute to a higher selling price. If the buyer is only interested in the lowest possible price, and you represent a marketer committed to a value added sales strategy, consider withdrawing from negotiations.

Concerns Related to Time

If a prospect says, "I want time to think it over," you may be encountering concerns related to time. Resistance related to time is often referred to as the **stall**. D. Forbes Ley, author of *The Best Seller*, states that a stall signals conflict. He says, "The conflict is the agony of indecision between the desire to have your product versus feelings of uncertainty and anxiety."[21] A stall usually means the customer does not yet perceive the benefits of buying now. In most cases the stall indicates that the prospect has both positive and negative feelings about your product. Consider using questions to determine the negative feelings: "Is it my company that concerns you?" "Do you have any concerns about our warranty program?" "Does anyone else need to approve this purchase?"

It is all right to be persuasive if the prospect can truly benefit from buying now. If the price may soon rise, or if the item may not be available in the future, then you should provide this information. You must, however, present this information sincerely and accurately. It is never proper to distort the truth in the hope of getting the order.

Randall Murphy, President of Acclivus Corporation, explains the steps in a successful negotiation to a group of salespeople enrolled in his popular sales negotiation seminar. Courtesy Acclivus Corporation.

Table 12.1

Objections are often requests for more information to justify the buying decision. Objections can tell us a lot about the real source of hesitation and what type of information the customer is seeking.

OBJECTION	SOURCE OF HESITATION	REQUEST FOR . . .
"Price too high"	Perceived cost versus benefit	Value articulation
"Think about it"	Afraid to make a bad decision	Create comfort, provide proof
"Talk to boss"	Unable to justify decision	Risk reduction, benefit review
"Need more quotes"	Unsure you're their best option	Targeted solutions, value
"Set with current provider"	Doesn't see benefit of change	Differentiation
"Bad history"	Past experience is affecting current view	Offer proof of change

Adapted from "Hide-and-Seek," a table from Nancy J. Stephens, "Objections Are a 'Yes' About to Happen," *Selling* November 1998, p. 3.

GENERAL STRATEGIES FOR NEGOTIATING BUYER CONCERNS

The successful negotiation of buyer concerns is based in large part on understanding human behavior. This knowledge, coupled with a good measure of common sense, helps us overcome most buyer concerns. It is also helpful to be aware of general methods for negotiating buyer resistance.

Anticipate Buyer Concerns

Many salespeople such as Sherry Binger, at the Stouffer Esmeralda Resort, have learned to anticipate certain problems and forestall them with a well-planned and well-executed presentation. Although buyer concerns are by no means insurmountable, it is a good idea to take preventative measures whenever possible. By anticipating problems we can approach the prospect with greater confidence and often save valuable time.

Know the Value of What You Are Offering

It is important that we know what is of real value to the customer, and not consider value only in terms of purchase price. The real value of what you are offering may be a value-added intangible such as superior product knowledge, good credit terms, or prompt delivery. An important aspect of the negotiation process is discovering what is of utmost importance to the buyer. The focus of personal selling today should be the mutual search for value. This process is called **added-value negotiating** because it seeks to add more value to any sale so both the salesperson and the customer feel comfortable.[22] Some salespeople make the mistake of offering a lower price the moment buyer concerns surface. In the customer's mind, price may be of secondary importance compared with the quality of service after the sale. As noted previously, do not be in a hurry to make price concessions.

Many salespeople have learned to anticipate certain problems and forestall them with a well-planned and well-executed presentation.

Prepare for Negotiations

It helps to classify possible resistance with the aid of a negotiations worksheet. To illustrate how this form works, let us review an example from the food industry. Mary Turner is a salesperson for Durkee Famous Foods. She represents more than 350 products. Mary calls on supermarkets daily and offers assistance in the areas of ordering and merchandising. Recently, her company decided to offer retail food stores an allowance of $1 per case of olives if the store purchased 15 or more cases. Prior to talking with her customers about this offer, Mary sat down and developed a negotiations worksheet, shown in Fig. 12.4. We cannot anticipate every possible problem, but it is possible to identify the most common problems that are likely to arise. The negotiations worksheet can be a useful tool.

Understand the Problem

We already have noted that the prospect occasionally misunderstands the salesperson. It is just as easy for the salesperson to misunderstand the prospect. Therefore, an important step in dealing with a problem is to make sure you understand it. Be certain that both you and the prospect are clear on the true nature of what needs to be negotiated. When the prospect begins talking, listen carefully without interrupting, even when you think you know what the prospect is going to say. It is only common courtesy to give people the opportunity to express their point of view. With probing questions, you can fine-tune your understanding of the problem.

Create Alternative Solutions

When the prospect finishes talking, it is a good practice to validate the problem, using a confirmation question. This helps to isolate the true problem and reduce the chance of misunderstanding. The confirmation question might sound like this: "I think I understand your

| Negotiations Worksheet | | |
Customer's concern	Type of concern	Possible response
"Fifteen cases of olives will take up valuable space in my receiving room. It is already crowded."	Need	**Combination Direct denial/Superior benefit** "You will not have to face that problem. With the aid of our merchandising plan you can display 10 cases immediately on the sales floor. Only five cases will become reserve stock. You should move all 15 cases in about two weeks."
"This is a poor time of the year to buy a large order of olives. People are not buying olives at this time."	Time	**Combination Indirect denial/Third party testimony** "I agree that it has been a problem in the past, but consumer attitudes seem to be changing. We have found that olives sell well all year long if displayed properly. More people are using olives in the preparation of omelets, pizza, and other dishes. Of course, most relish trays feature olives. We will supply you with point-of-purchase material that provides kitchen-tested ways to use this high-profit item."
"I have to stay within my budget."	Price	**Superior benefit** "As you know, olives represent a high-profit item. The average margin is 26 percent. With the addition of our $1.00 per case allowance the margin will rise to about 30 percent. This order will give you a good return on your investment."
"I am very satisfied with my present supplier."	Source	**Combination question/Trial order** "What can I do to get you to take just a trial order?"

Figure 12.4

Before the presentation it is important to prepare a negotiations worksheet.

concern. You feel the warranty does not provide you with sufficient protection. Is this correct?" By taking time to ask this question you accomplish two important objectives. First, you are giving personal attention to the problem, which pleases the customer. Second, you gain time to think about the best possible response.

The best possible response is very often an alternative solution. Many of today's customers do not want to hear that there is only one way or a single solution. In the age of information, people have less time to manage their work and their lives, so they expect new levels of flexibility. In the area of computers, Gateway, Dell, Compaq, and several other companies were quick to respond to this trend. Some of today's most successful companies recognize that customers expect options.[23]

Find Some Point of Agreement

Negotiating buying problems is a little like the art of diplomacy. It helps to know what points of agreement exist. This saves time and helps establish a closer bond between you and the prospect. At some point during the presentation, you might summarize by using a confirmation question: "Let us see if I fully understand your position. You think our product is well constructed and will provide the reliability you are looking for. Also, you believe our price is fair. Am I correct on these two points?"

Once all the areas of agreement have been identified, there may be surprisingly few points of disagreement. The prospect suddenly sees that the advantages of ownership far outweigh the disadvantages. Now that the air is cleared, both the salesperson and the customer can give their full attention to any remaining points of disagreement.

Do Not Destroy Your Relationship Strategy with Anger

In most situations the relationship between the salesperson and the prospect contains the seeds of conflict and disagreement. Negotiations can get emotional. Conflict can arise when the salesperson and prospect fail to agree on need, price, credit terms, or other factors. When the customer becomes impatient or angry, the salesperson must be careful not to fuel this emotion. Most people's natural response when under attack is to defend themselves or to counterattack. Both of these tactics usually fuel an upward spiral of heated disagreement.[24] If you want to earn the customer's trust and respect, avoid becoming defensive and argumentative. Ask questions and keep the customer talking so you learn more about the true nature of the problem. Also, listen to what the customer is saying. Listening without defending helps to defuse any anger.[25]

➤➤ *Building Relationships in a Diverse World*

NEGOTIATING ACROSS CULTURES

Negotiations in the international area vary from one country to another because of cultural differences. German buyers are more apt to look you in the eye and tell you what they do not like about your product. Japanese buyers, on the other hand, do not want to embarrass you and therefore bury their concerns beneath several layers of courtesy. In China, now the largest market in the world for American products, negotiations are more straightforward. People who have been doing business in China for many years suggest a very direct approach to negotiations. However, do not become antagonistic. Do get involved in native business rituals that are intended to create a friendly atmosphere.

When we enter into negotiations in foreign countries, it is important to understand and accommodate the customer's culture. You may not get every detail exactly right, but you win respect by trying. In most cases you don't have the luxury of making mistakes and learning from experience. Seek advice from someone who has firsthand experience with the culture.

Selling in certain cultures often requires more time in bonding and building rapport. Several meetings may be needed to lay the groundwork for the actual sale.

In some cultures no may not mean no and yes may not mean yes. Take time to validate your understanding so that you know exactly what has been accepted or rejected.[b]

SPECIFIC METHODS OF NEGOTIATING BUYER CONCERNS

There are seven specific methods of negotiating buyer concerns. In analyzing each problem we should try to determine which method can be most effective. In most cases we can use a combination of the following methods to negotiate buyer concerns.

Direct Denial

Direct denial involves refuting the opinion or belief of a prospect. The direct denial of a problem is considered a high-risk method of negotiating buyer concerns. Therefore, you should use it with care. People do not like to be told they are wrong. Even when the facts prove the prospect is wrong, resentment can build if we fail to handle the situation properly.

When a prospect offers buyer resistance that is not valid, we sometimes have no option other than to openly disagree. If the person is misinformed, we must provide accurate information. For example, if the customer questions the product's quality, meet the concern head-on with whatever proof seems appropriate. It is almost never proper to ignore misinformation. High-performance salespeople counter inaccurate responses from the prospect promptly and directly.

The manner in which you state the denial is of major importance. Use a win–win approach. Be firm and sincere in stating your beliefs, but do not be offensive. Above all, do not patronize the prospect. A "know-it-all" attitude can be irritating.

Indirect Denial

Sometimes the prospect's concern is completely valid, or at least accurate to a large degree. This method is referred to as the **indirect denial**. The best approach is to bend a little and acknowledge that the prospect is at least partially correct. After all, if you offered a product that is objection proof, you would likely have no competitors. Every product has a shortcoming or limitation.[26] The success of this method is based in part on the need most people have to feel that their views are worthwhile. For this reason the indirect denial method is the most widely used. An exchange that features the use of this approach follows. The salesperson is a key account sales representative for Pacific Bell Directory.[27]

Salesperson: The total cost of placing your six- by eight-inch ad in the yellow pages of five different Pacific Bell directories is $32,000.

Prospect: As a builder I want to reach people who are planning to build a home. I am afraid my ad will be lost among the hundreds of ads featured in your directories.

Salesperson: Yes, I agree the yellow pages in our directories do feature hundreds of ads, but the section for general contractors features less than 30 ads. Our design staff can prepare an ad that can be highly visible and can set your company apart from ads placed by other contractors.

Note that the salesperson used the words, "Yes, I agree . . ." to reduce the impact of denial. The prospect is less likely to feel her point of view has been totally disproved.

FEEL–FELT–FOUND

Successful salespeople are sensitive to clues that indicate the client feels something is wrong. One way to empathize with the client's concerns is to use the "feel–felt–found" strategy. Here is how it works. Assume the customer is concerned about the complexity of the microcomputer, and says, "I do not think I can ever learn how to operate that thing."

Your response might be, "I understand how you *feel*, Mr. Pearson. Many of my customers *felt* the same way, until they started using the PC-120 and *found* it quite easy to master."[28]

Questions

Another effective way to negotiate buyer resistance is to convert the problem into a question. Let us say that a prospect wants to trade used office equipment for new equipment but objects to the low trade-in allowance. The salesperson responds in this way: "Do you agree that our trade-in allowance, which is slightly lower than what you expected, will be more than offset by the extra service and dependability of our company?"

Suppose a prospect interested in purchasing four new tires objects to the price, which is about $20 higher per set than the price of a competing firm. The salesperson uses a question to minimize the price difference: "Do you agree that the convenience of our nationwide dealer network more than offsets the small price difference?" In this example the question is designed to encourage the tire buyer to weigh the disadvantage of a slightly higher price against the advantage of a national system of dealers who can provide convenient service. Questions often motivate the prospect to think in more depth about the salesperson's offer. Prior to a sales presentation, make a list of the concerns you expect to hear from the prospect, and next to each one list the questions you can use to minimize it.

Superior Benefit

Sometimes the customer raises a problem that cannot be answered with a denial. For example: "Your copy machine does not feature an automatic document feed mechanism. This means that our employees will have to spend more time at the machine." You should acknowledge the valid objection and then discuss one or more superior benefits: "We have not included the automatic feature because it is less reliable than the manual approach. As you know, downtime is not only costly but also inconvenient." A **superior benefit** is a benefit that in most cases outweighs the customer's specific concern.

The product demonstration is one of the most convincing ways to overcome buyer concerns.

►► CUSTOMER RELATIONSHIP MANAGEMENT WITH TECHNOLOGY

AUTOMATED SORTING AND PRODUCTIVITY

The notes of a busy salesperson soon can become extensive. Paper notes make it difficult, if not impossible, to cross-reference important information within those notes. The notes in a customer relationship management (CRM) system gives salespeople immediate access to records containing needed words or phrases. This offers users many advantages, including a method of quickly finding information about buyers with similar interests or concerns. (See the exercise, Finding Keywords in a CRM Database, at p. 281 for more information.)

Demonstration

If you are familiar with your product as well as that of your competition, this method of negotiating buyer resistance is easy to use. You know the competitive advantages of your product and can discuss these features with confidence.

The product demonstration is one of the most convincing ways to overcome buyer skepticism. With the aid of an effective demonstration you can overcome specific concerns.

Sometimes a second demonstration is needed to overcome buyer skepticism. This demonstration can provide additional proof. High-achieving sales personnel know when and how to use proof to overcome buyer resistance.

Trial Offer

A **trial offer** involves giving the prospect an opportunity to try the product without making a purchase commitment. The trial offer (especially with new products) is popular with customers because they can get fully acquainted with your product without making a major commitment. Assume that a buyer for a large restaurant chain says, "I am sure you have a good cooking oil, but we are happy with our present brand. We have had no complaints from our managers." In response to this comment you might say, "I can understand your reluctance to try our product. However, I do believe our oil is the finest on the market. With your permission I would like to ship you 30 gallons of our oil at no cost. You can use our product at selected restaurants and evaluate the results. If our oil does not provide you with superior results, you are under no obligation to place an order."

In the case of office equipment the customer may be given the opportunity to use the product on a trial basis. An office manager might respond to the salesperson who sells dictation equipment in this manner: "I would not feel comfortable talking to a machine." In response to this issue a salesperson might say, "I can understand how you feel. How about using one of our demonstration models for a few days?"

Third-Party Testimony

Studies indicate that the favorable testimony of a neutral third party can be an effective method of responding to buyer resistance. Let us assume that the owner of a small business states that he can get along without a personal computer. The salesperson might respond in this manner: "Many small business owners think the way you do. However, once they use a personal computer (PC), they find it to be an invaluable aid. Mark Williams, owner of

Williams Hardware, says that his PC saves him several hours a week. Plus, he has improved the accuracy of his record keeping." Third-party testimony provides a positive way to solve certain types of buying problems. The positive experiences of a neutral third party almost never trigger an argument with the prospect.

COMBINATION METHODS

As noted previously, consultative selling is characterized by flexibility. A combination of methods sometimes proves to be the best way to deal with buyer resistance. For example, an indirect denial might be followed by a question: "The cost of our business security system is a little higher than the competition. The price I have quoted reflects the high-quality materials used to develop our system. Wouldn't you feel better entrusting your security needs to a firm with more than 25 years of experience in the business security field?" In this situation the salesperson also might consider combining the indirect denial with an offer to arrange a demonstration of the security system.

Summary

Sales resistance is natural and should be welcomed as an opportunity to learn more about how to satisfy the prospect's needs. Buyers' concerns often provide salespeople with precisely the information they need to close a sale.

Concerns may arise from a variety of reasons, some related to the content or manner of the presentation strategy and others related to the prospect's own concerns. Whatever the reasons, the salesperson should *negotiate* sales resistance with the proper attitude, never making too much or too little of the prospect's concerns.

General strategies for negotiating buyer concerns include anticipating it, knowing the value of what you are offering, preparing for negotiations, understanding the problem, creating alternate solutions, finding some point of agreement, and avoiding anger.

The best strategy for negotiating sales resistance is to anticipate it and preplan methods to answer the prospect's concerns. If a salesperson uses a negotiations worksheet, then it can be much easier to deal with buyer concerns.

We discuss the various types of problems likely to surface during the sales presentation. Most objections can be placed in one of five categories: need, product, source, price, and time.

Specific methods and combinations of methods of negotiating resistance vary depending on the particular combination of salesperson, product, and prospect. We have described several common methods, but you should remember that practice in applying them is essential and that there is room for a great deal of creative imagination in developing variations or additional methods. With careful preparation and practice, negotiating the most common types of buyer concerns should become a stimulating challenge to each salesperson's professional growth.

KEY TERMS

Negotiation

Stall

Added-Value Negotiating

Direct Denial

Indirect Denial

Superior Benefit

Trial Offer

Review Questions

1. Explain why a salesperson should welcome buyer concerns.

2. List the common types of buyer resistance that might surface in a presentation.

3. How does the negotiations worksheet form help the salesperson prepare to negotiate buyer concerns?

4. Explain the value of using a confirmation question as a general strategy for negotiating buyer concerns.

5. List seven general strategies for negotiating buyer resistance.

6. John Ruskin (see p. 271) says that it is unwise to pay too much when making a purchase, but it is worse to pay too little. Do you agree or disagree with this statement? Explain.

7. What is usually the most common reason prospects give for not buying? How can salespeople deal effectively with this type of concern?

8. Professional buyers often learn to use specific negotiation tactics in dealing with salespeople. List and describe two tactics that are commonly used today.

9. When a customer says, "I want time to think it over," what type of resistance is the salesperson encountering? Suggest ways to overcome this type of buyer concern.

10. What are some positive ways to cope with the loyalty objection?

Application Exercises

1. During an interview with a prospective employer the interviewer raises the objection that you are not qualified for the job for which you are applying. On the basis of your observation you do not believe the interviewer fully understands the amount of experience you have or that you really have the ability to perform the job requirements. Write how you would overcome the objection the interviewer has raised.

2. Your negotiation of sales resistance can be compared in part with how you manage interpersonal conflicts. In learning how to deal with conflicts constructively the first step is to become aware of your present and past style of managing conflict. Think back over the interpersonal conflicts you may have been involved in during the past few years. These conflicts may be with customers, friends, parents, spouse, teachers, boss, or subordinates. In the space provided, list the five major conflicts you can remember and how you resolved them.

CONFLICT	RESOLUTION OF CONFLICT
1.	
2.	
3.	
4.	
5.	

Analyze your basic style of conflict management from these five examples. Do you tend to back away from conflicts (the "flight method" of conflict resolution), or do you look for conflict and stand your ground no matter what happens (the "fight method" of conflict resolution)? Would salespeople who have a flight style of handling objections close many sales? How about the salesperson who has a fight style? Which style would the salesperson who always used the direct denial method of negotiating tend to possess—flight or fight? Is the indirect denial a fight, a flight, or a somewhere in between style? Explain.

3. Assume you have decided to sell your own home. During an open house a prospect, whom you are showing through the house, begins to criticize every major selling point about your home.

a. You have taken excellent care of your home, believe it to be a good home, and have done a lot of special projects to make it more enjoyable. What will be your emotional reaction to this prospect's criticisms? Should you express this emotional reaction?

b. Underneath this surface criticism you think this prospect is really interested in buying your home. How would you negotiate the sales resistance she is showing?

4. Acclivus Corporation (www.acclivus.com) is a leading supplier of sales training programs. As noted in this chapter, one of their most popular programs is the Acclivus Sales Negotiation System. Access the Acclivus home page on the Internet, and click on the "capabilities" link. Study the information on the Negotiation training program. Also, click on the Advertising screen and study the Acclivus "R3evolution" concept. What is this concept? Click on the "Success Stories" screen and examine what organizations say about the negotiation training they have received.

CRM APPLICATION EXERCISE

Finding Keywords in a CRM Database

During sales training this week, your sales manager, Becky Kemley, led a discussion about negotiating buyer resistance and managing objections. The discussion included methods of identifying and responding to price concerns. You wish to find those contacts who might have a price objection so that you can better prepare for working with them. Using the ACT! software, access all records containing the word "price" by selecting Lookup, Keyword, type "price," and check Notes; and then press Enter. After searching, ACT! displays three records in which price is an issue. Print contact reports for these three records by selecting Report, Contact Report, Active Lookup, Printer, and OK.

CASE PROBLEM

Each year public and private organizations send thousands of employees to meetings held at hotels, motels, convention centers, conference centers, and resorts. These meetings represent a multimillion dollar business in the United States. Some of the largest providers of meeting space and related services are catering to clients in new and exciting ways. The Stouffer Esmeralda Resort hotel (introduced at the beginning of this chapter) provides a good example of such a destination. The goal of this hotel is to provide guests with an experience they can talk about the rest of their lives. The hotel offers 560 deluxe guest rooms, several suites, soundproof meeting rooms with state-of-the-art audiovisual technology, and continuous break service that can accommodate any agenda. Lavish customized meal events are a specialty of the Esmeralda Resort. Guests enjoy use of a championship golf course; tennis courts; swimming pools; and a fitness center complete with whirlpools, saunas, weight room, and aerobic classes. Several restaurants and lounges are available to guests.

In an ideal situation Sherry Binger, sales manager, likes to guide prospects on a site inspection of her property. This tour, in some ways, fulfills the function of a sales demonstration. Throughout the tour she describes special amenities and services offered by the hotel. She also uses this time to get better acquainted with the needs of the prospect. Once the tour is completed she escorts the prospect back to her office and completes the needs assessment. Next, she prepares a detailed sales proposal. In most cases the proposal is presented to the prospect at a second meeting. The proposal needs to contain accurate and complete facts because when signed, it becomes a legally enforceable sales contract.

Rarely is the sales proposal accepted without modification. Professional meeting planners are experienced negotiators and press hard for concessions. Some have completed training programs developed for professional buyers. The concessions requested may include a lower guest room rate, lower meal costs, complimentary suites, or a complimentary event such as a wine and cheese reception or a theme party.

Of course, some buyer resistance is not easily identified. Sherry Binger says that she follows three steps in dealing with buyer concerns:

1. *Locate the resistance.* Some prospects are reluctant to accept a sales proposal, but the reason may be unclear. Sherry has discovered in some cases that small groups are concerned about the sheer size of the Esmeralda. They wonder if a small group can receive the same personalized attention given to a large group. Once this perception is uncovered, Sherry knows how to deal with it.
2. *Clarify the resistance.* If a prospect says, "I like your facilities, but your prices are a little high," then the salesperson must clarify the meaning of this objection. Is the prospect seeking a major price concession or a small price concession?
3. *Overcome the objection.* Sherry says, "You must be prepared for negotiations and know the value of what you are offering." The resort must earn a profit, so concessions can be made only after careful consideration of the bottom line.

Sherry has discovered that the best way to negotiate buyer concerns is to make sure both the prospect and the resort feel like winners once the negotiations are finalized. If either party feels like a loser, a long-term partnership will not be possible. Refer to the opening paragraph of this chapter for more information.

Questions

1. If you were selling convention services for a hotel located in a large city, what types of buyer concerns would you expect from a new prospect?
2. Let us assume that you are representing the Stouffer Esmeralda Resort Hotel and you are meeting with a new prospect in her office. She is a busy meeting planner who does not want to visit your property until she has a meeting with you. What are some tools that you might use during the sales presentation? What proof devices might you use to support your claims?
3. If you meet with a professional buyer who is trained in negotiation, what tactics can you expect the person to use? How would you respond to each of these tactics?

CRM CASE STUDY

Negotiating Resistance

Becky Kemley has asked you to review Pat Silva's former prospect accounts. She wants you to look for accounts with which you might anticipate objections during a presentation.

Questions

1. Which account might voice a time objection and say, "We want to put off our decision for now," and how would you propose dealing with this objection?
2. Which account is most likely to try to get you to agree to a lower price and how would you respond?
3. Which account might you anticipate would use the phrase "we want to shop around for a good solid supplier." What would be your response?

PARTNER SELLING A ROLE PLAY/SIMULATION
(see Appendix 3, p. 406)

DEVELOPING A PRESENTATION STRATEGY—NEGOTIATING

Refer to *sales memorandum 3* and strategically plan to anticipate and negotiate any objections or concerns your customer may have to your presentation. You should prepare a negotiations worksheet to organize this part of your presentation.

The instructions for item 2e directs you to prepare negotiations for the time, price, source, and product objections. You note that your price is approximately $200 more than your customer budgeted for this meeting. You have to be very effective in negotiating a value-added strategy because your convention center is not a low-price supplier (see Chapter 6 on value-added product strategies).

During the presentation you should use proof devices from the product strategy materials provided in *employment memorandum 1* to negotiate concerns you anticipate. You also may want to use a calculator to negotiate any financial arrangements such as savings on parking, airport transportation, etc. Using spreadsheet software you may want to prepare graphs to illustrate competitive pricing. Place these materials in the front pocket of your three-ring binder (portfolio) so that you can easily access them during your presentation. You may want to secure another person to be your customer, instructing them to voice the objections you have anticipated, and then you respond with your negotiation strategies. This experience can provide you with the opportunity to rehearse your negotiation strategies.

Closing the Sale and Confirming the Partnership

*D*ana Bengtson, sales representative for Ryder Commercial Leasing & Services (www.ryder.com), understands the importance of patience in selling. It took him two years to convince Burris Foods, a Delaware-based food distributor, to replace its in-house truck fleet with leased trucks from Ryder. Soon after his first contact he arranged for efficiency studies of Burris's existing transportation system. With this information he was able to demonstrate the cost advantages of leasing. Although he seemed to be moving toward a close, Burris officials let it be known that they did not want to continue talks about leasing, at least for the time being. Bengtson realized it was time to slow down negotiations and be patient. In his words, it was time to "do nothing." Later Bengtson resumed his closing efforts. He sent Burris officials articles on long-term vehicle leasing and information on the food distribution business. He restructured his proposal to make it more appealing. After six more months of hard work, he was rewarded with a seven-year lease agreement worth $3 million annually to Ryder. Dana Bengtson closed this sale because he knew when to speed up and when to slow down negotiations.[1]

DEVELOPING AN ATTITUDE TOWARD CLOSING THE SALE

The excitement and personal satisfaction Dana Bengtson feels after closing a sale are common among both new and experienced salespeople. When the prospect says yes, the salesperson receives both a personal and an economic reward. The amount of personal satisfaction received on closing the sale depends on the salesperson's attitude toward the product. Salespeople who believe strongly in their product enjoy converting prospects to customers. They also look forward to a continuing partnership with the new customer.

The Six–Step Presentation Plan	
Step One: APPROACH	☑ Review Strategic/Consultative Selling Model. ☑ Initiate customer contact.
Step Two: PRESENTATION	☑ Determine prospect needs. ☑ Select product or service. ☑ Initiate sales presentation.
Step Three: DEMONSTRATION	☑ Decide what to demonstrate. ☑ Select selling tools. ☑ Initiate demonstration.
Step Four: NEGOTIATION	☑ Anticipate buyer concerns. ☑ Plan negotiating methods. ☑ Initiate double–win negotiations.
Step Five: CLOSE	☐ Plan appropriate closing methods. ☐ Recognize closing clues. ☐ Initiate closing methods.
Step Six: SERVICING THE SALE	☐ Suggestion selling. ☐ Follow through. ☐ Follow-up calls.
Service, retail, wholesale, and manufacturer selling.	

Figure **13.1**
Effective closing methods require careful planning.

Closing the sale is less difficult if each detail is handled properly throughout the sales presentation. A strategically prepared salesperson approaches the close with confidence (Fig. 13.1). Closing is usually more difficult when some aspect of the sales presentation has not been handled properly. Maybe a negative first impression still lingers in the prospect's mind. Perhaps the sales demonstration did not go smoothly. Maybe sales resistance was not negotiated effectively. These and other factors can serve as barriers to closing the sale.

Some sales are lost because the salesperson attempts to close too early or too late. Sometimes, salespeople try to close before the prospect is ready to buy. An early closing attempt may be interpreted as "pressure" selling. We must take care to avoid giving the prospect a feeling of anxiety about being sold something.

It is also possible to close too late by ignoring obvious closing clues. Sometimes, salespeople keep on talking long after buyers have decided to make the purchase. When this happens, customer attitudes sometimes change, and sales are lost.

Another barrier to closing the sale is the early "retreat." When the buyer says no, the salesperson may give up too soon. These and other barriers are discussed in this chapter.

Looking at Closing from the Prospect's Point of View

Closing the sale is no doubt easier if you look at this aspect of selling from the prospect's point of view. Recognize the concerns that may surface in the person's mind.

Closing should be viewed as part of the selling process—the logical outcome of a well-planned presentation strategy.

Do I really need this product?

Does this product measure up to the competition?

Should I postpone buying?

Will this supplier stand behind the product?

What will my friends think if I buy this item?

These may be genuine concerns that could prevent the buyer from saying yes to your proposal. It is best to anticipate these concerns and develop a strategic sales presentation that can eliminate them.

Determination is the Key

Joe Batten, author of the popular sales training film, *Ask for the Order and Get It*, believes that determination is a major key to success in personal selling. He describes determination as a firm, unyielding stand never to let a sale you have worked to make go unasked for. Determination prevents you from taking a quick no for an answer. Determination keeps you from mistaking a customer's doubt for refusal, recognizing that the word no may mean "no for now," or "no based on what I currently know."[a]

Closing the Sale—The Beginning of the Partnership

Closing should be viewed as part of the selling process—the logical outcome of a well-planned presentation strategy. There is a building process that begins with an interesting approach and need discovery. It continues with effective product selection and presentation of benefits that build desire for the product. After a well-planned demonstration and after dealing with sales resistance, it is time to ask for the sale. Closing should be thought of as the beginning of a long-term partnership.

The image of a salesperson who makes a quick pitch, writes up an order, and disappears has faded into history. In the new information age economy the customer realizes the need for a partner, someone to be there when needed, to consistently advise, and to help solve problems on a continuing basis.[2]

GUIDELINES FOR CLOSING THE SALE

A number of factors increase the odds that you will close the sale (Fig. 13.2). These guidelines for closing the sale have universal application in the field of selling.

Focus on Dominant Buying Motives

Most salespeople incorporate the outstanding benefits of their product into the sales presentation. This is only natural. However, be alert to the *one* benefit that generates the most excitement. The buying motive that is of greatest interest deserves the greatest emphasis. Vince Peters, director of sales training and development for Wyeth-Ayerst International, tells his 8,000 pharmaceutical salespeople that the key to closing ". . . is to find out exactly what a prospect is looking for".[3]

Zig Ziglar, author of *Secrets of Closing the Sale*, reminds us that when closing, it is important to give prospects a reason to buy, or some information so that they can act in their own best interests. He says, "This helps you move closing from being *selfish* on your part to being *helpful* to the prospect."[4] To apply this premise, focus your close on the point of greatest interest, and give the prospect a reason for buying.

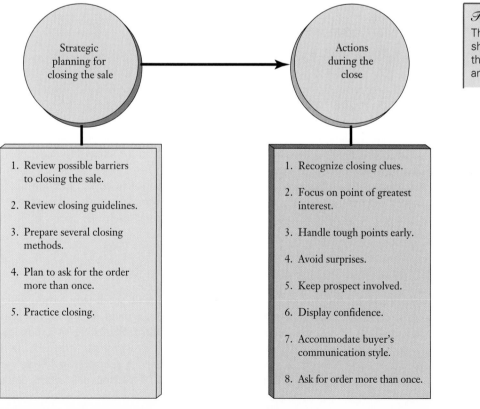

Strategic planning for closing the sale

1. Review possible barriers to closing the sale.
2. Review closing guidelines.
3. Prepare several closing methods.
4. Plan to ask for the order more than once.
5. Practice closing.

Actions during the close

1. Recognize closing clues.
2. Focus on point of greatest interest.
3. Handle tough points early.
4. Avoid surprises.
5. Keep prospect involved.
6. Display confidence.
7. Accommodate buyer's communication style.
8. Ask for order more than once.

Figure **13.2**
The presentation strategy should include reviewing these guidelines for closing and confirming the sale.

Negotiating the Tough Points Before Attempting the Close

Many products have what might be thought of as an Achilles heel. In other words, the product is vulnerable, or appears to be vulnerable, in one or more areas. Negotiate a win–win solution to the tough points before you attempt to close the sale. Such factors can lose the sale if you ignore them. The close should be a positive phase of the sales presentation. This is not the time to deal with a controversial issue or problem.

In the case of Maytag washing machines, Hickey-Freeman–hand-tailored suits, Lexus automobiles, or Ritz-Carlton conference facilities, the Achilles heel may be price. Each of these products may seem expensive in comparison with competing ones. People who sell them find ways to establish the value of their product before attempting the close.

Longer Selling Cycles Require More Patience

Longer selling cycles have become a fact of life. One reason for this change is that more people are involved in purchasing some products. The purchase of highly technical products such as computers, security equipment, and robotics may involve persons from many areas of the organization. In some cases the buyer has more options than in the past. Customers who have more options than in the past are likely to take more time to make a buying decision. This is especially true in the case of expensive products.

The partnership between Vixel Corporation, a small developer of high-speed Fibre Channel storage interconnect solutions, and computer giant Compaq, is a case study in patient selling. The sale was closed after a series of meetings covering four years. Compaq wanted to establish a long-term partnership with a company that was customer-driven. David Brancato, director of sales for Vixel's Houston office, says, "You have to focus on the relationship with Compaq, sell the company more than the products.[5]

Avoid Surprises at the Close

Some salespeople make the mistake of waiting until the close to reveal information that may come as a surprise to the prospect. For example, the salesperson quotes a price but is not specific concerning what the price includes. Let us assume that the price of a central air-conditioning unit is $1,800. The prospect believes that the price is competitive in relation to similar units on the market and is ready to sign the order form. Then the salesperson mentions casually that the installation charge is an extra $225. The prospect had assumed that the $1,800 fee included installation. Suddenly, the extra fee looms as a major obstacle to closing the sale.

The surprise might come in the form of an accessory that costs extra, terms of the warranty, customer service limitations, or some other issue. Do not let a last-minute surprise damage the relationship and threaten the completion of a sale.

Do Not Isolate the Prospect during the Sale

Adults are self-directing people. They are most comfortable when they have a voice in matters that influence their lives. Do not forget this important point at the time you attempt to close. Involve the customer in the close if at all possible. Sometimes it is possible to involve the prospect in some type of "doing" activity. The prospect might be asked to hold the sales proposal as the salesperson explains the details. A salesperson selling carpet might hand the prospect a sample case and ask the person to pick out her favorite color.

You can achieve involvement with questions. You might summarize points of agreement with carefully phrased confirmation-type questions. Some examples are

"Ms. Hansen, you seem to agree that this model combines good looks with durability. Is that right?"

"Mr. Walker, you do agree that your current electric bills are too high. Is that right?"

You also might let the prospect summarize the positive aspects of your product. This might be done by using the following types of questions:

"What features of our product do you like best?"

"What aspects of our customer service program do you find most appealing?"

Display a High Degree of Self-Confidence at the Close

Do you believe in your product? Do you believe in your company? Have you identified a genuine need? If you can answer yes to each of these questions, then there is no need to display timidity. Look the prospect in the eye, and ask for the order. Do not be apologetic at this important point in the sales presentation. The salesperson who confidently asks for the sale is displaying the boldness that often is needed in personal selling.

Ask for the Order More than Once

Too often, salespeople make the mistake of not asking for the order or asking just once. If the prospect says no, they give up. Michael LeBoeuf, author of *How to Win Customers and Keep Them for Life*, reports that almost two thirds of all sales calls conclude without the salesperson asking for the order. He also says that a majority of all customers say no four times before saying yes.[6] Some of the most productive salespeople asked for the order three, four, or even five times. A surprising number of yes responses come on the fourth or fifth attempt. Of course, not all these closing attempts necessarily came during one call.

Many customers think more highly of you if you have the courage to ask for the order. Do not be timid. If you beat around the bush, they may begin to question your commitment to the product. If you are fearful of asking for the order, or ask once and give up, you may never achieve success in personal selling.

Recognize Closing Clues

As the sales presentation progresses, you need to be alert to closing clues (sometimes called buying signals). A **closing clue** is an indication, either verbal or nonverbal, that the prospect is preparing to make a buying decision. It is a form of feedback, which is so important in selling. When you detect a closing clue, it may be time to attempt a close.

Many closing clues are quite subtle and may be missed if you are not alert. This is especially true in the case of nonverbal buying signals. If you pay careful attention—with your eyes and your ears—many prospects may tell you how to close the sale. As we have noted earlier in this text, one of the most important personality traits salespeople need is empathy, the ability to sense what the other person is feeling. In this section we review some of the most common verbal and nonverbal clues.

➤➤ Building Quality Partnerships

An Inspiring Example

Ben Feldman was an unlikely candidate to earn the title "Greatest Life-Insurance Salesperson in History." He talked softly and hesitantly, and had a deceptively sleepy appearance. He was so shy that he once insisted on standing behind a screen when he spoke to an audience of fellow insurance salespeople. This quiet demeanor seemed to appeal to most customers because he closed thousands of sales. He joined New York Life Insurance Company in the early 1940s and soon started making his mark. In the 1950s, he became the first agent to write a million dollars in new business a month. In the 1960s, he was the first salesperson to write a million a week. When he was in his prime, Feldman's income approached $5 million a year.

He sold life insurance by talking about life, not death. He focused his attention on owners of small industrial corporations. Feldman appealed to their need to protect their assets with large amounts of life insurance. He would show prospects his "tax book," a loose-leaf binder that contained the financial histories of people whose businesses or property had to be sold because they died without enough life insurance to pay estate taxes. Taped inside were a $1,000 bill and a few pennies. He would point to the pennies and say, "For these you can get this"—the bill. This sales tool helped him close many sales.

In 1993, New York Life marked Ben Feldman's 50th year with the company by proclaiming "Feldman's February." The company initiated a national competition in which agents were encouraged to sell their best to honor Feldman. The winner of the Feldman February competition was Ben Feldman. Working the phones as he recovered from a health problem, he recorded sales of over $15 million.[b]

VERBAL CLUES

Closing clues come in many forms. Spoken words (verbal clues) are usually the easiest to perceive. These clues can be divided into three categories: (1) questions, (2) recognitions, and (3) requirements.

Questions One of the least subtle buying signals is the question. You might attempt a trial close after responding to one of the following questions:

> "Do you have a credit plan to cover this purchase?"
>
> "What type of warranty do you provide?"
>
> "How soon can our company get delivery?"

Recognitions A recognition is any positive statement concerning your product or some factor related to the sale, such as credit terms or delivery date. Some examples follow:

> "We like the quality control system you have recommended."
>
> "I have always wanted to own a boat like this."
>
> "Your delivery schedule fits our plans."

Requirements Sometimes, customers outline a condition that must be met before they can buy. If you are able to meet this requirement, it may be a good time to try a trial close. Some requirements that the prospect might voice are

> "We will need shipment within two weeks."
>
> "Our staff will need to be trained in how to use this equipment."
>
> "All our equipment must be certified by the plant safety officer."

In some cases, verbal buying clues do not jump out at you. Important buying signals may be interwoven into normal conversation. Listen closely whenever the prospect is talking.

NONVERBAL CLUES

Nonverbal buying clues are even more difficult to detect. Once detected, this type of signal is not easy to interpret. Nevertheless, you should be alert to body movement, facial expression, and tone of voice. Some actions follow that suggest the prospect may be prepared to purchase the product.[7]

The prospect's facial expression changes. Suddenly, the person's eyes widen, and genuine interest is clear in the facial expression.

The prospect begins showing agreement by nodding.

The prospect leans forward and appears to be intent on hearing your message.

The prospect begins to examine the product or study the sales literature intently.

When you observe or sense one of these nonverbal buying clues, do not hesitate to ask for the order. Keep in mind that the modern approach to selling holds that there may be several opportunities to close throughout the sales presentation. Important buying signals may surface at any time. Do not miss them.

SPECIFIC METHODS FOR CLOSING THE SALE

There is no *best* closing method. Your best bet is to preplan several closing methods and use the ones that seem appropriate (Fig. 13.3). Given the complex nature of many sales, it is often a good idea to be prepared to use a combination of closing methods. Do keep in mind that your goal is not only to close the sale but also to develop a long-term partnership. A win–win closing strategy results in repeat business and the opportunity to obtain referrals.

Trial Close

Charles B. Roth, noted sales consultant, once said, "Start your presentation on a closing action, continue it on a closing action, and end it on a closing action." This may be overdoing it a little, but Mr. Roth does make an important point. You should not postpone attempts to close until your sales presentation is completed.

A **trial close**, also known as a *minor point close*, is a closing attempt made at an opportune time during the sales presentation to encourage the customer to reveal readiness or unwillingness to buy. When you are reasonably sure that the prospect is about to make a decision but is being held back by natural caution, the trial close may be appropriate. It is a good way to test the buyer's attitude toward the actual purchase. A trial close often is presented in the form of a probing or confirmation question. Here are some examples:

"We can arrange an August first shipment. Would this date be satisfactory?"

"Which do you prefer, the dark green or the blue finish?"

"Would you rather begin this plan on July first or July fifteenth?"

"Do you want one of our staff members to supervise the installation?"

"Will a $250 down payment be possible at this time?"

Some salespeople use the trial close more than once during the sales presentation. After the salesperson presents a feature, converts that feature to a buyer benefit, and confirms the prospect's agreement that the benefit is important, it would be appropriate to use a trial close.[8]

Closing Worksheet		
Closing clue (prospect)	Closing method	Closing statement (salesperson)
"That sounds fine."	**Direct appeal close**	"Good, may I get your signature on this order form?"
"What kind of financing do you offer?"	**Multiple options close**	"We have two financing methods available: 90-day open credit or two-year–long-term financing. Which of these do you prefer?"
"Well, we don't have large amounts of cash available at this time."	**Assumption close**	"Based on your cash position, I would recommend you consider our lease–purchase plan. This plan allows you to pay a very small initial amount at this time and keep the cash you now have for your everyday business expenses. I will be happy to write up your order on the lease–purchase plan."
The prospect completes a careful reading of the proposal and communicates (nonverbal clue) a look of satisfaction.	**Combination summary of benefits/direct appeal close**	"That solution surpasses your quality requirements, meets your time deadlines, and provides your accounting department with the details they requested. Can you get your chief financial officer's signature on the order?"

Figure **13.3**

Preparing for the close requires the preplanning of several closing methods. Research indicates that in many selling situations several closing attempts may be necessary.

In broader terms, it would be appropriate to attempt a trial close after steps two, three, or four of the six-step presentation plan (Fig. 13.4).

Summary-of-Benefits Close

Let us assume that you have discussed and demonstrated the major benefits of your product and you detect considerable buyer interest. However, you have covered a great deal of material. There is a chance that the prospect is not able to put the entire picture together without your help. At this point you should provide a concise summary of the most important buyer benefits. Your goal in the **summary-of-benefits close** is to reemphasize the benefits that can help bring about a favorable decision. For maximum sales success, focus on those benefits that satisfy the personal concerns of the buyer.[9]

Let us see how this closing method works in the hospitality industry. Terry Hall, sales manager of the Emory Hotel, recently called on Mr. Ray Busch, director of marketing for a large corporation. Near the end of the sales presentation, Terry summarized the major bene-

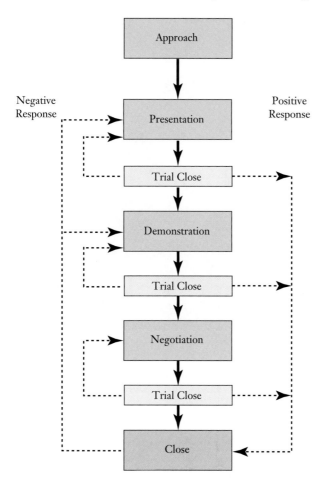

fits in this manner: "Mr. Busch, we can provide you with a conference room that will seat 200 people comfortably and four smaller rooms for the workshops you have planned. Our staff will serve a noon lunch, and the cost will be less than $11 per person. Finally, we will see that each of your employees receives a pad of paper, a pen, and a copy of the conference program. Should I go ahead and reserve these facilities for November 24?" In the process of reviewing all the important points you provide the buyer with a positive picture of the proposal.

Assumption Close

The **assumption close** assumes the customer is going to buy.[10] This closing approach comes near the end of the planned presentation. If you have identified a genuine need, presented your solutions in terms of buyer benefits, presented an effective sales demonstration, and negotiated buyer concerns satisfactorily, it may be natural to assume the person is ready to buy. In the assumption close you actually assume that the prospect already has bought the product and then ask one or more questions about a minor point. Some examples may include

"Do you want this purchase added to your charge account?"

"Will next Friday be OK for delivery, or will you need it sooner?"

In place of asking a question the salesperson may start an activity such as writing up the order. The order might be completed and handed to the prospect along with a pen. The salesperson says, "Can I get your signature here?" or some similar statement. This must be

The assumption close assumes the customer is going to buy. You are confident that the prospect is ready to buy and you are only bringing the selling–buying process to a close.

done with a positive mental attitude. You are confident that the prospect is ready to buy and you are only bringing the selling–buying process to a close.

Special Concession Close

The **special concession close** offers the buyer an extra incentive for acting immediately. A special inducement is offered if the prospect agrees to sign the order. The concession may be part of a low-price strategy such as a sale price, a quantity discount, a more liberal credit plan, or an added feature that the prospect did not anticipate.

You should use this closing approach with care, because some customers are skeptical of concessions. This is especially true when the concession comes after the salesperson has made what appears to be the final offer. Let us assume that a customer is interested in buying a certain piano. The salesperson says in a firm voice, "The price is $5,800." The customer says, "The price seems awfully high." After a few minutes of discussion the customer seems to be losing interest in the purchase. The salesperson says, "I think that price is firm, but let me check with the boss." A few minutes later the salesperson returns and says, "You are in luck. We can cut the price by $400."

What may be the impact of the $400 price concession? It may be the factor that motivates the buyer to say yes. On the other hand, it may have a negative influence on the person's attitude. Some thoughts that might surface in the prospect's mind follow:

I wonder why the salesperson had to discuss the price with the boss.

Why was the lower price not quoted in the first place?

Maybe if I start to leave, the salesperson will lower the price again.

If he is willing to lower the price, maybe there is something wrong with the product.

If the $5,400 figure provides the store with an adequate profit margin, it may be best to quote this price in the first place. It is difficult to establish specific guidelines for every selling situation, but a good rule of thumb is to avoid "gimmicks." Today's better educated buyer is not fooled easily.

Multiple Options Close

In many selling situations it is a good idea to provide the prospect with options regarding product configuration, delivery options, and price. This is especially true when you are dealing with the price conscious transactional buyer. As noted in the previous chapter, today's customer expects new levels of flexibility. In the **multiple options close**, allow the person to examine several different options, and try to assess the degree of interest in each one. As you near the point where a close seems appropriate, remove some of the options. This reduces confusion and indecision.

You often see the multiple options close used in office equipment sales. If a small business owner wants to purchase a copy machine, most vendors offer several models for consideration. Let us assume that the prospect has examined four models and seems to be uncertain about which one would be the best choice. The salesperson might determine which copier is least appealing and eliminate it as an option. Now the prospect can choose between three copiers. If the prospect seems to favor one copier, it would be appropriate to ask for the order.

When using the multiple options close, follow these simple steps:

1. Configure more than one product solution.
2. Cease presenting product options when it appears that the prospect has been given ample selection. Too many choices can result in confusion and indecision.
3. Remove products (or features) that the prospect does not seem genuinely interested in and concentrate on the options the prospect seems to be interested in.

Direct Appeal Close

The **direct appeal close** has the advantages of clarity and simplicity. This close involves simply asking for the order in a straightforward manner. It is the most direct closing approach, and many buyers find it attractive. Realistically, most customers expect salespeople to ask for the sale.

The direct appeal should not, of course, come too early. It should not be used until the prospect has displayed a definite interest in the product or service. The salesperson also must gain the prospect's respect before initiating this appeal. Once you make the direct appeal, stop talking. Raymond Slesinski, Digital Equipment sales trainer, tells his trainees, "After asking a closing question, do not speak, even if the prospect doesn't answer quickly." His advice is to give the prospect time to think about your offer.[11]

A variation of the direct appeal close involves use of a question to determine how close the customer is to making a buying decision. The question might be, "How close are we to closing the sale?" This direct question calls for a direct answer. The customer is encouraged to reflect on the progress of the sale.[12]

Combination Closes

In some cases the most effective close is one that combines two or more of the closing methods we have discussed. To illustrate, let us observe Colleen White as she attempts to close a sale in the office of a buyer for a large department store. Colleen represents a firm that manufactures a wide range of leather clothing and accessories. Near the end of her planned presentation she senses that the prospect is quite interested in her products but seems reluctant to make a decision.

This is how Colleen handles the close: "Ms. Taylor, I have described two benefits that seem especially important to you. First, you agree that this line will be popular with the fashion conscious shoppers your store caters to. Second, you indicated that the prices I quoted will allow you excellent profit margins. If we process your order now, you will have the merchandise in time for the pre-Christmas buying period. We can guarantee the delivery at this point." Notice that this close starts with a summary of benefits close and ends with a special concession.

PRACTICE CLOSING

Your success in selling can depend in large part on learning how to make these six closing methods work for you. You may not master these approaches in a few days or a few weeks, but you can speed up the learning process with preparation and practice. Role playing is the best known way to experience the feelings that accompany closing, and to practice the skills needed to close sales. To prepare the role play, anticipate various closing scenarios and then prepare a written script of the drama.[13] Find someone (your sales manager, friend, or spouse) to play the role of the customer and give that person a script to act out. Practice the role plays in front of a video recorder, and then sit back and observe your performance. The video monitor provides excellent feedback. Use the closing worksheet (see Fig. 13.3) to prepare for practice sessions. You need to learn these methods so well that you can use them without consciously thinking about them.

One of the most important outcomes of practice is increased self-confidence. Think about Larry Wilson's views on the importance of confidence: "Fear of failure and fear of rejection are the most significant barriers to success and fulfillment in selling."[14]

CONFIRMING THE PARTNERSHIP WHEN THE BUYER SAYS YES

Congratulations! You have closed the sale and have established the beginning of what you hope will be a long and satisfying partnership with the customer. Before preparing to leave, be sure that all details related to the purchase agreement are completed. Check all particulars with the buyer, and then ask for a signature if necessary.

Once the sale has been closed, it is important to take time to reassure the customer. This is the **confirmation step** in closing the sale. Before you leave, reassure the customer by pointing out that she has made the correct decision, and describe the satisfaction that will come with ownership of the product. The reason for doing this is to resell the buyer and to prevent buyer's remorse. **Buyer's remorse** is an emotional response that can take various forms such as feelings of regret, fear, or anxiety.[15] It's common to wonder whether or not we have made the right decision. Compliment the person for making a wise decision. Once the sale is closed, the customer may be required to justify the purchase to others. Your words of reassurance can be helpful.

Before leaving, thank the customer for the order. This is very important. Everyone likes to think that a purchase is appreciated. No one should believe that a purchase is taken for granted. Even a small order deserves words of appreciation. In many cases a follow-up–thank-you letter is appropriate.

In several previous chapters we note that a satisfied customer is one of the best sources of new prospects. Never hesitate to ask, "Do you know anyone else who might benefit from owning this product?" or a similar question. Some customers may even agree to write an introductory letter on your behalf.

After you complete the sale, you should do all that is possible to make sure the customer receives maximum satisfaction from the purchase. This may require a detailed explanation of how to operate and maintain the product. Some sales representatives make it a practice to be present when the product is delivered. They want to make sure the cus-

Beth Manning, Jody Sprock Interiors & Associates
119 19th Street, Suite 202
West Des Moines, Iowa 50265-4226
515-225-9253   Fax 515-225-9386

Letter of Agreement

Beth Manning Jody Sprock Interiors (BMJSI) is pleased to be of service to you in designing and beautifying the interior of your design project. Our design service is described in the following contract agreement.

DESIGN SERVICES: The designer may perform the following services for the client:
      Schematic Design - Space Planning - Budget Estimates
      Design Development - Product and Finish Specification
      Procurement - Administration - Installation - Design Execution

A. DESIGN SERVICES - PURCHASING THROUGH *BMJSI* - RETAINER
Client shall pay in advance a retainer of $565.00. This is estimated to cover approximately 7 1/2 hours of design time (This includes driving time.). The $565.00 retainer will be applied to your final invoice as a credit, if procurement occurs through *BMJSI* as planned. When a minimum $2500.00 purchase is made within a three month period, the retainer will be credited to a final product invoice. If a minimum $2500.00 purchase is not made within a three month period, the retainer will be used as hourly compensation. In the event that specified products are purchased elsewhere or if a portion of the job that the designer has done research and development on is not completed, the designer will be compensated at an hourly rate ($75.00) for services/time rendered. A detailed account of the designer's hours will be charged and billed to client if the project does not proceed as planned. When a minimum sale of $2500.00 per project occurs, the hourly fee will be waived.

B. DESIGN/CONSULTATION SERVICES ONLY - NO PROCUREMENT THROUGH BMJSI
An advance retainer of $375.00 will be collected in order to begin work on the project. This covers approximately 5 hours of design research and development. Clients using design services only will be billed at an hourly rate of $75.00 (This includes driving time.). Billing will be after each appointment. Payment is due within 10 days or prior to the next appointment. *Billable design services* may include: SPACE PLANNING, DESIGN PLANNING, COLOR GUIDELINING, PHASE PLANNING, SHOPPING SERVICES, ACCESSORIZING, PROJECT MANAGEMENT, PRODUCT SPECIFICATION, BID PREPARATION.
OTHER: _____

C. TRIP CHARGE
A trip allowance will be billed for out of town job sites.

D. WARRANTIES AND WORKMANSHIP
We wish to inform you that by using a professional design firm you are guaranteed:
1. Professional coordination of fabrics and furnishings and concern for your needs first.
2. Prompt, professional follow-up if problems do arise.
3. Recommended resources that maintain the highest standards of workmanship.

BMJSI is not responsible for:
1. Work by third parties not engaged by *BMJSI*.
2. Warranties not provided by our manufacturers and resources.

CLIENT: _____ DATE: _____

DESIGNER: _____ DATE: _____

"SPECIALIZING IN LIFE STYLE DESIGN"

After the buyer says yes be sure that all details related to the purchase agreement are completed, and then ask for a signature. A signature is required on this "Letter of Agreement."

Before leaving, thank the customer for the order. This is very important. Everyone likes to think that a purchase is appreciated.

tomer does not have any problems with the new product. How to "service" a sale properly is described fully in Chapter 14.

What to Do When the Buyer Says No

High-performance salespeople learn to manage disappointment. Abraham Zalezik, professor emeritus at the Harvard Business School, says that the way we handle disappointment is often more important in reaching success than our focus on success itself. Learning to cope with disappointment forces people to learn more about themselves and better manage future disappointments.[16]

Never treat a lost sale as a defeat. When you adopt the win–win relationship strategy, there is never a winner and a loser. When the sales interview is over, both the customer and salesperson should feel like winners. A strong display of disappointment or resentment is likely to close the door to future sales.

Faced with the possibility of a failed presentation strategy, some salespeople abandon their relationship and customer strategies and turn to selling methods that are unethical, illegal, or both. Sometimes, sales representatives imply that if the prospect postpones signing the order, the item may not be available. If in fact the company has a large surplus of these products, the salesperson has been dishonest. Another unethical practice is suggesting that the price may increase sharply soon, when in all likelihood the price will not change. If the customer finds out later that your information was not correct, you are likely to lose the opportunity for repeat business.

In some selling situations it is proper to reopen the presentation. If you are preparing to leave and think of an effective approach to closing the sale, do not hesitate to use it. You might recall an important point that was overlooked earlier. For example, you might want to review a testimonial from a satisfied customer. A third-party opinion might reopen the door and set the stage for the close.

➤➤ Selling in Action

NO NEED FOR PRICE CONCESSIONS

Kevin Altman and Brian Shaw have very little in common in terms of the products they sell, but they do share a common view of price concessions. Neither of these successful sales representatives would consider using a price concession to close a sale. Shaw works for Young Minds, Incorporated, a company that makes CD-ROM mass product systems and mass storage systems for UNIX and Windows NT. He never reduces his price because he believes this tactic devalues his product in the eyes of the customer. Shaw's product is much more expensive than the competition, but he believes the product's unique features justify the higher price. Altman, a senior account executive for AM FM Broadcasting, a group of radio stations based in Fresno, California, avoids the price issue by using a value-added strategy. Altman provides customers with the factual information (demographics and audience profiles) they need to make an informed buying decision. He is viewed by his clients as a consultant, an important source of qualitative data.

Prepare the Prospect for Contact with the Competition

Some prospects refuse to buy because they want to take a close look at the competing products. This response is not unusual in the field of selling. You should do everything possible to help the customer make an intelligent comparison.

It is always a good practice to review your product's strong points one more time. Give special emphasis to areas in which your product has a superior advantage over the competition. To illustrate, let us assume you are selling a commercial quality copy machine designed for high-volume users. The prospect seems to like your product but insists on looking at a competing product before making a buying decision. At this point you should review the exclusive features of your product and encourage the customer to remember these points when making a comparison. Make it easy for the person to buy your product at some future date.

Follow-up telephone calls can be used to provide the prospect with additional information needed to make a buying decision.

►► CUSTOMER RELATIONSHIP MANAGEMENT WITH TECHNOLOGY

ADDING AND DELETING PROSPECTS

Prospect and customer databases are continually changing. Promotions, transfers, mergers, and many other events require additions and deletions in a salesperson's automated data. Most customer relationship management (CRM) software makes this an easy process and warns users against the inadvertent removal of an account. (See the exercise, Adding and Deleting Prospects, at p. 302 for more information.)

Analyze Lost Sales

When you experience a no-sale call, try to benefit from the experience. A lost sale can be a good learning experience. Take a good, objective look at your presentation, and try to identify any weaknesses. Were you able to arouse genuine interest early? Did you ask well-thought-out questions? Was the sales demonstration handled properly? Were you able to deal effectively with buyer resistance? If you do pinpoint a weakness, consider how to avoid this problem in the future. When you experience a no-sale call, salvage as much as possible from the experience. If you anticipate a return call, do record any new information you have learned about the prospect. This might include personal information, company information, or purchase priorities. Callbacks frequently yield good results, so avoid the temptation to give up after a single call on a prospect.

Do not spend *too much* time analyzing lost sales. Jack Falvey, author and sales consultant, says that we get no's for many unknown or subjective reasons, so a time-consuming study of every no-sale call may not be cost effective. He cautions salespeople to avoid dwelling on rejection and to keep moving forward.[17] Learning how to deal with no's is an important key to success in selling.

Summary

Closing the sale is usually not difficult if everything is handled properly throughout the sales presentation. When the sales presentation is well organized and well delivered, the close is part of the process that results in a sale.

The salesperson must be alert to *closing clues* from the prospect. These clues fall into two categories: verbal and nonverbal. Verbal clues are the easiest to recognize, but they may be subtle as well. Again it is important to be an attentive listener. The recognition of nonverbal clues is more difficult, but practice in careful observation helps in detecting them.

Several closing methods may be necessary to get the prospect to make a buying decision; therefore it is wise for the salesperson to preplan several closes. These closing methods should be chosen from the list provided in this chapter and then customized to fit the product and the type of buyer with whom the salesperson is dealing. In some selling situations the use of *combination closes* is very effective.

The professional salesperson is not discouraged or offended if the sale is not closed. Every effort should be made to be of further assistance to the prospect—the sale might be closed on another call. Even if the sale is lost, the experience may be valuable if analyzed to learn from it.

KEY TERMS

Closing Clue
Trial Close
Summary-of-Benefits Close
Assumption Close
Special Concession Close

Multiple Options Close
Direct Appeal Close
Combination Closes
Confirmation Step
Buyer's Remorse

REVIEW QUESTIONS

1. List some aspects of the sales presentation that can make closing and confirming the sale difficult to achieve.
2. Explain why sales cycles are longer today. How should salespeople respond to this trend?
3. What guidelines should a salesperson follow for closing the sale?
4. Why is it important to look at closing from the prospect's point of view?
5. What three verbal clues can the prospect use to indicate that it is time to close the sale? For what nonverbal clues should the salesperson be alert?
6. Explain how the multiple options close might be used in the sale of men's and women's suits.
7. Is there a best method to use in closing the sale? Explain.
8. What is meant by a trial close? When should a salesperson attempt a trial close?
9. Explain the summary-of-benefits close.
10. What confirming steps should a salesperson follow when the customer says yes? What should be done when the customer says no?

APPLICATION EXERCISES

1. Which of the following statements, often made by prospects, would you interpret as buying signals?
   a. "How much would the payments be?"
   b. "Tell me about your service department."
   c. "The company already has an older model that seems good enough."
   d. "We do not have enough cash flow right now."
   e. "How much would you allow me for my old model?"
   f. "I do not need one."
   g. "How does that switch work?"
   h. "When would I have to pay for it?"
2. You are an accountant who owns and operates an accounting service. You have been contacted by the president of an advertising agency about the possibility of your auditing his business on a regular basis. The president has indicated that he investigated other accounting firms and thinks they price their services too high. With the knowledge you have about the other firms you know you are in a strong competitive position. Also, you realize his account would be profitable for your firm. You really would like to capture this account. How will you close the deal? List and describe two closing methods you might use in this situation.

3. Ryder Commercial Leasing and Services is the topic of the opening material in this chapter. Access this company's Web site at http.//www.ryder.com/ and view the information provided. Examine articles in the company news section, and determine if any of this information would be helpful in closing the sale. Examine the business services section. Does it appear that Ryder is able to partner with its potential customers?

CRM Application Exercise

Adding and Deleting Prospects

Adding and deleting contacts is easy with the ACT! software, as it is with most CRM software. Create a Contact record for a B. H. Rivera by selecting Edit, New Contact or by pressing the Insert key (Ins on some keyboards). This displays a blank record that can be completed by selecting fields with the mouse or by using the Tab key to move from field to field. In the Company field, type "Graphic Forms" and type 3195556194 (no hyphens) into the Phone field. The address is "2134 Martin Luther King"; and Atlanta, GA, and 61740 are City, State, and Zip.

Most CRM software permits you to save time and avoid errors by selecting field data from menus. For example, point at the ID/Status field label and double-click with your mouse on the label, not the field. A menu of choices should appear. Another method to obtain this menu is to place the cursor in the field and press the F2 function key. From this menu, select Prospect as the ID/Status for the B. H. Rivera record.

You have just added a new record to the ACT! database. The demonstration version of the ACT! software version limits the number of contacts to 25. The full version of ACT! has no such limit. Do not enter more than 25 contacts into this demonstration version. Print this new record by selecting Report, Contact Report, Active Contact, Printer, and OK.

To remove a contact, select Edit, Delete Contact. The window is displayed with a box for Contact, Lookup, and Cancel. Picking Contact causes the individual record to be deleted, Lookup deletes all records currently being looked up, and Cancel terminates the procedure. Choosing to delete a record causes a warning window to be displayed. This window asks if you are sure that you wish to delete the contact. Caution is advised when deleting records or using the delete function. Pressing the F1 function key displays the appropriate help screen.

Case Problem

Ruan and Clark Distributing is a respected wholesale broker of building products, including a quality line of carpeting. Three years ago, Bob Thompson graduated from college and accepted a sales position with Ruan and Clark as the representative for the carpet line.

During the past six months, Bob has been calling on Woodside Building and Supply Company, one of the firms in his territory. Woodside already carries carpet lines from several of Bob's competitors. Woodside dominates its trading area in several product lines, including carpet. Bob has called on the buyer, Jim Cooney, four times; however, he has not been able to close the sale. Recently, Ruan and Clark took a new line of carpet that Bob felt offered his dealers an excellent buy.

In calling Woodside for the fifth time, Bob decided to use the new product line to try to close the sale. The following sales presentation took place:

Bob: Hello, Jim. It's good to see you.

Jim: (In a warm, friendly tone of voice) Good to see you again, Bob, but I'll tell you right up front I don't have a budget to buy additional goods! I would like to find out what you have, but even if you *gave* me a roll of carpet, I wouldn't be able to find a place here to store it.

Bob: I'm sorry to hear that, because we have just added another product line that we think is going to revolutionize the carpet industry. (Bob shows Jim a sample of the new line — a toast color with alternating rows of cut and uncut yarn.) Our carpet mill took the popular traditional candy stripe, built it up to a higher quality, and changed its styling to appeal to more of your customers. In short, with this new toast-colored, 10-year-guaranteed carpet you no longer have to compete with your competitors on the same product. This can give your salespeople a strong competitive advantage in their sales presentation. Our sales forecasting indicates that within 12 months this new product will take over 25 percent of the traditional market.

Jim: Bob, this is an appealing line.

Bob: (Handing the sample to Jim) Because of our mill's innovation in construction, you get a much better feel in the surface yarns, don't you?

Jim: Yes, it does feel good.

Bob: This construction feature, along with the improved rubber backing, gives your customers a better quality piece of goods. In addition, Jim, the mill has been able to hold the price on these goods to a competitive level. What do you think of it?

Jim: (Inspecting the goods a second time) I like it, Bob, but as I said before . . .

Bob: (Breaking in and focusing on the space problem) Jim. I can appreciate your space problem, but I am in a position to ship you as little as one roll now, so you can get into the market immediately and find out how well this product is suited for your situation.

Jim: (Showing more interest) Well, I would like to try it, but I just cannot see how I can do it today.

Bob: That is too bad, Jim, because we are running this new line at a special introductory price. The regular price on these goods is $4.89 a yard, but we are introducing it at $3.99. (Bob feels he now has Jim wanting the goods; however, he thinks Jim may want to put the sale off until later.)

Jim: That is a good price, Bob, but I am just . . .

Bob: (Interrupting Jim) Also, we will pay the freight at $3.99, which will save you an additional 15 percent. (Bob really wants to open the Woodside account because of the high sales Woodside can experience and the future profitability his company can achieve. Under any other circumstances he would never have offered to pay the freight at this price.)

Jim: (In a quiet voice) That sure sounds like something I should take advantage of.

Questions

1. Based on the information given, do you think this sales call can be closed?
2. Assume you are Bob. After Jim's last comment, which close would you use next? Why?
3. What appeared to be the major obstacle to closing this sale?
4. Did Jim give any closing clues? Identify them.
5. Did Bob use any trial closes? Identify them.
6. What did you like and what did you dislike about the way Bob attempted to close this sale?

CRM CASE STUDY

Forecasting the Close

You are interested in discovering what your commissions may be for the next few months, just from Pat Silva's former accounts. To do this, you review the information on each Contact record. There are four fields on the first page of the Contact Screen from which you can forecast your expected sales: Network Need, Likelihood, Dollar Amount, and

Date Close. When working with these accounts, Pat entered the information found in each of these fields. In the Network Need field, Pat entered the type of network that the prospect might order. In the Likelihood field, Pat estimated the percentage of possibility that the account might place an order (0.80 means 80%). The Dollar Amount field refers to how much Pat thought the account would spend and the month Pat believed they would order is in the Date Close field (01/31 means January).

You can estimate each month's likely sales by multiplying the Dollar Amount field number times the Likelihood field percentage number. An 80% chance of a $100,000 sale is a forecast of $80,000 in sales. If the Date Close field for several accounts is 12/31, you can calculate the sales for that month (December) by totaling the forecasts for each account. For an estimate of your commission income, multiply each month's forecast by 10%.

Pat did not show that any forecasted sales were 100%. Pat recognized that the sales might not close, the amount anticipated (Dollar Amount) might not be achieved, and the close might not take place during the month projected. Pat knew that these prospects would not close themselves; certain steps would have to be taken to increase the possibility that the prospect would place an order. To collect your commissions, you have to discover the steps most likely to close these sales.

Questions

1. What would your commission income be for all Pat's accounts if you closed them as Pat forecasted?
2. What kind of special concession might be necessary to close the sale with Quality Builders?
3. What kind of close may be necessary to get an order from Computerized Labs?
4. What kind of close would be appropriate for the Lakeside Clinic?

PARTNERSHIP/SELLING: A ROLE PLAY/SIMULATION
(see Appendix 3, p. 406)

DEVELOPING A PRESENTATION STRATEGY—CLOSING THE SALE

Refer to *sales memorandum 3* and strategically plan to close the sale with your customer. To consider the sale closed you need to secure the signature of your customer on the sales proposal form. This guarantees your customer the accommodations listed on the form. These accommodations may change depending on the final number of people attending your customer's convention. This is an important point to keep in mind when closing the sale; however, you still must get the signature to guarantee the accommodations.

Follow the instructions carefully, and prepare a closing worksheet listing at least four closes using the methods outlined in this chapter. Two of these methods should include the summary of the benefits, and the direct appeal. Remember it is not the policy of your convention center to cut prices, so your methods should include value-added strategies.

Use proof devices to make your closes more convincing and place them in the front pocket of your three-ring binder/portfolio for easy access during your presentation. You may want to secure another person to be your customer, and practice the closing strategies you have developed.

Servicing the Sale and Building the Partnership

When you finish reading this chapter, you should be able to

1. Explain how to build long-term partnerships with customer service

2. Describe current developments in customer service

3. List and describe the major customer service methods that strengthen the partnership

4. Explain how to work effectively with customer support personnel

5. Explain how to deal effectively with complaints

*N*ever underestimate the power of indifference. This time-proven fundamental has universal support in the business community, yet many sales and marketing professionals still do things that give the customer an "emotional" slap in the face. Aurora Pucciarello, CEO of Dallas-based Max Distribution, describes how a valued customer was lost due to indifference. Near the end of a lucrative three-year contract, the client indicated a desire to renew it. All she and her sales staff had to do was complete a basic proposal. "We were told to just fill out the same numbers as before. We thought great, we've got them in our pocket." The proposal was filed away and forgotten. Later a phone call from the client let Pucciarello know she had missed the proposal deadline and lost the business. This client accounted for 10 percent of her total sales. She cried that day.[1]

BUILDING LONG-TERM PARTNERSHIPS WITH CUSTOMER SERVICE

Customer service is the key to building customer loyalty. In the past some organizations were able to survive without fully embracing this fundamental, but times have changed. In a world of increased global competition and narrowing profit margins, customer retention through value-based initiatives can mean the difference between increasing or eroding

Figure 14.1

Servicing the sale involves three steps: suggestion selling, follow-through, and follow-up calls.

The Six–Step Presentation Plan	
Step One: APPROACH	☑ Review Strategic/Consultative Selling Model. ☑ Initiate customer contact.
Step Two: PRESENTATION	☑ Determine prospect needs. ☑ Select product or service. ☑ Initiate sales presentation.
Step Three: DEMONSTRATION	☑ Decide what to demonstrate. ☑ Select selling tools. ☑ Initiate demonstration.
Step Four: NEGOTIATION	☑ Anticipate buyer concerns. ☑ Plan negotiating methods. ☑ Initiate double–win negotiations.
Step Five: CLOSE	☑ Plan appropriate closing methods. ☑ Recognize closing clues. ☑ Initiate closing methods.
Step Six: SERVICING THE SALE	☐ Suggestion selling. ☐ Follow through. ☐ Follow-up calls.
Service, retail, wholesale, and manufacturer selling.	

market share. Progressive marketers are searching for ways to differentiate their service from competitors and to build emotional loyalty through value.[2]

Customer service can be defined as those activities that enhance or facilitate the purchase and use of the product. In good times and bad, quality customer service builds profits by attracting new accounts and keeping old ones active. The point of view that "service pays" is accepted by successful firms that have adopted the marketing concept and seek to establish long-term partnerships with customers.

A sales organization that can develop a reputation for servicing each sale (Figure 14.1) is sought out by customers who want a long-term partner to help them with their buying needs. Satisfied customers represent an "auxiliary" sales force—a group of people who recommend customer-driven organizations to others. If customers are pleased with the service that they receive after the sale, be assured that they tell other people. Research shows that when someone has a good customer service experience, he tells an average of six people; when he has an outstanding experience, he tells twice as many.[3]

Responding to Increased Postsale Customer Expectations

People buy expectations, not products, according to Ted Levitt, author of *The Marketing Imagination*. They buy the expectations of benefits you promised. Once the customer buys your product, expectations increase. Levitt points out that after the sale is closed, the buyer's attitude changes.

A follow-up phone call to thank the customer and find out if he or she is pleased with the product strengthens the relationship after the sale.

The fact of buying changes the buyer. He expects the seller to remember the purchase as having been a favor bestowed on him by the buyer, not as something earned by the seller. Hence it is wrong to assume that to have gained an account gives you an advantage by virtue of having gotten "a foot in the door." The opposite is increasingly the case. If the buyer views the sale as a favor conferred by him on the seller, then he in effect debits the seller's account. The seller owes him one. The seller is in the position of having to rebuild his relationship from a deficit position.[4]

Increased customer expectations, after the sale is closed, require a strategic plan for servicing the sale. Certain aspects of the relationship, product, and customer strategies can have a positive influence on the customer's heightened expectations.

How do we respond to a customer who has increased expectations? First, we should be certain our customer strategy is on target. We must fully understand the needs and wants of the customer. What is the customer trying to accomplish and how can you help the person do it better? Successful salespeople are driven by a close-to-the customer orientation and they frequently test their assumptions concerning levels of customer satisfaction. In some cases this means asking the customer questions that might make the salesperson uncomfortable. The answers to these questions serve as an early warning system for matters that are going wrong.[5] Unresolved postsale problems open the door to competitors.

Second, we should reexamine our product strategy. In some cases we can enhance customer satisfaction by suggesting related products or services. If the product is expensive, we can follow through and offer assistance in making credit arrangements. If the product is complex, we can make suggestions concerning use and maintenance. Each of these forms of assistance may add value to the sale.

High Cost of Customer Attrition

Financial institutions, public utilities, airlines, retail stores, restaurants, manufacturers, and wholesalers face the problem of gaining and retaining the patronage of clients and customers. These companies realize that keeping a customer happy is a good strategy. To

Carl Sewell lives, sleeps, eats, and breathes his obsession with customer service and the result is a half-billion-dollar dealership that is the envy of almost everyone in the automobile business.

regain a lost customer can be four to five times more expensive than keeping a current customer satisfied.[6]

There is no longer any doubt that poor service is the primary cause of customer attrition. A surprisingly small number of customers (12–15 percent) are lost due to product dissatisfaction. No more than 10–15 percent of lost customers leave due to price considerations. Most research indicates that from 50 to 70 percent of customer attrition is due to poor service.[7] A carefully developed strategic plan to reduce customer defection pays big dividends.

Carl Sewell, Chairman of Sewell Automotive Companies with dealerships in Dallas, Fort Worth, New Orleans, and San Antonio, has fully embraced the customer-for-life philosophy of doing business. He lives, sleeps, eats, and breathes his obsession with customer service and the result is a half-billion-dollar dealership that is the envy of almost everyone in the automobile business.[8]

CURRENT DEVELOPMENTS IN CUSTOMER SERVICE

Bill Gates, in his book *Business @ The Speed of Thought* predicts that in the new millennium customer service may become the primary value-added function.[9] He recognizes that customer service is the primary method of building and extending the partnership.

Customer-friendly, computer based systems frequently are used to enhance customer service.

Customer service, in its many forms, nourishes the partnership and keeps it alive. The age of information has ushered in a series of customer service initiatives that affect the daily work of salespeople. We discuss three of these current developments.

▶ *Salespeople are spending more time monitoring customer satisfaction.* There is a growing trend in which companies rely on their salespeople to continually monitor their customers' needs, concerns, and future plans. In the past many salespeople would live or die by the number of sales closed and too little attention was given to service after the sale. Eastman Chemical Company in Kingsport, Tennessee, provides a good example of a company that involves its salespeople in the customer service process. Eastman developed the "customer advocacy" program that is designed to objectively measure customer satisfaction levels, and to give salespeople the responsibility for improving and maintaining that performance. Members of the sales force conduct ongoing surveys to assess levels of customer satisfaction. The survey form is delivered by a salesperson who emphasizes the importance of helping Eastman improve sales and service performance.[10]

Salespeople who have direct contact with the customer are in an excellent position to assess the health of the partnership. Mack Hanan, author of *Consultative Selling*, encourages salespeople to seek answers to several questions:[11] Is the customer still growing because of your products and your expertise? How much more growth can take place in the future? How much is the partner growing you? In other words, is your company benefiting enough from the partnership? When the partnership involves a strategic alliance, answers to these questions are especially important.

▶ *Customer knowledge is viewed by sales and sales support personnel as an important key to improving customer service.* Bob Johnson, vice president of Information Technology Services Marketing Association, says that the ability to manage your customer knowledge is the number-one lesson for anyone who wants to build customer loyalty:[12]

> If you can't capture, manage and leverage customer history (as well as information regarding current and future needs), you can forget about loyalty. Limited knowledge management capability fosters the sense that the company has no real interest in the customer—or his repeat patronage.

Once you acquire knowledge about your customer, you can tailor your customer service initiatives to develop a more productive and cost-effective partnership. Sanwa Bank California, headquartered in Los Angeles, uses customer knowledge to determine what type of service may be beneficial for each customer. Customers use money in many different ways, and the bank offers a complex line of products and services. Sales representatives at Sanwa can access a computerized customer database for any bank customer in a matter of seconds.[13]

▶ *Customer-friendly, computer-based systems frequently are used to enhance customer service.* Computers give both the salesperson and the customer ready access to information and problem-solving alternatives. In the future human involvement in service may shift from routine, low-value tasks to a high-value, personal consultancy on important customer problems or desires.[14] We may see greater use of technology to enhance information sharing. General Electric has begun to create a very large extranet for its 12 operating units. An **extranet** is a private Internet site that enables several companies to securely share information and conduct business.[15]

➤➤ BUILDING QUALITY PARTNERSHIPS

THE MOMENT OF MAGIC

Tony Alessandra, a well-known sales trainer and consultant, says that there are three possible outcomes when a customer does business with an organization.

The moment of truth. In these selling situations the customer's expectations were met. Nothing happened to disappoint the customer, and the salesperson did not do anything to surpass the customer's expectations. The customer is apt to have somewhat neutral feelings about her relationship with the salesperson. The moment of truth usually does not build customer loyalty.

The moment of misery. This is the outcome of a selling situation where the customer's expectations were not met. The customer may feel a sense of disappointment or even anger. Many customers who experience the moment of misery may share their feelings with others and often make a decision to "fire" the salesperson.

The moment of magic. This is the outcome of a sale where the customer received more than he expected. The salesperson surpassed the customer's expectations by going the extra mile and providing a level of service that added value to the customer–salesperson relationship. This extra effort is likely to establish a foundation for increased customer loyalty.[a]

The "Moment of Magic" is the outcome of a sale where the customer receives more than he expected. Value-added customer service strategies often produce this outcome.

CUSTOMER SERVICE METHODS THAT STRENGTHEN THE PARTNERSHIP

Sales & Marketing Management magazine states that customer service encompasses all activities that enhance or facilitate the sale and use of one's product or service. The skills required to service a sale are different from those required prior to the sale (Fig. 14.2). High-performance sales personnel do not abdicate responsibility for delivery, installation,

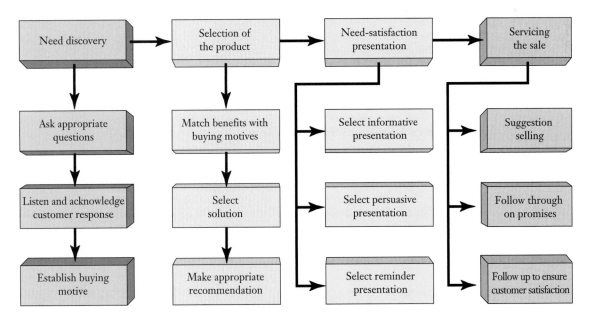

Figure 14.2

The completed Consultative Sales Presentation Guide illustrates the ways in which high-performance salespeople use value-added strategies to service the sale and build repeat business and referrals. Customer service provides many opportunities to strengthen the partnership.

warranty interpretation, or other customer service responsibilities. They continue to strengthen the partnership with suggestion selling, follow-through on promises, and follow-up on activities.

Adding Value with Suggestion Selling

Suggestion selling is an important form of customer service. This is the process of suggesting merchandise or services that are related to the main item sold to the customer. The suggestion is made when, in the salesperson's judgment, the added item can provide the customer with additional satisfaction.

The salesperson who is genuinely interested in helping customers solve their problems can enhance the relationship with suggestion selling. Some of the best ways to engage in suggestion selling follow.

Suggest Related Items In some cases there are related products or services that may add to the customer's satisfaction. To illustrate, let us look at the sale of town houses. Many real estate firms offer the customer a basic dwelling plus a choice of options. The option list might include a fireplace, a screened patio, or an outdoor gas grill. As another example, selling related merchandise at an auto agency is quite common. Most customers can choose from a long list of options including special trim, upscale stereo systems, antilock braking system, and hosts of other items. Suggestion selling is no less important when selling services. For example, a travel agent has many opportunities to use suggestion selling. Let us assume that a customer purchases a two-week vacation in Germany. The agent can offer to book hotel reservations or schedule a guided tour. Another related product would be a rental car. Sometimes a new product is simply not "right" without related merchandise. A new business suit may not look right without a new shirt and tie. An executive training program held at a fine hotel can be enhanced with a refreshment break featuring a variety of soft drinks, fresh coffee, and freshly baked pastries. That new stereo receiver may not sound right until it is matched with a set of quality speakers.

Suggest New Items New products and services are being introduced at a record pace. Some are brand-new features, while others are variations of existing items. Many buyers need help in keeping up with new product introductions. In most cases the salesperson who already has established a relationship with the customer is in the best position to introduce new products. Frank Smith, successful direct sales representative for Institutional Food House, a distributor based in South Carolina, mentions new items when making routine sales calls on his accounts. His goal is to introduce two or three new items during each visit. He also holds new product presentations once a month.[9]

Suggest a Larger Quantity The customer can benefit in several ways from buying a larger quantity. Economy is one of the most common benefits. Many companies offer a discount on large orders. A grocer may be offered a 10-case shipment at $9.90 a case. If the person buys 15 cases, the price is $0.60 per case cheaper. In the retail food business a price reduction of this amount is significant. Sometimes a large order is a good hedge against rising prices. The prices of oil, sugar, paper, antifreeze, and other products also have increased. When a salesperson is sure that prices will rise in the near future, it is a good policy to suggest a larger quantity. Convenience is another value-added benefit associated with large orders. The customer is saved the inconvenience of running out of the item at a critical time.

Suggest Better Quality Products Quality can be described as the degree of excellence inherent within a product or service. Many firms offer the customer a choice of products that varies in terms of quality and price. This is a good marketing strategy because most people like to have a choice when making a purchase. Also, higher priced products often

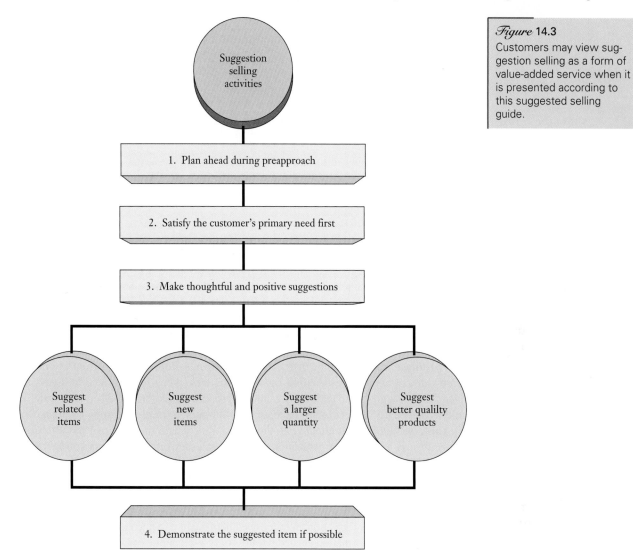

Figure 14.3
Customers may view suggestion selling as a form of value-added service when it is presented according to this suggested selling guide.

provide the customer with added value. The effort to sell better quality goods is known as *trading up,* or *upgrading,* in the field of selling. It is an important selling method that often benefits the customer. The higher priced item may be the best buy when such factors as durability, comfort, or trade-in value are considered.

HOW AND WHEN TO USE SUGGESTION SELLING

Customers may view suggestion selling as a form of value-added service when it is presented correctly. There is a right way and a wrong way to make suggestions. Some guidelines to follow include (Fig. 14.3):

1. *Plan for suggestion selling during the preapproach step.* Before meeting with the customer, develop a suggestion selling plan that includes your objectives for this important dimension of selling. This may involve recording a list of items that you might suggest after you close the sale. Suggestion selling is easier when you are prepared.

2. *Make suggestions after you have first satisfied the customer's primary need.* If you make suggestions too early, the customer may become confused or fail to give your proposal full attention.

3. *Make your suggestion thoughtful and positive.* "We just received a new order of silk ties that would go well with your new shirt. Let me show you the collection." Avoid questions like, "Can we ship anything else?" This question invites a negative response.

4. *Demonstrate the suggested item if at all possible, or use sales tools to build interest.* If you have suggested a shirt to go with a new suit, allow the customer to see it next to the suit. In industrial selling, show the customer a sample, or at least a picture if the actual product is not available.

Suggestion selling is a means of providing value-added service. When you use it correctly, customers thank you for your thoughtfulness and extra service. It is also a proven sales-building strategy. Use it often.

Cross-Selling Used to Grow Sales

We have seen an increase in the use of cross-selling to grow sales volume. **Cross-selling** involves selling products that are not directly related to products that you have sold to an established customer. A bank customer who has a home equity loan might be contacted and asked to consider purchase of a mutual fund. The customer who has purchased a town house might be a candidate for a security service. Quick & Reilly, a nationwide financial services company, has trained its 600 customer service representatives to use cross-selling when customers call concerning their current investments. Representatives from 118 offices nationwide completed cross-selling training programs. They learned how to assess the caller's financial goals and to develop a tailored proposal of products and services. Quick & Reilly achieved a 35 percent sales increase after developing the cross-selling program.[16]

Cross-selling is most effective in those situations where the customer has a positive attitude toward the selling organization. Also, the salesperson (or customer service representative) must propose only products that are tailored to solve the specific problem the customer has confirmed. If cross-selling fulfills a genuine customer need, the result may be a stronger partnership.

Cross-selling has become a major phenomenon in the age of information. Customers often have too much information and they need help deciding which information has value. In many cases, the information needed requires only a telephone call. A well-informed and well-trained customer service representative can strengthen the partnership.

Adding Value with Follow-Through

A major key to an effective customer service strategy is follow-through on assurances and promises that were part of the sales presentation. Did your sales presentation include claims for superior performance; promises of speedy delivery; assistance with credit arrangements; and guaranteed factory assistance with installation, training, and service?

Most sales presentations are made up of claims and promises that the company can fulfill. However, fulfillment of these claims depends to a large degree on after-sale action. Postsale follow-through is the key to holding that customer you worked so hard to develop.

COMMON POSTSALE PROBLEMS

Every salesperson should become familiar with the most common postsale problem areas. Identify the leading problem areas in your company, and be aware of possible solutions. Many studies indicate that customer-related problems after the sale are most likely to be in one of the areas that follow.

Salespeople often assist with credit arrangements and provide counsel to prospective customers.

Making Credit Arrangements Credit has become a common way to finance purchases. This is true of industrial products, real estate, automobiles, home appliances, and many other products. Closing the sale often depends on your ability to develop and present attractive credit plans to the customer. Even if you do not get directly involved in the firm's credit and collection activities, you must be familiar with how the company handles these matters. Salespeople need to establish a relationship with the credit department and learn how credit analysts make their decisions.[17]

Several agencies can supply up-to-date credit information. A credit bureau is available in most large cities. The national firm of Dun & Bradstreet, Incorporated publishes credit books for each state. Sometimes, local bank personnel can provide helpful information.

Making credit decisions gets a lot tougher when you are conducting business in foreign countries. Overseas transactions can be complex, and in some cases there is little recourse if a customer does not pay. Doron Weissman, president of Overseas Brokers, a freight forwarder and export brokerage firm in Great Neck, New York, says, "When I sell my services, I automatically qualify the account to make sure they're financially able to meet my demands. If not, I move on."[18]

Timely Deliveries Many organizations are adding value with on-time deliveries. A late delivery can be a problem for both the supplier and the customer. To illustrate, let us assume that the supplier is a manufacturer of small appliances and the customer is a department store chain. A late delivery may mean lost sales due to out-of-stock conditions, cancellation of the order by the department store, or loss of future sales.

The causes of late delivery may be beyond your control. It is not your fault if the plant closes because of labor trouble or weather conditions. It is your responsibility, however, to keep the customer informed of any delays. You also can take steps to prevent a delay. Check to be sure your order was processed correctly. Follow up to see if the order was shipped on time. Above all, keep the customer informed of any delays.

Proper Installation Buyer satisfaction is often related to proper installation of the product. This is true of consumer products such as security systems, central air-conditioning, solar heating systems, and carpeting. It also is true of industrial products such as electronic data processing equipment and air quality control systems. Some salespeople believe it is to their advantage to supervise product installation. They then are able to spot installation problems. Others make it a practice to follow up on the installation to be sure no problems exist.

Tom Peters believes there is one asset that can appreciate over the years. That asset is the well-served customer, who becomes the most significant sustainer of the business, the lifetime customer.

Creating the Lifetime Customer

When we build a plant or purchase a computer—when we acquire just about any new asset—by accounting conventions, it begins to depreciate on day one. But there is one asset that can *appreciate* over the years. That asset is the well-served customer, who becomes the most significant sustainer of the business, the lifetime customer.

Tom Peters

Customer Training in the Use or Care of the Product For certain industries it is essential that users be skilled in how to use the new product. This is true of office duplication equipment, electronic cash registers, farm implements, and many other products. Technology has become so complex that many suppliers must provide training as part of the follow-up to ensure customer satisfaction. Most organizations that sell microcomputers and other types of electronic equipment for office use now schedule training classes to ensure that customers can properly use and care for the products. These companies believe that users must be skilled in handling their equipment.

Price Changes Price changes do not need to be a serious problem if they are handled correctly. The salesperson is responsible for maintaining an up-to-date price list. As your company issues price changes, record them accurately. Customers expect you to quote the correct price the first time.

PREVENTING POSTSALE PROBLEMS

There are ways to prevent postsale problems. The key is conscientious follow-up to be sure everything has been handled properly. Get to know the people who operate your shipping and installation department. They are responsible for getting the right merchandise shipped and installed on time, and it is important that they understand your customers' needs.

Become acquainted with people in the credit department. Be sure that they maintain a good, businesslike relationship with your customers. This is a delicate area; even small mistakes (a "pay now" notice sent too early, for example) can cause hurt feelings. If your company uses a customer support staff to resolve postsale problems, be sure to get acquainted with people who provide this service.

Adding Value with Customer Follow-Up

Customer follow-up methods usually have two major objectives. One is to express appreciation for the purchase and thus enhance the relationship established during the sales presentation. You no doubt thanked the customer at the time the sale was closed, but it would not hurt to say thank-you again a few days later. The second purpose of the follow-up is to determine if the customer is satisfied with the purchase. Both of these methods can strengthen the buyer–seller relationship and build a partnership that results in additional sales.

In survey after survey, poor service and lack of follow-up after the sale are given as primary reasons people stop buying from us. Most customers are sensitive to indifferent treatment by the sales representative. With this fact in mind you should approach follow-up in a systematic and businesslike way. There are five follow-up methods.

PERSONAL VISIT

This is usually the most costly follow-up method, but it may produce the best results. It is the only strategy that allows face-to-face, two-way communication. When you take time to make a personal visit, the customer knows that you really care.

Use the personal follow-up to keep the customer informed of new developments, new products, or new applications. This information may pave the way for additional sales. When you do make a personal visit, do not stay too long. Accomplish the purpose of your visit as quickly as possible, and then excuse yourself.

TELEPHONE CALL

The telephone provides a quick and efficient way to follow up a sale. A salesperson can easily make 10 or 12 phone calls in a single hour, and the cost can be minimal. If you plan to send a thank-you card or letter, follow it up with a thank-you call. The personal appeal of the phone call increases the effectiveness of the written correspondence. The telephone call has one major advantage over written correspondence. It allows for a two-way exchange of information. Once an account is well established, you may be able to obtain repeat sales by telephone.

►► CUSTOMER RELATIONSHIP MANAGEMENT WITH TECHNOLOGY

CONFIRMING IMMEDIATELY

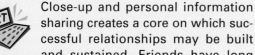

Close-up and personal information sharing creates a core on which successful relationships may be built and sustained. Friends have long supplemented their personal visits with notes, letters, and telephone calls.

Contemporary technology offers new ways to save time in addition to enhancing and extending relationship-rich communications. Enlightened salespeople use the fax and computer modem as fast, thus effective, methods to give information to their customers. The Fax function can be particularly useful to quickly convey temporary messages such as those that confirm, affirm, or verify. (See the exercise, Correspondence with CRM, at p. 323 for more information.)

E-MAIL MESSAGE

In many cases it is a lot quicker to send an e-mail message than to make a phone call. Salespeople report that they waste a lot of time playing "phone tag." Some customers prefer e-mail messages and may become irritated if you do not adhere to their wishes. If you know that a customer is not in the habit of checking her e-mail all that often, use the telephone as a back-up method. When in doubt, use parallel channels of communication.

LETTER OR CARD

Written correspondence is an inexpensive and convenient form of customer follow-up. Letters and cards can be used to thank the customer for the order and to promise continued service. Some companies encourage their salespeople to use a formal letter typed on company stationery. Other companies have designed special thank-you cards, which are signed and sent routinely after a sale is closed. The salesperson may enclose a business card. These thank-you cards do have one major limitation: They are mass-produced and therefore lack the personal touch so important to customer satisfaction.

CALL REPORT

The **call report** is a form that serves as a communications link with persons who can assist with customer service. The format varies, but generally it is a simple form with only four or five spaces. The sample call report form that appears in the text is used by a company that installs security systems at banks and other financial institutions.

A form like this is one solution to the problem of communication between the company personnel and the customer. It is a method of follow-through that triggers the desired action. It is simple, yet businesslike.

Follow-up programs can be as creative or as ingenious as you wish according to Nancy Friedman, president of a national telephone training company. She suggests you customize your follow-up program to meet the needs of your customer.[19] Every sales organization competes on value, so you must continually think of new ways to add value. Creative use of your interpersonal communication skills can keep your messages fresh and personalized. Keep in mind that people buy both from the head and the heart. Let customers know how much you care about their business.[20] You can use these five methods independently or in combination. Your main consideration should be some type of appropriate follow-up that (1) tells customers you appreciate their business and (2) determines if they are satisfied with the purchase.

The Call Report

Date: October 26, 200_
To: Walt Higgins, service engineer
From: Diane Ray, sales representative

Action Promised: Visit the First National Bank of Middleberg within the next week to check on installation of our security system.

Assistance Needed: System B-420 was installed at the First National Bank of Middleberg on October 24. As per our agreement, you should make a follow-up call to check the installation of the system and provide bank personnel with a Form 82 certification checklist. The form should be given to Mr. Kurt Heller, president.

Copies to: Mr. Kurt Heller

Preplan Your Service Strategy

Servicing the sale is a very important dimension of personal selling, so a certain amount of preplanning is essential. It helps to preplan your service strategy for each of the three areas we have discussed: suggestion selling, follow-through, and follow-up. You cannot anticipate every aspect of the service, but you can preplan important ways to add value once the sale is closed. Develop a servicing-the-sale worksheet, shown in Figure 14.4, prior to each sales presentation.

Servicing-the-Sale Worksheet	
Method of Adding Value	What You Will Say or Do
Suggestion Selling Suggest the purchase of global positioning system (GPS) technology to enhance use of seed research equipment.	"GPS technology will enable you to track all your research and plot the findings on your computer screen."
Follow-Through Set up a secured Web site or extranet so client can track the production and delivery of the custom engineered seed research equipment.	Set up the secured Web site in a timely manner and then contact the customer when it is operational. Explain how to access the Web site and review the benefits of using this source of assistance.
Schedule training for persons who will be using the new technology.	Send training schedule to customer and confirm the dates with a follow-up call.
Follow-Up Send a thank-you letter to each member of the team that made the purchase decision.	Express sincere appreciation for the purchase and explain the steps you will take to ensure a long-term partnership.
Check to be certain that the training was effective.	Visit the customer's research facility and talk with the employees who completed the training. Answer questions and provide additional assistance as needed.

Figure 14.4

Suggestion selling, follow-through on assurances and promises, and customer follow-up methods must be carefully planned. Use of this worksheet can help you preplan ways to add value.

PARTNERSHIP BUILDING STRATEGIES SHOULD ENCOMPASS ALL KEY PEOPLE

Some salespeople do a great job of communicating with the prospect but ignore other key people involved in the sale. To illustrate how serious this problem can be, let us look at the approach used by Jill Bisignano, a sales representative for a major restaurant supply firm. Jill had called on Bellino's Italian Restaurant for several years. Although she was always very friendly to Nick Bellino, she treated the other employees with nearly total indifference. One day she called on Nick and was surprised to learn that he was retiring and had decided to sell his restaurant to two longtime employees.

As you might expect, it did not take the new owners long to find another supplier. Jill lost a large account because she failed to develop a good personal relationship with other key employees. It pays to be nice to everyone.

Here is a partial list of people in your company and in the prospect's company who can influence both initial and repeat sales.

1. *Receptionist.* Some salespeople simply do not use common sense when dealing with the receptionist. This person has daily contact with your customer and may schedule most or all calls. To repeatedly forget this individual's name or display indifference in other ways may cost you dearly. Display a friendly but businesslike attitude toward this person. Do not be patronizing or aloof.
2. *Technical personnel.* Some products must be cleaned, lubricated, or adjusted on a regular basis. Take time to get acquainted with the people who perform these duties. Answer their questions, share technical information with them if necessary, and show appreciation for the work they are doing.
3. *Stock clerks or receiving clerks.* People working in the receiving room are often responsible for pricing incoming merchandise and making sure that these items are stored properly. They also may be responsible for stock rotation and processing damage claims.

►► Selling in Action

EFFECTIVE DESIGN AND USE OF THE BUSINESS CARD

The business card continues to be a powerful tool for salespeople. It provides a personal touch in our high-tech world. The business card is a convenient way to communicate important information to customers, sales support personnel, and others. When you develop your business card, keep these tips in mind.

- Use eye-catching items such as your picture, your company logo, raised letters, colors, and textured paper. The card should be tasteful and pleasing to the eye.
- The card should feature all current contact information such as your e-mail address, telephone numbers, and mailing address.

- Consider using both sides of the card. You might print your customer service philosophy on the back of the card or list the products you sell.

Give your cards generously to anyone who might need to contact you later. Always offer your business card when networking. The card is useful when the contact tells others about your products or services.[c]

4. *Management personnel.* Although you may be working closely with someone at the departmental or division level, do not forget the person who has the final authority and responsibility for this area. Spend time with management personnel occasionally and be alert to any concerns they may have.

This is not a complete list of the people you may need to depend on for support. There may well be other key people who influence sales. Always look beyond the customer to see who else might have a vested interest in the sale.

PARTNERING WITH AN UNHAPPY CUSTOMER

We have learned more about the impact of customer complaints through research that indicates unhappy customers often do not initiate a verbal or written complaint. This means that postsale problems may not come to the attention of salespeople or other personnel within the organization. We also know that unhappy customers do share their negative experiences with other people. A dissatisfied customer often tells 8–10 people about his problem.[21] A double loss occurs when the customer stops buying our products and takes steps to discourage other people from buying our products. When complaints do surface, we should view the problem as an opportunity to strengthen the business relationship. To achieve this goal, follow these suggestions.

1. *Give customers every opportunity to disclose their feelings.* Companies noted for outstanding customer service rely heavily on telephone systems—like toll-free "hotlines" to ensure easy access. At Federal Express, Cadillac Division of General Motors, and IBM, to name a few companies, specially trained advisors answer the calls and offer assistance. When a customer purchases a Ford vehicle, the salesperson introduces the customer to service staff who play a key role in providing postsale service. The goal is to personalize the relationhip with another member of the service team. Ford has discovered that after-sale contact builds a perception of value.[22] When customers do complain, by telephone or in person, encourage them to express all their anger and frustration. Do not interrupt. Do not become defensive. Do not make any judgments until you have heard all the facts as the customer sees them.[23] If they stop talking, try to get them to talk some more. Most of us feel better once we have had the opportunity to express our concerns fully.

2. *As the customer is talking, listen carefully and attentively.* You need accurate information to solve the problem. One of the biggest barriers to effective listening is emotion. Do not become angry, and do not get into an argument. Once you feel the customer has fully vented, paraphrase what she said to prove you cared enough to listen.[24]

3. *Keep in mind that it does not really matter whether a complaint is real or perceived.* If the customer is upset, you should be polite and sympathetic. Do not yield to the temptation to say, "You do not really have a problem." Remember, problems exist when customers perceive they exist.[25]

4. *Do not alibi.* Avoid the temptation to blame the shipping department, the installation crew, or anyone else associated with your company. Never tear down the company you work for. The problem has been placed in your hands, and you must accept responsibility for handling it. "Passing the buck" only leaves the customer with a feeling of helplessness.

5. *Politely share with the customer your point of view concerning the problem's cause.* At least explain what you think happened. The customer deserves an explanation. At this point a sincere apology is usually appropriate.

6. *Decide what action must be taken to remedy the problem.* Take action quickly and offer a value-added atonement. Don't just do what is expected, but delight the customer by exceeding his expectations. Winning customer loyalty today means going beyond making it right.[26]

The value of customer complaints can emerge in two forms. First, complaints can be a source of important information that may be difficult to obtain by other means. Second, customer complaints provide unique opportunities for companies to *prove* their commitment to service. Loyalty builds in the customer's mind if you do a good job of solving her problem.[27]

Summary

Servicing the sale is a major dimension of the selling process, with the objectives of providing maximum customer satisfaction and establishing a long-term partnership. Good service ensures that the product meets the customer's needs, and also satisfies the needs for security and recognition discussed in Chapter 7 (see Maslow's hierarchy of needs.) A reputation for good service is essential in attracting new accounts and keeping old ones. The goal is to develop lifetime customers. We review several current developments in *customer service*. Salespeople are spending more time monitoring customer satisfaction. Customer knowledge is an important key to improving customer service, and computer-based systems are being used to enhance customer service.

The customer service strategy is made up of three activities: adding value with *suggestion selling*, adding value with follow through, and adding value with customer follow-up. These activities create a positive impression of the salesperson and the company, which results in increased patronage buying.

A salesperson depends on the support of many other people in servicing a sale. Maintaining good relationships with support staff members who help service your accounts is well worth the time and energy required. This chapter also includes information on ways to effectively solve the customer's problem. Regular and objective self-evaluation is also a valuable practice. Efficient performance of the functions involved in customer service is important to ensure continuing customer satisfaction and should be a matter of professional pride.

KEY TERMS

Customer Service	Cross-Selling
Extranet	Call Report
Suggestion Selling	

REVIEW QUESTIONS

1. What two powerful motivators can a salesperson appeal to with a well-planned customer service program? Explain the significance of each one.
2. Define customer service. List the activities associated with this phase of personal selling.

3. Explain how suggestion selling fits into the definition of customer service. How does suggestion selling differ from cross-selling?

4. Explain some of the reasons customer service is considered a profit stimulator.

5. List and describe three current developments in customer service.

6. How does credit become a part of servicing the sale?

7. This chapter describes the value of the lifetime customer. Is it realistic to believe that people will become lifetime customers in our very competitive marketplace?

8. List and describe five customer follow-up methods.

9. What types of customer service problems might be prevented with the use of a call report?

10. Briefly describe the design elements of an effective business card.

APPLICATION EXERCISES

1. You are a salesperson working in the paint department at a Home Depot store. A customer has just purchased 15 gallons of house paint. Assume that your store carries everything in the painting line, and list as many items as you can think of that could be used for suggestion selling. Explain how your suggestions of these items could be a service to the customer.

2. You work as a wholesale salesperson for a plumbing supply company. One of your customers, a contractor, has an open line of credit with your company for $10,000 worth of products. He is currently at his limit; however, he is not overdue. He just received word that he has been awarded a $40,000 plumbing contract at the local airport. The contract requires that he supply $9,000 worth of plumbing products. Your customer does not have the cash to pay for the additional products. He informs you that unless you can provide him with some type of financing, he may lose the contract. He says that he can pay you when he finishes his next job in 60 days. Explain what you will do.

3. You have just interviewed for a job that you really would like to have. You have heard it is a good idea to follow up an interview with a thank-you note or letter and an indication of your enthusiasm for the position. Select the strategy you will use for your follow-up, and explain why you chose it.

4. Using your search engine, examine the Internet for information on customer satisfaction. Type in "customer satisfaction" + selling. Are you surprised by the number of queries on this subject? Examine some of the queries related to what customers have said about specific company customer service programs.

CRM APPLICATION EXERCISE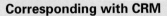

Corresponding with CRM

Waiting for a client who forgot an appointment can be very time consuming. The client who promptly receives a faxed reminder note is more likely to remember and honor a commitment to meet. Quickly confirming an agreement reached by telephone is easy for customer relationship management (CRM) systems such as ACT!. Look up the contact Ian Program, select <u>W</u>rite, and <u>F</u>ax Cover. This displays the fax cover sheet that by itself may be used to convey a short confirmation message. Position the cursor at Subject and type "Lunch," and then press Enter twice and type "I look forward to lunch with you Friday noon at Jimmy's." Select File Print (Ctrl+ P) to print the fax cover note. If your computer is running fax software, you could send the fax cover note directly to your client's fax machine.

CASE PROBLEM

If you spend time visiting highly successful companies such as Federal Express, Southwest Airlines, or Motorola, you learn about a series of rituals, stories, and heroes that express the organizations' "corporate culture." Often the heroes you hear about are employees who provided some form of customer service that was "beyond the call of duty." Ginger Trumfio, assistant editor of *Sales & Marketing Management*, says that keeping customers happy and coming back requires more than smiles and thank-yous. She believes that building customer loyalty requires outrageous service:

> . . . in today's business climate salespeople need to do more than follow up on promises, meet deadlines, and create win–win situations to keep clients happy—and coming back. Salespeople need to be outrageous, shocking, even death-defying.

Outrageous? Shocking? Death-defying? Does good customer service really require this much effort? Trumfio contacted several sales forces to find examples of outrageous service. Three examples follow.

Example one. The industry standard for morning express air carrier deliveries had been 10:30 A.M. Xerox Corporation had a critical need to get emergency parts to its technicians much earlier. Airborne Express carefully studied Xerox's needs and developed a plan to guarantee delivery times across the United States ranging from 8:00 to 9:30 A.M. Airborne has taken several steps to track Xerox packages throughout the process of delivery. For example, the scanner of every driver has been coded to beep and read "Xerox" when there is a Xerox package to be delivered. Once drivers realize they have an urgent package, the load plan is prioritized to make that delivery first.

Example two. Tony Heineman, account executive at KTUL Channel 8 in Tulsa, Oklahoma, describes a telephone conversation he had with the media buyer for a local company. He immediately detected that she was in a bad mood, so he asked her what was wrong. She explained that nearly every media representative in town had called that day to inquire about the details of a large media buy her company was about to make. Heineman sensed that something else might be bothering the buyer and asked, "What's *really* wrong?" He discovered that she was concerned about car repairs that she needed but could not afford. He said, without hesitation, "Don't move, I'm on my way." Heineman jumped in his car and drove to his client's office. He picked up her car and took it to a friend who is a mechanic at a local dealer. The mechanic agreed to repair the car at no charge. The next day he returned the car to his client who was both happy and relieved.

Example three. David Lubelkin, president of Industrial Edge USA, an apartment house supply company in Orange, New Jersey, gave outrageous service during a winter snowstorm. On a cold January day, after a major snowstorm, he received a call from a desperate customer who needed 60 pounds of rock salt to be delivered to a property located 100 miles away. Predictions of sleet and icy rain threatened to bring traffic to a halt. Knowing that his delivery trucks were already on the road and not due back until late in the day, Lubelkin promised to deliver the salt needed by the customer. He quickly met with company CEO Stephen Weitraub and a decision was made to rent a truck for the delivery. The trip, normally a one and a half hour drive turned into a four and a half hour crawl at an average speed of 20 miles per hour. After dropping off the salt, the return trip took even longer. It was 10:00 P.M. when they finally returned to the office.[28]

Questions

1. Do you agree that outrageous service is needed to build customer loyalty? Explain.

2. Is there a downside to outrageous service after the sale? Reflect on the three preceding examples as you answer this question.

3. How might these acts of outrageous service influence the organization's "corporate culture"?

4. Would you consider following through on assurances and promises, and customer follow-up to be examples of outrageous customer service? Explain.

CRM CASE STUDY

Servicing the Sale with CRM

You have taken over a number of accounts of another salesperson, Pat Silva. Most of these accounts are prospects, which means that they have not yet purchased from SimNet. Two accounts did purchase networks from Pat: Ms. Karen Murray of Murray D'Zines, and Ms. Judith Albright, owner of Piccadilly Studio. You now want to be sure that these sales are well serviced.

Questions

1. Whom should you speak with, within SimNet, before following through and contacting each of the customers? What would you need to discover?

2. What will be your follow-up strategy for each customer?

3. Does the fact that these customers initiated their orders (they were not sold the products, they bought them) influence your follow-up strategy?

4. Might other customers or prospects be affected by your service activities? How would this influence your activities? Could customer service be your competitive edge?

5. Do you see any suggestion selling opportunities with these two accounts? Which *suggestion* selling methods should you consider?

PARTNERSHIP SELLING: A ROLE PLAY/SIMULATION
(see Appendix 3, p. 406)

DEVELOPING A PRESENTATION STRATEGY—SERVICING THE SALE

Refer to *sales memorandum 3*, and strategically plan to service the sale with your customer. After closing the sale (getting the customer's signature) there are several steps to add value and build customer confidence and satisfaction. These steps are important to providing total quality customer service and should provide for repeat sales and a list of referred customers.

Follow the instructions in item 2g of your presentation plan. You need to schedule a future appointment to telephone or personally call and confirm the number of people attending the convention, and final room and menu needs (see convention center policies). Also, during this conversation you may suggest beverages for breaks, audiovisual needs, and any other items that can make this an outstanding convention for your customer.

You should have your calendar available to suggest and write down dates and times for this future contact. Any special materials such as a calendar can be placed in the back pocket of your portfolio. You may want to secure another person to be your customer and practice the customer service strategies you have prepared.

At this point you should be strategically prepared to make the presentation outlined in *sales memorandum 3* to your customer. Your instructor will provide you with further instructions.

MANAGEMENT OF SELF AND OTHERS

➤ Personal selling requires a great deal of self-discipline and self-direction. Chapter 15 examines the four dimensions of self-management. Chapter 16 introduces communication style bias and explains how to build strong relationships with style flexing. The final chapter examines the fundamentals of sales force management.

By knowing our own communication style, we get to know ourselves better. And we get along with others better as we develop the ability to recognize—and respond to—their styles.

PAUL MOK AND
DUDLEY LYNCH

CHAPTER 15

Management of Self: The Key to Greater Sales Productivity

When you finish reading this chapter, you should be able to

1. Discuss the four dimensions of self-management

2. List and describe time management strategies

3. Explain factors that contribute to improved territory management

4. Identify and discuss common elements of a records management system

5. Discuss stress management practices

Julio Melara, born to Honduran immigrant parents, made work the centerpiece of his life at an early age. Throughout high school he cut grass, worked as a busboy, delivered newspapers, and sold newspaper subscriptions. While attending college he worked as a courier with *New Orleans City Business*, a local business newspaper. By age 23 he was top producer and head of national sales. Later he left the newspaper and went into radio advertising sales. By age 28, Melara broke all sales records at WWL and became the radio's first million-dollar producer. He is a self-motivated person who says that he has learned a great deal from such books as *The Power of Positive Thinking* by Norman Vincent Peale. He is also someone who believes in management of self. Goal setting is the central theme of Melara's sales philosophy. He believes that written goals (personal and professional) facilitate growth and success.[1]

A salesperson is much like the individual who owns and operates a business. The successful sales representative, like the successful entrepreneur, depends on good self-management. Both of them must keep their own records, use self-discipline in scheduling their time, and analyze their own performance.

High-performance salespeople and successful entrepreneurs have one more characteristic in common. They realize that all development is really self-development.[2]

Goal setting is the central theme of Julio Melara's sales philosophy. He believes that written goals (personal and professional) facilitate growth and success.

MANAGEMENT OF SELF—A FOUR-DIMENSIONAL PROCESS

What makes a salesperson successful? Some people believe the most important factor is hard work. This is only partly true. Some people work hard but do not accomplish much. They lack purpose and direction. This lack of organization results in wasted time and energy.

Wasting time and energy is the key to failure in the age of information. Many salespeople are drowning in information and the flood of messages each day leaves little time to think and reflect. Sales and sales support personnel, like most other knowledge workers, are working under tighter deadlines. The response time to customer inquiries has been shortened and customers are less tolerant of delays.

In this chapter we approach management of self as a four-dimensional process consisting of the following components:

1. *Time management.* There are only about 250 business days per year. Within each day there is only so much time to devote to selling. Selling hours are extremely valuable. A group of 1,300 salespeople were asked to evaluate 16 challenges they face in their work. "Not enough time" was rated number 1 and "Achieving balance between work and family" was rated number 2. "Dealing with information overload" was ranked number 3.[3]

2. *Territory management.* A sales territory is a group of customers and prospective customers assigned to a single salesperson. Every territory is unique. Some territories consist of one or two counties, while others encompass several states. The number of accounts within each territory also varies. Today, territory management is becoming less of an art and more of a science.

3. *Records management.* Every salesperson must maintain a certain number of records. These records help to "systematize" data collection and storage. A wise salesperson never relies on memory. Some of the most common records include planning calendars, prospect forms, call reports, summary reports, and expense reports.

4. *Stress management.* A certain amount of stress comes with many selling positions. Some salespeople have learned how to take stressful situations in stride. Others allow stress to trigger anger and frustration. Learning to cope with various stressors that surface in the daily life of a salesperson is an important part of the self-management process.

TIME MANAGEMENT

A salesperson can increase sales volume in two major ways. One is to improve selling effectiveness, and the other is to spend more time in face-to-face selling situations. The latter objective can be achieved best through improved time and territory management.

Improving the management of both time and territory is a high-priority concern in the field of selling. These two closely related functions represent major challenges for salespeople.

Let us first look closely at the area of time management. There is definitely a close relationship between sales volume and number of customer contacts made by the salesperson. You have to make calls to get results.

Time-Consuming Activities

Some salespeople who have kept careful records of how they spend their time each day are surprised to learn how little is spent in face-to-face selling situations. The major time-consuming activities in personal selling are travel, time spent waiting to see a customer, com-

Agency Sales Magazine, September 1997.

pletion of sales records, casual conversation, time spent on customer follow-through and follow-up, and time spent in face-to-face selling. Salespeople need to carefully examine each of these activities and determine whether too much or too little time is spent in any area. One way to assess time use is to keep a time log. This involves recording, at the end of every hour, the activities in which they were engaged during that time.[4] At the end of the week, add up the number of minutes spent on the various activities and ask yourself, "Is this the best use of my time?"

Once you have tabulated the results of your time log, it should be easy to identify the "time wasters." Pick one or two of the most wasteful areas, and then make plans to correct the problem. Set realistic goals that can be achieved. Keep in mind that wasting time is usually a habit. To manage your time more effectively, you need to form new habits.

Time Management Methods

Sound time management methods can pave the way to greater sales productivity. The starting point is forming a new attitude toward time conservation. You must view time as a scarce resource not to be wasted. The timesaving strategies presented here are not new, nor are they unique. They are being used by time-conscious people in all walks of life.

DEVELOP A SERIES OF PERSONAL GOALS

According to Alan Lakein, author of *How to Get Control of Your Time and Your Life,* the most important aspect of time management is knowing what your goals are. He is referring to all goals—career goals, family goals, and life goals. People who cannot or do not sit down and write out exactly what they want from life lack direction.

The goal-setting process requires that you be clear about what you want to accomplish. If your goal is too general or vague, progress toward achieving that goal is difficult to observe. Goals such as "I want to be a success" or "I desire good health" are much too

> Most people who achieve success in selling have a strong work ethic. They are "self-starters" who are committed to more than the 8-hour day or the 40-hour week.

general. Goals also should reflect the values that govern your life. For example, if one of your governing values is "I love my family," then you may commit yourself to spending quality time with family members.

Goals have a great deal of psychological value to people in selling. Sales goals, for example, can serve as a strong motivational force. To illustrate, let us assume that Mary Paulson, sales representative for a cosmetic manufacturer, decides to increase her sales by 15 percent over the previous year. She now has a specific goal to aim for and can begin identifying specific ways to achieve the new goal. Goals often help us form new habits.

PREPARE A DAILY "TO DO" LIST

Sales professionals who complete the time management course offered by Franklin Covey are encouraged to engage in event control. This involves planning and prioritizing events every day.[5] Start each day by thinking about what you hope to accomplish. Then write down the activities (Fig. 15.1). Putting your thoughts on paper forces you to clarify your thinking. Moff D. Warren, president of Intellective Innovations, says, "If you write down exactly what needs to be done, not only does it make you psychologically ready for the day but also it helps you think broadly as you develop strategies for your business."[6] It is much easier to coordinate activities written in black and white than to try to carry them around in your head.

Now you should rank these activities from most important to least important. Make sure that daily activities are related to attaining the goals you have established. Begin each day with the highest priority task. Resist the urge to relegate the tasks you dislike to the bottom of the list.[7]

Preparing a daily "to do" list should become a habit. Try not to let busy-work crowd planning out of your schedule. After all, preparation of a to do list usually requires only five to ten minutes. This small investment of time can pay big dividends.

MAINTAIN A PLANNING CALENDAR

Ideally, a salesperson needs a single place to record daily appointments (personal and business), deadlines, and tasks. Unfortunately, many salespeople write daily tasks on any slip of paper they can find—backs of envelopes, three-by-five cards, napkins, or Post-it notes.

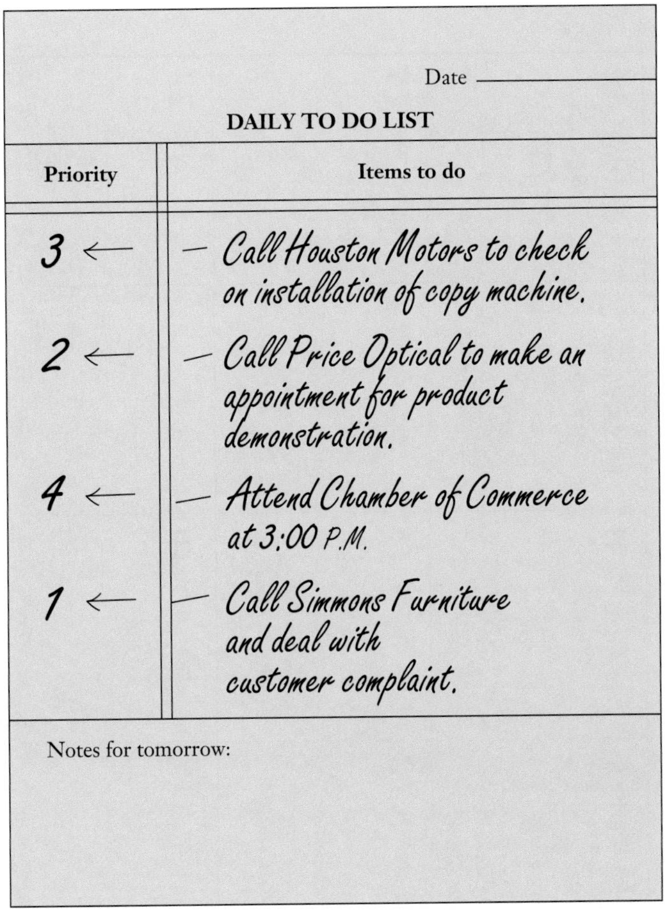

DAILY TO DO LIST	Date _____

Priority	Items to do
3 ←	— *Call Houston Motors to check on installation of copy machine.*
2 ←	— *Call Price Optical to make an appointment for product demonstration.*
4 ←	— *Attend Chamber of Commerce at 3:00 P.M.*
1 ←	— *Call Simmons Furniture and deal with customer complaint.*

Notes for tomorrow:

Figure 15.1
A daily list of activities can help us set priorities and save time. Today this list is recorded electronically in most CRM systems. The list is one of the first things salespeople see when they access the software each day.

Hyrum W. Smith, author of *The 10 Natural Laws of Successful Time and Life Management*, calls these pieces of paper "floaters."

> They just float around until you either follow through on them or lose them. It's a terribly disorganized method for someone who wants to gain greater control of his or her life.[8]

The use of floaters often leads to the loss of critical information, missed appointments, and lack of focus. Select a planning calendar design (the Franklin Covey Day Planner is one option) that can bring efficiency to your daily planning efforts. You should be able to determine at a glance what is coming up in the days and weeks ahead (Fig. 15.2).

Some salespeople are using electronic pocket organizers to store hundreds of names, addresses, and phone numbers. These organizers can be used to keep track of appointments and serve as a perpetual calendar. You simply key in a birthday or anniversary, and a gentle beep jogs your memory on the appropriate date. The electronic organizer also can be used to keep track of appointments.

ORGANIZE YOUR SELLING TOOLS

You can save valuable time by finding ways to organize sales literature, business cards, order blanks, samples, and other items needed during a sales call. You may waste time on a callback because some item was not available during your first call. You may even lose a sale because you forgot or misplaced a key selling tool.

If you have a great deal of paperwork, invest in one or more file cabinets. Some salespeople purchase small, lightweight cardboard file boxes to keep their materials organized.

June '02

NOTES

MAY 2002

S	M	T	W	T	F	S
			1	2	3	4
5	6	7	8	9	10	11
12	13	14	15	16	17	18
19	20	21	22	23	24	25
26	27	28	29	30	31	

JULY 2002

S	M	T	W	T	F	S
	1	2	3	4	5	6
7	8	9	10	11	12	13
14	15	16	17	18	19	20
21	22	23	24	25	26	27
28	29	30	31			

SUNDAY	MONDAY	TUESDAY	WEDNESDAY	THURSDAY	FRIDAY	SATURDAY
						1
2	**3**	**4** 10:30 Wheat First Securities 12:00 Lunch with Ray Williams 3:00 Farrell's Service Center	**5** 9:00 Demonstration at Charter Federal 11:00 Demo at Mills, Inc. 3:30 Meet with Helen Sisson	**6** 9:00 Austin & Son Storage 10:30 Demo at CMP Sporting Goods 1:00 Attend Computer Trade Show	**7** 9:00 Sales Meeting at Imperial Motor Lodge 1:30 Demo at Omega Homes	**8** 10:00 Take Dana to soccer game
9	**10** 8:00 to 12:00 Sales Training 1:30 Meet with M.I.S. staff at Mission College	**11** 9:30 Park Realty 11:00 White Tire Service 2:00 Demo at Ritter Seafood	**12** 9:00 Demonstration at Ross accounting services 11:00 Prospecting 2:30 Meet with technical support staff	**13** 8:30 Meet with Helen Hunt 12:00 Lunch with Tim 1:00 Demo at Collins Wholesale 4:00 Parent-Teacher conference	**14** 9:00 Demo at National Bank 1:00 to 5:00 Update sales records	**15** 9:00 10-K run (starts at YMCA building)
16	**17**	**18**	**19**	**20**	**21**	**22**

Figure 15.2
MONTHLY PLANNING CALENDAR SAMPLE

Shown are 12 days of a monthly planning calendar for a computer service sales representative. Monthly planning calendars such as this one are now a key function of most CRM systems.

These boxes can be placed easily in your car trunk and moved from one sales call to another. The orderly arrangement of selling tools is just one more method of time conservation.

The key to regular use of the four timesaving techniques described previously is *commitment*. Unless you are convinced that efficient time management is important, you will probably find it difficult to adopt these new habits. A salesperson who fully accepts the "time is money" philosophy uses these techniques routinely.

Saving Time with Telephones, Facsimile (Fax) Machines, E-Mail, and Electronic Data Interchange

As the cost of a sales call increases, more and more salespeople are asking the question, "Is this trip necessary?" In many situations a telephone call can replace a personal visit. The telephone call may be especially useful in dealing with accounts that are marginal in terms of profitability. Some customers actually prefer telephone contact for certain types of business transactions. Some situations in which the phone call is appropriate follow:

Call the customer in advance to make an appointment. You save time, and the customer knows when to expect you.

Use the telephone to keep the customer informed. A phone call provides instant communication with customers at a low cost.

Build customer goodwill with a follow-up phone call. Make it a practice to call customers to thank them for buying your product and determine if the customer is satisfied with the purchase.

Some customers prefer to be contacted by e-mail and it would be a mistake to ignore their preference. Busy people often discourage telephone calls as a means of minimizing interruptions. They review e-mail messages only at specific times of the day.

Voice mail automated telephone systems are now being used by companies of all sizes. These systems not only answer the phone and take messages but also provide information-retrieval systems that are accessible by telephone. This technology is especially useful for salespeople who need to exchange information with others.[9] For many salespeo-

The cellular telephone has become a convenient and timesaving sales tool.

►► Customer Relationship Management with Technology

Islands of Information

Companies often use many different software programs that contain information about customers. The firm may have customer purchase and payment history in its accounting system. Customer service problems may be recorded in the service department's software. A help desk program may be used by people in customer support.

The company's salespeople may be using one software program to manage their contacts with customer personnel, another program to prepare quotes, and yet another for correspondence with customers. To reduce these "islands" of customer information, more companies are finding ways to merge this information or to acquire software that performs more than one of these functions. Some customer relationship management (CRM) systems are combining a number of these functions into one integrated package.

ple the cellular car telephone has become a convenient and timesaving sales tool. A pager also can be used to facilitate communication with customers and the main office.

The fax machine takes telecommunication a step further. With the aid of a fax machine, salespeople can send and receive documents in seconds, using standard public or cellular telephone lines. Detailed designs, charts, and graphs can be transmitted across the nation or around the world.

Electronic Data Interchange (EDI) provides a fast and efficient way of exchanging common documents such as purchase orders, invoices, sales reports, and fund transfers. EDI is meeting the needs of companies that no longer want to transfer information on paper. In today's fast-paced world, if you only do business on paper, some firms do not buy your products. Most Fortune 500 companies are using EDI today.[10]

TERRITORY MANAGEMENT

Many marketing organizations have found it helpful to break down the total market into manageable units called sales territories. A **territory** is the geographic area where prospects and customers reside. Although some firms have developed territories solely on the basis of geographic considerations, a more common approach is to establish a territory on the basis of classes of customers. Territories are often classified according to sales potential. Some marketers assign sales representatives to key industries. The Ottawa *Citizen* newspaper divided the paper's customer base into major business lines such as real estate and automotive.[11] Regardless of how the sales territory is established, it is essentially a specific number of present and potential accounts that can be called on conveniently.

With the aid of a fax machine, salespeople can send and receive documents in seconds.

What Does Territory Management Involve?

To appreciate fully the many facets of territory management, it is helpful to examine a typical selling situation. Put yourself in the shoes of a salesperson who has just accepted a position with a firm that manufactures a line of high-quality tools. You are responsible for

➤➤ Selling in Action

BALANCING CAREER AND FAMILY

Women today know that they will probably be working for pay for part or all of their adult lives. Most will also perform multiple roles that can be stressful and tiring. Many women who work full-time in sales also assume the responsibilities of wife and mother. Ellyn Foltz, vice president of sales and marketing for Dataline Incorporated, maintains a fully equipped personal computer (PC) and Internet hookup at her home. She gets up early and usually spends about 90 minutes on her work while family members are eating breakfast. In the evening, she logs on and completes two or three hours of work after her son is in bed. Foltz has structured her life so that she does not have to make "impossible choices" between work and family. She turned down a high-profile job that would have required constant travel.

Jill Doran, director of national accounts for National Car Rental, says that her employer gives her the tools and support she needs to maintain balance in her life. She received 10 weeks of maternity leave for each of her children and has the freedom to work from her home part of each week. When she is at home, Doran checks her phone mail and e-mail frequently to be sure she is responsive to each of her national accounts. She records everything in her Daytimer to avoid work–family conflicts.

As women struggle to balance career and family choices, many employers are doing more to help. Women, as well as men, who work in sales often have the option of spending part of every week working at home.[a]

a territory that covers six counties. The territory includes 88 auto supply firms that carry your line of tools. It also includes 38 stores that do not carry your tools. On the basis of this limited information, how would you carry out your selling duties? To answer this question, it is necessary to follow these steps.

STEP 1 — CLASSIFY ALL CUSTOMERS

If you classify customers according to potential sales volume, then you must answer two questions: What is the dollar amount of the firm's current purchases? What amount of additional sales might be developed with greater selling effort? Store A may be purchasing $3,000 worth of tools each year, but potential sales for this firm amount to $5,000. Store B currently purchases $2,000 worth of tools a year, and potential sales amount to $2,500. In this example, store A clearly deserves more time than store B.

It is important to realize that a small number of accounts may provide a majority of the sales volume. Many companies get 75–80 percent of their sales volume from 20 to 25 percent of their total number of customers. The problem lies in accurately identifying which accounts and prospects fall into the top 20–25 percent category. Once this information is available, you can develop customer classification data that can be used to establish the frequency of calls.

The typical sales territory is constantly changing, so the realignment of territories from time to time is necessary. A division of AT&T based in Albany, New York, uses MapInfo ProAlign software to realign its sales territories. Accounts are segmented based on industry, size, dollar volume, and complexity. The sales manager enters a variety of account information and then produces maps that show accounts in different configurations.[12]

With the aid of mapping software salespeople can perform rapid analysis of sales opportunities in Europe.

STEP 2—DEVELOP A ROUTING AND SCHEDULING PLAN

Many salespeople have found that travel is one of their most time-consuming nonselling activities. A great deal of time also can be wasted just waiting to see a customer. The primary objective of a sales routing and scheduling plan is to increase actual selling by reducing time spent traveling between accounts and time spent waiting to see customers.

If a salesperson called only on established accounts and spent the same amount of time with each customer, routing and scheduling would not be difficult. In most cases, however, you need to consider other variables. For example, you may be expected to develop new accounts on a regular basis. In this case, you must adjust your schedule to accommodate calls on prospects. Another variable involves customer service. Some salespeople devote considerable time to adjusting warranty claims, solving customer problems, and paying goodwill visits.

There are no precise rules to observe in establishing a sales routing and scheduling plan, but the following guiding principles apply to nearly all selling situations:

1. Obtain or create a map of your territory, and mark the location of present accounts with pins or marking pen. Each account might be color coded according to sales potential. This gives you a picture of the entire territory. Many companies are using mapping software to create a territory picture that can be viewed on the computer screen. With the aid of Geographic Information System mapping software, sales people can perform a rapid analysis of sales opportunities in a geographic area and create a territory plan.[13]
2. If your territory is quite large, consider organizing it into smaller subdivisions. You can then plan work in terms of several trading areas that make up the entire territory.
3. Develop a routing plan for a specific period of time. This might be a one- or two-week period. Once the plan is firm, notify customers by telephone, letter, or e-mail of your anticipated arrival time.
4. Develop a schedule that accommodates your customers' needs. Some customers appreciate getting calls on a certain day of the week or at a certain hour of the day. Try to schedule your calls in accordance with their wishes.
5. Think ahead, and establish one or more tentative calls in case you have some extra time. If your sales calls take less time than expected or if there is an unexpected cancellation, you need optional calls to fill in the void.
6. Decide how frequently to call on the basis of sales potential. Give the greatest attention to the most profitable customers.

Sales Call Plans

You can use information from the routing and scheduling plan to develop a **sales call plan**. This proposal is a weekly action plan, usually initiated by the sales manager. Its primary purpose is to ensure efficient and effective account coverage.

The form most sales managers use is similar to Figure 15.3. One section of the form is used to record planned calls. A parallel section is for completed calls. Additional space is provided for the names of firms called on.

The sales manager usually presents the sales call plan to individual members of the sales staff. The plan's success depends on how realistic the goals are in the eyes of the sales staff, how persuasive the sales manager is, and what type of training accompanies the plan's introduction. It is not unusual for members of the sales force to respond with comments such as, "My territory is different," "Do not put me in a procedural straitjacket," or "My territory cannot be organized." The sales manager must not only present the plan in a convincing manner but also provide training that helps each salesperson implement the plan successfully.

Sales Call Plan

Salesperson _____   For week ending _____

Territory _____   Days worked _____

Planned Calls	**Total Completed Calls**

Number of planned calls _____   Number of calls only _____

Number of planned
presentations _____   Number of presentations _____

Number of planned
telephone calls _____   Number of telephone calls _____

Account Category Planning   Number of orders _____

  A. Account calls _____   Total miles traveled _____

  B. Account calls _____   A. Account calls _____

  C. Account calls _____   B. Account calls _____

                                              C. Account calls _____

Companies called on	Address	Date	Customer rating	Comments about call

Figure 15.3
SALES CALL PLAN

RECORDS MANAGEMENT

Although some salespeople complain that paperwork is too time consuming and reduces the amount of time available for actual selling, others recognize that accurate, up-to-date records actually save time. Their work is better organized, and quick accessibility to information often makes it possible to close more sales and improve customer service.

A good record-keeping system gives salespeople useful information with which to check their own progress. For instance, an examination of sales call plans at the end of the day provides a review of who was called on and what was accomplished. The company also benefits from complete and accurate records. Reports from the field help management make important decisions. A company with a large sales force operating throughout a wide geographic area relies heavily on information sent to the home office.

A good record-keeping system gives salespeople useful information that can be used to enhance service to customers.

Common Records Kept by Salespeople

A good policy is never to require a record that is not absolutely necessary. The only records worth keeping are those that provide positive benefits to the customer, the salesperson, or the personnel who work in sales-supporting areas of the company. Each record should be brief, easy to complete, and free of requests for useless detail. Where possible the format should provide for the use of check marks as a substitute for written responses. Completing sales record forms should not be a major burden.

What records should you keep? The answer to this question varies depending on the type of selling position. Some of the most common records salespeople keep are described in this section.

CUSTOMER AND PROSPECT CARD FILES

Most salespeople find it helpful to keep records of customers and prospects. Each of these cards has space for name, address, and phone number. Other information recorded might be the buyer's personal characteristics, the names of people who might influence the purchase, or appropriate times to make calls. Of course, many salespeople have replaced their card files with computerized record systems.

CALL REPORTS

The call report (also called activity report) is a variation of the sales call plan described earlier in this chapter. It is used to record information about the people you have called on and about what took place. The call report is one of the most basic records used in the field of selling. It provides a summary of what happened during the call and an indication of what future action is required. The call report (daily and weekly) featured in Figure 15.4 is typical of those used in the field.

We are seeing less emphasis on call reports that require only numbers (calls made each day, number of proposals written, etc.). Companies that emphasize consultative selling are requesting more personal information on the customer (information that expands

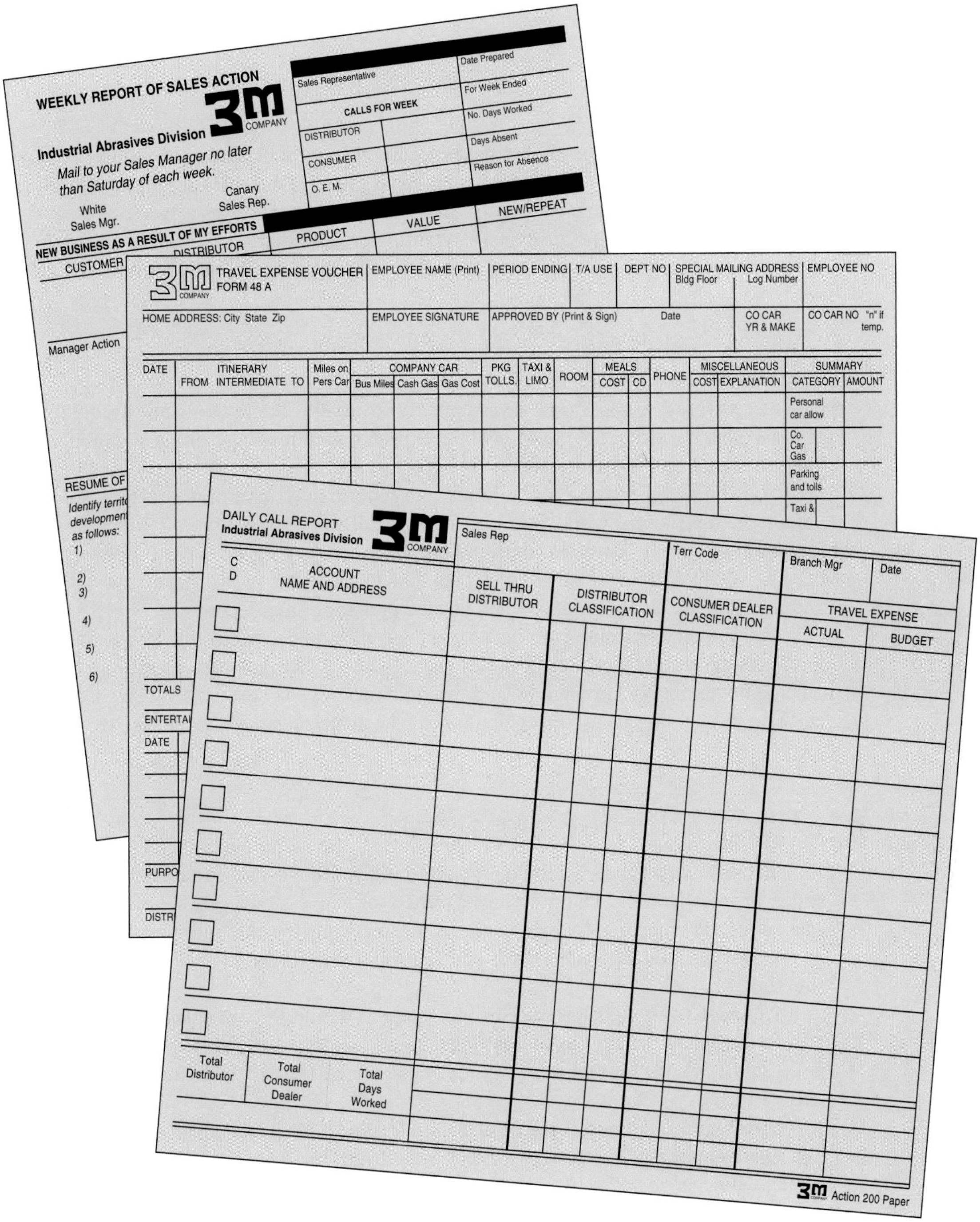

WEEKLY REPORT OF SALES ACTION
3M COMPANY
Industrial Abrasives Division
Mail to your Sales Manager no later than Saturday of each week.
White Sales Mgr.
Canary Sales Rep.
Sales Representative
Date Prepared
For Week Ended
CALLS FOR WEEK
No. Days Worked
DISTRIBUTOR
Days Absent
CONSUMER
Reason for Absence
O. E. M.
NEW BUSINESS AS A RESULT OF MY EFFORTS
CUSTOMER
DISTRIBUTOR
PRODUCT
VALUE
NEW/REPEAT
Manager Action
RESUME OF
Identify territ
development
as follows:
1)
2)
3)
4)
5)
6)

3M COMPANY TRAVEL EXPENSE VOUCHER FORM 48 A
EMPLOYEE NAME (Print)
PERIOD ENDING
T/A USE
DEPT NO
SPECIAL MAILING ADDRESS Bldg Floor Log Number
EMPLOYEE NO
HOME ADDRESS: City State Zip
EMPLOYEE SIGNATURE
APPROVED BY (Print & Sign)
Date
CO CAR YR & MAKE
CO CAR NO "n" if temp.
DATE
ITINERARY FROM INTERMEDIATE TO
Miles on Pers Car
COMPANY CAR Bus Miles Cash Gas Gas Cost
PKG TOLLS.
TAXI & LIMO
ROOM
MEALS COST CD
PHONE
MISCELLANEOUS COST EXPLANATION
SUMMARY CATEGORY AMOUNT
Personal car allow
Co. Car Gas
Parking and tolls
Taxi &
TOTALS
ENTERTAI
DATE
PURPO
DISTR

DAILY CALL REPORT
Industrial Abrasives Division
3M COMPANY
Sales Rep
Terr Code
Branch Mgr
Date
C D
ACCOUNT NAME AND ADDRESS
SELL THRU DISTRIBUTOR
DISTRIBUTOR CLASSIFICATION
CONSUMER DEALER CLASSIFICATION
TRAVEL EXPENSE
ACTUAL
BUDGET
Total Distributor
Total Consumer Dealer
Total Days Worked
3M Action 200 Paper

Figure 15.4

CALL REPORT, EXPENSE VOUCHER, AND WEEKLY SALES REPORT

These are three of the most common records kept by 3M salespeople. Many salespeople process these forms via electronic mail.

the customer profile) and more information on the customer's short- and long-range buying plans.[14]

EXPENSE RECORDS

Both your company and the government agencies that monitor business expenses require a record of selling expenses. These usually include such items as meals, lodging, travel, and in some cases entertainment expenses. Several expense reporting software packages are now available to streamline the expense reporting process. Automated expense reports save the salesperson a great deal of time and allow them to get reimbursed while still on the road.

SALES RECORDS

The records used to report sales vary greatly in design. Some companies require daily reports, others weekly ones. As you would expect, one primary use of the sales report is to analyze salespeople's performance.

You can take certain steps to improve a reporting system. Some records should be completed right away, while you can easily recall the information. Accuracy is always important. It can be embarrassing to have an order sent to the wrong address simply because you have transposed a figure. Take time to proofread forms for accuracy. Neatness and legibility are also important when you are preparing sales records.

You should reexamine your territory management plan continually. Update it often so it reflects the current status of your various accounts. When possible, use a portable computer and appropriate software to improve your records management system. Computers can help you achieve increased selling time and enhance customer service.

STRESS MANAGEMENT

Personal selling produces a certain amount of stress. This is due in part to the nonroutine nature of sales work. Each day brings a variety of new experiences, some of which may cause stress. Prospecting, for example, can be threatening to some salespeople. Long hours on the job, the loss of leisure time, and too little time for family members also can be stressful.

Although "variety is the spice of life," there is a limit to how much diversity one can cope with. One of the keys to success in selling is learning how to bring order to the many facets of the job. We also must be physically and mentally prepared to handle work-related stress.

Stress can be defined as the behavioral adjustment to change that affects you psychologically and physically. It is a process by which your mind and body mobilize energy for coping with change and challenge.[15] Repeated or prolonged stress can trigger a variety of warning signs. Physical signs might take the form of headaches, loss of appetite, hypertension, or fatigue. Psychological symptoms include anxiety, depression, irritability, and reduced interest in personal relationships.[16] The latter problem can be a serious barrier to success in sales. Some stress is beneficial because it helps keep us motivated, but too much stress can be unhealthy if left unchecked.

Stress might be caused by trying to figure out ways to meet a sales quota or schedule travel throughout a sales territory. Missed appointments, presentations before large groups, and lack of feedback concerning your performance also can create stress. Ironically, some of the timesaving tools used by salespeople (fax machines, car phones, and e-mail) make it difficult for them to escape the pressures of their job. Many salespeople feel they are "on call" 24 hours a day.

As noted in Chapter 1, information surplus has replaced information scarcity as an important new problem in the age of information. A growing number of knowledge workers report tension with colleagues, loss of job satisfaction, and strained personal relationships as a result of information overload. Too much information also crowds out quiet moments needed to restore balance in our lives.[17]

It is not possible to eliminate stress from your life, but you can adopt stress management strategies that can help you cope with the stress in your life. Three stress management strategies are discussed next.

Maintain an Optimistic Outlook

Researchers evaluated the coping strategies of 101 salespeople from three companies. They found that those who face job-related stress with an optimistic outlook fared better than those with a pessimistic attitude. The research team found that optimists used "problem-focused" coping strategies, while pessimists used "emotion-focused" techniques. The optimistic salespeople most frequently focused on various ways to solve the problem. Pessimists were more likely to try avoiding the problem and direct their feelings toward other people.[18]

Practice Healthy Emotional Expression

When stress occurs, you may undergo physiological and psychological changes. The heartbeat quickens, the blood pressure rises, and tension builds. To relieve the pressure, you may choose a *fight* or *flight* response. Fighting the problem may mean unleashing an avalanche of harsh words or ignoring the other person. These reactions, of course, are not recommended. This behavior may damage relationships with team members, customers, or customer support personnel.

Flight is the act of running away from the problem. Instead of facing the issue squarely, you decide to turn your back on it. The flight response is usually not satisfactory; the problem seldom goes away by itself. If you feel stress from an impractical quota, talk to your sales manager and try to get the quota reduced. Don't just give in to the feeling of being overwhelmed. If you are spending too much time away from family, take a close look at your territory management plan and try to develop a more efficient way to make sale calls.

Maintain a Healthy Lifestyle

An effective exercise program—jogging, tennis, golf, racquetball, walking, or some other favorite exercise—can "burn off" the harmful chemicals that build up in your bloodstream after a prolonged period of stress. Salespeople at Owens Corning in Toledo, Ohio, formed a sales wellness advisory team (SWAT). The team organized a health screening for Owen's 600 salespeople and instituted an incentive program that rewarded those who reached exercise goals.[19] The food you eat can play a critical role in helping you manage stress. Health experts agree that the typical American diet—high in saturated fats, refined sugar, additives, caffeine, and even too much protein—is the wrong menu for coping with stress. Leisure time also can provide you with the opportunity to relax and get rid of work-related stress. Mike McGinnity, director of sales and marketing at the Excelsior Hotel in Little Rock, Arkansas, encourages his salespeople to take full advantage of vacations. He helps them organize their work load so they are able to fully enjoy their vacations.[20]

Increasingly, in the age of information, physical exercise is a very important part of a strategic stress management program.

An Action Plan to Reduce Stress

1. Take 15 minutes.
2. Make two columns on a piece of paper. Write "Work" at the top of one, "Personal" at the top of the other. Write down all the things that are driving you crazy.
3. Underline the most important items on the lists.
4. Separate them into "chronic" and "acute."
5. For each one, ask yourself: What do I need to do to reduce the stress arising from this factor *right now*? Some answers could be as simple as "Get a good night's sleep."
6. Take action.[b]

One additional way to handle stress is to come to work rested and relaxed. Dr. Louis E. Kopolow, an expert in the field of stress management, says, "The best strategy for avoiding stress is to learn how to relax."[21] Fatigue reduces your tolerance for dealing with stressful situations. How much sleep do you need each night? The number of hours of sleep required for good health varies from person to person, but seven or eight hours seems to be about right for most people. The critical test is if you feel rested in the morning and prepared to deal with the day's activities.

In many respects, salespeople must possess the same self-discipline as a professional athlete. Sales work can be physically demanding. Lack of proper rest, poor eating habits, excessive drinking, and failure to exercise properly can reduce one's ability to deal with stress and strain.

▶▶ Building Quality Partnerships

Four Moderators of Stress

The stress-related tension that surfaces in our lives can be a barrier to effective interpersonal relations. The psychological problems that can result from too much stress are anxiety, depression, instability, and reduced interest in personal relationships. The authors of *The One-Minute Manager Gets Fit* have identified four moderators of stress. When these four are in good working order, they can help prevent stress from turning into strain.

1. *Autonomy* is a sense we get on weekends of being able to do what we want. Autonomy also can be working independently or having the necessary skills and qualifications to be able to move from one job to another.

2. *Connectedness* relates to the ties we have with those around us. People with a high sense of connectedness believe they have strong, positive relationships in all areas—at home, at work, and in the community.

3. *Perspective* has to do with the meaning of life—the direction, the purpose, the passion that you feel for what you are doing. It keeps you from letting little things get you down. Because you are looking at the big picture, normal strains of daily life do not get blown out of proportion.

4. *Tone* is your energy level, your physical well-being and appearance, and how you feel about your body. By having better tone a person can definitely improve self-esteem and, in doing so, help moderate stress.[c]

Summary

In this chapter we describe management of self as a four-dimensional process. It involves time management, territory management, records management, and stress management.

All salespeople can learn more about their products and improve their selling skills. However, there is no way to expand time. Our only option is to find ways to improve time and territory management. The four timesaving techniques discussed in this chapter should be used by every salesperson. When used on a regular basis, they can set the stage for more face-to-face selling time.

The first step in territory management is classification of all customers according to sales volume or some other appropriate criteria. You normally should spend the most time with accounts that have the greatest sales potential. The second step requires developing a routing and scheduling plan. This plan should reduce time spent traveling between accounts. In some cases you can substitute telephone calls or e-mail messages for personal calls.

A good record-keeping system provides many advantages. Accurate, up-to-date records can actually save time because work is better organized. The company also benefits because sales reports provide an important communication link with members of the sales force. Today, computers are used to develop more efficient record-keeping systems.

There is a certain amount of stress associated with sales work. This is due in part to the nonroutine nature of personal selling. Salespeople must learn to cope with the factors that upset their equilibrium. Three stress management strategies are discussed.

KEY TERMS

Territory   Stress
Sales Call Plan

REVIEW QUESTIONS

1. Describe how a salesperson is much like the individual who owns and operates a business.
2. Management of self has been described as a four-dimensional process. Describe each dimension.
3. What are the two major ways a salesperson can increase sales volume?
4. How can a salesperson use a time log to improve time management?
5. List four techniques the salesperson should use to make better use of valuable selling time.
6. Effective territory management involves two major steps. What are they?
7. What is a *sales call plan*? Explain how it is used.
8. Describe the most common records kept by salespeople.
9. What is the definition of *stress*? What are some indicators of stress?
10. The Building Quality Partnerships box on p. 344 describes four moderators of stress. Which of these four moderators do you think is most important for persons employed in the sales field? Explain.

APPLICATION EXERCISES

1. The key to successful time management lies in thinking and planning ahead. You must become conscious of yourself and decide what you want from your time. You can manage your time only when you have a clear picture of what is going on within and around you. To assess the quality of your working time, it might be helpful to keep a careful record for a certain amount of time showing exactly how you have used your day. Over this period of time, write down everything you have done and how long it took. Next you can appraise your use of time and decide whether or not your time was put to good use. Some pertinent questions you might ask yourself in appraising your use of time are suggested by the following "time analysis questions":

   a. What items am I spending too much time on?

   b. What items am I spending too little time on?

   c. What items offer the most important opportunities for saving time?

   d. What am I doing that does not need to be done at all?

   e. How can I avoid overusing the time of others?

   f. What are some other suggestions?

2. Deciding on a goal can be the most crucial decision of your life. It is more damaging not to have a goal than it is not to reach a goal. It is generally agreed that the major cause of failure is the lack of a well-defined purpose. A successful life results not from chance, but from a succession of successful days. Prepare a list for the following categories:

   Career goals
   1.
   2.
   3.

   Family goals
   1.
   2.
   3.

   Educational goals
   1.
   2.
   3.

   Interpersonal relationship goals
   1.
   2.
   3.

3. Interview someone you know who uses a planning calendar. What kind is it— pocket, desk, or some other type? How long has the person been using it? How important is the calendar to daily, weekly, monthly, and yearly planning? Has the person ever considered discontinuing its use? What are the person's suggestions for someone who does not use one? Write your answer.

4. Time management is an important part of a successful salesperson's job. Using your search engine, examine the Internet for information on time management. Type in "time management" + selling. Examine the training products and services available on this topic.

CASE PROBLEM

Julio Melara, introduced at the beginning of this chapter, has achieved success in three different sales and marketing positions in the fields of radio broadcasting and publishing. At age 31 he holds the position of executive vice president of the $10 million New Orleans Publishing Group and publisher of *New Orleans Magazine* (www.neworleansmagazine.com). He is convinced that success comes to those who have the right attitude and the will to win. Now that he has proved himself in two very competitive fields, Melara is ready to share the beliefs and success principles that made a difference in his own career. His success formula is made of five elements.

1. You have to believe you can achieve your dreams and desires. He likes to quote a verse from the book of Proverbs that says, "As a man thinketh, so he is." Put another way, "If you believe, you will achieve." Salespeople tend to behave in a way that supports their own ideas of how successful or unsuccessful they will be. Those who have serious doubts about their capabilities tend to reduce their efforts or give up altogether when faced with major challenges.

2. Put all your goals in writing. A written goal, reviewed daily, is much more likely to be achieved. Melara says that a written goal keeps the vision in front of you. Many salespeople avoid setting goals because they do not understand the importance of this self-improvement method. As we make and keep commitments to ourselves, we begin to establish a greater sense of self-confidence and self-control. For many salespeople, goals become an integral part of their plan to break old habits or form new ones.

3. Get all the education and information that you can. Melara is fond of saying, "You'll never earn more unless you learn more." In recent years, most salespeople have had to develop expertise in the area of computer technology. Knowledge of the customer's business is not an option if you want to build a strong partnership. Developing expertise in appropriate areas can result in increased self-confidence.

4. Commit to excellence in everything that you do. There is an interconnection among the many areas of work and family. Melara believes that salespeople must fulfill both work and family responsibilities. Many sales and marketing organizations have found that family problems are linked to employee problems such as tardiness, absenteeism, and low productivity. Of course, problems at work often have a negative influence on one's personal life.

5. Protect your enthusiasm. Melara says, "Watch the friends you hang out with, the people you associate with, and the television programs you watch." Enthusiasm for work and work-related activities is often fragile. The negative views of a co-worker or a friend can erode our enthusiasm. One of the best defenses against loss of enthusiasm is to maintain positive expectations about the future.

Questions

1. Which of these elements can make the most important contribution to a career in personal selling? Explain.

2. Reflect on your own approach to accomplishing tasks and select two of Melara's elements you would find easy to adopt. Then select two elements that you would find difficult to adopt. Explain your choices.

3. How might goal setting be used in conjunction with time management?

4. How might a commitment to excellence improve the processes of territory management and records management?

5. Do you agree or disagree that the people you associate with can influence your enthusiasm?

CRM CASE STUDY

Managing Yourself with CRM

A key objective in managing your time is to confirm that, at any time, you are working on your highest priorities. Contacting prospective customers is the highest priority for most salespeople. The next challenge is to decide in which order prospects should be contacted. Many salespeople prioritize their accounts on the basis of their value, the amount that they are likely to spend with the sales organization.

Questions

1. On the basis of the dollar amount Pat Silva estimated that each account might spend, in what order would you contact the prospects in the ACT! database?

2. If you were to rank these prospects on the basis of your sales commission, would this priority list be different than the list developed in question 1? If so, why?

3. There are several ways that this list of prospects could be prioritized, for example, by date, dollar amount, or commission. Which of these rankings is best?

16

Communication Styles: Managing the Relationship Process

When you finish reading this chapter, you should be able to

1. Discuss communication-style bias and how it influences the relationship process

2. Explain the benefits derived from an understanding of communication styles

3. Identify the two major dimensions of the communication-style model

4. List and describe the four major communication styles in the communication-style model

5. Learn how to identify your preferred communication style and that of your customer

6. Learn to overcome communication-style bias and build strong selling relationships with style flexing

LEARNING OBJECTIVES

The headline of the *Wall Street Journal* article says, "NationsBank's McColl Masters the Soft Sell." Some bankers across America who have been involved in negotiations with the hard-charging chief executive officer (CEO) of NationsBank Corporation find the news hard to believe. NationsBank has acquired many smaller banks in recent years and has earned the reputation as the most aggressive acquirer in Banking. Hugh McColl long has been known as an executive who displays an aggressive and demanding communication style. Yet people who have had recent dealings with him note a change in his demeanor. One banking executive said, "I've known Hugh a long time. There's no question he's more polished than before." Another banking executive said, "I couldn't have dealt with a more soft-spoken and impeccable gentleman." He seems to have mastered the art of the soft sell. Mr. McColl himself attributes his demeanor to personal selling. "I've been a successful salesman for a long, long period of time. So I've always been willing to make concessions on things to make something happen."[1]

Hugh McColl appears to display the characteristics of the *Director* communication style. The Director style is one of the four styles of communication discussed in this chapter. McColl also seems to be displaying communication-style flexibility, a deliberate attempt to adjust one's communication style to meet the needs of the other person.

COMMUNICATION STYLES—AN INTRODUCTION TO MANAGING SELLING RELATIONSHIPS

Almost everyone has had the pleasant experience of meeting someone for the first time and developing instant mutual rapport. There seems to be a quality about some people that makes you like them instantaneously—a basis for understanding that is difficult to explain. On the other hand, we can all recall meeting people who "turn us off" almost immediately. Why does this happen during the initial contact? To answer this question, we must understand a unique form of bias that can surface in almost any social or business setting. The information presented in this chapter can help you reduce tension and increase trust in all types of business relationships.

Communication-Style Bias

Bias in various forms is quite common in our society. In fact, local, state, and national governments have passed many laws to curb blatant forms of racial, age, and sex bias. We also observe some degree of regional bias when people from various parts of the country meet.

The most frequently occurring form of bias is not commonly understood in our society. What has been labeled **communication-style bias** is a state of mind that almost every one of us experiences from time to time, but we usually find it difficult to explain the symptoms. Communication-style bias develops when we have contact with another person whose communication style is different from our own. For example, a purchasing agent was overheard saying, "I do not know what it is, but I just do not like that sales representative." The agent was no doubt experiencing communication-style bias but could not easily describe the feeling.

Your communication style is the "you" that is on display every day—the outer pattern of behavior that others see. If your style is very different from the other person's, it may be difficult for the two of you to develop rapport. All of us have had the experience of saying or doing something that was perfectly acceptable to a friend or co-worker and being surprised when the same behavior irritated someone else. However, aside from admitting that this happens, most of us are unable to draw meaningful conclusions from these experiences to help us perform more effectively with people in the future.[2]

In recent years, thousands of sales professionals have learned to manage their selling relationships more effectively through the study of communication styles. Books, such as *People Styles at Work* by Robert Bolton and Dorothy Grover Bolton, and *The Versatile Salesperson* by Roger Wenschlag, serve as good references. Many training companies offer seminars that provide enrollees with a practical understanding of communication-style theory and practice. This practical theory of human behavior, based on research by the Swiss psychoanalyst Carl Jung and others, helps them achieve improved sales productivity. The psychology of behavior patterns is a practical blend of concepts taken from the fields of psychology, communication, and sociology.

Communication-Style Principles

The theory of behavioral- or communication-style bias is based on a number of underlying principles. A review of these principles can be beneficial before we examine specific styles.

1. *Individual differences exist and are important.* It is quite obvious that we all differ in terms of physical characteristics such as height, shoe size, facial features, and

body build, but the most interesting differences are those patterns of behavior that are unique to each of us. Each of us displays an individual combination of nonverbal characteristics. Voice patterns, eye movement, facial expression, and posture are some of the components of our communication style. Additional characteristics are discussed later in this chapter.

2. *A communication style is a way of thinking and behaving.* It is not an ability, but instead, a preferred way of using abilities one has. This distinction is very important. An ability refers to how well someone can do something. A style refers to how someone likes to do something.[3]

3. *Individual style differences tend to be stable.* Our communication style is based on a combination of hereditary and environmental factors. Our style is somewhat original at the time of birth; it takes on additional individuality during the first three to five years of life. By the time we enter elementary school, the teacher should be able to identify our communication style. This style remains fairly constant throughout life.

4. *There is a finite number of styles.* Most people display one of several clusters of similar behaviors, and this allows us to identify a small number of behavioral categories. By combining a series of descriptors we can develop a single "label" that describes a person's most preferred communication style.

5. *Everyone makes judgments about people based on communication style.* As noted in Chapter 3, when people meet you for the first time, they form an immediate and distinct impression of you. This impression tends to influence how others communicate with you.

The ability to identify another person's communication style, and to know how and when to adapt your own preferred style to it, can afford you a crucial advantage in dealing with people. Differences between people can be a source of friction. The ability to "speak the other person's language" is an important relationship–management skill.[4]

Group sales presentations can be very challenging because in most cases you are attempting to relate to several different communication styles.

➤➤ BUILDING QUALITY PARTNERSHIPS

LIFO DEVELOPS NEW GOLDEN RULE

Communication-style principles and practices serve as the foundation for High-Performance Selling, a sales training program offered by Stuart Atkins Incorporated (SAi), a California-based training company. This training program is a version of LIFO Training that has been completed by 2 million people in over 10,000 organizations. LIFO training invites self-examination and promotes self-development. At the beginning of the High-Performance Selling program enrollees complete the LIFO Survey. This self-scoring instrument helps each participant identify her most preferred communication style and her least preferred communication style. There are four basic styles or ways of seeing problems, people, and situations. The most preferred style represents the person's primary selling strengths. These are the factors that contribute the most to one's success in selling. Our least preferred style represents a source of untapped strengths that can be used to increase sales.

The High-Performance Selling program reminds us that often we are selling products and services to a person who has a different preferred style than our own. If we always rely on our major selling strengths (most preferred style) we will not achieve our full potential. This is especially true if the customer's most preferred style is our least preferred style. Salespeople often overuse their favorite selling strengths to the point of unproductive excess.

High-Performance Selling provides an emphatic reminder that customers have communication style preferences. If we can identify the customers' most preferred style, we can adjust our approach to meet their needs. Most of us have been taught to use the Golden Rule, which means, "Do unto others as you would have them do unto you." In recognition of the fact that not everybody wants to be sold the same way, the creators of High-Performance Selling developed a new golden rule for salespeople: Do unto others as they want to be done unto.[a]

Improving Your Relationship – Management Skills

Anyone who is considering a career in selling can benefit greatly from the study of communication styles. These concepts provide a practical method of classifying people according to communication style and give the salesperson a distinct advantage in the marketplace. A salesperson who understands communication-style classification methods and learns how to apply them can avoid common mistakes that threaten interpersonal relations with customers. Awareness of these methods greatly reduces the possibility of tension arising during the sales call. Tony Alessandra and Michael O'Connor, authors of *People Smart*, state, "If we don't think first of the other person, we run the risk of unintentionally imposing a tension-filled win–lose or lose–lose relationship on them."[5]

The first major goal of this chapter is to help you better understand your own most preferred communication style. The second goal is to help you develop greater understanding and appreciation for styles that are different from your own. The third goal is to help you manage your selling relationships more effectively by learning to adapt your style to fit the communication style of the customer. This practice is called "style flexing."

COMMUNICATION-STYLE MODEL

This section introduces you to the four basic communication styles. One of these will surface as your most preferred style. The communication-style model that defines these styles is based on two important dimensions of human behavior: dominance and sociability. We look at the dominance continuum first.

Dominance Continuum

Dominance can be defined as the tendency to control or prevail over others.[6] Dominant people tend to be quite competitive. They also tend to offer opinions readily and be decisive and determined. Each of us falls somewhere on the dominance continuum illustrated by Figure 16.1.

A person classified as being high in dominance is generally a "take charge" type of person who makes a position clear to others. A person classified as being low in dominance is usually more reserved, unassertive, and easygoing. Dominance has been recognized as a universal behavioral characteristic. David W. Johnson developed the Interpersonal Pattern Exercise to help people achieve greater interpersonal effectiveness. He believes that people fall into two dominance categories:

1. *Low dominance.* These people have a tendency to be quite cooperative and eager to assist others. They tend to be low in assertiveness.
2. *High dominance.* These people tend to give advice freely and frequently initiate demands. They are more aggressive in dealing with others.[7]

The first step in determining your most preferred communication style is to identify where you fall on the dominance continuum. Do you tend to rank low or high on this scale? To answer this question, complete the Dominance Indicator form in Table 16.1. Rate yourself on each scale by placing a check mark on the continuum at the point that represents how you perceive yourself. If most of your check marks fall to the right of center, you are someone who is high in dominance. If most of your check marks fall to the left of center, you are someone who is low in dominance. Is there any best place to be on the dominance continuum? The answer is no. Successful salespeople can be found at all points along the continuum.

Sociability Continuum

Sociability reflects the amount of control we exert over our emotional expressiveness.[8] People who are high in sociability tend to express their feelings freely, while people who are low in this dimension tend to control their feelings. Each of us falls somewhere on the sociability continuum illustrated in Figure 16.2.

Sociability is also a universal behavioral characteristic. It can be defined as the tendency to seek and enjoy interaction with others. Charles Margerison, author of *How to*

Low  High

Figure 16.1
The first step in determining your most preferred communication style is to identify where you are on the dominance continuum.

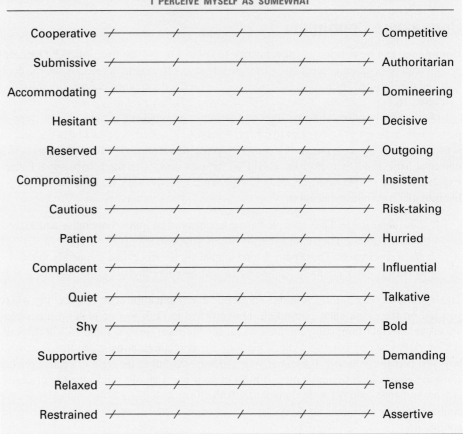

Table 16.1 **DOMINANCE INDICATOR**

Rate yourself on each scale by placing a check mark on the continuum at the point that represents how you perceive yourself.

I PERCEIVE MYSELF AS SOMEWHAT

Cooperative	Competitive
Submissive	Authoritarian
Accommodating	Domineering
Hesitant	Decisive
Reserved	Outgoing
Compromising	Insistent
Cautious	Risk-taking
Patient	Hurried
Complacent	Influential
Quiet	Talkative
Shy	Bold
Supportive	Demanding
Relaxed	Tense
Restrained	Assertive

High

Low

Figure 16.2
The second step in determining your most preferred communication style is to identify where you are on the sociability continuum.

Assess Your Managerial Style, says that high sociability is an indication of a person's preference to interact with other people. He says that low sociability is an indicator of a person's desire to work in an environment where the person has more time alone instead of having to make conversation with others.[9] The person who is classified as being low in the area of sociability is more reserved and formal in social relationships.

The second step in determining your most preferred communication style is to identify where you fall on the sociability continuum. To answer this question, complete the Sociability Indicator form shown in Table 16.2. Rate yourself on each scale by placing a check mark on the continuum at the point that represents how you perceive yourself. If most of your check marks fall to the right of center, you are someone who is high in sociability. If most of your check marks fall to the left of center, you are someone who is low in sociability. Keep in mind that there is no best place to be. Successful salespeople can be found at all points along this continuum.

Table 16.2	SOCIABILITY INDICATOR

Rate yourself on each scale by placing a check mark on the continuum at the point that represents how you perceive yourself.

I PERCEIVE MYSELF AS SOMEWHAT

Disciplined	Easygoing
Controlled	Expressive
Serious	Lighthearted
Methodical	Unstructured
Calculating	Spontaneous
Guarded	Open
Stalwart	Humorous
Aloof	Friendly
Formal	Casual
Reserved	Attention-seeking
Cautious	Carefree
Conforming	Unconventional
Reticent	Dramatic
Restrained	Impulsive

With the aid of the dominance and sociability continuums we are now prepared to discuss a relatively simple communication-style classification plan that has practical application in the field of selling. We describe the four basic styles: Emotive, Director, Reflective, and Supportive.

Four Styles of Communication

By combining the two dimensions of human behavior, dominance and sociability, we can form a partial outline of the communication-style model (Fig. 16.3). Dominance is represented by the horizontal axis, and sociability is represented by the vertical axis. Once the two dimensions of human behavior are combined, the framework for communication-style classification is established.

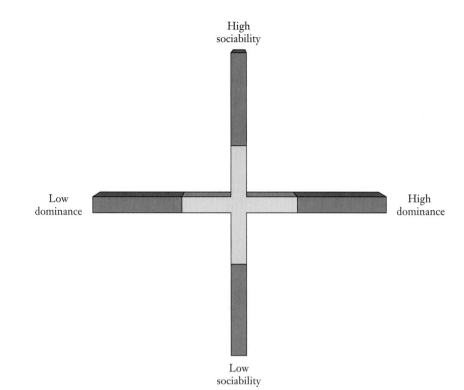

Figure **16.3**
When the dominance and sociability dimensions of human behavior are combined, the framework for communication-style classification is established.

EMOTIVE STYLE

The upper right-hand quadrant of Figure 16.4 defines a style that combines high sociability and high dominance. We call this the **Emotive style.** Emotive people like Jesse Jackson and Jay Leno usually stand out in a crowd. They are expressive and willing to spend time maintaining and enjoying a large number of relationships.[10] Oprah Winfrey, the well-known television personality, and talk show host David Letterman provide excellent models of the Emotive communication style. Sandra Bullock provides still another example. They are outspoken, enthusiastic, and stimulating. Larry King, popular talk show host, and Bill Clinton also project the Emotive communication style. The Emotive person wants to create a social relationship quickly and usually feels more comfortable in an informal atmosphere. Some of the verbal and nonverbal clues that identify the Emotive person follow:

1. *Appears quite active.* This person gives the appearance of being busy. A person who combines high dominance and high sociability is often restless. The Emotive person is likely to express feelings with vigorous movements of the hands and a rapid speech pattern.
2. *Takes the social initiative in most cases.* Emotives are the classic extraverts. When two people meet for the first time, the Emotive person is more apt to initiate and maintain the conversation as well as to initiate the handshake. Emotives rate high in both directness and openness.
3. *Likes to encourage informality.* The Emotive person moves to a "first name" basis as soon as possible (too soon in some cases). Even the way this person sits in a chair communicates a preference for a relaxed, informal social setting.
4. *Expresses emotional opinions.* Emotive people generally do not hide their feelings. They often express opinions dramatically and impulsively.

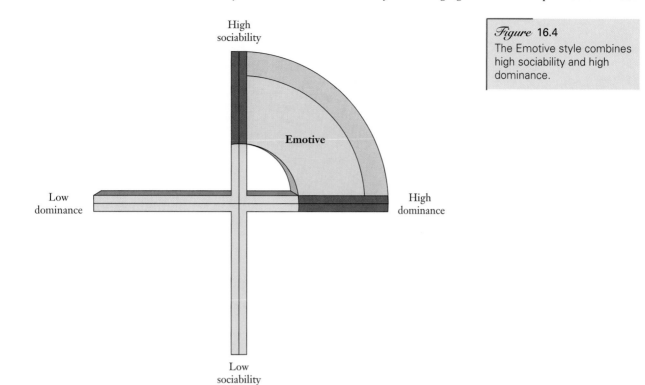

Figure 16.4
The Emotive style combines high sociability and high dominance.

KEY WORDS FOR THE EMOTIVE STYLE

Sociable	Unstructured
Spontaneous	Excitable
Zestful	Personable
Stimulating	Persuasive
Emotional	Dynamic

Emotive people like Oprah Winfrey are enthusiastic, outspoken, and stimulating.

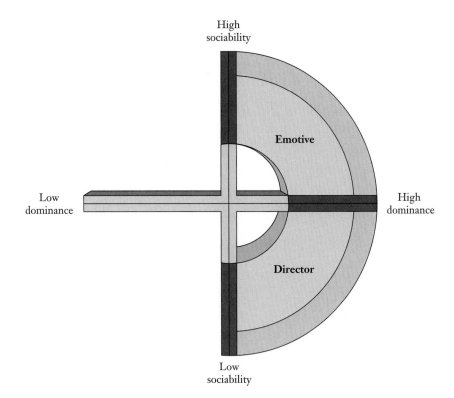

DIRECTOR STYLE

The lower right-hand quadrant defines a style that combines high dominance and low sociability. We will call this the **Director style** (Fig. 16.5).

To understand the nature of people who display the Director communication style, picture in your mind's eye the director of a Hollywood film. The person you see is giving orders in a loud voice and is generally in charge of every facet of the operation. Everyone on the set knows this person is in charge. Although the common stereotyped image of the Hollywood film director is probably exaggerated, this example is helpful as you attempt to become familiar with the Director style.

Lee Iacocca, Sam Donaldson (television commentator), and Bob Dole project the Director style. Lou Gerstner, IBM's CEO, Jesse Ventura, Governor of Minnesota, and Barbara Walters, television commentator, typify this communication style. These people have been described as frank, demanding, aggressive, and determined.

In the field of selling you will encounter a number of customers who are Directors. How can you identify these people? What verbal and nonverbal clues can we observe? A few of the behaviors displayed by Directors follow:

1. *Appears to be quite busy.* The Director generally does not like to waste time and wants to get right to the point. General Norman Schwarzkopf and Judge Judy Sheindlin of the *Judge Judy* television show display this behavior.
2. *May give the impression of not listening.* In most cases the Director feels more comfortable talking than listening.
3. *Displays a serious attitude.* A person who is low in sociability usually communicates a lack of warmth and is apt to be quite businesslike and impersonal. Mike Wallace, one of the stars on the popular *60 Minutes* television show, seldom smiles, or displays warmth.
4. *Likes to maintain control.* The person who is high on the Dominance continuum likes to maintain control. During meetings the Director seeks to control the agenda.[11]

Bob Dole is known for his frank, demanding, and aggressive communication style.

KEY WORDS FOR THE DIRECTOR STYLE

Aggressive	Determined
Intense	Frank
Requiring	Opinionated
Pushy	Impatient
Serious	Bold

REFLECTIVE STYLE

The lower left-hand quadrant of the communication-style model features a combination of low dominance and low sociability (Fig. 16.6). People who regularly display this behavior are classified as having the **Reflective style**.

The Reflective person tends to examine all the facts carefully before arriving at a decision. Like a cautious scientist, this individual wants to gather all available information and weigh it carefully before taking a position. The reflective type is usually a stickler for detail.[12] The late physicist, Albert Einstein, fits the description. Dr. Joyce Brothers (psychologist), former U.S. President Jimmy Carter, and Alan Greenspan (chairman of the Federal Reserve) also display the characteristics of the Reflective type.

The Reflective communication style combines low dominance and low sociability; therefore, people with this classification tend to be reserved and cautious. Some additional behaviors that characterize this style follow:

1. *Controls emotional expression.* Reflective people tend to curb emotional expression and are less likely to display warmth openly.
2. *Displays a preference for orderliness.* The Reflective person enjoys a highly structured environment and generally feels frustration when confronted with unexpected events.
3. *Tends to express measured opinions.* The Reflective individual usually does not express dramatic opinions. This communication style is characterized by disciplined, businesslike actions.
4. *Seems difficult to get to know.* The Reflective person tends to be somewhat formal in social relationships and therefore is viewed as aloof by many people.

Persons with the Reflective style, such as former president Jimmy Carter, tend to control their emotions and examine all the facts when making a decision.

Figure **16.6**
The Reflective style com-
bines low dominance and
low sociability.

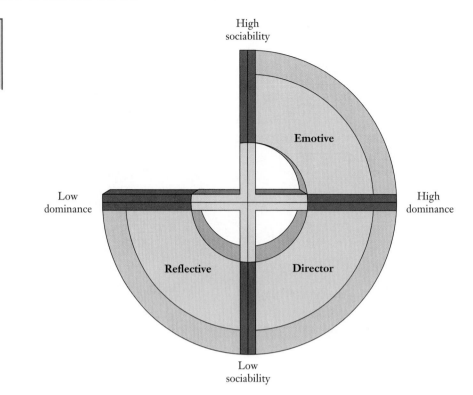

In a selling situation the Reflective customer does not want to move too fast. This person wants the facts presented in an orderly and unemotional manner and does not want to waste a lot of time socializing.

KEY WORDS FOR THE REFLECTIVE STYLE

Precise	Scientific
Deliberate	Preoccupied
Questioning	Serious
Disciplined	Industrious
Aloof	Stuffy

SUPPORTIVE STYLE

The upper left-hand quadrant shows a combination of low dominance and high sociability (Fig. 16.7). This communication style is called the **Supportive style** because these people find it easy to listen and usually do not express their views in a forceful manner. Former U.S. President Gerald Ford and the late Princess Di; and entertainers Meryl Streep, Kevin Costner, Mary Tyler Moore, and Patrick Duffy display the characteristics of the Supportive style.

KEY WORDS FOR THE SUPPORTIVE STYLE

Lighthearted	Patient
Reserved	Sensitive
Passive	Relaxed
Warm	Compliant
Docile	Softhearted

Low visibility generally characterizes the lifestyle of Supportive people. They complete their tasks in a quiet, unassuming manner and seldom draw attention to what they have accomplished. In terms of assertiveness, persons with the Supportive style rank quite

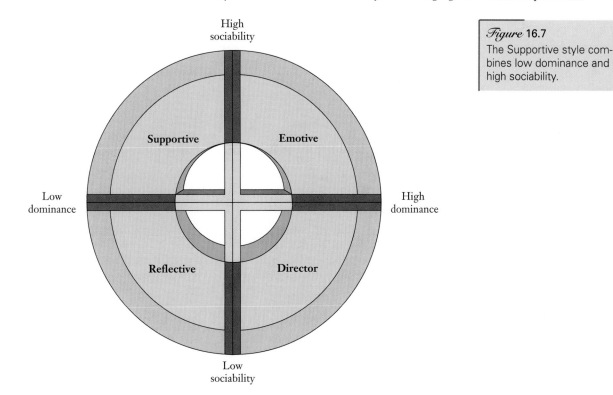

Figure 16.7
The Supportive style combines low dominance and high sociability.

low. Someone who ranks high on the dominance continuum might view the Supportive individual as being too easygoing. Other behaviors that commonly characterize the Supportive person follow:

1. *Gives the appearance of being quiet and reserved.* People with the Supportive behavioral style can easily display their feelings, but not in the assertive manner common to the Emotive individual.
2. *Listens attentively to other people.* In selling, good listening skills can be a real asset. This talent comes naturally to the Supportive person.
3. *Tends to avoid the use of power.* Whereas the Director may rely on power to accomplish tasks, the Supportive person is more likely to rely on friendly persuasion.
4. *Makes decisions in a thoughtful and deliberate manner.* The Supportive person usually takes longer to make a decision.

Popularity of the Four-Style Model

We are endlessly fascinated by ourselves, and this helps explain the growing popularity of the four-style model presented in this chapter. To satisfy this insatiable appetite for information many training and development companies offer training programs that present the four social or communication styles. Figure 16.8 features the approximate equivalents of the four styles presented in this chapter.

Determining Your Communication Style

You now have enough information to identify your own communication style. If your location on the dominance continuum is right of center and your position on the sociability continuum is below the center mark, you fall into the Director quadrant. If your location on

Figure 16.8
The four basic communication styles have been used in a wide range of training programs. For comparison purposes the approximate equivalents to the four communication styles discussed in this chapter are listed.

Supportive (Manning/Reece) Amiable (Wilson Learning) Supportive-Giving (Stuart Atkins Inc.) Relater (People Smarts) Steadiness (Personal Profile System)	Emotive (Manning/Reece) Expressive (Wilson Learning) Adapting-Dealing (Stuart Atkins Inc.) Socializer (People Smarts) Influencing (Personal Profile System)
Reflective (Manning/Reece) Analytical (Wilson Learning) Conserving-Holding (Stuart Atkins Inc.) Thinker (People Smarts) Cautiousness/Compliance (Personal Profile System)	Director (Manning/Reece) Driver (Wilson Learning) Controlling-Taking (Stuart Atkins Inc.) Director (People Smarts) Dominance (Personal Profile System)

the dominance continuum is left of center and your position on the sociability continuum is above the center mark, then your most preferred style is Supportive. Likewise, low dominance matched with low sociability forms the Reflective communication style, and high dominance matched with high sociability forms the Emotive style.

Of course, all of us display some characteristics of the Emotive, Director, Reflective, and Supportive communication styles. However, one of the four styles is usually predominant and readily detectable.[13]

Some people who study the communication-style model for the first time may initially experience feelings of frustration. They find it hard to believe that one's behavioral style tends to remain quite uniform throughout life. People often say, "I am a different person each day!" It is certainly true that we sometimes feel different from day to day, but our most preferred style remains stable.

The Supportive person might say, "I sometimes get very upset and tell people what I am thinking. I can be a Director when I want to be!" There is no argument here. Just because you have a preferred communication style does not mean you never display the behavioral characteristics of another style. Some people use different styles

The nonverbal gestures displayed by this customer indicate a preference for the Reflective Communication style.

in different contexts and in different relationships.[14] Reflective people sometimes display Emotive behavior, and Emotive people sometimes display Reflective behavior. We are saying that each person has one most preferred and habitually used communication style.

MANAGING COMMUNICATION-STYLE BIAS

The most important reason for our discussion of communication styles is this: Communication-style bias is a barrier to success in selling. This form of bias is a common problem in sales work simply because salespeople deal with people from all four quadrants. You cannot select potential customers on the basis of their communication style. You must be able to develop rapport with people from each of the four quadrants. When people of different styles work together but don't adjust to one another, serious problems can develop.[15]

How Communication-Style Bias Develops

To illustrate how communication-style bias develops in a sales situation, let us observe a sales call involving two people with different communication styles. Mary Wheeler entered the office of Dick Harrington with a feeling of optimism. She was sure that her product would save Mr. Harrington's company several hundred dollars a year. She had done her homework and was 99 percent certain that the sale would be closed. Thirty minutes after meeting Mr. Harrington she was walking out of his office without the order. What went wrong?

Mary Wheeler is an "all business" type who is Director in terms of communication style. Her sales calls are typically fast paced and focused. She entered the office of Mr. Harrington, a new prospect, and immediately began to talk business. Mr. Harrington interrupted to ask if she wanted coffee. She declined the offer and continued her sales presentation. Mr. Harrington asked Mary if she enjoyed selling. After a quick glance at her watch, she responded by saying that selling was a rewarding career and then quickly returned to her sales presentation.

Mr. Harrington's communication style is Supportive. He feels uncomfortable doing business with strangers and likes slow-paced interactions with people. He felt tension when Mary failed to establish a social relationship. He also felt she was moving at a pace that was too fast. If she had spent a few minutes socializing with Mr. Harrington, his preferred approach to communication would have become apparent. The "all business" approach she used would be more appropriate for the Director or Reflective communication style.

One of the most important steps in mastering the sales process is for the salesperson to adapt his selling behavior to the customer's communication style. Communication is *always* the responsibility of the salesperson. This is not a responsibility that can be shared.[16]

Developing Style Flexibility

When people are introduced to communication styles for the first time, they often label certain styles as being "more favorable" or "less favorable" for selling careers. The truth is, there is no one best place to be on the communication-style model because there are no best types of personality.[17] As noted previously, a style refers to how someone likes to do something, not how well someone can do something. Successful salespeople come from all four quadrants. What these high achievers have in common is style flexibility.

➤➤ CUSTOMER RELATIONSHIP MANAGEMENT WITH TECHNOLOGY

BEING PREPARED

Customer relationship management (CRM) software empowers a salesperson with information essential to continue a relationship. The software can be used to record, retain, and produce personal information including such factors as marital status, names and ages of children, and individual preferences. Before placing a call, the salesperson might review the database information to refresh her memory about the prospect. This can be especially helpful when preparing to talk with someone with a specific communication style. (See the exercise, Identifying Communication Styles, at p 370 for more information.)

MATURE AND IMMATURE BEHAVIOR

There is a mature and an immature side to each behavioral style. Let us examine the Emotive style to illustrate this point. People with this style are open, personable individuals who seem genuinely friendly. The natural enthusiasm displayed by the mature Emotive is refreshing. On the other hand, an Emotive person may be too talkative and too emotional and may lack the ability to listen to others; this is the immature side of the Emotive communication style.

You recall that we use the words *industrious* and *precise* to describe the Reflective style. These are words that apply to the mature side of the Reflective person. We also use the words *aloof* and *stuffy*. These words describe the immature side of the Reflective.

The good news is that we all have the potential for developing the mature side of our communication style. Our most preferred communication style does not change, but matures as we mature.

STRENGTH—WEAKNESS PARADOX

It is a fact of life that your greatest strength can become your greatest weakness. If your most preferred style is Reflective, people are likely to respect your well-disciplined approach to life as one of your strengths. However, this strength can become a weakness if it is exaggerated. The Reflective person can be too serious, too questioning, and too inflexible. Robert Haas, chairman of Levi Strauss & Company, is known for extraordinary (some say obsessive) attention to detail. Those who work with him say an offhand conversation can sound like a lecture. This Reflective, however, has the ability to flex his style. Levi's employees are fiercely loyal to Haas and describe him as compassionate to a fault.[18]

People with the Director style are open and frank. They express their true feelings in a direct manner. In most cases we appreciate candor, but we do not like to be around people who are too straightforward or too blunt in expressing their views. Albert J. "Chain-Saw Al" Dunlap, former CEO of Sunbeam Corporation, was famous for his booming voice, abruptness, propensity for dominating discussions, and strong opinions.[19] When people come across as *opinionated*, they tend to antagonize others. We should avoid pushing our strengths to the point of unproductive excess.[20]

To illustrate how strengths become weaknesses in excess, let us add more detail to our communication-style model. Note that it now features three zones that radiate out from the center (Fig. 16.9). These dimensions might be thought of as intensity zones.

Zone one People who fall within this zone display their unique behavioral characteristics with less intensity than those in zone two. The Emotive person, for example, is moderately high on the dominance continuum and moderately low on the sociability continuum. As

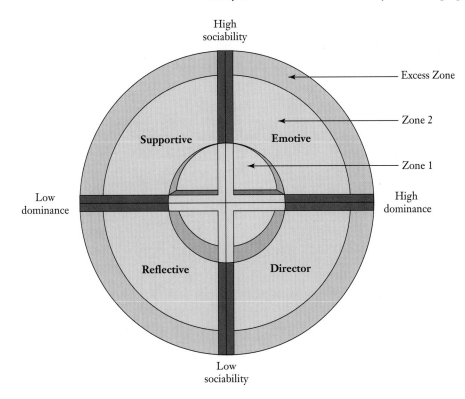

Figure 16.9
The completed communication-style model provides important insights needed to manage the relationship process in selling.

you might expect, zone one communication styles are more difficult to identify because there is less intensity in both dimensions (dominance and sociability).

Zone two   Persons who fall within this zone display their unique behavioral characteristics with greater intensity than persons in zone one. The zone two Reflective, for example, falls within the lowest quartile of the dominance continuum and the lowest quartile of the sociability continuum.

The boundary line that separates zone one and zone two should not be seen as a permanent barrier restricting change in intensity. Under certain circumstances we should abandon our most preferred style temporarily. A deliberate move from zone one to zone two, or vice versa, is called style flexing.

Excess zone   The excess zone is characterized by a high degree of intensity and rigidity. When people allow themselves to drift into this zone, they become very inflexible, which is often interpreted by others as a form of bias toward their style. In addition, the strengths of the inflexible person become weaknesses. Extreme intensity in any quadrant is bound to threaten interpersonal relations.

We are apt to move into the excess zone and exaggerate our style characteristics under stressful conditions. Stress tends to bring out the worst in many people. Some of the behaviors that salespeople and customers may display when they are in the excess zone follow:

Emotive style	Expresses highly emotional opinions
	Stops listening to the other person
	Tries too hard to promote own point of view
	Becomes outspoken to the point of being offensive
	Uses exaggerated gestures and facial expressions to make a point
Director style	Gets impatient with the other person
	Becomes dictatorial and bossy
	Does not admit being wrong

The excess zone is characterized by a high degree of intensity and rigidity. We are more apt to move into the excess zone under very stressful conditions.

	Becomes extremely competitive
	Is cold and unfeeling when dealing with people
Reflective style	Becomes stiff and formal
	Is unwilling to make a decision
	Avoids displaying any type of emotion
	Displays a strong dislike for change
	Is overly interested in detail
Supportive style	Agrees with everyone
	Is unable to take a strong stand
	Becomes overly anxious to win approval of others
	Tries to comfort everyone
	Constantly seeks reassurance

DEVELOPING COMMUNICATION-STYLE FLEXIBILITY

Style flexing is the deliberate attempt to adjust one's communication style to accommodate the needs of the other person. You are attempting to communicate with the other person on her own "channel." Ron Willingham, in his book *Integrity Selling*, reminds us, "People are more apt to buy from you when they perceive you view the world as they view the world."[21] In a selling situation you should try to determine the customer's most preferred style and flex your own accordingly. If your preferred communication style is Director, and your customer is a Supportive, try to be more personal and warmer in your presentation. Once you know the customer's style, flexing your style can make the difference between a presentation that falters, and one that exceeds your expectations.[22] Style sensitivity and flexing are not developed overnight, of course. It takes practice.

Throughout the preapproach you should learn as much as possible about the customer and try to determine his style. Once you are in the presence of the customer watch and listen for clues that reveal his predominant style.

When you are meeting with a customer do not become preoccupied analyzing the person's style. If you are trying hard to analyze the person's style, you may not listen closely enough to what she is trying to tell you. If you are truly tuned into the customer, you can absorb many clues that help you determine her style. After the sales call, analyze the communication and record your findings. Use this information to plan your next contact with the customer.[23] Listen closely to the customer's tone of voice. A Supportive person sounds warm and friendly. The Reflective customer's voice is more likely to be cautious and deliberate. Pay particular attention to gestures. The Emotive individual uses his hands to communicate thoughts and ideas. The Director also uses gestures to communicate but is more controlled and less spontaneous. The Reflective person appears more relaxed, less intense. The Emotive individual is an open, impulsive communicator, while the Reflective person is quite cautious. The Supportive type is personal and friendly, while the Reflective person may seem difficult to get to know. To avoid relationship tension, consider the following suggestions for each of the four styles.

Selling to Emotives

If you are attempting to sell products to an Emotive person, keep in mind the need to move at a pace that holds the attention of the prospect. Be enthusiastic, and avoid an approach that is too stiff and formal. Take time to establish goodwill and build relationships. Do not place too much emphasis on the facts and details. To deal effectively with Emotive people, plan actions that provide support for their opinions, ideas, and dreams.[24] Plan to ask questions concerning their opinions and ideas, but be prepared to help them get "back on track" if they move too far away from the topic. Maintain good eye contact and, above all, be a good listener.

Selling to Directors

The key to relating to Directors is to keep the relationship as businesslike as possible. Developing a strong personal relationship is not a high priority for Directors. In other words, friendship is not usually a condition for a good working relationship. Your goal is to be as efficient, time disciplined, and well organized as possible; and to provide appropriate facts, figures, and success probabilities. Most Directors are goal-oriented people, so try to identify their primary objectives and then determine ways to support and help with these objectives. Early in the sales presentation, ask specific questions and carefully note responses. Look for specific points you can respond to when it is time to present your proposals.

Selling to Reflectives

The Reflective person responds in a positive way to a thoughtful, well-organized approach. Arrive at meetings on time and be well prepared. In most cases it is not necessary to spend a great deal of time building a social relationship. Reflective people appreciate a no-nonsense, businesslike approach to personal selling. Use specific questions that show clear direction. Once you have information concerning the prospect's needs, present your proposal in a slow, deliberate way. Provide as much documentation as possible. Do not be in too big a hurry to close the sale. Never pressure the Reflective person to make quick decisions.

Selling to Supportives

Take time to build a social relationship with the Supportive person. Spend time learning about the matters that are important in this individual's life—family, hobbies, and major interests. Listen carefully to personal opinions and feelings. Supportive individuals like to

➤➤ *Building Relationships in a Diverse World*

VERSATILITY IS KEY

One way to increase sales and enjoy selling more is to reduce the tension between you and the prospect. Personal selling is almost never a tension-free activity, but there are effective ways to control the tension that is likely to surface during the selling process. Dr. David Merrill, one of the early pioneers in development of communication style instruments and training programs, uses the term *versatility* to describe our ability to control the tension we create in others. He believes it is important to understand your preferred communication style, but you also must be willing to control personal behavior patterns and adapt to the people with whom you have contact. In jobs such as selling, which require a high degree of interpersonal effectiveness, versatility can be the key to success.

Roger Wenschlag, author of *The Versatile Salesperson,* defines versatility as, "The degree to which a salesperson is perceived as developing and maintaining buyer comfort throughout the sales process." This does not mean you must become "another person" and display behaviors that make you uncomfortable. However, you should be able to temporarily adjust your behavior to fit the buyer's style. Versatility displayed by the salesperson sends the message, "I care about the relationship."

Versatility has another benefit according to Tony Alessandra, author of *People Smarts.* He notes that this quality enables you to interact more productively with difficult people.

The wonderful feature about versatility is that it can be learned. We can learn to control what we say and do to make others more comfortable.[b]

conduct business with sales personnel who are professional but friendly. Therefore, study their feelings and emotional needs as well as their technical and business needs. Throughout the presentation, provide personal assurances and support for their views. If you disagree with a Supportive person, curb the desire to disagree too assertively; Supportive people dislike interpersonal conflict. Give them the time to comprehend your proposal. Patience is important.

As you develop your communication-style identification skills and become more adept at style flexing, you are better able to manage the relationship process. With these skills you should be able to open more accounts, sell more to established customers, and more effectively meet the pressures of competition. Most important, your customers view you as a person better able to understand and meet their needs.

Word of Caution

It is tempting to put a label on someone and then assume the label tells you everything you need to know about that person. If you want to build an effective partnering type of relationship with a prospect, you must acquire additional information about that person. Stuart Atkins, a respected authority on communication styles and author of *The Name of Your Game* says that it requires real effort to look beyond the label and to experience the whole person as a dynamic process.[25] You also must be careful not to let the label you place on yourself become the justification for your own inflexible behavior. Try not to let the label justify or reinforce why you are unable or unwilling to communicate effectively with others.[26]

Summary

The primary objective of this chapter is to introduce *communication-style bias* and examine the implications of this concept for salespeople. Many sales are lost because salespeople fail to communicate effectively with the prospect. Communication-style bias contributes to this problem. Every salesperson who is willing to develop style sensitivity and engage in appropriate *style flexing* can minimize one of the most common barriers to success in selling.

The communication-style model is based on two continuums that assess two major aspects of human behavior: *dominance* and *sociability*. By combining them as horizontal and vertical continuums we create quadrants that define four styles of communication. We have called these the *Emotive, Director, Reflective,* and *Supportive styles.* With practice in observation you should be able to increase your sensitivity to other people's styles. Practice in self-awareness and self-control give you the ability to flex your own style and help others to feel at ease.

KEY TERMS

Communication-Style Bias   Director Style
Dominance   Reflective Style
Sociability   Supportive Style
Emotive Style   Style Flexing

REVIEW QUESTIONS

1. What is the most prominent form of bias in our society? Explain.
2. Describe the five major principles that support communication-style theory.
3. What are the benefits to the salesperson who understands communication style?
4. What two dimensions of human behavior are used to identify communication style?
5. Describe the person who tends to be high in sociability.
6. What are the four communication styles? Develop a brief description of each of the styles.
7. What is the reaction of most people who study communication styles for the first time? Why does this reaction surface?
8. What is the major reason for introducing communication styles in a textbook on selling?
9. Explain the statement, "Your greatest strength can become your greatest weakness."
10. The Building Relationships in a Diverse World box on p. 368 suggests that we should try to control what we say and do to make others more comfortable. Is it realistic to expect salespeople to follow this advice? Explain your answer.

APPLICATION EXERCISES

1. Oprah Winfrey has been referred to as one of America's best talk show hosts.
   a. On the dominance continuum, mark where you think her television personality belongs.

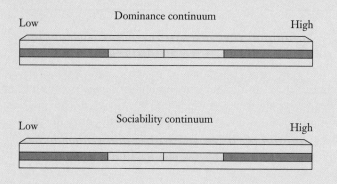

b. On the sociability continuum, mark where you believe her television personality belongs.

c. Using the two continuums to form the communication-style model, what is Oprah Winfrey's television communication style? Does Oprah Winfrey possess style flexibility? Explain this in terms of (i) the different styles of guests on her program and (ii) her apparent popularity with millions of people.

d. Describe Oprah Winfrey's personality using statements and terms from this chapter.

e. Have you ever observed Oprah Winfrey slipping into her excess zone? Explain.

2. Many salespeople, after being introduced to communication-style psychology, attempt to categorize each of their customers. They report that their relationships become mutually more enjoyable and productive. Select five people whom you know quite well (supervisor, subordinate, customer, teacher, friend, or members of your family). Using the two behavioral continuums in this chapter, determine these people's communication styles. Using your own descriptive terminology in conjunction with terminology in this chapter, develop a descriptive behavioral profile of each of these people. Explain how this information can improve your relationship with each of these people.

3. Self-awareness is important in personal selling. As we get to know ourselves, we can identify barriers to acceptance by others. Once you have identified your most preferred communication style, you have taken a big step in the direction of self-awareness. If you have not yet determined your most preferred communication style, take a few minutes to complete the Dominance Indicator form (see Table 16.1) and the Sociability Indicator form (see Table 16.2). Follow the instructions provided on pp. 353–354.

4. Myers-Briggs Personality Types and Jungian Personality Types are two very popular descriptions of the material in this chapter. Using your search engine, access the Internet sites that refer to these concepts. Type in "Jungian" + personality profiles to access the Jungian personality types. To access the Myers-Briggs types, type in "Myers-Briggs" + personality profiles. Does the number of queries indicate anything about the validity and popularity of these theories? Examine specific queries about both of these theories. Do you see the relationship between these two theories and the material in this chapter?

CRM APPLICATION EXERCISE

Identifying Communication Styles

Pat Silva carefully recorded the communication styles of most of the people in the database; and identified the prospects as Emotive, Director, Reflective, or Supportive. If you feel like talking to an Emotive, you can find them by selecting Lookup, Keyword, type "Emotive", check Notes, and press Enter. After searching, ACT! displays four records of people who Pat identified as Emotives. Print these notes by selecting Report, Contact Report, Active Lookup, Printer, and Enter.

CASE PROBLEM

Ray Perkins has been employed at Grant Real Estate for almost two years. Prior to receiving his real estate license he was a property manager with a large real estate agency in another community. During his first year with Grant, he was assigned to the residential property division and sold properties totaling $825,000. He then requested and received a transfer to the commercial division.

Three months ago, Ray obtained a commercial listing that consisted of 26 acres of land near a growing residential neighborhood. The land is zoned commercial and appears to be ideally suited for a medium-sized shopping center. Ray prepared a detailed prospectus and sent it to Harold Maynard, president of Mondale Growth Corporation, a firm specializing in development of shopping centers. One week later he received a letter from Mr. Maynard requesting more information. Shortly after receiving Ray's response, Mr. Maynard called to set up an appointment to inspect the property. A time and date were finalized, and Ray agreed to meet his plane and conduct a tour of the property.

Ray is a quiet, amiable person who displays the Supportive communication style. Friends say that they like to spend time with him because he is a good listener.

Questions

1. If Mr. Maynard displays the characteristics of the Director communication style, how should Ray conduct himself during the meeting? Be specific as you describe those behaviors that would be admired by Mr. Maynard.
2. If Mr. Maynard wants to build rapport with Ray Perkins, what behavior should he display?
3. It is not a good idea to put a label on someone and then assume the label tells us everything about the person. As Ray attempts to build rapport with Mr. Maynard, what other personal characteristics should he try to identify?

CRM CASE STUDY

Preparing to Communicate with CRM

Becky Kemley has asked for a meeting to discuss your relationship strategy with your accounts. One of the topics she wishes to cover is your plan for approaching people on the basis of their differing communication styles.

Questions

1. Should you use a formal or an informal approach to Colleen Landers of Landers Engineering?
2. Should you focus on building a strong personal relationship with Karen Murray of Murray D'Zines?
3. Should you press Sam Pearlman Computerized Labs to make a purchasing decision?
4. Will a friendly and sociable approach work well with Dwayne Ortega of Big Tex Auto Sales?

Management of the Sales Force

$\mathcal{S}$ ome sales managers work hard to maintain a competitive spirit among members of their sales force. Marga McNally, vice president of sales for WRC-TV, an NBC-owned station in Washington, DC, takes a different approach. She works hard to build a sense of team effort and shared accomplishment among her 11 salespeople. McNally's management style emphasizes brainstorming and teamwork. She says, "I want salespeople who will be competitive going out the door and collaborative when they come back in the door." McNally wants her salespeople to share winning sales strategies, critique each other, and help work out what is best for the customer. She believes the best way to build a partnership with customers is to discover solutions that are right for the customer and not just right for her TV station. This is accomplished by listening without any preconceived notions. "We take a pad and pencil with us on customer calls rather than a canned presentation. Then we come back and brainstorm together on how to respond."[1]

McNally has adopted a leadership style that is very effective in the age of information. She recognizes that shared participation in problem solving and decision making is the key to individual growth and development. Collaboration also helps members of her sales team discover solutions that result in stronger partnerships with customers. She recognizes that one of the major values that has surfaced throughout the past decade is teamwork over individualism. To be an effective "team facilitator" she knows that coaching is an important part of being a leader.

SALES MANAGEMENT FUNCTIONS

Salespeople frequently have the opportunity to advance to a management position. The first promotion for many is to the position of sales manager. Those who achieve success at this level may advance to management positions that offer even greater challenge and increased economic rewards.

The **sales manager** typically performs the functions of recruiting, training, organizing, and supervising the sales force. In companies that use team selling the sales manager must possess the knowledge and skills needed to create effective teams.[2] Managing the sales force is an external management function, focused on bringing in orders and revenue

Besides supervising the sales force, sales managers often are involved in establishing sales quotas, developing long- and short-term forecasts, and seeing that goals are achieved.

from outside the company. However, it also requires coordination and cooperation with almost every internal department including marketing, finance, and distribution.[3]

The sales manager's duties vary somewhat from one marketing organization to another. Today's sales manager is more likely to function in a virtual office environment. Sales force automation permits salespeople to receive data on their laptops or their home computers. The use of other technology—videoconferencing, teleconferencing, e-mail, and voice mail—reduces the need for frequent face-to-face contact with members of the sales team.[4]

Sales managers maintain a steady flow of information to salespeople and also provide a variety of selling tools and aids. Successful sales managers also help salespeople cope with the rapid change and uncertainty that permeates today's business environment.[5]

Sales managers can have a dramatic influence on the salespeople they supervise. Depending on the leadership qualities adopted, sales managers can have an advantageous, neutral, or even detrimental effect on the performance of sales subordinates.[6]

Effective leadership has been discussed in hundreds of books and articles. A careful review of this material indicates that most successful supervisory–management personnel have certain behaviors in common. Writers of this material agree that there are two important dimensions of effective leadership.[7] We shall label these dimensions *structure* and *consideration.*

Structure

Sales managers who display **structure** clearly define their own duties and those of the sales staff. They assume an active role in directing their subordinates' work. Policies and procedures are clearly defined, and subordinates know what is expected of them.

An effective sales manager provides regular feedback. All employees want to know "where they stand" with the manager.

Salespeople also know how well they are doing because the structured supervisor evaluates their productivity and provides feedback. Members of the sales force usually appreciate the predictable nature of the highly structured sales manager. The following behaviors provide evidence of structure:

1. *Planning takes place on a regular basis.* The effective sales manager thinks ahead and decides what to do in the future. Strategic planning is the process of determining the company's current position in the market; determining where you want to be and when; and making decisions on how to secure the position you want.[8] Strategic planning gives meaning and direction to the sales force.

2. *Expectations are clearly communicated.* Expectations of sales managers can have a positive impact on the performance of salespeople. In most cases high expectations lead to high performance.[9]

3. *Decisions are made promptly and firmly.* An effective sales manager is willing and able to make decisions in a timely way. An ineffective manager often postpones important decisions, hoping the problem will go away. Of course, most decisions cannot be made until all the facts are available. A good sales manager keeps the lines of communication open and involves subordinates in making the truly important decisions.

4. *Performance of salespeople is appraised regularly.* All employees want to know "where they stand" with the manager. An effective sales manager provides regular feedback. When a salesperson is not performing up to established standards, the sales manager takes immediate action.

Although structure is an important aspect of sales management, too much structure can sometimes create problems. In an effort to become better organized and more systematized, some sales organizations have developed detailed policies and procedures that rob salespeople of time and energy. Filling out endless reports and forms, for example, can cause unnecessary frustration and may reduce productivity.[10]

Consideration

A sales manager who displays the dimension of **consideration** is more likely to have relationships with salespeople that are characterized by mutual trust, respect for salespeople's ideas, and consideration for their feelings. A climate of good two-way communication usually exists between the manager and the employee. The following behaviors provide evidence of consideration:

1. *Regular and effective communication receives a high priority.* Whenever possible the effective manager engages in face-to-face communication with salespeople. They do not rely entirely on memos, letters, or sales reports for information sharing, but arrange face-to-face meetings. John Morrone, vice president of sales for Pitney Bowes Management Services, frequently travels with his salespeople. He says, "My claim to fame is reaching out and touching people."[11] The effective sales manager is a good listener and creates an atmosphere of cooperation and understanding.
2. *Each salesperson is treated as an individual.* The sales manager takes a personal interest in each member of the sales force. No one is treated like a "number." The interest is genuine, not artificial. The effective sales manager does not endanger effectiveness by showing favoritism to anyone.
3. *Good performance is rewarded often.* Positive reinforcement is one of the strongest morale-building factors in the work environment. Ken Blanchard, co-author of *The One Minute Manager,* says, "The key to developing people will always be to concentrate on catching them doing something right instead of blaming them for doing something wrong."[12] Recognition for a job well done is always appreciated.

Coaching for Peak Performance

Sales managers who develop a leadership style that combines structure and consideration behaviors possess the skills needed to be an effective coach. **Coaching** is an interpersonal process between the sales manager and the salesperson in which the manager helps the salesperson improve performance in a specific area. The coaching process has two primary areas of focus: helping the salesperson recognize the need to improve his or her performance and developing the salesperson's commitment to improve performance.[13]

Coaching is often used to correct a specific performance problem such as ineffective prospecting, poorly developed sales presentations, or failure to provide service after the sale. An outline for a coaching strategy involves four-steps.[14] Step one in the coaching process involves documentation of performance problems. In some cases the best approach is to observe and assess performance during actual sales calls. Step two involves getting the salesperson to recognize and agree that there is a need to improve performance in a specific area. Sales managers should never assume the salesperson sees the problem in the same way they do. Step three involves exploring solutions. At this point it's often best to let the salesperson suggest ways to improve performance. Step four involves getting a commitment from the salesperson to take action. This step may involve development of a contract (written or verbal) that clarifies the coaching goals, approaches, and outcomes. A major goal of coaching meetings is to improve performance, while enabling sales managers and salespeople to maintain a relationship based on mutual respect and trust.

Positive reinforcement is one of the strongest ways to build morale. Effective managers reward their subordinates for good performance.

RECRUITMENT AND SELECTION OF SALESPEOPLE

Careful recruitment and selection of salespeople is very important. This is one of the most significant tasks sales managers perform. When they hire the wrong person, several problems may arise.

> If the new salesperson is not a top producer, the business must absorb the cost of low productivity.

> If the new employee is not able to provide good service, regular customers may be lost. Established customers represent one of the firm's most valuable assets.

> If the new employee quits after a few months or must be fired, the business suffers an economic loss. The money invested in salary, benefits, travel expenses, and training can be significant. It can cost anywhere from $10,000 to $100,000 a year in terms of training, salary, and benefits, and lost productivity when the wrong person is hired.[15]

Successful salespeople are often difficult to identify. The selection of sales personnel today is, however, more of a "science" and less of an "art." Sales managers no longer need to rely on "gut feelings." The ability to identify sales aptitude accurately can be acquired. Many progressive sales organizations recognize the need to help sales managers develop the interviewing skills necessary to make profitable hiring decisions. It is impossible to avoid occasionally hiring a poor performer, but sales managers can improve their average by using some established recruitment and selection guidelines.

Determine Actual Job Requirements

To decide what type of applicant is needed, the manager should first outline the duties the person should perform. The sales manager must have a clear picture of the job requirements before beginning the recruitment process.

Some sales managers make every effort to discover the success factors that contribute to the achievements of their high-performance salespeople. Success factors are the skills, knowledge, abilities, and behaviors considered critical for successful performance.[16] This information may be collected by use of interviews with salespeople or customers, by observing the salesperson during sales calls, or by some other method.

After a careful study of the duties the salesperson should perform and identification of the success factors, a job description should be prepared. A job description is an explanation of what the salesperson will do and under what conditions the work will be performed. It is a good idea to spell out in as much detail as possible the abilities and qualities that the applicant needs to be successful. This can be accomplished by answering a few basic questions about the position.

1. Will the person be developing new sales territory or assuming responsibility for an established territory?
2. Is the product or service well established, or is it new to the marketplace?
3. Will the salesperson work under the sales manager's close supervision or independently?
4. What amount of travel is required? What are the likelihoods of eventual transfer and promotion?

Once the job description is prepared, the foundation has been established to determine the type of person to be hired. There is no substitute for knowing what the job requires.

Search Out Applicants from Several Sources

To identify the best possible person, it is usually best to seek applicants from more than one source. As a rule of thumb, try to interview three or more applicants for each opening. Some suggested sources of new employees follow:

1. *Candidates within the company.* One of the first places to look is within your own company. Is there someone in accounting, engineering, customer service, or some other area who aspires to a sales position? These people have the advantage of being thoroughly familiar with the company's product offering, policies, operations, and what it takes to please the customer.[17]
2. *College and university students.* Many business firms are turning to college and university campuses to recruit salespeople. Placement offices are usually cooperative and often publicize openings.
3. *Trade and newspaper advertisements.* A carefully prepared newspaper advertisement often attracts well-qualified job applicants. A well-written ad should describe the job requirements *and* spell out the opportunities. All information should be accurate. The ad should "sell" the position, but it should not exaggerate its benefits.
4. *Employment agencies and listings.* Nearly 2,000 public employment offices are located throughout the United States. These offices recruit applicants and screen them according to your specifications. There is no charge for this service. There are also many private employment agencies. These firms specialize in matching applicants to the job and usually do some initial screening for employers. A fee is assessed for the services these agencies provide.
5. *Internet.* Many companies are using the Internet to recruit for sales positions. Two popular Web sites are Monster.com and careermosaic.

Select the Best Qualified Applicant

Once you have identified qualified applicants, the next step is to select the best person. This is becoming more difficult as products become more complex, customers become more sophisticated, and competitors become more aggressive. Selecting the best qualified applicant is never easy, but there are some qualifications and characteristics that all sales managers should look for. One of the most important qualities is a high level of interest and enthusiasm for the job and high degree of self-motivation. Salespeople have to be self-starters. Barry Farber, president of Farber Training Systems, says that he would hire a salesperson without experience or knowledge of the industry who is willing to give 110 percent versus someone who has experience and is highly skilled, but who is not motivated.[18]

Some sales managers use a performance activity to identify the self-motivated person. Alan Gold of The Office Place, an office supply and equipment dealer in Anchorage, Alaska, conducts one interview to make a general assessment of the candidate. If the person seems to have potential, he sets a date for a second interview. He gives the candidate a product ID number and tells the person to be prepared to make a presentation on that product at their next meeting. The candidate's motivational level is measured by the efforts made to obtain enough information about the product and the company to prepare a good presentation.[19]

Reliability is another quality to search for. Do not hesitate to check references to determine police records, problems at previous jobs, or patterns of instability. The applicant for a sales position must be able to earn your complete trust.

➤➤ Selling in Action

ARE YOU READY FOR THE SALES INTERVIEW?

The personal interview is an important part of the selection process when filling sales positions. When companies use a series of interviews, the first one often is used to eliminate unacceptable candidates—those who lack maturity, lack enthusiasm, or display poor appearance. Subsequent interviews are used to match people to job qualifications. At Hewlett Packard, candidates may have as many as six interviews with various people. At Smith Kline, a team approach is used so candidates do not learn the "right" answers from one interview to the next.

While interviews vary from one company or interviewer to another, there are some popular questions and requests that you should be prepared to handle:

- Tell me about yourself.
- Describe the sales process as you understand it.

- What books have you read recently on selling or for personal development?
- What is your greatest weakness? Strength?
- What was the most boring job you ever had, and how did you handle it?
- How do you feel about your present (or previous) employer?
- What was the biggest contribution you made to your last employer?
- Sell me this pen (ashtray, laptop computer, lamp).
- Why should we hire you?

Some employers also ask you to complete a test to demonstrate your written communication skills, or your ability to handle "the numbers." These are both important skills for a sales professional.[a]

One of the greatest challenges is hiring salespeople who can develop a close, trusting, long-term relationship with customers. As we have noted previously, the manner in which salespeople establish, build, and maintain relationships is no longer an incidental aspect of personal selling. Mike Mitchell, vice president of human resources for Tiffany & Company, says, "We look for people who feel a great sense of purpose in serving our customers. You can train people to be consultative in their approach to the point that they master the mechanics of the sales process, but you can't teach someone to care."[20]

Experts in the field of employment testing say that psychological tests can be helpful as an element of the hiring process. Psychological assessments can provide objective information about a candidate's skills and abilities. One example is the Sales Achievement Predictor developed by Western Psychological Services. This instrument assesses self-confidence, competitiveness, and other qualities deemed important in sales.[21] Test results always should be used *in conjunction* with information obtained from the interview with the candidate and the findings of reference checks.

ORIENTATION AND TRAINING

Once you have selected the best qualified salesperson, two steps should be taken to ensure that this person becomes a productive member of your staff. First, give the new employee a thorough orientation to your business operation. Provide the orientation *before* the person begins working. This should include a review of your company's history, philosophy of doing business, mission statement, business policies, compensation plan, and other important information.

Sales training that is carefully planned and executed can make a major contribution to the performance of every salesperson.

Second, initiate a training program to help the person achieve success. Sales training that is carefully planned and executed can make a major contribution to the performance of every salesperson. Study results indicate that salespeople have a more positive view about their job situation, greater commitment, and improved performance when their sales managers clarify their job role, how to execute their tasks, and how their needs can be satisfied with successful job performance.[22]

Even salespeople with great potential are handicapped when the company fails to provide adequate training. Keep in mind that in the absence of formal training, employees develop their own approaches to performing tasks.

Many sales managers believe that new salespeople (those with no prior sales experience) need special attention during the orientation and training period. One expert said, "They must be managed differently, compensated differently, and gradually converted to the ranks of experienced sales professionals. It is often an 18-month process."[23]

The size of the firm should not dictate the scope of the training program. Even the smallest marketing organization should have a formal sales training program. This program should have three dimensions:

1. Knowledge of the product line, company marketing strategies, territory information, and related areas
2. Attitude toward the company, the company's products and services, and the customers to be served
3. Skill in applying personal selling principles and practices—the "doing" part of the sales training program

An important part of the sales training program is foundation level instruction. This aspect of sales training focuses on the *basics.* If salespeople are to plan and execute a sales call successfully, they must first master certain fundamental selling skills—the skills that form the foundation for everything salespeople do in their careers. The steps that make up the Six-Step Presentation Plan (approach, presentation, demonstration, negotiation, close, and servicing the sale) represent fundamental selling skills (see Fig. 14.1).

>> BUILDING QUALITY PARTNERSHIPS

WINNING THROUGH TEAMWORK

There is no shortage of motivational speakers who can fire up your sales force. One of the most popular speakers these days is Pat Riley, the successful coach who guided the Los Angeles Lakers to four National Basketball Association championships and later coached the New York Knicks and Miami Heat. Hundreds of Fortune 500 companies have paid $25,000 to have him inspire their sales and marketing personnel. He likes to discuss with audiences the ideas presented in his book titled *The Winner Within: A Life Plan for Team Players.* Drawing on his experience on the basketball court, Riley talks about the universal importance of cooperation and teamwork. The sales manager who wants to get the best performance from a sales force must understand one important principle of human behavior:

> It all has to start with trust. A good manager is tough, compassionate, and deals with the truth each day. People working for that kind of leader will recognize those qualities and allow themselves to be infiltrated with a team concept.

Riley tells his audiences that success does not happen without dedication, goals, and ability to work together. He also believes that all salespeople should be rewarded for their effort. Riley encourages sales managers to develop effective compensation plans.[b]

SALES FORCE MOTIVATION

It is helpful to note the difference between internal and external motivation. An **internal motivation** is an intrinsic reward that occurs when a duty or task is performed. If a salesperson enjoys calling on customers and solving their problems, this activity is in itself rewarding, and the salesperson is likely to be self-motivated.[24] Internal motivation is likely to be triggered when sales positions provide an opportunity for achievement and individual growth. **External motivation** is an action taken by another person that involves rewards or other forms of reinforcement that cause the worker to behave in ways to ensure receipt of the award.[25] A cash bonus given to salespeople who achieve a sales goal provides an example of external motivation. Experts on motivation agree that organizations should attempt to provide a mix of external rewards and internal satisfaction.

A basic contention among too many sales managers has been that sales productivity can be improved by staging more elaborate sales contests, giving more expensive recognition awards, or picking truly exotic meeting locations. This point of view ignores the merits of internal motivation. One of the foremost critics of external rewards is Alfie Kohn, author of *No Contest: The Case against Competition* and *Punished by Rewards: The Trouble with Gold Stars, Incentive Plans, A's and Other Bribes*. Kohn states that a reward system that forces people to compete for awards or recognition may undermine cooperation and teamwork. In addition, he says that reward plans often create a situation where some salespeople are winners and some are losers. Kohn further declares, "For each person who wins, there are many others who carry with them the feeling of having lost."[26]

In many cases, intrinsic motivators (achievement, challenge, responsibility, advancement, growth, enjoyment of work itself, and involvement) have a longer term effect on employee attitudes than extrinsic motivators (contests, prizes, quotas, and money). A salesperson who is intrinsically satisfied in the job will work willingly at high-performance levels.

Although criticisms of external rewards have a great deal of merit, the fact remains that large numbers of organizations continue to achieve positive results with carefully developed incentive programs. It is possible to design programs that have long-range benefits for both the organization and the individual employee. Kirby Bonds, the San Francisco regional sales manager for Avis Rent-A-Car's corporate sales division, has used sales contests to identify new accounts, build business within existing accounts, and generate endorsement letters from satisfied customers. Bonds keeps contest time frames short so more of his salespeople have an opportunity to win.[27]

Because people bring different interests, drives, and values to the workplace, they react differently to attempts at motivation. When possible, motivation strategies should reflect the needs of the sales force. If a salesperson is not making very much money, then a cash incentive may be an effective reward. An experienced salesperson who is earning a lot of money in salary and commission might be motivated by an exciting travel or merchandise incentive. High-performing salespeople employed by Hormel Foods Corporation were rewarded with a 1950s themed road rally in Southern Florida, complete with motorcycles and convertibles. People who are involved in a unique travel event often feel more valued and appreciated.[28]

Some sales managers are discovering that simply asking salespeople for their opinions and then following up on their suggestions, where appropriate, are excellent ways to motivate them. Effective communication is one of the most important qualities that salespeople desire from their sales manager.[29]

Many sales managers have discovered the value of communicating positive expectations to their salespeople. They recognize that most people can be greatly influenced by the expectations of others. Goethe gave sales managers some good advice when he said, "If you treat a man as he is, he will remain as he is; if you treat him as if he were what he could

Experts on motivation agree that organizations should provide salespeople with a mix of external rewards and internal satisfaction. The Achievement Award featured in this advertisement is an example of an external reward.

►► CUSTOMER RELATIONSHIP MANAGEMENT WITH TECHNOLOGY

STAYING INFORMED

A key role of the sales manager is to provide a steady flow of information and advice to salespeople. Salespeople look to their managers for information about market trends, products, company policies, and assistance with their accounts. Customer relationship management (CRM) software improves and enhances the flow of information between managers and the sales force. The same features that are used to enrich communications with customers also support the sales organization's internal communications. With direct access to a shared CRM database, for example, a sales manager can review relationships with accounts in "real time" by examining a salesperson's notes at any time. This makes it possible for the manager to enter advice about an account directly into that account's record. (See the exercise, Receiving Advice through CRM, at p. 387 for more information.)

be, he will become what he could be." With the aid of effective supervision practices and job enrichment it is possible to release the motivation within each salesperson.

COMPENSATION PLANS

Compensation plans for salespeople combine direct monetary payments (salary and commissions); and indirect monetary payments such as paid vacations, pensions, and insurance plans. Compensation practices vary greatly throughout the field of selling. Furthermore, sales managers are constantly searching for the "perfect" sales force compensation plan. Of course, the perfect plan does not exist. Each plan must be chosen to suit the specific type of selling job, the objectives of the firm's marketing program, and the type of customer served.

Recognition for success in sales can be an effective form of external motivation.

We are beginning to see some trends in the area of sales force compensation. A growing number of companies are linking sales pay to customer satisfaction. The consulting firm of Hewitt Associates says that 27 percent of companies use some measure of customer service in the sales-incentive programs.[30] Many companies are following the lead of DuPont, Digital Equipment, Data General, and Tandem Computers in developing teams made up of sales representatives, engineers, and technicians. In response to this trend we are seeing the use of team compensation plans.[31] Selecting a fair method of compensation for team members is a dilemma for many companies. Team development and outcomes may suffer if equitable compensation plans are not developed.[32]

In the field of selling there are five basic compensation plans. Here is a description of each:

Straight commission plan. The only direct monetary compensation comes from sales. No sales, no income. Salespeople under this plan are very conscious of their sales. Lack of job security can be a strong inducement to produce results. However, these people also may concentrate more on immediate sales than on long-term customer development.

Commission plan with a draw provision or guaranteed salary. This plan has about the same impact on salespeople as the straight commission plan. However, it gives them more financial security.

Commission with a draw or guaranteed salary plus a bonus. This plan offers more direct financial security than the first two plans. Therefore, salespeople may adhere more to the company's objectives. The bonus may be based on sales or profits.

Fixed salary plus bonus. Salespeople functioning under this compensation plan tend to be more company centered and to have a fairly high degree of financial security if their salary is competitive. The bonus incentive helps motivate people under this plan.

Straight salary. Salespeople who work under this compensation plan are usually more company centered and have financial security.

According to *Dartnell's 29th Sales Force Compensation Survey 1996–1997*, over 75 percent of the companies participating in the survey used some form of compensation plan that combined base salary and incentive.[33] The salary plus bonus and salary plus commission plans are both quite popular.

As might be expected, many companies are experimenting with some variation of these basic plans. In some situations, salespeople are rewarded for achieving a specific objective such as developing new accounts or improving the quality of customer service. Awards in the form of cash or points that can be used to "purchase" prizes can be used. Award programs can be styled to suit a variety of sales objectives:

Specific product movement. Bonus points can be given for the sale of certain items during specified "push" selling periods.

Percentage sales increase. Sales levels can be established with points that are given only when those levels are reached.

Establish new accounts. A block of points can be awarded for opening a new account or for introducing new products through the existing outlets.

Increase sales activity. For each salesperson, points can be awarded based on the number of calls.[34]

There is no easy way to develop an effective compensation plan. There are, however, some important guidelines for your efforts to develop a good plan. First, be sure that your sales and marketing objectives are defined in detail. The plan should complement these goals. If sales and marketing objectives are in conflict with the compensation plan, problems surely arise.

Second, the compensation plan should be field tested before full implementation. Several questions should be answered: Is the new plan easy to administer? How does the proposed plan differ in terms of payout compared with the existing plan?

Third, explain the compensation plan carefully to the sales force. Misunderstanding may generate distrust of the plan. Keep in mind that some salespeople may see change as a threat.

Fourth, change the compensation plan when conditions in the marketplace warrant change. One reason for the poor showing of many plans is that firms fail to revise their plan as the business grows and market conditions change.[35] Review the compensation plan at least annually to ensure that it's aligned with conditions in the marketplace and the company's overall marketing strategy.

ASSESSING SALES FORCE PRODUCTIVITY

As the cost of maintaining a sales force increases, sales managers must give more attention to measuring productivity. The goal is to analyze the profitability of each salesperson's sales volume. This task is complicated because sales territories, customers, and business conditions vary.

The problem of measuring sales force productivity is more complicated than might appear at first glance. In most cases, sales volume alone does not tell you how much profit or loss you are making on the sales of each member of the sales force. A small manufacturer was losing money until he analyzed the profitability of sales generated by each person. He found that one salesperson created a loss on almost every order. This salesperson was concentrating on a market that had become so competitive that she had to reduce the markup to make sales.

Some sales managers view the frequency of calls as an indicator of success. This information is only helpful when compared with the profit earned on each account. The number of calls made on an account should bear some relationship to the sales and profit potential of that account. In some cases it is possible to maintain small accounts without frequent personal calls.

To compare a salesperson's current productivity with the past also can be misleading. Changes in products, prices, competition, and assignments make comparisons with the past unfair—sometimes to the salesperson, sometimes to the company. It is better to measure cumulative quarterly, semiannual, or annual results in relation to established goals.

Some sales managers use performance evaluation criteria that communicate to the sales force which elements of their jobs are most important and how they are doing in each area. Evaluating salespeople involves defining the bases on which they are to be evaluated, developing performance standards to determine the acceptable level of performance desired on each base, monitoring actual performance, and giving salespeople feedback on their performance.[36] Some of the most common criteria for assessing the productivity of salespeople are listed as follows:

Quantitative Criteria

Sales volume in dollars

Sales volume compared with previous year's sales

Sales volume by product or product line

Number of new accounts opened

Amount of new account sales

Net profit dollars

Number of customer calls

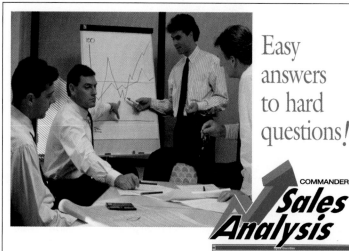

Customer relationship management programs such as Commander Profit help the sales manager assess key sales force productivity measurements.

Qualitative Criteria

Attitude

Product knowledge

Communication skills

Personal appearance

Customer goodwill generated

Selling skills

Initiative

In most cases it is best to emphasize assessment criteria that can be expressed in numbers (quantitative). The preceding quantitative items are especially significant when accompanied by target dates. For example, you might assess the number of new accounts opened during a six-month period. Of course, a sales manager should not ignore the other criteria listed here. The other items can affect a salesperson's productivity, and you do have to make judgments in these areas.

Some sales managers ask their salespeople to complete a self-evaluation as part of the overall evaluation process. Many salespeople believe that self-evaluation contributes to their personal development.[37]

Summary

Many capable salespeople have advanced to the position of *sales manager*. This job involves such diverse duties as recruiting, selecting, training, and supervising salespeople. Some sales managers are concerned solely with the management of salespeople; others have responsibility for additional marketing functions such as advertising and market research.

The sales manager is part of the management team and therefore must be concerned with leadership. An effective sales manager is an effective leader. Although the qualities of effective leaders are subject to debate, most research tells us that such people display two dimensions: *structure* and *consideration*. Sales managers who develop a leadership style that combines structure and consideration possess the skills needed to be an effective *coach*.

Many sales managers are involved directly or indirectly in recruiting and selecting salespeople. This is an important responsibility, because mistakes can be costly. A portion of the company's profit picture and the firm's image can be influenced positively or negatively by each member of the sales force.

Training and motivating salespeople are almost daily concerns of the sales manager. Training should always be viewed as an investment in human resources. Training helps members of the sales force reach their fullest potential.

We discuss the difference between *internal* and *external motivation*. In many cases intrinsic motivators (achievement, challenge, responsibility, involvement, and enjoyment of work itself) have a longer term effect on employee attitudes than extrinsic motivators (contests, prizes, and money). Sales managers need to discover the individual differences between salespeople to select the most effective motivation strategies.

The most common *compensation plans* are discussed. Compensation plans should be field tested before full implementation.

Assessing sales force productivity is a major responsibility of the sales manager. Sales managers use both quantitative and qualitative criteria.

KEY TERMS

Sales Manager
Structure
Consideration
Coaching

Internal Motivation
External Motivation
Compensation Plans

REVIEW QUESTIONS

1. What is the sales manager's primary responsibility?
2. Are all sales managers' duties the same? Explain.
3. What are the two main leadership qualities displayed by most successful sales managers? Define and explain each of these qualities.
4. List and describe the four basic steps involved in coaching.
5. What is a job description? Explain the importance of job descriptions in selecting salespeople.
6. What are four sources of recruiting new salespeople?

7. What should sales managers look for in selecting new salespeople? Describe at least three important qualities.

8. What are some common criticisms of external rewards?

9. List and describe the five basic compensation plans for salespeople.

10. What are the *best* criteria for measuring a salesperson's performance? List additional criteria that should be considered in evaluating individual performance.

APPLICATION EXERCISES

1. Assume that you are a manager of a wholesale electrical supply business. Sales have increased to a level where you need to hire another salesperson. What sources can you use in recruiting a good professional salesperson? What criteria can you use in selecting the person you hire?

2. Carefully analyze the following types of selling positions:
   a. A territory selling position for a national manufacturer that requires the salesperson to provide customer service to a large number of accounts plus open up several new accounts each month
   b. A retail sales position in the cosmetics department of a department store
   c. An automobile salesperson who sells and leases new and used cars
   d. A real estate salesperson who sells residential real estate

   Assuming that each of the preceding positions is full time, identify the type of compensation plan you think is best for each. Supply an explanation for each of your answers.

3. Schedule an appointment with two sales managers. Interview each of them, using the following questions as a guide:
   a. What are your functions as a sales manager?
   b. How do the functions of a sales manager differ from those of a salesperson?
   c. What criteria do you use in selecting salespeople?
   d. What kinds of training programs do you have for new salespeople?
   e. What method of compensation do you use for your salespeople?
   f. How do you evaluate the performance of your salespeople?
   g. What personal qualities are important for becoming a sales manager?

   Write the answers to these questions. Summarize the similarities and differences of the sales managers' responses.

4. The Internet lists many sources of training in the field of sales management. Using your search engine, type in "sales management." How many queries did you find? Examine one or more of the training programs and list the topics that are covered. Compare this list of topics with the material presented in this chapter.

CRM APPLICATION EXERCISE

Receiving Advice through CRM

Becky Kemley, your sales manager at SimNet Systems, regularly reviews your progress with accounts by examining your notes. She recently entered into one of your records a note about an account's debt problems. Find her note and the two accounts she refers to by selecting Lookup, Keyword, type "debt," check Notes, and press Enter. Print the information contained in these records by selecting Report, Contact Report, Active Lookup, Printer, and Enter.

Case Problem

One of the more interesting developments in sales force management is the use of customer feedback to improve the performance of salespeople. Most of these programs are relatively new and go by a variety of names such as *360 degree feedback, customer-conscious compensation*, and *customer satisfaction rewards*. Organizations that have adopted this assessment strategy believe salespeople can benefit from feedback collected from the customers they serve. Also, information collected can be used by the company to improve customer service.

The use of customer-driven evaluation programs is on the increase because of the rising regard for the role of sales at many companies. Tom Mott, a consultant with Hewitt Associates, says, "Salespeople who were volume pushers are now becoming the manager of their company's relationship with the customer." Mott points out that customer feedback is likely to reflect on the performance of the salesperson and the performance of the company. If problems surface in either area, customer dissatisfaction may surface.

Data collection methodology is not uniform at this point. Some companies use telephone surveys while others use mailed questionnaires. IBM has experimented with a series of in-person meetings that bring together corporate customers, their IBM sales representatives, and the salesperson's boss.

Some salespeople have not welcomed the use of customer evaluations. Maryann Cirenza, senior account executive at Teleport Communications Group (TCG) of New York, said that she felt betrayed when she saw the questionnaire the company was sending to her customers. One of the questions asked, "Does your sales rep know your industry?" Cirenza said, "I thought the company was checking up on me." Later her anger subsided when she learned the survey was not simply a monitoring system but a trial run for a new compensation plan. After field testing the surveys, TCG used customer feedback to set bonuses. Cirenza was actually rewarded for good customer service by earning a bonus of about 20 percent of her base pay. Greg Buseman, a Chicago-based IBM salesman, believes the shift to compensation through customer feedback has improved personal selling at his company. He now spends more time understanding the customer's business and learning to be a problem solver for his clients.[38]

Questions

1. Should the customer be given a major voice in determining how salespeople are performing? Explain.
2. Should sales force compensation be linked to customer feedback? What are the advantages and disadvantages of this approach?
3. Assume you are a sales manager preparing to develop and implement a customer feedback system. How might you gain support for this system from members of your salespeople? What data collection method would you use?
4. Research indicates that customers rank "understanding of our business" as an important criterion used to evaluate salespeople. Why is this criterion ranked so high?

Finding Employment: A Personalized Marketing Plan for the Age of Information

The principles of strategic/consultative selling can be used to prepare a personalized marketing plan to secure a high-paying, professional career position. In Chapter 1 we identify the marketing concept. This concept states that a good marketing program begins with research. After finding out the "what, where, when, why, and how much" during research, the marketing mix is developed (Fig. A.1). In designing a marketing mix, the elements of product, place, promotion, and pricing are coordinated to satisfy the job seeker's needs uncovered during the research phase. The following material describes the steps that should be followed to develop a personal marketing plan for securing a job.

Research Phase

During the research step of the personal marketing plan, the emphasis is on information gathering: (1) what type of career the individual is seeking, (2) what the market (in which that position exists) is looking for in applicants, and (3) what the market is willing to pay (Fig. A.2). This information is the starting point for the development of the rest of the personal marketing plan. Securing this basic information is fundamental to the personal marketing plan. Job seeking without this important first step is a waste of time. Many job seekers do not start with this first step and consequently fail to find a rewarding career position.

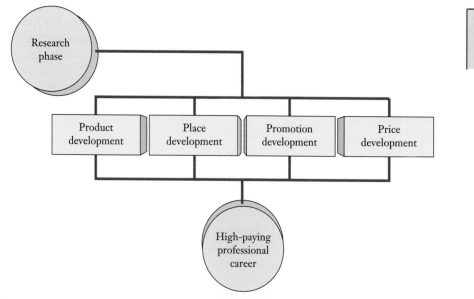

Figure A.1
THE EMPLOYMENT
MARKETING MIX

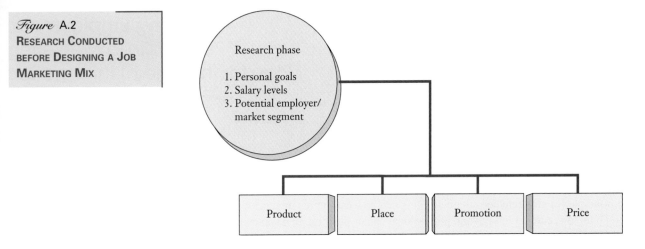

Figure A.2
RESEARCH CONDUCTED BEFORE DESIGNING A JOB MARKETING MIX

Deciding what you want to achieve in your career begins with a great deal of reflection on who you are and what you want to accomplish. Your future productivity and fulfillment depend on finding employment that matches your personal beliefs and preferences. How important is it for you to earn a great deal of money early in your career? Do you want to work for a company that maintains high ethical standards? How important is it to achieve balance between time spent at work and leisure time? Do you find travel to be an energizing experience? Finding answers to these and other questions can help you set goals that are aligned with your values. The development of intermediate (one to two years) goals and long-range (three to five years) goals is an important part of your personal marketing plan.

Realistic income goals should be researched and established for each of these time segments (Fig. A.3). This information is extremely important because most interviewers ask about income goals during the interview.

The next phase of the research process is to determine in which industries (market segments) the career opportunities exist that complement the goals you have set. This is called market segmentation. A preliminary list of 20 or more companies should be prepared. Later this list can be turned into a prospect list.

The final part of the research process is to determine what qualities the particular market segment wants in the people it selects for employees. In determining the hiring motives (see Chapter 7 on buying motives), does the market look for quantitative backgrounds, such as a minimum number of years of education or a minimum number of years of experience? Does it look for qualitative background, such as a positive attitude (see Chapter 3), a professional image (see Chapter 3), or certain communication skills? During this stage it is important to find out which of these qualities or combination of qualities the potential employer (market segment) is looking for, because the design of the marketing mix is based on these findings.

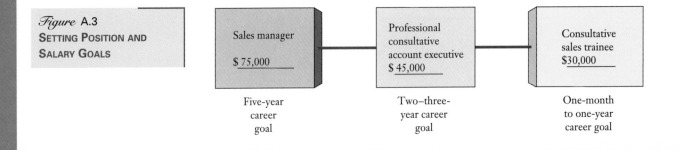

Figure A.3
SETTING POSITION AND SALARY GOALS

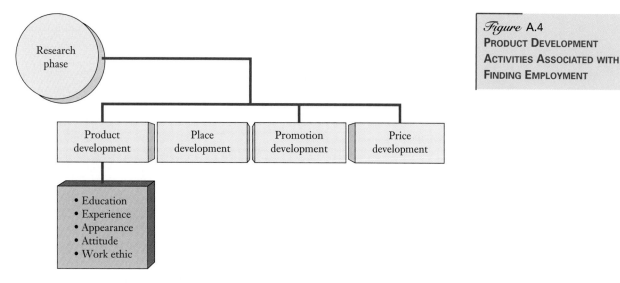

Figure A.4
**PRODUCT DEVELOPMENT
ACTIVITIES ASSOCIATED WITH
FINDING EMPLOYMENT**

Product Development

After the research phase of the personal marketing plan is complete, the next step is the development of the marketing mix. This begins with a product development program—documenting the proper amount and kind of education and job experience, fostering an appropriate appearance (packaging) and attitude, and work ethic (Fig. A.4).

It is important to take each of these areas of development and convert it into a benefit that helps the prospective employer or market segment achieve its objectives. For example, being elected an officer of a social or professional organization often means that the individual has a high-energy level, tends to get along well with people, and is respected by peers (benefits). These are all important benefits that help a prospective employer meet quotas and profit objectives (see Chapters 5 and 6).

Place Development

The next phase of the personal marketing mix consists of developing a sophisticated prospect base (see Chapter 8). The prospect base is made up of potential employers who offer career positions corresponding to the career goals set in the research phase. This prospect list should include the company name, address, telephone number, names and titles of individuals to be contacted concerning employment, and other background information on the company (Fig. A.5). The number of prospects depends on the desired size of

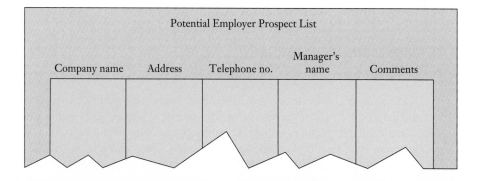

Figure A.5
**PLACE DEVELOPMENT
THROUGH USING A PROSPECT
LIST**

the market to be contacted. Job seekers using direct mail marketing plans may contact up to 200 prospects, while telephone and direct contact personal marketing plans begin with about 20 potential employers.

Source of Potential Employers

The easiest source of potential employers to add to the prospect list is probably the classified section of the newspaper; however, "seldom does anything good come easy," and the newspaper is generally not the best source of prospective employers. In many cases either the best positions advertised in the newspaper are informally filled before they are advertised or the competition for them is extremely keen. It is not uncommon for a company to receive from 100 to 150 resumés for jobs offering competitive salaries. In other cases, companies mass merchandise jobs that are unattractive and difficult to fill. While newspapers should not be overlooked in developing a prospect list, it is wise to use them with caution.

The Internet is an excellent place to start your search for job openings. More than half of the companies use the Internet for job postings. The use of on-line salary surveys can help you determine potential earnings. The Bureau of Labor Statistics (www.bls.gov) is good source of Web-based salary data. JobStar California (www.jobstar.org) provides links to 300 salary surveys.[1] Consider starting your job search with a visit to the Web sites that follow:[2]

Careerbuilder.com This site links you to 25 on-line career centers. The site offers 80 job categories.

Jobsearch.org This site, a product of the U.S. Department of Labor, contains over a million job openings.

Monster.com Job seekers can find over 250,000 job listings and a database of 1 million resumés.

Hotjobs.com Job seekers can post their resumé on this site and then control which companies are allowed to view it.

Headhunter.net This site provides job seekers with specific categories, which include geography, salary, travel requirements, and experience.

In addition to these sites, most trade organizations and many companies have their own on-line list of job openings.

To build a good list of prospective employers, use directories, referrals, friends, acquaintances, and cold calls (Fig. A.6). Most jobs can be found by visiting job fairs, talking to recruiters, networking with friends and acquaintances, and knocking on doors. (See Chapter 8 for information on these methods.)

Do not include in your list only companies with existing job vacancies. Research shows that companies frequently have openings that are not actively being recruited. Turnover also creates openings, and many firms go back into applicant files to fill these openings. In addition, many companies create openings, especially for trainees, when a well-qualified person applies for a career-oriented position.

Promotion Development

Developing the promotional element of the personal marketing program consists of creating an effective resumé (advertisement), writing good application and thank-you letters (sales promotion), and conducting convincing job interviews (sales presentation) (Fig. A.7). The rules for developing each of these promotional concepts are much different at the professional-career level than at part-time and entry levels. They also tend to be different for acquiring a position in the private business sector than in public employment. The

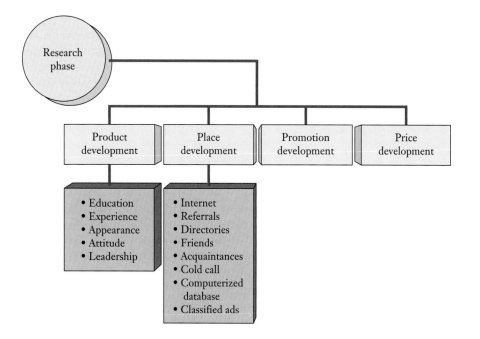

Figure A.6
SOURCES FOR DEVELOPING A PROSPECTIVE EMPLOYER LIST

following promotional principles relate mainly to the professional-career level in private business, although many also apply to securing entry level, part-time, or public employment positions.

The Resumé

Creating a good resumé should be thought of as creating an advertisement. It should be a professional, business-oriented selling aid that stands out even though it is part of a pile of 20 or more resumés. It should attract attention and interest, as a good advertisement does when a reader is looking through a magazine and stops to study one of the ads. The

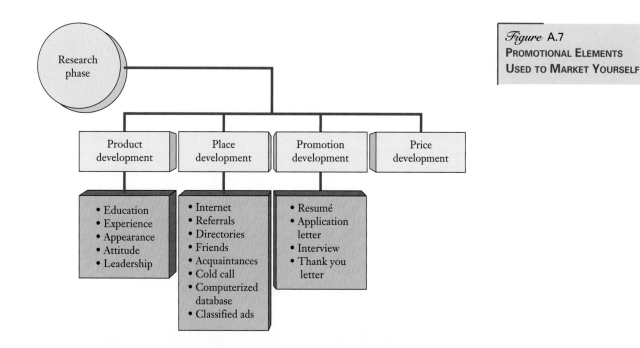

Figure A.7
PROMOTIONAL ELEMENTS USED TO MARKET YOURSELF

resumé should be long enough (one to two pages, depending on depth of background) and well-written, supplying benefits so that it gets the prospective interviewer to desire and take action to set up a personal interview. The Microsoft Word program provides several resumé wizards to use when developing your resumé. You may want to consider posting your resumé on line. This can be accomplished by using **CareerSite.com**, **Monster.com**, or some other site. Many firms request resumés via e-mail. The letter of application and thank-you letter also should take the interviewer's mind through the mental steps in the buying process—attention, interest, desire, conviction, and action (see Chapter 7).

CYNTHIA ELIZABETH SMITH

Current Address	**Permanent Address**
1305 34th Street	617 Hail Street
Des Moines, Iowa 50311	Rockport, Illinois 60202
(515) 277–4753	(312) 246–3872

Objectives: To secure a growth-oriented sales position in the wholesale, service, or manufacturing industries

Primary Skills: Have acquired background skills in selling, buying computers, and management at Drake through classroom work and On the Job Training

Possess progressive work experience in retail, from a small specialty store to a large department store

Have the ability to understand and apply creative design concepts through my previous classroom experience

Have the ability to work effectively and harmoniously with a wide range of people

Have the ability to rapidly learn new techniques and concepts

Summary: Twenty-one-year-old college graduate with a degree in marketing; enjoy working with people; willing to work hard to achieve success in chosen career

WORK EXPERIENCE

1999–Present Von Maurs, Des Moines, Iowa

Started in a Retail Management Trainee position; duties and responsibilities include Professional Selling, Visual Merchandising, Buying and Inventory; exposure to a broad variety of management and supervisory philosophies

1999 Mark Henri Ltd., Des Moines, Iowa

Started as a fashion consultant for a small women's specialty store, which is an affiliate of Seiferts; learned basic store procedures, selling and display techniques; worked part-time during the summer while attending college

1999 Temporary Manpower, Chicago, Illinois

Temporary office service, which consisted of working as a librarian for an accounting firm, Author Young and Company; also as a receptionist for Loyola Law School; worked during the summer while attending evening classes

1997–98 Evanston Park District, Glen Ellyn, Illinois

Park District Counselor, taught safety to young children, instructed crafts, and coached a girl's softball team; also worked as a receptionist at the main office

1996 Maloney's Restaurant, Lombard, Illinois

Hostess at a restaurant; seated customers, cleaned tables, and ran the register; worked during the summer

EDUCATION

Drake University, Des Moines, Iowa

Graduated with a B.S.B.A. in Marketing and an emphasis in Art and Design; major areas of study include Selling, Sales and Promotion, Marketing, Marketing Management, Accounting, Economics, and Consumer Behavior; earned a G.P.A. of 3.3

Completed an internship study program at Von Maurs, at Valley West Mall in Des Moines, Iowa; major emphasis included learning different store procedures

Graduated from Glenbard West High School, in Glen Ellyn, Illinois

ORGANIZATIONS, ACTIVITIES, and INTERESTS

College:

Member of Kappa Kappa Gamma Social Sorority

Vice President and Charter Member of Marketing Club—attended a large number of personal and professional development seminars

Greek Week representative

Panhellenic Representative

Director of house Variety Show

Registrar of Kappa Kappa Gamma

Little Sister of Sigma Alpha Epsilon

Intramural Football

Honors and Awards:

Alpha Lambda Delta Freshman Honor Society

Dean's list for three semesters

The Interview

The interview should be viewed as a strategic/consultative sales presentation (see Chapters 9–14). The applicant should be well prepared with preapproach information such as determination of goals, answers to challenging questions (negotiating objections), clear understanding of personal qualities and benefits, and knowledge of the interviewer and the company. When meeting the interviewer, a good first impression (good social contact) must be made. Transition from social contact to need discovery (finding out precisely what the company is looking for in an applicant) should be preplanned with well-chosen questions. Effective listening results in productive two-way communication that maintains positive impressions. Effective listening also helps determine which parts of the interviewee's background (benefits) should be stressed. If for some reason the interviewer has not seen the resumé, the interviewee should offer it at this point to review the selling points made so far. Closing questions should be preplanned by the interviewee. These might include questions such as, "When do you plan to fill this position?" or "May I call you back on Friday?" Courtesy closing statements such as, "Thank you very much for an informative interview" or "I appreciate the time you spent with me, and I enjoyed our visit very much" should be preplanned. It is important to follow up the interview with a thank-you letter. This letter can be sent via e-mail or through normal mail delivery.

Price Development

Price development involves salary negotiations. Adequate preinterviewing preparation is important for effective salary negotiations (Fig. A.8). The following guidelines should be followed during salary negotiations:

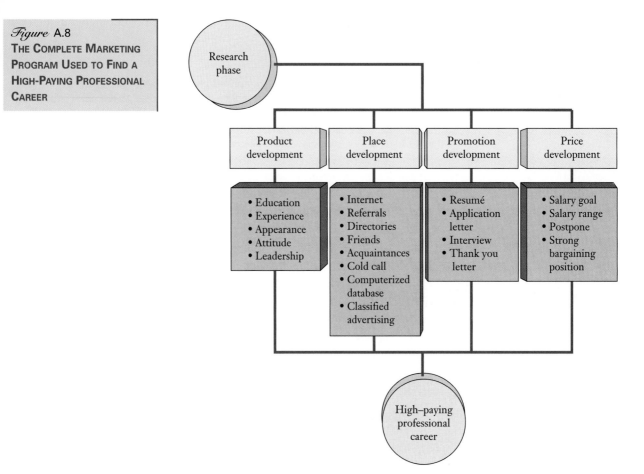

Figure A.8
THE COMPLETE MARKETING
PROGRAM USED TO FIND A
HIGH-PAYING PROFESSIONAL
CAREER

1. Determine the amount of money you want to make during the first year of employment. Convert this to a range with a difference from $3,000 to $5,000 (*example:* from $25,000 to $30,000).
2. Try to find out what salary range the position pays before the interview. As noted previously, the Internet can be your link to a large number of salary surveys.
3. Plan to state that while starting salary is important, it is more important to know what can be made during the first year, given an excellent review.
4. As a general rule, if possible, postpone salary discussions until a job offer is made. This maintains a better bargaining position.
5. Position yourself in a strong bargaining position with a good personal marketing program.
   a. Have goals well thought out and be able to articulate them clearly.
   b. Have outstanding references.
   c. Have outstanding written materials that show achievement and accomplishment.
   d. Possess good knowledge of industry, company, product personnel, and salary ranges.
   e. Be currently employed with no sense of urgency to leave.
   f. Sell credentials first and discuss salary second.
   g. Indicate your knowledge of how to get a job.
   h. Become effective in face-to-face selling situations.

Summary

From the employer's viewpoint the decision to accept the personal marketing plan of a career-oriented job seeker is a major one. An employee who stays with a company five to seven years can be paid from $200,000 to $350,000 in salary (five to seven years times an average annual salary of $40,000). The $200,000–$350,000 salary plus the cost of benefits is the price the employer is paying for the marketing plan. When you make an analogy between the price of a human resource and the purchase of a piece of equipment, it becomes apparent that this is a large purchase. Therefore, a company is going to carefully examine all dimensions of the purchase.

A job seeker with knowledge of the hiring and employment process realizes the dollar value of the purchase an employer is making and designs a professional personal marketing plan with this in mind. The personal marketing plan emphasizes a high-quality professional approach to identifying the right product, positioning it in the right places with the right quality and quantity of promotion, and the right price.

Use of Customer Relationship Management (CRM) Software (ACT!)

A Special Note to the Student

Selling Today now offers you a unique opportunity to learn the reason modern software is helping to redefine sales and marketing.

You can download and use a scaled-down version of the popular ACT! software, which more than 3 million salespeople use to build relationships with their customers. The software is easy to use and includes information about more than 20 customers. You can experience first-hand how salespeople today gain the sales advantage with this new category of software.

Beginning in chapter one you will find simple, easy to follow, instructions on using this software to store and access a wide variety of business and personal information about your customers. You will discover the convenience of using this software to stay in touch with people.

The ACT! software includes important customer information that you will use in your CRM case study assignments for Chapters 8–14. You will access the information in your ACT database to approach, present, demonstrate, negotiate, close and service more than $1.2 million dollars worth of sales volume.

Effectively using information technology, especially CRM, will give you a career advantage in today's highly-competitive workplace. After mastering the exercises provided, you can report your CRM experience on your resumé.

Instructions for Downloading and Using the Customer Relationship Management (CRM) Software

The software that you will be using is a demonstration version of ACT!, the leading Customer Relationship Management (CRM) software. This version is limited in that no more than 25 contacts may be entered. Today, the ACT! 2000 program is much more robust, extensive, and powerful and can manage thousands of contacts.

The software that you need is found on the Web site *www.prenhall.com/manningreece*. When you view the Web page with your browser, you will find a button labeled CRM. Selecting this button will cause the page with the software to be displayed. That page will identify the link that you will choose to begin the downloading process.

The software that you will download is a special compressed (zipped) version. Called case_act.exe, this software file first needs to be copied to your computer then decompressed (unzipped). When decompressed, a number of files will be created that consume nearly 3 megabytes of memory, so you will need that much space available on your hard disk drive. The software is designed to be used with any version of Windows.

Experienced Users

If you are a computer user experienced with downloading and launching software, you should have no difficulty with this executable file. You can download to your hard disk drive and launch the software by double-clicking on it or using the Run command on the Windows Start menu. The launch pop-up window (see below) should be self-explanatory. The program will create a new folder (c:\actcase), decompress, load, and start running.

Inexperienced Users

If you are not familiar with downloading software, point at the case_act.exe file on the Web site with your cursor and click the RIGHT mouse button. If your browser is Microsoft's Internet Explorer, select the menu choice, "Save Target As." If you are using a Netscape browser, your choice will be "Save Link As." If you are using Netscape and it displays an "Unknown File Type" message, select the "Save File" button. If you are using another browser, consult its users' guide for instructions.

Once you choose to download, or save the file, a window will be displayed that asks where you want to save the file. You can save this file anywhere on your hard disk drive and you want to be sure to remember where you saved it. It is recommended that you save it to your C:\ drive (see below).

Save to C: →

Save As...		? ☒
Save in: 🖴 My computer (C:)		

📁 _Accounting	📁 _My Documents	📁 _Program Fi
📁 _ACT! 2000	📁 _My Download Files	📁 _Saleslogix
📁 _Internet Explorer	📁 _My Files	📁 _Scanner
📁 _Microsoft Exchange	📁 _Netscape	📁 _Temp
📁 _Microsoft Office	📁 _Palm Pilot	📁 _ToDo
📁 _Mouse	📁 _Printer	📁 _Windows

File name:	case_act.exe	Save
Save as type:	All Files (*.*)	Cancel

Special Download Challenges

Filters

Some networks have a "filter" installed that prevents individual computer users from downloading software from the Internet. In other cases some networked systems will not allow the downloading of software files as large as ACT!. If you encounter difficulty downloading this software on a Networked computer system, consult your system administrator about these limitations. To download this software, you may need to use a computer without these limitations.

Diskette Version

A special diskette version of the software is available if you want to download to one computer and use the software on another computer. For example, if you want to download at a university computer center, then take the software home. This version has been reduced in size so as to fit on a $3\frac{1}{2}$ inch floppy diskette and is so identified on the Web site. This version of the software does not include the Help (F1 Key) functions that are described in the text.

　　To download the special diskette version, follow the above instructions and save the file to a $3\frac{1}{2}$ inch floppy diskette that is known as the A: drive (see window).

You will need a formatted $3\frac{1}{2}$ inch, 1.44 megabyte IBM-compatible diskette that has no other file on it. You can also select the diskette drive by typing "A:\" in front of case_act.exe in the above File name field.

Launching the Software

Once you have saved the case_act.exe file on your hard disk drive or diskette, it is easy to launch the program. The easiest way is to click the Windows Start button, then select Run, and enter "c:\case_act.exe" if you saved the file on the C:\ drive. If you saved it elsewhere on your hard disk drive, use the browse button to find it. When the file is displayed in the Run dialog box (window), click OK.

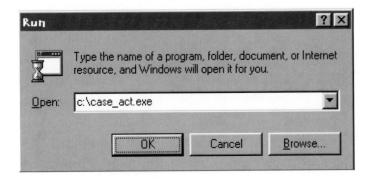

The following window will be displayed.

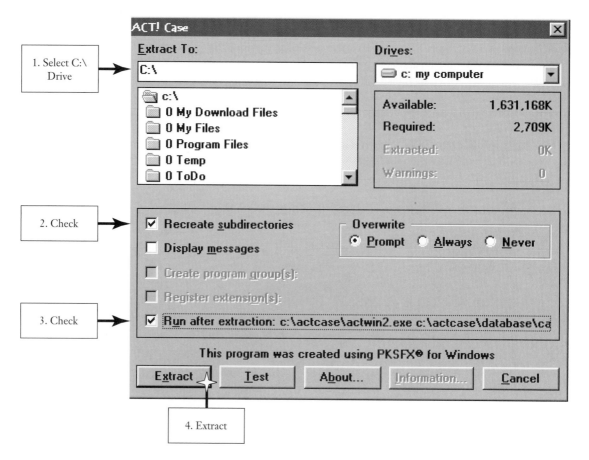

Confirm that 1, 2, and 3 above are displayed on your computer the same as in the above image. Click on 4, the button labeled Extract, and a new folder, ActCase, will be created on your computer, the files will be decompressed (unzipped), and the program will begin running. The first window that you see should look similar to the following.

Software Status. The program on your hard disk drive can be run as many times as you need. After completing the Sales Automation Case Study, you may choose to leave the demonstration software on your hard disk drive or you may remove it. If you saved the downloaded file on a diskette, you can reload the software from the diskette at any time. If you need another copy of the software, you may download it again from the Selling-Today.com Web page.

Finding the Downloaded File

If you downloaded the file but cannot find it on your hard disk drive, you can use Window's Find utility to search for it. Select the Windows Start button, then choose Find, and Files or Folders and enter case_act.exe.

![Find: All Files dialog box. Tabs: Name & Location, Date, Advanced. Named: case_act.exe. Containing text: (blank). Look in: C:\. Include subfolders checked. Buttons: Find Now, Stop, New Search, Browse.]

When this search utility finds and displays the file, simply select the file (case_act.exe) with your cursor and double click.

Understanding the Software

ACT! is a Windows-based program and uses the standard Windows features. It is "menu driven," which means that you can operate the program by selecting from lists of choices. The main menu is displayed at the top of the screen as above displayed.

The screen that displays the information about a customer is referred to as the contact screen. ACT! has two contact screens that can be toggled by pressing the F6 function key.

You can use the arrows on the Rolodex icon (see inset) to move among the records. A single arrow moves to the next record and a double arrow displays the first (up) or last (down) record in the database. You can also use the PageUp and PageDown keys to move between records. The records are in alphabetical order, by company name. The first record (double arrow up) in the database is for Able Profit Machines, Inc.

21 of 21

Most records contain notes taken by the previous salesperson, Pat Silva. To display these notes, press the F9 function key. When you are through examining a note, you can press the Escape key (to save changes, select File Close). The notes for the Able Profit Machines company follow on page 405.

Using the Act! Software with the CRM References Throughout the Book

With the instructions provided above, you can complete any of the references to CRM located throughout the book. These references include the following:

CRM WITH TECHNOLOGY INSIGHTS. These insights, located within the chapter, describe how salespeople are using CRM software today to build relationships with customers.

CRM APPLICATION EXERCISES. These application exercises located at the end of the chapter provide you instructions for learning how to use the software, and gain expertise. Detailed instructions lead you through the important functions salespeople use to develop, build, and maintain relationships with customers.

CRM CASE STUDY. The case study provides you with a database of customers supplied by a previous salesperson. You assume the role of a newly hired salesperson and with the information supplied, create relationship, product, customer, and presentation strategies to manage the sales activities in the territory your are assigned. Questions are supplied to help you plan your activities. The CRM case study starts in Chapter 8 and continues through Chapter 14.

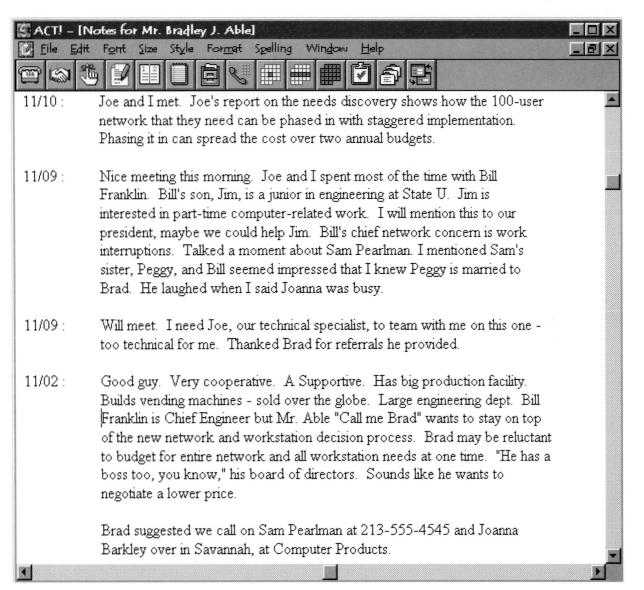

ACT! – [Notes for Mr. Bradley J. Able]

File   Edit   Font   Size   Style   Format   Spelling   Window   Help

11/10 :   Joe and I met. Joe's report on the needs discovery shows how the 100-user network that they need can be phased in with staggered implementation. Phasing it in can spread the cost over two annual budgets.

11/09 :   Nice meeting this morning. Joe and I spent most of the time with Bill Franklin. Bill's son, Jim, is a junior in engineering at State U. Jim is interested in part-time computer-related work. I will mention this to our president, maybe we could help Jim. Bill's chief network concern is work interruptions. Talked a moment about Sam Pearlman. I mentioned Sam's sister, Peggy, and Bill seemed impressed that I knew Peggy is married to Brad. He laughed when I said Joanna was busy.

11/09 :   Will meet. I need Joe, our technical specialist, to team with me on this one - too technical for me. Thanked Brad for referrals he provided.

11/02 :   Good guy. Very cooperative. A Supportive. Has big production facility. Builds vending machines - sold over the globe. Large engineering dept. Bill Franklin is Chief Engineer but Mr. Able "Call me Brad" wants to stay on top of the new network and workstation decision process. Brad may be reluctant to budget for entire network and all workstation needs at one time. "He has a boss too, you know," his board of directors. Sounds like he wants to negotiate a lower price.

Brad suggested we call on Sam Pearlman at 213-555-4545 and Joanna Barkley over in Savannah, at Computer Products.

Table of Contents

A Special Note to the Student: Use of the Role Play/Simulation Appendix

This role play/simulation provides an opportunity to apply the principles that serve as a foundation for the four broad strategic areas of personal selling: relationship, product, customer, and presentation strategies. The activities are designed to take you from "learning about" selling to "learning to do" selling.

You will start as a convention center sales and marketing department trainee. Your sales manager will supply you with memos that will assist you in learning about your product, competition, customers, and presentations. You will be supplied many sales tools including photos, awards, schedules, menus, floor plans, references, company policies, electronic sales proposal/product configurators (see pp. 417–450) and sales planning worksheets.

The first memo on p. 411 provides background information about your product, company, industry, and competition. As a trainee your first sales and marketing assignment (see memo on p. 447) will be to create an electronic sales proposal and cover sales letter. This activity will give you an opportunity to apply information presented in Chapter 5.

After successfully communicating with your first customer, and being promoted to account executive, you are instructed by your sales manager in memos on pp. 452–453 to plan and conduct your first face to face contact with another potential customer. The primary objective of this first contact is to establish a relationship with your customer.

The next memo from your sales manager on pp. 456–457 requests that you use your questioning skills to conduct a needs analysis involving the customer you previously contacted. Your customer, who was favorably impressed as a result of your first meeting, has called and requested a meeting to talk about an important convention being planned.

The last memo on pp. 460–461 assists you in creating and presenting a proposal that meets your customer's needs. You will create a portfolio presentation using the awards, photos, price lists, menus, references, floor plans, and schedules provided.

Introduction

Salespeople today are working hard to become more effective in such important areas as person-to-person communications, needs analysis, interpersonal relations, and decision making. This role play/simulation will help you develop these critical selling skills. You will assume the role of a new sales trainee employed by the Park Inn International Convention Center.

Part I:

Developing a Sales-Oriented Product Strategy will challenge you to acquire the necessary product information needed to be an effective sales representative for the Park Inn (see Chapters 5 and 6). Your sales manager, T. J. McKee, will describe your new trainee position in an employment memorandum. Your instructions will include the study of materials featured on the following pages, viewing a video that describes the convention facilities and services provided by a competitor, and role playing the request made in a T. J. McKee customer service/sales memorandum.

Part II:

Developing a Relationship Strategy is another major challenge in personal selling. An employment memorandum will inform you of a promotion to an account executive position. A sales memorandum will inform you of your assignment to accounts in a specific market segment. Part II also involves a role play on the development of a relationship with a new customer in your market segment (see Chapters 3 and 9). Your call objective will be to acquire background information on your new customer, who may have a need for your services.

Part III:

Understanding Your Customer's Buying Strategy involves a needs analysis role play (see Chapters 7 and 10). You will again meet with the customer who has indicated an interest in scheduling a business conference at your convention center. During this meeting you will acquire information to complete Part IV, which involves preparation for the sales presentation.

Part IV:

Developing a Presentation Strategy will involve preparation of a sales proposal and a *portfolio* presentation (see Chapters 10–14). This section also involves a third role play with the customer. During the role play you will reestablish your relationship with the customer, present your proposal, negotiate customer concerns, and attempt to close and service the sale.

Throughout completion of the role play/simulation, you will be guided by the employment and sales memoranda (from the sales manager) and instructions and additional forms provided by your instructor.

As you complete this simulation activity, note that the principles and practices you are learning to use have application in nearly all personal selling situations.

General Instructions for Role Playing

Overview

The primary goal of a simulation in personal selling should be to strike a balance between just enough detail to focus on the process of selling and not so much as to drown in an ocean of facts. Either too much detail or too little detail can develop anxiety in role play participants. *Partnership Selling* is designed to minimize anxiety by including only the facts needed to focus on learning the processes involved in high-performance selling.

Some anxiety will occur, however, because you are asked to perform under pressure (in terms of building relationships, securing strategic information, changing people's thinking, and getting them to take action). Learning to perform in an environment full of genuine, but nonthreatening pressure, affords you the opportunity to practice your selling skills so you will be prepared for real-world selling anxiety.

The following suggestions for role playing will help you develop the ability to perform under stress.

Instructions for Salesperson Role Plays

1. Be well prepared with product knowledge.
2. Read information for each role play ahead of time.
3. Follow specific instructions carefully.
4. Attempt to sense both the context and the facts of the situation presented.
5. Conduct a mental rehearsal. See yourself successfully conducting and completing the role play.
6. Be prepared to take notes during the role play.
7. After the role play, take note of your feelings and mentally put them into the context of what just occurred.
8. Be prepared to discuss your reaction to what occurred during the role play.

Instructions for Customer Role Plays

1. Read the instructions carefully. Be sure to note both the role play instructions and the information you are about to share.
2. Attempt to sense both the context of the buying situation and the individual facts presented in the instructions.
3. Let the salesperson initiate greetings, conversations, and concluding actions. React appropriately.
4. Supply only the customer information presented in the background description.
5. Supply customer information in a positive manner.
6. Do not attempt to throw the salesperson off track.

PARK INN
INTERNATIONAL™

EMPLOYMENT MEMORANDUM 1

To: **New Convention Sales Center Trainees**
From: **T. J. McKee, Sales Manager**
Re: **Your New Sales Training Program—"Developing a Product Selling Strategy"**

I am extremely happy that you accepted our offer to join the Sales and Marketing Department. Enclosed is a copy of your new position description (see p. 414). Your first assignment as a trainee will be to learn about our product and what we have recently done to provide *total quality* customer service. *To apply what you are learning, I would like you to follow up on a customer service request I recently received. (See memo p. 447.)* You will use the following product information to complete the assignment:

AN AWARD-WINNING UPDATE (See pp. 417–419)

We have recently completed a *$2.8 million investment in our convention center.* This customer service investment included renovating all guest rooms and suites, lobby and front desk area, meeting rooms, restaurant and lounge, and enclosure of the swimming pool. Enclosed is a copy of the "Regional Architect's Award" which our facility won. We are the only facility in the Metro Area to have been presented with this award.

MEETING AND BANQUET ROOMS (See pp. 433–437)

The Park Inn offers convention planners just over *8,000 square feet of award-winning meeting space* in attractive, newly renovated meeting and banquet rooms. Our Central Park East and West rooms are conveniently located on the lobby level of the hotel. Each of these rooms can accommodate 180 people in a theater-style setting or 80 in a classroom-style setting. They also have a divider wall which can be retracted and, with the combined rooms, can accommodate up to 370 people.

   The Top of the Park provides a spectacular view of the city through windows that surround that ballroom. This unique room, located on the top floor, can accommodate 225 classroom style, 350 banquet style, or 450 people theater style. Also located in the Top of the Park is a revolving platform area which slowly moves, giving guests a 360 degree panoramic view of the city. The Parkview Room, which is also located on the top floor of the hotel, can accommodate 150 people theater style and 80 people classroom style.

   In addition for *groups booking forty rooms or more, we provide one luxurious suite **free**.* This suite features a meeting room, bedroom, wet bar with refrigerator, and jacuzzi.

   Be sure your clients understand that our meeting rooms *need to be reserved.* The first organization to sign a sales proposal for a specific date has the designated rooms guaranteed.

GUEST ROOM DECOR AND RATES (See pp. 429 and 437)

Our recent renovation included complete redecoration of all 250 of our large and spacious guest rooms. This includes all new furniture, wallcoverings, drapes, bedspreads, and carpets. Our interior designer succeeded in creating a comfortable, attractive, restful atmosphere. *Seventy of our rooms are designated nonsmoking.*

(continued)

ROOM RATES *(continued)*

	REGULAR RATES	*GROUP RATES*	*SAVINGS*
Single	$88	$78	$10
Double	$98	$88	$10
Triple	$106	$96	$10
Quad	$114	$104	$10

A comparison of competitive room, parking, and transportation rates are presented on p. 437.

BANQUET MEALS (See pp. 423–427)

Our executive chef, Ricardo Guido, recently won the *National Restaurant Association's "Outstanding Chef of the Year" Award.* His winning entry consisted of the three chicken entrees featured on the enclosed menus. Ricardo served as Executive Chef at the five-star rated Williamsburg Inn in Williamsburg, Virginia before we convinced him to join us six months ago. He personally oversees all our food and beverage operations. Ricardo, in my opinion, is one of the outstanding chefs in the country. His expertise and commitment to total quality customer service will help develop long-term relationships with our customers.

The enclosed dinner selections are only suggestions. We will design a special menu for your clients if they wish. A 16% gratuity or service charge is added to all group meal functions.

HOTEL/MOTEL AND SALES TAXES

All room rates are subject to the *local hotel/motel room tax, which is an additional 8%. In addition, all billings must have a 4% sales tax added. (The sales tax is not added to the hotel/motel tax and does not apply to gratuities.)*

LOCATION, TRANSPORTATION, AND PARKING (See map on p. 421)

We are located in a dynamic growing metropolitan area of over 400,000 people. With *convenient access, just off of Interstate 237 at the downtown exits,* we are within a block of the nationally recognized climate controlled skywalk system. This five-mile system is connected to theaters, excellent shopping, the civic center, the metropolitan convention center, and a large selection of ethnic and fast-food restaurants. Our location offers guests the privacy they deserve during their meetings, yet is close enough to downtown to enjoy all the excitement.

Free *courtesy van transportation* (also known as limousine service) is provided for our overnight guests to and from the airport, as well as anywhere in the downtown area. This service saves our guests who arrive by plane from *$8.00 to $10.00 each way.*

Guests who will be driving to the hotel will find over *300 parking spaces* available to them at *no charge*. Unlike other downtown properties, our free parking saves guests up to *$6.00 per day* in parking fees. For security purposes, we have closed-circuit camera systems in the parking lot and underground parking areas.

VALUE-ADDED GUEST SERVICES AND AMENITIES

Our convention center owners have invested heavily in the facility to provide our clients with *total quality service*, unmatched by our competition. Additional value-added services and amenities include:

- A large *indoor pool, sundeck, sauna, whirlpool, and complimentary Nautilus exercise room* in an attractive tropical atmosphere (see p. 431)
- "Cafe in the Park" featuring 24-hour continental cuisine seven days a week
- "Pub in the Park" where friendly people meet, featuring *free hors d'oeuvres* Monday through Friday, 5 to 7 P.M.
- Cable television with HBO
- A.V. rental of most equipment in-house, at a nominal fee (see p. 439)
- *Free coffee and donuts or rolls* in the lobby each morning from 6 to 8 A.M.
- A team of *well-trained, dedicated, and friendly associates* providing total quality front desk, food, and guest services
- Express check in
- Electronic key entry system
- Hair dryer, iron, and ironing board in each room
- Data port capabilities for lap top computers in each room
- Desk in each room
- Video message retrieval
- Voice mail
- On command video (choice of 50 new release movies)

SALES LITERATURE (See pp. 417–450)

Included in your product training materials are photos, references, letters, room schedules, sales proposals, and other information that you will use in your written proposals and verbal sales presentations. When you move into outside sales, you should use these tools to create effective sales portfolios.

TOTAL QUALITY COMMITMENT

Our convention center is committed to *total quality customer service. Our Partnership Style of Customer Service and Selling* is an extension of our total quality process. The Total Quality Customer Glossary provides definitions of terms that describe our total quality process (see p. 416).

The Hotel and Convention center industry is mature and well established. Our sales and customer service plan is to *establish strong relationships, focus on solving customer problems, provide total quality customer service, and become a long-term hotel and convention center partner with our clients*. By utilizing this type of selling and customer service, your compensation and our sales revenue will both increase substantially.

TJM:ESS
Enclosures

PARK INN
I N T E R N A T I O N A L™

POSITION DESCRIPTION — CONVENTION CENTER ACCOUNT EXECUTIVE

COMPANY DESCRIPTION

The Park Inn Convention Center is a total quality, full-service equal opportunity employment convention center that has recently made large investments in the physical facility, the food and beverage department, and sales department. Company culture includes an effective and enthusiastic team approach to creating *total quality* value-added solutions for customers in a very competitive industry. The primary sales promotion tool is *Partnership Selling* with extensive marketing support in the form of photos, reference letters, team selling, etc. The company goal is to increase revenues 20 percent in the coming year by providing outstanding customer service.

SUCCESSFUL ACCOUNT EXECUTIVE WILL

1. Acquire necessary convention center company, product, industry, and competitive information through company training program
2. Be committed to a total quality customer service process
3. Develop a list of potential prospects in the assigned target market
4. Develop long-term total quality selling relationships that focus on solving the meeting planner's convention center needs
5. Achieve a sales volume of $700,000 to $800,000 annually

WORKING RELATIONSHIPS

Reports to: Sales Manager
Works with: Internal Support Team including Food Service, Housekeeping and Operations, Customer Service and Front Desk; External Relationships including customers, professional associations, and industry personnel

SPECIFIC REQUIREMENTS

1. Must project a positive and professional sales image
2. Must be able to establish and maintain long-term relationships
3. Must be goal oriented with a plan for self-improvement
4. Must be flexible to deal effectively with a wide range of customers
5. Must be good at asking questions and listening effectively
6. Must be accurate and creative in developing customer solutions
7. Must be clear and persuasive in communicating and negotiating solutions
8. Must be good at closing the sale
9. Must follow through on promises and assurances
10. Must have math skills necessary for figuring sales proposals

SPECIFIC REWARDS

1. Attractive compensation package that includes base salary, a commission of 10 percent of sales, bonuses, and an attractive fringe benefit package
2. Pride in working for an organization that practices total quality management in employee relations and customer service
3. Extensive sales and educational support
4. Opportunity for growth and advancement

EOE/AA/TQM

TOTAL QUALITY CUSTOMER SERVICE GLOSSARY

DIRFT—DO IT RIGHT THE FIRST TIME means being prepared, asking the right questions, selecting the right solutions, and making effective presentations. This creates repeats and referrals.

QIP—QUALITY IMPROVEMENT PROCESS means always striving to better serve our customers resulting in high-quality, long-term relationships.

TQM—TOTAL QUALITY MANAGEMENT means the commitment to support and empower people to deliver legendary customer service.

QIT—QUALITY IMPROVEMENT TEAM means a team approach to deliver outstanding customer service.

COQ—COST OF QUALITY means the ultimate lowering of cost by providing outstanding service the first time, so as to build a list of repeat and referred customers.

PONC—PRICE OF NONCONFORMANCE means the high cost of not meeting high standards. This results in correcting problems and losing customers. PONC also causes longer sales cycles and higher sales costs.

POC—PRICE OF CONFORMANCE means the lower costs of providing outstanding customer service, and achieving a list of repeat or referral customers.

WIIFM—WHAT IS IN IT FOR ME means the psychic and monetary rewards in the form of personal enjoyment, higher salaries, commissions, or bonuses caused by delivering outstanding customer service.

QES—QUALITY EDUCATION SYSTEMS means internal and external educational activities designed to improve the quality of customer service.

YOU—THE MOST IMPORTANT PART OF QUALITY means the on-going program of self-improvement that results in outstanding customer service, and personal and financial growth.

THE ALL NEW PARK INN

**(With an award winning
2.8 million dollar renovation)**

▶ Use the sales information on the reverse side of this page to position your convention center and the $2.8 million renovation in the mind of your customer.

REGIONAL ARCHITECTS ASSOCIATION

"Excellence in Renovation Design"

PRESENTED TO:

Park Inn International

With Special Recognition for Creating an Outstanding
Convention Environment.

Presented on the Eleventh Day of March, 200_.

Patricia Bennett
President, Regional Architects Association

Allen Rogge
Chairperson, Design Selection Committee

▶ Use the sales information on the reverse side of this page to demonstrate and describe the award for "Creating an Outstanding Convention Environment" and explain that it was given with regard to the quality of the meeting rooms, guest rooms, ambiance of lobby and restaurant, and the pool area.

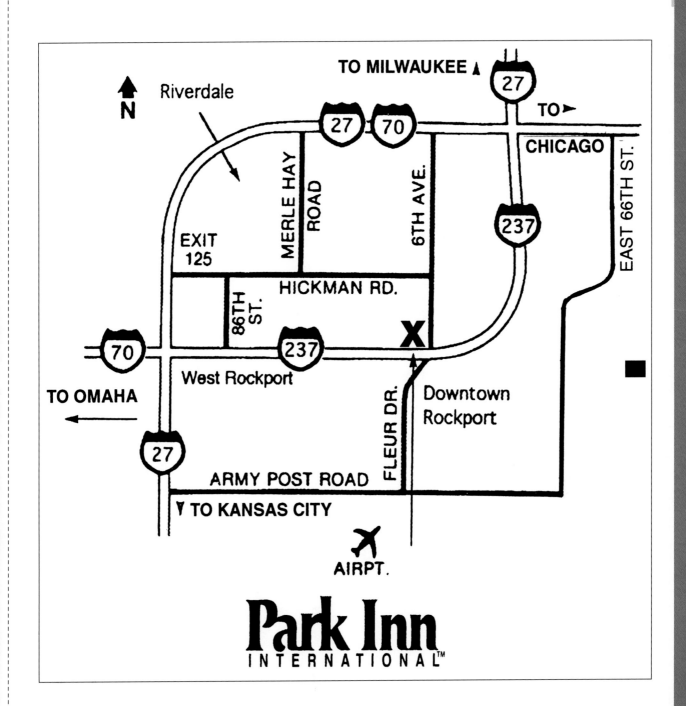

CONVENIENT, EASY TO FIND LOCATION WITH "FREE" PARKING

Conveniently located at I-237 and 6th Ave.
Just 8 miles from Rockport International Airport

▶ Use the sales information on the reverse side of this page to illustrate the ease and convenience of your customers locating and traveling to the Convention Center.

OUTSTANDING FOOD SERVICE
**Personally Supervised by Award-Winning
"Executive Chef of the Year"
Ricardo Guido**

▶ Use the sales information on the reverse side of this page to introduce and explain the "outstanding food service" that will be personally supervised by Executive Chef of the Year Ricardo Guido.

NATIONAL RESTAURANT ASSOCIATION

EXECUTIVE CHEF OF THE YEAR

AWARDED TO:

Ricardo Guido

PRESENTED ON THE ELEVENTH DAY OF APRIL, 200_.

Patricia Reed
PRESIDENT, NATIONAL RESTAURANT ASSOCIATION

Ella Reed
CONFERENCE CHAIRPERSON

▶ Use the sales information on the reverse side of this page to explain the benefits of having an award-winning executive chef and describe his background.

BANQUET STYLE MENU SELECTIONS

**All selections include tossed greens with choice of dressing,
choice of potato (baked, oven browned, au gratin, or mashed),
rice or buttered noodles, rolls with butter,
coffee, decaffeinated coffee, tea, or iced tea.**

ENTREES

CHICKEN WELLINGTON—Boneless breast of chicken topped with a
mushroom mixture, wrapped in puff pastry shell and baked to a golden brown $17.95

CHICKEN BREAST TERIYAKI—Marinated boneless breast of chicken
grilled and topped with our *special* teriyaki sauce $17.95

CHICKEN BREAST NEW ORLEANS—Baked boneless breast of chicken,
garnished with peppers, mushrooms, onions, and Monterey Jack cheese $17.95

BROILED NEW YORK STRIP STEAK—Center cut New York strip steak
broiled to perfection, topped with our own seasoned herb butter $23.50

BROILED FILET MIGNON—A steak from the center cut tenderloin,
broiled and served with a rich red wine sauce $24.50

SLICED PORK LOIN WITH MUSTARD SAUCE—Boneless loin of pork
oven roasted and sliced, served with a mustard sauce $18.95

GRILLED PORK CHOP—A thick cut of pork grilled to juicy perfection $18.95

BROILED ORANGE ROUGHY—A filet of orange roughy broiled
and covered with basil-lemon sauce $18.95

BROILED HALIBUT STEAK—Tender flaky halibut cut into steaks
and broiled in lemon-butter served with fresh lemon slices $19.95

* BUFFET STYLE meals are available. Approval of pricing on Buffet Style servings must
be made by the Executive Chef.

Prices do not include 16% service charge or Sales Tax.

▶ Use the sales information on the reverse side of this page to explain and configure the menus available for banquet style meals.

ATTRACTIVE, COMFORTABLE GUEST ROOMS

(All new furnishings, HBO in every room, free *USA Today* weekday delivery, no telephone access charges for 800 and credit card calls, and data port capabilities for lap top computers)

▶ Use the sales information on the reverse side of this page to explain and illustrate the attractive and comfortable guest rooms. Remind customers that the rooms were a major factor in receiving the Architect's Award.

A TROPICAL PARADISE

For relaxation after a day's work—
attractive pool, sauna, whirlpool, sundeck,
and Nautilus fitness center

▶ Use the sales information on the reverse side of this page to explain and illustrate the benefits of the totally renovated and redesigned pool, with the sauna, whirlpool, sundeck and Nautilus Fitness Center.

BRIGHT, COMFORTABLE, AND STRATEGICALLY ARRANGED MEETING ROOMS

Everything you need for outstanding meetings

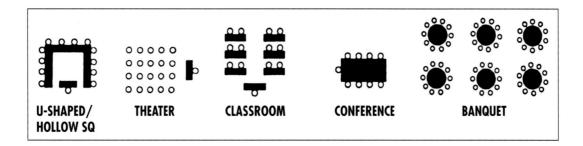

U-SHAPED/HOLLOW SQ   THEATER   CLASSROOM   CONFERENCE   BANQUET

▶ Use the sales information on the reverse side of this page to illustrate the attractiveness of the newly remodeled meeting rooms, which were another important factor in receiving the Architect's Award. Also, use this form to explain and illustrate the various seating arrrangements for meeting rooms.

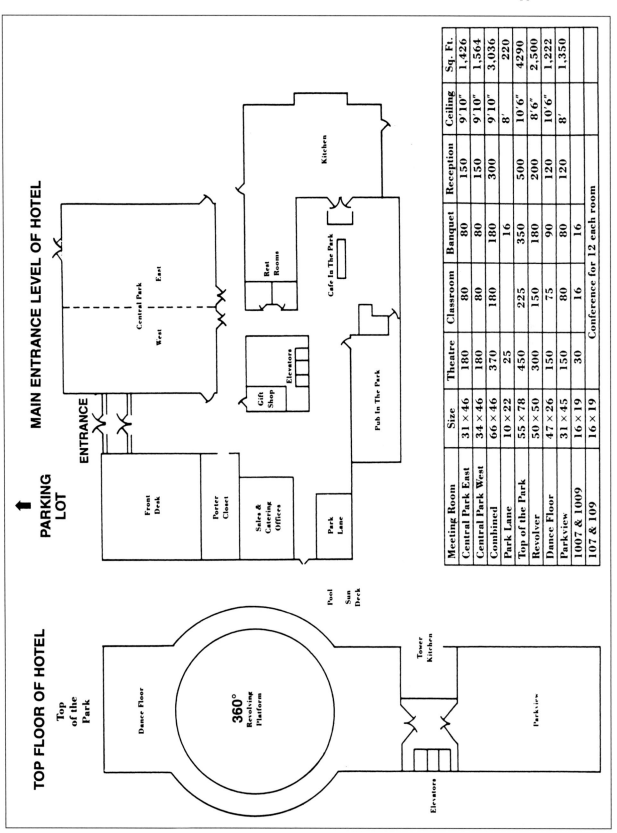

MAIN ENTRANCE LEVEL OF HOTEL

PARKING LOT

ENTRANCE

Front Desk

Porter Closet

Sales & Catering Offices

Park Lane

Central Park

West | East

Gift Shop

Elevators

Rest Rooms

Pub In The Park

Cafe In The Park

Kitchen

TOP FLOOR OF HOTEL

Top of the Park

Dance Floor

360° Revolving Platform

Pool

Sun Deck

Tower Kitchen

Elevators

Parkview

Meeting Room	Size	Theatre	Classroom	Banquet	Reception	Ceiling	Sq. Ft.
Central Park East	31 × 46	180	80	80	150	9'10"	1,426
Central Park West	34 × 46	180	80	80	150	9'10"	1,564
Combined	66 × 46	370	180	180	300	9'10"	3,036
Park Lane	10 × 22	25		16		8'	220
Top of the Park	55 × 78	450	225	350	500	10'6"	4290
Revolver	50 × 50	300	150	180	200	8'6"	2,500
Dance Floor	47 × 26	150	75	90	120	10'6"	1,222
Parkview	31 × 45	150	80	80	120	8'	1,350
1007 & 1009	16 × 19	30	16	16			
107 & 109	16 × 19	Conference for 12 each room					

▶ Use the sales information on the reverse side of this page to illustrate the location and layout of the meeting rooms in the convention center. Also, use this information to configure and explain the various sizes and capacities for each style of seating in the meeting rooms for your customers.

METRO AREA COMPETITIVE SURVEY
QUOTED GROUP RATES (IN DOLLARS) FOR HOTEL/MOTEL GUEST ROOMS

HOTEL/MOTEL	*SINGLE*	*DOUBLE*	*DAILY PARKING*	*AIRPORT TRANS.*
Park Inn	**78**	**88**	**Free**	**Free**
Marriott	80	90	6	10 each way
Sheraton	85	105	6	12 each way
Hilton	80	100	7	9 each way
Embassy	82	103	6	8 each way
Guest Quarters	84	104	Free	8 each way
Carlton	75	95	8	3 each way
Saboe	75	85	Free	12 each way
Chesterfield	70	80	Free	13 each way
Best Western	65	70	Free	15 each way
Days Inn	60	65	Free	12 each way
Sunset Inn	55	n/a	Free	12 each way

MEETING ROOM RATES

SQUARE FEET	*MEETING ROOM*	*4 HOURS*	*8 HOURS*	*24 HOURS*
4,290	**Top of the Park**	$400	$600	$900
1,426	**Central Park East**	$150	$200	$300
1,564	**Central Park West**	$160	$200	$300
3,036	**Combined Central Park**	$300	$400	$500
220	**Park Lane**	$ 25	$ 40	$ 60
2,500	**Revolver**	$300	$500	$700
1,222	**Dance Floor**	$100	$175	$275
1,350	**Park View**	$110	$185	$300
304	**1,007 and 1,009**	$ 40	$ 60	$ 80
304	**107 and 109**	$ 40	$ 60	$ 80

- Meeting room rental charges based on set changes at 12:00 noon, 5:00 P.M., or 10:00 P.M.
- For groups of 20 or more who are reserving 20 or more guest rooms or scheduling 20 or more banquet meals, rental rates will be waived for rooms up to 1,600 square feet for up to 8 hours of use per day.
- For groups of 50 or more who are reserving 50 or more guest rooms or scheduling 50 or more banquet meals, rental rates will be waived for all rooms for up to 24 hours of use.

▶ Use the sales information on the reverse side of this page to configure and demonstrate the prices for the convention center as well as the competing convention centers in the Rockport area. Note the pricing for daily parking and transportation to and from the Rockport Airport. These prices are collected weekly and distributed to all sales and marketing personnel.

▶ Also, use the sales information at the bottom of the page to configure and explain the pricing and policies with regard to charges for use of the meeting rooms. Explain that convention center's policies with regard to pricing and use of meeting rooms are very competitive with the charges of other centers in the Rockport area.

AUDIO VISUAL PRESENTATIONS GUIDE

These are the most popular audio/visual equipment items. If you require special equipment and services not listed. Please let us know. We'll do the rest!

AUDIO VISUAL EQUIPMENT PACKAGES

Saves Money • Saves Time

35mm Slides

Kodak Ektagraphic III 35mm Slide projector package features a projection stand or cart, 4" to 8" zoom lens, wireless remote control, spare 80 slide tray, all extension AC cords safely taped. Select Screens Below.

35mm Slide Projector Package $45.00

Recommended by
Professional Meeting Planners:

Complete speaker freedom with

Laser Pointer $27.50
Wireless Microphone $80.00
Groups over 75 people:
Special Zoom Lens $11.00

Video VCR/Monitor

VHS 1/2" or U-MATIC 3/4" Player/Recorder package features a roll-around 54" projection cart, a 27" full-function color video monitor/receiver. All cable connections. AC extension cords safely taped.

*VHS 1/2" $150.00
3/4" U-MATIC $185.00

Recommended by
Professional Meeting Planners:

More visibility for large groups with additional 27" video, monitor and cart, includes cables and connectors. Each $90.00
Full House Sound $27.50

LCD Video Projection

LCD* Proxima Video Projector $500.00
Color Video Projector Projects Full Color Video or Computer Images up to SVGA. Recommended for larger groups. Select Screen Below.

Overhead Projectors

Popular overhead projector package with super-wide overhead projector featuring automatic spare lamp changer. All AC extension cords safely taped. Select Screens Below.

Overhead Projector Package $40.00

Recommended by
Professional Meeting Planners:

Complete speaker freedom with

Laser Pointer $27.50
Wireless Microphone $80.00

LCD Panel Projection

Color Computer Data Panel $325.00
Full Color Panel Projects Computer Images on a 6'–10' Projection Screen with Hi-Intensity Overhead Projector. Select Screen Below.

Full Motion Video Projection

CRT Projector with VCR $550.00
Color video projector projects full motion video on screen. Recommended for larger groups. Select screen below.

AUDIO VISUAL EQUIPMENT Á LA CARTE

Motion Picture Projection

16mm Autoload projector w/2" prime lens with stand $40.00

Hi-Intensity Overhead Projector

4000 Lumen projector for LCD computer
Data panel or larger groups $65.00

Meeting Accessories

Laser Pointer $27.50
Flip Chart Easel (No Pen) $14.00
Flip Chart Rental w/Markers $22.00
Projection carts and stands $16.50
Meeting accessories such as acetate rolls and sheets are available on request.

Video Equipment

Camcorder with tripod $120.00
VCR $60.00

Audio Equipment

Cassette Player/Recorder $40.00
CD Player $40.00
Portable CD/Cassette Player $40.00

AV Technician Services

AV Tech is on site for installation and dismantle. Requirements for exclusive event management will be charged these hourly rates:
Monday through Friday, 7am-5pm $30.00
Evenings, Weekdays, and Holidays $40.00

Microphones

Microphone, wired $22.00
Lavaliere, wired $22.00
Wireless microphone (Hand held or Lavaliere) $80.00
Sound patch to house system $27.50
4 Channel mixer $27.50

Screens

6' × 6' Tripod $22.00
8' × 8' Tripod $27.50
10' × 10' Cradle $55.00
*7 1/2' × 10' Fast Fold $80.00
*9' × 12' Fast Fold $110.00
*(Front or rear projection)
Fast fold drape kits included.

▶ Use the sales information on the reverse side of this page to sell, configure, and explain the availability of audio visual equipment available to customers scheduling meetings in the convention center. This equipment must be reserved in advance of the scheduled date to guarantee availability.

THE PRINCIPAL COMPANY

1900 Grand Avenue
Rockport, IL 50322

December 15, 200_

Carroll Parez, General Manager
The Park Inn
555 West Side Street
Rockport, IL 50310

Dear Carroll:

On behalf of our employees I thank you and your associates for the wonderful time we had at the Park Inn during our convention last month. Enclosed is a check for $22,991.23 to pay the invoice for the meeting costs.

The hospitality that we received during our time there was unparalleled. The friendliness and dedication of the staff simply made our time so enjoyable we hated to leave.

The Chicken New Orleans was superb. Our *heartfelt thanks to Chef Ricardo Guido* for creating the best meals we have ever had at a convention.

Without reservation I will direct anyone looking for convention space to your award-winning property. The group who gave you the award certainly knew what was important to convention planners. You may count on us to return in the future.

Sincerely,

Reggie Regan

Reggie Regan, Vice President
Field Sales Division

Enclosures:
Schedule for our next eight convention dates
Check
Service Evaluation

ss

▶ Use this reference letter with customers to support the outstanding service we strive to provide to ALL of our convention center customers. Note the friendliness and dedication of the center staff, the quality of the food service, the reference to the award, and the enclosures regarding repeat business involving eight more meeting dates and the check in the amount of $22,991.23.

REFERENCES

COMPANY/ADDRESS	TELEPHONE NO.	DATE OF BOOKING
Association of Business and Industry 2425 Hubbell Mr. James Warner (Director)	265–8181	July 1–2
Acme Supply Company 2531 Dean Linn Compiano (Training Manager)	265–9831	July 14
Rotary International 1230 Executive Towers Mr. Roger Shannon (Executive Director)	792–4616	July 28–29
Archway Cookie Company Boone Industrial Park Mr. Bill Sorenson (Sales Manager)	432–4084	August 9
West College 4821 College Parkway Toni Bush (Athletic Director)	283–4142	September 9–11
Travelers Insurance Company 1452 29th Mr. Richard Wiese (Training Manager)	223–7500	November 14
Meredith Corporation 1716 Locust Mrs. Carol Rains (Public Relations)	284–2654	November 23–24
Pioneer Hi-Bred Incorporated 5700 Merle Highway Mrs. Sheri Sitterly (Administrative Services)	272–3660	December 12–13

▶ Use the sales information on the reverse side of this page to supply a list of successful business people, who can be contacted regarding the quality of food and service they received at previous meetings they have scheduled at the convention center.

CONVENTION CENTER POLICIES AND GENERAL INFORMATION

FOOD AND BEVERAGE

- A 16% gratuity or service charge and applicable sales tax will be added to all food and beverage purchases. Any group requesting a tax exemption must submit their Certificate of Exemption prior to the event.

- There is a $25 setup fee for each meal function of 25 persons or less.

GUARANTEES

- The Convention Center will require your menus and meeting room requirements no later than two weeks before your meeting or food function.
- Convention Center facilities are guaranteed on a "first confirmed, first served" basis.

- A meal guarantee is required 48 hours prior to your function. This guarantee is the minimum your group will be charged for the function. If no guarantee is received by the catering office, we will then consider your last number of attendees as the guarantee. We will be prepared to serve 5% over your guaranteed number.

BANQUET AND MEETING ROOMS

- As other groups may be utilizing the same room prior to or following your function, please adhere to the times agreed on. Should your time schedule change, please contact the Catering Office, and every effort will be made to accommodate you.

- Function rooms are assigned by the room number of people anticipated. If attendance drops or increases, please contact the Catering Office to ensure proper assignment of rooms.

AUDIO VISUAL SERVICES

- A wide selection of audio visual equipment and services is available on a rental basis. See Audio Visual presentation guide for details.

▶ Use the sales information on the reverse side of this page to carefully explain the policies and general information on the operation of the convention center. Please note the 16% gratuity, and the $25 setup fee for certain meals. Also, note the policies and guarantees that are required for menus, meeting rooms, and meals.

PARK INN
INTERNATIONAL™

CUSTOMER SERVICE/SALES MEMORANDUM 1

To: **Convention Sales Trainee**
From: **T. J. McKee, Sales Manager**
Re: **Assistance with a Customer Request**

A new prospect called and requested that we immediately submit a proposal for a planned Rockport meeting. Please review the profile in our automated database (printed as follows).

CONTACT REPORT

Name: Graphic Forms	Address: 2134 Martin Luther King
Contact: B. H. Rivera	:
Phone: 314–619–4879	:
Title: President	City: Atlanta
Sec:	State: GA
Dear: B. H. Rivera	ZIP: 61740

◄ **CONTACT SCREEN**

(McKee) Visited with B. H. Rivera on the phone. Seemed very interested. Nice emotive person. Has a son, Matt, attending West College. Also knew Toni Bush of West, who is an excellent account of ours. B. H. wants a proposal ASAP to cover the following buying conditions:
1. Ten single guest rooms for two nights—Friday and Saturday
2. A meeting room for 20 people, classroom style, Friday and Saturday from 2 to 6 P.M.
3. Dinner for 20, banquet style, at 6 P.M. each night
   Friday: Grilled Pork Chops
   Saturday: Broiled Orange Roughy
4. A swimming pool

◄ **NOTES WINDOW**

Complete the following customer service/sales assignment using the material in your product sales training program (pp. 417–450) and the forms on the next two pages. (See Chapters 5 and 6 on Developing a Product Strategy.)
1. *Complete the sales proposal worksheet (p. 449).*
   Our sales proposal needs to contain accurate and complete facts because when signed, it becomes a legally enforceable sales contract. All the product and pricing guidelines have been supplied in your sales training materials. You should sign your name with your new job title "Account Executive" in the lower left-hand corner of the form.
2. *Write a sales letter (p. 450).*
   Prepare a letter that custom fits and positions the benefits that will appeal to B. H. Rivera. Be sure to list any sales literature you will be sending under the Enclosure section of your letter. (Use business letter format on p. 441.)

Make file copies of everything you prepare so our food and beverage, housekeeping, and accounting departments will have them available.

We should send or fax the proposal, cover letter, and sales literature by tomorrow afternoon.

Thank you.

Enclosures

PARK INN
INTERNATIONAL™

SALES PROPOSAL

Customer Name: _____ Title: _____

Organization Name: _____ Telephone: _____

Address: _____

Date(s) of Meetings: _____

Kind of Meetings: _____

Buying Conditions (What the customer needs—be specific): _____

_____

_____

A. Meal Functions Needed

	Time	Description	Quantity	Price	Total
Meal 1					
Meal 2					
Other		(Beverages, set up fees, etc.)			

Total _____

Sales Tax _____

Service Charge _____

Total Meal Cost _____

B. Meeting and Banquet Rooms and Equipment Needed (describe time, date, and cost)

Total _____

Sales Tax _____

Total Meeting/Banquet Rooms and Equipment Charges _____

C. Guest Rooms Needed

Number of Rooms Needed	Description (dates, locations, special conditions)	Group Rate Per Room	Total Cost

Total _____

Room Tax _____

Sales Tax _____

D. Total Customer Costs (from above)

Total Guest Room Charges _____

A. $_____ plus B. $_____ plus C. $_____ equals **Total Charges** $_____

_____ _____
Authorized Signature   Date

_____ _____
Customer Signature   Date

_____
Title

_____
Title

555 West Side Street, Rockport, IL 50322
618-225-0925   Fax 618-225-9386

PARK INN

I N T E R N A T I O N A L™

EMPLOYMENT MEMORANDUM 2

To: **New Convention Center Account Executives**
From: **T. J. McKee, Sales Manager**
Re: **Your New Sales Assignment**

Congratulations on successfully completing your training program, and receiving your new appointment. You will find three challenges as you partner with your accounts.

Your *first challenge will be establishing relationships* with your customers. This will require that you do strategic planning before you can call on your client for the first time. Make sure your initial meetings focus on subjects of interest to your customer.

Your *second major challenge will be to gain a complete and accurate understanding of your customer's needs.* You should prepare to ask good questions, take detailed and accurate notes, and confirm your customer's and your own understanding of their need. This process is a part of our total quality management program which strives to provide total quality customer service.

Your *third challenge as an account executive will be to make good presentations.* Our industry, as most others these days, is competitive and is characterized by many look-alike products and some price cutting. Always *organize and deliver good presentations* that focus on (1) providing solutions to immediate and long-term customer needs, (2) negotiating double-win solutions to customer concerns, and (3) closing sales that keep our facility full. This approach will give you a competitive edge and help you maintain high-quality, long-term profitable relationships.

Effectively meeting these challenges will also require that you have a program of *self-improvement.* This will enhance your career as an account executive.

Attached you will find a memorandum on an account I would like you to develop. Please follow the instructions included, and provide me with appropriate feedback on your progress. I look forward to working with you on this account.

P. S. I want to compliment you on your excellent work on the B. H. Rivera account. B. H. called while you were attending a training meeting and said that your proposal and letter looked very good. Their organization was impressed with our facility, the apparent quality of our food, and your letter. Their organization will be scheduling a total of *eleven more meetings* at our convention center during the next twelve months if everything works the way you describe it. Each of these sales will be reflected in your *commission checks.* Great work.

PARK INN
INTERNATIONAL™

SALES MEMORANDUM 1A

To: **Association Account Sales**
From: **T. J. McKee, Sales Manager**
Re: **Developing the Erin Adkins YWCA Account (Call 1, Establishing a Relationship Strategy)**

My sales assistant has called Erin Adkins, chairperson of the YWCA Physical Fitness Week program (see following contact report), and set up an appointment for you on Monday at 1:00 P.M. in Erin's office. During your first sales call with Erin, your call objectives will be to (1) Establish a strong relationship, (2) Share an appealing benefit of our property to create customer interest, (3) Find out if your customer is planning any conventions in the future.

As we discussed during your training class, using Erin Adkins' prospect information presented below and the sales tools in your product strategy materials, your presentation plan should be to (see Chapters 3 and 9)

1. Use compliments, comments on observations, or search for mutual acquaintances to determine which topics Erin wants to talk about (Erin will only want to talk about three of these topics). This should set the stage for a good relationship.
2. Take notes on the topics of interest to Erin so we can add them to our customer information data bank for future calls. (Erin will share three new items of information on each topic of interest, if you acknowledge interest.)
3. Show and describe an appealing and unique benefit of our facility so we will be considered for Erin's future convention needs. (Consider using the Architect's Award, p. 419.)
4. Discuss any conventions Erin may be planning.
5. Schedule a call back appointment.

Name: YWCA	Address:	16 Ruan Center
Contact: Erin Adkins	:	
Phone: 515-555-3740	:	
Title: Chairperson, Physical Fitness Programs	City:	Rockport
Sec:	State:	IL
Dear: Erin	ZIP:	50322

◀ **CONTACT SCREEN**

(McKee) Toni Bush, the Athletic Director of West College, supplied the following information about Erin Adkins:
1. Toni and Erin have a close relationship.
2. Erin just designed and built a new home.
3. Erin appears in local TV advertising about the YWCA.
Toni reports that in Erin's office you will observe the following:
4. An autographed picture of the Chicago Bulls basketball team
5. A Schwinn Air-dyne Fitness Cycle

◀ **NOTES WINDOW**

Comments, Compliments, and Questions	**Notes on New Items of Interest to Customer**
(Toni Bush suggested you mention his name.)	1. (Example) Toni Bush is my cousin
	2.
	3.
	1.
	2.
	3.
	1.
	2.
	3.

PARK INN
I N T E R N A T I O N A L™

SALES MEMORANDUM 1B

To: **Corporate Account Sales**
From: **T. J. McKee, Sales Manager**
Re: **Developing the Leigh Combs, Epic Design Systems Account (Call 1, Establishing a Relationship Strategy)**

My sales assistant has called Epic Design Systems (see following contact report) and set up an appointment for you on Monday at 1:00 P.M. in Leigh's office. During your first sales call with Leigh, your call objectives will be to (1) Establish a strong relationship, (2) Share an appealing benefit of our property to create customer interest, (3) Find out if your customer is planning any conventions in the future.

As we discussed during your training class, using Leigh Comb's prospect information presented below and the sales tools in your product strategy materials, your presentation plan should be to (see Chapters 3 and 9)

1. Use compliments, comments on observations, or search for mutual acquaintances to determine which topics Leigh wants to talk about (Leigh will only want to talk about three of these topics). This should set the stage for a good relationship.
2. Take notes on the topics of interest to Leigh so we can add them to our customer information data bank for future calls. (Leigh will share three new items of information on each topic of interest, if you verbally or nonverbally acknowledge interest.)
3. Show and describe an appealing and unique benefit of our facility so we will be considered for Leigh's future convention needs. (Consider using the Executive Chef's Award, p. 425.)
4. Discuss any conventions Leigh may be planning.
5. Schedule a call back appointment.

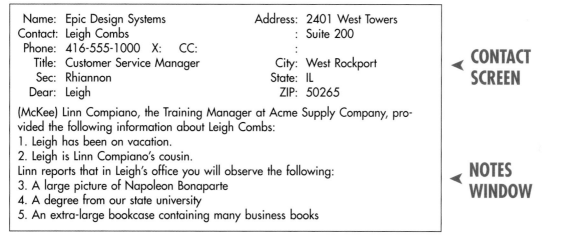

Name: Epic Design Systems	Address: 2401 West Towers	◄ **CONTACT SCREEN**
Contact: Leigh Combs	: Suite 200	
Phone: 416-555-1000 X: CC:	:	
Title: Customer Service Manager	City: West Rockport	
Sec: Rhiannon	State: IL	
Dear: Leigh	ZIP: 50265	

(McKee) Linn Compiano, the Training Manager at Acme Supply Company, provided the following information about Leigh Combs:
1. Leigh has been on vacation.
2. Leigh is Linn Compiano's cousin.
Linn reports that in Leigh's office you will observe the following:
3. A large picture of Napoleon Bonaparte
4. A degree from our state university
5. An extra-large bookcase containing many business books

◄ **NOTES WINDOW**

Comments, Compliments, and Questions	Notes on New Items of Interest to Customer
(Linn Compiano mentioned that Leigh Combs just returned from a very enjoyable vacation.)	1. (Example) Spent one week in California 2. 3.
	1. 2. 3.
	1. 2. 3.

PRESALE PLAN WORKSHEET

SALES CALL 1 — ESTABLISHING A RELATIONSHIP

Name:_____

Your appointment for your first call is scheduled for (1) _____ at (2) _____

P.M. Your appointment was set up by (3) _____. On entering your prospect's office, you

will need to (4) _____ yourself, (5) _____ hands, and explain your

(6) _____ objectives. Your next step will be to make a (7) _____,

(8) _____, or do a search for mutual acquaintances or interests. When your customer opens

up and shares new information, you are instructed to (9) _____ _____ and

take (10) _____. If you are successful in getting your customer to talk about things in which

(s)he is interested, you should receive (11) _____ new pieces of relationship information.

At the appropriate time during your call you will convert attention from the (12) _____

to showing a (13) _____ device and presenting a (14) _____

_____, to interest your customer in your convention center. In completing your call

(15) _____ you are asked to (16) _____ _____ if your cus-

tomer is planning any future (17) _____. If you have not received a total of

(18) _____ new pieces of relationship information, you should go back and talk about things

of interest to your customer. The (19) _____ screen on the contact report provides factual

information about your prospect while the (20) _____ _____ contains

information that reflects your customer's interests. Erin Adkins is involved with the (21)

_____. Erin also knows (22) _____ _____

of West College. Leigh Combs is a (23) _____ _____ manager

and has just returned from (24) _____. There are at least two important items to (25)

_____ in both Erin's and Leigh's office.

ASSESSMENT FORM 1
RELATIONSHIP STRATEGY

Salesperson's Name:_____

Date:_____

Assessment Item	Excellent		Average		Poor	Did Not Do
1. Conducted good verbal introductions (shared full name, title, and company name)	10	9	8	7	6	0
2. Made good nonverbal introduction (good entrance, carriage, handshake, and seating posture)	10	9	8	7	6	0
3. Communicated call objectives (shared why salesperson was calling)	10	9	8	7	6	0
4. Verbalized effective comments and compliments (sincerely made comments and compliments on five relationship topics)	10	9	8	7	6	0
5. Kept conversation focused on customer topics (acknowledged new information provided by customer)	10	9	8	7	6	0
6. Took effective nondistractive notes (was organized and prepared to take notes)	10	9	8	7	6	0
7. Attractively showed material on convention center (was well prepared with a proof device)	10	9	8	7	6	0
8. Made effective benefit statement (made a benefit statement that appealed to customer)	10	9	8	7	6	0
9. Effectively inquired about convention needs (asked good questions about future needs)	10	9	8	7	6	0
10. Effectively thanked customer (communicated appreciation, said thank-you, indicated interest in prospect future business)	10	9	8	7	6	0

Relationship Presentation:_____

Total Points

Your Name:_____

Return this form to salesperson and discuss your reaction to this presentation!

PARK INN
I N T E R N A T I O N A L™

SALES MEMORANDUM 2A

To: **Association Account Salesperson**
From: **T. J. McKee, Sales Manager**
Re: **Erin Adkins Account—phone call from customer**
         (Call 2, Discovering a Customer's Buying Strategy)

Erin Adkins from the YWCA, whom you called on recently, left a message for you to stop in about a program they are planning. Congratulations on making that first call so effectively. Apparently, you established a good relationship.

As we discussed in your training program, your *call objectives* should be to

1. Reestablish your relationship
2. Discover Erin's buying conditions (the what, why, who, when, and what price needs), so we can custom fit a program for them
3. Set up an appointment to present your solution

Also, as we discussed, your *presentation plan* for this call should include (see Chapters 7 and 10)

1. In advance of your meeting, prepare general *information-gathering questions* to get your customer talking and to achieve your call objectives. (Use our form that follows.)
2. Later in your meeting, use *probing and confirmation questions* to clarify and confirm Erin's and your own perception of each buying condition.
3. During your sales meeting, write down each of Erin's buying conditions. (Use our form that follows.)
4. To end your first meeting, use your notes to construct a *summary-confirmation question* to clarify and confirm all six of Erin's buying conditions.
5. Schedule a call back appointment to make your presentation and present your proposal.

Good luck!

INFORMATION-GATHERING QUESTIONS	NOTES ON BUYING CONDITIONS
(Example: Can you share with me what you had in mind?)	(Example: Needs a small meeting room)
	1.
	2.
	3.
	4.
	5.
	6.

PARK INN
INTERNATIONAL™

SALES MEMORANDUM 2B

To: **Corporate Account Salesperson**
From: **T. J. McKee, Sales Manager**
Re: **Leigh Combs Account—phone call from customer**
           (Call 2, Discovering a Customer's Buying Strategy)

Leigh Combs from Epic Design Systems, whom you called on recently, left a message for you to stop in about a program they are planning. Congratulations on making that first call so effectively. Apparently, you established a good relationship.

As we discussed in your training program, your *call objectives* should be to

1. Reestablish your relationship
2. Discover Leigh's buying conditions (the what, why, who, when, and what price needs), so we can custom fit a program for them
3. Set up an appointment to present your solution

Also, as we discussed, your *presentation plan* for this call should include (see Chapters 7 and 10)

1. In advance of your meeting, prepare general *information-gathering questions* designed to get your customer talking and to achieve your call objectives. (Use our form below.)
2. Later in your meeting, use *probing and confirmation questions* to clarify and confirm Leigh's and your own perceptions of each buying condition.
3. During your sales meeting, write down each of Leigh's buying conditions. (Use our form below.)
4. To end your first meeting, use your notes to construct a *summary-confirmation question* to clarify and confirm all six of Leigh's buying conditions.
5. Schedule a call back appointment to make your presentation and present your proposal.

INFORMATION-GATHERING QUESTIONS	NOTES ON BUYING CONDITIONS
(Example: Can you share with me what you had in mind?)	(Example: Needs a small meeting room)
	1.
	2.
	3.
	4.
	5.
	6.

PRESALE PLAN WORKSHEET

SALES CALL 2 — DISCOVERING A CUSTOMER STRATEGY

Name:_____

In call 2, your first objective is to (1) _____ _____ _____. To do this you should plan

to visit about (2) _____ information you acquired in call (3) _____.

Because your (4) _____ requested this meeting, you probably do not have to state your

(5) _____ _____ at the beginning of the call. The reason this meeting

was requested is because you apparently did a good job of (6) _____ the

_____ in call 1. In discovering your customer's needs (buying conditions) "what" refers

to services your customer needs and (7) _____ _____ refers to the

budget that your customer has. (8) _____ refers to the people coming, and

(9) _____ refers to the reason for the meeting. To secure general information you

should use (10) _____-_____ questions, and to get the details you should

use (11) _____ questions. (12) _____ questions check your

customer's and (13) _____ _____ perceptions. (14)

_____-_____ questions are used to summarize and check a list of things the

customer needs. Active listening requires that you (15) _____ _____ so you have

a record to work from in custom fitting a solution. You will also use your (16) _____

to construct your (17) _____-_____ question. When you have re-

ceived (18) _____ buying conditions from your customer you will be prepared to set up an

(19) _____ to come back and make a (20) _____. Your second call

objective is to (21) _____, and your third call objective is to schedule an (22)

_____. Erin Adkins is in the (23) _____ accounts market, and Leigh

Combs is in the (24) _____ accounts market.

ASSESSMENT FORM 2

CUSTOMER STRATEGY

Salesperson's Name:_____

Date:_____

Assessment Item	Excellent		Average		Poor	Did Not Do
1. Effectively reestablished relationship (made enthusiastic comments about information from first meeting)	10	9	8	7	6	0
2. Communicated positive body language (entrance, carriage, handshake, and seating)	10	9	8	7	6	0
3. Communicated positive verbal language (used positive words, showed enthusiasm with well-modulated voice)	10	9	8	7	6	0
4. Used customer's name effectively (used name at least three times)	10	9	8	7	6	0
5. Asked quality information-gathering questions (seemed prepared, questions were general and open ended)	10	9	8	7	6	0
6. Asked quality probing questions (followed up to secure all details)	10	9	8	7	6	0
7. Verified custom needs with good confirmation questions (wanted to be correct in interpreting customer needs)	10	9	8	7	6	0
8. Appeared to take effective notes (was organized and nondistracting, used notes in confirming needs)	10	9	8	7	6	0
9. Effectively set up next appointment (requested another meeting; suggested and wrote down date, time, and place)	10	9	8	7	6	0
10. Effectively thanked customer (communicated appreciation, said thank you, indicated enthusiasm for next meeting)	10	9	8	7	6	0

Discovering Customer Needs Presentation:_____

Total Points

Return this form to salesperson and discuss your reaction to this presentation!

Your Name:_____

PARK INN
I N T E R N A T I O N A L™

SALES MEMORANDUM 3A

To: **Association Account Sales**
From: **T. J. McKee, Sales Manager**
Re: **Your recent meeting on the Erin Adkins Account**
          (Call 3, Developing a Presentation Strategy)

Congratulations on doing such a thorough job of discovering Erin's buying conditions. I found that your list of buying conditions includes the kind of customer information important to increasing our sales and partnering with our clients. I would like to see a copy of Erin's proposal when you complete it.

Reviewing what we discussed during your training, your next call objectives are

1. Make a persuasive sales presentation that custom fits your proposal to Erin's needs
2. Negotiate any concerns Erin may have
3. Close and confirm the sale
4. Build repeat and referral business

Also, as we discussed, your *presentation plan* for this call should be to

1. Prepare and price a product solution that meets Erin's needs. *Complete the Sales Proposal Worksheet* (p. 465).
2. Before your sales call, prepare a *portfolio* presentation (see model on p. 464) that follows these guidelines.
   a. Review the relationship information, and prepare for those topics you will discuss.
   b. Prepare a summary-confirmation question that verifies the buying conditions secured in your second call (see Chapter 10).
   c. Select sales tools (proof devices), and create feature/benefit selling statements that appeal to Erin's buying conditions (see Chapter 11).
   d. Plan confirmation questions that verify Erin's acceptance of your solution to each buying condition. *Complete Strategic Planning Form A* (p. 469) for items b, c, and d.
   e. Prepare to negotiate the time, price, source, and product objections. *Complete Strategic Planning Form B* (p. 470) (see Chapter 12).
   f. Prepare at least four closing methods in addition to the summary of benefits. *Complete Strategic Planning Form C* (p. 471) (see Chapter 13).
   g. Plan methods to service the sale. Follow up by scheduling an appointment between now and the convention date (telephone call or personal visit) to follow through on guarantees concerning rooms and meals, suggestions about audio visual needs, and any possible changes in the convention schedule. *Complete Strategic Planning Form D* (p. 472) (see Chapter 14).
3. During the sales call reestablish the relationship, and using your portfolio presentation
   a. Confirm all of Erin's previous buying conditions
   b. Match a proof device and feature/benefit selling statement with each buying condition
   c. Confirm Erin's acceptance to each of your proposed benefit statements
   d. Negotiate any sales resistance
   e. Close the sale
   f. Service the sale to get repeats and referrals

Good luck!

PARK INN
I N T E R N A T I O N A L™

SALES MEMORANDUM 3B

To: **Corporate Account Sales**
From: **T. J. McKee, Sales Manager**
Re: **Your recent meeting on the Leigh Combs Account**
(Call 3, Developing a Presentation Strategy)

Congratulations on doing such a thorough job of discovering Leigh's buying conditions. I found that your list of buying conditions includes the kind of customer information important to increasing our sales and partnering with our clients. I would like to see a copy of Leigh's proposal when you complete it.

Reviewing what we discussed during your training, your next *call objectives* are

1. Make a persuasive sales presentation that custom fits your proposal to Leigh's needs
2. Negotiate any concerns Leigh may have
3. Close and confirm the sale
4. Build repeat and referral business

Also, as we discussed, your *presentation plan* for this call should be to

1. Prepare and price a product solution that meets Leigh's needs. *Complete the Sales Proposal Worksheet* (p. 465).
2. Before your sales call, prepare a *portfolio* presentation (see model on p. 464) that follows these guidelines:
   a. Review the relationship information, and prepare for those topics you will discuss.
   b. Prepare a summary-confirmation question that verifies the buying conditions secured in your second call (see Chapter 10).
   c. Select sales tools (proof devices), and create feature/benefit selling statements that appeal to Leigh's buying conditions (see Chapter 11).
   d. Plan confirmation questions that verify Leigh's acceptance of your solution to each buying condition. *Complete Strategic Planning Form A* (p. 469) for items b, c, and d.
   e. Prepare to negotiate the time, price, source, and product objections. *Complete Strategic Planning Form B* (p. 470) (see Chapter 12).
   f. Prepare at least four closing methods in addition to the summary-of-benefits close. *Complete Strategic Planning Form C* (p. 471) (see Chapter 13).
   g. Plan methods to service the sale. Follow up by scheduling an appointment between now and the convention date (telephone call or personal visit) to follow through on guarantees concerning rooms and meals, suggestions about audio visual needs, and any possible changes in the convention schedule. *Complete Strategic Planning Form D* (p. 472) (see Chapter 14).
3. During the sales call reestablish the relationship, and using your portfolio presentation
   a. Confirm all of Leigh's previous buying conditions
   b. Match a proof device and feature/benefit selling statement with each buying condition
   c. Confirm Leigh's acceptance to each of your proposed benefit statements
   d. Negotiate any sales resistance
   e. Close the sale
   f. Service the sale to get repeats and referrals

Good luck!

PRESALE PLAN WORKSHEET

SALES CALL 3 — DEVELOPING A PRESENTATION

Name:_____

In opening your third sales call, your first activity should be to (1) _____ the relationship. To do this you will comment on topics discussed in call number (2) _____. After this step, you will make a (3) _____ type presentation. The first page in your presentation will be a (4) _____ of items discovered in call (5) _____. To present this you will use a (6) _____ _____ question. If your customer (7) _____ you will return to the (8) _____ (9) _____ condition, repeat it, and show a (10) _____ _____ from your (11) _____ strategy materials. In describing what you have shown, you will make one or more (12) _____ statements, and then you will use a (13) _____ _____ to see if your customer agrees and likes your solution. If your customer disagrees with any of your (14) _____ statements or raises a concern, you have an (15) _____ to overcome or (16) _____. If your customer agrees you will proceed on through all (17) _____ buying conditions. After you have successfully gone through all the buying instruc-tions, you are instructed to summarize the (18) _____ and (19) _____ the sale. Prior to the customer signing your sales proposal, you will need to overcome the (20) _____ concerns. After addressing each concern you should try to (21) _____ the sale. Overcoming these concerns is best accomplished by you (22) _____ them and preparing ahead of time. After closing you will (23) _____ _____ _____ by scheduling an (24) _____ to follow up on meeting details, such as (25) _____ concerning rooms and meals.

ASSESSMENT FORM 3

PRESENTATION STRATEGY

Salesperson's Name:_____

Date:_____

Assessment Item	Excellent		Average		Poor		Did Not Do
1. Reestablished a good relationship (talked sincerely and enthusiastically about topics of interest to customer) Comments:	10	9	8	7	6		0
2. Confirmed needs from previous meeting Comments:	10	9	8	7	6		0
3. Made solution sound appealing (used nontechnical, customer-oriented benefit statements) Comments:	10	9	8	7	6		0
4. Used proof devices to prove sales appeals (made product sound appealing) Comments:	10	9	8	7	6		0
5. Verified customer's understanding of solution Comments:	10	9	8	7	6		0
6. Negotiated price objection (established high value to price impression) Comments:	10	9	8	7	6		0
7. Negotiated time objection (Created need to sign now using empathy) Comments:	10	9	8	7	6		0
8. Negotiated source objection (knew the competition well) Comments:	10	9	8	7	6		0
9. Asked for the order, closed sale (attempted to close after each objection) Comments:	10	9	8	7	6		0
10. Serviced the sale (established relationship that would result in referrals or repeat sales opportunities) Comments:	10	9	8	7	6		0

_____

Presentation Points

| Overall quality of sales portfolio and proof devices | | 25 | 20 | 15 | 0 | 5 | 0 |

Comments:

_____

Total Points

Return this form to salesperson and discuss your reaction to this presentation!

Your Name:_____

PORTFOLIO PRESENTATION MODEL

Three-ring binder with pockets recommended

PAGE 1
Summary of Customer's
Buying Conditions
1.
2.
3.
4.
5.
6.
(confirmation question)

PAGE 2
Buying Condition
1

PAGE 3
Proof Devices
(could be more than one)

(state benefits, ask
confirmation question)

PAGE 4
Buying Condition
2

PAGE 5
Proof Devices

(state benefits, ask
confirmation question)

PAGE 6
Buying Condition
3

PAGE 7
Proof Devices

(state benefits, ask
confirmation question)

PAGE 8
Buying Condition
4

PAGE 9
Proof Devices

(state benefits, ask
confirmation question)

PAGE 10
Buying Condition
5

PAGE 11
Proof Devices

(state benefits, ask
confirmation question)

PAGE 12
Buying Condition
6

PAGE 13
Proof Devices

(state benefits, ask
confirmation question)

PAGE 14
Summary of Benefits
1.
2.
3.
4.
5.
6.
(trial close)

**FRONT POCKET
MATERIALS**
Additional value-added
pages as needed to over-
come sales resistance
and close the sale

**BACK POCKET
MATERIALS**
Additional value-added
pages as needed to
service the sale

PARK INN
INTERNATIONAL™

SALES PROPOSAL

Customer Name: _____ Title: _____

Organization Name: _____ Telephone: _____

Address: _____

Date(s) of Meetings: _____

Kind of Meetings: _____

Buying Conditions (What the customer needs—be specific): _____

_____

_____

A. Meal Functions Needed

	Time	Description	Quantity	Price	Total
Meal 1					
Meal 2					
Other		(Beverages, setup fees, etc.)			

Total _____

Sales Tax _____

Service Charge _____

Total Meal Cost _____

B. Meeting and Banquet Rooms and Equipment Needed
(Describe time, date, and cost)

Total _____

Sales Tax _____

Total Meeting/Banquet Rooms and Equipment Charges _____

C. Guest Rooms Needed

Number of Rooms Needed	Description (dates, locations, special conditions)	Group Rate Per Room	Total Cost

Total _____

Room Tax _____

Sales Tax _____

Total Guest Room Charges _____

D. Total Customer Costs (from above)

A. $_____ plus **B.** $_____ plus **C.** $_____ equals **Total Charges** $ _____

Authorized Signature _____ Date _____

Customer Signature _____ Date _____

Title _____

Title _____

PARK INN
INTERNATIONAL™

555 West Side Street, Rockport, IL 50322
618-225-0925   Fax 618-225-9386

MEETING AND BANQUET ROOM SCHEDULE OF EVENTS

1ST THURSDAY OF NEXT MONTH

Central Park East
    Open—Expect confirmation tomorrow

Top of the Park
    Open—Expect confirmation tomorrow

Central Park West
    Open—Expect confirmation tomorrow

Revolver
    Open

Park Lane
    10:00 A.M. C of C Membership Committee
    2:00 P.M. County Central Planning Committee

Dance Floor
    7:00 P.M. IBM Dinner and Dance

Parkview
    Open—Expect confirmation tomorrow

1007 and 1009
    11:00 A.M. Advertising Prof's Luncheon
    7:00 P.M. IBM Communication Seminar

107 and 109
    10:00 A.M.—Expect confirmation tomorrow

ATTENTION: Phone 225-0925, ext. 8512
immediately to confirm reservations.

▶ Use the scheduling information on the reverse of this page to illustrate to your customers that reservations for rooms must be scheduled as soon as possible. All guest and meeting room reservations are guaranteed on a "first come first signed" basis with the customer's signature on a sales proposal. Once a room has been reserved on a signed sales form, it is no longer available. Upon receiving a signature, sales and marketing personnel should immediately phone, fax, or e-mail this information to the reservations department. Noting that a possible meeting may be confirmed does not constitute a signed reservation.

STRATEGIC SALES PLANNING FORM A

MATCHING BUYING CONDITIONS WITH PROOF DEVICES AND FEATURE/BENEFITS

BUYING CONDITION *You indicated you wanted . . .*	PROOF DEVICE *Here is . . .*	FEATURE *which has (have) . . .*	BENEFIT *which means to you . . .*	CONFIRMATION QUESTION *What do you think?*
1. ____ (number) guest rooms	A picture of one of our guest rooms (see p. 428)	Just been remodeled	Your people will enjoy clean, comfortable, spacious, and attractive surroundings	Is that what you had in mind?
2.				
3.				
4.				
5.				
6.				

Optional Role Play 3-A Instructions (see Chapters 10 and 11)

Step 1 Prepare your presentation plan by completing the above form.

Step 2 Organize your presentation plan by placing the above information on $8\frac{1}{2}'' \times 11''$ sheets of paper according to the portfolio presentation plan on page 464. Select proof devices from the product strategy materials presented on pages 417–450 and the completed proposal on page 465.

Step 3 Using the portfolio materials you have prepared, pair off with another student who will play the role of your customer. Review your customer's buying conditions, present your solutions with benefit statements, prove your sales appeals with demonstrations, secure your customer's reactions and summarize the benefits presented. Discuss your customer's reactions to your presentation. This exercise will help you prepare for call 3.

STRATEGIC PLANNING FORM B

ANTICIPATING AND NEGOTIATING SALES RESISTANCE WORKSHEET

PART I	ANTICIPATING SALES RESISTANCE	PART II	NEGOTIATING SALES RESISTANCE
Type	What Customer Might Say	Methods*	What You Will Say (Include Proof Devices you will use)
Time	"I would like to take a day to think over your proposal."	Indirect denial	"I understand, but . . . ." (Show p. 467, Schedule of Events.)
Price	"That price is way over my budget."		
Source	"I'm going to check with the Marriott."		
Product	"I'm concerned about the size of your meeting rooms."		

Optional Role Play 3-B Instructions

Using the preceding material you have prepared, pair off with another student who will play the role of your customer. Provide your customer with the material in Part I and instruct her to raise sales resistance in any order she chooses. Playing the role of the salesperson, you will respond with the material you prepared in Part II. Continue the dialogue until all the types of sales resistance have been successfully negotiated. Discuss with your customer her reaction to your methods of successfully negotiating the different types of sales resistance. This exercise will help you prepare for Sales Call 3.

*Method of Negotiating Sales Resistance: (see Chapter 12)

- Direct Denial
- Indirect Denial
- Question
- Third Party
- Superior Benefit
- Demonstration
- Trial Offer
- Feel, Felt, Found

STRATEGIC PLANNING FORM C

CLOSING AND CONFIRMING THE SALE WORKSHEET

PART I	PART II	
Verbal and Nonverbal Closing Clues	Method of Closing*	What You Will Say (Include proof devices you will use)
Agreement with each benefit	Summary of the benefits and direct appeal	"Let me review what we have talked about . . . . May I get your signature?" (Use p. 465, Sales Proposal.)
Agreement after an objection to price, time, or source	Assumption	
Appears enthusiastic and impatient	Trial close and assumption	
Agreement with all benefits but will not under any circumstances go over budget	Special concession	

Optional Role Play 3-C Instructions

Using the preceding material you have prepared, pair off with another student who will play the role of your customer. Provide your customer with the appropriate closing clues from Part I and instruct him to provide verbal or non-verbal closing clues in any order he chooses. Playing the role of the salesperson, you will respond with the material you prepared in Part II. Continue the dialogue until you have responded to all the anticipated closing clues. Discuss with your customer his reaction to your methods of successfully closing and confirming the sale. This exercise will help you prepare for Sales Call 3.

*Method of Closing the Sale (see Chapter 13)

- Trial Close
- Summary of the Benefits
- Assumption
- Special Concession
- Multiple Option
- Direct Appeal

STRATEGIC PLANNING FORM D

SERVICING THE SALE WORKSHEET

PART I	PART II
What You Will Do to Add Value to the Sale	What You Will Say or Write to Add Value to the Sale
1. Schedule appointments to confirm rooms and final counts on meals. Dates Time 1_____ 1_____ 2_____ 2_____	"I would like to call to confirm . . . ." (Show p. 445, Convention Center Policies, and write date and time on your calendar.)
2. Make suggestions during next meeting about audio visual equipment, beverages for breaks, etc.	
3. Provide personal assurances concerning your continuing efforts to make the meeting an outstanding success.	
4. Prepare thank-you letter concerning call 3.	

Optional Role Play 3-D Instructions

Using the preceding material you have prepared, pair off with another student who will play the role of your customer. Using the topics identified in Part I, verbally present what you have prepared in Part II on this form. Discuss with your customer her reaction to your methods of servicing the sale. This exercise will help you prepare for Sales Call 3.

Method of Servicing the Sale (see Chapter 14)

- Suggestion Selling
- Follow through on Promises and Obligations
- Follow up to ensure Customer Satisfaction

Chapter 1

1. Interview with Scott Daley, Director of Marketing, on July 13, 1999; interview with Celeste Berouty, National Sales Manager, Wet Suit Division, on August 6, 1999.
2. Lucy McCauley, "Voices: The State of the New Economy," *Fast Company*, September 1999, p. 124.
3. Stan Davis and Christopher Meyer, *Blur: The Speed of Change in the Connected Economy* (New York: Addison-Wesley, 1998), p. 9.
4. David Shenk, *Data Smog* (New York: HarperEdge, 1997), pp. 27–29.
5. Chad Kaydo, "America's Best Sales Forces," *Sales & Marketing Management*, October 1997, p. 61.
6. William D. Perreault and E. Jerome McCarthy, *Basic Marketing: A Managerial Approach*, 12th ed. (Homewood, IL: Irwin, 1996), p. 45.
7. William J. Stanton, B. J. Walker, and M. J. Etzell, *Fundamentals of Marketing*, 10th ed. (New York: McGraw-Hill, 1994), p. 464.
8. Dennis Fox, "Ringing Up Prospects," *Sales & Marketing Management*, March 1993), pp. 75–77.
9. Robert M. Peterson, George H. Lucas, and Patrick L. Schul, "Forming Consultative Trade Alliances: Walking the Walk in the New Selling Environment," *NAMA Journal*, Spring 1998, p. 11; Beth Belton, "Technology Is Changing Face of U.S. Sales Force," *USA Today*, February 9, 1999, p. 2A.
10. Leslie Agnello-Dean, "Converting Salespeople to Consultant/Advisors," *Sales & Marketing Training*, March–April 1990, p. 18.
11. William M. Pride and O. C. Ferrell, *Marketing*, 10th ed. (Boston: Houghton Mifflin, 1997), p. 518.
12. Robert B. Miller and Stephen E. Heiman, *Strategic Selling* (New York: Warren Books, 1985), p. 26.
13. "Menu Analysis: Key to the Sale," *Institutional Distribution*, May 15, 1990, pp. 122–124.
14. Fiona Gibb, "The New Sales Basics," *Sales & Marketing Management*, April 1995, p. 81.
15. John O'Toole, "Get Inside Your Clients Skin," *Selling*, May 1995, p. 77.
16. Francy Blackwood, "Equal, But Not Separate," *Selling*, June 1996, pp. 74–75; "Books & Videos," *Training*, February 1996, p. 62.
17. Stephen Hagg, Maeve Cummings and James Dawkins, *Management Information Systems for the Information Age* (New York: Irwin McGraw-Hill, 1998), p. 15.
18. Ginger Conlon, "Business With a Capital E," *Sales & Marketing Management*, August 1999, p. 80.
19. John Heinrich, "Relationship Selling," *Personal Selling Power*, May–June 1995, p. 32.
20. Geoffrey Brewer, "The Customer Stops Here," *Sales & Marketing Management*, March 1998, pp. 31–32.
21. Donna Fenn, "Details, Details, Details,: *Inc.*, July 1997, p. 107; Rosabeth Moss Kanter, "The Power of Partnering," *Sales & Marketing Management*, June 1997, p. 26.
22. Robert M. Peterson, George H. Lucas, and Patrick L. Schul, "Forming Consultative Trade Alliances: Walking the Walk in the New Selling Environment," *NAMA Journal*, Spring 1998, p. 11.

Source for Boxed Feature

a   James Champy, "Selling to Tomorrow's Customer," *Sales & Marketing Management*, March 1999, p. 28; Neil Rachman and John DeVincentis, *Rethinking the Sales Force*, New York: McGraw Hill, 1999, pp. 11 and 104.

Chapter 2

1. Todd Natenberg, "Why I Chose Sales over Journalism," *Selling*, June 1997, p. 16.
2. Charles Butler, "Why the Bad Rap?" *Sales and Marketing Management*, June 1996, p. 64.
3. Bryan Gruley, "Inside the Dream: A High-Tech Start-Up Begs for Cash and Life," *Wall Street Journal*, October 13, 1998, pp. A1 and A14.
4. Stanley Marcus, "Sales School," *Fast Company*, November 1998, p. 105.
5. Thomas A. Stewart, "Knowledge, the Appreciating Commodity," *Fortune*, October 12, 1998, p. 18.
6. John Naisbitt, *Megatrends* (New York: Warner Books, 1982), p. 18.
7. Christopher Caggiano, "Sign of the Cross-Training Times," *Inc.*, December 1998, pp. 122–123.
8. Malcolm Fleschner, "The Little Pickup that Could," *Personal Selling Power*, April 1993, pp. 28–29.
9. "Hidden Sellers," *Success*, May 1993, p. 23.
10. Harry Beckwith, *Selling the Invisible* (New York: Warner Books, 1997), p. 38.
11. Allan S. Boress, *The I Hate Selling Book* (New York: AMACOM, 1995), p. 8.
12. Linda Corman, "Look Who's Selling Now," *Selling*, July–August 1996, pp. 46–53.
13. Ibid., p. 53.
14. Joshua Harris Prager, "Start-Ups Drop Despite Strong Economy," *Wall Street Journal*, January 28, 1999, p. A2.
15. James Koch, "Portrait of the CEO as Salesman," *Inc.*, March 1988, p. 45.
16. Beth Belton, "Technology Is Changing Face of U.S. Sales Force," *USA Today*, February 9, 1999, p. A2.
17. Mary Sykes Wylie, "Free," *Networker*, January–February 1998, p. 25.
18. *Statistical Abstract of the United States*, 1998, 118th ed. (Washington, DC: U.S. Department of Commerce, 1998), p. 418.
19. "A Career in Sales," *Selling Power*, October 1997, p. 12; "Selling Sales to Students," *Sales & Marketing Management*, January 1998, p. 15.
20. "The Selling Power 400," *Selling Power*, September 1998, p. 70.
21. Ken Liebeskind, "Sporting Chance," *Selling Power*, June 1998, pp. 14–16.
22. "Help Wanted," *Sales & Marketing Management*, July 1998, p. 14.
23. Eli Jones, Jesse N. Moore, Andrea J. S. Stanaland, and Rosalind A. J. Wyatt, "Salesperson Race and Gender and the Access and Legitimacy Paradigm: Does Difference Make a Difference," *The Journal of Personal Selling & Sales Management*, Fall 1998, p. 71.
24. "Big Deal Worth the Price," *Selling*, July–August 1996, p. 14.
25. Francy Blackwood, "Five Hot Fields," *Selling*, July–August 1995, p. 49.
26. Ibid., pp. 54–56.
27. Leonard Berry, "Stores with a Future," *Retailing Issues Letter*, March 1995, p. 2.
28. Erika Rasmusson, "The Death of Retail?" *Sales & Marketing Management*, March 1999, p. 17.
29. Francy Blackwood, "Selling With vs. Selling To," *Selling*, December 1995, pp. 28–29.

30. Beth Belton, "Technology Is Changing Face of U.S. Sales Force," *USA Today*, February 9, 1999, p. A2.

31. "Industry Report 1998," *Training*, October 1998, p. 55.

32. News release issued by Certified Marketing Services, Inc. September 6, 1996.

Sources for Boxed Features

a Gene Koretz, "Women Swell the Workforce," *Business Week*, November 4, 1996, p. 32; Naomi Freundlich, "Maybe Working Women Can't Have It All," *Business Week*, September 15, 1997, pp. 19–22; Keith H. Hammonds, "She Works Hard for the Money," *Business Week*, May 22, 1995, p. 54; Anne Fisher, "Overseas, U.S. Businesswomen May Have the Edge," *Fortune*, September 28, 1998, p. 304.

b Michele Marchetti, "Sales Training Even a Rep Could Love," *Sales & Marketing Management*, June 1998, p. 70.

Chapter 3

1. *Sales Talk: Communication Styles* (Pasadena, CA: Intelecom).

2. Daniel Goleman, *Working with Emotional Intelligence* (New York: Bantam Books, 1998), pp. 24–28, 317.

3. L. B. Gschwandtner and Gerhard Gschwandtner, "Balancing Act," *Selling Power*, June 1996, p. 24.

4. Ibid.

5. Denis Waitley, *Empires of the Mind* (New York: William Morrow, 1995), p. 3.

6. Jonathan J. Ward, "Foolish Inconsistency," *Sales & Marketing Management*, March 1993, p. 32.

7. J. D. Power and Associates, *Fact Sheet*, Los Angeles, CA, 1993.

8. "Partnering: The Heart of Selling Today" (Des Moines, IA: American Media Incorporated, 1990).

9. Paul S. Goldner, "How to Set the Playing Field," *Selling*, April 1998, p. 9.

10. Larry Wilson, "Selling in the 90s" (Chicago: Nightingale Conant, 1988), p. 35.

11. William Keenan Jr., "Customer Satisfaction Builds Business," *Selling*, March 1998, p. 12.

12. Madelyn Callahan, "Teaching the Sales Relationship," *Training and Development*, December 1992, p. 35.

13. Maxwell Maltz, *Psycho-Cybernetics* (Englewood Cliffs, NJ: Prentice-Hall, 1960), p. 2.

14. "The Keys to Good Selling," *Sales & Marketing Management*, January 1990, p. 32.

15. Nathaniel Branden, *Self-Esteem at Work* (San Francisco: Jossey-Bass, 1998), pp. 20–21.

16. Denis Waitley, *The Double Win* (Old Tappan, NJ: Fleming H. Revell, 1985), p. 31.

17. Robert B. Miller and Stephen E. Heiman, *Strategic Selling* (New York: Warner Books, 1985), p. 60.

18. "The Strength of Character," *Royal Bank Letter* (Royal Bank of Canada, May–June 1988), p. 1.

19. Eli Jones, Jesse N. Moore, Andrea J. S. Stanaland, and Rosalind A. J. Wyatt, "Salesperson Race and Gender and the Access and Legitimacy Paradigm: Does Difference Make a Difference," *Journal of Personal Selling and Sales Management*, Fall 1998, p. 74.

20. Ginger Trumfio, "More than Words," *Sales & Marketing Management*, April 1994, p. 55.

21. "Get to the Truth of the Message," *The Pryor Report*, Vol. VI, No. 1A, p. 7.

22. Susan Bixler, *The Professional Image* (New York: Putnam Publishing Group, 1984), p. 216.

23. Barbara Pachter and Marjorie Brody, *Complete Business Etiquette Handbook* (New York: Prentice-Hall, 1995), p. 14.

24. Adapted from Leonard Zunin, *Contact: The First Four Minutes* (New York: Nash Publishing, Ballantine Books, 1972), p. 109.

25. "Name that Customer," *Personal Selling Power*, January–February 1993, p. 48.

26. Deborah Blum, "Face It!" *Psychology Today*, September–October 1998, pp. 32–69.

27. John T. Molloy, *Dress for Success* (New York: Peter H. Wyden, 1975); *The Woman's Dress for Success Book* (Chicago: Follet, 1977); and *Live for Success* (New York: Morrow, 1981).

28. Anne M. Phaneuf, "Decoding Dress Codes," *Sales & Marketing Management*, September 1995, p. 139.

29. Susan Bixler and Nancy Nix-Rice, *The New Professional Image*, Adams Media Corporation, 1997, p. 11–15; Barbara Pachter and Marjorie Brody, *Complete Business Etiquette Handbook* (New York: Prentice-Hall, 1995), p. 72.

30. Paul Galanti, "Talking Motivates—Communication Makes Things Happen," *Personal Selling Power*, November–December 1995, p. 88.

31. Susan Berkley, "Hone Your Sharpest Sales Weapon," *Sales & Field Force Automation*, July 1997, p. 24.

32. Barry L. Reece and Rhonda Brandt, *Effective Human Relations in Organizations*, 7th ed. (Boston: Houghton Mifflin, 1999), p. 293.

33. "Sales-Related Book Picked in Top Ten for Shaping America's Culture," *Des Moines Register*, April 3, 1985, p. 3.

34. L. B. Gschwandtner, "Mary Lou Retton," *Personal Selling Power*, 15th Anniversary Issue, 1995, p. 99.

35. Shad Helmstetter, *What to Say When You Talk to Yourself* (New York: Pocket Books, 1982), p. 72.

Sources for Boxed Features

a Robert McGarvey and Scott Smith, "Etiquette 101," *Training*, September 1993, p. 51; Ann C. Humphries, "Errors Steal Power from Power Lunch," *San Jose Mercury News*, November 4, 1990, p. 2; Erika Rasmusson, "Beyond Miss Manners," *Sales & Marketing Management*, August 1997, p. 84.

b Gerald A. Michaelson, "Build Relationships by 'Making Deposits,'" *Selling*, August 1997, p. 7.

Chapter 4

1. Leslie Scism, "Some Agents 'Churn' Life-Insurance Policies, Hurt Their Customers," *Wall Street Journal*, January 3, 1995, p. 1.

2. "Can Art Ryan Move 'The Rock'?" *Business Week*, August 5, 1996, p. 70; Leslie Scism, "Prudential Cleanup in Wake of Scandals Hurts Insurance Sales," *Wall Street Journal*, November 17, 1997, p. A-1; Deborah Lohse, "Suits Settled by Prudential for $62 Million," *Wall Street Journal*, February 16, 1999, p. C-1.

3. Vivian Arnold, B. June Schmidt, and Randall L. Wells, "Ethics Instruction in the Classrooms of Business Educators," *Delta Pi Epsilon Journal*, Vol. 38, No.4, Fall 1996, p. 185.

4. Stephen R. Covey, *The Seven Habits of Highly Effective People* (New York: Simon & Schuster, 1989), p. 18.

5. "Nearly Half of Workers Take Unethical Actions—Survey," *Des Moines Register*, April 7, 1997, p. 18B.

6. Patrick Smith, "You Have a Job, But How About a Life?" *Business Week*, November 16, 1998, p. 30.

7. Julia Lawlor, "Stepping Over the Line," *Sales & Marketing Management*, October, 1995, pp. 90–101.

8. Charles H. Melville, "Pistols at Dawn," *Agency Sales Magazine*, June 1997, pp. 10–11.

9. Dawn Marie Driscoll, "Don't Confuse Legal and Ethical Standards," *Business Week*, July–August 1996, p. 44.

10. Thomas J. Peters and Robert H. Waterman Jr., *In Search of Excellence* (New York: Harper & Row, 1982), p. 6.

11. Mary Ellen Egan, "Old Enough to Know Better," *Business Ethics*, January–February 1995, p. 19.

12. "Rivalries, Law Policies Take a Toll on Ethics," *Wall Street Journal*, March 22, 1990, p. B-1.

13. Corinne McLaughlin, "Workplace Spirituality Transforming Organizations from the Inside Out," *The Inner Edge*, August–September 1998, p. 26.

14. Michele Krebs, "All the Marketing Men," *Autoweek*, February 16, 1998, p. 11.

15. Dena Bunis, "Sex in Business: Scandal Generates Concerns," *Roanoke Times & World News*, August 12, 1990, p. D-9.

16. Fiona Gibb, "To Give or Not to Give," *Sales & Marketing Management*, September 1994, pp. 136–139.

17. Linda Corman, "The 13 Sins of Selling," *Selling*, September 1994, p. 77.

18. Steven Sack, "Watch the Words," *Sales & Marketing Management*, July 1, 1985, p. 56.

19. Ibid.

20. Rob Zeiger, "Sex, Sales & Stereotypes," *Sales & Marketing Management*, July 1995, pp. 52–53.

21. Barry L. Reece and Rhonda Brandt, *Effective Human Relations in Organization*, 7th ed. (Boston: Houghton Mifflin, 1999), p. 123.

22. Ron Willingham, *Integrity Selling* (New York: Doubleday, 1987), p. xv.

23. Ron Willingham, "Four Traits All Highly Successful Salespeople Have in Common," Phoenix, AZ, 1998 (audio tape presentation).

24. Carol Wheeler, "Getting the Edge on Ethics," *Executive Female*, May–June 1996, p. 47.

25. Ron Willingham, *Integrity Selling* (New York: Doubleday, 1987), p. xv.

26. Ibid.

27. Sharon Drew Morgan, *Selling with Integrity* (San Francisco, Berrett-Koehler, 1997), pp. 25–27.

28. Ibid., pp. 27–28.

29. Tom Peters, *Thriving on Chaos* (New York: Alfred A. Knopf, 1988), p. 521.

30. Gerhard Gschwandtner, "Lies and Deception in Selling," *Personal Selling Power*, 15th Anniversary Issue, 1995, p. 62.

31. Price Pritchett, *The Ethics of Excellence* (Dallas, TX: Pritchett & Associates, Inc., no copyright), p. 18.

32. Ibid., p. 14.

Sources for Boxed Features

a   Jeff Kemp, "Rules to Live by on and off the Field," *Imprimis*, July 1998, p. 3.

b   Glenn R. Simpson, "Foreign Deals Rely on Bribes, U.S. Contends," *Wall Street Journal*, February 23, 1999, p. A-3; Chitra Ragavans, "Let the Scandal Inquiries Begin, *U.S. News & World Report*, January 11, 1999, p. 33.

Chapter 5

1. *In Position: Product Selling Strategies* (Pasadena, CA: Intelecom).

2. Erick Schonfeld, "The Customized, Digitized, Have-It-Your-Economy," *Fortune*, September 28, 1998, p. 116.

3. Don Peppers and Martha Rogers, "Don't Drown Customers in Choices," *Selling Power*, November–December 1998, p. 24.

4. "Mutual Fund Investors Have 7,607 Choices," *San Jose Mercury News*, May 7, 1995, p. 50.

5. John Fellows, "A Decent Proposal.," *Personal Selling Power*, November–December 1995, p. 56.

6. Adapted from John Fellows, "A Decent Proposal." *Personal Selling Power*, November–December 1995, p. 56.

7. Joseph Conlin, "The Write Staff," *Sales & Marketing Management*, January 1998, p. 73.

8. Jim Morgan, "The Best Sales Reps Will Take on Their Bosses for You," *Purchasing*, November 7, 1996, pp. 50–52.

9. "97 Ways to Sell More in '96," *Selling*, January–February 1996, p. 53.

10. Robert Levering and Milton Moskowitz, *The 100 Best Companies to Work for in America* (New York: New American Library, 1993), p. 343; Ann Goodman, "In Patagonia," *Sky*, April 1999, pp. 107–111.

11. Interview with Michelle A. Reece, The Certified Medical Representatives Institute, Inc., Roanoke, VA, July 19, 1996.

12. Sarah Lorge, "Can ISO Certification Boost Sales?" *Sales & Marketing Management*, April 1998, p. 19.

13. Ian Gelenter, "Build Satisfaction with a Service Contract," *Selling*, May 1998, p. 7.

14. Robert Levering and Milton Moskowitz, *The 100 Best Companies to Work for in America* (New York: New York Library, 1993), p. 373.

15. Michael R. Williams and Jill S. Attaway, "Exploring Salespersons' Customer Orientation as a Mediator of Organizational Culture's Influence on Buyer–Seller Relationships," *Journal of Personal Selling & Sales Management*, Fall 1996, pp. 33–52.

16. "Grassroots Problem Solving," *Inc.*, March 1996, p. 92.

17. Alan Test, "The Scoop on the Competition," *Personal Selling Power*, November–December 1995, p. 38.

18. "Best Advice," *Sales & Marketing Management*, January 1990, p. 34.

19. "Power Tools," *Sales & Marketing Management*, March 1999, p. 50; Matt Purdue, "Networked With . . . Chip Herbert," *Sales & Field Force Automation*, January 1998, p. 18.

20. Andy Cohen, "Long-Distance Learning," *Sales & Marketing Management*, June 1996, p. 55.

21. "Group Selling," *Success*, May 1990, p. 29.

22. Robert McMath and Thom Forbes, "Look Before You Leap," *Entrepreneur*, April 1998, pp. 135–139.

23. Jerry Vass, "Ten Expensive Selling Errors," *Agency Sales Magazine*, July 1998, pp. 38–39.

24. Adopted from "Benchmarking the Sales Function," a report based on a study of 100 salespeople from small, medium, and large businesses, conducted by Ron Volper Group, White Plains, NY, 1996. Summary presented in the June 1997 issue of *Inc.*, p. 96.

Source for Boxed Feature

a   Edwin McDowell, "Ritz-Carlton's Keys to Good Service," *New York Times*, March 31, 1993, p. D-1; Jennifer Walsh, "The Pursuit of a Benchmark: How Nissan/Infiniti Developed Its Service Standard," *Multinational Business,* The Economist Intelligence Unit, New York,

NY, Winter 1992–93, pp. 24–25; "Ritz-Carlton Hotel Company Receives ASTD Corporate Award," *American Society for Training and Development*, Alexandria, VA, May 10, 1993, pp. 1–3.

Chapter 6

1. Ginger Conlon, "Time for a Shakeup," *Sales & Marketing*, October 1998, p. 40.
2. William M. Pride and O. C. Ferrell, *Marketing: Concepts and Strategies*, 10th ed. (Boston: Houghton Mifflin, 1997), p. 217.
3 D. Lee Carpenter, "Return on Innovation—the Power of Being Different," *Retailing Issues Letter*, May 1998, p. 3.
4. Teri Lammers, "The Open-Book Travel Analysis," *Inc.*, July 1992, p. 95.
5. Tom Peters, *Thriving on Chaos* (New York: Alfred A. Knopf, 1988), pp. 89–91.
6. Edward O. Welles, "Virtual Realities," *Inc.*, August 1993, pp. 50–58; "Evolution of the Professional Entrepreneur," *The State of Small Business 1997* (published in *Inc.* magazine), p. 52.
7. Carl K. Clayton, "Sell Quality, Service, Your Company, Yourself," *Personal Selling Power*, January–February 1990, p. 47.
8. J. Thomas Russell and W. Ronald Lane, *Kleppner's Advertising Procedure* (Englewood Cliffs, NJ: Prentice-Hall, 1996), pp. 46–47.
9. Andy Cohen, "Starting Over," *Sales & Marketing Management*, September 1995, pp. 40–41.
10. Lawrence Ladin, "Selling Innovation: Tips for Commercial Success," *Wall Street Journal*, March 20, 1995, p. A-14.
11. "Sales Support Is Northwestern's No. 1 Policy," *Sales & Marketing Management*, June 1987, p. 66.
12. Michael D. Mondello, "Naming Your Price," *Inc.*, July 1992, p. 82.
13. Michael Treacy, "You Need a Value Discipline—But Which One?" *Fortune*, April 17, 1995, p. 195.
14. Robert Shulman and Richard Miniter, "Discounting is No Bargain," *Wall Street Journal*, December 7, 1998, p. A-30.
15. Albert D. Bates, "Pricing for Profit," *Retailing Issues Letter*, Vol. II, No. 8, September 1990, p. 2.

16. Chad Kaydo, "Jumping on a Hot Market," *Sales & Marketing Management*, October 1998, p. 15.
17. Thomas Petzinger Jr., "This Former Salesman Treats Development Like a Sacred Cow," *Wall Street Journal*, September 29, 1995, p. B-1.
18. Malcolm Fleschner and Charles Lee Browne, "Value Sells," *Selling Power*, March 1996, pp. 48–52.
19. "How to Win Customers and Influence Profits," *Norwest Business Advantage*, January–February 1998, p. 9.
20. Malcolm Fleschner, "We Want to Be the Biggest Small Company Around," *Selling Power*, April 1999, p. 48–52.
21. Adapted from a model described in "Marketing Success through Differentiation—of Anything," *Harvard Business Review*, January–February, 1980.
22. Tom Peters, *Thriving on Chaos*, (New York: Alfred A. Knopf, 1988), p. 92.
23. Joanna Johnson, "A New Perspective on Marketing," *Construction Dimensions*, April 1990, p. 14.
24. Ted Levitt, *Marketing Imagination* (New York: Free Press, 1983), p. 80.
25. Ibid., p. 81.
26. Thomas A. Stewart, "A Satisfied Customer Isn't Enough," *Fortune*, July 21, 1997, pp. 112–113.
27. "Business Bulletin," *Wall Street Journal*, September 24, 1998, p. A-1.
28. Madalyn Callahan, "Tending the Sales Relationship," *Training and Development*, December 1992, p. 32.
29. Larry Wilson, *Changing the Game: The New Way to Sell* (New York: Simon & Schuster, 1987), p. 200.
30. Ibid., p. 201.
31. "Marilyn Carlson Nelson, Carlson Companies CEO," *Fast Company*, November 1998, p. 108.
32. Ted Levitt, *Marketing Imagination* (New York: Free Press, 1983), p. 84.
33. Francy Blackwood, "The Concept that Sells," *Selling*, March 1995, pp. 34–36.
34. Sue Shellenbarger, "The New Pace of Work Makes Taking a Break for Child Care Scarier," *Wall Street Journal*, May 19, 1999, p. B-1.
35. William C. Symonds, "Build a Better Mousetrap Is no Claptrap," *Business Week*, February 1, 1999, p. 47.
36. Stan Davis and Christopher Meyer, *Blur: The Speed of Change in the Connected Economy* (New York: Addison-Wesley, 1998), p. 47.

Sources for Boxed Features

a   Adapted from discussion in Leonard L. Berry, A. Parasuraman, and Valerie A. Zeithaml, "The Service-Quality Puzzle," *Business Horizons*, September–October 1988, pp. 35–43; Robert Kreitner, *Management*, 5th ed. (Boston: Houghton Mifflin, 1992), pp. 613–14.
b   Rhonda M. Abrams, "Problem for Pros: Knowing How Much to Charge," *The Des Moines Register*, January 26, 1998, p. 2-B.

Case Credits

Francy Blackwood, "The Concept that Sells," *Selling*, March 1995, pp. 34–36; *Systems Furniture Overview*, Steelcase Incorporated, November 1995, pp. 48–50.

Chapter 7

1. *Step by Step: The Buying Process* (Pasadena, CA: Intelecom).
2. "Six Selling Rules," *Training and Development Journal*, March 1988, p. 40.
3. Michael Hammer and James Champy, *Reengineering the Corporation: A Manifest for Business Revolution* (New York: Harper Business, 1993), p. 18.
4. Tom Peters and Nancy Austin, *A Passion for Excellence* (New York: Random House, 1985), p. 71.
5. "How Well Do You Know Your Customers?" *Sales & Field Force Automation*, January 1999, p. 141.
6. Stan Davis and Christopher Meyer, *Blur: The Speed of Change in the Connected Economy* (New York: Addison-Wesley, 1998), p. 16.
7. Stanley Brown, "This is No Psyche Job," *Sales & Marketing Management*, March 1995, p. 32.
8. "Belonging Satisfies Basic Human Need," *Menninger Letter*, August 1995, p. 6.
9. Amy Dunkin, "Buoying Women Investors," *Business Week*, February 27, 1995, p. 126.
10. Ibid.
11. Barry L. Reece and Rhonda Brandt, *Effective Human Relations in Organizations*, 7th ed. (Boston: Houghton Mifflin, 1999), p. 180.
12. William M. Pride and O. C. Ferrell, *Marketing*, 10th ed. (Boston: Houghton Mifflin, 1997), pp. 143–148.
13. Douglas A. Bernstein, Alison Clark-

Stewart, Edward J. Roy, and Christopher D. Wickens, *Psychology*, 4th ed. (Boston: Houghton Mifflin, 1997), p. 570.

14. William F. Schoell and Joseph P. Guillinan, *Marketing* (Boston: Allyn & Bacon, 1992), p. 164.

15. "Met Life Targets the Rich," *Des Moines Register*, June 5, 1993, p. 10.

16. Douglas A. Bernstein, Alison Clark-Stewart, Edward J. Roy, and Christopher D. Wickens, *Psychology*, 4th ed. (Boston: Houghton Mifflin, 1997), p. 21.

17. Craig Calhoun, Donald Light, and Suzanne Keller, *Sociology*, 6th ed. (New York: McGraw-Hill, 1994), p. 8.

18. George A. Torres, "Culture—A Matter of Semantics," *NSPST Newspost*, Winter 1997, pp. 14–16.

19. William M. Pride and O. C. Ferrell, *Marketing: Concepts and Strategies*, 10th ed. (Boston: Houghton Mifflin, 1997), p. 139.

20. "Focusing with Al Ries," *Sales & Field Force Automation*, July 1997, p. 120.

21. Phil Kline, "Dominant Buying Motive Is the Result of Strong Emotions," *Marketing News*, May 24, 1993, p. 4.

22. Stan Davis and Christopher Meyer, *Blur: The Speed of Change in the Connected Economy* (New York: Addison-Wesley, 1998), p. 52.

23. Hal Lancaster, "It's Time to Stop Promoting Yourself and Start Listening," *Wall Street Journal*, June, 1997, p. B-1.

24. "A Selling Guide to Bentonville," *Selling*, April 1994, p. 70.

25. Bill Sharfman, "The Power of Information and Quality," *Autoweek*, February 1996, p. 97.

26. Stuart F. Brown, "How Great Machines Are Born," *Fortune*, March 1, 1999, pp. 164J–164R.

27. "The Front Lines of Business," *Selling*, February 1997, p. 16.

28. "Consultative Selling," *Training*, May 1998, p. 80.

29. Tom Peters and Nancy Austin, *A Passion for Excellence* (New York: Random House, 1985), p. 45.

30. Michael Hammer and Steven A. Stanton, "The Power of Reflection," *Fortune*, November 24, 1997, pp. 291–294.

31. Jack Falvey, "How the Best Get Better," *Selling*, April 1998, p. 13.

32. "How Well Do You Know Your Customers?" *Sales & Field Force Automation*, January 1999 (supplement to the January issue).

Sources for Boxed Features

a Adopted from Jeffery Ball, "But How Does It Make You Feel?" *Wall Street Journal*, May 3, 1999, pp. B-1 and B-4; Joseph E. DeMatio, "2001 Chrysler PT Cruiser," *Automobile Magazine*, June 1999, pp. 76–82.

b Patricia 'cia' Rodemann, "Selling to the New Demographics," *Wall Paper*, February 1996, pp. 22–25; Barry L. Reece and Rhonda Brandt, *Effective Human Relations in Organizations* (Boston: Houghton Mifflin, 1999), pp. 388–389; Marlene L. Rossman, *Multicultural Marketing* (New York: AMCOM, 1994).

Chapter 8

1. ACT! Demonstration video, Symantec Corporation, Cupertino, CA, 1994; Stephen H. Wildstrom, "Can Your Rolodex Do This?" *Business Week*, May 27, 1996, p. 18.

2. Don Peppers, Martha Rogers, and Bob Dorf, "Is Your Company Ready for One-to-One Marketing?" *Harvard Business Review*, January–February 1999, pp. 151–154.

3. Gerhard Gschwandtner, "Thoughts to Sell By," *Personal Selling Power*, 15th Anniversary Issue, 1995, p. 122.

4. Dorothy Leeds, "Where Are the Real Decision Makers?" *Personal Selling Power*, March 1993, p. 62.

5. Gerhard Gschwandtner, "The Funnel Concept," *Personal Selling Power*, May–June 1993, p. 22.

6. Bob Donath, "Fire Your Big Customers? Maybe You Should," *Marketing News*, June 21, 1999, p. 9.

7. Gerhard Gschwandtner, "The Funnel Concept," *Personal Selling Power*, 15th Anniversary Issue, 1995, p. 23.

8. Zig Ziglar, *Ziglar on Selling* (New York: Ballantine Books, 1991), pp. 70–71.

9. Paul S. Goldner, "The Ten Commandments of Prospecting," *Selling*, April 1997, p. 12.

10. Roger Pell, "It's a Fact . . . Qualified Referrals Bring More Sales to Your Company," *Personal Selling Power*, January–February 1990, p. 30.

11. Thomas Petzinger Jr., "Selling a 'Killer App' Is a Far Tougher Job than Dreaming It Up," *Wall Street Journal*, April 3, 1998, p. B-1.

12. "How Significant Are Trade Shows to Your Marketing Efforts?" *Sales & Marketing Management*, August 1992, p. 22.

13. "Advertising Scores High in Lead Generation," *Sales & Marketing Management*, April 1994, p. 25.

14. Jan Gelman, "What Are You Waiting For?" *Selling*, July–August 1996, pp. 32–39.

15. David Haskin, "Simplified Selling," *Success Selling*, May 1997, p. 68.

16. Alan Test, "Cold Calls Are Hot," *Agency Sales Magazine*, September 1995, p. 28.

17. Maxwell Maltz, Dan S. Kennedy, William T. Brooks, Matt Oechsli, Jeff Paul, and Pamela Yellen, *Zero-Resistance Selling* (Paramus, NJ: Prentice-Hall, 1998), p. 167.

18. Anne Baber and Lynne Waymon, "No-Nonsense Networking," *Your Company*, Summer 1993, p. 34.

19. Michele Marchetti, "Do You Have the Knack for Networking?" *Sales & Marketing Management*, January 1996, p. 30.

20. Maxwell Maltz, Dan S. Kennedy, William T. Brooks, Matt Oechsli, Jeff Paul, and Pamela Yellen, *Zero-Resistance Selling* (Paramus, NJ: Prentice-Hall, 1998), pp. 179–180.

21. "Hitting It Out of the Ballpark" *Inc.*, February 1996, p. 93.

22. Chad Kaydo, "Teach Your Clients Well," *Sales & Marketing Management*, April 1998, p. 83.

23. William F. Schoell and Joseph P. Guiltinan, *Marketing* (Boston: Allyn & Bacon 1992), p. 29.

24. Tracy Emerick, "The Trouble with Leads," *Sales & Marketing Management*, December 1992, p. 58.

25. Harvey Mackay, *Swim with the Sharks* (New York: William Morrow, 1988), pp. 43, 44.

26. Tricia Campbell, "Managing Leads," *Sales & Marketing Management*, December 1998, p. 38.

27. Geoffrey Brewer, "Selling to Senior Executives," *Sales & Marketing Management*, July 1996, p. 43.

28. Gerald A. Michaelson, "Selling to the Top," *Selling*, October 1998, p. 7.

29. "Prospecting Is Where the Gold Is," *Institutional Distribution*, May 15, 1990, pp. 70–72.

30. Jack Stack, "A Passion for Forecasting," *Inc.*, 1997, pp. 37–38.

Sources for Boxed Features

a   Sarah Lorge, "The Best Way to Prospect," *Sales & Marketing Management*, January 1998, p. 80.

b   Barbara Siskind, *Seminars to Build Your Business* (North Vancouver, BC: Self-Counsel Press, 1998); pp. 9–12; Sheldon Gordon, "Punch Up Your Profits," *Profit*, May 1999, pp. 17–22.

Chapter 9

1. *Going the Distance: The Consultative Sales Presentation* (Pasadena, CA: Intelecom).
2. Francy Blackwood, "From Salesperson to Consultant: The Race Will Go to Those with Vision," *Selling*, July–August 1995, p. 55.
3. Regina Eisman, "Justifying Your Incentive Program," *Sales & Marketing Management*, April 1993, p. 52.
4. Malcolm Fleschner, "Too Busy to Buy," *Selling Power*, March 1999, p. 36.
5. Malcolm Fleschner, "Anatomy of a Sale," *Selling Power*, April 1998, p. 76.
6. "Set the Agenda," *Personal Selling Power*, May–June, 1995, p. 79.
7. David Greising, "The Newest Wrinkle in Buying Suits," *Business Week*, April 16, 1990, p. 96.
8. Sandy Miller, "Hot Topics & Trends," *Selling Power*, April 1998, p. 73.
9. Dawn R. Detter-Schmelz and Rosemary Ramsey, "A Conceptualization of the Functions and Roles of Formalized Selling and Buying Teams," *Journal of Personal Selling & Sales Management*, Spring 1995, pp. 47, 48.
10. Charles Butler, "Why the Bad Rap?" *Sales & Marketing Management*, June 1996, p. 66.
11. Henry Canaday, "Teaming with Sales," *Selling Power*, May 1998, pp. 94–102.
12. James F. O'Hara, "Successful Selling to Buying Committees," *Selling*, February 1998, p. 8.
13. "97 Ways to Sell More in '96," *Selling*, January–February 1996, p. 50.
14. Alex Markels, "Memo 4/8/97, FYI: Messages Inundate Offices," *Wall Street Journal*, April 7, 1997, p. B-1.
15. Stan Davis and Christopher Meyer, *Blur: The Speed of Change in the Connected Economy* (New York: Addison-Wesley, 1998), pp. 167, 237.
16. Francy Blackwood, "Did You Sell $5 Million Last Year?" *Selling*, October 1995, pp. 44–53.

17. John Fellows, "Your Foot in the Door," *Selling Power*, March 1996, pp. 64–65.
18. Adapted from Art Sobczak, "Please, Call Me Back!" *Selling*, March 1999, p. 12.
19. Ibid.
20. Susan Bixler and Nancy Nix-Rice, *The New Professional Image* (Holbrook, MA: Adams Media Corporation, 1997), p. 3.
21. Melissa Campanelli, "Sound the Alarm," *Sales & Marketing Management*, December 1994, pp. 20–25.
22. James E. Lukaszewski and P. Ridgeway, "To Put Your Best Foot Forward, Start by Taking These 21 Simple Steps," *Sales & Marketing Management*, June 1990, p. 84.
23. Abner Littel, "Selling to Women Revs up Car Sales," *Personal Selling Power*, July–August, 1990, p. 50.
24. "Six Great Upselling Questions," *Personal Selling Power*, April 1993, p. 44.
25. Art Sobczak, "Dealing with the 'Bad-Timing' Brush-Off," *Selling Power*, January–February 1999, p. 14.
26. "Confront Call Reluctance," *Personal Selling Power*, September 1995, p. 46.
27. Alan Farnham, "Are You Smart Enough to Keep Your Job?" *Fortune*, January 15, 1996, pp. 34–42.
28 "The Disappointment Trap," *Selling Power*, January–February 1999, p. 14.

Sources for Boxed Features

a   Jay Winchester, "Ripe for Change," *Sales & Marketing Management*, August 1998, p. 81.

b   Barry L. Reece and Rhonda Brandt, *Effective Human Relations in Organizations*, 7th ed. (Boston: Houghton Mifflin, 1999), pp. 52–54; Charlene Marmer Solomon, "Global Operations Demand that HR Rethink Diversity," *Personnel Journal*, July 1994, p. 44; Lennie Copeland and Lewis Griggs, *Going International* (New York: Random House, 1985), p. 54.

Chapter 10

1. Betty Wiesendanger, "Reading His Customers Right," *Selling*, September 1996, p. 60.
2. Ibid., pp. 60–62.
3. "97 Ways to Sell More in '96," *Selling*, January–February 1996, p. 50.

4. Thomas Petzinger Jr., "At Deere They Know a Mad Scientist May Be a Firm's Biggest Asset," *Wall Street Journal*, July 14, 1995, p. B-1.
5. James Champy, "Selling to Tomorrow's Customer," *Sales & Marketing Management*, March 1999, p. 28.
6. Kevin Daley, "Socrates on a Sales Call," *Marketing News*, May 6, 1996, p. 4.
7. Gail Gabriell, "Dialogue Selling," *Success*, May 1993, p. 34.
8. "Questions Are the Answer," *Selling Power Sales Achiever*, January–February 1999, p. 8.
9. Dorothy Leeds, "The Art of Asking Questions," *Training and Development*, January 1993, p. 58.
10. "How to Ask the Right Questions," *Agency Sales Magazine*, June 1990, p. 64.
11. "Getting into the Habit," *Sales & Marketing Management*, May 1996, p. 68.
12. Cynthia Crossen, "The Crucial Question for the Noisy Times May Just Be: Huh?" *Wall Street Journal*, July 10, 1997, p. A-1.
13. Joseph A. DeVito, *The Interpersonal Communication Book*, 4th ed. (New York: Harper & Row, 1986), p. 52.
14. Barry L. Reece and Rhonda Brandt, *Effective Human Relations in Organizations*, 7th ed. (Boston: Houghton Mifflin, 1999), p. 45.
15. Matthew McKay, Martha Davis, and Patrick Fanning, *Messages: The Communications Skills Book* (Oakland, CA: New Harbinger, 1995), p. 15.
16. Robert A. Lupe Jr., "Improving Your Listening Ability," *Supervisory Management*, June 1992, p. 7.
17. Ginger Trumfio, "Ready! Set! Sell!" *Sales & Marketing Management*, February 1994, p. 84.
18. "Presentation-Wise, We've Lost Our Tails," *Sales & Field Force Automation*, July 1999, p. 4.
19. Robert Frank, "Frito-Lay Devours Snack-Food Business," *Wall Street Journal*, October 27, 1995, p. B-1.
20. Janny Scott, "Gotcha! Americans Are Finding It Harder and Harder to Escape the Weapons of Persuasion," *Roanoke Times & World News*, August 8, 1993, p. A-1.
21. "Eye Contact: the Overlooked Presentation Tool," *Sales & Marketing Management*, December 1998, p. 80.
22. Richard Whitely, "Do Selling and

Quality Mix?" *Sales & Marketing Management*, October 1993, p. 70.

23. Stephanie G. Sherman and V. Clayton Sherman, *Make Yourself Memorable* (New York: AMACOM, 1996), pp. 58–59.

24. Art Sobczak, "How to Sell with Sizzle Stories," *Selling*, November 1998, p. 12.

25. Thomas A. Stewart, "The Cunning Plots of Leadership," *Fortune*, September 7, 1998, pp. 165–66.

26. "97 Ways to Sell More in '96," *Selling*, January–February 1996, p. 52.

27. Michele Marchetti, "That's the Craziest Thing I Ever Heard," *Sales & Marketing Management*, November 1995, p. 77.

28. Chad Kaydo, "Lights! Camera! Sales!" *Sales & Marketing Management*, February 1998, p. 111.

29. Neil Rachman and John DeVinventis, *Rethinking the Sales Force* (New York: McGrawHill, 1999), p. 17.

Sources for Boxed Features

a   Neil Rackham, *Spin Selling* (New York: McGraw-Hill, 1988), pp. 67–89; "Tip of the Month," *Selling*, July 1998, p. 1; Dana Ray, "United They Sell," *Selling Power*, November–December 1998, pp. 19–21.

Chapter 11

1. Thomas Petzinger Jr. "Selling Golden Voices, An Entrepreneur Gets a Lesson in Technology," *Wall Street Journal*, February 19, 1999, p. B-1.

2. Larry Tuck, "Presentations that Cut through the Information Clutter," *Sales & Field Force Automation*, June 1999, p. 86.

3. Ken Taylor, "Help Your Audience Visualize Your Message," *Selling*, April 1998, p. 10.

4. Lambeth Hochwald, "Simplify," *Sales & Marketing Management*, June 1998, pp. 66–67.

5. David Peoples, *Selling to the Top* (New York: John Wiley & Sons, 1993), p. 197.

6. Tom Hopkins, "Demonstrating Property to Your Clients," *Real Estate Professional*, January–February 1996, p. 70.

7. Steve Heimoff, "Taking the Road Less Traveled," *Wine Spectator*, October 31, 1990, pp. 67–70; Jeff Morgan, "Geyser Peak's Turnaround," *Wine Spectator*, November 15, 1995, pp. 37–40.

8. Brandon Mitchener, "Mercedes Dealers Offer New Kind of Test Drive," *Wall Street Journal*, March 26, 1998, p. B-8.

9. "Country-Wide Creativity," *Selling Power*, April 1998, p. 58.

10. Douglas A. Bernstein, Alison Clarke-Stewart, Edward J. Roy, and Christopher D. Wilkens, *Psychology*, 4th ed. (Boston: Houghton Mifflin, 1997), p. 327.

11. Harold H. Bloomfield and Robert K. Cooper, *The Power of 5* (Emmaus, PA: Rodale Press, 1995), p. 196.

12. Merrie Spaeth, "Prop up Your Speaking Skills," *Wall Street Journal*, July 1, 1996, p. A-14.

13. Joseph B. White, "New Ergonomic Chairs Battle to Save the Backs of Workers, for Big Bucks," *Wall Street Journal*, June 8, 1999, p. B-4B.

14. Lambeth Hochwald, "Simplify," *Sales & Marketing Management*, June 1998, pp. 65–66.

15. "Seeing Is Believing," *Inc.*, July 1990, p. 95.

16. Ginger Trumfio, "Ready! Set! Sell!" *Sales & Marketing Management*, February 1995, pp. 82–84.

17. David Ranii, "Dermabond's Debut Disappoints," *News & Observer*, July 31, 1999, p. D-1.

18. Dana Ray, "Presentations," *Selling Power Source Book*, 1999, p. 66.

19. "Hugging the Curves of the Info Highway," *Sales & Field Force Automation*, July 1999, p. 12.

20. Gerald L. Manning and Jack W. Linge, *Selling-Today.Com* (Upper Saddle River, NJ: Prentice-Hall, 1998), p. 34.

21. Malcolm Campbell, "All in a Days Presentation," *Selling Power*, November–December 1998, pp. 91–93.

22. Francy Blackwood, "Present Your Best Case," *Selling*, January–February 1995, pp. 26–28.

23. "The Presentation Paper Trail," *Sales & Marketing Management*, March 1995, p. 49.

Sources for Boxed Features

a   Marc Hequet, "Giving Good Feedback," *Training*, September 1994, p. 74; Molly McGinn, "On Your Own," *News & Observer*, June 27, 1999; Polly Labarre, "Unit of One," *Fast Company*, June 1999, p. 103.

b   Michael Chylewski, "Memorable Sale," *Selling Power*, January–February 1999, p. 22.

Chapter 12

1. *Breaking through: Dealing with Buyer Resistance* (Pasadena, CA: Intelecom).

2. Hal Lancaster, "You Have to Negotiate for Everything in Life, So Get Good at It," *Wall Street Journal*, January 27, 1998, p. B-1.

3. Ron Willingham, *Integrity Selling* (Garden City, NJ: Doubleday, 1987), p. 100.

4. Tom Reiley, "Step up Your Negotiating Success," *Personal Selling Power*, April 1990, p. 40.

5. "Powers of Persuasion," *Fortune*, October 12, 1998, p.162

6. Gregg Crawford, "Let's Negotiate," *Sales & Marketing Management*, November 1995, pp. 28–29.

7. "The Readers Forum," *Personal Selling Power*, January–February 1993, p. 12.

8. Sarah Mahoney, "Competing against a Long-Term Supplier," *Selling*, June 1998, p. 10.

9. John O'Toole, "Inside the Mind of a Buyer," *Selling*, October 1994, p. 75.

10. Homer Smith, "How to Cope with Buyers Who Are Trained in Negotiation," *Personal Selling Power*, September 1988, p. 37.

11. Ibid.

12. Robert Adler, Benson Rosen, and Elliot Silverstein, "Thrust and Parry," *Training & Development*, March 1996, p. 47.

13. Homer Smith, "How to Cope with Buyers Who Are Trained in Negotiation," *Personal Selling Power*, September 1988, p. 37.

14. Robert Adler, Benson Rosen, and Elliot Silverstein, "Thrust and Parry," *Training & Development*, March 1996, p. 44.

15. Joseph Conlin, "Negotiating Their Way to the Top," *Sales & Marketing Management*, April 1996, p. 58.

16. "Salespeople Can Be Their Own Worst Enemies," *Competitive Advantage*, 1996, p. 5.

17. Same Deep and Lyle Sussman, *Close the Deal: Smart Moves for Selling* (Reading, MA: Perseus Books, 1999), p. 225.

18. Roland M. Sandell, "Five Sure-Fire Methods to Overcome Objections to Price," *American Salesman*, October 1976, p. 38.

19. Alan Test, "Answering the Price Objection," *Agency Sales Magazine*, April 1996, pp. 56–57.

20. Joseph Conlin, "Negotiating Their

Way to the Top," *Sales & Marketing Management*, April 1996, p. 62.

21. D. Forbes Ley, "The Stall—A Decision Not to Make a Decision," *Selling Advantage* (Malvern, PA: Progressive Business Publications, 1995), pp. 1–2.

22. Steve Albrecht, "Added-Value Negotiating," *Training & Development*, July 1996, pp. 5–6.

23. John R. Graham, "Do You Know What Your Customer's Expect? *Selling*, January 1998, pp. 8–9.

24. Thomas C. Keiser, "Negotiating with a Customer You Can't Afford to Lose," *Harvard Business Review*, November–December 1988, p. 31.

25. Ibid.

26. Jeff Keller, "Objections? No Problem," *Selling Power*, September 1996, pp. 44–45.

27. Adapted from Nanci McCann, "Irate over Rates," *Selling*, July–August 1996, p. 25.

28. Tony Allessandra and Jim Catheart, "Turn Objections into Sales."

Sources for Boxed Features

a   Hal Lancaster, "You Have to Negotiate for Everything in Life, So get Good at It," *Wall Street Journal*, January 27, 1998, p. B-1; Amy Lindgren, "Want Raise? Don't Daydream; Polish Your Negotiating Skills," *Des Moines Register*, April 26, 1998, p. 1L.

b   Sarah Lubman, "Round and Round," *Wall Street Journal*, December 10, 1993, p. R-3; Urban C. Lehner, "Native Intelligence," *Wall Street Journal*, December 10, 1993, p. R-16; "Getting to Yes, Chinese Style," *Sales & Marketing Management*, July 1996, pp. 44–45; Sam Deep and Lyle Sussman, *Close the Deal* (Reading, MA: Perseus Books, 1999), pp. 279–81.

Chapter 13

1. Linda Corman, "The Slow and Steady Ryder Racer," *Selling*, January–February, 1996, pp. 56–58.

2. "How to Prosper in the New Economy," *Personal Selling Power*, January–February 1993, p. 52.

3. Andy Cohen, "Are Your Reps Afraid to Close?" *Sales & Marketing Management*, March 1996, p. 43.

4. Zig Ziglar, *Secrets of Closing the Sale* (New York: Fleming H. Revelle, 1984), p. 51.

5. Erika Rasmusson, "Dealing with the Big Guys," *Sales & Marketing Management*, November 1997, p. 16.

6. Graham Denton, "The Single Biggest Closing Mistake," Graham Denton Skills Center (Web page) May 4, 1999, p. 1.

7. "The Closing Moment," *Personal Selling*, October 1995, p. 48.

8. Len D'Innocenzo, "How to Close a Sale," *Personal Selling Power*, March 1990, p. 23.

9. James F. O'Hara, "The Silent Barriers to Closing the Sale," *Selling*, May 1997, p. 9.

10. Kerry L. Johnson, *Sales Magic* (New York: William Morrow, 1994), pp. 192–193.

11. "Salestalk," *Sales & Marketing Management*, May 1990, p. 116.

12. "Selling Tips," *Selling*, May 1999, p. 13.

13. Mel Silberman, *Active Training* (New York: Maxwell Macmillan Canada, 1990), pp. 96–99.

14. Larry Wilson, *Changing the Game: The New Way to Sell* (New York: Simon & Schuster, 1987), p. 104.

15. Dian Hymer, "How Can I Cure Buyer's Remorse," *Purchasing a New Home* (Web page), January 16, 1998, p. 1.

16. Gerhard Gschwandtner, "Dealing with Disappoinment," *Selling Power*, March 1998, p. 10.

17. Jack Falvey, "Adventures in No-Man's Land," *Selling*, April 1996, pp. 83–84.

Sources for Boxed Features

a   *Training Guide: Ask for the Order and Get It* (Des Moines, IA: Creative Media Division, Batten Batten Hudson and Swab, 1977), p. 3.

b   Linda Corman, "The Best Salesman Who Ever Lived," *Selling*, June 1994, pp. 44–53; Gerald L. Manning and Barry L. Reece, *Selling Today* (Boston: Allyn & Bacon, 1984), pp. 64–65 (personal interview with Ben Feldman).

c   "Top This! What to Do When a Prospect Has a Lower Quote from Your Competition," *Professional Selling*, July 10, 1998, p. 4.

Chapter 14

1. Susan Greco, "Five Ways to Blow a Sale," *Inc.*, September 1996, p. 101.

2. Bob Johnson, "Loyalty Lessons from

the Pros," *Customer Support Management*, July–August 1999, p. 115.

3. Ibid.

4. Theodore Levitt, *The Marketing Imagination* (New York: Macmillan, 1983), pp. 117–118.

5. Hal Lancaster, "Giving Good Service, Never an Easy Task, Is Getting a Lot Harder," *Wall Street Journal*, June 9, 1998, p. B-1.

6. Geoffrey Brewer, "The Customer Stops Here," *Sales & Marketing Management*, March 1998, pp. 31–32.

7. "Why Customers Leave," *Sales & Marketing Management*, May 1998, p. 86; Tom Peters, *The Circle of Innovation* (New York: Vintage Books, 1997), pp. 138–39.

8. Tom Peters, *The Circle of Innovation* (New York: Vintage Books, 1997), p. 464.

9. Bill Gates, *Business @ The Speed of Thought* (New York: Warner Books, 1999), p. 67.

10. Sarah Mahoney, "Look at Sales through Your Customer's Eyes," *Selling*, March 1997, pp. 1–2.

11. Mack Hanan, *Consultative Selling*, 3rd ed. (New York: AMACOM, 1985), pp. 121–22.

12. Bob Johnson, "Loyalty Lesson from the Pros," *Customer Support Management*, July–August 1999, p. 116.

13. Jim Dey, "Who Is Your Customer?" *Customer Support Management*, July–August 1999, pp. 63–70.

14. Bill Gates, *Business @ The Speed of Thought* (New York: Warner Books, 1999), p. 67.

15. Ibid., p. 218.

16. Melinda Ligos, "The Joys of Cross-Selling," *Sales & Marketing Management*, August 1998, p. 75.

17. Chad Kaydo, "An Unlikely Sales Ally," *Sales & Marketing Management*, January 1999, p. 69.

18. Sally J. Silberman, "An Eye for Finance," *Sales & Marketing Management*, April 1996, p. 26.

19. "Customer Care—Phone Feedback," *Inc.*, June 1993, p. 30.

20. Andrea Nierenberg, "Eight Ways to Stay Top of Mind," *Selling*, April 1998, p. 7.

21. "Inspirations from Michele," *Inspiring Solutions*, February 1999, p. 3.

22. Bob Johnson, "Loyalty Lessons from the Pros," *Customer Support Management*, July–August 1999, p. 115.

23. Bradley E. Wesner, "From Complaint to Opportunity," *Selling Power*, May 1996, p. 62.

24. Sam Deep and Lyle Sussman, *Close*

the Deal: Smart Moves for Selling* (Reading, MA: Perseus Books 1999), p. 252.

25. Bradley E. Wesner, "From Complaint to Opportunity," *Selling Power*, May 1996, p. 62.

26. Gerald A. Michaelson, "When Things Go Wrong, Make It Right," *Selling*, March 1997, p. 12.

27. Michael Abrams and Matthew Paese, "Wining and Dining the Whiners," *Sales & Marketing Management*, February 1993, p. 73.

28. Adopted from Ginger Trumfio, "Anything for a Client," *Sales & Marketing Management*, June 1994, pp. 102–5; Michael Traecy and Fred Wiersma, *Discipline of Market Leaders* (Reading, MA: Addison-Wesley 1995), pp. 144–52.

Sources for Boxed Features

a   "Relationships with Customers Must Be Job Number 1," *Food-Service Distributor*, July 1989, p. 74; Joan O. Fredericks and James M. Salter II, "Beyond Customer Satisfaction," *Management Review*, May 1995, pp. 29–32.

b   Tom Peters, "Creating the Lifetime Customer," *Insight*, January 1988, p. 29.

c   Byran Ziegler, "Your Business Card Can Be Powerful Tool," *The Des Moines Register*, August 2, 1999, p. 17-B.

Chapter 15

1. Dana Ray, "The Secret of Success," *Personal Selling Power*, November–December 1995, pp. 80–83.

2. "Sales Agency Management #17," *Agency Sales Magazine*, September 1990, p. 56.

3. "Data Trends," *Selling*, June 1999, p. 1.

4. Barry J. Farber, "Not Enough Hours in the Day," *Sales & Marketing Management*, July 1995, pp. 28–29.

5. Ed Brown, "Stephen Covey's New One-Day Seminar," *Fortune*, January 1999, p. 138.

6. "You Said It," *Sales & Marketing Management*, July 1990, p. 24.

7. Robert H. Tardiff, "Control Your Time," *Personal Selling Power*, May–June 1995, pp. 72–73.

8. Hyrum W. Smith, *The 10 Natural Laws of Successful Time and Life Management* (New York: Warner Books, 1994), p. 108.

9. "Voice-Mail: Helping to Increase Executive Efficiency," *Black Enterprise*, March 1990, p. 35.

10. Thomas J. Wall, "The ABCs of EDI," *SMT*, June 1996, pp. 30–32.

11. Michele Marchetti, "Territories: For Optimal Performance, Segment Your Customer Base by Industry," *Sales & Marketing Management*, December 1998, p. 35.

12. Ken Liebeskind, "Where Is Everyone?" *Selling Power*, March 1998, p. 35.

13. Rich Bohn, "Territory Management: Mapping Better Sales," *Sales & Field Force Automation*, April 1998, p. 76.

14. Nancy Arnott, "Brake out of the Grid!" *Sales & Marketing Management*, July 1994, p. 68–75.

15. Arnold A. Lazarus and Clifford N. Lazarus, *The 60-Second Shrink* (San Luis Obispo, California: Impact Publishers, 1997), p. 86; Howard I. Glazer, *Getting in Touch with Stress Management* (American Telephone and Telegraph, 1988), p. 2.

16. Barry L. Reece and Rhonda Brandt, *Effective Human Relations in Organizations*, 7th ed. (Boston: Houghton Mifflin, 1999), p. 370.

17. David Shenk, "Data Smog," *Perdid*, Spring 1999, pp. 5–7.

18. "Optimism Slows Job Stress," *Menninger Letter*, May 1993, pp. 1, 2.

19. Sandra Lotz Fisher, "Stress — Will You Cope or Crack?" *Selling*, May 1996, p. 31.

20. Geoffrey Brewer, "Person-to-Person," *Sales & Marketing Management*, December 1995, p. 29.

21. Louis E. Kopolow, "Plain Talk About . . . Handling Stress," *Agency Sales Magazine*, August 1990, p. 59.

Sources for Boxed Features

a   Michael Adams, "Family Matters," *Sales & Marketing Management*, March 1998, pp. 61–65.

b   Sandra Lotz Fisher, "Stress — Will You Cope or Crack?" *Selling*, May 1996, p. 29.

c   Kenneth Blanchard, D. W. Edington, and Marjorie Blanchard, *The One-Minute Manager Gets Fit* (New York: William Morrow, 1986), pp. 25–28.

Chapter 16

1. Nikhil Deogun and Martha Brannigan, "NationsBank's McColl Masters the Soft Sell," *Wall Street Journal*, September 2, 1997, p. B-1.

2. David W. Merrill and Roger H. Reid, *Personal Styles and Effective Performance* (Radnor, PA: Chilton Book, 1981), p. 1.

3. Robert J. Sternberg, *Thinking Styles* (New York: Cambridge University Press, 1997), p. 8.

4. Robert M. Hecht, *Office Systems*, February 1990, p. 26.

5. Tony Alessandra and Michael J. O'Connor, *People Smart* (LaJolla, CA: Keynote Publishing, 1990), p. 10.

6. The dominance factor was described in an early book by William M. Marston, *The Emotions of Normal People* (New York: Harcourt, 1928). Research conducted by Rolfe LaForge and Robert F. Suczek resulted in the development of the Interpersonal Checklist (ICL) that features a dominant–submissive scale. A person who receives a high score on the ICL tends to lead, persuade, and control others. The Interpersonal Identity Profile, developed by David W. Merrill and James W. Taylor, features a factor called "assertiveness." Persons classified as being high in assertiveness tend to have strong opinions, make quick decisions, and be directive when dealing with people. Persons classified as being low in assertiveness tend to voice moderate opinions, make thoughtful decisions, and be supportive when dealing with others.

7. David W. Johnson, *Reaching Out — Interpersonal Effectiveness and Self-Actualization*, 2nd ed. (Englewood Cliffs, NJ: Prentice-Hall, 1981), p. 44.

8. The research conducted by LaForge and Suczek resulted in identification of the hostile–loving continuum, which is similar to the sociability continuum. Their Interpersonal Checklist features this scale. L. L. Thurstone and T. G. Thurstone developed the Thurstone Temperament Schedule, which provides an assessment of a "sociable" factor. Persons with high scores in this area enjoy the company of others and make friends easily. The Interpersonal Identity Profile developed by Merrill and Taylor contains an objectivity continuum. A person with low objectivity is seen as attention seeking, involved with the feelings of others, informal, and casual in social relationships. A person who is high in objectivity appears to be somewhat indifferent toward the feelings of others. This

person is formal in social relationships.

9. Charles Margerison, *How to Assess Your Managerial Style* (New York: AMACOM, A Division of American Management Association, 1979), p. 49.

10. Pierce J. Howard and Jane M. Howard, "Buddy, Can You Paradigm?" *Training & Development*, September 1995, p. 31.

11. Sam Deep and Lyle Sussman, *Close the Deal* (Reading, MA: Perseus Books, 1999), p. 157.

12. Len D'innocenzo and Jack Cullen, "Chameleon Management," *Personal Selling Power*, January–February 1995, p. 61.

13. Rod Nichols, "How to Sell to Different Personality Types," *Personal Selling Power*, November–December 1992, p. 46.

14. Stuart Atkins, *How to Get the Most from Styles-Based Training* (Beverly Hills, CA: Stuart Atkins, 1996), p. 1.

15. Robert Bolton and Dorothy Grover Bolton, *People Styles at Work* (New York: AMACOM, 1996), p. 65.

16. John Emery, "Mastering Vital Steps," *Business Outlook*, November 3, 1986, p. 14.

17. Tony Alessandra and Michael J. O'Connor, *People Smart* (LaJolla, CA: Keynote Publishing, 1990), p. 15.

18. Nina Munk, "How Levi's Trashed a Great American Brand," *Fortune*, April 12, 1999, p. 85.

19. Martha Brannigan, "If 'Chain-Saw Al' Is Listening In, Can't Sunbeam's Board Hang Up?" *Wall Street Journal*, August 5, 1998, p. B-1.

20. Stuart Atkins, *How to Get the Most from Styles-Based Training* (Beverly Hills, CA: Stuart Atkins, 1996), p. 3.

21. Ron Willingham, *Integrity Selling* (New York: Doubleday, 1987) pp. 21–23.

22. Eric F. Douglas, *Straight Talk* (Palo Alto, CA: Davies-Black Publishing, 1998), p. 92.

23. Ron Willingham, *Integrity Selling* (New York: Doubleday, 1987), pp. 21–23.

24. David W. Merrill and Roger H. Reid, *Personal Styles and Effective Performance* (Radnor, PA: Chilton Book, 1981), pp. 134, 135.

25. Stuart Atkins, *The Name of the Game* (Beverly Hills, CA: Ellis & Stewart, 1981), p. 51.

26. Chris Lee, "What's Your Style," *Training*, May 1991, p. 28.

Sources for Boxed Features

a   Stuart Atkins, *LIFO Personality Digest* (Beverly Hills, CA: Stuart Atkins, 1991), p. 126; *High Performance Selling* (Beverly Hills, CA: Stuart Atkins), pp. 1–10.

b   Roger Wenschlag, *The Versatile Salesperson* (New York: John Wiley & Sons, 1989), pp. 165–71; Malcolm Fleschner, "The Adaptability Factor," *Selling Power*, January–February 1997, pp. 54–56; Rod Nichols, "How to Sell to Different Personality Types," *Personal Selling Power*, November–December 1992, pp. 46–47; David M. Merrill and Roger Reid, *Personal Styles and Effective Performance* (Radnor, PA: Chilton Book, 1981), p. 2; Tony Alessandra, *People Smarts* (San Diego, CA: (Pfeiffer & Company, 1994), p. 55.

Chapter 17

1. William Keenan Jr., "These 10 Managers Show They Have What It Takes to Lead and Succeed," *Sales & Marketing Management*, August 1995, pp. 38–39.

2. Gilbert A. Churchill Jr. and J. Paul Peter, *Marketing*, 2nd ed. (New York: Irwin McGraw-Hill, 1998), p. 515.

3. Jack Falvey, "Fly by Night, Sell by Day," *Wall Street Journal*, June 9, 1997, p. A-18.

4. William Keenan Jr., "Death of the Sales Manager," *Sales & Marketing Management*, April 1998, pp. 72–79.

5. Sally J. Silberman, "Troubling Transitions," *Sales & Marketing Management*, February 1996, pp. 20–21.

6. Alan J. Dubinsky, Francis J. Yammarino, Marvin A. Jolson, and William D. Strangler, "Transformational Leadership: An Initial Investigation in Sales Management," *Journal of Personal Selling & Sales Management*, Spring 1995, pp. 17–29.

7. These dimensions are described in Edwin A. Fleischman, *Manual for Leadership Opinion Questionnaire* (Chicago: Science Research Associates, 1960), p. 3.

8. Phillip Gelman, "The Good Sales Manager," *Personal Selling Power*, January–February, 1993, p. 56.

9. Alison Furnham, "Expect Good Work and You'll Get It," *Executive Female*, September–October 14, 1996, pp. 13–16.

10. Jack Falvey, "The Absolute Basics of

Sales Force Management," *Sales & Marketing Management*, August 1990, p. 8.

11. Sarah Lorge, "In the Box," *Sales & Marketing Management*, April 1998, p. 15.

12. Ken Blanchard, "3 Secrets of the One Minute Manager," *Personal Selling Power*, March 1993, p. 48.

13. Kenneth R. Phillips, "The Achilles' Heel of Coaching," *Training & Development*, March 1998, p. 41.

14. Ibid., pp. 41–44.

15. Barry J. Farber, "On the Lookout," *Sales & Marketing Management*, October 1995, pp. 34–35.

16. Richard J. Mirabile, "The Power of Job Analysis," *Training*, April 1990, p. 70.

17. Paul Tulenko, "The Key Role of Selling," *San Jose Mercury News*, August 23, 1992, PC-1.

18. William Keenan Jr., "Who Has the Right Stuff?" *Sales & Marketing Management*, August 1993, p. 28.

19. Ibid., p. 28.

20. Gerhard Gschwandtner, "A Jewel of a Company," *Personal Selling Power*, March 1995, p. 17.

21. Haidee Allerton, "News You Can Use," *Training & Development*, March 1996, p. 9.

22. Alan J. Dubinsky, Francis J. Yammarino, Marvin A. Jolson, and William D. Spangler, "Transformational Leadership: An Initial Investigation in Sales Management," *Journal of Personal Selling & Sales Management*, Spring 1995, p. 27.

23. Jack Falvey, "The Care and Feeding of New Salespeople," *Sales & Marketing Management*, February 1990, p. 22.

24. Barry L. Reece and Rhonda Brandt, *Effective Human Relations in Organizations*, 7th ed. (Boston: Houghton Mifflin, 1999), p. 174.

25. Ibid., p. 153.

26. Alfie Kohn, "Why Incentive Plans Cannot Work," *Harvard Business Review*, September–October 1993, pp. 58–59.

27. "Selling with Sales Contest," *Sales & Marketing Management*, June 1995, p. 35.

28. Nora Wood, "What Motivates Best," *Sales & Marketing Management*, September 1998, pp. 71–78.

29. Andy Cohen, "The Right Stuff," *Sales & Marketing Management*, January 1999, p. 15.

30. "Labor Letter," *Wall Street Journal*, March 29, 1994, p. 1.

31. Ibid.
32. Dawn R. Deeter-Schmelz and Rosemary Ramsey, "A Conceptualization of the Functions and Roles of Formalized Selling and Buying Teams," *Journal of Personal Selling & Sales Management*, Spring 1995, p. 58.
33. William Keenan Jr, "Sales Compensation 1996–1997," Supplement to *Selling*, February 1997.
34. "Point Incentive Sales Programs," *SBR Update*, Vol. I, No. 4.
35. Roger Ricklefs, "Enterprise," *Wall Street Journal*, March 6, 1990, p. B-1.
36. Donald W. Jackson Jr., John L. Schlacter, and William G. Wolfe, "Examining the Bases Utilized for Evaluating Salespeople's Performance," *Journal of Personal Selling & Sales Management*, February 1995, p. 57.
37. "Survey of Sales Evaluation Process—What Works, What Doesn't," *Selling Power*, September 1999, p. 115.
38. Lisa Holton, "Look Who's in on Your Performance Review," *Selling*, January–February 1995, pp. 47–55; Barry L. Reece and Rhonda Brandt, *Effective Human Relations in Organizations* (Boston: Houghton Mifflin, 1999), p. 200; "Customer Ratings Are Misleading," *Selling*, November 1996, p. 1.

Sources for Boxed Features

[a] Douglas J. Dalrymple and William L. Cron, *Sales Management: Concepts and Cases* (New York: John Wiley & Sons, 1998), pp. 344–47; William Keenan, "Time Is Everything," *Sales & Management*, August 1993, p. 61.

[b] Kerry Rottenberger-Murtha, "How to Play above the Rim," *Sales & Marketing Management*, September 1993, pp. 28–29.

Appendix 1

1. Kim Clark, "Why It Pays to Quit," *U.S. News & World Report*, November 1, 1999, pp. 74–92.
2. Joel Palmer, "Job Hunting on the Web," *Des Moines Business Record*, October 18, 1999, pp. 22–23.

A

added-value negotiating A negotiating process where both the seller and the customer search for mutual value so both feel more comfortable after a sale.

active listening The process of sending back to the person what you as a listener think the individual meant, both in terms of content and in terms of feelings. It involves taking into consideration both verbal and nonverbal signals.

approach The first contact with the prospect, either face-to-face or by telephone. The approach has three objectives: to build rapport with the prospect, to capture the person's full attention, and to generate interest in the product you are selling.

assumption close After the salesperson identifies a genuine need, presents solutions in terms of buyer benefits, conducts an effective sales demonstration, and negotiates buyer resistance satisfactorily, the assumption is that the prospect has already bought the product. The closing activity is based on the assumption that a buying decision has already been made.

B

body language A form of nonverbal communication that has been defined as "messages without words" and "silent messages."

bridge statement A transitional phrase that connects a statement of features with a statement of benefits. This method permits customers to connect the features of your product to the benefits they will receive.

buyer action theory The five mental steps—attention, interest, desire, conviction, and action—that lead to a buying decision. This is a widely accepted theory in selling, advertising, and display that explains how customers buy.

buyer's remorse Feelings of regret, fear, or anxiety that a buyer may feel after placing an order.

buyer resolution theory A selling theory that recognizes a purchase will be made only after the prospect has made five buying decisions involving specific affirmative responses to the following items: need, product, source, price, and time.

buying conditions Those circumstances that must be available or fulfilled before the sale can be closed.

buying motives An aroused need, drive, or desire that initiates the sequence of events that may lead to a purchase.

C

call report A written summary that provides information on a sales call to people in the sales organization so that follow-up action will be taken when necessary.

caveat emptor A philosophy that states, "Let the buyer beware." The buyer is expected to examine the product and presentation carefully. Once the transaction is concluded, the business relationship ends for all practical purposes.

character Your personal standards of behavior, including your honesty and integrity. Your character is based on your internal values and the resulting judgments you make about what is right and what is wrong.

closing clue An indication, either verbal or nonverbal, that the prospect is preparing to make a buying decision.

coaching An interpersonal process between a sales manager and a salesperson in which the manager helps the salesperson improve performance in a specific area.

cold calling A method of prospecting in which the salesperson selects a group of people who may or may not be actual prospects and then calls on each one.

combination close With the combination close, the salesperson tries to use two or more closing methods at the same time.

commodity A product that is nearly identical or appears to be the same as competing products in the customer's mind.

communication-style bias A state of mind we often experience when we have contact with another person whose communication style is different from our own.

compensation plans Pay plans for salespeople that combine direct monetary pay and indirect monetary payments such as paid vacations, pensions, and insurance plans.

confirmation questions A type of question used throughout the sales presentation to find out if the message is getting through to the prospect. It checks both the prospect's level of understanding and the prospect's agreement with the presentation's claims.

confirmation step Reassuring the customer after the sale has been closed, pointing out that he has made the correct decision. This may involve describing the satisfaction of owning the product.

consideration Sales managers displaying consideration are more likely to have relationships with salespeople that are characterized by mutual trust, respect for the salesperson's ideas, and consideration for their feelings.

consultative-style selling An approach to personal selling that is an extension of the marketing concept. Emphasis is placed on need identification, need satisfaction, and the building of a relationship that results in repeat business.

cross selling Selling products to an established customer that are not directly related to products the customer has already bought.

culture The arts, beliefs, institutions, transmitted behavior patterns, and thoughts of a community or population.

customer service All those activities enhancing or facilitating the sale and use of a product or service, including suggestion selling, delivery and installation, assistance with warranty or service contract, securing credit arrangements, and making postsale courtesy calls.

customer service representative These people process reservations, accept orders by phone or by other means, deliver products, handle customer complaints, provide technical assistance, and assist salespeople.

customer strategy A carefully conceived plan that will result in maximum customer responsiveness.

D

demonstration A sales and marketing technique that adds sensory appeal to the product. It attracts the customer's attention, stimulates interest, and creates desire.

detail salesperson A salesperson representing a manufacturer, whose primary goal is to develop goodwill and stimulate demand for a product or product line. This person usually assists the customer by improving the customer's ability to sell the product.

direct appeal close Involves simply asking for the order in a straightforward manner. It is the most direct closing approach.

direct denial Involves refuting prospect's opinion or belief. The direct denial of a problem is considered a high-risk method of negotiating buyer resistance.

Director style A communication style that displays the following characteristics: appears to be businesslike, displays a serious attitude, and voices strong opinions.

dominant buying motive The buying motive that has the greatest influence on a customer's buying decision.

dominance Reflects the tendency to influence or exert one's will over others in a relationship. Each of us falls somewhere on this continuum.

double win The view that "if I help you win, I win too."

E

electronic commerce The use of information technology to facilitate the exchange of goods and services between buyers and sellers. For the sales organization, it can support both external activities such as personal selling, and internal activities such as customer service.

emotional buying motives Those motives that prompt the prospect to act as a result of an appeal to some sentiment or passion.

emotional intelligence The capacity for recognizing our own feelings and those of others, for motivating ourselves, and for managing emotions well in ourselves and in our relationships.

emotional links The connectors that link the salesperson's message to the customer's internal emotions and increase the chance of closing a sale—for example, quality improvement, on-time delivery, service, innovation.

Emotive style A communication style that displays the following characteristics: appears to be quite active, takes the social initiative in most cases, likes to encourage informality, and expresses emotional opinions.

entry-level sales representative Anyone who is learning about the company's products, services, and policies, as well as proven sales techniques, in preparation for a sales assignment.

esteem needs The desire to feel worthy in the eyes of others, to develop a sense of personal worth and adequacy or a feeling of competence and importance.

ethics Rules of conduct used to determine what is good or bad. They are moral principles or values concerned with what ought to be done—a person's adherence to honesty and fairness.

expected product Everything that represents the customer's minimal expectations.

external motivation Action (taken by another person) that involves rewards or other forms of reinforcement that cause the worker to behave in ways to ensure receipt of the reward.

extranet This is a private Internet site that enables several companies to securely share information and conduct business.

F

field salesperson A salesperson employed by a manufacturer who handles well-established products that require a minimum of creative selling. The position usually does not require a high degree of technical knowledge.

G

generic product Describes only the basic substantive product being sold.

group influences Buyer behavior is influenced by the people around us. Group influences are the forces that other people exert on buying behavior.

I

indirect denial Often used when the prospect's concern is completely valid, or at least accurate to a large degree. The salesperson bends a little and acknowledges that the prospect is at least partially correct.

information-gathering questions Questions used to collect certain basic information from the prospect. These questions help the salesperson to acquire facts about the prospect that

may reveal the person's need for the product or service.

informative presentation Emphasizes factual information that is often taken from technical reports, company-prepared sales literature, or written testimonials from people who have used the product.

inside salesperson A salesperson employed by a wholesaler who solicits orders over the telephone. In addition to extensive product knowledge, the inside salesperson must be skilled in customer relations, merchandising, and suggestion selling.

integrity Part of your character. It is what you have when your behavior is in accordance with your professed standards and personal code of moral values.

intermediate sales representative A salesperson who has broad knowledge of the company's products and services and sells in a specifically assigned territory. She maintains contact with established customers and develops new prospects.

internal motivation An intrinsic reward that occurs when a duty or task is performed.

interpersonal value Win-win relationship building with the customer that results from keeping that person's best interest always at the forefront.

M

marketing concept A belief that the business firm should dedicate all its policies, planning, and operation to the satisfaction of the customer; a belief that the final result of all business activity should be to earn a profit by satisfying the customer.

marketing mix The combination of elements (product, promotion, place, and price) that creates continuing customer satisfaction for a business.

multicall sales presentations A standard practice in some industries where products are complex and buying decisions are made by more than one person. The purpose of the first call is to collect and analyze certain basic information that is used to develop a specific proposal.

multiple options close With the multiple options close, the salesperson gives the prospect several options to consider and tries to assess the prospect's degree of interest in each.

N

need discovery The salesperson establishing two-way communication by asking appropriate questions and listening carefully to the customer's responses.

need-satisfaction theory A selling theory that positions the salesperson as a consultant whose objective is to solve buying problems for customers. This theory is consistent with the marketing concept of discovering customer needs and then providing satisfaction, while at the same time making a profit.

negotiation Working to reach an agreement that is mutually satisfactory to both buyer and seller.

networking Networking is the practice of making and using contacts. It involves people meeting people and profiting from the connection.

O

organizational culture A collection of beliefs, behaviors, and work patterns held in common by people employed by a specific firm.

outside salesperson A salesperson, employed by a wholesaler, who must have knowledge of many products and be able to serve as a consultant to the customer on product or service applications. This position usually requires an in-depth understanding of the customer's operation.

P

partnering A strategically developed, high-quality relationship that focuses on solving the customer's buying problem.

patronage buying motives A motive that causes the prospect to buy a product from one particular company rather than another. Typical patronage buying motives include superior service, attractive decor, product selection, and competence of the salesperson.

perception A process whereby we receive stimuli (information) through our five senses and then assign meaning to them.

personal selling Involves person-to-person communication with a prospect. It is a process of developing relationships; discovering customer needs; matching appropriate products with these needs; and communicating benefits through informing, reminding, or persuading.

personal selling philosophy Involves three things: full acceptance of the marketing concept, developing an appreciation for the expanding role of personal selling in our competitive national and international markets, and assuming the role of problem solver or partner in helping customers to make complex buying decisions.

persuasion The act of presenting product appeals so as to influence the prospect's beliefs, attitudes, or behavior.

persuasive presentation A sales strategy that influences the prospect's beliefs, attitudes, or behavior; and encourages buyer action.

physiological needs Primary needs or physical needs, including the need for food, water, sleep, clothing, and shelter.

portfolio A portable case or loose-leaf binder containing a wide variety of sales-supporting materials. It is used to add visual life to the sales message and to prove claims.

potential product Refers to what may remain to be done, that is, what is possible.

preapproach Activities that precede the actual sales call and set the stage for a personalized sales approach, tailored to the specific needs of the prospect. This involves the planning necessary for the actual meeting with a prospect.

presentation strategy A well-conceived plan that includes three prescriptions: establishing objectives for the sales presentation; preparing the presale presentation plan needed to meet these objectives; and renewing one's commitment to providing outstanding customer service.

probing questions Help the salesperson to uncover the prospect's perceptions or opinions.

product One element of the marketing mix. The term product should be broadly interpreted to encompass goods, services, and ideas.

product benefit A feature that provides the customer with personal advantage or gain. This usually answers the question, "How will the customer benefit from owning or using the product?"

product buying motives Reasons that cause the prospect to buy one particular product brand or label over another. Typical product buying motives include brand preference, quality preference, price preference, and design or engineering preference.

product configuration If the customer has complex buying needs, then the salesperson may have to bring together many different parts of the company's product mix in order to develop a custom-fitted solution. The product selection process is often referred to as product configuration.

product development Testing, modifying, and retesting an idea for a product several times before offering it to the customer.

product feature Anything that a customer can feel, see, taste, smell, or measure to answer the question, "What is it?" Features include technical facts about such aspects as craftsmanship, durability, design, and economy of operation.

product life cycle Stages of a product from the time it is first introduced to the market until it is taken off the market, including the stages of introduction, growth, maturity, and decline.

product positioning Refers to decisions, activities, and communication strategies that are directed toward trying to create and maintain a firm's intended product concept in the customer's mind.

product strategy A well-conceived plan that emphasizes acquiring extensive product knowledge, learning to select and communicate appropriate product benefits that will appeal to the customer, and positioning the product.

promotional allowance A price reduction given to a customer who participates in an advertising or sales support program.

prospect Someone who has three basic qualifications. First, the person must have a need for the product or service. Second, the individual must be able to afford the purchase. Third, the person must be authorized to purchase the product.

prospect base A list of current customers and potential customers.

prospecting A systematic process of identifying potential customers.

psychic income Consists of factors that provide psychological rewards; helps to satisfy these needs and motivates us to achieve higher levels of performance.

Q

qualifying   Examining the prospect list to identify the people who are most apt to buy a product.

quality control   The evaluation or testing of products against established standards. This has important sales appeal when used by the salesperson to convince a prospect of a product's quality.

quantifying the solution   The process of determining if a sales proposal adds value. Quantifying the solution is especially important in situations where the purchase represents a major buying decision.

quantity discount   A price reduction made to encourage a larger volume purchase than would otherwise be expected.

R

rational buying motives   Prompt the prospect to act because of an appeal to the prospect's reason or better judgment; include profit potential, quality, and availability of technical assistance. Generally these result from an objective review of available information.

reciprocity   A mutual exchange of benefits, as when a firm buys products from its own customers.

reference group   Two or more people who have well-established interpersonal communications and tend to influence the values, attitudes, and buying behaviors of one another. They act as a point of comparison and a source of information for a prospective buyer.

referral   A prospect who has been recommended by a current customer or by someone who is familiar with the product.

Reflective style   A communication style that displays the following characteristics: controls emotional expression, displays a preference for orderliness, tends to express measured opinions, and seems difficult to get to know.

relationship selling   Salespeople who have adopted relationship selling working hard to build and nourish long-term partnerships. They rely on a personal, customized approach to each customer.

relationship strategy   A well-thought-out plan for establishing, building, and maintaining quality relationships.

reminder presentation   Sometimes called the reinforcement presentation. This assumes that the prospect has already been involved in an informative or persuasive presentation. The customer understands at least the basic product features and buyer benefits.

retail salesperson   Salesperson who is employed at the retail level to help prospects solve buying problems. This person is usually involved in selling higher priced, technical, and specialty retail products.

role   A set of characteristics and expected social behaviors based on the expectations of others. All the roles we assume may influence our buying behavior.

routing   The procedure used to determine which customers and prospects will be visited during a certain period of time.

S

sales automation   A term used to describe those technologies used to improve communications in a sales organization and improve customer responsiveness. These activities are used to improve the productivity of the sales force and the sales support personnel.

sales call plan   A plan developed with information taken from the routing and scheduling plan. The primary purpose of the plan is to ensure efficient and effective account coverage.

sales call reluctance   The fear of making contact with the customer.

sales engineer   A person who must have detailed and precise technical knowledge and the ability to discuss the technical aspects of his products. He sometimes introduces new products that represent a breakthrough in technology.

sales forecast   Outlines expected sales for a specific product or service to a specific target group over a specific period of time.

sales manager   The person who is responsible for hiring, training, and directing sales personnel.

satisfactions   The positive benefits that customers seek when making a purchase. Satisfactions arise from the product itself, from the company that makes or distributes the product, and from the salesperson who sells and services the product.

security needs   These needs represent our desire to be free from danger and uncertainty.

self-actualization   The need for self-fulfillment; a full tapping of one's potential to meet a goal; the need to be everything one is capable of being. This is one of the needs in Maslow's hierarchy.

self-image   A set of ideas, attitudes, and feelings you have about yourself that influences the way you relate to others.

self-talk   An effort to override past negative mental programming by erasing or replacing it with conscious, positive new directions. It is one way to get rid of barriers to goal achievement.

senior sales representative   A salesperson at the highest nonsupervisory level of selling responsibility. She is completely familiar with the company's products, services, and policies; usually has years of experience; and is assigned to major accounts and territories.

six-step presentation plan   Preparation involving consideration of those activities that will take place during the sales presentation.

sociability   Reflects the amount of control one exerts over emotional expressiveness. People who are high in sociability tend to express their feelings freely, while people who are low on this continuum tend to control their feelings.

social class   A group of people who are similar in income, wealth, educational background, and occupational prestige.

social needs   Needs that reflect a person's desire for affection, identification with a group, and approval from others.

special concession close   Offers the buyer something extra for acting immediately.

stall   Resistance related to time. A stall usually means the customer does not yet perceive the benefits of buying now.

strategic alliance   These alliances are achieved by teaming up with another company whose products or services fit well with your own.

strategic market plan   Takes into consideration all the major functional areas of the business that must be coordinated, such as production, promotion, finance, and personnel.

strategies   The things that salespeople do as the result of pre-call planning to ensure they call on the right people, at the right time, and with the right tactics to achieve positive results.

stress The response of the body or mind to demands on it, in the form of either physiological or psychological strain.

structure Sales managers clearly defining their own duties and those of the sales staff. They assume an active role in directing their subordinates.

style flexing The deliberate attempt to adjust one's communication style to accommodate the needs of the other person.

subculture Within many cultures the groups whose members share ideals and beliefs that differ from those held by the wider society of which they are a part.

suggestion selling The process of suggesting merchandise or services that are related to the main item being sold to the customer. This is an important form of customer service.

summary-confirmation questions Questions used to clarify and confirm buying conditions.

summary-of-benefits close Involves summarizing the most important buyer benefits, reemphasizing the benefits that will help bring about a favorable decision.

superior benefit A benefit that will, in most cases, outweigh the customer's specific concern.

Supportive style A communication style that displays the following characteristics: appears quiet and reserved, listens attentively to other people, tends to avoid the use of power, and makes decisions in a thoughtful and deliberate manner.

T

tactics Techniques, practices, or methods salespeople use during face-to-face interactions with customers.

target market A well-defined set of present and potential customers that an organization attempts to serve.

telemarketing The practice of marketing goods and services through telephone contact.

telesales The process of using the telephone to acquire information about the customer, determine needs, suggest solutions, negotiate buyer resistance, close the sale, and service the sale.

territory The geographic area where prospects and customers reside.

time-period pricing Adjusting up or down during specific times to spur or acknowledge changes in demand.

transactional selling Type of selling focused on getting an order, without consideration of building long-term customer relationships.

trial close A closing attempt made at an opportune time during the sales presentation to encourage the customer to reveal readiness or unwillingness to buy.

trial offer Involves giving the prospect an opportunity to try the product without making a purchase commitment.

U

unconscious expectations Certain views concerning appropriate dress.

V

value-added strategies Adding value to a product with a cluster of intangibles such as better trained salespeople, increased levels of courtesy, dependable product deliveries, better service after the sale, and innovations that truly improve the product's value in the customer's eyes.

value-added product Product that exists when salespeople offer the customer more than they expect.

W

wardrobe engineering Combining the elements of psychology, fashion, sociology, and art into clothing selection.

Web site A collection of Web pages maintained by a single person or organization. It is accessible to anyone with a computer and a modem.

written proposals A specific plan of action based on the facts, assumptions, and supporting documentation included in the sales presentation. Written proposals vary in terms of format and content.

Chapter 2

Fig. 2.1: Source: *Selling*, February 1997, p. 4.

Chapter 3

Fig. 3.3: Adapted from a list of losers, winners, and double winners, in *The Double Win* by Denis Waitley. **Fig. 3.4:** Source: Moravian Study of Nonverbal Communication.

Chapter 5

Fig. 5.2: Courtesy of RYKO Manufacturing Co. **Fig. 5.3:** Courtesy of Gear for Sports International, Inc.

Chapter 15

Fig. 15.4: Used with the permission of 3M Corp.

Advertisement Credits:

p. 19: Courtesy of Cushman & Wakefield, Inc. **p. 21:** Courtesy of SalesLogix Corporation. **p. 42:** Xerox Corporation, Customer Education Services, © 1999. Designed by dkn Marketing, California. **p. 65:** Courtesy of Pivotal. **p. 72:** Courtesy of CMSI. **p. 74:** Courtesy of Minnesota Mutual. **p. 99:** Courtesy of Doubletree Hotels. **p. 106:** Courtesy of Rich's Products. **p. 109:** Courtesy of the Idaho Potato Commission. **p. 119:** Courtesy of Lexus. **p. 125:** Courtesy of RYKO Manufacturing Co. **p. 128:** Courtesy of ALMACO. **p. 133:** Courtesy of General Mills. **p. 148:** Courtesy of Goldmine Software Corporation. **p. 150:** Courtesy of the Intel Corporation. **p. 151:** Courtesy of Environmental Systems Research Institute. **p. 153:** Courtesy of Driscoll Strawberry Associates, Inc. **p. 172:** Courtesy of Thomas Publishing Company. **p. 175:** Courtesy of American Business Information. **p. 179:** Courtesy of CogniTech Corp. **p. 180:** Courtesy of CogniTech Corp. **p. 181:** Courtesy of CogniTech Corp. **p. 193:** Courtesy of Proxima. **p. 225:** Courtesy of Texas Instruments. **p. 232:** Courtesy of the Microsoft Corporation. **p. 246:** Courtesy of Bell Helicopter Textron. **p. 254:** Reprinted by permission from Microsoft Corporation. **p. 255:** Courtesy of Iowa Realty, and affiliate of Mid American Services. **p. 257:** Courtesy of Mitsubishi Electronics America, Inc. **p. 297:** Courtesy of Beth Manning, Jody Sprock Interiors & Associates. **p. 308:** Courtesy of Sewell Automotive Companies. **p. 381:** Courtesy of Metal Decor, A division of Associates Engraving Co., Inc. **p. 385:** Courtesy of ComShare, Inc.

Photo Credits:

p. 4: AP/World Wide Photos. **p. 6:** © The New Yorker Collection 1998. Robert Mankoff from cartoonbank.com. All Rights Reserved. **p. 7:** VCG/FPG. **p. 9:** PhotoEdit. **p. 12:** Sepp Seitz/Woodfin Camp & Associates. **p. 13:** John Colletti/Allyn & Bacon. **p. 18:** John Colletti/Allyn & Bacon. **p. 28:** Stanley Marcus Consultants. **p. 28:** Aaron Strong/Liaison Agency, Inc. **p. 34:** SuperStock, Inc. **p. 35:** Page Chichester. **p. 36:** John Curtis/Offshoot. **p. 40:** Frank Siteman/Omni-Photo Communications. **p. 41:** Chris Ryan/Masterfile Corporation. **p. 51:** SuperStock, Inc. **p. 52:** Romilly Lockyer/The Image Bank. **p. 56:** Terry Vine/Stone. **p. 58:** SuperStock, Inc. **p. 61:** FPG International LLC. **p. 63:** Fisher/Thatcher/Stone. **p. 66:** FPG International LLC. **p. 78:** Steve Niedorf/The Image Bank. **p. 80:** Reprinted by permission of United Feature Syndicate, Inc. **p. 80:** Steve Gottlieb/FPG International. **p. 84:** FPG International LLC. **p. 93:** Jose L. Pelaez/The Stock Market. **p. 101:** Index Stock Imagery, Inc. **p. 103:** Courtesy of Xerox. **p. 104:** Tony Freeman/PhotoEdit. **p. 107:** Michael Rosenfield/Tony Stone Images. **p. 108:** Copyright 1982, G.B. Trudeau. Reprinted with permission of Universal Press Syndicate. All rights reserved. **p. 118:** Courtesy of Walden Paddlers, Inc. **p. 126:** © 2000 Edgar Argo. **p. 127:** AP/World Wide Photos. **p. 129:** Rene Macura/AP/World Wide Photos. **p. 131:** Bob Daemrich/Stock, Boston. **p. 145:** SuperStock, Inc. **p. 152:** FPG International LLC. **p. 154:** FPG International LLC. **p. 155:** © The New Yorker Collection 1998. Marisa Acocella from cartoonbank.com. All Rights Reserved. **p. 174:** Jose L. Pelaez/The Stock Market. **p. 182:** Govin-Sorel/Stone.

p. 194: David Joel/Tony Stone Images. **p. 195:** Masterfile Corporation. **p. 198:** SuperStock, Inc. **p. 201:** From the Wall Street Journal by permission of Cartoon Features Syndicate. **p. 201:** Mike Malyszko/FPG International. **p. 205:** Monkmeyer Press. **p. 216:** Jose Pelaez/The Stock Market. **p. 219:** Reprinted with special permission of King Features Syndicate. **p. 220:** Jeffrey Shaw. **p. 224:** Jose L. Pelaez/The Stock Market. **p. 226:** Institutional Distribution Magazine. **p. 227:** Copyright © Cathy Guisewite. Reprinted with permission of Universal Press Syndicate. All rights reserved. **p. 233:** Index Stock Photography, Inc. **p. 243:** Richard Pasley, Stock, Boston. **p. 248:** SuperStock, Inc. **p. 250:** Pictor . **p. 250:** Courtesy of Rich Tennant. **p. 252:** SuperStock, Inc. **p. 253:** Index Stock Imagery, Inc. **p. 264:** SuperStock, Inc. **p. 266:** Reprinted by permission of Roz Chast. **p. 271:** Courtesy of Acclivus Corporation. **p. 273:** Tony May/Stone. **p. 277:** Sam Sargent/Gamma-Liaison, Inc. **p. 286:** Reid Ken/FPG International LLC. **p. 294:** Tim Pannell/Sharpshooters. **p. 298:** Timothy Shonnard/Stone. **p. 299:** Kevin Altman. **p. 307:** SuperStock, Inc. **p. 309:** AP/World Wide Photos. **p. 311:** Alessandra & Associates. **p. 315:** SuperStock, Inc. **p. 316:** Toby Talbot/AP/World Wide Photos. **p. 330:** Donn Young Photography, Inc. **p. 331:** © 2000 Edgar Argo. **p. 332:** SuperStock, Inc. **p. 335:** Michael Paras/Photographic Resources. **p. 336:** Jose L. Pelaez/The Stock Market. **p. 338:** Stephen Agricola/Stock, Boston. **p. 340:** Dana White/PhotoEdit. **p. 343:** David Mautson/Stone. **p. 351:** Bruce Ayres/Stone. **p. 357:** Harpo Production/AP/World Wide Photos. **p. 359:** Steven Starr/Stock, Boston. **p. 359:** Courtesy of the White House Photo Office. **p. 362:** SuperStock, Inc. **p. 366:** Charles Thatcher/Stone. **p. 373:** FPG International LLC. **p. 374:** Michael Newman/PhotoEdit. **p. 376:** Tom McCarthy/Unicorn Stock Photos. **p. 379:** Fisher/Thatcher/Stone. **p. 382:** Jose L. Pelaez/The Stock Market. **p. 417:** Park Inn International. **p. 421:** Park Inn International. **p. 423:** Park Inn International. **p. 429:** Park Inn International. **p. 431:** Park Inn International. **p. 433:** Park Inn International.

Note: Boldface pages locate figures; italicized pages locate tables.

Note: Boldface pages locate figures; italicized pages locate tables.

Featured Material

BUILDING RELATIONSHIPS IN A DIVERSE WORLD

Opportunities for Women in Sales
Business Etiquette Fosters Quality
   Relationships
Bribes Sometimes Influence Foreign Deals
World-Class Quality at Ritz-Carlton
Keeping Pace with a Changing Customer Base
Selling Across Cultures
Do You Need a Voice Coach?
Negotiating Across Cultures
Versatility is Key

SELLING IN ACTION

Pitney Bowes' Certification Sets High Standards
Building Relationships with Frequent Deposits
Honesty from a Quarterback's Perspective
Pricing Your Professional Fees
Developing a "Segment Buster"
Seminar Selling
No Tech to High Tech
Tracking Down a Sale
No Need for Price Concessions
Effective Design and Use of the Business Card
Balancing Career and Family
Are You Ready for the Sales Interview?

BUILDING QUALITY PARTNERSHIPS

How Do Customers Judge Service Quality?
Recommended Reading
Solving Customer Problems Using a Multiple
   Question Approach
Developing Professional - Looking Printed
   Materials
Applying Negotiation Skills in the Job Market
An Inspiring Example
The Moment of Magic
Four Moderators of Stress
LIFO Develops New Golden Rule
Winning Through Teamwork
Prospecting with Your Partners